Frommer's

W9-CXN-348

Sicily

2nd Edition

by Darwin Porter & Danforth Prince

Here's what the critics say about Frommer's:

"Amazingly easy to use. Very portable, very complete."
—*Booklist*

"Detailed, accurate, and easy-to-read information for all price ranges."
—*Glamour Magazine*

"Hotel information is close to encyclopedic."
—*Des Moines Sunday Register*

"Frommer's Guides have a way of giving you a real feel for a place."
—*Knight Ridder Newspapers*

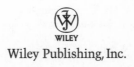

WILEY
Wiley Publishing, Inc.

About the Authors

As a team of veteran travel writers, **Darwin Porter** and **Danforth Prince** have produced numerous titles for Frommer's, including best-selling guides to Italy, France, the Caribbean, England, and Germany. Porter, a former bureau chief of the *Miami Herald,* is also a Hollywood biographer. His most recent releases are *The Secret Life of Humphrey Bogart* and *Katharine the Great,* the latter a close-up of the private life of the late Katharine Hepburn. Prince was formerly employed by the Paris bureau of the *New York Times* and is today the president of Blood Moon Productions and other media-related firms.

Published by:

Wiley Publishing, Inc.

111 River St.
Hoboken, NJ 07030-5774

ISBN-13: 978-0-7645-7458-0
ISBN-10: 0-7645-7458-2

Editor: Leslie Shen
Production Editor: Blair J. Pottenger
Cartographer: Nick Trotter
Photo Editor: Richard Fox
Production by Wiley Indianapolis Composition Services

Front cover photo: Family gathered at a table in Lipari, in the Aeolian Islands
Back cover photo: Sicily: Greek temple in the flowering field

For information on our other products and services or to obtain technical support, please contact our Customer Care Department within the U.S. at 800/762-2974, outside the U.S. at 317/572-3993 or fax 317/572-4002.

Wiley also publishes its books in a variety of electronic formats. Some content that appears in print may not be available in electronic formats.

Manufactured in the United States of America

5 4 3 2

Contents

List of Maps

An Invitation to the Reader

In researching this book, we discovered many wonderful places—hotels, restaurants, shops, and more. We're sure you'll find others. Please tell us about them, so we can share the information with your fellow travelers in upcoming editions. If you were disappointed with a recommendation, we'd love to know that, too. Please write to:

Frommer's Sicily, 2nd Edition
Wiley Publishing, Inc. • 111 River St. • Hoboken, NJ 07030-5774

An Additional Note

Please be advised that travel information is subject to change at any time—and this is especially true of prices. We therefore suggest that you write or call ahead for confirmation when making your travel plans. The authors, editors, and publisher cannot be held responsible for the experiences of readers while traveling. Your safety is important to us, however, so we encourage you to stay alert and be aware of your surroundings. Keep a close eye on cameras, purses, and wallets, all favorite targets of thieves and pickpockets.

Other Great Guides for Your Trip:

Frommer's Italy

Frommer's Northern Italy

Frommer's Rome

Frommer's Rome Past & Present

Frommer's Florence, Tuscany & Umbria

Frommer's Italy from $70 a Day

Frommer's Portable Venice

Frommer's Star Ratings, Icons & Abbreviations

Every hotel, restaurant, and attraction listing in this guide has been ranked for quality, value, service, amenities, and special features using a **star-rating system.** In country, state, and regional guides, we also rate towns and regions to help you narrow down your choices and budget your time accordingly. Hotels and restaurants are rated on a scale of zero (recommended) to three stars (exceptional). Attractions, shopping, nightlife, towns, and regions are rated according to the following scale: zero stars (recommended), one star (highly recommended), two stars (very highly recommended), and three stars (must-see).

In addition to the star-rating system, we also use seven **feature icons** that point you to the great deals, in-the-know advice, and unique experiences that separate travelers from tourists. Throughout the book, look for:

Finds	Special finds—those places only insiders know about
Fun Fact	Fun facts—details that make travelers more informed and their trips more fun
Kids	Best bets for kids and advice for the whole family
Moments	Special moments—those experiences that memories are made of
Overrated	Places or experiences not worth your time or money
Tips	Insider tips—great ways to save time and money
Value	Great values—where to get the best deals

The following **abbreviations** are used for credit cards:

AE	American Express	DISC	Discover	V	Visa
DC	Diners Club	MC	MasterCard		

Frommers.com

Now that you have the guidebook to a great trip, visit our website at **www.frommers.com** for travel information on more than 3,000 destinations. With features updated regularly, we give you instant access to the most current trip-planning information available. At Frommers.com, you'll also find the best prices on airfares, accommodations, and car rentals—and you can even book travel online through our travel booking partners. At Frommers.com, you'll also find the following:

- Online updates to our most popular guidebooks
- Vacation sweepstakes and contest giveaways
- Newsletter highlighting the hottest travel trends
- Online travel message boards with featured travel discussions

What's New in Sicily

Situated at the center of the Mediterranean, the island of Sicily was once one of the great centers of civilization in the Western world. Everything here is different from the Italian mainland, even the hybrid Sicilian dialect and the many place names tinged with Arabic in memory of the island's long-ago conquerors. The Greeks, the Romans, the Muslims, the Normans, and the Spaniards all passed through here and left their marks; much of that ancient past remains. But Sicily is also modern—and forever changing. Here are some of the latest developments.

PALERMO The hotel scene here is relatively stabilized, but two new restaurants have made headlines. **Il Mulinazzo,** S.S. 121, Località Bolognetta Nord, Villafrati (© 091-8724870), has become the best restaurant on the island and one of the finest south of Rome. With its finely tuned Sicilian cuisine, it is near perfect—both in the preparation of its food and in the use of quality ingredients. Giving it some competition is **I Ristorantino,** Piazzale Alcide De Gasperi 19 (© 091-512861), which offers one of Palermo's best Sicilian and Mediterranean cuisines. The creative menu is well crafted; sample such marvelous dishes as lobster tortellini with cherry tomatoes. See chapter 3.

USTICA This volcanic offshore island's **Hotel Clelia,** Via Sindaco I, 29 (© 091-8449039; www.hotel clelia.it), long a simple *pensione,* has been vastly upgraded and given three-star status by the government. Its prices remain reasonable, but it's now one of the better addresses for those seeking comfortable living on their visit to this remote island. Soundproof windows and modern plumbing have improved living conditions here considerably.

Also on Ustica, a local eatery, **Schiticchio,** Via de Tre Mulini (© 091-8449662), came into prominence in summer 2004 when it was one of the most fully booked restaurants on the island. Relatively modest, it serves good homemade food from the freshest ingredients— mainly regional dishes with a focus on fresh fish and shellfish. See chapter 5.

CEFALÙ More readers are discovering this north-coast town's **Hotel Tourist,** Lungomare Giardina (© 0921-421750), than any other hotel in the vicinity. The inn was extensively renovated in 2003, making it an even more attractive choice for visitors basing themselves in Cefalù. Word quickly got out about this affordable option, located a 10-minute walk from the center of town. Try to get one of the well-furnished guest rooms with a balcony opening onto a seascape. See chapter 6.

TAORMINA In Sicily's more elegant resort, a down-home restaurant is rising to the fore: **Osteria Nero D'Avola,** Vico de Spuches 8 (© 0942-628874), which not only serves some of the most affordable food in town, but also some of the best. The chef changes the menu daily, shopping for the freshest ingredients at the marketplace. His cooks prepare finely honed Sicilian fare backed up by a wine *carte* of some 200 different vintages. See chapter 8.

CATANIA Way back in 1968, Giuseppe La Rosa established **La Siciliana,** Viale Marco Polo 52A (© **095-376400**), in the north of the city. In 2004, it suddenly became the dining address of choice for many locals, who've also recommended it to visitors to Catania. Today, Vito and Salvo, sons of Guiseppe, have brought renewed energy to this old favorite, which is beginning to attract discriminating diners to its inviting precincts for the fine Sicilian cuisine. Everything tastes fresh and homemade, just the way locals like it. See chapter 9.

SYRACUSE An old *palazzo* in the heart of the monument-loaded island of Ortygia has been turned into **B&B Airone,** Via Maestranza 111 (© **0931-69005**), one of the city's most inviting bed-and-breakfasts. It's simple but comfortable here, and the hospitality of the owners and their affordable prices keep the place full. See chapter 10.

PIAZZA ARMERINA The sleepy taste buds of this provincial inland town are being awakened by an intriguing choice, **Al Fogher,** Contrada Bellia, Strada Statale 117 (© **0935-684123**), which has opened 3km (1¾ miles) north of the center. Its wine cellar, with some 400 different vintages, is the best in this part of the island, and the Sicilian food is creative, beautifully seasoned and flavored, and prepared to perfection.

Incidentally, thanks to quite a lot of international publicity in travel magazines in 2004, more and more visitors to Piazza Armerina are budgeting time for a side trip to the old town of **Caltagirone,** lying 30km (18 miles) to the southeast. It is the center of earthenware potteries, and buyers are flocking here to wander through its old-fashioned shops. See chapter 11.

AGRIGENTO Visitors exploring the world's most impressive Greek ruins, at the Valley of the Temples, are heading 2km (1¼ miles) southwest of the center to a new and inviting hotel that opens onto the Mediterranean. **Hotel Kaos,** Contrada Cumbo, Villaggio Pirandello (© **0922-598622**), was formed by converting the residence of a nobleman into this well-run lodging, and absorbing some of the original outbuildings as well. It has immediately become a family favorite, with an on-site outdoor swimming pool and two tennis courts. See chapter 12.

TRAPANI This is the major city along the western coast of the island, and, for many, their center for exploring the nearby towns of Erice and wine-producing Marsala. The dining situation in Trapani has improved considerably with the opening of **P & G,** a Sicilian and seafood restaurant at Via Spalti 1 (© **0923-547701**). Located near the train station, the restaurant lies across from the public gardens of Villa Margherita. It is clearly the best choice in town, specializing in market-fresh ingredients and succulent homemade pastas. See chapter 13.

The Best of Sicily

The largest island in the Mediterranean Sea, Sicily is a land of beauty, mystery, and world-class monuments. It's an exotic mix of bloodlines and architecture from medieval Normandy, Aragonese Spain, Moorish North Africa, ancient Greece, Phoenicia, and Rome. Much of the island's raw, primitive nature has faded in modern times, as thousands of newfangled cars clog the narrow lanes of its biggest city, **Palermo.** Poverty remains widespread, yet the age-old stranglehold of the Mafia seems less certain thanks to the increasingly vocal protests of an outraged public. On the eastern edge of the island is **Mount Etna,** the highest active volcano in Europe. Many of Sicily's larger urban areas (**Trapani, Catania,** and **Messina**) are relatively unattractive, but areas of ravishing beauty and eerie historical interest are found in the cities of **Syracuse, Taormina, Agrigento,** and **Selinunte.** Sicily's ancient ruins are rivaled only by those of Rome itself. Agrigento's **Valley of the Temples,** for example, is worth the trip alone.

1 The Best Travel Experiences

- **Walking Among the Dead:** Outside Palermo, the Catacombe dei Cappuccini amazingly preserve the lifelike corpses of some 8,000 Palermitans entombed here from the late 16th century until 1920, when the last victim, a 2-year-old *bambina,* was laid to rest. In dimly lit, murky, subterranean corridors, you can wander among these mummies. It's a gory sight, but it's absolutely fascinating. See p. 91.
- **Wandering Palermo's La Kalsa:** The ancient quarter of La Kalsa, created during the city's Arab domination, is as close as Sicily comes to having a casbah typical of the North African cities to the south. This densely populated district of narrow streets and markets provides a view of local Sicilian life unlike anywhere else on the island. To make your experience more authentic, purchase some *babbaluci* from one of the many vendors. (These are marinated baby snails sold in paper cornets for devouring on the spot.) Head for Piazza della Kalsa, the heart of the quarter, and the day is yours. See p. 91.
- **Encountering the Sicilian Apennines:** The island isn't all coastline, even though most visitors rarely dip into the hinterlands. For a close-up view of life as lived in the "Sicilian Alps," head inland to explore Sicily's greatest national park, Parco Naturale Regionale delle Madonie, sprawling across 39,679 hectares (98,007 acres). Castles dotting the park's lofty villages evoke the Middle Ages; the town of Cefalù makes the best base. This area is the breadbasket of Sicily, so you'll pass through pretty farms and vineyards. Fields ideal for a summertime picnic give way to downhill skiers in winter. See p. 151.
- **Climbing the Volcano:** Follow in the footsteps of the "disgraced"

Ingrid Bergman, who came here in 1949 with her lover and director, Roberto Rossellini, to make the ill-fated film *Stromboli.* On the Aeolian island of Stromboli, the most spectacular of its archipelago, you can witness showers of flaring rock and sparks from its volcano. For the most dramatic viewings, visit at night, when you can witness up close the channels from which the lava flows toward the sea along *sciara del fuoco,* or "trails of fire." At the top, you'll be treated to fiery explosions, a great show that's gone on for centuries. Just wear something over your coiffure so that you, too, don't light up the night. See p. 171.

- **Cooling Off in Gole dell'Alcantara:** Often visited from Taormina en route to Mount Etna, the Alcantara lava gorges are the best place to experience almost freezing waters when the temperatures in eastern Sicily soar from May to September. These gorges were carved by a river of the same name into rock-hard basalt, the creation of one of Mount Etna's ancient eruptions. You can rent thigh-length boots, but many prefer to take along a bathing suit. This wonderland is the place to be a kid again: There's nothing quite like splashing around in these cooling waters. See p. 182.

- **Visiting Medieval Erice:** This once heavily fortified and walled mountain town, left over from the Middle Ages, is suspended 755m (2,478 ft.) above sea level. Ancients called the city Eryx, and a glorious golden temple dedicated to Aphrodite at the pinnacle of the town was like a gleaming lighthouse for ancient mariners. You can wander its cobblestone streets and peer into flower-filled courtyards along twisting lanes. Nothing seems as foreboding as a walk down a *vanelle,* an alley so narrow that only one person can pass at a time. Many Sicilian men journey here looking for a wife, as the women of Erice have been considered the most beautiful in Sicily for centuries. See p. 290.

2 The Most Romantic Getaways

- **Atelier Sul Mare** (Castel di Tusa; ✆ **0921-334295**): Far off the beaten path is the most iconoclastic hotel on the island, created by an artist who has anointed himself the "Ambassador to Beauty." Some of the rooms are the creative statements of renowned artists who lived on the premises for months and made their rooms works of art. See p. 153.

- **Palazzo San Domenico** (Taormina; ✆ **0942-613111**): No other hotel in Sicily offers the sweeping majesty of this time-tested icon whose rooms were installed in a 15th-century monastery. Grand comfort on a deluxe level goes hand-in-hand with such charming ecclesiastical touches as Madonnas in wall niches and centuries-old depictions of saints praying in ecstasy. See p. 185.

- **Hotel Villa Sonia** (Castelmola; ✆ **0942-28082**): High above the resort of Taormina, this 1974 old-style villa is a true retreat for escapists. It's a cozy, tranquil nest, with beautiful public areas and rooms opening onto spectacular views. Its restaurant is so excellent, you won't want to leave the premises at night. See p. 189.

- **Villa del Bosco** (Catania; ✆ **095-7335100**): Few island hotels evoke the stately aristocratic life of the 19th century as does this estate, 5km (3 miles) south of the center of Catania. Once a private home, it has been successfully converted into a first-class hotel that often attracts celebrities. Its on-site restaurant is another reason to stay here. See p. 208.

- **Eremo della Giubiliana** (Ragusa; © **0932-669119**): A stone-built estate in sunny isolation, this is a baronial compound of refinement and grace. A stay here is like a visit to the grand country estate of some Sicilian *don* of the non-Mafia type. All the luxuries of the 21st century are found here, as well as fine dining, but the aura is definitely Old World. See p. 266.

- **Foresteria Baglio della Luna** (Agrigento; © **0922-511061**): This is one of the grandest country inns of Sicily, meticulously restored by an antiques dealer and turned into a glamorous oasis of style, comfort, and elegance. Agrigento never had such a stylish place to stay. See p. 279.

3 The Best Museums

- **Galleria Regionale della Sicilia** (Palermo; © **091-6230011**): This is the most magnificent collection of regional art in all of Sicily—in fact, the gallery is one of the finest in Italy. Housed in the Catalán-Gothic Palazzo Abatellis, its superb collections trace Sicilian painting and sculpture from the 13th to the 18th century. Some of its paintings, such as *Triumph of Death* from 1449, are among the most impressive masterpieces in the south of Italy. See p. 87.

- **Museo Archeologico Regionale** (Palermo; © **091-6116805**): One of the greatest archaeological museums in Italy is filled with a virtual "British Museum" collection of rare finds that is particularly rich in artifacts from the Greek and Roman colonizations of the island. The metopes dug up from the city of Selinunte alone are worth a visit. See p. 90.

- **Museo Mandralisca** (Cefalù; © **0921-421547**): Come here for no other reason than to gaze in wonder at Antonello da Messina's *Portrait of an Unknown Man,* painted in 1465. It is the masterpiece of this great Sicilian artist. While here, check out the other art treasures of this regional museum, including everything from a Chinese puzzle in ivory to a vase from the 4th century B.C. See p. 147.

- **Museo Regionale** (Messina; © **090-361292**): A former silk mill has been successfully converted into one of the island's most impressive regional museums, one that contains Sicily's greatest collection of art from the 15th to the 17th century. See p. 140.

- **Museo Civico** (Termini Imerese; © **091-8128279**): Housed in a 14th-century *palazzo* (palace) is one of the finest regional museums in Sicily, devoted to art and archaeology. The Hellenistic and Roman pottery are among its greatest treasures; the museum is also rich in medieval and Renaissance art. See p. 155.

- **Museo Archeologico Eoliano** (Lipari; © **090-9880174**): One of the great archaeological museums of Italy lies hidden away on the volcanic Aeolian island of Lipari. Among its many celebrated exhibits are a stunning collection of ancient vases, many from the 4th century B.C., and a magnificent trove of theatrical masks unearthed from tombs of the same era. See p. 162.

- **Museo Civico Belliniano** (Catania; © **095-7150535**): This museum pays homage to the composer Vincenzo Bellini, who was born here in 1801. The rather drab five-room apartment evokes old Catania and is filled with Bellini memorabilia, including original folios of his operas, his death mask, and even the coffin in which his body was transferred from Paris. See p. 217.

- **Museo Archeologico Regionale Paolo Orsi** (Syracuse; © **0931-464022**): This is a showcase for some of the most important archaeological finds of southern Italy. Especially intriguing are the showrooms devoted to the Greek colonization of Sicily, including the celebrated *Landolina Venus.* See p. 240.

- **Museo Regionale di Arte Mediovale e Moderna** (Syracuse; © **0931-69511**): One of Sicily's greatest art collections is housed in the 13th-century Palazzo Bellomo. The collections are finest in the painting and decorative arts of southeastern Sicily and include such masterpieces as *The Burial of St. Lucia,* by Caravaggio. See p. 245.

4 The Best Cathedrals & Churches

- **Chiesa di Santa Cita/Oratorio del Rosario di Santa Cita** (Palermo): The church of Santa Cita, bombed in World War II, is visited mainly for its stunning oratory, representing the crowning architectural achievement of sculptor Giacomo Serpotta, who labored on it between 1686 and 1718. His cherubs and angels are a real romp. See p. 92.

- **Oratorio del Rosario di San Domenico** (Palermo): This 16th-century oratory is the stunning achievement of sculptor and baroque decorator extraordinaire Giacomo Serpotta. To many, it is the equal of the also glorious Santa Cita oratory (see below). Serpotta's stucco designs are among the greatest in southern Italy. See p. 93.

- **Oratorio di San Lorenzo** (Palermo): This is yet another great oratory that shows the magnificent decoration of master sculptor Giacomo Serpotta, who created this masterpiece between 1698 and 1710. See p. 93.

- **Monreale Duomo** (Monreale): This grand cathedral represents the pinnacle of the glory of Arabo-Norman art and architecture. Launched in 1174 by William II, the Duomo is the most stunning of the Norman churches of Sicily, the mosaics in its interior rivaling those of the celebrated Cappella Palatina in Palermo. See p. 122.

- **Duomo** (Cefalù): One of Sicily's most magnificent Norman cathedrals, built by Roger II, stands in this charming little north-coast town. The cathedral is known for its grand array of Byzantine-Norman mosaics, completed in 1148. They are a virtual tour de force of this type of painstaking art. See p. 147.

- **Duomo** (Catania): Dedicated to the martyred St. Agatha, this cathedral was built on the orders of Roger I, the Norman king, and was largely destroyed in the earthquake that devastated Catania in 1693. What was left was redesigned with parts that survived the catastrophe. The great opera composer Bellini is buried here, as are several Aragonese kings. See p. 216.

5 The Best & Most Evocative Ruins

- **Tyndaris** (Capo Tindari): Tyndaris was a bustling place at its founding by Dionysius the Elder in 396 B.C. Later destroyed by pillaging conquerors, Tyndaris has now been unearthed, and the ruins of everything from a basilica to a Roman theater can be seen. The view of the sea is reason enough to visit. See p. 154.

- **Teatro Greco** (Taormina): Opening onto a view of Mount Etna in the background, this Greek amphitheater was hewn out of a rocky slope on Mount Tauro. What you see today is what's left after destruction by the Arabs in the 10th century. See p. 180.

- **Ortygia Island** (Syracuse): Famous in Greek mythology, this island is filled with ancient ruins such as the Tempio di Apollo, the Greek temple dedicated to Apollo that dates from the 6th century B.C. and the oldest peripteral (having a single row of columns) Doric temple still left in the world. See p. 244.

- **Parco Archeologico della Neapolis** (Syracuse): Two of the greatest attractions of Sicily—both from the world of the ancients—lie in this city in southeastern Sicily. The Greek Theater is one of the great theaters of the classical period still remaining. The other attraction is the Latomia del Paradiso, or the "Ear of Dionysius," the most famous of the ancient quarries of Syracuse. See p. 238.

- **Villa Romana del Casale** (Piazza Armerina): This is one of the grandest of all Roman villas to have survived from the classical era. It contains a total of 40 rooms "carpeted" with the most magnificent mosaics in western Europe. Its most reproduced mosaics are those of 10 young women dressed in strapless two-piece bikinis that would not be out of style today. See p. 270.

- **Valle dei Templi** (Agrigento): Containing the largest and greatest collection of ancient Greek ruins in the world, the "Valley of the Temples," outside the city of Agrigento, opens onto the southern coast of Sicily. The temples are especially stunning at night, when they're floodlit. The most impressive ones are those dedicated to Juno and to Concord. The latter is the most magnificent of all, with 13 wind-eroded columns still standing. See p. 274.

- **Selinunte's Archaeological Garden** (Selinunte, west of Agrigento): Guy de Maupassant called these ruins an "immense heap of fallen columns," and so they are, but they are also the remains of one of the greatest colonies of ancient Greece. The temples date from the 6th century to the 5th century B.C. See p. 286.

- **Tempio di Segesta** (Segesta): One of the world's most perfectly preserved monuments from antiquity, Tempio di Segesta was constructed in the 5th century B.C. Amazingly, 36 of its Doric columns still stand. A visit to this remote site in western Sicily also gives you a chance to see a large Greek theater in ruins. See p. 289.

6 The Best Beaches

- **Mondello Lido** (Mondello): This is where the citizens of Palermo flock on summer days to escape the stifling heat of the capital city. In Sicily, Mondello Lido is outclassed in fashion only by the beaches at the foot of Taormina. Its wide, sandy beaches extend for 2km (1¼ miles) from Monte Pellegrino to Monte Gallo. See p. 124.

- **Mortelle:** The best sands in northeast Sicily are found at the resort of Mortelle, which is where the Messinese themselves go to escape the scalding heat in their capital. The resort lies 12km (7½ miles) north of Messina at the northeast tip of the island. The area is filled with good sandy beaches, so you can take your pick. The best-accessorized strip is Lido dei Tirreno. See p. 144.

- **Spiaggia Sabbie Nere** (Vulcano): Completely off the beaten trail, "Black Sands Beach" is the finest in the Aeolian archipelago—that is, once you get over the fact that its sands are black and not powdery white. Beaching it here is something to tell the folks back home. See p. 168.

- **Lido Mazzarò** (Taormina): The best-equipped beach in Sicily, Lido Mazzarò is also one of the finest, a favorite sea-bordering strip of sand and gravel once frequented by the stars of Hollywood's Golden Age and still as interesting as ever. A 15-minute cable-car ride down from the medieval town of Taormina, the beach is a hot spot from April to October. Bars and restaurants border the sands. See p. 180.

- **Giardini-Naxos:** Situated on the waterfront near Taormina, Giardini-Naxos is one of the most sophisticated seaside resorts of Sicily. The sandy beach, one of the island's best, lies between Capo Taormina in the northwest and Capo Schisò in the south. It may lack Taormina's medieval charm, but it's filled with good hotels, fine swimming, and excellent restaurants. See p. 196.

- **Marina di Ragusa:** Southeastern Sicily has a number of beaches, some of them quite tacky, but Marina di Ragusa is the best of the lot. This is quite an appealing area, and if Ragusa is too hot in summer, you might drop anchor at a hotel here and visit the ancient city on a day trip. The resort also has the best ice-cream bars, pubs, and watersports in the area. See p. 263.

7 The Best Walks

- **Old Palermo:** In the heart of this ancient city, you can take a walk into history that in 3 hours will bring you by some of the Sicilian capital's most fabled monuments and into some of its most charming squares, such as Piazza Pretoria. You'll marvel that so much of the antique still remains, yet at the same time enjoy watching the locals go about their daily lives past monuments that in some cases were left over by the Arabs or the Normans. See p. 104.

- **Ustica:** In just 3 to 4 hours, you can circumnavigate the small island of Ustica, which rises out of the waters of the Tyrrhenian Sea 57km (36 miles) northwest of Palermo (reached by boat). The best hike on this volcanic island is the coastal path north of the main settlement. The local tourist office will provide a map. You'll pass along steep cliffs, part of a Marine Reserve, and be rewarded with some of the most stunning sea views in this part of the world. At some point, you can strip down and cool off from your walk by going swimming. See p. 128.

- **Parco Naturale Regionale delle Madonie:** This park, which begins 6km (3¾ miles) south of the coastal town of Cefalù, is too vast to explore by foot unless you have days. It comprises 39,679 hectares (8,007 acres) in all. But you can take a full-day excursion to walk through what has been called a "botanic paradise," containing more than half the species known on the island. Our favorite part of the walk centers around the village of Santuario di Gibilmanna, from whose belvederes you'll have the most panoramic views of the island. From here, you can walk all the way to the idyllic town of Castelbuno, coming to a rest at its historic Piazza Margherita. See p. 151.

- **Vulcano:** This is the most visited of the offshore Aeolian Islands. In ancient times, it was known as Thermessa and was believed to be the home of the god Vulcan, but also the gateway to Hades. Its big attraction is the Gran Cratere, which hasn't erupted since 1890. The walk to reach the peak of this crater is one of the most heavily trod in the islands. Allow about 3 hours for the trek there and back. For your effort, you'll be rewarded with the greatest of all views, not only of Vulcano, but of the other Aeolian Islands as well. See p. 167.

- **Old Catania:** Overshadowed by Mount Etna, Catania is the second-largest and one of the most historic cities of Sicily. A walk through the heart of Catania is the best way to explore its monuments. But it's not all history:

You'll also get to take in the sights of the bustling outdoor market in the historic core. It will take about 4½ hours, however, to cover just the highlights of the monuments, including the "Fountain of 10 Rivers" and the ancient Duomo which was built after the great earthquake of 1902. See p. 222.

- **Valley of the Temples:** Our favorite walk in all of Sicily is along the Valley of the Temples, in the city of Agrigento. This is one of the most memorable and evocative sights of the ancient world. You won't find such impressive Greek ruins even in Greece itself. We prefer to walk among these ruins either at dawn or sunset. Naturally, their mysterious aura is heightened even more in springtime, when all the wildflowers are bursting into bloom. The highlight of your walk will be the Tempio della Concordia (Concord), the best preserved Greek ruins in the world. See p. 274.

8 The Best Luxury Hotels

- **Villa Igiea Grand Hotel** (Palermo; © **091-6312111**): This old villa, built at the turn of the 20th century in the Art Nouveau style, is the grandest address in Palermo. Surrounded by a park overlooking the sea, it provides an old-world atmosphere but has all the modern comforts. See p. 68.

- **Grand Hotel Liberty** (Messina; © **090-6409436**): This is one of the grandest hotels on the eastern coast of Sicily. It was transformed in the mid-1990s into a bastion of comfort and tranquillity, with some of the island's best and plushest bedrooms. A stay here is a beautiful way to visit "messy" Messina. See p. 141.

- **Villa Meligunis** (Lipari; © **090-9812426**): This hotel is as good as it gets in the volcanic Aeolian

islands. A restored cluster of 17th-century fishermen's cottages forms the nucleus of the compound. All modern conveniences in this remote outpost have been added. See p. 164.

- **Grand Hotel Timeo** (Taormina; © **0942-23801**): Liz Taylor and Richard Burton have long vamoosed, but this deluxe hotel still attracts the rich and famous who want to enjoy the stately comfort of a 19th-century neoclassical villa near Taormina's Greek theater. It's lighthearted and baronial at the same time. See p. 185.

- **Excelsior Grand Hotel** (Catania; © **095-7476111**): This is the leading hotel of Sicily's second city, a monument to the modernism of *la dolce vita* days of the 1950s. The city may be in decay, but the hotel is completely up-to-date, housing its guests in luxury and comfort. See p. 208.

- **Grand Hotel** (Syracuse; ✆ **0931-464600**): This turn-of-the-20th-century hotel is so old, it's new again, following a major upgrade

and renovation in the 1990s. Its stately, old-fashioned charm has been preserved, but its comforts are definitely 21st century. It's the best place to stay if you plan to visit the archaeological gardens of Syracuse. See p. 246.

9 The Best Moderately Priced Hotels

- **Palazzo Excelsior** (Palermo; ✆ 091-6256176): With its faded 19th-century nostalgia, this is a very appealing choice lying on the most prestigious street of Palermo, but in an isolated spot. Much of the interior is appealingly dowdy. It's not for everyone, but it attracts those discerning guests who like staying in a living museum. See p. 73.
- **Hotel Grotta Azzurra** (Ustica; ✆ 091-8449396): This remote island off the northern coast of Sicily is home to a lush, resort-style Mediterranean retreat, set on a wide plateau above the ocean. The prices are most affordable. See p. 132.
- **Villa Fabbiano** (Taormina; ✆ 0942-626058): Romantically positioned in a hilltop village, this affordable hotel is a little gem. You're in a beautiful setting amid good furnishings, but you'll pay only a fraction of the price

charged by nearby competitors such as the deluxe Grand Hotel Timeo. See p. 188.

- **Villa Mora** (Giardini-Naxos; ✆ 0942-51839): With even its bedrooms opening onto views of the Ionian Sea, this is the ultimate beachfront retreat for those who prefer to be right on the water and not anchored in the hilltop village of Taormina above. This small hotel is an oasis of charm and tranquillity, with good rooms and pleasantly aromatic Sicilian cuisine. See p. 198.
- **Hotel Moderno** (Erice; ✆ 0923-869300): In spite of its dull and misleading name, this is quite a good hotel in Sicily's most enchanting medieval town. Rooms are located in an attractively decorated main building or in a newer annex. All units have hints of 19th-century styling and open onto private balconies or terraces with views in all directions. See p. 293.

10 The Best Restaurants

- **Il Mulinazzo** (Palermo; ✆ 091-8724870): Serious foodies make the trek 45 minutes from the center of Palermo, as Il Mulinazzo is currently hailed by Italian food critics as the best restaurant on the island. Its meticulously crafted Sicilian haute cuisine is a pleasure to both the palate and the eye. From the service to the market-fresh ingredients, everything about this place is top-notch. See p. 77.

- **I Ristorantino** (Palermo; ✆ 091-512861): This newcomer is hailed by some Italian critics for its classic and authentic Sicilian and Mediterranean cuisine. Francesco Inzerillo presents a creative menu that uses his imagination, yet also keeps alive his favorite old-time recipes. See p. 78.
- **La Scuderia** (Palermo; ✆ 091-520323): Set at the foot of Monte Pellegrino, 5km (3 miles) north of

the city, this is Palermo's grandest restaurant, with superb international and Italian cuisine. Talented chefs turn out a tempting array of dishes prepared with market-fresh ingredients and served on the town's prettiest terrace. See p. 78.

- **Charleston Le Terrazze** (Mondello; ✆ **091-450171**): Located in Palermo's fashionable beach resort, this restaurant serves a better cuisine than that found in the capital city itself. It's housed in a building from 1913. The chefs use the finest ingredients in preparing the Sicilian and international cuisine. See p. 128.

- **Osteria del Duomo** (Cefalù; ✆ **0921-421838**): Its location across from the town's most famous cathedral is touristy, but this first-rate restaurant is anything but. It's a bastion of some of the north coast's grandest cuisine, specializing in sophisticated Sicilian fare along with a discreet offering of international dishes that have attracted world celebrities. See p. 150.

- **Casa Grugno** (Taormina; ✆ **0942-21208**): Taormina has never had such a temple of gastronomy. One of the most exciting restaurants in Sicily is the culinary showcase for Andrea Zangerl, an Austria-born chef. His modern takes on Sicilian cuisine and sublime international dishes draw the world to his doorstep. See p. 190.

- **Le Zagare** (Catania; ✆ **095-7476111**): There is no finer Grand Hotel–style dining on the eastern coast of Sicily than at this citadel of haute cuisine, serving the best of island dishes along with a

well-chosen sampling of Continental recipes. The baroque city around it may be in decay, but the good life still holds forth here. See p. 213.

- **Osteria I Tre Bicchieri** (Catania; ✆ **095-7153540**): Upon opening in 2002, this quickly became Catania's finest restaurant. Naples-born *Wunderkind* and chef Laquinangelo Carmine has won immediate acceptance with his succulent Continental cuisine. He's known especially for his preparation of Mediterranean fish. See p. 214.

- **Il Barocco** (Noto; ✆ **0931-835999**): Your finest dining in this ancient but decaying town west of Syracuse is at this restaurant, housed in a building that was converted from an 18th-century stable block for a historic palace nearby. Today, it's the setting for excellent Sicilian dishes, especially seafood from the Ionian Sea. See p. 267.

- **Locanda Don Serafino** (Ragusa; ✆ **0932-248778**): One of the finest restaurants in southern Sicily is set inside the cellars of a 17th-century palace. The Sicilian cuisine, based on market-fresh products, is elegantly presented here—dishes are designed to appeal to the most discerning of tastes. See p. 268.

- **Ristorante Il Dehor** (Agrigento; ✆ **0922-511061**): In a grand villa of a hotel, Foresteria Baglio della Luna, this is one of the best restaurants in all of Sicily, serving refined Sicilian and international cuisine. Winning rave reviews from the press in Europe, this place will tempt you with an array of fixed-price menus from its very talented chef. See p. 284.

11 The Best Down-Home Trattorie

- **Lo Scudiero** (Palermo; ✆ **091-581628**): The capital's finest moderately priced *trattoria* is set across from the landmark Politeamo Theater. Honest, straightforward

Sicilian food is served here at very affordable prices. See p. 79.

- **Bye Bye Blues** (Mondello; ✆ **091-6841415**): Though the name doesn't sound very Sicilian, this is one of the best places to go for true island cooking. A casual, relaxed place outside Palermo, this trattoria is run by a husband-and-wife team who are passionate about feeding you well from the island's bounty. See p. 127.

- **E Pulera** (Lipari; ℭ 090-9811158): For some of the best Aeolian cooking, head here for time-tested recipes and some of the best fish specialties in the island chain, including a delectable fishermen's soup. No one makes a better swordfish ragout than these folks. See p. 165.

- **Granduca** (Taormina; ℭ 0942-24983): The most atmospheric choice in this chic resort looks like an antiques store with potted plants. It also contains an alluring terrace with panoramic views. But most people come here for the excellent food and repertoire of Sicilian and Italian specialties. See p. 192.

- **La Grotta di Carmelo** (Acireale; ℭ 095-7648153): The setting looks touristy and gimmicky, as you dine in a cave carved into a rock-face wall. Forget that it's constructed of black-lava rock from Mount Etna; the restaurant serves really good food, both seafood and typical Sicilian fare. Much of the fish is brought in daily from the Ionian Sea. See p. 233.

- **Don Camillo** (Syracuse; ℭ 0931-67133): One of the city's finest and most affordable dining rooms was constructed on the foundation of a 15th-century monastery. The cuisine of seafood and Sicilian recipes is among the most creative in town. It's a charmer. See p. 252.

- **Monte San Giuliano** (Erice; ℭ 0923-869595): In the medieval hilltop village of Erice, the most spectacular in Sicily, you can dine at this undiscovered garden hideaway after making your way through narrow, labyrinthine streets. Most of the foodstuffs are plucked from the sea. Some of the dishes, such as a seafood couscous, are inspired by North Africa. See p. 293.

Planning Your Trip to Sicily

To see most of Sicily's highlights, plan on spending at least 5 to 7 days and moving a few times. Everything is very spread out—Sicily is the largest island in the Mediterranean, 177km (110 miles) north to south and 281km (175 miles) wide. Taormina, the most popular resort, is a great place to relax and play in the sun for a couple of days; from here you can also visit Mount Etna. The town is rather isolated in the east, however, so it may not be the best base for seeing the island's other highlights. The quickest and most efficient way to see the majority of Sicily is to fly into Palermo, rent a car, and travel east to Taormina; then return your car and fly back to the mainland from Catania. (Conversely, you can fly into Catania, perhaps from Rome, and end your itinerary in Palermo, returning the car there before flying back to Rome.)

This chapter is devoted to the where, when, and how of your trip—the advance planning required to get it together and take it on the road.

1 The Regions in Brief

A predominantly mountainous island, Sicily is separated from the mainland by the Straits of Messina. Culturally there is an even wider gap between Italy and its semi-autonomous island, Sicily, which feels a world apart.

This is a land of tempestuous elements, including active volcanoes and torrential rivers that can flood during the winter rainy season and dry up in the scorching summer months. While northern Sicily enjoys a milder clime, southern Sicily is often profoundly affected by the hot winds known as *sirocco* blowing in from the deserts of North Africa.

Sicily lies at the confluence of a trio of seas—in fact, the Greeks called it *Sikelia,* or "three points." The northern coast opens onto the Tyrrhenian Sea, the eastern coast (Catania and Taormina) onto the Ionian Sea, and the southern coast onto the Sicilian Sea.

Sicily also controls a string of offshore islands, including Ustica, off the coast of Palermo; the Aeolians (mainly Stromboli, Vulcano, and Lipari); and the Egadis, lying off the cities of Marsala and Trapani on the west coast. Lonely Pantelleria lies off the western coast, and the southernmost Pelagians are almost in North Africa. Here's a rundown of the cities and regions covered in this guide.

AEOLIAN ISLANDS From the mud baths of Vulcano to the fiery explosions from the crater on Stromboli, the Aeolian Islands *(Isole Eolie)* are mysterious and exciting places to be, different from anything else in Italy. Awash in the Tyrrhenian Sea, these islands lie off the northern coast and are within easy reach of the port of Milazzo by hydrofoil or ferryboat. The three main islands to visit are **Vulcano** (closest to the Sicilian mainland), **Lipari** (where most of the tourist facilities are found), and **Stromboli** (still actively volcanic). Those travelers with unlimited time can also make day trips to such lesser islands as **Panarea, Filicudi, Salina,** and **Alicudi.**

Sicily

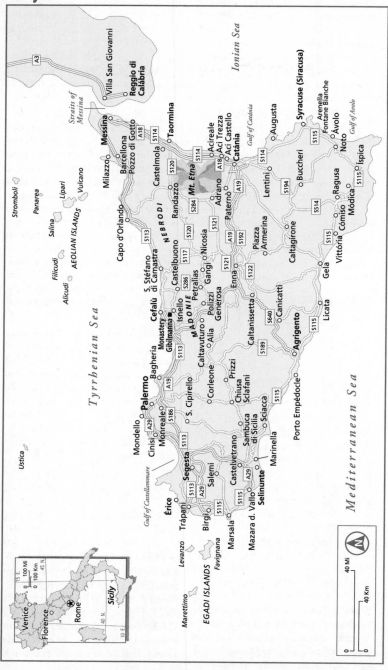

AGRIGENTO Located on the southern coastline of Sicily, Agrigento was one of the most important centers of Magna Graecia, and its **Valle dei Templi (Valley of the Temples),** a mammoth array of temple ruins, is reason enough to go to Sicily. The home of the 5th-century philosopher Empedocles and of the playwright Luigi Pirandello, Agrigento was destroyed by Carthage in 406 B.C. But those invading armies left plenty of ruins for us to explore today. The town's Doric temples date from the 6th century to the 5th century B.C. and were erected to such deities as Hercules, Juno, and Jupiter.

CATANIA The second city of Sicily opens onto the Gulf of Catania, lying at the foot of the southern slopes of Mount Etna, a volcano that has rained lava down on it for centuries. One of the oldest cities of Sicily, it dates from the 8th century B.C. Massively rebuilt after destruction by an earthquake in 1693, Catania today is called the "baroque city." You'll either love this massive sprawl or hate it. We love it, as did such hometown boys as the composer Vincenzo Bellini (1801–35).

MESSINA Overlooking the Straits of Messina on the northeast coast of Sicily, the city of Messina is for most visitors the gateway into Sicily. Although it's possible to fly into Palermo, most people arrive by hydrofoil or ferryboat from the Italian mainland, disembarking at the port of Messina, where rail and bus connections can be made to other parts of Sicily. Shakespeare used the city as a setting for *Much Ado About Nothing,* although he never actually laid eyes on it. Messina today is a modern city, having been rebuilt after many disasters.

MOUNT ETNA This is Sicily's greatest natural attraction and its highest mountain, and it's also the largest volcano in Europe and one of the most active in the world. The ancient Greeks viewed it as the home of Vulcan, god of fire, and home of the Cyclops, the one-eyed monster. Much of its surrounding landscape is covered with solidified lava, a surface for skiing in winter and hiking terrain in summer. The crater is dangerously active, so you always feel a sense of adventure, or even danger, while touring or hiking in the area.

PALERMO The island's largest city and its capital is also filled with the most sightseeing treasures. Palermo opens onto the Gulf of Palermo on the northwest coast of Sicily, the largest settlement in Conca d'Oro, a fertile land planted with citrus. Founded by the Phoenicians, it contains innumerable fine monuments, particularly in the baroque vein, along with an array of art that spans the centuries. It's difficult to navigate and crime-laden, but like its sister city Naples, it's worth the effort for those who don't mind a certain inconvenience.

PIAZZA ARMERINA This is not a piazza (square) but an actual town, and a spectacularly sited one as well, lying inland in central Sicily. It is visited mainly by those who want to see the famous Roman hunting lodge from the 4th century B.C. The mosaics found here are among the most spectacular in the world; they even include some bathing beauties in bikinis.

RAGUSA Set on the southern slope of the Iblei mountain range, Ragusa lies inland from the sea and is one of the most intriguing cities in the southeastern sector of the island. It's actually two cities in one, Ragusa Ibla and Ragusa Superiore. Of medieval origin, with narrow twisting lanes, the old city, which suffered a major earthquake in 1693, retained much of its appearance when it was rebuilt.

SEGESTA & SELINUNTE Your journey of discovery through Sicily should include these ancient ruins.

Segesta lies in western Sicily in a setting of rolling hills. Its claim to fame is a Doric temple built around 430 B.C., with its 36 limestone columns still intact. On the southern coast, Selinunte was once a rival to Segesta until it was destroyed by Hannibal and the Carthaginians. Like Agrigento and Syracuse, Selinunte is visited for its impressive and scattered ruins of temple columns that speak of former glory.

SYRACUSE Called *Siracusa* in Italian, this historic city, founded by the Greeks in the 8th century B.C., lies on the southeastern coast of the island. After Taormina and Palermo, it is the third-most-visited city in Sicily. Filled with medieval streets but with an essentially baroque aura in architecture, its main draws are its classical ruins and works of art. These include a Greek theater and a Roman amphitheater, both from the 3rd century B.C.

TAORMINA Sicily's grandest resort, first publicized by Goethe in 1787, has over time drawn a steady stream of celebrities, ranging from Oscar Wilde to Marlene Dietrich. Situated atop Monte Tauro, Taormina is not on the beach, but good sandy strips are easily reached along its eastern flanks. In spite of the hordes who descend on it every year from April to October, Taormina retains some of its medieval aura.

TRAPANI & ERICE The major city on the western coast, Trapani lies in the northwest, opening onto the Egadi archipelago of three islands. It offers superior transportation links to the rest of Sicily and easy road links to Palermo. Trapani was founded by the Greeks, though eventually it fell to the Romans. The medieval hill town of Erice, to its immediate north, has far more antique charm, and if you have only a day to spend in the west, devote it to touring Erice. But if you have the time, Trapani and its monuments make for an intriguing day of sightseeing as well.

2 Visitor Information

For information before you go, contact the Italian Government Tourist Board (www.italiantourism.com).

In the United States: 630 Fifth Ave., Suite 1565, New York, NY 10111 (© **212/245-4822;** fax 212/586-9249); 500 N. Michigan Ave., Suite 2240, Chicago, IL 60611 (© **312/644-0996;** fax 312/644-3019); and 12400 Wilshire Blvd., Suite 550, Los Angeles, CA 90025 (© **310/820-1898;** fax 310/820-6357).

In Canada: 175 Bloor St. E., South Tower, Suite 907, Toronto, ON, M4W 3R8 (© **416/925-4882;** fax 416/925-4799).

In the United Kingdom: 1 Princes St., London W1R 8AY (© **020/7408-1254;** fax 020/7493-6695).

You can also write directly (in English or Italian) to the provincial or local tourist boards of the areas you plan to visit. Provincial tourist boards (**Ente Provinciale per il Turismo**) operate in the principal towns of the provinces. Local tourist boards (**Azienda Autonoma di Soggiorno e Turismo**) operate in all places of tourist interest; you can get a list from the Italian Government Tourist Office.

If you are in Sicily and need to get information, call toll-free © **800-117700** (only within Italy). If you are calling from another country, dial © **06/874190 07.** This service is available daily from 8am to 11pm in five languages; it dispenses information concerning transportation, health assistance, events, museums, safety, hotels, and information points.

Online, check out the Italian Government Tourist Board's site, **www. italiantourism.com**, and the Italian State Tourism Board's site, **www.enit.it**.

3 Entry Requirements & Customs

ENTRY REQUIREMENTS

U.S., Canadian, U.K., Irish, Australian, and New Zealand citizens with a **valid passport** don't need a visa to enter Italy or Sicily if they don't expect to stay more than 90 days and don't expect to work there. If after entering Italy you want to stay more than 90 days, you can apply for a permit for an extra 90 days, which as a rule is granted immediately. Go to the nearest *questura* (police headquarters) or to your home country's consulate. If your passport is lost or stolen, head to your consulate as soon as possible for a replacement.

For information on how to get a passport, go to "Passports" in the "Fast Facts" section of this chapter (p. 57) —the websites listed provide downloadable passport applications as well as the current fees for processing passport applications. For an up-to-date country-by-country listing of passport requirements around the world, go to the Web page of the U.S. State Department at **http://travel.state.gov**.

CUSTOMS

WHAT YOU CAN BRING INTO ITALY OR SICILY Foreign visitors can bring along most items for personal use duty-free, including fishing tackle, a pair of skis, two tennis racquets, a baby carriage, two hand cameras with 10 rolls of film, and 400 cigarettes or a quantity of cigars or pipe tobacco not exceeding 500 grams (l.1 lb.). There are strict limits on importing alcoholic beverages: 2 liters of still table wine or 1 liter of alcohol over 22% volume. However, for alcohol bought tax-paid, limits are much more liberal than in other countries of the European Union.

WHAT YOU CAN TAKE HOME FROM ITALY OR SICILY Rules governing what you can bring back duty-free vary from country to country and are subject to change, but they're generally posted on the Web.

Returning U.S. citizens who have been away for 48 hours or more are allowed to bring back, once every 30 days, $800 worth of merchandise duty-free. You'll be charged a flat rate of duty on the next $1,000 worth of purchases. On mailed gifts, the duty-free limit is $200. Be sure to have your receipts or purchases handy to expedite the declaration process. *Note:* If you owe duty, you are required to pay on your arrival in the United States, either by cash, personal check, government or traveler's check, or money order, and in some locations, a Visa or MasterCard.

To avoid having to pay duty on foreign-made personal items you owned before you left on your trip, bring along a bill of sale, insurance policy, jeweler's appraisal, or receipts of purchase. Or you can register items that can be readily identified by a permanently affixed

---

Tips Passport Savvy

Allow plenty of time before your trip to apply for a passport; processing normally takes 3 weeks but can take longer during busy periods (especially spring). And keep in mind that if you need a passport in a hurry, you'll pay a higher processing fee. When traveling, safeguard your passport in an inconspicuous, inaccessible place like a money belt and keep a copy of the critical pages with your passport number in a separate place. If you lose your passport, visit the nearest consulate or embassy of your native country as soon as possible for a replacement.

serial number or marking—think laptop computers, cameras, and CD players—with Customs before you leave. Take the items to the nearest Customs office or register them with Customs at the airport from which you're departing. You'll receive, at no cost, a Certificate of Registration, which allows duty-free entry for the life of the item.

With some exceptions, you cannot bring fresh fruits and vegetables into the United States. For specifics on what you can bring back, download the invaluable free pamphlet *Know Before You Go* online at **www.cbp.gov**. Or call **U.S. Customs & Border Protection (CBP)** at © 877/287-8667 to request the pamphlet.

For a clear summary of Canadian rules, write for the booklet *I Declare,* issued by the **Canada Border Services Agency** (© **800/461-9999** in Canada, or 204/983-3500; www.cbsa-asfc.gc.ca). Canada allows its citizens a C$750 exemption. You're allowed to bring back duty-free one carton of cigarettes, 1 can of tobacco, 40 imperial ounces of liquor, and 50 cigars. In addition, you're allowed to mail gifts to Canada valued at less than C$60 a day, provided they're unsolicited and don't contain alcohol or tobacco (write on the package "Unsolicited gift, under $60 value"). All valuables should be declared on the Y-38 form before departure from Canada, including serial numbers of valuables you already own, such as expensive foreign cameras. *Note:* The C$750 exemption can only be used once a year and only after an absence of 7 days.

If you're a citizen of the United Kingdom, contact **HM Customs & Excise** at © **0845/010-9000** (from outside the U.K., 020/8929-0152), or go to www.hmce.gov.uk. Citizens of the U.K. who are returning from a European Union (E.U.) country will go through a separate Customs Exit especially for E.U. travelers. In essence, there is no limit on what you can bring back from an E.U. country, as long as the items are for personal use (this includes gifts), and you have already paid the necessary duty and tax. However, Customs law sets out guidance levels. If you bring in more than these levels, you may be asked to prove that the goods are for your own use. Guidance levels on goods bought in the E.U. for your own use are 3,200 cigarettes, 200 cigars, 400 cigarillos, 3 kilograms of smoking tobacco, 10 liters of spirits, 90 liters of wine, 20 liters of fortified wine (such as port or sherry), and 110 liters of beer.

Citizens of **Ireland** should contact the **Revenue Commissioner** at © **01/679-27-77**, or go to www.revenue.ie.

The duty-free allowance in **Australia** is A$400 or, for those under 18, A$200. Citizens can bring in 250 cigarettes or 250 grams of loose tobacco, and 1,125 milliliters of alcohol. If you're returning with valuables you already own, such as foreign-made cameras, you should file form B263. A helpful brochure available from Australian consulates or Customs offices is *Know Before You Go.* For information, call the **Australian Customs Service** at © **1300/363-263,** or go to www.customs.gov.au.

The duty-free allowance for **New Zealand** is NZ$700. Citizens over 17 can bring in 200 cigarettes, 50 cigars, or 250 grams of tobacco (or a mixture of all three if their combined weight doesn't exceed 250g); plus 4.5 liters of wine and beer, or 1.125 liters of liquor. Fill out a certificate of export, listing the valuables you are taking out of the country; that way, you can bring them back without paying duty. Most questions are answered in a free pamphlet available at New Zealand consulates and Customs offices: *New Zealand Customs Guide for Travellers, Notice no. 4.* For information, contact **New Zealand Customs** at © **04/473-6099** or 0800/428-786, or go to www.customs.govt.nz.

4 Money

CURRENCY

The **euro,** the new single European currency, became the official currency of Italy and 11 other participating countries on January 1, 1999.

However, the euro didn't go into general circulation until early 2002. The old currency, the Italian lira, disappeared into history on March 1, 2002, replaced by the euro, whose official abbreviation is "EUR." The symbol of the euro is a stylized *E: €.* Exchange rates of participating countries are locked into a common currency fluctuating against the dollar.

For more details on the euro, check out **www.europa.eu.int/euro**.

It's best to exchange currency or traveler's checks at a bank, and not at an exchange bureau, hotel, or shop. Currency and traveler's checks (for which you'll receive a better rate than cash) can be exchanged at all principal airports and at some travel agencies, such as American Express and Thomas Cook. Note the rates and ask about commission fees; it can sometimes pay to shop around.

Exchange rates are always more favorable at the point of arrival. Nevertheless, it's often helpful to exchange at least some money before leaving home (standing in line at the exchange bureau of the Palermo airport isn't fun after a long flight). You can exchange money at your local American Express or Thomas Cook office or your bank. If you're far away from a bank with currency-exchange services, American Express offers traveler's checks and foreign currency, though with a $15 order fee and additional shipping costs, at www.americanexpress.com or ℂ **800/807-6233.**

ATMS

ATMs are prevalent in all Sicilian cities and even in smaller towns. ATMs are linked to a national network that most likely includes your bank at home. The **Cirrus** (ℂ **800/ 424-7787;** www.mastercard.com) and **PLUS** (ℂ **800/843-7587;** www.visa. com) networks span the globe; look at the back of your bank card to see which network you're on, and then call or check online for ATM locations at your destination. Or just search out any machine with your network's symbol emblazoned on it.

Important note: Make sure your personal identification number (PIN) will work in Sicily. You'll need a 4-digit code (a 6-digit code won't work), so if you have a 6-digit code you'll have to go into your bank and get a new PIN for the trip. If you're unsure about this, contact Cirrus or PLUS. Be sure to also check the daily withdrawal limit before you depart.

(Tips   Dear Visa: I'm Off to Palermo!

Some credit card companies recommend that you notify them of any impending trip abroad so that they don't become suspicious when the card is used numerous times in a foreign destination and block your charges. Even if you don't call your credit card company in advance, you can always call the card's toll-free emergency number if a charge is refused—a good reason to carry the phone number with you. But perhaps the most important lesson here is to carry more than one card with you on your trip; a card might not work for any number of reasons, so having a backup is the smart way to go.

Foreign Currencies vs. the U.S. Dollar

Conversion ratios between the U.S. dollar and other currencies fluctuate, and these differences could affect the relative cost of your holiday. The figures reflected in the chart below are valid at press time, but might not be accurate by the time of your departure. This chart is useful for conversions of small amounts of money, but if you're planning on major transactions, check for more updated rates prior to making any serious commitments.

The U.S. Dollar & the Euro   At press time, 1 U.S. dollar is worth approximately .83€. (Inversely stated, that means 1€ equals approximately $1.20.)

The British Pound, the U.S. Dollar & the Euro   At press time, 1 pound equals approximately $1.85 or 1.50€.

The Canadian Dollar, the U.S. Dollar & the Euro   At press time, 1 Canadian dollar equals approximately 76¢ or .61€.

Euro	US$	UK£	Canadian$	Euro	US$	UK£	Canadian$
1.00	1.20	0.67	1.63	75	90.00	50.25	122.25
2.00	2.40	1.34	3.26	100	120.00	67.00	163.00
3.00	3.60	2.01	4.89	125	150.00	83.75	203.75
4.00	4.80	2.68	6.52	150	180.00	100.50	244.50
5.00	6.00	3.35	8.15	175	210.00	117.25	285.25
6.00	7.20	4.02	9.78	200	240.00	134.00	326.00
7.00	8.40	4.69	11.41	225	270.00	150.75	366.75
8.00	9.60	5.36	13.04	250	300.00	167.50	407.50
9.00	10.80	6.03	14.67	275	330.00	184.25	448.25
10.00	12.00	6.70	16.30	300	360.00	201.00	489.00
15.00	18.00	10.05	24.45	350	420.00	234.50	570.50
20.00	24.00	13.40	32.60	400	480.00	268.00	652.00
25.00	30.00	16.75	40.75	500	600.00	335.00	815.00
50.00	60.00	33.50	81.50	1000	1200.00	670.00	1630.00

TRAVELER'S CHECKS

These days, traveler's checks are less necessary because most Sicilian cities and towns have 24-hour ATMs, allowing you to withdraw small amounts of cash as needed. But if you prefer the security of the tried and true, you might want to stick with traveler's checks—provided that you don't mind showing an ID every time you want to cash a check.

You can get traveler's checks at almost any bank. **American Express** offers denominations of $20, $50, $100, $500, and (for cardholders only) $1,000. You'll pay a service charge ranging from 1% to 4%. You can also get American Express traveler's checks over the phone by calling ⓒ **800/721-9768;** Amex gold and platinum cardholders who use this number are exempt from the 1% fee.

Visa offers traveler's checks at Citibank locations nationwide, as well as at several other banks. The service charge ranges between 1.5% and 2%; checks come in denominations of $20, $50, $100, $500, and $1,000. Call

© **800/732-1322** for information. AAA members can obtain Visa checks without a fee at most AAA offices or by calling © **866/339-3378.**

MasterCard also offers traveler's checks. Call © **800/223-9920** for a location near you.

CREDIT CARDS

Credit cards are a safe way to carry money: They also provide a convenient record of all your expenses, and they generally offer relatively good exchange rates. You can also withdraw cash advances from your credit cards at banks or ATMs, provided you know your PIN. If you've forgotten yours, or didn't even know you had one, call the number on the back of your credit card and ask the bank to send it to you. It usually takes 5 to 7 business days, though some banks will provide the number over the phone if you tell them your mother's maiden name or some other personal information. Keep in mind that when you use your credit card abroad, most banks assess a 2% fee above the 1% fee charged by Visa or MasterCard or American Express for currency conversion on credit charges. But credit cards still may be the smart way to go when you factor in things like exorbitant ATM fees and higher traveler's check exchange rates and service fees.

5 When to Go

April to June and **late September to October** are the best months for traveling in Sicily—temperatures are usually mild and crowds aren't quite so intense. Starting in mid-June, the summer rush really picks up, and from **July to mid-September** the country teems with visitors. **August** is the worst month: Not only does it get uncomfortably hot, muggy, and crowded, but the entire island goes on vacation at least from August 15 to 31—and many Sicilians take off the entire month. Numerous hotels, restaurants, and shops are closed (except at the spas, beaches, and islands, where you'll find 70% of the vacationing Sicilians). From **late October to Easter,** most attractions go on reduced winter hours or are closed for renovation. Many hotels and restaurants take a month or two off between **November and February,** when spa and beach destinations become padlocked ghost towns, and it can get much colder than you'd expect. The almond trees blossom in February, especially along the southern coast, and Taormina and Mount Etna are celebrated for their riot of spring flowers. Easter is a time of major celebration on the island, with many traditional, religion-oriented festivals. **High season** on most airline routes to Rome/Palermo usually stretches from June to the beginning of September. This is the most expensive and most crowded time to travel. **Shoulder season** is from April to May, early September to October, and December 15 to 24. **Low season** is from November 1 to December 14 and December 25 to March 31.

WEATHER

It can be very hot in summery Sicily, especially inland. The high temperatures begin in May, often lasting until sometime in October. Winters are mild.

For the most part, it's drier in Sicily than in North America, so high temperatures don't seem as bad because the humidity is lower. On the islands, temperatures can stay in the 90s Fahrenheit (30s Celsius) for days, but nights are most often comfortably cooler.

> **Tips Quick ID**
>
> Tie a colorful ribbon or piece of yarn around your luggage handle, or slap a distinctive sticker on the side of your bag. This makes it less likely that someone will mistakenly appropriate it. And if your luggage gets lost, it will be easier to find.

Average Temperature & Rainfall in Palermo & Syracuse

	Jan	Feb	Mar	Apr	May	Jun	Jul	Aug	Sept	Oct	Nov	Dec
PALERMO												
Temp.(°F)	54	55	56	60	66	72	78	79	75	69	62	56
Temp.(°C)	12	13	13	16	19	22	26	26	24	21	17	13
Rainfall/in.	2.80	2.60	2.30	1.70	1.00	.50	.20	.50	1.60	3.90	3.70	3.20
SYRACUSE (SIRACUSA)												
Temp.(°F)	54	54	55	59	60	72	78	79	75	69	58	56
Temp.(°C)	12	12	13	15	16	22	26	26	24	21	14	13
Rainfall/in.	2.40	1.70	1.30	.70	.50	1.00	.10	.20	1.00	3.10	2.00	2.80

HOLIDAYS

Offices and shops in Sicily are closed on the following **national holidays:** January 1 (New Year's Day), Easter Monday, April 25 (Liberation Day), May 1 (Labor Day), July 15 (Santa Rosalia), August 15 (Assumption of the Virgin), November 1 (All Saints' Day), December 8 (Feast of the Immaculate Conception), December 25 (Christmas Day), and December 26 (Santo Stefano).

SICILY CALENDAR OF EVENTS

For major events for which tickets should be procured well before you arrive, check with **Keith Prowse** (© 800/223-6108; www.keith prowse.com).

January

Epiphania (Epiphany), Piana degli Albanesi. Located 29km (18 miles) from Palermo in one of the Albanian colonies founded at the end of the 15th century, the celebration of Epiphany is an ostentatious affair. A joyous procession of residents in traditional Albanian costumes parades through the streets. Call © **091-8571785** or go to www. pianalbanesi.it. January 6.

Carnevale, Acireale. Carnevale is celebrated all over Sicily, but this is the most beautiful event. In a town north of Catania, it's marked by a colorful parade of masked participants and giant floats. Lemons and oranges from nearby citrus fields are used in abundance, creating an aromatic atmosphere. It's a weeklong party of fun and revelry. Contact the Acireale tourist office at © **095-891999.** Third week in January.

February

Almond Blossom Festival, Agrigento. Literally thousands of almond trees are in bloom around the Valley of the Temples at this festival heralding the arrival of the first fruits of spring. In Phrygian myths, the almond tree was viewed as the "father of the world." The event is marked with music, beauty pageants, parades, and puppet shows. All kinds of sweets made with almonds are sold. Contact the Agrigento tourist office at © **0922-21899.** First half of February.

Feast of Saint Agata, Catania. Of pagan origin, this is a beautiful all-night religious celebration of the martyred patron saint of the city. A procession of candle-bearers called *candelore* parades through the city, accompanied by the mayor and his entourage in gilded horse-drawn carriages. High church officials add clouds of incense and all the requisite pomp and circumstance. There's also street theater and fireworks. Sweets based on centuries-old recipes from nunneries are sold. All-around mayhem prevails. Contact the Catania tourist office at © 095-730625. February 13 to 15.

April

The Dance of the Devils, Prizzi. Unique in Italy, a grotesque dance of the devils (*Il Ballo dei Diavoli*) takes place on Easter in this medieval town a 2-hour drive south of Palermo, deep in the Sicilian interior. The festival represents the age-old struggle between good and evil. Figures dressed as red devils, their faces covered with grotesque masks, parade through the streets, searching for souls to devour. Death is seen dressed in yellow and carrying a crossbow. All ends well when "angels" appear later to subdue the devils. Call © 091-8366510 or go to www.commune.prizzi.pa.it. Easter.

Holy Week Observances, island-wide. Processions and age-old ceremonies—some from pagan days, some from the Middle Ages—are staged in every city and town in Sicily. No matter where you are, you're likely to come across observances of this annual event. Particularly colorful and moving are the observances in Palermo and Catania along the coast. Trapani's procession of the *Misteri* is the island's most famous event staged during Holy Week. But the finest observance, in our view, is in the inland city of Caltagirone, a 2-hour drive southwest of Catania. Events are staged on such days as Holy Tuesday, Good Friday, and, of course, Easter Sunday itself. Local tourist offices can supply details. Week leading up to Easter.

May

Infiorata, Noto. The residents of this little southeastern town prepare a magnificent carpet of flowers along Via Nicolaci, in the historic core. Themes are taken from religion and mythology. The festival features crafts shows, performances of sacred music, and tours of religious sites, followed by dances and parades of flower-bedecked antique carriages. Check with the tourist office at © 0931-573779 for exact dates. Beginning of May.

June

Festa del Muzzini, Messina. *Muzzini* are ancient vases draped in silk that are carried in parades. This observance is actually a pagan rite to honor Demeter, the goddess of earth and fertility. It's rumored that many young women trying to have a child find themselves impregnated on the night of this celebration. Contact the Messina tourist office at © 090-674236. June 24.

July

The Feast of Santa Rosalia, Palermo. Holding a special place in the hearts of many residents, this festival is the most famous and popular in Sicily. During the week of the festival, Palermo becomes an open-air theater. The highlight is a 15m (50-ft.) high float known as the *carro,* which is paraded through the streets along with a statue of Santa Rosalia on a huge cart drawn by horses. Torchlight processions are conducted to the saint's shrine on Monte Pellegrino, where the saint is said to have appeared in a vision to a hunter. Bands, dancers, drums, religious choruses, , theatrical performances, sts (featuring everything from delectable tiny snails to fantastic gelato) characterize the event. Contact the Palermo tourist office at ℭ **091-583847.** July 10 to 15.

August

Ferragosto (Assumption Day). This national holiday virtually shuts down the island of Sicily, marking the event where Mary was said to have been "taken up and assumed into heaven." This event always includes a feast of pagan origin, street parades, and fairs with young girls dressed in virginal white, sitting on oxen carts, their virtue menacingly protected by spikes. They toss fruit at the spectators. This observance is at its most colorful in Palermo; you can call its local tourist office at ℭ **091-583847.** Mid-August.

Palio dei Normanni, Piazza Armerina. Sicily's Norman past is observed during this historic celebration in which locals dress in ancient costumes for parades. Even jousting takes place among knights in period costumes, looking like refugees from the pages of *Ivanhoe.* They fight against a puppet representing the dreaded Saracens. Contact the Piazza Armerina tourist office at ℭ **0935-680201.** Mid-August.

September

International Couscous Festival, San Vito Lo Capo. This annual event outside Trapani means 3 days of dancing to live music and a bounty of local foods. The couscous competition draws some of the best cooks in the world, including those from North Africa where the dish originated. You'll gain 10 pounds if you participate in all of the feasting. Contact the Trapani tourist office at ℭ **0923-27077.** Mid-September.

October

Maritime Festival, Porticello Santa Flavia. This festival takes place every year at a little fishing port to the east of Palermo. Sporting competitions include boat races among the fishermen. There's also a village festival dedicated to fish, a mainstay of the port's economy, especially the harvesting of anchovies and sardines. At night, there's a parade of boats illuminated with flaming torches, and an image of Maria is hauled to the water to be blessed. Naturally, stalls sell all the fish dishes you can consume. Contact the Palermo tourist office at ℭ **091-583847.** First Sunday in October.

November

Tutti Santi (All Saints' Day), island-wide. This ancient observance is celebrated all over Sicily as a national holiday including the "Day of the Dead." It's the Sicilian version of Halloween, in which the spirits of the dead are said to roam about. Originally more pagan in origin, it was tamed by the Catholic Church with the introduction of saints who are celebrated. Children are dressed in costumes for parades around the main squares of various towns. Pastry shops prepare a delectable confection, the ominously named "bones of the dead." Check with local tourist offices. November 1 and 2.

December

Christmas Fair, Syracuse. The major holiday fair of the south is conducted in this ancient city, which boasts the island's most colorful Christmas market. Many islanders drive for miles to purchase gifts here, including sweets, clothing, special embroidery, ornaments, and other items. It's conducted in the Epipoli section of Syracuse. Contact the Syracuse tourist office at ℭ **0931-67710.** From the second Saturday in December to December 21.

6 Travel Insurance

Since Sicily is far from home for most of us, and because a number of things could go wrong—lost luggage, trip cancellation, a medical emergency—consider the following types of insurance.

Check your existing insurance policies and credit card coverage before you buy travel insurance. You may already be covered for lost luggage, canceled tickets, or medical expenses.

The cost of travel insurance varies widely, depending on the cost and length of your trip, your age and health, and the type of trip you're taking.

TRIP-CANCELLATION INSURANCE Trip-cancellation insurance helps you get your money back if you have to back out of a trip, if you have to go home early, or if your travel supplier goes bankrupt. Allowed reasons for cancellation can range from sickness to natural disasters to the State Department declaring your destination unsafe for travel. In this unstable world, trip-cancellation insurance is a good buy if you're getting tickets well in advance—who knows what the state of the world, or of your airline, will be in 9 months? Insurance policy details vary, so read the fine print—and especially make sure that your airline is on the list of carriers covered in case of bankruptcy. A good resource is **"Travel Guard Alerts,"** a list of companies considered high-risk by Travel Guard International (see website below). Protect yourself further by paying for the insurance with a credit card—by law, consumers can get their money back on goods and services not received if they report the loss within 60 days after the charge is listed on their credit card statement.

Note: Many tour operators, particularly those offering trips to remote or high-risk areas, include insurance in the cost of the trip or can arrange insurance policies through a partnering provider, a convenient and often cost-effective way for the traveler to obtain insurance.

Make sure the tour company is a reputable one, however: Some experts suggest you avoid buying insurance from the tour or cruise company you're traveling with, saying it's better to buy from a "third party" insurer than to put all your money in one place.

For more information, contact one of the following recommended insurers: **Access America** (© 866/807-3982; www.accessamerica.com); **Travel Guard International** (© 800/826-4919; www.travelguard.com); **Travel Insured International** (© 800/243-3174; www.travelinsured.com); and **Travelex Insurance Services** (© 888/457-4602; www.travelexinsurance.com).

MEDICAL INSURANCE For travel overseas, most health plans (including Medicare and Medicaid) do not provide coverage, and the ones that do often require you to pay for services upfront and reimburse you only after you return home. Even if your plan does cover overseas treatment, most out-of-country hospitals make you pay your bills upfront, and send you a refund only after you've returned home and filed the necessary paperwork with your insurance company. As a safety net, you may want to buy travel medical insurance, particularly if you're traveling to a remote or high-risk area where emergency evacuation is a possible scenario.

If you require additional medical insurance, try **MEDEX Assistance** (© 410/453-6300; www.medexassist. com) or **Travel Assistance International** (© 800/821-2828; www.travel assistance.com; for general information on services, call the company's Worldwide Assistance Services, Inc., at © 800/777-8710).

LOST-LUGGAGE INSURANCE On international flights (including U.S. portions of international trips), baggage coverage is limited to approximately

$9.07 per pound, up to approximately $635 per checked bag. If you plan to check items more valuable than the standard liability, see if your valuables are covered by your homeowner's policy, get baggage insurance as part of your comprehensive travel-insurance package, or buy Travel Guard's "Bag-Trak" product. Don't buy insurance at the airport, as it's usually overpriced. Be sure to take any valuables or irreplaceable items with you in your carry-on luggage, as many valuables (including books, money, and electronics) aren't covered by airline policies.

If your luggage is lost, immediately file a lost-luggage claim at the airport, detailing the luggage contents. For most airlines, you must report delayed, damaged, or lost baggage within 4 hours of arrival. The airlines are required to deliver luggage, once found, directly to your house or destination for free.

7 Health & Safety

STAYING HEALTHY

In general, Sicily is viewed as a "safe" destination, although problems, of course, can and do occur anywhere. You don't need to get shots; most foodstuffs are safe; and the water in cities and towns is potable. If you're concerned, drink bottled water. It's easy to get a prescription filled in towns and cities, and nearly all places contain English-speaking doctors at hospitals with well-trained medical staffs. In other words, Sicily is part of the civilized world.

Before you go, contact the **International Association for Medical Assistance to Travelers (IAMAT)** (© 716/754-4883 or, in Canada, 416/652-0137; www.iamat.org) for tips on travel and health concerns in the countries you're visiting, and lists of local, English-speaking doctors. The United States **Centers for Disease Control and Prevention** (© 800/311-3435; www.cdc.gov) provides up-to-date information on health hazards by region or country and offers tips on food safety.

WHAT TO DO IF YOU GET SICK AWAY FROM HOME

If you suffer from a chronic illness, consult your doctor before your departure. For conditions like epilepsy, diabetes, or heart problems, wear a **MedicAlert identification tag** (© 888/633-4298; www.medicalert. org), which will immediately alert doctors to your condition and give them access to your records through MedicAlert's 24-hour hot line.

Pack **prescription medications** in your carry-on luggage, and carry prescription medications in their original containers, with pharmacy labels—otherwise they won't make it through airport security. Also bring along copies of your prescriptions in case you lose your pills or run out. Carry the generic name of prescription medicines, in case a local pharmacist is unfamiliar with the brand name. Don't forget an extra pair of contact lenses or prescription glasses.

In case of **emergency,** dial © 113 for the police, or © 112 for the *Carabinieri* (army police corps): They can call an ambulance or help you in many ways. If your situation is life-threatening, go to the *pronto soccorso* (emergency department) at the local hospital.

Many, but hardly all, doctors in Sicily speak English. If you get sick, consider asking your hotel concierge to recommend a local doctor—even his or her own. You can also try the emergency room at a local hospital. Many hospitals also have walk-in clinics for emergency cases that are not life-threatening; you may not get immediate attention, but you won't pay the high price of an emergency-room visit. In the chapters that follow,

Avoiding "Economy-Class Syndrome"

Deep vein thrombosis, or as it's known in the world of flying, "economy-class syndrome," is a blood clot that develops in a deep vein. It's a potentially deadly condition that can be caused by sitting in cramped conditions—such as an airplane cabin—for too long. During a flight (especially a long-haul flight), get up, walk around, and stretch your legs every 60 to 90 minutes to keep your blood flowing. Other preventative measures include frequent flexing of the legs while sitting, drinking lots of water, and avoiding alcohol and sleeping pills. If you have a history of deep vein thrombosis, heart disease, or another condition that puts you at high risk, some experts recommend wearing compression stockings or taking anticoagulants when you fly; always ask your physician about the best course for you. Symptoms of deep vein thrombosis include leg pain or swelling, or even shortness of breath.

we list hospitals and emergency numbers under "Fast Facts" in the sections on various cities.

Under the Italian national health-care system, you're eligible only for free *emergency* care. If you're admitted to a hospital as an in-patient, even from an accident and an emergency, you're required to pay (unless you're a resident of the European Economic Area). You're also required to pay for follow-up care.

If you do end up paying for health care, especially if you're admitted to a hospital for any reason, some health-insurance plans and HMOs will cover at least part of the out-of-country hospital visits and procedures. Be prepared to pay the bills upfront at the time of care, however. You'll get a refund after you've returned to your country and filed all the paperwork.

STAYING SAFE

Don't think you'll be at the mercy of the Mafia the moment you step foot in Sicily, as popular belief around the world suggests. The Mafia is virtually invisible.

You'll face more danger from petty thieves such as pickpockets than you will from the *Cosa Nostra. Scippatori,* or purse snatchers and pickpockets, are the curse of such cities as Palermo, Messina, and Catania.

Country towns, of course, are far safer. Avoid walking on dark streets in the old towns of Sicily at night. Even during the day, relatively deserted inner-city streets can put you at risk of robbery. Although many tourists are robbed, violence against visitors is rare.

Never leave valuables in a car, and never travel with your car unlocked. A U.S. State Department travel advisory warns that every car (whether parked, stopped at a traffic light, or even moving) can be a potential target for armed robbery. In these uncertain times, it is always prudent to check the U.S. State Department's travel advisories at http://travel.state.gov.

8 Specialized Travel Resources

TRAVELERS WITH DISABILITIES

Sicily is hardly in the vanguard of catering to travelers with disabilities. Only the most expensive first-class or deluxe hotels have facilities that accommodate persons with disabilities.

The narrow, cobblestone streets of Sicily's cities and villages, most of which date back to the Middle Ages, weren't built for people who get around in wheelchairs. Hysterical drivers and impossible parking don't help much either. Even if you're an Olympic athlete, getting across a street in the face of speeding traffic in Palermo is risky at any time.

We recommend that those with disabilities consider visiting Sicily on an organized tour specifically geared to provide assistance, which is vitally needed.

Many travel agencies offer customized tours and itineraries for travelers with disabilities. **Flying Wheels Travel** (② 507/451-5005; www.flying wheelstravel.com) offers escorted tours in minivans with lifts. **Access-Able Travel Source** (② 303/232-2979; www.access-able.com) offers extensive access information and advice for traveling around the world with disabilities. **Accessible Journeys** (② 800/846-4537 or 610/521-0339; www.disability travel.com) caters specifically to slow walkers and wheelchair travelers and their families and friends.

Organizations that offer assistance to disabled travelers include **MossRehab** (www.mossresourcenet.org), which provides a library of accessible-travel resources online; **SATH (Society for Accessible Travel & Hospitality)** (② 212/447-7284; www.sath.org; annual membership fees: $45 adults, $30 seniors and students), which offers a wealth of travel resources for all types of disabilities and informed recommendations on destinations, access guides, travel agents, tour operators, vehicle rentals, and companion services; and the **American Foundation for the Blind (AFB)** (② 800/232-5463; www.afb.org), a referral resource for the blind or visually impaired that includes information on traveling with Seeing Eye dogs.

For more information specifically targeted to travelers with disabilities, the community website **iCan** (www. icanonline.net/channels/travel/index. cfm) has destination guides and several regular columns on accessible travel. Also check out the quarterly magazine **Emerging Horizons** ($14.95 per year, $19.95 outside the U.S.; www. emerginghorizons.com); and **Open World Magazine,** published by SATH (see above; subscription: $13 per year, $21 outside the U.S.).

British travelers can contact the **Royal Association for Disability and Rehabilitation (RADAR)** (② 020/7250-3222; www.radar.org.uk), which publishes three holiday "fact packs" that provide information on holiday planning, insurance, finances, transportation, and specialized accommodations. Another good resource is **Holiday Care Service** (② 0845/124-9971; www.holidaycare.org.uk), a national charity that advises on accessible accommodations for the elderly and persons with disabilities; annual membership is £37 ($61).

GAY & LESBIAN TRAVELERS

Even though Italy has had rather liberal legislation regarding homosexuality since 1861, Sicily remains one of the major bastions of homophobia in Europe. Some of the islanders express anti-gay attitudes that might belong more appropriately to the Middle Ages. Open displays of affection between same-sex couples meets with obvious disapproval by intolerant islanders.

Don't be misled: Sicilian men are often very affectionate, linking arms with one another and kissing on the cheeks to say hello or bid goodbye. This is how straight men behave, and such affection is not to be construed as overtly sexual.

There are few gay businesses in Sicily. If you're gay and still want to go, your best bet is the more sophisticated resort of Taormina, following in the footsteps of past visitors like Tennessee Williams and his longtime companion, Frank Merlo.

If you really want a gay holiday in Italy, Sicily may not be for you.

Consider *la dolce vita* as lived on the Isle of Capri (see *Frommer's Italy*, Wiley Publishing, Inc.).

If you have your heart set on Sicily, however, the following resources may be helpful.

The **International Gay and Lesbian Travel Association (IGLTA)** (© 800/448-8550 or 954/776-2626; www.iglta.org) is the trade association for the gay and lesbian travel industry, and offers an online directory of gay- and lesbian-friendly travel businesses; go to its website and click on "Members."

Many agencies offer tours and travel itineraries specifically for gay and lesbian travelers. **Above and Beyond Tours** (© 800/397-2681; www.abovebeyondtours.com) is the exclusive gay and lesbian tour operator for United Airlines. **Now, Voyager** (© 800/255-6951; www.nowvoyager. com) is a well-known San Francisco–based gay-owned and -operated travel service. **Olivia Cruises & Resorts** (© 800/631-6277; www.olivia.com) charters entire resorts and ships for exclusive lesbian vacations and offers smaller group experiences for both gay and lesbian travelers.

The following travel guides are available at most travel bookstores and gay and lesbian bookstores, or you can order them from the bookstore **Giovanni's Room,** 1145 Pine St., Philadelphia, PA 19107 (© 215/923-2960; www.giovannisroom.com): *Frommer's Gay & Lesbian Europe* (www.frommers.com), an excellent travel resource; *Out and About* (© 800/929-2268; www.outand about.com), which offers guidebooks and a newsletter ($20/yr; 10 issues) packed with solid information on the global gay and lesbian scene; *Spartacus International Gay Guide* (Bruno Gmünder Verlag; www.spartacus world.com/gayguide) and *Odysseus: The International Gay Travel Planner* (Odysseus Enterprises Ltd.), both

good, annual English-language guidebooks focused on gay men; the *Damron* guides (www.damron.com), with separate, annual books for gay men and lesbians; and *Gay Travel A to Z: The World of Gay & Lesbian Travel Options at Your Fingertips,* by Marianne Ferrari (Ferrari International; Box 35575, Phoenix, AZ 85069), a very good gay and lesbian guidebook series.

SENIOR TRAVEL

Mention the fact that you're a senior when you first make your travel reservations; all major airlines and many Sicilian hotels offer discounts for seniors.

Members of **AARP** (formerly known as the American Association of Retired Persons), 601 E St. NW, Washington, DC 20049 (© 888/687-2277; www.aarp.org), get discounts on hotels, airfares, and car rentals. AARP offers members a wide range of benefits, including *AARP: The Magazine* and a monthly newsletter. Anyone over 50 can join.

Many reliable organizations target the 50-plus market. **Elderhostel** (© 877/426-8056; www.elderhostel. org) arranges study programs for those 55 and over (and a spouse or companion of any age) in more than 80 countries around the world, including Italy. Most courses last 2 to 4 weeks abroad, and many include airfare, accommodations in university dormitories or modest inns, meals, and tuition. **ElderTreks** (© 800/741-7956; www. eldertreks.com) offers small-group tours to off-the-beaten-path or adventure-travel locations, restricted to travelers 50 and older.

Recommended publications offering travel resources and discounts for seniors include: the quarterly magazine *Travel 50 & Beyond* (www.travel 50andbeyond.com); *Travel Unlimited: Uncommon Adventures for the Mature Traveler* (Avalon); *101 Tips for Mature Travelers,* available from

Traveling with Minors

It's always wise to have plenty of documentation when traveling with kids in today's world. To prevent international child abduction, E.U. governments have initiated specific procedures at entry and exit points. These often (but not always) include requiring documentary evidence of your relationship, as well as permission for the child's travel from the parent or guardian not present. Every child must have his or her own passport. To obtain a passport, the child *must* be present, in person, at the issuing center. Both parents must be present as well; if not, then a notarized statement from the absent parent is required. Parents or guardians can get questions answered by calling the **National Passport Information Center** (© 877/487-2778), Monday through Friday between 8am and 8pm.

Grand Circle Travel (© **800/221-2610** or 617/350-7500; www.gct.com); and *Unbelievably Good Deals and Great Adventures That You Absolutely Can't Get Unless You're Over 50* (McGraw-Hill), by Joann Rattner Heilman.

FAMILY TRAVEL

Throughout this guide, look for our kid-friendly icons. Sicilians may love *bambini*, but don't offer a lot of special amenities for them. For example, a kids' menu in a restaurant is a rarity. You can, however, request a half portion *(mezza porzione)*, and most waiters will oblige. Most Sicilian hoteliers will let children 12 and under stay for free in a room with a parent. Sometimes this requires a little negotiation at the reception desk.

At attractions, inquire if a kids' discount is available; Italians call it *sconto bambino*. European Community youths under 18 get a big break: They're admitted free to all state-run museums.

Babysitting services are available through most hotel desks or by going to the local tourist office in the town where you're staying. Many hotels have children's game rooms and playgrounds.

Recommended family travel websites include **Family Travel Forum** (www.familytravelforum.com), a comprehensive site that offers customized

trip planning; **Family Travel Network** (www.familytravelnetwork.com), an award-winning site that offers travel features, deals, and tips; **Traveling Internationally with Your Kids** (www.travelwithyourkids.com), a comprehensive site offering sound advice for international travel with children; and **Family Travel Files** (www.thefamilytravelfiles.com), which offers an online magazine and a directory of off-the-beaten-path tours and tour operators for families.

WOMEN TRAVELERS

Women traveling alone in macho Sicily will want to exercise caution and be wary of pickpockets and purse snatchers.

Women travelers may also want to check out the award-winning website **Journeywoman** (www.journeywoman.com), a "real life" women's travel information network where you can sign up for a free e-mail newsletter and get advice on everything from etiquette to dress to safety. The guide *Safety and Security for Women Who Travel*, by Sheila Swan and Peter Laufer (Travelers' Tales, Inc.), also offers commonsense tips on safe travel.

STUDENT TRAVEL

If you're planning to travel outside the U.S., you'd be wise to arm yourself with an **International Student Identity Card (ISIC)**, which offers substantial savings on rail passes, plane tickets, and entrance fees. It also provides you with basic health and life insurance and a 24-hour help line. The card is available for $22 from **STA Travel** (℗ **800/781-4040** in North America; www.sta.com or www.statravel.com), the biggest student travel agency in the world. If you're no longer a student but are still under 26, you can get an **International Youth Travel Card (IYTC)** for the same price from the same people, which entitles you to some discounts (but not on museum admissions).

(**Note:** In 2002, STA Travel bought competitors **Council Travel** and **USIT Campus** after they went bankrupt. Some offices still operate under the Council name, but they're owned by STA.) **Travel CUTS** (℗ **800/667-2887** or 416/614-2887; www.travel cuts.com) offers similar services for both Canadians and U.S. residents. Irish students may prefer to turn to **USIT** (℗ **01/602-1600;** www.usit now.ie), an Ireland-based specialist in student, youth, and independent travel.

9 Planning Your Trip Online

SURFING FOR AIRFARES

The "big three" online travel agencies, **Expedia.com, Travelocity,** and **Orbitz** sell most of the air tickets bought on the Internet. (Canadian travelers should try expedia.ca and Travelocity.ca; U.K. residents can go for expedia.co.uk and opodo.co.uk.) Each has different business deals with the airlines and may offer different fares on the same flights, so it's wise to shop around. Expedia and Travelocity will also send you **e-mail notification** when a cheap fare becomes available to your favorite destination. Of the smaller travel agency websites, **SideStep** (www.sidestep.com) has gotten the best reviews from Frommer's authors. It's a browser add-on that purports to "search 140 sites at once," but in reality only beats competitors' fares as often as other sites do.

Also remember to check **airline websites,** especially those for low-fare carriers, whose fares are often misreported or simply missing from travel agency websites. Even with major airlines, you can often shave a few bucks from a fare by booking directly through the airline and avoiding a travel agency's transaction fee. But you'll get these discounts only by **booking online:** Most airlines now offer online-only fares that even their phone agents know nothing about.

For the websites of airlines that fly to and from your destination, go to "Getting There," on p. 36.

Great **last-minute deals** are available through free weekly e-mail services provided directly by the airlines. Most of these are announced on Tuesday or Wednesday and must be purchased online. Most are only valid for travel that weekend, but some can be booked weeks or months in advance. Sign up for weekly e-mail alerts at airline websites or check mega-sites that compile comprehensive lists of last-minute specials, such as **Smarter Living** (www.smarterliving.com). For last-minute trips, **lastminute.com** in Europe often has better air-and-hotel package deals than the major-label sites. A website listing numerous bargain sites and airlines around the world is **www.itravelnet.com**.

If you're willing to give up some control over your flight details, use what is called an **opaque fare service** like **Priceline** (www.priceline.com; www.priceline.co.uk for Europeans) or its smaller competitor **Hotwire** (www.hotwire.com). Both offer rock-bottom prices in exchange for travel on a "mystery airline" at a mysterious time of day, often with a mysterious change of planes en route. The mystery airlines are all major, well-known carriers. The airlines' routing computers have gotten a lot better than they used to be, but your chances of getting a 6am or 11pm flight are pretty high. Hotwire tells you flight prices before you buy; Priceline usually has better deals than Hotwire, but you have to play its "name our price" game. If you're new at this, the helpful folks at **BiddingForTravel** (www.biddingfortravel.com) do a good job of demystifying Priceline's prices and strategies. Priceline and Hotwire are great for flights between the U.S. and Europe. *Note:* In 2004, Priceline added non-opaque service to its roster. You now have the option to pick exact flights, times, and airlines from a list of offers—or opt to bid on opaque fares as before.

For much more about airfares and savvy air-travel tips and advice, pick up a copy of *Frommer's Fly Safe, Fly Smart* (Wiley Publishing, Inc.).

SURFING FOR HOTELS

Shopping online for hotels is generally done one of two ways: by booking through the hotel's own website or through an independent booking agency (or a fare-service agency like Priceline; see below). These Internet hotel agencies have multiplied in mind-boggling numbers of late, competing for the business of millions of consumers surfing for accommodations around the world. This competitiveness can be a boon to consumers who have the patience and time to shop and compare the websites for good deals—but shop they must, for prices can vary considerably from site to site. And keep in mind that hotels at the top of a site's listing may be there for no other reason than that they paid money to get the placement.

Of the "big three" sites, **Expedia.com** offers a long list of special deals and "virtual tours" of available rooms so you can see what you're paying for (a feature that helps counter the claims that the best rooms are often held back from bargain booking

websites). **Travelocity** posts unvarnished customer reviews and ranks its properties according to the AAA rating system. Also reliable are **Hotels.com** and **Quikbook.com.** An excellent free program, **TravelAxe** (www.travelaxe.net), can help you search multiple hotel sites at once, even ones you may never have heard of—and conveniently lists the total price of the room, including taxes and service charges. Another booking site, **Travelweb** (www.travelweb.com), is partly owned by the hotels it represents (including the Hilton, Hyatt, and Starwood chains) and is therefore plugged directly into the hotels' reservations systems—unlike independent online agencies, which have to fax or e-mail reservation requests to the hotel, a good portion of which get misplaced in the shuffle. More than once, travelers have arrived at a hotel only to be told that they have no reservation. To be fair, many of the major sites are undergoing improvements in service and ease of use, and Expedia will soon be able to plug directly into the reservations systems of many hotel chains—none of which can be bad news for consumers. In the meantime, it's a good idea to **get a confirmation number** and **make a printout** of any online booking transaction.

In the opaque website category, **Priceline** and **Hotwire** are even better for hotels than for airfares; with both, you're allowed to pick the neighborhood and quality level of your hotel before offering up your money. Priceline's hotel product even covers Europe, though it's much better at getting five-star lodging for three-star prices than at finding anything at the bottom of the scale. On the downside, many hotels stick Priceline guests in their least desirable rooms. Be sure to go to the BiddingForTravel website (see above) before bidding on a hotel room on Priceline; it features a fairly up-to-date list of hotels that Priceline uses in major cities. For both Priceline

Frommers.com: The Complete Travel Resource

For an excellent travel-planning resource, we highly recommend **Frommers.com** (www.frommers.com), voted Best Travel Site by *PC Magazine*. We're a little biased, of course, but we guarantee that you'll find the travel tips, reviews, monthly vacation giveaways, bookstore, and online-booking capabilities thoroughly indispensable. Among the special features are our popular **Destinations** section, where you'll get expert travel tips, hotel and dining recommendations, and advice on the sights to see for more than 3,500 destinations around the globe; the **Frommers.com Newsletter,** with the latest deals, travel trends, and money-saving secrets; our **Community** area featuring **Message Boards,** where Frommer's readers post queries and share advice (sometimes even our authors show up to answer questions); and our **Photo Center,** where you can post and share vacation shots. When your research is done, the **Online Reservations System** (www. frommers.com/book_a_trip) takes you to Frommer's preferred online partners for booking your vacation at affordable prices.

and Hotwire, you pay upfront, and the fee is nonrefundable. *Note:* Some hotels do not provide loyalty program credits or points or other frequent-stay amenities when you book a room through opaque online services.

SURFING FOR RENTAL CARS

For booking rental cars online, the best deals are usually found at rental-car company websites, although all the major online travel agencies also offer rental-car reservations services. Priceline and Hotwire work well for rental cars, too; the only "mystery" is which major rental company you get, and for most travelers the difference between Hertz, Avis, and Budget is negligible.

10 The 21st-Century Traveler

INTERNET ACCESS AWAY FROM HOME

Travelers have any number of ways to check their e-mail and access the Internet on the road. Of course, using your own laptop—or even a PDA (personal digital assistant) or electronic organizer with a modem—gives you the most flexibility. But if you don't have a computer, you can still access your e-mail and even your office computer from cybercafes.

WITHOUT YOUR OWN COMPUTER

It's hard nowadays to find a city that *doesn't* have a few cybercafes. Although there's no definitive directory for cybercafes—these are independent businesses, after all—two places to start looking are **www.cybercaptive. com** and **www.cybercafe.com.** See "Fast Facts" under various cities in later chapters for listings of cybercafes.

Aside from formal cybercafes, most **youth hostels** nowadays have at least one computer with Internet access. And most **public libraries** across the world offer Internet access free or for a small charge. Avoid **hotel business centers,** unless you're willing to pay exorbitant rates.

Most major airports now have **Internet kiosks** scattered throughout their gates. These kiosks, which you'll also see in shopping malls, hotel lobbies, and tourist offices around the world, give you basic Web access for a per-minute fee that's usually higher than cybercafe prices. The kiosks' clunkiness and high prices mean they should be avoided whenever possible.

To retrieve your e-mail, ask your **Internet Service Provider (ISP)** if it has a Web-based interface tied to your existing e-mail account. If your ISP doesn't have such an interface, you can use a free service such as **mail2web** (www.mail2web.com) to view and reply to your home e-mail. For more flexibility, you may want to open a free, Web-based e-mail account with **Yahoo! Mail** (http://mail.yahoo.com). (Microsoft's Hotmail is another popular option, but Hotmail has severe spam problems.) Your home ISP may be able to forward your e-mail to the Web-based account automatically.

If you need to access files on your office computer, look into a service called **GoToMyPC** (www.gotomypc. com). The service provides a Web-based interface for you to access and manipulate a distant PC from anywhere—even a cybercafe—provided your "target" PC is on and has an always-on connection to the Internet (such as with a cable modem). The service offers top-quality security, but if you're worried about hackers, use your own laptop rather than a cybercafe to access the GoToMyPC system.

WITH YOUR OWN COMPUTER

Wi-fi (wireless fidelity) is the buzzword in computer access, and more and more hotels, cafes, and retailers are signing on as wireless "hotspots" from which you can get high-speed connection without cable wires, networking hardware, or a phone line (see below). You can get Wi-fi connection in one of several ways. Many laptops sold in the last year have built-in Wi-fi capability (an 802.11b wireless Ethernet connection). Mac owners have their own networking technology, Apple AirPort. For those with older computers, an 802.11b/**Wi-fi card** (around $50) can be plugged into your laptop. You sign up for wireless access service much as you do cellphone service, through a plan offered by one of several commercial companies that have made wireless service available in airports, hotel lobbies, and coffee shops.

There are also places that provide **free wireless networks** in cities around the world. To locate these free hotspots, go to **www.personaltelco. net/index.cgi/WirelessCommunities**.

If Wi-fi is not available at your destination, most business-class hotels throughout the world offer dataports for laptop modems, and a few thousand hotels in Europe now offer free high-speed Internet access using an Ethernet network cable. You can bring your own cables, but most hotels rent them for around $10. **Call your hotel in advance** to see what your options are.

In addition, major ISPs have **local access numbers** around the world, allowing you to go online by simply placing a local call. Check your ISP's website or call its toll-free number and ask how you can use your current account away from home, and how much it will cost.

Wherever you go, bring a **connection kit** of the right power, phone adapters, a spare phone cord, and a spare Ethernet network cable—or find out whether your hotel supplies them to guests.

USING A CELLPHONE OUTSIDE THE U.S.

The three letters that define much of the world's **wireless capabilities** are GSM (Global System for Mobiles), a big, seamless network that makes for easy cross-border cellphone use throughout Europe and dozens of other countries worldwide. In the U.S., T-Mobile, AT&T Wireless, and

Cingular use this quasi-universal system; in Canada, Microcell and some Rogers customers are GSM, and all Europeans and most Australians use GSM.

If your cellphone is on a GSM system, and you have a world-capable multi-band phone such as many (but not all) Sony Ericsson, Motorola, or Samsung models, you can make and receive calls across civilized areas on much of the globe. Just call your wireless operator and ask for "international roaming" to be activated on your account. Unfortunately, per-minute charges can be high—usually $1 to $1.50 in Europe.

That's why it's important to buy an "unlocked" world phone from the get-go. Many cellphone operators sell "locked" phones that restrict you from using any other removable computer memory phone chip (called a **SIM card**) other than the ones they supply. Having an unlocked phone allows you to install a cheap, prepaid SIM card (found at a local retailer) in your destination country. (Show your phone to the salesperson; not all phones work on all networks.) You'll get a local phone number—and much, much

lower calling rates. Getting an already locked phone unlocked can be a complicated process, but it can be done; just call your cellular operator and say you'll be going abroad for several months and want to use the phone with a local provider.

For many, **renting a phone** is a good idea. While you can rent a phone from any number of overseas sites, including kiosks at airports and at car-rental agencies, we suggest renting the phone before you leave home. That way you can give loved ones and business associates your new number, make sure the phone works, and take the phone wherever you go—especially helpful for overseas trips through several countries, where local phone-rental agencies often bill in local currency and may not let you take the phone to another country.

Phone rental isn't cheap. You'll usually pay $40 to $50 per week, plus airtime fees of at least a dollar a minute. If you're traveling to Europe, though, local rental companies often offer free incoming calls within their home country, which can save you big bucks. The bottom line: Shop around.

Digital Photography on the Road

Many travelers are going digital these days when it comes to taking vacation photographs. Not only are digital cameras left relatively unscathed by airport X-rays, but with digital equipment you don't need to lug armloads of film with you as you travel. In fact, nowadays you don't even need to carry your laptop to download the day's images to make room for more. With a **media storage card,** sold by all major camera dealers, you can store hundreds of images in your camera. These "memory" cards come in different configurations—from memory sticks to flash cards to secure digital cards—and different storage capacities (the more megabytes of memory, the more images a card can hold) and range in price from $30 to over $200. (**Note:** Each camera model works with a specific type of card, so you'll need to determine which storage card is compatible with your camera.) When you get home, you can print the images out on your own color printer or take the storage card to a camera store, drugstore, or chain retailer. Or have the images developed online with a service like **Snapfish** (www.snapfish.com) for something like 25¢ a shot. See also "Flying with Film & Video," p. 44.

Two good wireless rental companies are **InTouch USA** (© 800/872-7626; www.intouchglobal.com) and **Road-Post** (© 888/290-1606 or 905/272-5665; www.roadpost.com). Give them your itinerary, and they'll tell you what wireless products you need. InTouch will also, for free, advise you on whether your existing phone will work overseas; simply call © 703/222-7161 between 9am and 4pm EST, or go to http://intouchglobal.com/travel.htm.

For trips of more than a few weeks spent in one country, **buying a phone** becomes economically attractive, as many nations have cheap, no-questions-asked prepaid phone systems. Once you arrive at your destination, stop by a local cellphone shop and get the cheapest package; you'll probably pay less than $100 for a phone and a starter calling card. Local calls may be as low as 10¢ per minute, and in many countries incoming calls are free.

11 Getting There

BY PLANE

High season for most airlines' routes to Sicily is usually from June to the beginning of September. This is the most expensive and most crowded time to travel. **Shoulder season** is from April to May, early September to October, and December 15 to 24. **Low season** is from November 1 to December 14 and December 25 to March 31.

There are no direct flights to Sicily. Most visitors fly first to Milan or Rome, then take a connecting flight to Sicily, most often using Palermo as their gateway to the island.

In the western part of the island, planes arrive at the **Aeroporto Falcone & Borsellino,** 31km (19 miles) west of Palermo at Punta Raisl. In the east, planes land at Catania's **Aeroporto Fontanarossa,** 7km (4½ miles) south of the center of town. For Palermo airport information, call © 091-7020111 daily between 5:30am and 9:30pm, and for the Catania airport, call © 095-723-9111 daily between 8am and midnight.

Chances are you'll use **Alitalia** (© 800/223-5730 in the U.S., or © 8488-65643 for domestic flights within Italy; www.alitaliausa.com) for the Sicilian flights. For Alitalia flight information in Palermo, call © 091-7020313 daily between 5:30am and 7:30pm; in Catania, call © 095-7569111 daily between 5am and 9pm.

Alitalia operates at least 17 flights a day from Rome to Palermo and about 13 from Milan. There is one direct flight a day from Turin to Palermo (far more if you stop over in Milan or Rome and make a connecting flight). For most visitors who are already in the south of Italy, the daily flight from Naples to Palermo is the most heavily booked. There are also six daily flights from Bologna to Palermo.

Alitalia also operates 12 daily flights from Rome to Catania. There are an additional eight flights a day that stop first in Naples. From Milan to Catania, there are 16 direct flights daily, or nine with stops in Rome. From Turin, Alitalia offers two direct flights to Catania (or 16 with stops in Rome). From Bologna, the airline flies three times daily to Catania, or 16 times with stops in Rome or Naples.

Meridiana (© 06-65953880 in Rome, or 091-6512587 in Palermo; www.meridiana.it) is the second major carrier serving Sicily. The airline shares some of its flights and reservations functions with Alitalia (see above). Most of Meridiana's flights to Sicily operate between Rome and Palermo (four direct flights daily) and can be booked separately or as part of a transatlantic itinerary through Alitalia.

Tips **Cutting Air Costs**

Regardless of how you opt to fly, it's cheaper for transatlantic passengers to have a flight to Palermo written into their overall ticket when booking a flight to Italy from North America. If you book a flight to Palermo once you've arrived in Italy, it will cost much more.

In addition to its flights from Rome to Palermo, Meridiana offers two direct daily flights from Milan to Catania; one direct daily flight from Bologna to Palermo (three direct flights from Bologna to Catania); and one direct flight from Verona to Palermo (two direct flights from Verona to Catania). Surprisingly, Meridiana doesn't fly from Rome to Catania or from Naples to Catania.

From late March to late October, **Air Malta** (© **866/357-4155** in the U.S., or 356-21-662-211; www.air malta.com) offers two daily flights from Malta to Palermo, with a flying time of 50 minutes, and five daily flights from Malta to Catania, with a flying time of 45 minutes.

A final carrier serving Sicily is **Air One** (© **199-207080,** or 06-4885913 in Rome). It flies from Rome to Palermo five times a day, and from Rome to Catania five times a day. There are three daily flights from Milan to Palermo, and four flights from Milan to Catania. There is also a daily flight from Turin to Catania, and four flights daily from Turin to Palermo. From Pisa there are 20 flights daily: 10 to Palermo and 10 to Catania.

Of course, for North Americans to fly to Sicily from the mainland, you must first reach Italy.

FROM NORTH AMERICA Flying time to Rome from New York, Newark, or Boston is 8 hours; from Chicago, 10 hours; and from Los Angeles, 12½ hours. Flying time to Milan from New York, Newark, or Boston is 8 hours; from Chicago, 9¼ hours; and from Los Angeles, 11½ hours.

American Airlines (© **800/433-7300;** www.aa.com) offers daily nonstop flights to Rome from Chicago's O'Hare Airport, with other flights from all parts of American's vast network making connections in Chicago. **Continental** (© **800/525-0280;** www.continental.com) flies twice daily to Rome and Milan from its hub in Newark. **Delta** (© **800/241-4141;** www.delta.com) flies from New York's JFK Airport to Milan, Venice, and Rome; separate flights depart every evening. **US Airways** (© **800/428-4322;** www.usairways.com) offers one flight daily to Rome out of Philadelphia (you can connect through Philly from most major U.S. cities).

Air Canada (© **888/247-2262;** www.aircanada.ca) flies daily from Toronto to Rome. Two of the flights are nonstop; the others touch down en route in Montréal, depending on the schedule.

British Airways (© **800/AIR-WAYS;** www.britishairways.com), **Virgin Atlantic Airways** (© **800/862-8621;** www.virgin-atlantic.com), **Air France** (© **800/237-2747;** www. airfrance.com), **Northwest/KLM** (© **800/374-7747;** www.klm.com), and **Lufthansa** (© **800/399-LUFT;** www.lufthansa-usa.com) offer some attractive deals for anyone interested in combining a trip to Sicily with a stopover in, say, London, Paris, Amsterdam, or Germany.

Alitalia (© **800/223-5730;** www. alitaliausa.com) is the Italian national airline, with nonstop flights to Rome from North American cities including New York (JFK), Newark, Boston, Chicago, and Miami. Nonstop flights into Milan are from New York (JFK) and Newark. From Milan or Rome, Alitalia can easily book connecting domestic flights if your final destination is Sicily. Alitalia participates in the frequent-flier programs of other airlines, including Continental and US Airways.

FROM THE UNITED KINGDOM

Operated by the European Travel Network, **www.discount-tickets.com** is a great online source for regular and discounted airfares to destinations around the world. You can also use this site to compare rates and book accommodations, car rentals, and tours.

British newspapers are always full of classified ads touting slashed fares to Italy. One good source is *Time Out.* London's *Evening Standard* has a daily travel section, and the Sunday editions of almost any newspaper run many ads. Although competition is fierce, one well-recommended company that consolidates bulk ticket purchases and then passes the savings on to its consumers is **Trailfinders** (© 020/7937-5400; www.trailfinders. com). It offers access to tickets on such carriers as SAS, British Airways, and KLM.

From late March to early November, **British Airways** (© 0870/850-9850 in the U.K.; www.ba.com) now offers three daily direct flights from London's Gatwick Airport to Catania; flying time is 4 hours.

Both British Airways and **Alitalia** (© 0870/544-8259; www.alitaliausa. com) have frequent flights from London's Heathrow Airport to Rome, Milan, Venice, Pisa (the gateway to Florence), and Naples. Flying time from London to these cities is 2 to 3 hours. British Airways also has one direct flight a day from Manchester to Rome. Once on mainland Italy, you can make a connecting flight into Catania or Palermo, among other cities.

One of the fastest ways to get from the British Isles to Sicily is not via Alitalia or British Airways but through a smaller airline, **Meridiana** (© 01293/507527; www.meridiana. it), from London's Gatwick Airport. Meridiana maintains offices at 15 Charles II St. SW1, London (© 020/7730-3454). It flies twice daily to Palermo from Gatwick with a stopover in Florence. There is also one daily flight from Gatwick to Catania, plus another daily flight to Catania with a stopover in Florence.

GETTING THROUGH THE AIRPORT

With the federalization of airport security, security procedures at U.S. airports are more stable and consistent than ever. Generally, you'll be fine if you arrive at the airport **2 hours** before an international flight; if you show up late, tell an airline employee and she'll probably whisk you to the front of the line.

Bring a **current, government-issued photo ID** such as a passport. Keep your ID at the ready to show at check-in, the security checkpoint, and sometimes even the gate. (Children under 18 need government-issued photo IDs for international flights.)

Passengers with e-tickets can still beat the ticket-counter lines by using airport **electronic kiosks** or even **online check-in** from your home computer. Online check-in involves logging on to your airline's website, accessing your reservation, and printing out your boarding pass—and the airline may even offer you bonus miles to do so. If you're using a kiosk at the airport, bring your frequent-flier card or the credit card you used to book the ticket. Print out your boarding pass from the kiosk and simply proceed to the security checkpoint with your pass and a photo ID. If you're checking bags or looking to snag an exit-row seat, you will be able to do so using most airline kiosks.

Security checkpoint lines are getting shorter than they were during

2001 and 2002, but some doozies remain. If you have trouble standing for long periods of time, tell an airline employee; the airline will provide a wheelchair. Speed up security by **not wearing metal objects** such as big belt buckles. If you've got metallic body parts, a note from your doctor can prevent a long chat with the security screeners. Keep in mind that only **ticketed passengers** are allowed past security, except for folks escorting children or passengers with disabilities.

Federalization has stabilized **what you can carry on** and **what you can't.** The general rule is that sharp things are out, nail clippers are okay, and food and beverages must be passed through the X-ray machine—but that security screeners can't make you drink from your coffee cup. Bring food in your carry-on rather than checking it, as explosive-detection machines used on checked luggage have been known to mistake food (especially chocolate, for some reason) for bombs. Travelers are allowed one carry-on bag, plus a "personal item" such as a purse, briefcase, or laptop bag. Carry-on hoarders can stuff all sorts of things into a laptop bag; as long as it has a laptop in it, it's still considered a personal item. The Transportation Security Administration (TSA) has issued a list of restricted items; check its website (www.tsa.gov/public/index.jsp) for details.

Airport screeners may decide that your checked luggage needs to be searched by hand. You can now purchase luggage locks that allow screeners to open and re-lock a checked bag if hand-searching is necessary. Look for Travel Sentry certified locks at luggage or travel shops and Brookstone stores (you can buy them online at www.brookstone.com). These locks, approved by the TSA, can be opened by luggage inspectors with a special code or key. For more information on the locks, visit www.travelsentry.org. If you use something other than TSA-approved locks, your lock will be cut off your suitcase if a TSA agent needs to hand-search your luggage.

FLYING FOR LESS: TIPS FOR GETTING THE BEST AIRFARE

Passengers sharing the same airplane cabin rarely pay the same fare. Travelers who need to purchase tickets at the last minute, change their itinerary at a moment's notice, or fly one-way often get stuck paying the premium rate. Here are some ways to keep your airfare costs down.

- Passengers who can book their ticket **long in advance,** who can **stay over Saturday night,** or who **fly midweek** or **at less-trafficked hours** may pay a fraction of the full fare. If your schedule is flexible, say so, and ask if you can secure a cheaper fare by changing your flight plans.

- You can also save on airfares by keeping an eye out in local newspapers for **promotional specials** or **fare wars,** when airlines lower prices on their most popular routes. You rarely see fare wars offered for peak travel times, but if you can travel in the off season, you may snag a bargain.

- Search the **Internet** for cheap fares (see "Planning Your Trip Online," on p. 31).

- **Consolidators,** also known as bucket shops, are great sources for international tickets (though they usually can't beat the Internet on fares within North America). Start by looking in Sunday newspaper travel sections; U.S. travelers should focus on the *New York Times, Los Angeles Times,* and *Miami Herald.* For less-developed destinations, small travel agents who cater to immigrant communities in large cities often have the best deals. ***Beware:*** Bucket-shop tickets are usually nonrefundable or rigged with stiff cancellation penalties, often as high as 50% to 75% of the ticket price, and some put you on charter airlines, which may leave at inconvenient times and experience delays. Several reliable consolidators are worldwide and accessible online. **STA Travel** (© **800/781-4040;** www.sta.com) is now the world's leader in student travel, thanks to its purchase of Council Travel. It also offers good fares for travelers of all ages. **ELTExpress (Flights.com)** (© **516/228-4972;** www.elt express.com) started in Europe and has excellent fares worldwide, but particularly to that continent. It also has "local" websites in 12 countries. **FlyCheap** (© **800/FLY-CHEAP;** www.1800flycheap.com) is owned by package-holiday megalith MyTravel and so has especially good access to fares for sunny destinations. **Air Tickets Direct** (© **800/778-3447;** www. airticketsdirect.com) is based in Montréal.

- Join **frequent-flier clubs.** Accrue enough miles, and you'll be rewarded with free flights and elite status. It's free, and you'll get the best choice of seats, faster response to phone inquiries, and prompter service if your luggage is stolen, your flight is canceled or delayed, or if you want to change your seat.

You don't need to fly to build frequent-flier miles—**frequent-flier credit cards** can provide thousands of miles for doing your everyday shopping.

BY CAR

If you're already on the Continent, particularly in a neighboring country such as France or Austria, you may want to drive to Italy. However, you should make arrangements in advance with your car-rental company.

It's also possible to drive from London to Rome, a distance of 1,810km (1,124 miles), via Calais/Boulogne/Dunkirk, or 1,747km (1,085 miles) via Oostende/Zeebrugge, not counting channel crossings by hovercraft, ferry, or the Chunnel. Milan is some 644km (400 miles) closer to Britain than is Rome. If you cross over from England and arrive at one of the continental ports, you still face a 24-hour drive. Most drivers play it safe and budget 3 days for the journey.

Most of the roads from western Europe leading into Italy are toll-free, with some notable exceptions. If you use the Swiss superhighway network, you'll have to buy a special tax sticker at the frontier. You'll also pay to go through the St. Gotthard Tunnel into Italy. Crossings from France can be through the Mont Blanc Tunnel, for which you'll pay, or you can leave the French Riviera at Menton and drive directly into Italy along the Italian Riviera toward San Remo.

Travel in the Age of Bankruptcy

Airlines go bankrupt, so protect yourself by **buying your tickets with a credit card,** as the Fair Credit Billing Act guarantees that you can get your money back from the credit card company if a travel supplier goes under (and if you request the refund within 60 days of the bankruptcy). **Travel insurance** can also help, but make sure it covers against "carrier default" for your specific travel provider. And be aware that if a U.S. airline goes bust mid-trip, a 2001 federal law requires other carriers to take you to your destination (albeit on a space-available basis) for a fee of no more than $25, provided you rebook within 60 days of the cancellation.

If you don't want to drive such distances, ask a travel agent to book you on a Motorail arrangement in which the train carries your car. This service, however, is good only to Milan, as no car and sleeper expresses run the 644km (400 miles) south to Rome.

Warning: You won't save a lot of money by driving to Sicily from another European country. Once you cross the frontier into Italy, you'll face a staggering number of tolls for riding the *autostrade* (express highways). Not only that, but gasoline costs are among the highest in Europe. Count on a lot of time, at least 17 hours of straight driving from the Swiss or French border to Villa San Giovanni, the point from which the car-carrying ferries sail to Messina in eastern Sicily.

BY TRAIN

For many visitors, this is the most convenient way to reach Sicily from the Italian mainland. Trains with connections from all over Europe, including Rome and Naples, arrive at the port of Villa San Giovanni, near Reggio di Calabria, in southern Italy.

Trains roll onto enormous barges for the 1-hour crossing into eastern Sicily. Passengers remain in their seats during the short voyage across the Straits of Messina, eventually rolling back onto the tracks once they reach Sicily. The trip from Rome to Palermo takes 11 to 13 hours, depending on the speed of the train. The trip from Naples to Palermo takes 10 hours.

For fares and information within Italy, call ℂ **892021.** See individual town or city listings for more detailed train information and fares.

If you plan to travel a lot on the European or British railroads on your way to or from Sicily, you'd do well to secure the latest copy of the *Thomas Cook European Timetable of Railroads.* It's available online at **www.thomas cooktimetables.com.**

New electric trains have made travel between France and Italy faster and more comfortable than ever. France's high-speed **TGV** trains have cut travel time between Paris and Turin from 7 to 5½ hours and between Paris and Milan from 7½ to 6¾ hours. Italy's **ETR** trains currently run between Milan and Lyon, a 5-hour ride, with a stop in Turin.

RAIL PASSES FOR NORTH AMERICAN TRAVELERS

EURAILPASS   If you plan to travel extensively in Europe, the **Eurailpass** might be a good bet. It's valid for first-class rail travel in 17 European countries. With one ticket, you can travel whenever and wherever you please; more than 100,000 rail miles are at your disposal. Here's how it works: The pass is sold only in North America. A Eurailpass good for 15 days costs $588; a 21-day pass, $762; a 1-month pass, $946; a 2-month pass, $1,338; and a 3-month pass, $1,654.

If you're under 26, you can buy a **Eurail Youthpass,** which entitles you to unlimited second-class travel for 15 days ($414), 21 days ($534), 1 month ($664), 2 months ($938), or 3 months ($1,160).

Children under 4 travel free if they don't occupy a seat; all children under 12 who take up a seat are charged half-price.

Travelers considering buying a 15-day or 1-month pass should estimate rail distance before deciding whether a pass is worthwhile. To take full advantage of the tickets for 15 days or 1 month, you'd have to spend a great deal of time on the train. Eurailpass holders are entitled to substantial discounts on certain buses and ferries as well.

Eurail Saverpass offers a 15% discount to each person in a group of three or more people traveling together between April and September, or two people traveling together between October and March. The price of a Saverpass, valid all over Europe for first-class travel only, is $498 for 15 days, $648 for 21 days,

$804 for 1 month, $1,138 for 2 months, and $1,408 for 3 months. Even more freedom is offered by the **Saver Flexipass,** which is similar to the Eurail Saverpass except that you are not confined to consecutive-day travel. For travel over any 10 days within 2 months, the fare is $592; for any 15 days over 2 months, the fare is $778.

Eurail Flexipass allows even greater flexibility. It's valid in first class and offers the same privileges as the Eurailpass. However, it provides a number of individual travel days over a much longer period of consecutive days. Using this pass makes it possible to stay longer in one city and not lose a single day of travel. There are two Flexipasses: 10 days of travel within 2 months for $694, and 15 days of travel within 2 months for $914.

The **Eurail Youth Flexipass,** with many of the same qualifications and restrictions as the Eurail Flexipass, is sold only to travelers under 26. It allows 10 days of travel within 2 months for $488, 15 days of travel within 2 months for $642.

Travel agents in all towns and railway agents in such major cities as New York, Montréal, and Los Angeles sell all of these tickets. For Eurailpass and other European train information, call **RailEurope** ((C) **800/438-7245**) or go to **www.raileurope.com**.

RAIL PASSES FOR BRITISH & OTHER EUROPEAN TRAVELERS

If you plan to do a lot of exploring by train, you might prefer one of the three passes designed for unlimited travel within a designated region during a predetermined number of days. These passes are sold in Britain and several other European countries.

The **InterRail Pass** (www.raileurope.com) is available to passengers of any nationality, with some restrictions—passengers must be able to prove residency in a European or North African country (Morocco, Algeria, and Tunisia) for at least 6 months before buying the pass. It allows unlimited travel through Europe, except Albania and the republics of the former Soviet Union. Prices are complicated and vary depending on the countries you want to include. For pricing purposes, Europe is divided into eight zones; the cost depends on the number of zones you include. For those 25 and under, the most expensive option (£295/$546) allows 1 month of unlimited travel in all eight zones and is known to BritRail staff as a "global." The least expensive option (£119/$220) allows 16 days of travel within only one zone.

Passengers 25 and over can buy an **InterRail 26-Plus Pass.** The cost varies from £223 ($413) for 16 days to £415 ($768) for 1 month. Passengers must meet the same residency requirements that apply to the InterRail Pass (described above).

For information on buying individual rail tickets or any of the aforementioned passes, contact **National Rail Inquiries,** Victoria Station, London ((C) **08705/848-848** or 0845/748-4950). Tickets and passes are also available at any of the larger railway stations as well as select travel agencies throughout Britain and the rest of Europe.

BY BOAT & FERRY

As an island, Sicily is well linked via sea to mainland Italy. The major connection is from Villa San Giovanni in Calabria, the last mainland city approached before the ferry trip over to Messina, in eastern Sicily. Ferries *(traghetti)* depart frequently from Villa San Giovanni, making the trip of 12km (7½ miles) across the Straits. For complete details on the crossings, including fares, see p. 136. If you don't have a car, the fastest way to go is by hydrofoil from Reggio di Calabria.

If you're already in Naples, it's easy to go by sea from there to Palermo.

SNAV (© 081-425500; www.snav.it) operates hydrofoils that make 5-hour southern crossings to Sicily. There is also a car-carrying ferry service operated by **Traghetti Lines** (© 050-754492; www.traghetti.com), taking 11 hours to reach Palermo from Naples. Boat schedules are dependent on weather conditions. For details, see p. 63.

If you're in the north of Italy, you can also sail to Palermo from Genoa. **Grandi Navi Vedloci,** Via Fieschi 1 (© 010-589331), runs daily service to Palermo from July 8 to September 21 (Mon–Sat otherwise). The journey takes 20 hours and costs 101€ ($121) for foot passengers or 170€ ($204) per person for those bringing a vehicle. Ferries in Genoa depart from Nuovo Terminale Traghetti.

Grand Navi Veloci, Varco Galvali (© 0586-409804), operates ferries to Palermo from the port of Livorno. Three ferry departures a week make the 17-hour run. Foot passengers are charged 75€ ($90) one-way; a person in a vehicle pays 121€ ($145).

BY BUS

There is no direct bus service to Sicily from outside Italy. Europe's major bus carrier, **Eurolines** (© 0870/514-3219 in London), has its main office at Grosvenor Gardens, Victoria, London SW1. It runs buses to Rome in 33 hours. After that, you can take an Italian bus to Sicily unless you're completely exhausted. Buses leave England on Wednesday and Friday, heading for Milan and Rome. The cost ranges from £136 to £146 ($252–$270).

If you're in Rome and want to travel overland by bus into Sicily, you can book tickets at **Segesta,** Piazza della Repubblica (© 06-4819676; www.interbus.it). It has two departures daily from Rome's Piazza Tiburtina to Palermo; the trip takes 12 hours and costs 33€ ($40) one-way. The line also goes to Syracuse in 11 hours, with a one-way ticket costing 39€ ($47).

12 Packages for the Independent Traveler

Before you start your search for the lowest airfare, you may want to consider booking your flight as part of a travel package. Package tours are not the same thing as escorted tours. Package tours are simply a way to buy the airfare, accommodations, and other elements of your trip (such as car rentals, airport transfers, and sometimes even activities) at the same time and often at discounted prices—kind of like one-stop shopping. Packages are sold in bulk to tour operators—who resell them to the public at a cost that usually undercuts standard rates.

One good source of package deals is the **airlines** themselves. Most major airlines offer air/land packages, as do several big **online travel agencies** (such as Expedia, Travelocity, Orbitz, Site59, and Lastminute.com).

Package operators are often advertised in the travel section of your local Sunday newspaper. Or check ads in national travel magazines such as *Travel & Leisure, National Geographic Traveler,* and *Condé Nast Traveler.*

Package tours can vary by leaps and bounds. Some offer a better class of hotels than others. Some offer the same hotels for lower prices. Some offer flights on scheduled airlines, while others book charters. Some limit your choice of accommodations and travel days. You are often required to make a large payment upfront. On the plus side, packages can save you money, offering group prices but allowing for independent travel. Some even let you add on a few guided excursions or escorted day trips (also at prices lower than if you booked them yourself) without booking an entirely escorted tour.

Before you invest in a package tour, get some answers. Ask about the

Flying with Film & Video

Never pack film—exposed or unexposed—in checked bags, as the new, more powerful scanners in U.S. airports can fog film. The film you carry with you can be damaged by scanners as well. X-ray damage is cumulative; the faster the film, and the more times you put it through a scanner, the more likely the damage. Film under 800 ASA is usually safe for up to five scans. If you're taking your film through additional scans, U.S. regulations permit you to demand hand inspections. In international airports, you're at the mercy of airport officials. On international flights, store your film in transparent baggies, so you can remove it easily before you go through scanners. Keep in mind that airports are not the only places where your camera may be scanned: Highly trafficked attractions are X-raying visitors' bags with increasing frequency.

Most photo supply stores sell protective pouches designed to block damaging X-rays. The pouches fit both film and loaded cameras. They should protect your film in checked baggage, but they also may raise alarms and result in a hand inspection.

You'll have little to worry about if you're traveling with a **digital camera**. Unlike film, which is sensitive to light, the digital camera and storage cards are not affected by airport X-rays, according to Nikon. Still, if you plan to travel extensively, you may want to play it safe and hand-carry your digital equipment or ask that it be inspected by hand. See "Digital Photography on the Road," p. 35.

Carry-on scanners will not damage **videotape** in video cameras, but the magnetic fields emitted by the walk-through security gateways and hand-held inspection wands will. Always place your loaded camcorder on the screening conveyor belt or have it hand-inspected. Be sure your batteries are charged, as you may be required to turn the device on to ensure that it's what it appears to be.

accommodations choices and prices for each. Then look up the hotels' reviews in a Frommer's guide and check their rates online for your specific dates of travel. You'll also want to find out what type of room you get. If you need a certain type of room, ask for it; don't take whatever is thrown your way. Request a nonsmoking room, a quiet room, a room with a view, or whatever you fancy.

Finally, look for **hidden expenses.** Ask whether airport departure fees and taxes, for example, are included in the total cost.

13 Escorted General-Interest Tours

Escorted tours are structured group tours, with a group leader. The price usually includes everything from airfare to hotels, meals, tours, admission costs, and local transportation.

Many people derive a certain ease and security from escorted trips. Escorted tours—whether by bus, motor coach, train, or boat—let travelers sit back and enjoy their trip without having to spend lots of time behind the wheel or worrying about details. You know your costs upfront, and there are few surprises. Escorted tours can take you to the maximum number of sights in the minimum amount of time with the least amount of hassle—you don't have to sweat over the plotting and planning of a vacation schedule. Escorted tours are particularly convenient for people with limited mobility. They can also be a great way to make new friends.

On the downside, an escorted tour often requires a big deposit upfront, and lodging and dining choices are predetermined. You'll get little opportunity for serendipitous interactions with locals. The tours can be jam-packed with activities, leaving little room for individual sightseeing, whim, or adventure—plus they also often focus only on the heavily touristed sites, so you miss out on the lesser-known gems.

Before you invest in an escorted tour, ask about the **cancellation policy:** Is a deposit required? Can they cancel the trip if they don't get enough people? Do you get a refund if they cancel? If *you* cancel? How late can you cancel if you are unable to go? When do you pay in full? *Note:* If you choose an escorted tour, think strongly about purchasing trip-cancellation insurance, especially if the tour operator asks you to pay upfront (p. 25).

You'll want to get a complete **schedule** of the trip to find out how much sightseeing is planned each day and whether enough time has been allotted for relaxing or wandering solo.

The **size** of the group is also important to know upfront. Generally, the smaller the group, the more flexible the itinerary, and the less time you'll spend waiting for people to get on and off the bus. Find out the **demographics** of the group as well. What is the age range? What is the gender breakdown? Is this mostly a trip for couples or singles?

Discuss what is included in the **price.** You may have to pay for transportation to and from the airport. A box lunch may be included in an excursion, but drinks might cost extra. Tips may not be included. Find out if you will be charged if you decide to opt out of certain activities or meals.

Finally, if you plan to travel alone, you'll need to know if a **single supplement** will be charged and if the company can match you up with a roommate.

Italiatour, part of the Alitalia Group (© **800/845-3365;** www.italia tourusa.com), offers the best escorted tours of Sicily. The most attractive deal is a 9-day, 7-night jaunt from $2,099 round-trip that takes in such highlights as Catania, Ragusa, Agrigento, Palermo, and Giardini-Naxos (the latter the "beachfront" for Taormina). Of all the tours we've studied, this one best encapsulates the highlights. Because of the company's close link with Alitalia, the prices quoted are sometimes among the most reasonable on the market.

Amelia International (© **800/742-4591;** www.ameliainternational.com) specializes in Sicily and its Mediterranean neighbors. Custom-designed tours of Sicily last 11 days and cost from $5,200 per person, double occupancy (land charges only). You spend 4 nights in Palermo, 1 night in Agrigento, 2 nights in Syracuse, and 3 nights in Taormina. Highlights of the trip include visits to the Aeolian Islands, a journey to the medieval village of Erice, and a jeep ride along the craters of Mount Etna.

One of the biggest escorted-tour operators is **Perillo Tours** (© **800/431-1515;** www.perillotours.com). Since it was founded in 1945, it has sent more than a million travelers to Italy. Perillo's tours cost much less than you'd spend if you arranged a comparable trip yourself. Accommodations are in first-class hotels, and guides tend to be well qualified. Tours in Sicily also include time in southern Italy, including 3 nights in Rome and 3 nights in Sorrento. The swing through Sicily itself, part of a larger tour, usually takes in 2 nights in Palermo, 1 night in Agrigento, and 3 nights in Taormina.

Globus and Cosmos Tours, working jointly, comprise one of Perillo's top competitors. **Globus** (© **866/ 755-8581;** www.globusandcosmos. com) also offers a 14-day grand tour of Italy and Sicily. **Cosmos** (© **800/ 276-1241**), the budget branch of Globus, sells the same itineraries. These tours must be booked through a travel agent and not directly.

Yet another option is **Insight Vacations** (© **800/582-8380;** www.insight vacations.com), which features art tours. Its 10-day tour of Italy and Sicily includes stopovers at the seaside resort of Giardini-Naxos (below Taormina) and visits to the temples at Agrigento and the art treasures of Palermo.

For a luxury tour, consider **Abercrombie & Kent** (© **800/554-7016** or 630/954-2944; www.abercrombie kent.com). Its 12-day tour of southern Italy includes Palermo, Agrigento, Piazza Armerina, Syracuse, and Taormina, with the option of adding a few nights in Rome to the itinerary.

14 Special-Interest Trips

For many visitors, a themed tour is the best way to explore the island.

For those who'd like to cycle along volcanic craters and rugged coastlines, in sight of Greek ruins, an intriguing 10-day biking tour is offered by **VBT** (© **800/BIKE-TOUR;** www.vbt. com). It costs from $2,595 per person, including accommodations (airfare not included). Bike trips circle the craters of Mount Etna and go to Taormina and on to some of the Aeolian Islands, including Lipari and Salina.

Hikes through ancient Sicily are organized through **Mountain Travel-Sobek** (© **888/687-6235** or 510/594-6000; www.mtsobek.com). Depending on the number in your group, 9-day tours (land costs only) range from $3,790 to $4,090 per person. Hikes go through Palermo, Piazza Armerina, and the temples of Agrigento, and even include wine tasting in Corleone, of Mafia fame.

Backroads (© **800/462-2848** or 510/527-1555; www.backroads.com), runs a 6-day biking and walking trip through Sicily that incorporates a boat ride to the Aeolian island of Panarea. It even offers a family version of this trip that's suitable for children as young as 9 years old. Both trips are around $3,300 per person (land costs only), double occupancy.

Butterfield & Robinson (© **800/ 678-1147** or 416/864-1354; www. butterfield.com) operates a ship-based tour that takes in Sicily and the Aeolian Islands by 32-passenger private yacht. Days bring opportunities for hiking, swimming, snorkeling, and diving. The 9-day tour starts at $8,950 per person (airfare not included).

Smithsonian Journeys (© **877/ 338-8687** or 202/357-4700; www. smithsonianjourneys.org) features educational travel with guides who are experts in their fields. The 11-day "Crossroads of Cultures" trip aboard a private yacht visits Sicily, the Aeolian Islands, and Malta, while the 11-day "Legacy of Sicily" tour explores the island in greater depth.

Academic Tours (© **800/875-9171** or 718/417-8782; www.academic tours.com) is a real Sicilian specialist. It offers the best archaeological tours of Sicily, visiting such ancient cities and sites as Segesta, Erice, Selinunte, Piazza Armerina, Noto, and Syracuse. Typical prices for land arrangements are $1,899 in a double room for a 15-day tour.

To Grandmother's House We Go
(☏ 718/768-4662; www.togrand
mothershousewego.com) features
cooking and cultural tours of Sicily.
Cooking classes concentrate on simple, delicious food, and no more than
10 people participate at one time. The
tour comprises not only food, but also
historical sights as well as living history—that is, the shops of artisans, a
winery, a tuna fishery, and more.

15 Getting Around Sicily

BY PLANE

Unlike in mainland Italy, flying
around Sicily is rarely an option. Once
you've made a choice to fly into
Palermo as your western gateway or
Catania as your eastern gateway, the
train, the bus, or a rental car are the
chief means of getting about. There
are domestic flights from Palermo to
the Pélagie Islands, close to North
Africa, and to the island of Pantelleria,
also owned by Sicily.

BY TRAIN

Unless you're heading for remote
towns and villages in Sicily, riding the
rails is the best way to traverse the
island without a private rental car. All
of the major cities such as Palermo,
Catania, Messina, Syracuse, Agrigento,
Taormina, and Trapani have rail links.
Trains on weekends and holidays tend
to be crowded, so book in advance.

Train fares are generally very affordable in Sicily. See "By Train" listings
under the individual town and city
sections for trip times and point-to-
point fares. Trains are operated by **Fer-
rovie dello Stato (FS),** the Italian
State Railways. For general information on connections through Sicily,
call ☏ 892021 from anywhere on the
island or within Italy itself. For more
information, search the website at
www.ferrovie.it.

A **Trenitalia Pass** allows you to
travel on the days you select so you
can explore Sicily or Italy at your
leisure. For 4 days in 2 months, the
cost is $239 in first class or $191 in
second class. Additional rail days cost
$24 and $19, respectively. A budget
version of this pass is the **Trenitalia**
Pass Saver, requiring two people to
travel together at all times. This pass
costs $203 in first class or $163 in second class, with additional rail days
costing $20 and $16, respectively.
Again, the pass is valid for 4 days of
rail travel in 2 months.

A supplement must be paid to ride
on certain rapid trains, designated
ETR-450 or **Pendolino** trains.

You can buy all of these passes from
any travel agent or by calling ☏ 800/
848-7245. You can also call ☏ 800/
4EURAIL or 800/EUROSTAR.

As a rule of thumb, second-class
travel usually costs about two-thirds the
price of an equivalent first-class trip.
The relatively new **InterCity trains**
(designated **IC** on train schedules) are
modern, air-conditioned trains that
make limited stops; compared with the
cost of the far slower direct or regional
trains, the supplement can be steep, but
a second-class IC ticket will provide a
first-class experience.

An IC couchette (private fold-down
bed in a communal cabin) requires a
supplement above the price of first-
class travel. Children 4 to 11 receive a
discount of 50% off the adult fare,
and children 3 and under travel free
with a parent. Seniors and travelers
under 26 can also purchase discount
cards. Seat reservations are highly recommended during peak season and on
weekends or holidays; they must be
booked in advance.

Slower Sicilian trains—called
Diretto, Espresso, and **Interregion-
ale**—stop at only major towns or
cities. Try to avoid a Regionale train
(sometimes known as the Locale), as

they stop in every hamlet and take forever.

Available at ticket offices is an FS booklet, *Treno Sicilia,* updated twice annually and usually distributed free.

BY BUS

Where the train doesn't go, there is almost always a local bus to take you into the more remote villages and hinterlands, although you can generally go from city to city and town to town by bus as well. Bus fares are often more expensive than rail transportation. For individual city and town links, and for a general outline of fares, refer to the individual sections on cities and towns in later chapters.

The major bus company is **SAIS** (© 091-616028 in Palermo, or 095-536168 in Catania; www.saisauto linnee.it), offering service from Palermo to Messina, Catania, and Syracuse. **Cuffaro** (© 091-6161510) links Palermo in the north with Agrigento in the south. **Etna Trasporti** (© 095-530396) travels between Catania and Piazza Armerina and between Catania and Taormina. **Interbus** (© 095-536201) has service between the cities of Catania, Messina, Taormina, and Syracuse.

Sunday is a bad day to take the bus, as schedules are either curtailed or else shut down completely. Keep in mind that large cities can have a number of bus depots. In smaller towns, buses generally pull into one central square, often the rail station.

Tickets are most often purchased right on the bus. In bigger cities such as Palermo, you can buy a ticket in advance at the office of one of the local companies. That way, you'll be more confident that you'll have a seat.

Only the cities and larger towns offer a bus system to get you from point to point. Tickets for city buses are bought before boarding and must be validated once you hop on, or else you'll be fined up to 30€ ($36) on the spot.

Tickets are generally purchased at ticket booths, tobacco shops *(tabacchi),* or newspaper kiosks. Most city buses charge .75€ (90¢) for a ticket whose validity lasts 60 to 90 minutes. Sometimes a city will offer a 24-hour transit ticket that can save you money if you plan to use the bus network extensively.

BY CAR

U.S. and Canadian drivers don't need an **International Driver's License** to drive a rented car in Italy or Sicily. However, if you're driving a private car, you will need such a license.

You can apply for an International Driver's License at any **AAA** branch. You must be at least 18 and have two 2-by-2-inch photos and a photocopy of your U.S. driver's license with your AAA application form. The actual fee for the license can vary, depending on where it's issued. Remember that an International Driver's License is valid only if physically accompanied by your original driver's license and only if signed on the back.

To find the AAA office nearest you, call © 800/222-4357 or 407/444-4300, or go to www.aaa.com. In Canada, you can get the location of the **Canadian Automobile Association** office closest to you by calling © 613/247-0117 or going to www. caa.ca.

RENTALS Many of the loveliest parts of Sicily lie miles from the main cities, far away from the train stations. For sheer convenience and freedom, renting a car is usually the best way to explore the island. But you have to be a pretty aggressive and alert driver who won't be fazed by super-high speeds on the autostrada or by narrow streets in the cities and towns. Sicilian drivers have truly earned their reputation as bad but daring.

However, the legalities and contractual obligations of renting a car in Sicily (where accident and theft rates are very high) are a little complicated. To rent a car here, a driver must have nerves of steel, a sense of humor, a valid driver's license, and a valid passport, and must be (in most cases) more than 25 years old. Insurance is compulsory, though any reputable rental firm will arrange it in advance before you're even given the keys.

In some cases, slight discounts are offered to members of AAA or AARP. Be sure to ask.

It is generally cheaper to make arrangements for car rentals before you leave home. Of course, you can also rent a car once you arrive in Sicily. Although the price can vary greatly, depending on the vehicle, the average rental on the island costs from 47€ to 106€ ($56–$127) per day.

The main rental agencies in Sicily include **Avis** (© 800/331-1212; www.avis.com) and **Hertz** (© 800/654-3131; www.hertz.com). Avis has locations at Catania's Aeroporto Fontanarossa (© 095-340500), in Catania itself at Via Cagliari 101 (© 095-371413), at Palermo's Aeroporto Falcone-Borsellino (© 091-591684), and in Palermo at Via Francesco Crispi 115 (© 095-586940).

Hertz has locations at Catania's Aeroporto Fontanarossa (© 095-341595), in Catania at Via Toselli 16C (© 095-322560), at Palermo's Aeroporto Falcone-Borsellini (© 091-213112), and in Palermo at Via Messina 7E (© 091-331668).

U.S.-based companies specializing in European car rentals are **Auto Europe** (© 800/223-5555; www.autoeurope.com), **Europe by Car** (© 800/223-1516 or 212/581-3040; www.europebycar.com), and **Kemwel Holiday Auto** (© 800/678-0678; www.kemwel.com).

The major Italian car-rental firm, **Maggiore**, is found at Catania's Aeroporto Fontanarossa (© 095-340594) and in Catania itself at Via Conte Ruggero 139 (© 095-536927).

GASOLINE Gasoline *(benzina)* is expensive in Sicily. Be prepared for sticker shock every time you fill up even a medium-size car with *super benzina,* which has the octane rating appropriate for most of the cars you'll be able to rent. It's priced throughout the country at around 1.35€ ($1.60) per liter (about $5.10 per gal.). Gas stations on the autostrade are open 24 hours, but stations on regular roads are rarely open on Sunday; also, many close from noon to 3pm for lunch, and most shut down after 7pm. Make sure the pump registers zero before an attendant starts refilling your tank. A popular scam in Sicily is to fill your tank before resetting the meter, so you pay not only your bill but also the charges run up by the previous motorist.

DRIVING RULES The Italian Highway Code follows the Geneva Convention, and Sicily like the rest of Italy uses international road signs. Driving is on the right; passing is on the left. Violators of the highway code are fined; serious violations might also be punished by imprisonment. In cities and towns, the speed limit is 50kmph (31 mph). For all cars and motor vehicles on main roads and local roads, the limit is 90kmph (56 mph). For the autostrade, the limit is 130kmph (81 mph). Use the left lane only for passing. If a driver zooms up behind you on the autostrada with his or her lights on, that's your sign to get out of the way. Use of seat belts is compulsory.

BREAKDOWNS & ASSISTANCE The **Automobile Club Italiano (ACI)** does not offer free roadside emergency help to stranded motorists in Sicily. If you call the ACI emergency number (© 803-116) in the event of a breakdown, you must pay a minimum of 93€ ($112), plus another 39€ ($47) to have your car towed to the nearest garage, plus tax and .85€ ($1) per kilometer. So getting stranded in Sicily has a serious cost. Not only that, but 20% is added to the bill between 10pm and 6am and on Saturday and Sunday. ACI offices are at Via delle Alpi 6, in Palermo (© **091-300468**), and at Via Sabotino 1, in Catania (© **095-533324**).

SICILIAN ROADS The autostrada does not exist as extensively on Sicily as it does on the Italian mainland. The most traveled route is the A19 between Palermo and Catania, a convenient link between the island's two major cities. The other oft-traveled route is A20 going between Palermo and Messina. A18 links Messina and Catania on the eastern coast, whereas A29 goes from Palermo to the capital of the western coast, Trapani.

Sicily has nowhere near the burdensome tolls of mainland Italy, but there are some: For example, taking the autostrada from Messina to Catania costs 3€ ($3.60).

Unless you're traveling from main city to main city, you'll use the state roads, or *Strade statali,* single-lane and toll-free routes. To reach remote villages, you'll sometimes find yourself going along a country lane and watching out for goats.

BY TAXI

Taxi rates vary from town to town, but in general are pricey. In most cities, the meter begins at 3.50€ ($4.20), and then charges you 2.25€ ($2.70) for the first kilometer, plus another .65€ (80¢) per kilometer thereafter. There are supplements of 3€ ($3.60) from 10pm to 7am and on holidays. Depending on the size of the taxi, four or as many as five passengers are allowed. Taxis are found at all airport arrival terminals. In some cities, they can be called. When you reserve by phone, the taxi meter goes on when the cabbie pulls out of his station. In Sicily, taxis rarely stop if hailed on the street.

BY BICYCLE

Most Sicilian cities have bike-rental firms; otherwise, your hotel might help you make arrangements for one. Rentals in cities start at 10€ ($12) a day or 60€ ($72) a week. Even though helmets and lights are not legally required, they are prudent to have. It is forbidden to bike along the autostrade. Bikes are transported free on Sicilian ferries, but you must pay to carry them on most trains. Fast trains generally do not allow bikes, although conductors on IC trains let you put a bike in the baggage train for an extra 7€ ($8.40).

16 Tips on Accommodations

SAVING ON YOUR HOTEL ROOM

The **rack rate** is the maximum rate that a hotel charges for a room. Hardly anybody pays this price, however, except in high season or on holidays. To lower the cost of your room:

- **Ask about special rates or other discounts.** Always ask whether a room less expensive than the first one quoted is available, or whether any special rates apply to you. You may qualify for corporate, student, military, senior, AAA, or other discounts. Find out the hotel policy on children—do

kids stay free in the room or is there a special rate?

- **Dial direct.** When booking a room in a chain hotel, you'll often get a better deal by calling the individual hotel's reservations desk rather than the chain's main number.

- **Book online.** Many hotels offer Internet-only discounts, or supply rooms to Priceline, Hotwire, or Expedia at rates much lower than the ones you can get through the hotel itself. Shop around. And if you have special needs—a quiet room, a room with a view—call the hotel directly and make your needs known after you've booked online.

- **Remember the law of supply and demand.** Resort hotels are most crowded and therefore most expensive on weekends, so discounts are usually available for midweek stays. Business hotels in downtown locations are busiest during the week, so you can expect big discounts over the weekend. Many hotels have high-season and low-season prices, and booking the day after high season ends can mean big discounts.

- **Look into group or long-stay discounts.** If you come as part of a large group, you should be able to negotiate a bargain rate, since the hotel can then guarantee occupancy in a number of rooms. Likewise, if you're planning a long stay (at least 5 days), you might qualify for a discount. As a general rule, expect 1 night free after a 7-night stay.

- **Avoid excess charges and hidden costs.** When you book a room, ask whether the hotel charges for parking. Use your own cellphone, pay phones, or prepaid phone cards instead of dialing direct from hotel phones, which usually have exorbitant rates. And don't be tempted by the room's minibar offerings: Most hotels charge through the nose for water, soda, and snacks. Finally, ask about local taxes and service charges, which can increase the cost of a room by 15% or more. If a hotel insists upon tacking on a surprise "energy surcharge" that wasn't mentioned at check-in or a "resort fee" for amenities you didn't use, you can often make a case for getting it removed.

LANDING THE BEST ROOM

Somebody has to get the best room in the house. It might as well be you. You can start by joining the hotel's frequent-guest program, which may make you eligible for upgrades. Always ask about a corner room. They're often larger and quieter, with more windows and light, and they often cost the same as standard rooms. When you make your reservation, ask if the hotel is renovating; if it is, request a room away from the construction. Ask about nonsmoking rooms; rooms with views; quiet rooms away from elevators, restaurants, bars, and discos. Ask for a room that has been most recently renovated or redecorated. If you aren't happy with your room when you arrive, ask for another one. Most lodgings will be willing to accommodate you.

You may also want to ask the following questions before you book a room:

- What's the view like? Cost-conscious travelers may be willing to pay less for a back room facing the parking lot, especially if they don't plan to spend much time in their room.

- Does the room have air-conditioning or ceiling fans? Do the windows open? If they do, and the nighttime entertainment takes place alfresco, you may want to find out when the show is usually over.

- What's included in the price? Your room may be moderately priced, but if you're charged for beach chairs, towels, sports equipment, and other amenities, you could end up spending more than you bargained for.

- How far is the room from the beach and other amenities? If it's far, is there transportation to and from the beach, and is it free?

SUGGESTED ITINERARIES

If You Have 1 Week

Day 1 Fly or sail into Palermo and allow 1 day to recover from travel fatigue. If you recover sufficiently,

1 Week Suggested Itinerary

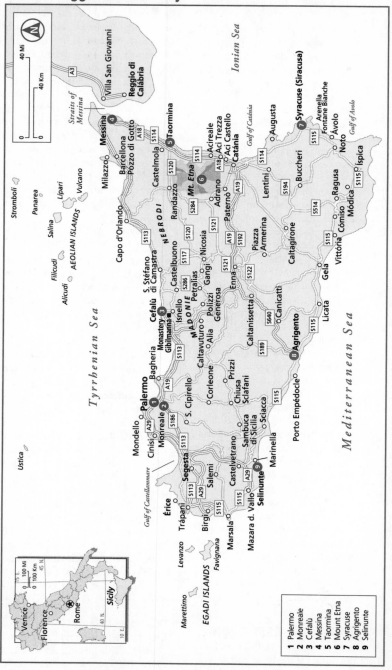

1 Palermo
2 Monreale
3 Cefalù
4 Messina
5 Taormina
6 Mount Etna
7 Syracuse
8 Agrigento
9 Selinunte

2 Week Suggested Itinerary

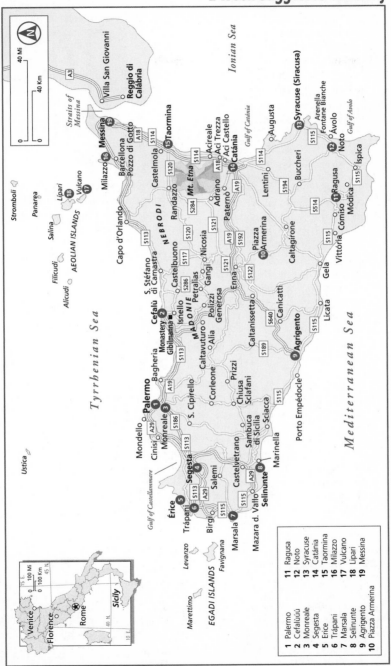

1 Palermo
2 Cefalùü
3 Monreale
4 Segesta
5 Erice
6 Trápani
7 Marsala
8 Selinunte
9 Agrigento
10 Piazza Armerina
11 Ragusa
12 Noto
13 Syracuse
14 Catánia
15 Taormina
16 Milazzo
17 Vulcano
18 Lipari
19 Messina

take our walking tour through old Palermo.

Day 2 Visit Palazzo dei Normanni and the Museo Archeológico Regionale in the morning. Head for Monreale and its mosaic-laden cathedral in the afternoon.

Day 3 Travel toward Messina for an overnight, but spend most of the day exploring Cefalù, dominated by its Romanesque Duomo.

Days 4 & 5 After Messina, head down the coastline to spend 2 nights in the medieval hilltop town of Taormina. One day can be spent discovering the town and getting in some beach time. On the final day from your base in Taormina, visit the volcanic slopes of Mount Etna.

Day 6 From Taormina, continue south to the ancient city of Syracuse, where you can spend the rest of the day wandering through its archaeological gardens. Overnight in this ancient place.

Day 7 After bidding adieu to Syracuse, head west for another ancient city, Agrigento, to explore its Valle di Templi (Valley of the Temples), which has some of the greatest Greek ruins in the world. With a little imagination, you'll know why Pindar called Agrigento "the most beautiful city built by mortal men." Overnight here before driving north the next day for your transportation links out of Palermo. If you have time in the morning, explore the ruins of the Greek temples at Selinunte before continuing on to Palermo and the end of your Sicilian sojourn.

If You Have 2 Weeks

Days 1 & 2 Fly into Palermo, where you can rent a car at the airport. The first day, explore the treasures of Palermo on foot. On the morning of the second day, take a drive east of Palermo to Cefalù,

returning right after lunch. In the afternoon, while still based in Palermo, head up to see the mosaics in the basilica of nearby Monreale, returning to Palermo for the night.

Day 3 Head southwest for Segesta in the morning, exploring its Greek ruins, which include Sicily's most magnificent ancient Greek temple. Then continue west to Erice, a medieval hill town, for the night.

Day 4 After a night in Erice, drive to the coastal city of Trapani for a morning visit. After taking in its sights, head south for an afternoon exploration of the wine-producing city of Marsala; overnight here.

Day 5 From Marsala, head along the southern coast of Sicily to see the ruins of Selinunte in the late morning and early afternoon. Since there are few good accommodations in the area, continue east to Agrigento for the night. On your first evening in town, wander around the illuminated Valley of the Temples.

Day 6 You can spend the entire day exploring the wonders of Agrigento. Its Valley of the Temples constitutes the best preserved remains of classical Greece—even Greece can't match the site. Spend yet another night in Agrigento.

Day 7 From Agrigento, cut cross-country to Piazza Armerina, viewing the fabulous mosaics in a Roman villa here before heading to Ragusa for the night.

Day 8 Explore Ragusa in the early morning, heading for the little city of Noto for the night. In the afternoon, wander around and take in the charm of Noto and its monuments. Overnight here in Noto.

Days 9 & 10 Continue east for a 2-night visit to Syracuse, once one of the great ancient capitals of Western civilization. You'll probably arrive in time for lunch. After your meal, you can explore some of the Greek and Roman ruins. But because Syracuse has so many attractions, devotees will want to spend at least another day, taking in not only the wonders left over from the ancient world, but also some of the finest examples of baroque art and architecture in Sicily.

Day 11   Head north to Catania, the most populated city along the eastern coastline. If you arrive in Catania with enough time, you can explore Mount Etna. Otherwise, tackle this volcano the following morning.

Day 12   North from Catania leads to Taormina, where you can catch up on some R&R, something that has been missing so far from this hectic itinerary. It would be ideal if you could spend a week in Taormina, but few visitors have that kind of time.

Days 13 & 14   The average visitor might want to end the tour in Taormina, perhaps taking the overnight train back to the mainland, arriving in Rome in the early morning. Visitors with more time can have yet another exciting adventure by driving north, bypassing the city of Messina, and continuing west to nearby Milazzo. Park the car here and take a ferryboat or hydrofoil to either Lipari or Vulcano, the two most fascinating of the famous Aeolian Islands. It's possible to spend 1 night on Lipari, the second night on Vulcano. In summer, reserve a room in advance before heading for the islands, as accommodations are extremely limited. After overnighting in the Aeolians, you can return to the port of Milazzo and head back east to Messina for your departure to the mainland of Italy.

FAST FACTS: Sicily

American Express Travel agencies representing Amex are found in large cities, including **La Duca Viaggi**, Viale Africa 14, in Catania (✆ 095-7222295); **La Duca Viaggi**, Via Don Bosco 39, in Taormina (✆ 0942-625255); and **Giovanni Ruggieri e Figli**, Emerico Armari 40, in Palermo (✆ 091-587144).

Business Hours Regular business hours are generally Monday through Saturday from 8 or 9am to 1pm and 4 to 7 or 8pm. The *riposo* (midafternoon closing) is observed in Sicily. If you're on the island in summer, when the heat is intense, you too may want to learn the custom of *riposo*, retreating back to your hotel for a long nap during the hottest part of the day. Banking hours vary from town to town, but in general are Monday through Friday from 8:30am to 1:20pm and 3 to 4pm.

Climate See "When to Go," p. 21.

Currency See "Money," p. 19.

Drugstores Every drugstore *(farmacia)* posts a list of those that are open at night and on Sunday.

Electricity The electricity in Sicily varies considerably. It's usually alternating current (AC); the cycle is 50Hz 220V. Check the exact local current at the hotel where you're staying. We recommend obtaining a transformer if you're carrying any electrical appliances. Plugs have prongs that are round, not flat; therefore, an adapter plug is also needed.

Embassies & Consulates There's a **U.S. Consulate** at Via Vaccarini 1, in Palermo (② **091-305857**). The nearest **U.S. Embassy** is in Rome, at Via Vittorio Veneto 119A (② **06-46-741**).

The **Canadian Embassy** is at Via G. B. de Rossi 27, in Rome (② **06-445-981**).

There's a **U.K. Consulate** at Via Cavour 117, in Palermo (② **091-326412**), and a **U.K. Embassy** at Via XX Settembre 80A, in Rome (② **06-422-00001**).

The **Irish Embassy** is at Piazza di Campitelli 3, in Rome (② **06-697-9121**). For consular queries, call ② **06-697-91211**.

The **Australian Embassy** is at Via Alessandria 215, in Rome (② **06-852-721**). The **New Zealand Embassy** is at Via Zara 28, in Rome (② **06-441-7171**).

Emergencies For the police, dial ② **113**; for an ambulance, ② **118**; and to report a fire, ② **115**. For road assistance, dial ② **116**. For a general crisis, call the *Carabinieri* (military-trained police force) at ② **112**.

Language Except in remote backwaters, Italian, of course, is the language of the land. (See p. 321 for a brief glossary of useful terms.) English is often understood at attractions such as museums and at most hotels and restaurants catering to foreigners. Even if not all of the staff speaks English at a particular establishment, such as a restaurant, sometimes at least one member of the staff does and can aid you. Most islanders also speak a Sicilian dialect. This is a patois comprised of words left over from various conquerors, including Arabic, Greek, French, and Spanish. It's a sort of linguistic amalgam, reflecting centuries of occupation (including American occupation).

Legal Aid The consulate of your country is the place to turn for legal aid, although offices can't interfere in the Italian legal process. They can, however, inform you of your rights and provide a list of attorneys. You'll have to pay for the attorney out of your pocket—there's no free legal assistance. If you're arrested for a drug offense, about all the consulate will do is notify a lawyer about your case and perhaps inform your family. If the problem is serious enough, most nationals will be referred to their embassies or consulates in Rome.

Liquor Laws Wine with meals has been a normal part of family life for hundreds of years in Sicily. Children are exposed to wine at an early age, and consumption of alcohol isn't anything out of the ordinary. There's no legal drinking age for buying or ordering alcohol. Alcohol is sold day and night throughout the year because there's almost no restriction on the sale of wine or liquor in Sicily.

Mail Mail delivery in Italy is notoriously bad. Your family and friends back home might receive your postcards in 1 week, or it could take 2 weeks (sometimes longer). Postcards, aerogrammes, and letters weighing up to 20 grams sent to the United States and Canada cost .75€ (90¢); to the United Kingdom, .60€ (70¢); and to Australia and New Zealand, .75€ (90¢). You can buy stamps at post offices and *tabacchi* (tobacco shops).

Newspapers & Magazines In major cities, hotels and news kiosks often carry the *International Herald Tribune* and *USA Today,* as well as other

English-language newspapers and magazines such as *Time* and *Newsweek*—but they're hard to find elsewhere. There are no English-language magazines or newspapers published in Sicily.

Passports **For Residents of the United States:** Whether you're applying in person or by mail, you can download passport applications from the U.S. State Department website at **http://travel.state.gov**. For general information, call the **National Passport Agency (② 202/647-0518)**. To find your regional passport office, either check the U.S. State Department website or call the **National Passport Information Center (② 900/225-5674)**; the fee is 55¢ per minute for automated information and $1.50 per minute for operator-assisted calls.

For Residents of Canada: Passport applications are available at travel agencies throughout Canada or from the central **Passport Office,** Department of Foreign Affairs and International Trade, Ottawa, ON K1A 0G3 **(② 800/567-6868;** www.ppt.gc.ca).

For Residents of the United Kingdom: To pick up an application for a standard 10-year passport (5-yr. passport for children under 16), visit your nearest passport office, major post office, or travel agency; contact the **United Kingdom Passport Service** at ② **0870/521-0410;** or go to www. ukpa.gov.uk.

For Residents of Ireland: You can apply for a 10-year passport at the **Passport Office,** Setanta Centre, Molesworth Street, Dublin 2 (② **01/671-1633;** www.irlgov.ie/iveagh). Those under 18 and over 65 must apply for a €12 ($14) 3-year passport. You can also apply at 1A South Mall, Cork **(② 021/272-525)** and at most main post offices.

For Residents of Australia: You can pick up an application from your local post office or any branch of Passports Australia, but you must schedule an interview at the passport office to present your application materials. Call the **Australian Passport Information Service** at ② **131-232,** or visit the website at www.passports.gov.au.

For Residents of New Zealand: You can pick up a passport application at any New Zealand Passports Office or download it from the website. Call the **Passports Office (② 0800/225-050** in New Zealand, or 04/474-8100) or go to www.passports.govt.nz.

Police Dial ② **113,** the all-purpose number for police emergency assistance in Italy.

Restrooms All airport and rail stations have toilets, often with attendants who expect to be tipped. Bars, clubs, restaurants, cafes, gas stations, and hotels have facilities as well. Public toilets are also found near many of the major sights. Usually they're designated *WC* (water closet), or *donne* (women) or *uomini* (men). The most confusing designation is *signori* (gentlemen) and *signore* (ladies), so watch that final *i* and *e!* Many public toilets charge a small fee or employ an attendant who expects a tip. Carry tissues in your pocket or purse—they come in handy.

Safety See "Heath & Safety," p. 26.

Taxes As a member of the European Union, Italy imposes a **value-added tax** (called **IVA** in Italy) on most goods and services. The tax that most affects visitors is the one imposed on hotel rates, which ranges from 9% in first- and second-class hotels to 19% in deluxe hotels.

Non-E.U. (European Union) citizens are entitled to a **refund of the IVA** if they spend more than 155€ ($186) at any one store, before tax. To claim your refund, request an invoice from the cashier at the store and take it to the Customs office *(dogana)* at the airport to have it stamped before you leave. *Note:* If you're going to another E.U. country before flying home, have it stamped at the airport Customs office of the last E.U. country you'll be in (for example, if you're flying home via Britain, have your Italian invoices stamped in London). Once back home, mail the stamped invoice (keep a photocopy for your records) back to the original vendor within 90 days of the purchase. The vendor will, sooner or later, send you a refund of the tax that you paid at the time of your purchase. Reputable stores view this as a matter of ordinary paperwork and are businesslike about it. Less-honorable stores might lose your dossier. It pays to deal with established vendors on large purchases. You can also request that the refund be credited to the credit card with which you made the purchase; this is usually faster.

Many shops are now part of the **"Tax Free for Tourists"** network (look for the sticker in the window). Stores participating in this network issue a check along with your invoice at the time of purchase. After you have the invoice stamped at Customs, you can redeem the check for cash directly at the Tax Free booth in the airport at Palermo or Catania, or mail it back in the envelope provided within 60 days.

Telephones To call Italy from the United States, dial the **international prefix, 011;** then Italy's **country code, 39;** and then the city code (for example, **091** for Palermo or **095** for Catania), which is now built into every number. Then dial the actual **phone number.**

A **local phone call** in Italy costs around .10€ (10¢). **Public phones** accept coins, precharged phone cards (*scheda* or *carta telefonica*), or both. You can buy a *carta telefonica* at any *tabacchi* (tobacco shop; most display a sign with a white т on a brown background) in increments of 2.50€ ($3), 5€ ($6), and 7.50€ ($9). To make a call, pick up the receiver and insert .10€ or your card (break off the corner first). Most phones have a digital display that'll tell you how much money you've inserted (or how much is left on the card). Dial the number, and don't forget to take the card with you after you hang up.

To call from one city code to another, dial the city code, complete with initial 0, and then dial the number. (Note that numbers in Sicily range from four to eight digits in length. Even when you're calling within the same city, you must dial that city's area code—including the zero. A Catanian calling another Catanian number must dial 095 before the local number.)

To dial direct internationally, dial 00 and then the country code, the area code, and the number. **Country codes** are as follows: the United States and Canada, 1; the United Kingdom, 44; Ireland, 353; Australia, 61; New Zealand, 64. Make international calls from a public phone, if possible, as hotels almost invariably charge ridiculously inflated rates for direct dial. Calls dialed directly are billed on the basis of the call's duration only. A reduced rate is applied Monday through Saturday from 11pm to 8am and all day Sunday. Direct-dial calls from the United States to Sicily are much cheaper, so arrange to be called at your hotel if possible.

Italy has recently introduced a series of **international phone cards** (*scheda telefonica internazionale*) for calling overseas. They come in increments of 50, 100, 200, and 400 *unita* (units), and they're usually available at *tabacchi* and bars. Each *unita* is worth .15€ of phone time; it costs 5 *unita* (.65€) per minute to call within Europe or to the United States or Canada, and 12 *unita* (1.55€) per minute to call Australia or New Zealand. You don't insert this card into the phone; merely dial ℂ **1740** and then *2 (star 2) for instructions in English, when prompted.

For free national telephone information (in Italian) in Italy, dial ℂ **12.** For international information, dial ℂ **176** but be prepared to pay .60€ (70¢) a shot.

To make collect or calling-card calls, drop in .10€ or insert your card and dial one of the numbers here; an American operator will shortly come on to assist you (because Sicily has yet to discover the joys of the touch-tone phone, you'll have to wait for the operator to come on). The following calling-card numbers work all over Italy: **AT&T,** ℂ 172-1011; **MCI,** ℂ 172-401; and **Sprint,** ℂ 172-1877. To make collect calls to a country besides the United States, dial ℂ **170** (free), and practice your Italian in order to relay the number to the Italian operator. Tell him or her that you want it *a carico del destinatario.*

Don't count on all Sicilian phones to have touch-tone service. You might not be able to access your voice-mail or answering machine from Sicily.

Time Zone Sicily is 6 hours ahead of Eastern Standard Time in the United States. Daylight saving time goes into effect in Italy each year from the end of March to the end of September.

Tipping In **hotels,** the service charge of 15% to 19% is already added to your bill. In addition, it's customary to tip the chambermaid .50€ (60¢) per day, the doorman (for calling a cab) .50€ (60¢), and the bellhop or porter 1.50€ to 2.50€ ($1.80 to $3) for carrying bags to your room. The concierge expects about 15% of his or her bill, as well as tips for extra services performed, which may include help with long-distance calls. In expensive hotels, these amounts are often doubled.

In **restaurants and cafes,** 15% is usually added to your bill to cover most charges. If you're not sure whether this has been done, ask, *"E incluso il servizio?"* (ay een-*cloo*-soh eel sair-*vee*-tsoh?). An additional tip isn't expected, but it's nice to leave the equivalent of an extra couple of dollars if you're pleased with the service. Restaurants are required by law to give customers official receipts. Checkroom attendants expect .75€ (90¢); washroom attendants, .35€ (40¢).

Taxi drivers expect at least 15% of the fare.

Water Most Sicilians take mineral water with their meals; however, tap water is safe everywhere, as are public drinking fountains. Unsafe sources will be marked ACQUA NON POTABILE. If tap water comes out cloudy, it's only the calcium or other minerals inherent in a water supply that often comes untreated from fresh springs.

Settling into Palermo

Through all its vicissitudes, Palermo has continued to capture the imagination of world travelers. In 1768, the German romantic poet Johann Wolfgang Goethe had to see Palermo to add the city to his knowledge of classical culture.

In Goethe's travel diary, *Italian Journey*, he described his arrival by sea and a magnificent setting at the foot of Monte Pellegrino, the "tops of trees swaying like vegetable glow-worms" and a haze tinting "all the shadows blue." So enraptured was Goethe with his first glimpse of Palermo that the captain had to urge him to disembark. Goethe had it right: The best way to appreciate Palermo for the first time is an arrival by sea. Once the poet went ashore, he decided that Palermo was "easy to grasp in its overall plan, but difficult to get to know in detail." That observation is still valid today.

As a city, Palermo is both loathed and adored by visitors, praised and condemned. It's a mixture of panache and poverty, a place of beauty that is hideously ugly in places, and a great city in which to wear a money belt and keep an eye on your camera. There are a lot safer places to be in the world than Palermo after dark.

Palermo's Arab-Norman buildings have no equal on the planet, and the entire city is a treasure trove of museums (often dusty, forgotten ones) and baroque oratories. Its outdoor markets, such as raucous Vucciria, evoke North Africa and are still dominated by the influence of the Arabs who departed centuries ago.

To feel the pulse of Palermo, visit one of these markets. We are eternally fascinated by the sea creatures sold—even Jacques Cousteau would have been amazed. We sigh at the beauty of mounds of purple artichokes, piles of blood-red oranges, and pyramids of oyster-white eggplant.

Get used to the roar of traffic and the wail of police sirens. Watch out for those cars racing down the street. Noise and pollution hang over the city as you ricochet your way among old monuments: Arab cupolas, Byzantine street markets, and Norman and baroque architectural gems that someone forgot to tear down a long time ago.

Its summers are oppressive—"not fit for habitation," in the words of one visitor—and its street scenes frenetic. Think Tangier or Algiers.

Palermo still bears the imprint of its former conquerors. What it's not is a typically European city, nor even an Italian one for that matter. As one of its 700,000 residents is quick to point out, "We're Sicilian—*not* Italian."

"Yes, yes, we have crime," a city official reluctantly admits, seemingly angered that we had raised the subject. "But it's mostly petty crime. We have an underground that exists on various levels. But give us some credit. For centuries Palermo knows how to absorb its villains well."

Palermo is old, and in spite of certain "beauty marks," it looks it. The Phoenicians established a trading post here in the 8th century B.C. In time Palermo became the Carthaginian center of Sicily. When the Roman conquest came in 254 B.C., Palermo went into decline, as the new conquerors shifted their power and trading to Syracuse on the east coast.

As the centuries moved inexorably forward, Palermo played host to what seemed like never-ending armies of invaders. The Vandals came, then the Ostrogoths, and by 831 the city had fallen to the Arabs. Although that seemed a disaster at the time, Palermo under the Arabs became one of the great emporiums of the Mediterranean, with splendid mosques and sumptuous palaces. It was the equal of Cairo in Egypt or Córdoba in Spain.

Even by the 11th century, with the Arabs in retreat, Palermo still flourished. By 1072, it had fallen to Roger de Hauteville, marking the beginning of the Norman period. Under his son, King Roger, who ruled from 1130 to 1154, Palermo entered its golden age, with Muslims, Christians, and Jews living in harmony and prosperity. There's a lot to be said for religious tolerance.

Under King Frederick, who ascended to the throne of Sicily in 1208, Palermo became the capital of the Holy Roman Empire. The grand age of Hohenstaufen rule ended in 1266 when the French Angevins came to the throne, launching a despotic rule that ended in the Rebellion of the Sicilian Vespers in 1282.

In the aftermath, the Spanish Aragonese came into power and influence in Palermo. The Aragonese preferred Naples over Palermo as a capital, and in their departure the power vacuum was filled with feudal families and religious orders.

Palermo was never to regain the power and prestige it enjoyed in its long-ago heyday. The city's decay and decline stretched on for centuries. Then an even worse disaster descended on it in 1943, when the city was targeted for massive bombardments by Allied air forces stationed in North Africa.

In the aftermath of the war, Palermo was reconstructed haphazardly. In the postwar years, the city's very name became a synonym for corruption under the Mafia. Over the past 10 years, the odious influence of this gang has been on the wane, but we suspect there are still plenty of aging *Godfather* types hiding out behind all those closely guarded compounds.

A number of city officials will admit (off the record, of course) that many of the funds allocated in Rome or by the European Union to "rescue" Palermo have ended up in the pockets of the Mafia. But the unheard-of actually happened some 20 years ago: A series of informers, at risk for their lives, came forward to squeal on the Mafia.

Palermo headlines blared that "the tide was turning" against the *Cosa Nostra*. The fight continued under Leoluca Orlando, the city's mayor from 1993 to 2001. He refused to have the city do business with companies he suspected of having links with the Mafia. Even his own Christian Democrat party disavowed him, but that didn't stop Orlando.

Along with the fight against crime, Palermo only belatedly came to realize the greatness of its architectural heritage. Interest in restoration has at long last arrived. The Teatro Massimo was restored and reopened in 1997, and old and historic quarters, such as Kalsa, are being restored and given a new lease on life with the opening of restaurants, galleries, and cafes. In Palermo, there is hope for the future.

An old-time resident, Giovanni Fatone, summed it up this way for us: "We have passion—sometimes— although it fades with age. We awake with energy but often lose strength in the scalding sun. We are warm and friendly but also rude and irksome when our mood changes quickly. We are a simple people but capable of great wisdom and sophistication when called upon. Palermo and its people are a controversial lot, and many bad things are said and written about us. But even our enemies agree on one point: We are the consumers of the pleasures of life."

1 Essentials

GETTING THERE

BY PLANE   Flights into Palermo from mainland Italy are obviously the fastest, most convenient links. Palermo's airport, **Punta Raisi/Falcone & Borsellino Airport,** is the island's largest, with the greatest number of flights; it's 31km (19 miles) west of Palermo on the A29 highway. For more detailed information on flights into Sicily, see p. 36. In Palermo, you can call ℂ 091-6019250 for information on domestic flights or ℂ 091-7020111 for international connections. Most likely you will be booked on a flight via Rome or Milan to your return destination.

From the airport, a local **bus** to Piazza Giulio Cesare (central train station) will cost 6€ ($7.20). A **taxi** is likely to charge at least 35€ ($42)—or more, if the driver thinks he can get away with it. It's also possible to rent a **car** at the airport (all the major firms are represented) and drive into Palermo. Allow 20 to 30 minutes—longer, if traffic is bad—to get to the center of town. See also "Getting Around," below.

BY TRAIN   Palermo has good rail links with the rest of Sicily and also to Italy. After a 3-hour ride from Messina, on the northeast coast, you'll arrive at Palermo's main terminal, **Stazione Centrale,** at Piazza Giulio Cesare (ℂ 091-6161844), which lies on the eastern side of town and is linked to the center by a network of buses or taxis. The ticket office here is open daily from 6:45am to 8:40pm, with luggage storage available.

The train ride from Catania, in the east, takes 3½ hours, with frequent departures throughout the day. From Trapani, in the west, it's a 2½-hour ride, with 11 trains arriving daily.

It's also possible to book trains from major Italian cities. From Rome, it's an 11-hour trip, with seven trains arriving per day. From Naples, visitors usually take the ferry, though the 9-hour train ride is also an option (there are about five trains daily).

Intra-island train tickets are cheap: 18€ ($22) from Catania; 11€ ($13) from Messina; 7€ ($8.40) from Agrigento; and 6.80€ ($8.15) from Trapani. The big rail haul from Rome costs 56€ ($67) one-way. For rail information for Sicily or Italy in general, call ℂ **892021.**

BY BUS   You can take a bus from Rome to Palermo, but we don't recommend it: The ride is long, dull, and boring. Palermo-bound buses leave Rome's Tiburtina station daily at 8am and 9pm; the trip takes 12 hours. For information, call **Segesta,** Via Balsamo 26 (ℂ **091-6167919**).

If you prefer bus travel, we'd suggest it for shorter hauls on the island itself. There are convenient links to major cities by **SAIS,** Via Balsamo 16 (ℂ **091-6166028**). From Messina, it takes 3¼ hours to reach Palermo; from Catania, 2½ hours. Segesta also has bus links to Trapani in the west, a 2-hour trip. **Cuffaro,** Via Balsamo 13 (ℂ **091-6161510**), runs between Palermo and the city of Agrigento in 2½ hours.

Tips **The Next Pocket Picked May Be Yours**

Palermo is home to some of the most skilled pickpockets on the Continent, so be especially alert. Don't flaunt jewelry, cameras, or wads of bills; women who carry handbags are particularly vulnerable to purse snatchers on Vespas. Park your car in a garage rather than on the street, and don't keep valuables inside. Police squads operate mobile centers throughout the town to help combat street crime.

The Palermo bus stations along Via Balsamo are adjacent to the rail station. The trip from Rome costs 38€ ($46), but most bus fares on the island are inexpensive. For example, the cost from Trapani is 6.20€ ($7.45); from Agrigento, 7.20€ ($8.65); from Catania, 12€ ($14); and from Messina, 13€ ($16).

BY CAR   Three *autostrade* (superhighways) link Palermo with the rest of Sicily. The most used routes are A19 from Catania or A20 from Messina. From the west, A29 comes in from Mazara del Vallo. In addition, two main highways link Palermo: SS113 from Trapani in the west or Messina in the east, and SS121 from Catania and Enna in the east. Palermo is cut off from mainland Italy. To reach it by car, you'll have to cross the Straits of Messina by ferries operated by FS, the state railway authority.

Once the ferry has landed at Messina, you'll still face a drive of 233km (145 miles) to Palermo. If you're planning to drive down from Naples or Rome, as many visitors do, prepare yourself for a long trip: 721km (448 miles) south from Naples, 934km (580 miles) south from Rome.

BY BOAT   This is our favorite way to get here from mainland Italy, since we always visit Palermo from Naples. From Naples, the most convenient service over to Palermo is provided by **SNAV** (© 081-4285555). The ferry trip takes 10½ hours and costs 30€ to 69€ ($36–$83) per person. A rival ferry is operated by **Tirrenia Lines** (© 199-123199), which takes 10½ hours and costs 38€ to 74€ ($46–$89). Schedules vary depending on weather conditions, so always call on the day of departure even if you've already confirmed your reservation the day before.

VISITOR INFORMATION

There are tourist offices at strategic points, including the Palermo airport (© **091-591698**) and the main train stations (© **091-6165914**). The principal office is the **Azienda Autonoma Turismo,** Piazza Castelnuovo 34 (© **091-583847**), open Monday through Friday from 8:30am to 2pm and 3 to 7pm, and Saturday from 9am to 1pm. When you stop in, ask for a good city map.

CITY LAYOUT

The capital of Sicily has both an Old City and a so-called New City. The hardest part to navigate is the sector lying north of the rail depot. The street plan of the Middle Ages is still in effect here, so it's easy to get lost.

Two main roads cut across medieval Palermo, the **Old City,** virtually "quartering it." The first is **Corso Vittorio Emanuele,** which begins at La Cala, the ancient harbor, and cuts southwest to the landmark Palazzo dei Normanni and the Duomo (the Palermo cathedral). Corso Vittorio Emanuele runs east/west through this ancient maze of streets known to the Arabs of long ago. The other street splitting the town into two sections is **Via Roma,** which runs north and south.

The Old City is split into quadrants at the **Quattro Canti,** the virtual heart of Palermo. This is the point where Vittorio Emanuele crosses **Via Maqueda,** an artery beginning to the west of the rail depot, heading northwest. Running roughly parallel to Via Maqueda to its east is **Via Roma,** which heads north from Piazza Giulio Césare. Via Roma and the much older Via Maqueda, virtually parallel streets, shoulder the burden of most of the inner city's heavy traffic.

La Kalsa, the medieval core of Palermo, lies to the southeast of the busy hub of Quattro Canti. The residential neighborhood of **Alberghiera** is to the southwest of Quattro Canti. This is the center of the sprawling Ballaro market. Like La Kalsa, Alberghiera was heavily bombed in World War II.

Chances are you'll have little reason to visit **Sincaldi,** the northwest quadrant, unless you want to go to the Capo market. The smallest of the districts of the quadrant is **Amalfitani,** the northeast sector. La Cala, the ancient harbor, eats up most of the space in the district.

Via Cavour divides the medieval core to the south and the **New City** to the north. In spite of its heavy traffic, the more modern section of Palermo is much easier to navigate. At the heart of this grid are the double squares of **Piazza Castelnuovo** and **Piazza Ruggero Séttimo.** Palermitans call this piazza maze **Piazza Politeama** (or just Politeama). At the double square, Via Ruggero Séttimo (a continuation of Via Maqueda; see above) crosses **Via Emerico Amari.**

Heading northwest from Politeama is Palermo's swankiest street, **Viale della Libertà,** home to smart stores and tony boutiques. It is also the street of many upmarket restaurants, bars, office blocks, and galleries. Libertà races its way to the southern tip of **Parco della Favorita.**

STREET MAPS   Even with a good map, you can get lost in the maze of central Palermo. The tourist office issues maps called "Carta Monumentale" that are sold all over Palermo. These are updated every year or so to take into account the many changes occurring in the city as it alters and restores itself. If you purchase a map, make sure it has a street index (some don't). Otherwise, you've wasted your money.

NEIGHBORHOODS IN BRIEF

Historically, the medieval quarters of Palermo were rigidly defined. You were born into one of the city quarters, you grew up there, married, had children, and died there. What you didn't do was intermarry with a man or woman from another quarter. When this was done, it met with social ostracism. Each quarter had its own dialect, palaces, markets, and shops. From an early age, children learned the boundaries of their quarter and stayed within it. Palermo today, of course, is hardly so rigidly confined, and its citizens move throughout the city. But Palermo still has its neighborhoods, beginning with La Kalsa.

La Kalsa The Saracens created this quarter; in Arabic, *Khalisa* means pure, but little was ever pure about La Kalsa. Only now is it awakening to tourism. Always an interesting section, evocative of a city in North Africa, it was viewed as extremely dangerous after dark. The opening of bars and restaurants has changed that pattern, though it's still not a place to wander blithely about at night. The center of La Kalsa was destroyed in 1943 by Allied bombers, and for

years in the postwar era it remained a large bomb site. Today, that bombed area has been turned into a green park, but the neighborhood still has plenty of narrow alleys and streets to get lost in. Kalsa lies to the east of Albergheria, moving toward the harbor, and to the south of Corso Vittorio Emanuele.

La Vucciria North of Kalsa and north of Corso Vittorio Emanuele, La Vucciria moves east toward the harbor and the ancient port of La

Cala. It is bordered to the west by the Palazzo dei Normanni and Porta Nuova and to the south by the bus terminal, Stazione Centrale. Its northern outpost is Piazza Verdi. Although famed mainly for its open-air market, Vucciria is also filled with monuments and is of major interest to art-loving visitors. This is the best known of all the quadrants that form the core of the medieval city. Like La Kalsa, it is still viewed as a dangerous place at night, especially along its dark maze of little alleyways. But few can resist a look at the market Leonardo Sciascia called a "hungry man's dream." In the book *Midnight in Sicily,* Peter Robb called it "the belly of Palermo and its heart, too."

Il Ballaro Most of this sector lies to the west of Kalsa and to the south of Il Capo, which begins north of Corso Vittorio Emanuele, the northern fringe of Ballaro. Ballaro is known mainly for its market lying to the west of Piazza Ballaro. This district is also home to one of Palermo's most elegant baroque squares, Piazza Bologni. A statue of the emperor Charles V stands in the heart of a rectangle of palaces decorated with coats-of-arms.

Il Capo One of the oldest quadrants of Palermo, Il Capo lies in the northwest, east of Vucciria and directly north of Ballaro. You've entered it once you cross north from Corso Vittorio Emanuele. Il Capo, too, is filled with decaying streets, alleys, and lanes occasionally broken by little pockets of greenery. Our favorite square here is Piazza del Monte, which is planted with trees and has a friendly neighborhood bar or two. The palaces are decaying, and there's not a lot of tourist interest here, but we still like to wander about with no particular goal other than to appreciate the neighborhood and wonder what

lives are led behind the rotting facades of all those once-noble *palazzi* (palaces). Eventually you'll come to Porta Carini, one of the major gates left over from the Middle Ages.

Albergheria South of Ballaro is this historic old district, bounded by Via Maqueda and Corso Vittorio Emanuele and lying to the northwest of the Stazione Centrale. Ripe in its decay, Albergheria is filled in part with palazzi, like all the other neighborhoods, particularly in the area that opens onto Via Maqueda. The most notable of these is the Palazzo Santa Croce, at the intersection of Via Maqueda and Via Bosco. Much of Albergheria's central area is absorbed by an open-air street market. The district is filled with a maze of narrow alleys and streets, and it also contains many fine churches (many in desperate need of funds). Several sections are very poor, and since poverty breeds crime, be sure to exercise caution both day and night. Much of the bomb damage from 1943 remains, simply because no one has ever had the money to fully restore the area.

New City As you head north of the medieval quarter, the streets grow broader but also more nondescript. The monumental and recently restored **Teatro Massimo,** at Piazza Verdi, marks the division between the Old City and the New City. Once Via Maqueda cuts through the medieval district, it becomes Via Ruggero Séttimo as it heads north through the modern town. This street explodes into the massive double squares at Piazza Politeama, site of Teatro Politeama Garibaldi. North of the square is Palermo's swankiest street, Viale della Libertà, shooting up toward Giardino Ingese.

GETTING AROUND

Parking is difficult in Palermo, and traffic horrendous. There are treasures to be found here, but getting around to see them is more than difficult.

BY BUS   The modernized bus system, once you learn to work it, is the best means of getting around the attractions on the periphery of Palermo, such as Monreale or Mondello. Most central lines cross Via Maqueda and its parallel street Via Roma, going through the quadrants of the old town. Other buses run east and west along the major dividing street, Corso Vittorio Emanuele.

In the New Town, Piazza Verdi, with its landmark Teatro Massimo, is a major hub, as is Piazza Politeama.

A ride on a municipal bus costs around 1€ ($1.20) and the ticket remains in effect for two hours, or else you can buy a full-day ticket for 3.35€ ($4). For information, call **AMAT,** Via Borrelli 16 (© **091-6902690**). Most passengers buy their tickets at tobacco shops *(tabacchi)* before boarding.

A tourist bus called *Giro Città* begins and ends its circuit at the landmark Teatro Politeama (the Emerico Amari side). It stops at many major monuments, including the Duomo and the Royal Palace. Departures are at 9am daily. Tickets are sold on board; there are no advance reservations. The cost is 11€ ($13) per person. Children under 12 are granted a 50% discount. For information, call © **091-6902690.**

BY TAXI   Getting around the inner core of Palermo by bus is very time-consuming and not easy, and driving a car around Palermo is a nightmare. In most cases, taxis are the best way to navigate the city center. Taxi stands are found at the main rail depot, at Piazza Verdi, at Piazza Indipendenza, and at Piazza Ruggero Séttimo, among other locations. The meter drops at 3.50€ ($4.20) and charges 2.25€ ($2.70) for the first kilometer, plus .65€ (80¢) per kilometer thereafter. If you can't find a taxi on the street, call © **091-513311** or 091-513374.

If you can afford it, consider renting a taxi for the day to explore Palermo attractions; it will cost 80€ to 90€ ($96–$108). Most drivers speak only a few words of English, but somehow they manage. You can request an English-speaking driver; perhaps one will be available. For further information on taxi sightseeing, call © **091-512737.**

ON FOOT   Palermo is a city designed for walking, especially to the museums, monuments, and palaces in the medieval core. But walking is exhausting and not at all practical if you want to take in attractions on the city's periphery. To go outside the center, rely on the network of buses (see above).

BY CAR   Driving around Palermo can be done, but is guaranteed to take years off your life. You may want to rent a car for side trips to places like Monreale, however. Rentals can be arranged at airport desks or at offices within central Palermo. The major firms include **Avis,** Punta Raisi Airport (© **091-591684**), and Via Francesco Crispi 115 (© **091-586940**). There are two leading Italian car-rental firms: **Maggiore** (© **091-591681**) is at the airport, with a branch at the Notarbartolo Railway Station (© **091-6810801**); **Sicily By Car** (© **091-591250**) is also at the airport, as well as at Via Stabile Mariano 6A (© **091-581045**). Rates average from 62€ to 70€ ($74–$84) per day.

Then there's parking. Parking spaces are like gold in central Palermo. One of the most convenient garages is **Garage Stazione Centrale** (© **091-6168297**), at the rail station, which charges 15€ ($18) per night (closed Sun). Two other convenient garages—identified simply by the word GARAGE—are at Via Stabile

10 ((C) **091-321667**), charging 15€ ($18) per night, and at Via Libertà 102 ((C) **091-305512**), charging 20€ ($24) per night.

BY ORGANIZED TOUR The best tours are offered by **CST (Compania Siciliana Turismo),** 124 Via Emerico Amari. You can visit its office in person to discuss your interests and see what is available on any given day. CST arranges trips to such sights in Palermo as Monte Pellegrino or the Capuchin Catacombs, but will also set up side trips to the Greek ruins at Segesta, or day trips to western coastal towns such as Erice and Trapani. CST can be contacted by fax at **091-582294,** or by email at cstmail@tin.it.

FAST FACTS: Palermo

American Express American Express services are available through a local agency, at **Giovanni Ruggieri e Figli,** Emerico Amari 40 ((C) **091-587144),** open Monday through Friday from 9am to 1pm and 4 to 7:30pm, Saturday from 9am to 1pm. Lose your card? Call (C) **06-72282** at once.

Bookstore The best offering of English-language titles is found at **Feltrinelli,** Via Maqueda 395 ((C) **091-587785),** open Monday through Saturday from 9am to 7pm.

Consulates There's a **U.S. Consulate** at Via Vaccarini 1 ((C) **091-305857),** open Monday through Friday from 9am to 1:30pm. There's also a **United Kingdom Consulate** at Via Cavour 117 ((C) **091-326412),** open Monday through Friday from 9am to 1pm.

Emergencies For the police, dial (C) **112;** for an ambulance, (C) **118;** and to report a fire, (C) **115.** For road assistance, dial (C) **116.** In a general crisis, call the *Carabinieri* at (C) **113.**

Hospital The most convenient emergency center is at **Ospedale Civico,** Via Carmelo Lazzaro ((C) **091-6661111).**

Internet Access Your most central bet is **Internett@mente,** Via S. Martino 3A ((C) **091-6121174),** which charges 3€ ($3.60) per half hour for its services; open Monday from 3 to 8pm, Tuesday through Saturday from 10am to 8pm. The best and biggest Internet cafe in Palermo is **Everalways Internet C@fè,** Corso Tukory 198 ((C) **091-217652).** It has 55 computers and charges 1.50€ ($1.80) per half hour; open Monday through Saturday from 9am to midnight.

Lost Property Check with **Ufficio Stranieri,** V. S. Lorenzo Colli 271A ((C) **091-6725111).** The train station has its own lost-and-found office: **Oggetti Rinvenuti** ((C) **091-6031111)** at the Stazione Centrale. Hours for both offices are daily from 9am to 1pm and 3 to 7pm.

Luggage Storage You can leave luggage at an office in the Stazione Centrale, open daily from 6am to 10pm. It charges 3€ ($3.60) per suitcase for 12 hours. For information, call (C) **091-6033040.**

Pharmacies Convenient pharmacies in the city center are found at the following addresses: Via Roma 1 ((C) **091-6162117);** Via Mariano Stabile 177 ((C) **091-334482);** and Via Principe di Belmonte 110 ((C) **091-581771).**

Police Dial (C) **112.**

Post Office The main post office is at Via Roma 320 (© **091-7535193**), open Monday through Friday from 8am to 7pm, Saturday from 8am to noon. Branches can be found at the train station (no phone), open Monday through Saturday from 8:30am to 1pm; and at the airport (© **091-212176**), open Monday through Friday from 8:30am to 3:30pm.

Transit Information Call the local bus company, **AMAT**, at © **091-6902690.**

Travel Agencies See **"American Express,"** above. Budget-oriented travelers can try **Wasteels**, Via Francesco Paolo di Blasi 14 (© **091-7308304**), open Monday through Saturday from 7:30am to 2:30pm.

2 Where to Stay

Hotels in Palermo come in all shapes, sizes, prices, and degrees of comfort, so you should not have trouble finding a room that suits both your desires and your pocketbook. You can live in first-class style or rather inexpensively; the city has more good and inexpensive accommodations than any other place in Sicily.

Because of the heat, July and August are the low season, whereas in such coastal resorts as Taormina those are the most expensive months to visit.

Budget hotels in Palermo are called *pensioni, locande,* or *alberghi,* and most of them lie at the southern frontiers of those two parallel streets, Via Maqueda and Via Roma. Women traveling alone will feel safer checking into hotels on one of the main arteries and not down some narrow side street in the medieval quarters.

VERY EXPENSIVE

Villa Igiea Grand Hotel ★★★   The best hotel in town, Villa Igiea, built at the turn of the 20th century, is a remarkable example of Sicilian Art Nouveau. It's in better shape and more comfortable than the also highly rated Grand Hotel et des Palmes, Palermo's other historic property. Once the private villa of the Fiorio family, whose claim to fame was coming up with the notion of putting tuna fish into a tin can, the villa hosts the moneyed elite of Sicily when they're in town for business or pleasure.

Located in the suburb of Acquasanta, 2.4km (1½ miles) north of the center and reached after you pass through a shabby district, the villa is surrounded by a park overlooking the sea. The old architecture has been preserved, including ceilings with stone vaults joining in an arch. Guest rooms contain valuable furnishings such as comfortable wrought-iron beds. Each unit has a bathroom with tub-shower combination. The villa also has a pool and tennis court. We like to wander the jasmine-scented gardens at night, admiring the ancient Greek temple near the water's edge. It's an evocative moment for Palermo.

Note: This hotel is at the edge of town, so you'll likely need to rent a car or take cabs, which can be expensive. It's the best lodging in the area, but inconvenient for those who like to get around on foot.

Salita Belmonte 43, Acquasanta, 90142 Palermo. © 091-6312111. Fax 091-547654. www.cormorano.net/sgas/villaigiea. 116 units. 163€–424€ ($196–$509) double; 421€–584€ ($505–$701) suite. Rates include breakfast. AE, DC, MC, V. Free parking. Bus: 139. **Amenities:** Dining room; bar; outdoor saltwater pool; tennis court; room service; babysitting; laundry service; dry cleaning; nonsmoking rooms; rooms for those w/limited mobility. *In room:* A/C, TV, dataport, minibar, hair dryer, safe.

EXPENSIVE

Astoria Palace Hotel ★★   Chances are good that if a CEO or even a president is bunking down in Palermo, he or she will be sheltered at this government-rated four-star selection. For sheer comfort and convenience, and not for those seeking an accommodation dripping with atmosphere, we consider Astoria Palace the number-two hotel in town, ranked just after the charming but less efficient Villa Igiea. Don't let the word "palace" fool you, however. The name comes from the fact that it's a behemoth, not some classic antique. It is the biggest hotel in town and the setting for many large conventions. It is our sincere hope that you won't be here during one; you'll feel more welcomed and will get better service if you don't have to share the place with hundreds of conventioneers.

The rooms have modern but elegant furnishings, and the bathrooms with tub and shower are kept in state-of-the-art condition. Not all rooms are spacious; some are rather boxlike with just a small window. If you can afford it, go for a junior suite, which will be far bigger and more comfortable. Naturally, the best units are those on the top floor where the view is less obstructed.

Via Monte Pellegrino 62, 90142 Palermo. ⓒ 091-6282111. Fax 091-6372178. www.ghshotels.it. 315 units. 177€ ($212) double; 235€ ($282) triple; 270€ ($324) suite. Rates include American buffet breakfast. AE, DC, MC, V. Free parking. Bus: 139 or 721. **Amenities:** 2 restaurants; bar; business center; room service; babysitting; laundry service; dry cleaning; nonsmoking rooms; valet. *In room:* A/C, TV, dataport, minibar, hair dryer.

Centrale Palace 🏨🏨
For atmosphere and comfort, we'd still give the edge to Villa Igiea or the Astoria Palace—but Centrale Palace is a close runner-up. No other lodging lies as close to the Duomo, the Quattro Canti, and the monumental medieval heart of Palermo. The core of the hotel is a 17th-century private home, although guest rooms occupy adjacent buildings that are newer. The lobby is daringly painted in vivid colors associated with the Italian Renaissance, such as terra cotta and intense blues.

The original palazzo was converted into a hotel in 1892 during Palermo's Belle Epoque Golden Age. Some period or Empire antiques are placed about to take the curse off the *moderno.* But many furnishings, especially those in the guest rooms, have more function than flair. Doubles are generally medium-size to spacious, with modernized bathrooms that mostly come with tub-shower combinations. The quietest rooms are on the side streets, and double-glazing on the front windows block but do not entirely keep out Palermo's horrific street noise. Our favorite perch is the top-floor dining room, taking in views over the Palermo rooftops to Monte Pellegrino.

Corso Vittorio Emanuele 327 (at Via Maqueda), 99134 Palermo. ⓒ 091-336666. Fax 091-334881. www. centralepalacehotel.it. 103 units. 233€–256€ ($280–$307) double; 269€–290€ ($323–$348) junior suite. Rates include buffet breakfast. AE, DC, MC, V. Parking 15€ ($18). Bus: 103, 104, or 105. **Amenities:** Restaurant; bar; gym; sauna; 24-hr. room service; babysitting; laundry service; dry cleaning; nonsmoking rooms; solarium; rooms for those w/limited mobility. *In room:* A/C, TV, dataport, minibar, hair dryer.

Grand Hotel et des Palmes 🏨
This is the most legendary hotel in Sicily, and it's still receiving guests even though its heyday is long past. For nostalgia buffs, however, there's nothing to top it. Since the 19th century, it has sheltered some of the island's most illustrious visitors, including Richard Wagner, who finished *Parsifal* here. The hotel has seen enough murders, suicides of poets, romantic but off-the-record liaisons, and aristocratic intrigue to fill a book the size of *War and Peace.* Classy furnishings, towering pillars, and antique chandeliers still evoke the greatness of a bygone era. The charm of this antique grande dame glows on its rooftop terrace as well.

Now used largely to house tour groups, the hotel carries on nobly with such drawbacks as an absolute lack of greenery and a location along one of the busiest streets of Palermo. Management is working to revive the place to its former glory, but it's an uphill battle, and a great deal depends on your room assignment.

Palermo Accommodations & Dining

While the public rooms are still glamorous, some guest rooms can be disappointingly simple. The best ones feature antiques, heavy Italian fabrics, stucco ceilings, and parquet floors.

Via Roma 398, 90139 Palermo. © 091-6028111. Fax 091-331545. www.amthotels.it. 183 units. 185€–225€ ($222–$270) double; 250€–300€ ($300–$360) suite. Rates include buffet breakfast. AE, DC, MC, V. Parking 15€ ($18). Bus: 101, 102, 103, 104, or 225. **Amenities:** Restaurant; bar; room service; babysitting; laundry service; dry cleaning; all nonsmoking rooms; solarium. *In room:* A/C, TV, dataport (in some units), minibar, hair dryer, safe.

Massimo Plaza Hotel ★ *Value*   Its major competitor, Principe di Villafranca, has better facilities, but we still applaud this little palazzo for its location in the historic center in front of the Teatro Massimo, reached after a steep climb up a flight of steps. It has a tasteful but subdued elegance that we like as well. The hotel oozes Sicilian style, from its welcoming atmosphere to its drawing-room-like bar; it also has a breakfast room and a reading room. Most small hotels in this category have cramped guest rooms, but the accommodations here are fairly spacious and comfortably furnished, each with a tub-and-shower bathroom and soundproofing against the curse of Palermo: traffic noise. The hotel has been refurbished as part of a general architectural restoration in the historic sector—but it still has no elevator.

Via Maqueda 437, 90133 Palermo. © 091-325657. Fax 091-325711. www.massimoplazahotel.com. 15 units. 192€ ($230) double; 230€ ($276) triple. AE, DC, MC, V. Parking 13€ ($16). Bus: 101 or 102. **Amenities:** Bar; babysitting; laundry service; dry cleaning; nonsmoking rooms; private beach. *In room:* A/C, TV, dataport, fridge, safe.

Principe di Villafranca ★★★ *Finds*   This charming 1998 property is the finest boutique-style hotel in Palermo. Stylish, intimate, and evocative of an elegant, unfussy private home, it occupies two floors of what was originally built as a low-rise apartment house. Its Sicilian theme includes enough antiques and architectural finesse to make you think the place is a lot older than it really is. Grace notes include Oriental rugs, marble floors, vaulted ceilings, and a baronial fireplace. The hotel and some of its neighbors were built within what was once one of Palermo's most beautiful gardens, the Ferriato, owned long ago by the princes of Villafranca.

Guest rooms are midsize to spacious, with tile, granite, and travertine bathrooms with tub and shower; Internet access; and a welcome variety of postmodern comfort and style. The excellent restaurant, Il Firriato, specializes in elegant Sicilian food. In the bar, notice the valuable Liberty-era writing desk crafted by Basile, one of the luminaries of his era.

Via G. Turrisi Colonna 4, 90141 Palermo. © 091-6118523. Fax 091-588705. www.principedivillafranca.it. 34 units. 185€ ($222) double; 268€ ($322) suite. Rates include buffet breakfast. AE, DC, MC, V. Free parking. Bus: 101 or 102. **Amenities:** Restaurant; bar; gym; 24-hr. room service; babysitting; laundry service; dry cleaning. *In room:* A/C, TV, minibar, hair dryer, safe.

MODERATE

Hotel Sport Club Portorais ★   This is the best and most appealing of the hotels near Palermo's airport, with very little of the aircraft noise you'd expect from such a location. Painted pink, and designed like a Mediterranean villa, it was built in the 1970s on a small bay lined with jagged boulders. Owned and operated by the Marchese family, it functions both as a resort and as an airport hotel, welcoming overnight guests who want to avoid the traffic congestion of Palermo on the morning of their departure.

Inside the hotel is a surprisingly interesting collection of art and antiques, including 18th- and 19th-century choir stalls, painted dowry chests, and an elaborately carved *portantina,* a cramped but gilded box with horizontal poles, wherein ladies used to be carried by hardworking members of their entourages. Many guests here spend their days beside the terraced, oval-shaped pool or at the private pebbly beach. The hotel's restaurant is excellent, and a dining pavilion opens directly onto a view of the sea. Rooms are high-ceilinged and airy, with Asian art, tiled bathrooms (mostly with showers but no tubs), and, in many cases, private terraces or loggias.

Via Piraineto 125, 90044 Carini (Palermo). © **091-8693481.** Fax 091-8693458. www.portorais.it. 44 units. 150€–180€ ($180–$216) double. Rates include breakfast. Free parking. AE, DC, MC, V. **Amenities:** Restaurant; bar; outdoor saltwater pool; gym; laundry service; dry cleaning. *In room:* A/C, TV, minibar.

Jolly Hotel Foro Italico ✦   Many hotels of charm and grace now compete for the position of the top five or six "best in town." Given the added competition, this 1960s chain hotel, once one of the best, is now much lower on the food chain. That doesn't mean that it's fallen off in standards. It's still the same well-organized, well-run hotel it always was. Its major selling point is that it's the only hotel in the center with a swimming pool—and on an August day in Palermo, that's one heck of a selling point. Its location overlooking the sea and the Foro Italico adds to its allure.

A few steps from the Villa Giulia, the Jolly is also close to the harbor and the rail station. As was the style in Italy in the 1960s, rooms tend to be small. They are comfortable, however, and well organized, with lots of built-ins, frequently renewed bed linens, and tiled bathrooms with showers. To escape the traffic noise, ask for one of the more tranquil units on the upper floors, which also have better views of the sea.

Via Foro Italico 22, 90133 Palermo. © **800/221-2626** in the U.S., 800/237-0319 in Canada, or 091-6165090. Fax 091-6161441. 237 units. 136€–172€ ($163–$206) double; 220€–274€ ($264–$329) suite. Rates include breakfast. Half board 34€ ($41) per person. AE, DC, MC, V. Parking 15€ ($18). Bus: 139. **Amenities:** Restaurant; bar; outdoor pool (seasonal); room service; laundry service; dry cleaning; nonsmoking rooms. *In room:* A/C, TV, minibar, hair dryer.

Palazzo Excelsior ✦   No hotel in Palermo evokes the faded nostalgia of the late 19th century as effectively as this one. Built in 1892, it sits in a quiet neighborhood at the northern end of the prestigious Via Libertà, in a site that's both convenient to major boulevards and isolated. You get the sense that you're in a living museum here—the kind of appealingly dowdy and very grand venue that hasn't yet been "gussied up" by teams of 21st-century decorators. The result is appropriately old-fashioned. Guest rooms benefited from a renovation last year, though retain a vague Liberty-style overlay despite their modernizations. The restaurant, where the staff is appropriately uniformed and formal, serves regional specialties.

Via Marchese Ugo 3, 90141 Palermo. © **091-6256176.** Fax 091-342139. www.excelsiorpalermo.it. 127 units. 185€–235€ ($222–$282) double; 240€–300€ ($288–$360) suite. Rates include buffet breakfast. AE, DC, MC, V. Free parking. Bus: 101, 104, 107, 108, or 806. **Amenities:** Restaurant; bar; room service; babysitting; laundry service; dry cleaning; nonsmoking rooms; rooms for those w/limited mobility. *In room:* A/C, TV, dataport, minibar, safe.

Politeama Palace Hotel   This is a very appealing hotel, with lots of regional charm and enough touches of international modernity to make tour groups from northern Europe feel at home. Built in 1977, and set behind an angular concrete facade, it rises nine stories above a point immediately adjacent to one of Palermo's most architecturally distinctive theaters, the Politeama, in the heart of the stylish Via Libertà district. Inside, expect a contemporary decor of polished granite, hardwood, leather, and Italian *moderno* styling. The most interesting rooms overlook the heroic bronze chariots on the nearby theater and the square that contains it. All units contain elaborate woodwork, gilt touches, original art, dignified friezes that evoke baronial life in 19th-century Sicily, and small- to medium-size tile or stone bathrooms with tub and shower. Some rooms have Jacuzzis as well.

Piazza Ruggiero Settimo 15, 90139 Palermo. ℂ 091-322777. Fax 091-6111589. www.hotelpoliteama.it. 94 units. 190€ ($228) double; 207€–250€ ($248–$300) suite. Rates include breakfast. AE, DC, MC, V. Bus: 101, 102, 103, or 104. **Amenities:** Restaurant; bar; babysitting; laundry service. *In room:* A/C, TV w/pay movies, dataport, minibar, hair dryer.

President Hotel   This eight-story concrete-and-glass structure rising above the harbor remains a reliable choice in Palermo. After a much-needed renovation in 2002, the President emerged as one of the better and more moderately priced options in town. You'll pass beneath a soaring arcade before entering the informal stone-trimmed lobby. The amenities here are simple but comfortable. There's little stylish about the small rooms, but they are well kept, as are the adjoining tiled bathrooms with tub-shower combinations. You needn't bother with the on-site restaurant and its clientele of tired businesspeople. All you have to do is walk out along the harbor to find a number of fine *trattorie* serving excellent fish.

Via Francesco Crispi 228, 90139 Palermo. ℂ 091-580733. Fax 091-611588. www.s-h-systems.co.uk/italy/palermo47099.html. 129 units. 103€–129€ ($124–$155) double. Rates include breakfast. AE, DC, MC, V. Parking 5€ ($6). Bus: 139. **Amenities:** Restaurant; bar; limited room service; laundry service; dry cleaning. *In room:* A/C, TV, minibar, hair dryer.

San Paolo Palace 𝒢   Built in 1990, this modern 14-story hotel offers serious competition to the Astoria Palace. Like the Astoria, San Paolo calls itself a "palace" hotel, which is hardly evocative of what it is: a large, sprawling, though welcoming high-rise. In fact, if you're returning from a trattoria with too much *vino* under your belt, you might confuse the two properties. One guest told us she'd stayed in a similar hotel along the west coast of Africa, which means San Paolo could be anywhere.

Overlooking the sea, between Capo Zafferano and Mount Pellegrino, the hotel is not without its charms, among them a roof-garden restaurant with a spectacular view. The government gives San Paolo three stars instead of the four reserved for the Astoria, which means its rooms are slightly cheaper, yet you get basically the same deal. Guest rooms open onto the most famous gulf in Sicily and are extremely comfortable, though not particularly stylish. There's a wide choice of different bed arrangements, from king-size to cozy "matrimonial." Located a few minutes' ride from the town center, the hotel is a favorite of business clients and, like the Astoria, attracts conventions, which are hardly ideal times to stay here. As for maintenance, management rightly concedes that "so far we manage with a face-lift, a tuck here and there," not the major corrective surgery of a total renovation.

Via Messina Marine 91, 90123 Palermo. ℂ 091-6211112. Fax 091-6215300. www.sanpaolopalace.it. 290 units. 135€ ($162) double; 190€ ($228) suite. Rates include breakfast. AE, DC, MC, V. Free parking. Bus: 221, 224, 225, 250, or 824. **Amenities:** 2 restaurants; bar; outdoor rooftop pool (seasonal); fitness center; room service; babysitting; laundry service; dry cleaning; nonsmoking rooms. *In room:* A/C, TV, dataport, minibar, hair dryer.

Villa D'Amato 𝒢 *Finds*   This little discovery, a completely renovated antique Sicilian villa opening onto the seafront, lies a 15-minute drive from the center. As a hotel, it is outclassed by Principe di Villafranca and Massimo Plaza Hotel, but it is not without its (considerable) charms. Set on its own parklike grounds, it is especially good for motorists who don't want to battle traffic in the heart of Palermo. We like it mainly for its gardens, a Mediterranean oasis. As you relax here, watching the plants grow, you'll be in Palermo but it won't feel like it. The guest rooms are completely comfortable, decorated in a sort of Italian Liberty style, yet they come off as rather plain. Small to midsize, each comes with a tiled bathroom with shower. The good Sicilian/international cuisine is another reason to book here.

Via Messina Marine 178–180, 90123 Palermo. ℂ/fax **091-6212767**. www.hotelvilladamato.it. 37 units. 120€ ($144) double; 162€ ($194) triple. Rates include buffet breakfast. AE, DC, MC, V. Free parking. Bus: 221, 224, 225, 250, or 824. **Amenities:** Restaurant; bar; room service; babysitting. *In room:* A/C, TV, minibar, safe.

INEXPENSIVE

Albergo Hotel Joli   Not to be confused with the Jolly chain, this is an inexpensive hotel on the third floor of a building on the beautiful old Piazza Florio. At the historic center of Palermo, it lies near the pricey Grand Hotel et des Palmes, a few blocks away from Piazza Castelnuovo. Of course, it's hardly comparable to des Palmes, which you might want to visit for a drink or a sumptuous meal. But if you're looking to save money and you don't demand elegance, this hotel, which was renovated in 2003, offers small to midsize guest rooms; they're a bit boxy and furnished simply though comfortably, with compact tiled bathrooms that contain shower-tub combinations. The best units come with small terraces overlooking the square. Convenient to both the port and the modern city, the hotel is also within walking distance of most points of historic interest. Considering its heartbeat location, the Albergo Joli provides a relatively tranquil setting.

Via Michele Amari 11, 90139 Palermo. ℂ/fax **091-6111765**. www.hoteljoli.com. 30 units. 108€ ($130) double; 130€ ($156) suite. Rates include breakfast. AE, DC, MC, V. Bus: 103, 106, or 108. **Amenities:** Breakfast room; bar; babysitting; laundry service; dry cleaning. *In room:* A/C, TV, dataport, hair dryer.

Albergo Mediterraneo   One of our preferred government-rated three-star hotels, this angular 1956 building sits on a narrow commercial street in a blandly modern neighborhood. The granite-sheathed lobby leads to six upper floors with wide hallways and spacious dimensions, evoking a well-designed contemporary hospital. Rooms are bigger than you might imagine, with a sense of calm but absent of a lot of unnecessary furniture. All come with private bathrooms—some with tubs, others with showers. Overall, this place is businesslike and highly recommendable.

Via Rosolino Pilo 43, 90139 Palermo. ℂ **091-581133**. Fax 091-586974. www.abmedpa.com. 106 units. 104€ ($125) double. Rate includes breakfast. AE, DC, MC, V. Bus: 101, 104, or 107. **Amenities:** Restaurant; bar. *In room:* A/C, TV, minibar, safe.

Albergo Sausele *(Value)*   This family-run inn stands out amid the depressing rail station–area hotels. It boasts high ceilings, globe lamps, modern art, and new modular furnishings. The staff is hospitable, as is the resident St. Bernard, Eva. Guest rooms with shower-only bathrooms are certainly small and modest, but are a pleasant choice. To avoid street noise, light sleepers should request a unit overlooking the peaceful courtyard. What makes this place special are the handcrafted and antique artifacts from around the world, collected by Giacomo Sausele on his travels.

Via Vincenzo Errante 12, 90127 Palermo. ℂ **091-6161308**. Fax 091-6167525. www.hotelsausele.it. 36 units. 78€ ($108) double; 123€ ($148) triple. Rates include breakfast. AE, DC, MC, V. Parking 10€ ($12). Bus: Any to Centrale Stazione. **Amenities:** Bar; 2 lounges. *In room:* A/C, TV, hair dryer.

Hotel Moderno ⭐ *(Value)*   One of the city's best cost-conscious options lies on the third and fourth floors of a stately-looking building that's among the grandest in its busy and highly congested neighborhood. Don't expect the same kind of grandeur inside that you see on the building's neoclassical exterior: You'll take a cramped elevator to the third-floor reception area, then proceed to a clean but very simple guest room. Each comes with a tiled, shower-only bathroom; lots of artwork; and not a great deal of direct sunlight. In view of the oppressive heat outside, and in light of the reasonable prices, few of this hotel's repeat visitors seem to mind.

Via Roma 276 (at Via Napoli), 90133 Palermo. Ⓒ **091-588683**. Fax 091-588260. 38 units. 75€ ($90) double. AE, DC, MC, V. Bus: 101, 102, 103, or 107. **Amenities:** Bar. *In room:* A/C, TV.

Hotel Posta   The street housing the Hotel Posta is narrow, claustrophobic, and flanked with buildings whose exteriors could use a good cleaning. But the location is within a short walk of the Mussolini-era post office, several massive and very important churches, and the hubbub of a nearby street market. Despite the unprepossessing approach to the Posta, it is a celebrated address among writers, singers, artists, and actors appearing in productions at the local landmark theaters of Palermo. The controversial playwright, actor, director, and political activist Dario Fo (winner of the 1997 Nobel Prize for Literature) is a frequent guest at the hotel, which has been run by the same family since the early 1920s. Renovated in 2002, the Posta is small, functional, and unfrilly, with a tiny lobby; it's an intriguing blend of hypermodern design and antique stonework. The simple, fairly spacious guest rooms are accessible via a tiny elevator and come with small bathrooms with showers.

Via A. Gagini 77, 90133 Palermo. Ⓒ **091-587338**. Fax 091-587347. 27 units. 100€ ($120) double. Rates include breakfast. AE, DC, MC, V. Bus: 101 or 104. **Amenities:** Nonsmoking rooms. *In room:* A/C, TV, minibar.

3 Where to Dine

Many restaurants in Palermo are close to the sea, from which emerges much of the bounty on the trattoria table. Pasta mixed with fresh sardines *(pasta con le sarde),* spaghetti with clams or mussels, and grilled fish and seafood are the items to order on most menus.

Most of the cuisine is Sicilian, although there's more diversity in Palermo than anywhere else in Sicily. Tunisian and Chinese food are the most popular foreign offerings, although you can also find Spanish, Greek, French, Italian, and even Brazilian fare if you search hard enough. Many local dishes still show the influence of Palermo's long-departed conquerors, the Arabs.

If you're a street-food fanatic, Palermo is your kind of town. As you walk along any section of the city, you'll encounter peddlers touting the local specialties, such delights as *panelle* (fritters made with chickpea flour) and *calzoni* (deep-fried meat- or cheese-filled pockets of dough).

If you're with Mrs. Petrillo from *The Golden Girls,* and you want something authentically Sicilian, head for a food stall with a large cast-iron pot turning out fresh buns stuffed with thin strips of calf's spleen and ricotta cheese. The hot sauce that goes with it will have your tongue begging for mercy.

Desserts are also sold on the street. Some of the best concoctions are holdovers from the days of Arab occupation, including sweetened ricotta with cinnamon, pistachios, candied fruit, and cloves.

Budget eateries crowd the Stazione Centrale, but we generally avoid these tourist traps. Some of the best restaurants are hidden in the medieval Kalsa sector, to which you may want to take a taxi at night to avoid walking along streets where muggings occur.

Since Palermitans tend to be late diners (though not as late as the Spanish), most restaurants don't open until 8pm.

BREAKFAST & PASTRIES   If your hotel doesn't serve breakfast (most do), or even if it does but on an a la carte menu, you might want to begin your experience in Palermo by going to almost any bar or *pasticceria* for morning coffee and pastries. Our favorites are **Bar Alba** (p. 81) and **Caffè Mazzara** (p. 115).

In the Medaglie d'Oro area, a great cake shop/bar is **La Dolceria Pasticceria Coga,** Via Gustavo Roccella 56 (© **091-596944**). One of the city's oldest and most famous cake shops, **Caffè Antico,** Via di Belmonte 115 (© **091-3292200**), in the Politeama area, turns out brioches, meringues, and croissants until midnight.

PIZZA PARLORS   The people of Palermo eat almost as much pizza as the Neapolitans. You should definitely sample the local pie, *pizza Palermitana,* made with bread crumbs, anchovies, pine nuts, olive oil, and cheese (and sometimes sausage, capers, olives, and grilled eggplant). Our favorite pizza joint is **Italia** (p. 84). **Antica Focacceria San Francesco** (p. 80) has been turning out pies fresh from the oven since 1834. A word to the frugal: A pizzeria is your cheapest option for a sit-down meal in Palermo; as such, they're packed on weekends, mostly with an under-25 crowd.

JUICE BARS   Not as plentiful as they once were, juice bars or kiosks used to line many of the city streets. They were—and some still are—an obligatory place to stop for a fruit ice. On a hot August day in Palermo, no one (in our view) has ever improved on lemon ice. For a change of pace, try a refreshing glass of sparkling water flavored with aniseed.

GELATERIE   These ice-cream shops are found all over Palermo, especially in the northern reaches of the city. Our favorite remains pistachio, although the flavors are more varied than the rainbow. Some gelato lovers even order ice cream for breakfast. The concoction is called *brioche con gelato,* or ice cream in a bun.

A1 Gelato 2, Via de Gasperi 15 (© **091-528299**), in the Libertà neighborhood, serves Palermo's best ice cream. It also has the largest array of flavors of any gelateria. If you're a true ice-cream devotee and feel you've had your favorite food in all known flavors, scan the list of selections here: You're in for a surprise or two.

VERY EXPENSIVE

Il Mulinazzo ⊛⊛⊛ SICILIAN   After several visits, we're beginning to believe what island foodies have been telling us all along: The restaurant of Nino Graziano (the chef) and his wife, Sabine Bour, is the best in Sicily. It's well worth the 45-minute drive from the center of Palermo to reach this elegant country house, where you'll dine in ultimate comfort and be attended to by the region's best-trained waitstaff.

Moments   Calling All Lovers of Sardines

As a city of the sea, Palermo is peopled with diners who enjoy the rich bounty of fish harvested off their coastline. The lowly sardine has a special place in their hearts, enjoying the same popularity as the codfish to the Portuguese. If you've had only tinned sardines up until now, try them fresh. The all-time favorite pasta dish in Palermo, *maccheroni con le sarde,* is made with fresh sardines and wild fennel.

The cuisine is meticulously crafted and backed up by a well-chosen wine *carte* of regional, national, and international selections. The chef takes superb ingredients to the limits of their innate possibilities, with a minimum of artifice and frills. The dishes of the day might include a sausage of fresh tuna flavored with mint, or perhaps a spicy *taglioni* (long pasta) with pesto. Freshly caught fish is a delight, cooked in a salt crust to seal in its juices and served on a platter of grilled vegetables. Fava-bean purée *(macco)* might be a staple dish of the poor, but in the hands of Nino it becomes something of wonder, especially when it's paired with scampi, ricotta, peppercorns, and fried basil.

S.S. 121, Località Bolognetta Nord, Villafrati. ⓒ **091-8724870.** Reservations required. Main courses 15€–19€ ($18–$23); fixed-price menus 55€–60€ ($66–$72). AE, DC, MC, V. Tues–Sat 1–2:30pm and 8–10:30pm; Sun 1–2:30pm. Closed Jan 10–24 and July 6–26. From Palermo, take the autostrada east toward Catania, exiting where it's marked "Agrigento-Villabate S.S. 121." Continue 17km (10½ miles). The restaurant is on the right side of S.S. 121.

EXPENSIVE

I Ristorantino ★★ SICILIAN/MEDITERRANEAN   This restaurant is justifiably celebrated for its finely honed cuisine. Francesco Inzerillo, hailed as the city's top chef by gourmet Italian guides, presides over an establishment that's not only elegant but also one of the most stunningly modern in the city. The menu is creative, although old-time favorites are also included. He won our hearts with mackerel with caper sauce and a winning soup of zucchini and fresh seafood. Try the lobster tortellini with cherry tomatoes or the well-crafted swordfish au gratin. Desserts are luscious, so save some room. The restaurant lies in the suburbs north of the center and is best reached by taxi.

Piazzale Alcide De Gasperi 19. ⓒ **091-512861.** Reservations required. Main courses 10€–18€ ($12–$22). AE, DC, MC, V. Tues–Sat 12:30–3:30pm and 8:30pm–midnight. Closed 2 weeks in Aug and Jan 1–7.

La Scuderia ★★★ INTERNATIONAL/ITALIAN   On our latest tour of Palermo dining rooms, La Scuderia surfaced at the top of our list. Dedicated professionals run this restaurant surrounded by trees at the foot of Monte Pellegrino, 5km (3 miles) north of the city center near the stadium at La Favorita. The talented chefs change the menu according to what looks good at the market; the ingredients, as always, are of top quality. The imaginative cuisine includes a mixed grill of fresh vegetables with a healthy dose of a Sicilian cheese called *caciocavallo; involtini* (roulade) of eggplant or veal; risotto with seafood; and *maccheroni Nettuno* (pasta studded with swordfish, eggplant, and tomato sauce). Everything is beautifully presented and served with typical Sicilian courtesy. In summer, the restaurant has one of the prettiest terraces in town, with tables sought after by lovers, families, and vacationing glamour queens alike.

Viale del Fante 9. ⓒ **091-520323.** Reservations recommended. Main courses 10€–13€ ($12–$16). AE, DC, MC, V. Mon–Sat 12:30–3pm and 8:30pm–midnight. Closed 2 weeks in Aug. Bus: 107 or 603.

MODERATE

Capricci di Sicilia *Value* SICILIAN   Great care goes into the traditional Palermo cuisine here; to go really local, order *polpette* (fishballs of fresh sardines). The pasta is often flavored with sardines and broccoli; the spaghetti with sea urchins is succulent; and the swordfish roulade is always dependable. This is one of the best places to sample *cassata Siciliana,* Sicily's fabled dessert. In warm weather, meals are served in a small garden. The central location is close to Piazza Politeama.

Via Instituto Pignatelli 6 (off Piazza Sturzo). ⓒ **091-327777.** Reservations recommended. Main courses 8€–15€ ($9.60–$18). AE, DC, MC, V. Sept–July Tues–Sun 12:30–3pm and 8pm–midnight; Aug Tues–Sun 8pm–midnight. Bus: 806 or 833.

Friends' Bar ⚜ SICILIAN   About 10km (6 miles) north of Palermo, this is one of the better restaurants in the region. Named after the four friends *(amici)* who opened it in the 1970s, it features an air-conditioned dining room and a gazebo-like structure that rises from a lush garden. A meal here is an event for many Sicilians, and a reservation (especially for the garden) might be hard to get. The antipasti, rich in marinated vegetables and grilled fish, are loaded onto a buffet table. The pastas tend to be strong, aromatic, and laced with such flavors as anchovies, fresh basil, and sardines. Grilled swordfish, calamari, and octopus are also a savory kettle of goodies. The house wine is redolent with the flavors and sunshine of southern Italy.

Via Filippo Brunelleschi 138, Michelangelo. ☏ **091-201401.** Reservations required. Main courses 10€–15€ ($12–$18). AE, DC, MC, V. Tues–Sun 10am–3pm and 7:30–11pm. Closed 3 weeks in Aug. Bus: 513, 540, or 675.

La Fenice SICILIAN   On the ground floor of the historic Palazzo Notarbartolo di Rosa, near Porta Felice in the Tribunali/Castellamare neighborhood, "The Phoenix" is a bastion of fine cuisine. But don't come here for pasta—they don't serve it, although they do offer some well-flavored rice dishes (especially a sublime rice salad). The old structure contains intimate dining rooms with stone walls and low ceilings; the waiters rush about with contagious enthusiasm, serving a menu that rarely varies. The grilled swordfish is a masterpiece; we also like the sausage *alla pizzaiola,* cooked with parsley-flavored tomatoes and onions. The grilled dishes go well with the Regaleali whites. After a *caffè,* go native, rinsing out your cup with anise liqueur.

Piazza Marina 52–53. ☏ **091-6162230.** Reservations recommended. Main courses 7€–10€ ($8.40–$12). AE, DC, MC, V. Sept–July daily 12:30–3pm and 8pm–midnight; Aug daily 7:30pm–midnight. Bus: 103, 105, or 225.

Le Delizie di Cagliostro ⚜ *Finds* SICILIAN/INTERNATIONAL   The restaurant that bears his name celebrates the dubious achievements of Sicily's most successful (and, ultimately, tragic) swindler, Giuseppe Balsamo (alias Count Cagliostro; 1743–95). His mystical mumbo-jumbo and sleight-of-hand looted the purses and pride of commoners and aristocrats (including Marie Antoinette) alike, earning him a respected place in the pantheon of noteworthy Sicilian rogues.

Set on a busy boulevard in a commercial neighborhood, the restaurant boasts vaulted 18th-century ceilings covered with *trompe l'oeil* frescoes. Once you get past the overweening presence of the ghost of the count, you can sit back and enjoy the cuisine. Market-fresh ingredients go into dishes such as risotto with shrimp, cream, and curry; mushroom-stuffed crepes; and that Palermo favorite, pasta with fresh sardines. The platter of grilled vegetables, their flavors enhanced with olive oil and balsamic vinegar, is succulent.

Corso Vittorio Emanuele 150. ☏ **091-332818.** Reservations recommended. Main courses 10€–15€ ($12–$18). AE, DC, MC, V. Daily noon–2pm and 7pm–midnight. Bus: 101, 102, or 105.

Lo Scudiero ⚜⚜ SICILIAN   Set directly across the busy street from the Teatro Politeamo Garibaldi (site of the Galleria d'Arte Moderno), this cozy restaurant and brasserie (its name translates as "The Shield Bearer") is not to be confused with the grander and more expensive restaurant with a roughly similar name out in the suburbs near the soccer stadium. Honest, straightforward, and unpretentious, it's favored by locals, many of whom work or live in the nearby Via Libertà neighborhood. Fine raw materials and skilled hands in the kitchen produce such tempting dishes as grilled swordfish flavored with garlic and a touch of mint. The fish served here is really fresh, as the owner buys it every day at the market. This place gets our vote for some of Palermo's best roulades, grilled veal rolls with a stuffing of ground salami and herbs. Vegetarians can opt for the medley of grilled vegetables with balsamic vinegar and olive oil.

Via Turati 7. ℂ 091-581628. Reservations recommended. Main courses 7.50€–15€ ($9–$18). AE, DC, MC, V. Mon–Sat 12:30–3pm and 7:30–11:30pm. Closed Aug 10–20. Bus: 101 or 107.

Ma Che Bontà ✰ *Finds* SICILIAN   Surely pasta dishes in Palermo don't get much better than this. The fettuccine arrived flavored with fresh mint, sautéed baby eggplant in virgin olive oil, and freshly caught swordfish. One platter contained two versions of ravioli: one stuffed with crabs, the other with sage-flavored mushrooms and rich cream. The tagliatelle was a taste sensation with tuna roe, almonds, pistachios, and fresh tomatoes. If you have room for a main course, stick to the fresh fish, such as tuna in a bittersweet sauce or swordfish roulades with an herb-flavored stuffing. "No! No! No!" everyone shouted at the suggestion of dessert—and then proceeded to devour the homemade cannoli and almond parfait with warm chocolate.

Viale Emilia 75. ℂ 091-511156. Reservations recommended. Main courses 6€–8€ ($7.20–$9.60). AE, DC, MC, V. Mon–Sat 1–3:30pm; daily 8–11:30pm.

Mi Manda Picone ✰ *Finds* SICILIAN   We like to come here for three reasons: to sample the excellent and well-chosen Sicilian wines, to enjoy the tasty food at affordable prices, and to admire the facade of that Romanesque gem, Chiesa di San Francesco, rising a few steps from the restaurant's entrance.

The specialty here is wine, mostly from Sicily (450 kinds), accompanied by platters of hearty, robust food. Sit on the terrace in front of the church or retreat to the woodsy, medieval-style interior, which once functioned as a stable. Light snacks include stuffed and deep-fried vegetables; a marvelous flan of fava beans and Pecorino cheese; fresh salads; and antipasti platters. More substantial fare includes grilled tuna or swordfish steaks with capers and black pepper.

Via Alessandro Paternostro 59 (Piazza San Francesco d'Assisi). ℂ 091-6160660. Reservations not necessary. Main courses 8€–13€ ($9.60–$16). AE, MC, V. Wine 3.50€–7.50€ ($4.20–$9) per glass. Mon–Sat 7:30–11pm. Bus: 103, 108, or 164.

Sottosopra ✰ ITALIAN/SICILIAN   One of Palermo's most avant-garde restaurants occupies a two-story storefront a few steps off the posh edges of the Via Libertà. Its minimalist stainless-steel and ebony decor is radically different from the interiors of more staid competitors; you'll find a serpentine bar, ostrich-skin upholstery, and a simultaneously formal and ultra-modern upstairs dining room. This vividly theatrical setting is presided over by the intensely social owner.

Menu items vary with the seasons. Expect artful preparations of Sicilian-style smoked and grilled fresh fish; a succulent spaghetti *ricci,* seasoned with sea urchins, tomatoes, and herbs; and fresh salads, including a tantalizing version made from arugula, pink grapefruit, avocado, scampi, and lobster.

Via XII Gennaio. ℂ 091-6124736. Reservations recommended. Main courses 10€–15€ ($12–$18). AE, DC, MC, V. Mon–Sat 1–3:30pm and 8:30pm–midnight. Bus: 101, 102, 103, or 106.

INEXPENSIVE

Antica Focacceria San Francesco ✰✰ *Kids* FOCACCIE/SICILIAN   All visitors need to make at least one stop at this local favorite, a tradition since 1834, in the Palazzo Reale/Monte di Pietà district. Nearly every kid in Palermo has feasted on its stuffed focaccia sandwiches and other inexpensive eats. High ceilings and marble floors evoke the era in which the eatery was born; the food has changed little since. You can still get *panino con la milza* (real hair-on-your-chest fare: a bread roll stuffed with slices of boiled spleen and melted cheese). The *panelle* (deep-fried chickpea fritters) are marvelous, as are the *arancini di riso* (rice balls stuffed with tomatoes and peas or mozzarella). Try the specialty, *focaccia farcita* (flat pizza baked with various fillings).

Via A. Paternostro 58. ⓒ **091-320264**. Reservations not needed. Sandwiches 3€–5€ ($3.60–$6); pastas 4.50€–6€ ($5.40–$7.20). AE, DC, MC, V. Daily 10am–midnight. Bus: 103, 105, or 225.

Antico Caffè Spiannato ⟨⟨ PASTRIES/SNACKS   Established in 1860, this is the most opulent cafe in its neighborhood. Set on a quiet, pedestrian-only street, it's the focal point for residents of the surrounding Via Libertà district, thanks to its lavish displays of sandwiches, pastries, and ice creams. Buy coffee at the bar and be tempted by the elaborate cannoli and almond cakes. If you're hungry, sit at a tiny table—either indoors or out—for one of the succulent *piatti di giorno.* (These include fresh salads, grills, and succulent pastas such as spaghetti with sea urchins.) In the evenings, the focus shifts from coffee to cocktails, and from pastries to platters. Live music entertains the nighttime crowd.

Via Principe di Belmonte 115. ⓒ **091-583231**. Pastries 1€–3€ ($1.20–$3.60); platters 3€–12€ ($3.60–$14). AE, DC, MC, V. Daily 7am–1am. Bus: 101, 104, 107, or 806.

Bar Alba ⟨ SICILIAN   This bar has been a Palermo institution since 1955. We were still in college when we were first taken here to sample *cassata Siciliana* on native soil. This is the famous regional dessert of candied fruit, marzipan, and sponge cake—it's a delight if you're not afraid of a diabetic coma. The home-made ice creams deserve an award, especially the creations made with pistachio, and the *frutta di Martorana* (fruits made of almond paste) will dazzle you. You can also go whole hog on savory dishes—their *arancine* (rice ball with ham and cheese), a typical Sicilian specialty, is the best in town. The location is at the top of Via della Libertà, near the entrance to La Favorita Park.

Piazza Don Bosco 7C. ⓒ **091-309016**. Reservations not needed. Pastries 1.50€–2€ ($1.80–$2.40). Main dishes 3.50€ ($4.20). AE, DC, MC, V. Tues–Sun 7:30am–11pm. Bus: 603 or 833.

Carillon SICILIAN   This well-established trattoria in the Libertà neighborhood is a refined choice. It takes its name from the old and new music boxes used to decorate the place. The terrace is open year-round, with large heaters keeping diners warm in winter. The dishes are properly cooked with real flavor, portions are large, and, on top of that, service is friendly and prompt. One of the most intriguing pasta dishes in Palermo is Carillon's spaghetti with shrimp, pumpkin flowers, and a hard ricotta cheese. Or try the pasta with swordfish, zucchini, mint, and tuna roe. For a bit of exotica, ask for grilled shrimp with strawberries (you heard that right), served with a béarnaise sauce.

Via Notarbartolo 12. ⓒ **091-343666**. Reservations recommended. Main courses 7€–10€ ($8.40–$12). AE, DC, MC, V. Tues–Sun 1–3pm and 8pm–midnight. Bus: 102, 103, or 702.

Casa del Brodo ⟨ SICILIAN   For more than a century, this Palermitan institution in the Palazzo Reale/Monte di Pietà neighborhood has handsomely fed some of the island's most discerning palates, such as the late Count Giuseppe Tasca of Almerita, once Sicily's premier vintner. In its two intimate, plainly decorated rooms, it attracts an equal number of locals and visitors, its atmosphere unchanged over the years.

With a name like "House of Broth," you could well imagine that broth is its specialty. And in truth, there is no kettle of broth finer in all of Sicily than that served here. But Casa del Brodo has many other dishes, too, including *macco di fave* (meatballs and tripe), a recipe that seems long forgotten in the kitchens of most Sicilians today. The one specialty we always order is *carni bolliti* (boiled meats). Trust us: It may not sound enticing, but it is a tantalizing assortment of tender, herb-flavored meats, especially good when preceded by a savory risotto with fresh asparagus.

Corso Vittorio Emanuele 175. ℂ 091-321655. Reservations recommended. Main courses 5€–15€ ($6–$18). DC, MC. V. Wed–Mon 12:30–3pm and 7:30–11pm. Bus: 103, 104, 105, 118, or 225. Closed Sun from June–Sept.

Cin-Cin ⭑⭑ *Finds* SICILIAN/CREOLE   One of the culinary treasures of Palermo, this is a favorite spot with locals. Pronounced "chin-chin," the restaurant's name is the Italian version of the toast "cheers!" and suggests the camaraderie found here behind an unpretentious facade. It's reached by going down a flight of steps off Via Libertà, in the section between the Giardino Inglese and the Teatro Politeama.

Some of the recipes have come down unchanged from Palermo's baroque period in the 19th century. Sample the seafood pastas, into which all sorts of sea creatures (shrimp, clams, mussels, sea urchins) are tossed with a succulent sauce. Sicilians often treat beef and lamb as sideshows to their antipasti, pastas, and seafood dishes, but here the chef gives full attention to turning out perfectly cooked and aromatically seasoned meats.

The owners, the Clemente family, once operated a restaurant in Baton Rouge, Louisiana, and Cin-Cin is the only restaurant in Sicily to offer such distinctly Louisiana dishes as oysters Rockefeller and chicken gumbo. Homemade Marsala and almond ice creams are a Cin-Cin specialty.

Via Manin 22, off Via Libertà. ℂ 091-6124095. Reservations recommended. Main courses 6€–15€ ($7.20–$18). AE, DC, MC, V. Sept–June Mon–Fri noon–3pm, Mon–Sat 8pm–midnight; July–Aug Mon–Fri noon–3:30pm. Bus: 101 or 107.

Cucina Papoff ⭑ *Finds* SICILIAN   With a name like "Papoff's Kitchen," you'll think you've landed in Bulgaria. The restaurant is named for its Bulgarian founder, but this friendly little trattoria actually serves some of the most traditional of all Sicilian dishes. The setting is an atmospheric 18th-century building with stone vaulting in the heart of Palermo, near Via Libertà and Politeama Piazza, just a few steps from the newly restored Teatro Massimo.

The basic recipes remain pretty much the same as they were 200 years ago. It was here that we became addicted to *maccu,* a creamy fava-bean soup flavored with wild fennel. We also fell for batter-fried cardoon florets with the nutty taste of the artichoke bottoms (only better). The stuffed radicchio is Palermo's best, as is the exquisite rabbit in red-wine sauce. You'll also see all those soul-food specialties that warm a Sicilian's heart, including *arancini di riso* (stuffed rice balls), potato croquettes, and *caponata* (eggplant salad). Although the wine *carte* has a number of European and even American selections, opt for one of the rare Sicilian vintages that are almost never found beyond the island's shores.

Via Isidoro La Lumia 32. ℂ 091-586460. Reservations recommended. Main courses 7€–12€ ($8.40–$14). AE, MC, V. Mon–Fri 1–3:30pm; Mon–Sat 8pm–midnight. Closed Aug. Bus: 101, 102, 104, or 106.

Hirsch ⭑ *Finds* GERMAN   A meal within Hirsch's rustic, wood-paneled interior provides a welcome change from a constant diet of Sicilian food. Except for the dusty sun-baked pavement outside and the palms and oleanders that line the street, you might imagine you're in Salzburg, thanks to the dark paneling, wrought iron, and *gemütlich* sense of kitsch that permeates the place. You'll find many of the time-tested Teutonic specialties here, including sauerbraten and Wiener schnitzel, as well as more exotic fare such as ostrich steaks and barbecued beef. And where else in Palermo can you order a fat roast goose? All of it tastes wonderful when accompanied by foaming steins of beer from the tap. Expect a table full of homesick Germans to be seated next to you.

Via Damiani Almeyda 32A. ℂ 091-347825. Main courses 6.50€–11€ ($7.80–$13). DC, MC, V. Tues–Sun 6pm–2am. Bus: 102, 103, 118, or 702.

Il Mirto e la Rosa ⊛ *Value* SICILIAN/VEGETARIAN   "The Myrtle and the Rose" is no longer a strict vegetarian restaurant. True, it still serves some of the most flavorful vegetarian dishes in Palermo, made with only the freshest harvests from the fields; but these days, its customers are also treated to an array of well-prepared meat and fish dishes. It's set in an interesting Liberty-style building from the turn-of-the-20th-century Belle Epoque days; a dining terrace is open in summer. The North African–inspired vegetable couscous is the best in town, as are any number of rice and pasta dishes with tantalizing sauces. We'd also rank the chef's veal Marsala as the best in Palermo. If you want generous portions and good flavor, order the delectable grilled steak Florentine. Seasonal produce is always emphasized on the menu.

Via Principe di Granatelli 30, off Piazza Florio. ℂ 091-324353. Reservations recommended. Main courses 7€–13€ ($8.40–$16). AE, DC, MC, V. Mon–Sat noon–3pm and 7–11pm. Closed Aug 25–31. Bus: 101, 102, or 103.

Le Pergamène *Value* ITALIAN/SICILIAN   This is one of two alfresco restaurants that sit adjacent to each another at the edge of a pleasant but not very well known public garden known as the Giardino Garibaldi, right at the point where the narrow streets of medieval Palermo open onto a network of 19th-century avenues and piazzas. The plastic armchairs of this restaurant are green, as opposed to the yellow chairs of the restaurant next door, with whom there's a friendly rivalry. The menu lists two dozen pizzas; pastas that include the ubiquitous *pasta alla Norma* made with eggplant, as well as a version with either smoked salmon or smoked swordfish; and main courses that focus on grilled steaks (beef, pork, and veal), roulades, and fresh fish.

Piazza Marina 48–49. ℂ 091-6166142. Reservations not necessary. Pizzas 3€–8€ ($3.60–$9.60); main courses 5.50€–12€ ($6.60–$14). Daily 5pm–2am. Bus: 103, 105, or 225.

Osteria Lo Bianco *Value* SICILIAN   The Sicily of yesterday lives on in this no-frills eatery frequented by street vendors and stevedores, with an occasional trucker dropping in. It's not everybody's antipasti, and if we were out on a date with the queen of England we'd take her somewhere else; but we like the joint, even with the rough treatment. The owner presides over the establishment with time-seasoned flair, a sort of Palermo version of the father of Eliza Doolittle in *My Fair Lady.* We've enjoyed his pasta with fresh sardines, although we find the pasta with potatoes too starchy. We were highly pleased with the spaghetti alla *ragù,* not having tasted such a rich version of the sauce since we'd departed Naples. And we were rewarded with the sweetest-tasting swordfish steak we've ever had in Sicily. Many diners come here just to make a meal out of *pasta nero di seppia* (pasta with a medley of seafood).

V. E. Amari 104. ℂ 091-585816. Reservations not accepted. Main courses 3.50€–6€ ($4.20–$7.20). No credit cards. Mon–Sat noon–3:30pm and 7:30–10:30pm. Bus: 101, 104, 106, 108, or 124.

Ristorante/Pizzeria Italia SICILIAN/ITALIAN Set on a narrow street that funnels into the piazza facing the elaborate 19th-century facade of the Teatro Massimo, this pizzeria-cum-taverna is fronted with an elaborate wrought-iron sign. Inside, you'll find a warren of tile-floored dining rooms, a prominent pizza oven, and a slightly bored staff that has been churning out pizzas since 1945. Despite that, the range of pizzas is gratifying, the beer cold. Begin with *bucatina* (a thick penne-style paste) with fresh sardines or else "to hell with the calories" spaghetti carbonara, followed by grilled steak, a North African–inspired couscous, and a medley of grilled vegetables. And if you're in the mood for spicy, consider *pizza Lucifer,* spiked with red-hot peppers and pepperoni.

Via Orologio 54. ℂ **091-589885.** Reservations not necessary. Main courses 5€–10€ ($6–$12); pizzas 4€–7€ ($4.80–$8.40); set menu 23€ ($28). MC, V. Daily 7:30pm–midnight. Bus: 101 or 103.

Santandrea 🔍 *(Finds* SEAFOOD/SICILIAN All of the bounty gathered at the Vucciria morning market is prepared with skill at this chic local favorite in the heart of La Kalsa. In fair weather, you can sit out on this old square to the south of Piazza San Domenico, looking at crumbling buildings from the 19th century. The waiter will recite the day's specials with obvious pleasure; go with the mixed antipasti, which always features fresh seafood. The pasta dishes are excellent, notably spaghetti prepared with sea urchins, a local delicacy, or spaghetti with fresh sardines. One of the habitués at an adjoining table confided to us, "For a Sicilian, a day without fresh sardines is like a life without sex." The homemade desserts, especially the black chocolate mousse, are some of Palermo's most luscious.

Piazza Sant'Andrea 4. ℂ **091-334999.** Reservations required. Main courses 7€–10€ ($8.40–$12). AE, DC, MC, V. Wed–Mon 1–3pm and 8pm–midnight. Closed Jan. Bus: 101, 103, 104, or 107.

Exploring Palermo

Although relatively neglected by the casual visitor to Italy, Palermo is one of the great art cities of Italy. It may not be the equal of Venice or Florence, but it is a treasure nonetheless.

Down through the ages, writers have tried to capture Palermo's singular allure. Vincenzo Consolo, in his *Strolling through Sicily*, was overcome with the city's rich red earth "with springs of water where the palm grove rises tall and slender."

The oasis he wrote of is largely swept away today. In its place is one of the more difficult cities in southern Italy to explore. There's just too much traffic and pollution, and getting around in summer is an often dusty, humid affair, and even a risky one as you try to avoid cars, buses, and motor scooters.

Yet in spite of its difficulties, those willing to go to the trouble to uncover Palermo's hidden treasures will find much to appreciate here. In exploring Palermo, expect both sensuous sunshine and somewhat sinister shadows.

The Phoenicians were taken with the setting of Palermo way back in the 7th century B.C. They called it Ziz, which meant "flower." Palermo hasn't experienced a golden age since the 9th century, when, under Arab conquerors, the city became one of the great centers of Islamic culture in the Western world.

In 1072, the Normans arrived, bringing a style that merged with the local residents' into a kind of "Arabo-Norman" period.

All subsequent conquerors added their own particular style and alterations to the city's skyline, contributing new layers to Palermo's rich cultural heritage. Frederick II of Swabia arrived in 1212, ushering in a time of intellectual development and prosperity. Following the Swabians came the Angevins, until the Spaniards drove them out. In the 18th century, the Bourbons of Naples arrived, embellishing everything with their baroque touch—not necessarily a good thing, as their architects and artisans destroyed much classical beauty.

Palermo spent most of the 20th century in decline, becoming a center for the notorious Mafia dons. It suffered severe damage in Allied air raids in 1943 and an earthquake in 1968. Much of its priceless medieval quarter has either been torn down or continues to decay.

Fortunately, matters are looking up these days, as more and more citizens are realizing what an artistic treasure Palermo is. Although not moving as fast as some preservationists would like, restoration is definitely in the air.

1 The Major Attractions

You should give Palermo at least 3 days, and even then you will have grasped only some of its highlights. If your time here is severely limited, you can attempt to visit the city's top 10 attractions in a very rushed 2 days. If you can't spare even that much time, and have only a day for the artistic monuments of Sicily's capital, here's how the top five sights rank on a very short A-list:

1. Palazzo dei Normanni/Cappella Palatina;
2. Galleria Regionale della Sicilia;
3. Museo Archeologico Regionale;
4. Catacombe dei Cappuccini; and
5. La Kalsa.

Palazzo dei Normanni (Palace of the Normans) ✹✹   This is Palermo's greatest attraction and Sicily's finest treasure trove. Allow 1½ hours and visit just this site if your time is really limited.

The history of the palace can be traced to the 9th century and the days of the Arab emirs and their harems, but probably goes back even further: The Arabs built the palace on an older Roman and Punic fortress. Over time it was abandoned by the Arabs, and the conquering Normans restored it into a sumptuous residence. The Normans came and went, and by the mid–16th century the palace was in serious decay until discovered anew by Spanish viceroys, who in 1555 began its rescue and once again turned it into a royal residence. Today it is the seat of Sicily's semi-autonomous regional government.

If you enter from Piazza Indipendenza, you'll be directed to the splendid **Cappella Palatina (Palatine Chapel)** ✹✹✹, representing the apex of the Arabo-Norman collective genius and built by Roger II from 1130 to 1140, when it was adorned with extraordinary Byzantine mosaics. You'd have to travel to Istanbul or Ravenna to encounter mosaics as awe-inspiring as these. The whole cycle constitutes the largest array of Islamic paintings to survive to the present day. Your appreciation of them, however, may be dimmed by the guardians trying to move people on their way, especially on days when too many tour-bus hordes arrive at the same time.

The chapel features a nave and two aisles divided by oval arches. The central area is surmounted by a hemispheric dome set on corner niches over a mosaic floor with walls of marble wainscoting. At the entrance to the nave is a mammoth **royal throne** encrusted in mosaics. Note the towering **Paschal candelabrum** ✹ carved with figures, wild animals, and acanthus leaves, a masterpiece that has come down from the 12th century.

Covering the central nave is a honeycomb stalactite wooden **muqarnas ceiling** ✹✹, a true masterpiece and the creation of Arab artisans brought from North Africa. They depicted scenes from daily life, including animal hunts and dances. Our favorite? The depiction of a "picnic" in a harem.

The mosaics were installed to teach the story of the Bible to an illiterate people. We're especially fond of Adam and Eve, each with the "forbidden fruit" in their mouths and greedily reaching for a second luscious piece. Ah, the symbolism.

There is no one set of mosaics to seek out: It is the sum total that adds to a miraculous artistic statement. Biblical scenes decorate the walls, with the image of Christ Pantocrator, surrounded by angels, on the cupola. The colors of the mosaics are vivid, the style realistic, the effect sometimes achieved by gold-backed tesserae and silver mosaic tiles. This mixed inlay makes the surfaces gleam in the soft light.

The mosaics in the nave are evocative of those at Monreale's Duomo (p. 122). If you don't have time to visit Monreale, you'll have seen the essence of this brilliant art here. Almond-eyed biblical characters from the Byzantine world create a panorama of epic pageantry, illustrating such Gospel scenes as the Nativity. The effect is enhanced by inlaid marble as well as by pillars made of granite shipped from the East.

Expect tight security as you wander around the **Royal Apartments** ✪✪ above, as this is still a seat of government. (On some days, visitors may not gain entrance at all.) You'll first enter **Salone d'Ercole,** from 1560, the chamber of the Sicilian Parliament. The salon is named for the mammoth frescoes, created by Giuseppe Velasquez in the 19th century, depicting the *Twelve Labours of Hercules.* Only six panels are visible (the others are concealed behind the gallery). The most dramatic scene is the slaying of the multi-headed Hydra of Lerna. You definitely won't want to adopt the three-headed dog, Cerberus, as your pet.

The most intriguing room of the apartments is the **Sala di Ruggero II,** where King Roger himself slumbered. It's decorated with 12th-century mosaics. Look for depictions of the peacock; it was said, symbolically, that the flesh of the peacock would never rot for eternity. A charmer is the **Hall of Mirrors,** sometimes called the "Yellow Hall" because of all its stunning candelabra.

One of the most splendid courts of Europe once held forth in other rooms of the Royal Apartments. Here the Western world met the mysteries of the East, as Latin scholars conversed and exchanged ideas with Arab astronomers. Regrettably, little is left of those golden days, when this was the most magnificent of European medieval courts.

Piazza del Parlamento. ℂ **091-7054317.** Admission 5€ ($6). Mon–Sat 8:30am–noon and 2–5pm; Sun 8am–noon. Bus: 104, 105, 108, 109, 110, 118, 304, or 309.

Galleria Regionale della Sicilia (Regional Gallery) ✪✪✪   This is the greatest gallery of regional art in Sicily and one the finest art galleries in all of Italy. It's housed in the **Palazzo Abatellis** ✪, itself an architectural treasure, a Catalan-Gothic structure with a Renaissance overlay designed by Matteo Carnelivari in 1490. Carnelivari constructed the building for Francesco Abatellis, the praetor of Palermo. After World War II bombings, the architect Carlo Scarpa restored the palazzo in 1954.

The superb collection shows the evolution of the arts in Sicily from the 13th to the 18th centuries. Sculpture predominates on the main floor. Beyond room 2, the former chapel contains the gallery's most celebrated work, the *Triumph of Death* ✪✪✪, dating from 1449 and of uncertain attribution (though it's sometimes credited to Pisanello). In all its gory magnificence, it portrays a horseback-riding skeleton (representing Death, of course) trampling his victims. The painter depicted himself in the fresco, seen with a pupil praying in vain for release from the horrors of Death. The modernity of this extraordinary work, including the details of the nose of the horse and the men and women in the full flush of their youth, is truly amazing, especially for its time.

The second masterpiece of the gallery lies at the end of the corridor exhibiting Arabic ceramics in room 4: the white-marble, slanted-eyed bust of *Eleanara di Aragona* ✪✪, by Francesco Laurana, who created it in the 15th century. This was Laurana's masterpiece.

The second-floor galleries are filled mainly with paintings from the Sicilian school, including a spectacular *Annunciation* ✪✪, the creation of Antonello da Messina, in room 11.

In the salon of Flemish paintings rests the celebrated *Triptych of Malvagna* ✪✪, the creation of Mabuse, whose real name was Jean Gossaert. His 1510 work depicts a Madonna and Bambino surrounded by singing angels with musical instruments.

Via Alloro 4, Palazzo Abatellis. ℂ **091-6230011.** Admission 4.50€ ($5.40) adults, 2€ ($2.40) children. Fri–Mon 9am–1:30pm; Tues–Thurs 9am–1:30pm and 2:30–7:30pm. Bus: 103, 105, or 139.

Airport

CUBA

Piazza
Indipendenza

ZISA

Colonna Rotta

Corso Re Ruggero

Via Piave

Viale delle Scienze

Corso Pisani

Corso Calatafimi

Corso

Alberto

Via Gaetano Mosca

Corso

Via dei Bene dettini

VILLA
BONANNO

Amedeo

Mercato
delle
Pulci

Palazzo di
Giustizia

Piazza
di Giustizia

Via Porta di Castro

Via Antonio Mongitore

Via Albergheria

Corso Tukory

Piazza della
Vittoria

Duomo

IL CAPO

Via del Celso

Via Sant' Agostino

Teatro
Massimo

IL BALLARO

Ballaro
Market

Via Vittorio

Via del Bosco

MEDIEVAL QUARTER

Via Volturno

Piazza
Verdi

Via

Maqueda

LA
VUCCIRIA

Via Bandiera

Via S. Basilio

Piazza
Bellini

Stazione
Centrale

Piazza
G. Cesare

Via

Roma

Emmanuele

Vucciria
Market

Piazza San
Domenico

Via Cavour

ALBERGHERIA

Via Garibaldi

Via Divisi

Via Squarcialupo

Via Lincoln

Via Alloro

Piazza
Magione

LA KALSA

ORTO
BOTANICO

Piazza
Marina

La
Cala

Via Sammuzzo

Foro Italico

TERRAZZA A MARE

Museo Archeologico Regionale (Regional Archaeological Museum) ⚑⚑⚑   This is one of the grandest archaeological museums in Italy, stuffed with artifacts from prehistoric times to the Roman era. Spread over several buildings, the oldest from the 13th century, the museum's collection includes major Sicilian finds from the Phoenician, Punic, Greek, Roman, and Saracen periods, with several noteworthy treasures from Egypt. Even though some of the exhibitions appear shabby and the museum is definitely not state-of-the-art, its treasures are worth wading through the dust to see.

You'll pass through small **cloisters** ⚑ on the ground floor, centered around a lovely hexagonal 16th-century fountain bearing a statue of Triton. In room 3 is some rare Phoenician art, including a pair of **sarcophagi** that date from the 5th century B.C.

In room 4 is the ***Pietra di Palermo,*** a black diorite slab known as the Rosetta Stone of Sicily. Dating back to 2700 B.C., and discovered in Egypt in the 19th century, it was intended for the British Museum. Somehow, because of red tape, it got left behind in Palermo. It contains carved hieroglyphics detailing information about the pharaohs, including the delivery of 40 shiploads of cedarwood to Snefru.

The most important treasures of the museum, in room 13, are the **metopes of Selinunte** ⚑⚑. These finds were unearthed at the temples of Selinunte, once one of the major cities of Magna Graecia (Greek colonies along the coast of southern Italy). The Selinunte sculptures are remarkable for their beauty, casting a light on the brilliance of Siceliot sculpture in general. Displayed are three magnificent metopes from Temple C, a quartet of splendid metopes from Temple E, and, in the center, a 5th-century bronze statue, **Ephebe of Selinunte** ⚑. These decorative friezes cover the period from the 6th century B.C. to the 5th century B.C., depicting such scenes as Perseus slaying Medusa, the Rape of Europa by Zeus, and Actaeon being transformed into a stag.

Etruscan antiquities grace rooms 14 to 17. Discoveries at the Tuscan town of Chisu, such as the unearthing of funereal *cippi* (stones), shed more light on these mysterious people. The **Oinochoe Vase,** from the 6th century B.C., is one of the most detailed artifacts of Etruscan blackened earthenware (called *bucchero*).

Other exhibit halls on the ground floor display underwater archaeology, with the most complete collection of **ancient anchors,** mostly Punic and Roman, in the world.

Finds from Greek and Roman sites in western Sicily are to be seen on the second floor in rooms 2 and 12. Here are more artifacts from Selinunte and other ancient Sicilian sites such as Marsala, Segesta, Imera, and Randazzo. These include **funereal aedicules** (openings framed by two columns, an entablature, and usually a pediment), **oil lamps,** and **votive terra cottas.**

In room 7 is a remarkable and rare series of large Roman bronzes, including the most impressive, a supremely realistic **bronze Ram** ⚑⚑, a Hellenistic work from Syracuse. It's certainly worth the climb up the steps. Another notable work here is ***Hercules Killing the Stag*** ⚑, discovered at Pompeii, a Roman copy of a Greek original from the 3rd century B.C. In room 8, the most remarkable sculpture is ***Satyr Filling a Drinking Cup*** ⚑, a Roman copy of a Praxitelean original.

On the third floor is a prehistoric collection along with Greek ceramics, plus Roman mosaics and frescoes. The highlight of the collection is panels illustrating **Orpheus with Wild Animals** ⚑, from the 3rd century A.D.

Piazza Olivella 24. ✆ **091-6116805.** Admission 4.50€ ($5.40) adults, 2€ ($2.40) children. Tues–Sat 8:30am–6:15pm; Sun 9am–1pm. Bus: 101, 102, 103, 104, or 107.

Catacombe dei Cappuccini (Catacombs of the Capuchins) ★★   If you've got a secret yearning to join mummified cadavers, and your tastes lean to the bizarre, you should spend at least an hour at these catacombs under the Capuchins Monastery.

Some 350 years ago, it was discovered that the catacombs contained a mysterious preservative that helped mummify the dead. As a result, Sicilians from nobles to maids—at least 8,000 in all—demanded to be buried here. The oldest corpses date from the late 16th century. The last corpse to be buried here was that of 2-year-old Rosalia Lombaro, who died in 1920. She still appears so lifelike that locals have dubbed her "Sleeping Beauty." Giuseppe Tommasi, prince of Lampedusa and author of one of the best-known works of Sicilian literature, *The Leopard,* was buried here in 1957. His body was not embalmed, but buried in the cemetery next to the catacombs instead.

Visitors can wander through the catacombs' dank corridors among the mummified bodies. Some faces are contorted as if posing for Edvard Munch's *The Scream.* Although many corpses are still remarkably preserved, time and gravity have been cruel to others. Some are downright creepy, with body parts such as jaws or hands missing.

Capuchins Monastery, Piazza Cappuccini 1. ℂ **091-212117.** Admission 1.50€ ($1.80). Daily 9am–noon and 3–5pm (until 7pm in summer). Closed holidays.

La Kalsa ★★   In Arabic, the name *Khalisa* means "pure," although that is about the last word we'd use to describe this colorful but seedy district. Left over from the Middle Ages, the crumbling Quartiere della Kalsa is the medieval core of Old Palermo and its most intriguing neighborhood in spite of all the decay, wartime destruction, and poverty.

Located in the southwestern section of the old city, La Kalsa was designed and constructed by Arab rulers as a walled city for the emir and his ministers. Already in serious decline before World War II, La Kalsa was heavily bombed in 1943 by Allied bombers seeking to conquer Sicily from Fascist control (the neighborhood was on the bombers' radar for its strategic location near the city's port). In the postwar era, La Kalsa sank into deeper misery and squalor.

When the Albanian nun Mother Teresa visited La Kalsa, she lectured the well-heeled Palermitani, telling them that since Palermo was as poor as a third-world country, "charity should begin at home." Today, after endless delays, Mother Teresa's words are finally being heard, and La Kalsa is slowly getting the restorative attention it deserves.

Tips Where Mafia Wannabes Get Street Smarts

La Kalsa is just as dangerous as it is fascinating. More and more foreigners are visiting at night, mainly to patronize some of the newly emerging restaurants—but still keep your wits about you. It's relatively safe to visit during the day, but even then, try not to walk around alone. Leave your valuables back in the hotel safe, hang on to your wallet, and take a taxi to your destination. Finally, never wander down dark, deserted labyrinthine streets: You may encounter street thugs, usually rejects from the Mafia, who want your money or valuables.

La Kalsa is bounded by the port of La Cala on one side and Via Garibaldi and Via Paternostro to the east and west, and by Corso Vittorio Emanuele and Via Lincoln to the north and south. One of its main thoroughfares is Via Butero.

A good place in the heart of the quarter to begin your rambling is the fancifully baroque church of **Santa Teresa alla Kalsa** (© **091-6171658**), which opens onto the center square, **Piazza della Kalsa.** The church was constructed between 1686 and 1706. Two orders of Corinthian columns grace its stately facade. If it's open, visit the luminous interior to see the impressive stuccoes of Giuseppe and Procopio Serpotta. To reach Piazza della Kalsa, enter near La Cala, the harbor, through Porta dei Greci, right off the busy thoroughfare, Foro Italico. Arm yourself with a good, detailed map before venturing into the quarter.

From Piazza della Kalsa, walk north along Via Torremuzza until you come to **Via Alloro,** La Kalsa's main street in the Middle Ages. Head west along this street for a close encounter with the decaying district. The elegant palaces of yesteryear have been destroyed, torn down, or burnt down; some are still standing, albeit most likely in a serious state of decay. One of the grandest extant palaces along Via Alloro is the **Palazzo Abatellis,** home today to the **Galleria Regionale della Sicilia** (p. 87).

After passing Palazzo Abatellis, you will shortly come to Via della Vetriera. At this point, head south for another close encounter with La Kalsa. This street will lead you to **Chiesa di Santa Maria dello Spasimo,** Via dello Spasimo (© **091-6161486**). A melancholy aura hangs over this church, originally constructed in the late Gothic style in 1506. This is the only example of the Northern Gothic style on the island. The walls went up, as did a soaring apse; but the builders abandoned the project and it was never roofed. Naturally, its interior was never finished either. Two towering ailanthus trees adopted it and now grow tall and proud. The church ruins make a marvelous venue for performances in summer.

For a final look at La Kalsa, bid adieu to Santa Maria dello Spasimo and head west across Piazza della Spasimo. This will lead into the Piazza Magione. From here, you can enjoy the facade of **La Magione** or the **Chiesa della Santa Trinità** (© **091-6170596**), an excellent example of a Norman church constructed in 1191 by the Cistercians. In 1197, Holy Roman Emperor Henry VI awarded it to the Teutonic Knights, who remained in control until 1492, when Pope Innocent VIII kicked them out of Italy. The knights are gone, but their marble funereal slabs can still be seen on the floor of the church's austere interior. The beautiful cloisters date from the founding of the original Cistercian monastery; they were severely damaged when the 1943 Allied air raids bombed the church.

Chiesa di Santa Cita/Oratorio del Rosario di Santa Cita ✹✹✹   The Oratory of the Rosary of St. Cita is a far greater artistic treasure than the church of St. Cita, on which Allied bombs rained in 1943. Only a glimmer of its former self, the church still contains a lovely **marble chancel arch** ✹ by Antonello

---

Tips   Street Eats: What, You Haven't Tasted *Babbaluci?*

Around the heart of La Kalsa, at Piazza della Kalsa, you can do as the locals do and indulge in a savory treat. Several vendors can be seen cooking and peddling *babbaluci,* a gourmet delicacy to the people of the district. These baby snails are marinated in virgin olive oil, chopped fresh parsley, and garlic; sprinkled with red pepper; and sold to passersby in paper containers called cornets.

Moments **The Church That Never Was**

One of the most evocative moments you can experience in Palermo is to stand in the church ruins of Santa Maria dello Spasimo on a dying summer day, watching the remains of this late Gothic building catch fire with the rays of the setting sun. This sight evokes the spirit of Raphael, who came here to paint his famous portrait of the anguish of the Madonna before the cross. You'll have to go to the Prado in Madrid to see the actual masterpiece, but the inspiration for it is right here in La Kalsa.

Gagini. Look for it in the presbytery. From 1517 to 1527, Gagini created other sculptures in the church, but they were damaged in the bombing. In the second chapel left of the choir is a **sarcophagus of Antonio Scirotta,** also the creation of Gagini. To the right of the presbytery is the lovely **Capella del Rosario** 𝕲, with its polychrome marquetry and intricate lacelike stuccowork. The sculpted reliefs here are by Gioacchino Vitaliano.

On the left side of the church, and entered through the church, is the **oratory,** the real reason to visit. This was the crowning achievement of the leading baroque decorator of his day, Giacomo Serpotta, who worked on it between 1686 and 1718. His cherubs and angels romp with abandon, delightfully climbing onto the window frames or spreading garlands of flowers in their path. They can also be seen sleeping, eating, and simply hugging their knees deep in thought.

The oratory is a virtual gallery of art containing everything from scenes of the flagellation to Jesus in the Garden at Gethsemane. The *Battle of Lepanto* bas-relief is meant to symbolize the horrors of war, while other panels depict such scenes as *The Mystery of the Rosary.* At the high altar is Carlo Maratta's *Virgin of the Rosary* (1690). Allegorical figures protect eight windows along the side walls.

Via Valverde 3. ✆ **091-332779.** Free admission (donation appreciated). Mon–Fri 9am–noon. Bus: 107.

Oratorio del Rosario di San Domenico 𝕲𝕲𝕲   Located in the area of the colorful open-air market, Mercato della Vucciria, the Oratory of the Rosary of St. Dominic was founded in the closing years of the 16th century by the Society of the Holy Rosary. Two of its most outstanding members were the sculptor Giacomo Serpotta and the painter Pietro Novelli, both of whom left a legacy of their artistic genius in this oratory.

In allure, this oratory is the equal of the Oratorio di San Lorenzo, which also displays Serpotta's artistic flavor. The sculptor excelled in the use of marble and polychrome, but it was in stucco that he earned his greatest fame. From 1714 to 1717, he decorated this second oratory with his delightfully expressive cherubs *(putti),* who are locked forever in a playground of happy antics.

Themes throughout the oratory are wide-ranging, depicting everything from Allegories of the Virtues to the Apocalypse of St. John. Particularly graphic is a depiction of a writhing "Devil Falling from Heaven." At the high altar is a masterpiece by Anthony van Dyck, *Madonna of the Rosary* (1628). Pietro Novelli frescoed the ceiling with the *Coronation of the Virgin.*

Via dei Bambinai. ✆ **091-332779.** Free admission. Mon 3–6pm; Tues–Fri 9am–1pm and 3–5:30pm; Sat 9am–1pm. Bus: 107.

Oratorio di San Lorenzo 𝕲𝕲𝕲   No longer as rich in treasures as it once was, the Oratory of San Lorenzo lies to the left of and faces the church of San

---

Fun Fact **The Mystery of the Stolen Painting**

In 1969, the art world learned in newspaper headlines that "the divine" Caravaggio's last large painting, *The Nativity,* had been stolen from the Oratory of San Lorenzo, where it once hung over the altar. Caravaggio created the work in 1609, a year before his death. No motive for the theft has ever been declared, and it is believed that the painting has been needlessly destroyed. The curator told us, "We keep hoping that one day it will come back to us, but as each day goes by, that hope grows dimmer and dimmer."

Francesco d'Assisi. A local Franciscan order, Compagnia di San Francesco, ordered this oratory constructed back in 1569. Its stunning mahogany pews, laced with mother-of-pearl, were created during the 18th century and rest on carved supports.

Of extraordinary elegance, the interior's **stucco decoration** 🎯🎯 is the masterpiece of Giacomo Serpotta, who worked on it between 1698 and 1710. It features a series of 10 symbolic statues, plus panels relating the details of the lives of St. Francis and St. Lawrence. Art historians have written of these wall paintings as "a cave of white coral." Some of the most expressive of the stuccoes depict the martyrdom of St. Lawrence. Paintings alternate with statues of the Virtues. In total contrast to the serene Virtues and the solemn nudes is the cavalcade of *putti,* who romp gaily, making soap bubbles or kissing one another.

Near the old port of La Cala, just south of Corso Vittorio Emanuele. Via dell'Immacolatella. © **091-332779.** Free admission. Mon–Sat 9am–noon. Bus: 101 or 102.

Duomo 🎯🎯   If too many cooks in the kitchen can spoil the broth, then too many architects turned Palermo's cathedral into a hodgepodge of styles. It is still a striking building, however, and well worth an hour or more of your time. Regrettably, the various styles—Greek-Roman, Norman, Arabic, Islamic—were not blended successfully with the overriding baroque overlay.

In 1184, during the Norman reign, the archbishop of Palermo, Gualtiero Offamiglio, launched the cathedral on the site of a Muslim mosque, which had been built over an early Christian basilica. Offamiglio was green with envy at the supremacy of the cathedral of Monreale. As the Palermo Duomo took shape, it became an architectural battleground for what was known as "The Battle of the Two Cathedrals."

Today, the facade is closed between two soaring towers with double lancet windows. The middle portal, dating from the 15th century, is enhanced by a double lancet with the Aragonese coat-of-arms. The four impressive campaniles (bell towers), date from the 14th century, the south and north porches from the 15th and 16th centuries.

But if anyone could be called the culprit for the cathedral's playground of styles, it is the Neapolitan architect Ferdinando Fuga, who went with the mood of his day and in 1771 and 1809 gave both the exterior and the interior of the Duomo a sweeping neoclassical style. In retrospect, he should have left well enough alone. The only section that the restorers didn't touch were the **apses** 🎯, which still retain their impressive geometric decoration.

The Duomo is also a pantheon of royalty. As you enter, the first chapel on the right contains six of the edifice's most impressive tombs, including that of Roger

II, the first king of Sicily, who died in 1154. He was crowned in the Duomo in 1130. His daughter Constance, who died in 1198, is buried here along with her husband, Henry VI, who died the year before. Henry VI was emperor of Germany and the son of Frederick Barbarossa. Their son, another emperor of Germany and king of Sicily, Frederick II, was also buried here in 1250, as was his wife, Constance of Aragón, who died in 1222. The last royal burial here, of Peter II, king of Sicily, was in 1342.

Accessed from the south transept, the **Tesoro,** or treasury, is a repository of rich vestments, silverware, chalices, holy vessels, altar cloths, and ivory engravings of Sicilian art of the 17th century. An oddity here is the bejeweled cap-like **crown of Constance of Aragón** ✿, designed by local craftsmen in the 12th century, and removed from her head when the tomb was opened in the 18th century. Other precious objects removed from the royal tombs are also on display here.

Piazza di Cattedrale, Corso Vittorio Emanuele. ✆ **091-334373.** Duomo: free (donation appreciated); crypt: 1€ ($1.20); treasury: 1€ ($1.20). Mon–Sat 8:30am–5:30pm. Bus: 103, 104, 108, 110, 118, or 139.

2 Other Great Churches

Chiesa del Gesù   Constructed in 1564, but extended and modified by several later architects, this was the first church in Sicily built by the Jesuits. Regrettably, it was another victim of the 1943 Allied air raids and had to be considerably restored at the end of World War II. Don't judge this church by its somber facade. Its **interior** ✿✿ is a triumph of baroque indulgence. Everywhere you look is an outstanding example of exuberant Sicilian baroque, with marble adornments, stucco reliefs, polychrome intarsia, and an array of paintings and sculpted works. All this overlay took centuries to complete.

The **frescoes** in the first bay of the vault of the nave are among the oldest pictorial decorations, created by Filippo Randazzo in 1743. The presbytery and apse also contain some of the original decorations, including sculptures by Gioacchino Vitaliano. Our favorite work of art here is the brilliant **chancel decor** ✿, the work of the Serpotta brothers. It's a romp of cherubs harvesting grapes, playing musical instruments, and holding torches and bouquets. Seek out the second chapel on the right as you enter to view paintings of **St. Philip of Agira** and the even more expressive **St. Paul the Hermit** ✿, both excellent examples of Pietro Novelli's work. The last figure depicted on the left in the St. Paul painting is actually a self-portrait of Novelli.

The magnificent porticoed courtyard gives access to the **Biblioteca Comunale,** the public library known as "Casa Professa." Filled with ancient manuscripts and incunabula, it also displays 300 portraits of illustrious men.

Piazza Casa Professa 21. ✆ **091-581880.** Free admission. Daily 7am–noon and 5–6:30pm. Bus: 101, 102, 103, 104, or 107.

Chiesa della Martorana/San Cataldo ✿✿   These two Norman churches stand side by side. If you have time for only one, make it La Martorana, as it is the most celebrated church in Palermo remaining from the Middle Ages. Visit it if only to see its series of spectacular **mosaics** ✿✿.

Named for Eloisa Martorana, who founded a nearby Benedictine convent in 1194, this church is dedicated not to her, but to Santa Maria dell'Ammiraglio (St. Mary of the Admiral). History was made here as well: It was in this church that Sicily's noblemen convened to offer the crown to Peter of Aragon.

Today's baroque facade regrettably conceals a Norman front. You enter through a beautiful combined portico and bell tower with a trio of ancient columns and double arch openings. The bell tower is original, dating from the 12th century. Once you go inside, you'll know that your time spent seeking out this church was worthwhile. The stunning mosaics were ordered in 1143 by George of Antioch, the admiral of King Roger and a man of Greek descent who loved mosaics, especially when they conformed, as these did, to the Byzantine iconography of his homeland. It's believed that the craftsmen who designed these mosaics also did the same for the Cappella Palatina. The mosaics are laid out on and around the columns that hold up the principal cupola. They're at their most beautiful in the morning light when the church opens.

Dominating the dome is a rendition of Christ, surrounded by a bevy of angels with the Madonna and the Apostles pictured off to the sides. Even with the passage of centuries the colors remain vibrantly golden, with streaks of spring green, ivory, azure blue, and what one art critic called "grape-red."

On a visit to La Martorana, you can obtain a key from the custodian sitting at a tiny table to your right as you enter the chapel. This key allows entry into the tiny **Chiesa di San Cataldo** next door. Also of Norman origin, it was founded by Maio of Bari, chancellor to William I. But because he died in 1160, the interior was never completed. The church is famous for its Saracenic red golf-ball domes. Sicilians liken these bulbous domes to a eunuch's hat.

Piazza Bellini 2, adjacent to Piazza Pretoria. (✆ **091-6161692.** Free admission. La Martorana: Mon–Sat 9:30am–1pm and 3:30–6:30pm; Sun 8:30am–1pm. San Cataldo: Tues–Sat 9am–5pm; Sat–Sun 9am–1pm. Bus: 101 or 102.

Chiesa di San Domenico

Although its oratory (p. 93) is a more intriguing artistic expression because of the delightful *putti* by Giacomo Serpotta, the Church of St. Dominic is one of the city's most remarkable baroque structures, its elegant baroque facade often depicted on postcards. It was constructed in 1640 to the design of the architect Andrea Cirrincione. The facade, however, wasn't added until 1726. Many antique buildings on the square were demolished to give this church more breathing room.

The facade rises in a trio of carefully ordered tiers, graced with both Corinthian and Doric pillars along with square pilasters that form a sort of picture frame for a statue of St. Dominic. Unlike the lavishly decorated oratory, the church has a severe interior that only emphasizes the beauty of the architecture. Its chapels, on the other hand, are richly decorated, forming a pantheon of tombs and cenotaphs of some of the more noble Sicilians, including Francesco Crispi, the former prime minister of Italy. The tomb of the painter, Pietro Novelli (1608–47), is in the north aisle.

Adjacent is the headquarters of the Sicilian Historical Society, with its own tiny **Museo del Risorgimento,** containing mementoes of Garibaldi. The fragmented 14th-century cloister was part of the first church erected on this site.

Piazza San Domenico. (✆ **091-584872.** Free admission. Mon–Fri 9–11:30am; Sat–Sun 5–7pm. Bus: 101.

Chiesa di San Francesco d'Assisi

Set in the medieval Kalsa district, north of Via Alloro, this church remains a gem in spite of earthquakes and the devastating bombardment by Allied planes in 1943. It was built between 1255 and 1277 as a shrine to St. Francis of Assisi. The church is known for its facade with a shallow porch and zigzag ornamentation. Its **rose window** ⟨ℛ⟩ is one of the finest in Sicily, and its flamboyant **Gothic portal** ⟨ℛ⟩ is from the original 13th-century structure.

After the 1943 bombardments, restorers set about to return the interior to its original medieval appearance, removing the overlay added by decorators who

---

Fun Fact **A Medieval Delicacy Lives On**

In the Middle Ages, every convent in Palermo specialized in creating a different kind of confectionery. Many of those old recipes are gone forever, but one of the most enduring is still sold at *pasticceria* all over the city: *frutta martorana,* named after the old Benedictine convent of La Martorana. Originally this marzipan was molded into various fruit and vegetable shapes. Today, these almond-paste sweetmeats resemble anything from cats to sailboats. The *frutta martorana* are most abundant in the bakeries before the feast day of All Saints, in early November.

---

found the neoclassical style more alluring. The interior today is rather austere, with a trio of cylindrical piers and wide Gothic arches. But it still has the light, airy sense of space evocative of Franciscan churches erected in medieval times.

A few notable works of art survive. In the north aisle, fourth chapel on the left, note the magnificent **arch** ⭐⭐, superbly sculpted by Pietro de Bonitate and Francesco Laurana in 1468. This arch was the earliest major Renaissance work in Sicily. The sanctuary has beautiful **choir stalls** carved by Paolo and Giovanni Gili in 1520.

It's best to tie in a visit to this church with a look at the **Oratorio di San Lorenzo,** which is virtually next door.

Piazza di San Francesco d'Assisi, off Via Paternostro. ✆ **091-6162819.** Free admission. Mon–Fri 7am–noon and 4:30–6pm; Sat 9am–noon. Bus: 101 or 102.

Chiesa di Sant'Agostino   Even if you don't go inside, you won't miss much. The **facade** ⭐ is the most beautiful part of this church, which was financed in the 13th century by two prominent Palermo dynasties, the Chiaramonte and Sciafani families. Both the lava-mosaic-enclosed main portal and the distinctive rose window are in the Norman architectural style.

In contrast to the classic medieval front is the interior, which was reconstructed with baroque adornment centuries later. Here you'll see the last stuccoes of followers of the Serpotta School, completed between 1711 and 1729. You can still see Serpotta's mark, a *serpe* (Sicilian for "lizard"). The medieval cloister was originally built in the Catalan Gothic style, surrounding a central fountain. Lying at a corner of the cloister, the chapter house preserves many of its original 13th-century architectural features. Embedded into the wall of the stairs leading from the church's side entrance is an ancient Roman tomb.

Sant'Agostino lies adjacent to **Mercato di Capo,** a busy street market and one of Palermo's more intriguing sights.

Via S. Agostino. ✆ **091-584632.** Free admission. Mon–Sat 7am–noon and 4–5:30pm; Sun 7am–noon. Bus: 225.

Chiesa S. Maria della Catena ⭐   No church is quite as evocative as Catena at sunset. The setting sun throws dramatic golds and ruby reds on its ancient facade. Situated in the old harbor district, called the *cala,* this Gothic-Catalan church with Renaissance elements dates back to the 15th century. The name *catena,* meaning "chain," comes from the long chain that was used to close the old port at night and that was attached to the church's outer wall.

The front of the church is elevated on a high flight of steps, with a spacious portico and a trio of arches. With its twin corner pilasters, this three-arched porch marries the Gothic with the Renaissance in its architectural style. Beneath the portico is a bas-relief **trio of portals** by Vincenzo Gagini, of the most famous artistic family in Sicily.

The **interior** ⚜ of the church is a work of beauty. A Gagini portal on the left side is graced with columns and single mullioned windows. A nave cuts through the interior with two side aisles separated by skinny Renaissance pillars.

A 14th-century Madonna and Child was discovered here in the 1980s. This work of art lies in the chapel on the right inside a 16th-century *baldacchino* (stone canopy). Wander through the east end with its elaborate Gothic decorative elements and double columns, and even a Roman sarcophagus. At the altar, symbolic chains represent the ancient port.

Piazza delle Dogane (Corso Vittorio Emanuele). ℂ **091-6077111.** Free admission. Mon–Fri 9am–1pm; Sun 11am–1pm. Closed Sat and Aug. Bus: 110, 118, 139, 224, 225, or 389.

La Gancia   Constructed in 1485 and dedicated to Santa Maria degli Angeli, this church stands next door to the Regional Gallery and can be easily visited at the same time. In the late Middle Ages, this was an enclave of the Franciscans. Much changed and altered over the centuries, the exterior of La Gancia contains a Gothic portal with a bas-relief on the arch. Inside, the nave is without aisles but contains a total of 16 side chapels and a marble floor in different hues.

The sculptor Giacomo Serpotta added baroque stucco decorations. The patterned **wooden ceiling** ⚜ is romantically painted with stars on a blue background. The chief treasure of La Gancia is a splendid **organ** ⚜⚜ by Raffaele della Valle that dates from the late 1500s, making it the oldest in Palermo. At the marble pulpit, look for the **relief tondi of the *Annunciation,*** the work of Antonello Gagini in the 16th century. As a curiosity, note the **novice monk** ⚜ peering over the top of a cornice in the chapel to the left of the main altar.

Via Alloro 27. ℂ **091-6165221.** Free admission. Mon–Sat 9:30am–noon and 3–6pm; Sun 10am–12:30pm. Bus: Linea Gialla (Yellow Line).

San Giovanni degli Eremiti ⚜⚜   This is one of the most famous of all the Arabo-Norman monuments still standing in Palermo. It is certainly the most romantic building remaining from the heyday of Norman Palermo. Since 1132, this church with its series of five red domes has remained one of the most characteristic landmarks on the Palermo skyline. It is located on the western edge of the Albergheria district.

With an atmosphere appropriate for the recluse it honors, St. John of the Hermits (now deconsecrated), this is one of the most idyllic spots in Palermo. A medieval veil hangs heavily in the gardens, with their citrus blossoms and flowers, especially on a hot summer day as you wander around the cloister.

A single nave divides the simple interior into two bays, surmounted by a dome. A small cupola tops the presbytery. The right-hand apse is covered by one of the red domes. Surrounding the left-hand apse is a bell tower with pointed windows; it, too, is crowned by one of the church's red domes.

The small late Norman **cloister** ⚜, with a Moorish cistern in the center, was part of the original Benedictine monastery that once stood here. It has little round arches supported by fine paired columns.

Via dei Benedettini 3. ℂ **091-6515019.** Admission 4.50€ ($5.40) adults, 2€ ($2.40) students, seniors, and children. Mon–Sat 9am–1pm and 3–7pm; Sun 9am–1pm. Bus: 109 or 318.

3 The Best of the Palaces

La Cuba ⚜   A less elaborate version of Zisa, and not as well preserved, "Cuba" is a Sicilian derivation of the Arabic *Ka'aba,* meaning "cube" or "square-shaped structure." It has nothing to do with the Caribbean island of the same name. Built in 1180 by King William II, it was a kind of summer palace with royal gardens where the court came to escape the heat. A tall building with a rectangular plan, it is another magnificent piece of Fatimid architecture. The interior of the original structure had a hall that rose the full height of the building and was covered by a dome.

Giovanni Boccaccio made La Cuba a setting in his tales of *The Decameron.* After it fell from royal use, it was privately owned, becoming a leper colony. When the Bourbons came to power, they turned it into a cavalry barracks. Today, La Cuba is part of a military barracks. Visitors can enter, but not photograph, the military grounds.

Corso Calatafimi 100 (in the Tukory Barracks opposite Via Quarto dei Mille). (𝄡 **091-590299.** Admission 2€ ($2.40). Mon–Sat 9am–7pm; Sun 9am–1pm. Bus: 105, 304, 309, 339, 364, 365, or 389.

La Zisa ⭐   Only the shell of the former Moorish palace remains, and its claims to resemble the Alhambra in Granada are so far-fetched as to be ridiculous. But an aura of *Arabian Nights* still lingers about the place. With a little imagination you can conjure up dancers who entertained the various sultans centuries ago.

Moorish craftsmen started the palace in 1166 under William I; it was finished in 1175 for his son, William II. La Zisa was the major building in a royal park that also embraced La Cuba. This beautifully landscaped park was called Genoard, meaning "terrestrial paradise," and was celebrated throughout Europe in the Middle Ages. The park was fenced in so that wild animals could roam about. Unfortunately, by the 16th century, the palace's heyday was all but a memory, and it was used as a depository for objects contaminated by the plague.

The structure you see today is high and compact. Two square towers flank the short sides of the castle. With its richness long stripped away, the interior is no longer remarkable, but you can still get some impression of the former sultan's palace. On the ground floor as you enter is the **Fountain Hall,** built on a cross plan. On the second floor is a good collection of Arabic art and artifacts.

Piazza Gugliemo il Buono (near Piazza Camporeale at the end of Via Dante). (𝄡 **091-6520269.** Admission 2.50€ ($3). Mon–Sat 9am–noon and 3–7pm; Sun 9am–1pm. Bus: 124.

Palazzo Mirto ⭐⭐   A visit to the nobleman's residence of the princes of Lanzi Filangeri is like a journey back in time. Though many of the other palazzi constructed at the same time lie rotting in the sun, this one is still relatively held together. Its history as a lavish abode dates back to the early 17th century; in 1982, the last surviving family member donated the palazzo to Sicily to preserve as a memorial to a vanished era.

Pause to take in the grace of the principal facade, with its double row of balconies, open to view on Via Lungarini. No other residence in Palermo can give you a better idea of a princely residence from the 18th and 19th centuries. As you enter the palazzo, look to the left, where magnificent **19th-century stables** ⭐ feature stalls and ornamental bronze horse heads. Take the fabulous red marble staircase up to the first floor, which is still decorated as it was when the last of the princes departed.

The first of the elegant drawing rooms is the **Sala degli Arazzi,** or tapestry hall, whose mythological scenes were painted by Giuseppe Velasco in 1804. Some of the salons open onto a patio garden with a flamboyant rococo fountain flanked by a pair of aviaries. Our favorite spot is the exquisite **Chinese sitting room** ⭐, with its *trompe l'oeil* ceiling, leather floor, and painted silk walls showing scenes from daily life. After dinner, the princes gathered here to smoke, talk, and play cards. As a note of curiosity, the next room has a series of remarkable Neapolitan plates from the 19th century, decorated with party costumes. At masked balls, each guest was assigned a plate that featured his or her costume. From the vestibule, you can visit another **smoking room** 🟊, this one painted and paneled with embossed leather. For a final bit of frippery, seek out the **Pompadour sitting room** 🟊, with a mosaic floor and silk walls embroidered with flowers, elegance so divine as to be decadent.

Via Merlo 2, off Piazza Marina. (C) 091-6164751. Free admission. Mon–Sat 9am–7pm; Sun 9am–1pm. Bus: 103, 105, or 139.

Villa Malfitano 🟊🟊 One of Palermo's great villa palaces, built in the Liberty style, sits within a spectacular **garden** 🟊🟊. The villa was constructed in 1886 by Joseph Whitaker, grandson of the famous English gentleman and wine merchant Ingham, who moved to Sicily in 1806 and made a fortune producing Marsala wine. Whitaker had trees shipped to Palermo from all over the world to plant around his villa. These included such rare species as Dragon's Blood, an enormous banyan tree and the only one found in Europe. Local high society flocked here for lavish parties, and even British royalty visited. In World War II, Gen. George Patton temporarily stayed here as he planned the invasion of southern Italy. The villa today is lavishly furnished with antiques and artifacts from all over the world. The **Sala d'Estate (Summer Room)** is particularly stunning, with *trompe l'oeil* frescoes covering the walls and ceiling.

Via Dante 167. (C) 091-6816133. Admission 6€ ($7.20). Mon–Sat 9am–1pm. Bus: 103, 106, 108, 122, 134, 164, or 824.

4 Other Great Museums

Civica Galleria d'Arte Moderna Empedocle Restivo 🟊 *Finds* Located on the second floor of Teatro Politeama, this little gallery of mostly 19th- and early-20th-century Sicilian art seems to be a local secret. Since 1910, the art-loving citizens of Palermo have been coming here to see works by home-grown artists. Be aware that few of the artists' names will be immediately recognizable to the international visitor, and some of the work is overly romanticized and a bit sappy.

But the museum does contain works by major artists. Look for pieces by Corrada Cagli, Carlo Carrà, Gino Severini, Giovanni Boldini, Antonio Mancini, and Domenico Morelli. Michele Catti, one of the finest landscape painters, is an artist of "long horizons," and his *Last Leaves* here is typical of his work. One of the most reproduced works of art from this museum is *Carusi,* by Onofrio Tomaselli. The figure on the left rests while those on the right are beasts of burden with heavy loads. The Sicilian portraits of Salvatore Lo Forte are especially realistic, and Sicilian patriotism is best evoked in the works of Erulo Eruli, whose masterpiece is *The Sicilian Vesper.* One of the most delightful sculptures is the marble *Faun,* by Trentacoste.

Via Turati 10. (C) 091-588951. Admission 3.10€ ($3.70) adults, free for children 17 and under and seniors 66 and over. Tues–Sat 9am–8pm; Sun 9am–1pm. Bus: 101, 102, 103, 106, 108, 124, or 134.

Museo della Fondazione Mormino This unusual, offbeat gallery is on the second floor of the Banco di Sicilia in the historic Villa Mormino. It displays the treasure trove accumulated by banking interests over the years, ranging from artwork to Greek artifacts to rare coins. The collection of Italian majolica from the 16th century to the 18th century is among the finest in Italy; there is also a vast array of Greek vases. Look for the magnificent but tiny Etruscan mirror with a relief of Silenus. Of equal interest is the terra-cotta statue of a young boy, dating from the 3rd century B.C. The final section displays coins and medals, many from the 1200s.

Viale Libertà 52. © 091-625519. Admission 4€ ($4.80) adults, 2€ ($2.40) children, students, and seniors. Mon–Fri 9am–1pm and 3–5pm; Sat 9am–1pm. Closed Aug. Bus: 101, 102, 702, or 704.

Museo Etnografico Pitré This is the attic of old Sicily, a virtual time capsule of the way life used to be lived on the island. Nearly everything that it documents has been virtually swept away in the past half century. Back in 1909, a great collector, Giuseppe Pitré, understood that the old ways were quickly vanishing, so he began to collect the tools of ordinary Sicilian life, accumulating some 4,000 objects that are today on exhibit at this museum.

Nothing is more evocative of old Sicily than the brightly painted, flamboyantly decorated **carts** ✩, which Sicilians call *carretti*. A family's social standing was judged by its carts: The more elaborate and intricate the decoration, the more important the family. The museum also displays an intriguing collection of puppets and a vast array of handicrafts, ranging from ceramic holy water fonts to painted masks to 19th-century lace dresses.

Parco della Favorita. © 091-7404890. Admission 5€ ($6) adults, free for children 17 and under and seniors 61 and over. Sat–Thurs 7:30am–7:30pm. Bus: 101 to Stadio Partanna, then change to 614 or 645.

Museo Internazionale delle Marionette (International Puppet Museum) ✩✩ *Kids* For those who are into puppets (or *pupi*, as the Sicilians say), this is the greatest museum of its kind in the world. In their shiny armor and with their stern expressions, these marionettes remain as an evocation of Norman Sicily, an era of legendary chivalry and troubadours. In the world of the puppet, the exploits of William the Bad (1120–66) and others live on, as do the legends of Charlemagne and the swashbuckling Saracen pirates. All of the puppets on display are handmade antiques, some of them centuries old, from Sicily as well as other parts of Italy. Most were used at one time in the *opera de pupi,* a local tradition fast dying out. The collection also includes puppets crafted in other parts of the world, notably Indonesia, India, and other countries from the Far East, as well as the English "Punch and Judy." The most outstanding artisan represented here is Gaspara Canino, who achieved fame with his theater puppets in the 1800s.

Piazzetta Niscemi 1. © 091-328060. Admission 4€ ($4.80) adults, 2.50€ ($3) children under 12. Mon–Fri 9am–1pm and 4–7pm; Sat 9am–1pm; Sun 10am–1pm. Bus: 103, 105, 139, or 225.

5 City Landmarks & Treasures

Fontana Pretoria ✩✩ In the heart of Palermo's loveliest square, **Piazza Pretoria** ✩✩, stands this magnificent fountain, the work of the Florentine sculptor Francesco Camilliani in 1554 and 1555. It overlooks the facades of the two churches on the square, S. Caterina and S. Giuseppe dei Teatini. This fountain is hardly subtle: It's adorned with depictions of allegories, animal heads, nymphs, monsters, ornamental staircases and balustrades, and, of course, gods and goddesses comprising an encyclopedia of Mount Olympus. One of the statuettes guarding the ramps is Ceres, the classical patroness of Sicily, depicted with a horn of plenty. The fountain is floodlit at night, a 24-hour sight.

Quattro Canti ✩ At the intersection of Via Vittorio Emanuele and Via Maqueda, the "Four Corners" of Palermo converge at a quartet of baroque palaces left over from the heyday of Spanish rule. The actual name of the square is Piazza

---

⟨ Fun Fact **Shocking, Outrageous, Disgraceful!**

When the **Fontana Pretoria** was first unveiled in 1575 at Piazza Pretoria, the outcry was so loud it could practically be heard across the city. Originally intended for a private Florentine villa and not a public square, the fountain is adorned with nude figures galore. In time, Palermitans learned to live with this "outrage," although they forever afterward referred to it as *Fontana della Vergogna,* or "Fountain of Shame."

Vigliena, although locals refer to it as Quattro Canti. Via Maqueda dates from the 1580s, when it converged with the ancient Via Càssaro, now called Vittorio Emanuele. The viceroy Vigliene ordered the construction of the four palaces at this crossroads, the buildings inspired by Rome's Quattro Fontane.

Each of the corners is decorated with a niche in three tiers. The first tier of each niche contains a fountain and a statue representing one of the four seasons. The second tier of each niche displays a statue of one of the Spanish viceroys. The third tier of each niche is dedicated to a statue of one of the patron saints of the city: Christina, Ninfa, Olivia, and Agata.

Unfortunately, Quattro Canti is no longer the meeting place of Palermitani as it was in the old days. Instead of creamy white buildings, think soot-blackened gray. And be careful when admiring the former beauty of the place, or you might be run down by a king of the road on a speeding Vespa.

6 Palermo's "Green Lungs": Parks & Gardens

The Arabs, a people who knew the joy of a green oasis, were the ones who introduced gardens into Palermo. The Normans extended the idea by creating parklands and summer palaces to escape the heat. Today, you can wander among gardens and greenery and encounter incredible banyan trees and other exotic plantings. If you have limited time to visit Palermo's parks, the most rewarding are Orto Botanico and Giardino Inglese, both described below.

GIARDINO GARIBALDI 🎄   In the very heart of Palermo, at Piazza Marina, lies this beautiful garden. Stunning **banyan trees** 🎄🎄, with their exposed, trunk-like "aerial" roots, grace this park along with fig trees and towering palms.

In the 16th century, Aragonese weddings and military victories were celebrated at **Piazza Marina.** Sadly, it was also the site of public executions. After a long period of neglect, Piazza Marina has been spruced up and is once again a gathering place for residents. At night, it's an animated square with outdoor tables spilling from several pizzerie.

The largest palace on the square is **Palazzo Chiaramonte** 🎄, constructed in 1307 for one of Sicily's noblest and richest dynasties during the Aragonese era. Its most attractive feature can be seen on its facade—two tiers of delightful **windows** 🎄🎄 with magnificent stone inlays. The palace is sometimes open for concerts.

GIARDINO INGLESE 🎄   The **English Gardens** lie to the north of the center, bordering Via della Libertà past Piazza Crispi. They were designed at the end of the 19th century. Always known as Palermo's prettiest little park, the gardens in the 1990s degenerated into a hangout for Palermo's drug-addicted population. Recently, however, the police have cracked down; unless conditions change, the park has been returned to its former self.

ORTO BOTANICO ✿✿   This is our favorite Palermo park, located at Via Abramo Lincoln 2B (✆ **091-6238241**). These botanical gardens were laid out in 1795; the circular water lily pond from 1796 is still here. If for no other reason, make a visit just to see the amazing **banyan tree** ✿✿, the tallest and most impressive specimen in the garden. This fig tree with its "aerial" roots is more than 150 years old.

The garden is known to botanists the world over thanks to the richness and variety of its plant species, which range from gigantic tropical plants to spiny kapok trees with their bottle-shaped trunks. Among the curiosities are the *Bombacaceae* and *Chorisias* plants shipped here in the late 19th century from South America. These have swollen and prickly trunks and in spring bloom with beautiful pink flowers that turn to a strange fruit. Upon ripening, the fruit bursts open and drops its seed on the ground along with a thick hair "padding." Locals once harvested this padding and used it like horsehair.

Admission to Orto Botanico is 3.50€ ($4.20). Hours are Monday through Friday from 9am to 6pm, Saturday and Sunday from 8:30am to 1:30pm (closes at 5pm in winter). Take bus no. 139, 211, 221, 224, 226, or 227. See below for a description of **Villa Giulia,** the park next door to the Orto Botanico.

PARCO DELLA FAVORITA   Reached by going 2.8km (1¾ miles) north of Palermo along Viale Diana is this large park at the foot of Monte Pellegrino. Parco della Favorita was part of an estate acquired in 1799 by Ferdinand of Bourbon, who came here after he was driven out of Naples by Napoleonic troops. He ordered that the land be laid out according to his rather Victorian taste. In time, it became the ruler's private hunting estate.

The fantastic **Palazzina Cinese (Chinese Palace)** built for Ferdinand is still standing. It was in this exotically decorated palace that the king, along with his wife, Maria Carolina, entertained Horatio Nelson and Lady Hamilton.

Note the marble fountain with a statue of Hercules. This is a copy of the celebrated *Farnese Hercules* that the king tried to abduct from Naples. Instead of the real thing, he got a copy.

In the 18th century, many noble families built summer villas around the park to escape the intense heat of the city. The most famous of these is **Villa Niscemi,** Piazza Niscemi (✆ **091-7494801**), a venue for occasional cultural events. The villa is sometimes open on Sundays from 9am to 1pm; call ahead to confirm.

VILLA BONANNO ✿   Behind the Palazzo dei Normanni lies Villa Bonanno, among the most beautiful public gardens of Palermo. Enter from Piazza della Vittoria. The city added palm trees in 1905, making the park look like an oasis in North Africa. Note the roof covering the ruins of a trio of ancient Roman houses, the only such artifacts of their kind left in Palermo. Villa Bonanno adjoins Piazza del Parlamento, with its mammoth statue of Philip V of the House of Bourbon.

VILLA GIULIA   Next door to the Orto Botanico, also opening onto Via Abramo Lincoln, is this Italianate oasis, created in 1778 and enlarged in 1866. This was the city's first public park and was named for its patron, Giulia Avalos Guevara, the wife of the ruling viceroy. Goethe came this way in 1787 and had much praise for the garden, which is also called "La Flora." Its beautiful trees and flowers are in better shape than the monuments. The best-known statue is called *Genius of Palermo,* by Marabitti.

7 Especially for Kids

Palermo is not the world's most child-friendly city. Because of roaring, dangerous traffic, it is difficult to walk the city's streets, especially the narrow ones, without constantly keeping an eye out for your *bambini*.

There is one attraction that kids adore in Palermo, however, and that's the **Museo Internazionale delle Marionette (International Puppet Museum)** (p. 101). Sicilians call their famous puppets *pupi*, and they are truly works of folkloric art. Delightful puppet shows are staged here on Fridays between 5 and 6pm. Puppet shows are also presented at **Teatro Ippogrifo,** Vicolo Ragusi 4 (✆ **091-329194;** bus: 225). These shows, costing from 5€ to 6€ ($6–$7.20) per ticket, are staged daily at 5:30pm, September through June only.

Each family who visits Palermo has to decide whether to take children to the **Catacombe dei Cappuccini** (p. 91), where mummified bodies and skeletons of some 8,000 Palermitans are on view. Young children in particular may be frightened by these ghoulish sights, including a baby girl who died in 1920, her corpse amazingly lifelike even today.

Away from the traffic, noise, and pollution of Palermo, the city's public parks offer refreshing interludes for families. Especially inviting is the landscaped oasis of the **Orto Botanico,** or botanical gardens (p. 103).

Another delight for families is a trip up to **Monte Pellegrino** (p. 116), a mountain that looms over north Palermo. With its greenery and parkland, the 600m (2,000-ft.) mountain evokes Yosemite. Keep in mind that the park is likely to be crowded on Sundays with Sicilian families in search of a respite from Palermo's smog.

Finally, if you're in Palermo on a summer day, you might want to escape the city altogether and head for **Mondello Lido,** with its long, sandy beaches. Even on a summer night, this is the place to be; many families can be seen walking along the water and ducking into one of the pizzerie when the kids get hungry. For more on Mondello Lido, see p. 124.

WALKING TOUR   OLD PALERMO

Start	San Giovanni degli Eremiti.
Finish	Piazza Marina.
Time	3 to 3½ hours. (Interior visits, of course, will consume far more time.)
Best Time	Daily from 8am to noon and 3 to 6pm, when many of the museums and churches are open.
Worst Time	During the lunch doldrums, from noon to 3pm, and after dark.

Begin your tour by the iron gates that protect the palm-shaded garden surrounding:

❶ San Giovanni degli Eremiti

The best known of all the Arabo-Norman monuments of Palermo, San Giovanni, at Via dei Benedettini, is a short block from roaring traffic arteries difficult to navigate. (*Tip:* To avoid walking through such heavy traffic, many visitors opt to take a taxi directly to the beginning of this walking tour.)

Five typically Arab domes reveal the origins of the Moorish craftsmen who constructed this monastery for Roger II in 1132. It honors St. John of the Hermits. The church's tranquil, beautiful gardens are devoted to such species as the pomegranate and the rose. The gardens lead to the ruins of the original Benedictine monastery that once stood here, a structure built in 581 for Pope Gregory the Great.

1 San Giovanni degli Eremiti

2 Palazzo dei Normanni

3 Villa Bonanno

4 Palazzo Arcivescovile

5 Duomo

6 Biblioteca Centrale
   della Regione Siciliana

7 Chiesa SS. Salvatore

🥄 Liberty Bar

8 Chiesa San Giuseppe dei Teatini

9 Quatro Canti (Four Corners)

10 Piazza Pretoria

11 Chiesa San Cataldo

12 Chiesa della Martorana

🥄 Pizzeria Bellini

13 Chiesa San Francesco di Assisi

14 Palazzo Mirto

15 Piazza Marina

After a visit, walk north toward the sound of roaring traffic coming from the nearby Piazza del Pinta. En route to the piazza, you'll pass a wall niche dedicated to Maria Addolorata, which is usually embellished with plants and fresh flowers.

Cross to the opposite side of Piazza del Pinta. From here, you'll see the severely dignified stone archway pierced with formidable doors, leading to:

❷ Palazzo dei Normanni

The chief attraction of Palermo, this mammoth palace and artistic treasure was constructed by the Arabs over the ruins of a Roman fort in the 11th century. Over time it was expanded and turned into the royal residence of Roger II, the Norman king. Much of the look of the present palace is from alterations it received from the 16th to the 17th century. The chief attraction inside is **Cappella Palatina,** a magnificent example of the Arabo-Norman artistic genius.

Exit from the compound's stately entrance gate (the same one you entered), walk about 50 paces downhill, and then turn left onto Via del Castione. You'll have trouble seeing a street sign at first.

From here, you'll skirt the Norman Palace's massive and sharply angled foundations. After 2 narrow and claustrophobic blocks, climb the first set of granite steps rising upward from Via del Castione's left side. This will lead you into a verdant garden, called:

❸ Villa Bonanno

Imbued with the scent of jasmine and oleander, this public park separates the rear entrance of the Palazzo dei Normanni from the Duomo compound you'll be visiting soon. Dotting the garden are monuments and effigies erected in honor of such Sicilian patriots as Caetano Bucceri and Pietro Gullo. If it's a hot day, this is an idyllic place to cool off.

Walk through the garden, exiting at its opposite end, which will lead you to:

❹ Palazzo Arcivescovile

Lying across the busy Via Bonello, a street of heavy traffic, only a portal survives from the palace constructed here in 1460. The present structure is from the 18th century. Originally the Museo Diocesano was founded here, housing artifacts from the cathedral and other works of art from churches about to be demolished. Since it's been closed for many years, the palace can be appreciated only from its outside.

As a slight detour from this walking tour, stroll down a narrow lane behind Palazzo Arcivescovile to the **Oratorio dei SS. Pietro e Paolo.** The interior contains stuccoes by Giacomo Serpotta and Domenico Castelli, plus a ceiling fresco by Filippo Tancredi. We've been able to see the interior of this oratory only one time over many years' worth of visits; it's been closed otherwise.

On the other side of Palazzo Arcivescovile on Via Bonello is the 16th-century **Loggia dell'Incoronazione,** with ancient columns and capitals that were incorporated into the present structure. The kings of Sicily used to "display" themselves to their subjects here following a coronation.

After viewing the palace, head east along the major artery, Corso Vittorio Emanuele. The sidewalk at this point becomes very narrow, barely passable, as cars roar by. The pavement will open within a short time onto a sweeping view of the:

❺ Duomo

At Piazza di Cattedrale, right off Corso Vittorio Emanuele, the cathedral of Palermo, dedicated to Our Lady of the Assumption, was built on the site of an early Christian basilica, which was later turned into a mosque by Arab rulers. Although launched in the 12th century, the cathedral has seen many architects and much rebuilding over the centuries. The cathedral today is a hodgepodge of styles, its baroque cupola added in the late 18th century.

After a look or a visit, continue east along Corso Vittorio Emanuele on narrow sidewalks until you come to:

⑥ Biblioteca Centrale della Regione Siciliana

Once a Jesuit college called Collegio Massimo dei Gesuiti, this building is today the home of Palermo's main public library, providing shelter for more than half a million volumes and many ancient manuscripts, including several from the 15th and 16th centuries. A double arcaded courtyard is its architectural centerpiece. It is entered by the portal of the adjacent Chiesa di S. Maria della Grotta.

Continue to head east along Corso Vittorio Emanuele until you come to the intersection of Via SS. Salvatore. If it's open, you can duck into the dark, shadowy recesses of:

⑦ Chiesa SS. Salvatore

Palermo has far greater churches than this, so feel free to settle for just a look at its facade. Built in 1682 by Paolo Amato, the church was severely damaged during the 1943 Allied air raids but has been restored, enough so that its oval interior is frequently a venue for weddings.

Our eastward trek continues along Corso Vittorio Emanuele to a point where the street widens into a square, the Piazza Bologni. It's time to:

TAKE A BREAK
The tables of **Liberty Bar,** Corso Vittorio Emanuele 350 (© 091-328929), spread out onto the square. Here you can have your fill of excellent espresso or cappuccino, delicious ice cream as only the Italians know how to make it, and even sandwiches or a pizza.

After a refueling stop, continue east for a short distance until you come to:

⑧ Chiesa San Giuseppe dei Teatini

Near Quattro Canti (see below), this lavishly decorated church was built by the Theatine congregation. The interior has a dancing baroque spirit, although the facade, not completed until 1844, is along more severe neoclassical lines. The cupola of the church is adorned with majolica tiles. If you go inside (hours are Mon–Sat 8:45–11:15am and 5–7pm, Sun 8:30am–1pm), you'll find a two-aisle nave. Flanking it are towering columns resting under a frescoed ceiling, holding up walls covered with a marble polychrome decoration. The main altar is constructed of semi-precious gems, and the chapels are lavishly frescoed with stucco decoration. The church was designed by Giacomo Besio of Genoa (1612–45).

At this point of the walking tour, you are in the very heart of Old Palermo at the famous:

⑨ Quattro Canti (Four Corners)

Corso Vittorio Emanuele intersects with Via Maqueda, the latter street a famous piece of Palermitano civic planning, carved out of the surrounding neighborhood in the 16th century by the Spanish viceroy.

Architecturally, Four Corners is a melting pot of Arabo-Norman magnificence, Palermitan baroque, and the work of craftsmen of the Middle Ages. Each sculpted angle of the Four Corners celebrates seasons, a patron saint, or a Spanish viceroy.

Directly east of this "crossroads" of Palermo lies:

⑩ Piazza Pretoria

This lovely square is Palermo's most famous. Its beautiful but controversial fountain, originally intended for a Tuscan villa, is bedecked with nude statues and mythological monsters—thus was called **Fontana della Vergogna,** or "fountain of shame," by outraged churchgoers. **San Giuseppe dei Teatini** is the church directly to the west; the eastern end of the square is flanked by **Chiesa Santa Catarina.** On the south axis stands **Palazzo Pretorio,** the

Let the Horse Lead the Way

Consider hiring one of the horse-drawn carriages that line up on the Via Maqueda at Piazza Pretoria. A 60-minute ride for up to four passengers costs 60€ ($72). In a style that's either romantic, nostalgic, or corny, depending on your point of view, it will haul you around for a view of the city's street life and a fast overview, from the outside, of monumental Palermo. For more information on carriage tours from a driver we find cooperative, call ℂ **380-5097646.**

city hall. Note the plaque on the front of the building commemorating Garibaldi's 1860 triumph, ending the Bourbon reign in Sicily.

Now walk to the southern edge of the Piazza Pretoria and go through the narrow gap between City Hall and the Church of Santa Catarina. A vista over the Piazza Bellini will open up before you. At its far end rise two of the most distinctive churches in Palermo, the first called:

❶ Chiesa San Cataldo

Standing side by side with Chiesa della Martorana (see below), this is one of two Norman churches in Palermo. The church, with its rose-colored cupolas, was founded in 1154 by Maio da Bari, the despised emir of William I. After a checkered history—the church was turned into a post office in the 19th century—San Cataldo today is the seat of the Knights of the Holy Sepulchre.

Next door to San Cataldo is:

❷ Chiesa della Martorana

With its handsome Norman bell tower, this is the more intriguing of the two churches. It is the loveliest Greek church remaining in Sicily. It was founded in 1143 by George of Antioch, called Roger II's "Emir of Emirs." Regrettably, the linear symmetry of the original Norman church is today covered by a baroque facade.

After this intense spate of church-going, you'll probably think it's time to:

 TAKE A BREAK
Pizzeria Bellini, Piazza Bellini 6 (ℂ **091-6165691**), is set directly at the base of the Church of San Cataldo, with a pleasant terrace that's shielded from the dust and congestion of the surrounding neighborhood by an evergreen hedge and latticework barrier. This is the kind of cafe where you almost fall into the chairs, then slug back a half liter of liquid refreshment. It doubles as a restaurant, in case you want a full meal, but most participants on this walking tour opt for gelato, a coffee, or a drink. Closed Mondays.

To resume the tour, retrace your steps along Via Maqueda north to Quattro Canti. Once at the Four Corners, continue east along Corso Vittorio Emanuele on the street's right-hand side. Here the neighborhood grows increasingly battered, commercial, and decrepit. In about 4 minutes, turn right onto Via Alessandro Paternostro, a narrow street 1 short block after Vicolo Madonna del Cassaro. Walk uphill along Via Alessandro Paternostro through a commercial section of shops. In less than 4 minutes, note the intricately carved Romanesque facade of the:

❸ Chiesa San Francesco d'Assisi

This is one of our favorite churches in Palermo, thanks to its dignified simplicity and unusual combination of Romanesque and baroque detailing, plus the sense you get that it's still very much involved in the day-to-day life of this ancient parish. First constructed in the 13th century, it was destroyed by Frederick II after he was excommunicated by the pope. A new church was constructed and completed in 1277, although it's seen much alteration over the years. A 1943 Allied bombing didn't help matters, either.

From the square directly in front of the church (Piazza di San Francesco d'Assisi), head east on the narrow, unmarked street on the right-hand side of the church as you face it. Walk 1½ short blocks until you reach:

⓮ Palazzo Mirto

This is your greatest opportunity in Old Palermo to visit a palace from yesterday and to see how a Sicilian noble family lived. Of the many other palaces in the neighborhood, most are closed to the public and still not restored. Palazzo Mirto miraculously remains as it was, with its original furnishings. It dates from the 18th century, having been built over earlier structures that went back to the 15th century.

After a visit, walk a few steps to the west into the broad 19th-century vistas of:

⓯ Piazza Marina

This is the largest square in Palermo. Its most significant architectural monument is **Palazzo Steri-Chiaramonte,** constructed in 1307 by one of Sicily's most influential noble families. The palace was built in a Gothic style with Arabo-Norman influences. In the middle of Piazza Marina is the **Giardino Garibaldi,** a beautiful park where you may want to wind down and enjoy the splashing waters of its central fountain.

8 City Markets & Shopping

Palermo is like a grand shopping bazaar. You'll find a little bit of everything here, including boutiques of high fashion. Many shoppers seek out the expert craftspeople known for their skill in producing any number of goods, especially beautiful coral jewelry. Embroidered fabrics are another specialty item. Some visitors come to Palermo just to purchase ceramics.

Palermo markets (see below) are the most colorful in southern Italy. At these markets, all the bounty of Sicily—fruits, vegetables, fish—is elegantly displayed. Since it is unlikely you will be staying in accommodations with kitchen facilities, the markets are mainly for sightseeing, although they do offer an array of clothing and crafts as well.

For the best shopping, head for **Via della Libertà,** north of the city's medieval core within a 19th-century residential neighborhood of town houses and mid-20th-century apartment buildings that evoke some of the more upscale residential sections of Barcelona.

⌠Moments Sugar Shock

You'll find traditional fruit-filled tarts as well as *cassata Siciliana* (tarts with a ricotta-based filling) at **Fratelli Magri,** Via Isidoro Carini 42 (① **091-584788**). The shop also makes other types of sweets, as well as gelato in the summer, but come here for the authentic high-calorie pastries. **I Peccatucci di Mamma Andrea,** Via Principe di Scordia 67 (① **091-334835**), a celebration of local confections, will tempt you with the bounty of Sicily's traditional desserts. The best examples are pralines, *torrone, panetoni,* segments of fruit dripping with Sicilian honey, marzipan, and an age-old specialty known as *ghirlande di croccantini* (hazelnut torte). Get ready for sugar shock and lots of local color. Bus: 122 or 124.

Within this same neighborhood, **Via Principe di Belmonte** is an all-pedestrian thoroughfare with many hip and elegant shops, as well as fashionable cafes such as Spinnato.

The two other principal shopping streets in the old town are **Via Roma** and **Via Maqueda.**

Monday morning is the worst time to shop, as nearly all stores are closed. Otherwise, general shopping hours are Monday through Friday from 9am to 1pm and from 3:30 to 7 or 7:30pm, Saturday from 4 to 8pm.

ART

Galleria Caravello   One of Palermo's largest and busiest galleries occupies the ground floor of a modern apartment building near the northern terminus of the Via di Libertà. It sells empty picture frames (the massively ornate and gilded kind) as well as contemporary-looking landscapes that will evoke Sicily and its vistas long after your return home. Via Marchese Ugo 64–70. (℃ **091-6251736.** Bus: 101, 102, 104, 106, 107, or 306.

BOOKS

Libreria Altro Quando   This is Palermo's most visible counterculture bookstore, with a definite allegiance to things revolutionary, socialist, feminist, gay-liberated, and ecologically and politically correct. Gay books tend to be shunted off to a mezzanine in back, which is accessible via a flight of hard-to-navigate stairs. Via Vittorio Emanuele 145. (℃ **091-6114732.** Bus: 103, 104, 105, 108, 110, 139, 224, 225, 389, or 824.

Libreria Kalós   From a cool, contemplative hideaway within a walled compound in the heart of Palermo's well-heeled Via Libertà district, this shop sells books, holds poetry readings, sponsors chamber-music recitals, and publishes some of the finest books in the world on Sicily's artistic and architectural heritage. Come here for books (mostly in Italian, less frequently in English or French) and insight into the arts and letters of this distinct southern Italian city. Via XX Settembre 56B. (℃ **091-322380.** Bus: 101 or 107.

CERAMICS

De Simone   For majolica-style stoneware, this old favorite, a family-run business, has been producing quality ware since the 1920s. It also offers some of the most tasteful ceramics and finest tiles in Palermo. Most tiles are painted with scenes of Sicilian country life, including seascapes and bird-filled landscapes. Also for sale are porcelain dinner and tea services, along with ceramic chandeliers. While visiting the shop, you can inquire about visits to the factory at Via Lanza de Scalea 698 ((℃ **091-6711005**), open Monday through Friday from 8am to 5pm. Via Gaetano Daita 13B. (℃ **091-584876.** Bus: 103, 106, 108, or 122.

Laboratoriao Italiano di Patricia Italiano 🕸   This is the sales outlet for the most dynamic and creative ceramic artists in Palermo. Set in the fashionable Via Libertà neighborhood, it sells inventories based on 19th-century Sicilian models, but always with a sophisticated, modern twist. The result is a shop that's often visited by owners of nearby beach houses and condos who stock up on jardinieres, planters, lace-edged bowls and platters, and holders for votive candles. We love the wall-mounted receptacles for holy water, priced at 40€ ($48); they show Madonnas, some of them black, "in conversation." Prices are lower than you'd expect. Via Principe di Villafranca 42. (℃ **091-320282.** Bus: 103.

DEPARTMENT STORES

Barone Confezioni-Abbigliamento-Corredi In business for some 6 decades, this is the best department store in Palermo. Its focus is mainly on moderately and inexpensively priced clothing, with lots of popular labels in evidence. The store carries sportswear and casual wear as well as more formal suits and dresses. Women's fashions are found on the main floor, with departments for kids and men one floor down. Via Abramo Lincoln 146. (✆ **091-6165626**. Bus: 139, 211, 221, 224, 226, 227, 231, 234, 250, or 971.

ECCLESIASTICAL OBJECTS

Postolato Liturgico For devout Catholics visiting from around the world, this store represents a treasure trove of church-related finery (or iconography, depending on your point of view). It's staffed by an international bevy of nuns, all in white habits, all of them members of the *Paoline Piedice* (Pious Disciples of the Divine Master) order. Inventories—some of them incredibly valuable—are usually displayed behind glass in a style that may remind you of a museum. You'll see chalices, monstrances, and medallions—some made of gold, others encrusted with gemstones—as well as some of the most gorgeous liturgical robes in Italy. Corso Vittorio Emmanuele 454. (✆ **091-6512467**. Bus: 103, 104, 105, 108, 110, or 118.

FABRICS

Giuseppe Gramuglia Traditional Sicilian decor—at least that inspired by the late 19th century—usually involves lots of fabric, in the form of rich-looking upholsteries and heavy curtains that block out the intense sunlight. If you want to duplicate this look in your own home, consider a visit to this store. Set at the corner of Palermo's most fashionable shopping street (Via Principe di Belmonte), it contains hundreds of bolts of fabric, in every conceivable pattern. It also sells decorative ropes, fringes, and tassels. Via Roma 412–414 (at Via Principe di Belmonte). (✆ **091-583262**. Bus: 104, 107, 122, 124, 224, or 225.

FASHIONS FOR MEN

Carieri & Carieri This is a store for serious menswear shoppers—and if you express the slightest interest, a member of its staff is likely to "adopt" you, leading you to selections in your size and along a wide spectrum of fashion-related statements. The only thing wrong with this store is its intimidatingly large size, which might confuse you (or delight you) when you first walk in. The staff is about as upscale and attentive as any you're likely to find in Palermo, and if there aren't a lot of other customers, they're likely to descend upon you, en masse, to attend to your needs. The selection of suits and office wear is very extensive— the best and classiest displays in town. Via E. Parisi 4. (✆ **091-321846**. Bus: 101, 102, 104, 106, 107, 306, or 309.

FASHIONS FOR WOMEN

Le Gi di Valentino Don't be fooled into thinking that the evening gown you buy here will be genuine (i.e., created by Valentino). What you'll get instead is a sense of fun, obscene amounts of silk taffeta arranged into tarty-looking flounces, and a genuine whimsy that might look fetchingly fabulous at a cocktail party back home. Clothes here manage to look "wenchy" and elegant at the same time, a real accomplishment if you're brave enough to wear them. Via Ruggiero Settimo 99–101. (✆ **091-324197**. Bus: 101, 102, 103, or 124.

Motivi The minimalist and often highly revealing clothing sold here might not be appropriate for any woman of a certain age, unless she's terribly pulled together, sexy, and well-preserved. But if you're adventurous or merely curious

---

Moments Sampling the Local Vino

Sicily's hot climate and volcanic soil nurture a wealth of vineyards, many of which produce simple table wines. Of the better vintages, the best-known is **Marsala,** a sweet dessert wine produced in both amber and ruby tones. One name that evokes years of winemaking traditions, thanks to the winery's skill at producing Cerasucio di Vittoria and Moscato di Pantelleria, is **Corvo Duca di Salaparuta,** a 19th-century winery in the hills above Palermo. For information, contact the **Casa Vinicola Duca di Salaparuta,** Via Nazionale, SS113, Casteldaccia, 90014 Palermo (© **091-953988**). If you'd like to visit, call ahead to make an appointment and get directions. *Note:* This winery produces the Moscato di Pantelleria wine but not Marsala, which is produced only in Marsala.

---

about what's going on design-wise with Sicilian 20-somethings, take a look. The clothing is appropriate for the beach, for the disco, or for merely riding around in cars with boys. The venue is trendy—perhaps too much so—and, at its best, fun. Via Ruggiero Settimo 109. © **091-322158.** Bus: 101, 102, 103, or 124.

FOOD

I Peccatucci di Mamma Andrea ⟨⟩   This small-scale boutique contains one of the most diverse collections of gastronomic abundance in Palermo, each item artfully wrapped into the kind of gift that will delight recipients back home. Elegant bottles contain liqueurs distilled from herbs or fruits you might never have thought suitable, such as almonds, basil, myrtle, fennel, figs, and rose petals. Jams and honeys showcase the agrarian bounty and aromas of Sicily. There is also an array of *peccatucci* ("small sins")—utterly delightful candies made from almond paste, sugar, and liqueur—that resemble fruit or sleeping cherubs. 67 Via Principe di Scordia. © **091-334835.** Bus: 101, 102, 103, 104, 107, 122, 124, 224, or 225.

FRAMES

Meli   These family owners have worked for more than a century turning out handcrafted tortoise-shell frames. They also specialize in reproductions of antique picture frames made of coral, along with jewel cases, stylish prints, etchings, and engravings from the 16th to the 19th century. Via Dante 294. © **091-6824213.** Bus: 103, 106, 108, or 122.

JEWELRY

Di Bella   This is one of the better jewelry stores of Palermo, operating in a location near the old Capo marketplace. Top names in watches are featured along with tastefully styled rings, necklaces, and bracelets. Via Carini 22. © **091-320818.** Bus: 104 or 107.

Fiorentino   A Palermo tradition since 1890, this jeweler is still going strong, offering both traditional and contemporary designs. The pieces are exquisite; there's also a vast array of gift items, silverware, and watches. The fashionable set along Via Libertà shop here. Via della Libertà. © **091-6047111.** Bus: 101, 102, 104, 106, 107, 303, 603, 702, 704, 721, 731, or 806.

LINENS

Frette   This company's wares are highly prized by those who favor high-thread-count sheets and butter-soft linens. Frette has been the royal purveyors of linens to everyone from the Pope to the former royal families of Italy. It offers sheets, tablecloths, towels, bedspreads, nightgowns, curtains, and tapestries, among other items. Via Ruggero Settimo 12. ℭ 091-585166. Bus: 101, 102, 103, or 124.

MARKETS

The Muslims were active traders, and Palermo's markets, which spill over into narrow alleys shaded by colorful awnings, still have an Arabic feel. Nothing else connects you with local life more than a visit to a bustling Palermo market.

The best, most famous market in Palermo is **La Vucciria** ✦✦. In Sicilian dialect, *vucciria* means "hubbub" or "voices," and that's what you'll hear here. The market spills onto the narrow side streets of Piazza San Domenico, off Via Roma between Corso Vittorio Emanuele and the San Domenico church. This is one of Europe's great casbah-like markets, with mountains of food ranging from fresh swordfish steaks to all sorts of meat and recently harvested produce, reflecting the bounty of the Sicilian countryside. The array of such items as wild fennel, long-stemmed artichokes, blood oranges, and giant octopus will astound you. This market trades Monday through Saturday until 2pm. Try to go before 10am, when it's at its most frenetic and colorful. The markets described below keep roughly the same hours.

If you're seized with market fever, you can also visit **Mercato di Capo,** a large street market that captures some of the spirit of the city's Saracen past. This market sprawls around the area of Chiesa di Sant'Agostino. Clothing stalls flank the streets of Via S. Agostino and Via Bandiera; the items here tend to be cheap and poorly made. More interesting is the food section off Via Volturno, which spreads along Via Beati Paoli and Via Porta Carini. The most colorful part of this market converges around Piazza Beati Paoli. The stalls wind toward the old gate, Porta Carini, that used to be a part of the city wall surrounding Palermo.

The third great market of Palermo is **Ballarò,** in the Albergheria district, roughly between Piazza Carmine leading to Piazza Casa Professa and Piazza S. Chiazra. This is mainly a food market, with mountains of fruits and vegetables along with fishmongers and hawkers of discount clothing.

MILITARY UNIFORMS

Romano Luigi, Sartoria Civile e Militare   This shop, along with three or four shops on either side, specializes in the uniforms and paraphernalia used by

---

Moments Feasting at the Markets

We like to visit the markets not only to look at the fabulous produce, but also to enjoy some of the tastiest snacks in Sicily. It's a great way to have lunch as you graze from stall to stall.

Some visitors stroll along while munching chopped **boiled octopus** (*purpu* in Sicilian) and delectable, freshly cooked **artichokes.** Naturally, there's plenty of **fresh bread** and luscious **vine-ripened fruit** as well.

You can also purchase absolutely delicious *panelle* (chickpea fritters) or *calzoni* (deep-fried meat- or cheese-filled pockets of dough). If you have an adventurous palate, dig in to a roll filled with beef spleen or tripe, called *pani cu' la meuza.* These pani are often topped with fresh ricotta or a velvety cheese known as *caciocavallo.* Hot sauce is sprinkled on at the last moment.

members of the Italian police and *Guardia Civile.* Ironically set directly across the street from shops that specialize in church vestments for the Catholic liturgy, it's a military fetishist's dream. Not everything can be (officially) sold to a layperson (such as some aspects of an official police officer's uniform), but the selection is intriguing for anyone who has ever completed a stint in the armed forces. Corso Vittorio Emanuele 453–455. © 091-324457. Bus: 104, 105, 108, 110, 118, 139, 224, 225, or 389.

PERFUMES & COSMETICS

Limoni   When it comes to toiletries and cosmetics for both women and men, Palermo shops don't get much better than this. Affiliated with one of Italy's most popular chains, this store features a wide array of scents. Many items are suitable as gifts. Corso Tukory 222. © 091-6514324. Bus: 103, 234, 246, or 318.

9 Palermo After Dark

For such a large city, Palermo has a dearth of nightlife. In the hot summer months, the townspeople parade along the waterfront of **Mondello Lido** to cool off (p. 12). Although they are improving somewhat, many Palermo areas with bars and taverns (such as La Kalsa or Alberghiera) are not safe for walking around at night. And some of the bars and taverns in the medieval core of Palermo have the life span of sickly butterflies. The safest places for drinking, making conversation, and meeting like-minded companions are the many bars in the deluxe and first-class hotels. They are also the most sanitary.

The liveliest squares at night—and the relatively safest because lots of people are here—are **Piazza Castelnuovo** and **Piazza Verdi.** Another "safe zone" is a pedestrian strip flanked by bars and cafes, many with sidewalk tables, along **Via Principe di Belmonte,** between Via Roma and Via Ruggero Settimo. Some of these bars have live pianists in summer. If you like the sound of things, drop in for a glass of wine or a beer.

If you're interested in the arts and cultural venues, stop by the tourist office (p. 63) and pick up a copy of *Palermo & Provincia Live,* which documents cafes and other venues offering live music in summer.

THE ARTS   Palermo is a cultural center of some note, with an opera and ballet season running from November to July. The principal venue for cultural presentations is the restored **Teatro Massimo** ⊛⊛, Via Maqueda (© 091-6053555), across from the Museo Archeologico. It boasts the largest indoor stage in Europe after the Paris Opera House. Francis Ford Coppola shot the climactic opera scene here for *The Godfather: Part III.* The theater was built between 1875 and 1897 in a neoclassical style, and reopened after a restoration in 1997 to celebrate its 100th birthday. During the **Festival di Verdura,** from late June to mid-August, many special presentations, most often with international performers, are presented here. Ticket prices range from 15€ to 80€ ($18–$96). The box office is open Tuesday through Sunday from 10am to 4pm. *Note:* The Teatro Massimo can be visited Tuesday through Sunday from 10am to 3:30pm. Visits cost 3€ ($3.60). Guided tours in English are given Tuesday through Saturday from 10am to 2pm and 3 to 4pm. Bus: 101, 102, 103, 104, 107, 122, or 225.

If you have only one night for theater in Palermo, make it the Teatro Massimo. However, **Politeama Garibaldi,** Piazza Ruggero Settimo (© 091-6053315), is also grandiose, and it, too, presents a wide season of operatic and orchestral performances. Again, the tourist office will have full details on what is being performed at the time of your visit. Bus: 101, 102, 103, or 124.

Finds The Local Nerve Center

While in Palermo, you might want to make **Kursaal Kalhesa,** Fort Umberto I 21 (© **091-6167630**), your official headquarters. It's a bee-hive of activity and a great way to meet locals, most of whom are young and fluent in English. Situated in a restored palace near Piazza Marina, this is where Sicily meets New York's SoHo. An attractive crowd congregates at the bar, which is flanked by discreetly lit stone walls and a bookstore-cum-lounge. You can read English-language newspapers, listen to live music, get online at the Internet cafe, or pick up tourist info at the travel agency.

For serious eating, head upstairs for Sicilian and Tunisian fare. The chef's delectable dishes are served in a cavernous room decorated with blue and white tiles; in warm weather, there's terrace dining. The best dishes include artichoke pasta with a radicchio cream sauce, lemon-fla-vored swordfish with shrimp, and the famous lentils grown on the island of Ustica and flavored with squid ink, a local delicacy. Main courses cost from 5€ to 10€ ($6–$12).

The Kursaal building is open Tuesday through Sunday from 11:30am to 2pm and 4pm to 1am. As one local told us, "It's where I always go to hang my hat, even if people don't wear hats anymore."

CAFES   We like to start off an evening by heading to the century-old **Caffè Mazzara,** Via Generale Magliocco (© **091-321443**), to sample wonderful ice cream, sip rich coffee, or try heady Sicilian wine. You'll run into us hanging out at the espresso bar and pastry shop on the street level. The cafe is open daily from 7:30am to 11pm. Bus: 101, 102, or 103.

DANCE CLUBS   Palermo's most popular dance clubs lie in the city's commercial center, although one good one is in north Palermo. The city's main club is **Candelai,** Via Candelai 65 (© **091-327151**). Mainstream rock blasts throughout the night in this crowded complex of gyrating 20-year-olds. The club is open Friday through Sunday from 8pm, with no set closing time. There is no cover, but it is necessary to buy a membership card (valid for a month) for 15€ ($18).

PUBS   One of our favorite pubs, **Nashville,** Via Belgio 4A (© **091-522980**), is a good place to spend an evening in fun company. You can order snacks or dessert here along with your drinks. A backdrop of rock, pop, or disco livens up the atmosphere. The pub attracts a mainly young crowd nightly from 8pm to 1:30am. Bus: 100, 164, 529, 544, or 616.

Villa Niscemi, Piazza Niscemi 55 (© **091-6880820**), has a rustic bar, plus overflowing sidewalk tables in summer. The pub also has musical instruments; if you're the master of one (or even if you're not), you can play an instrument and hopefully entertain the patrons. Live music is featured on Fridays. A crowd of mostly 25- to 45-year-olds patronizes the joint, open daily from 7pm to 3am. Closed Mondays in July and August. Bus: 614, 615, 645, or 837.

Agricantus, Via XX Settembre 82 (© **091-487117**), is one of the liveliest pubs in town. You never know what might be happening here on the night of your visit—perhaps classical music, jazz, pop, even theater. The pub attracts people of all ages Tuesday through Sunday from 8:30pm to 1:30am. Bus: 101 or 107.

GAY & LESBIAN   Gay and lesbian bars in Palermo are as scarce as a virgin at the *Playboy* mansion; most gay encounters occur on the streets, in cafes, and around squares. That said, gays and lesbians from 18 to 70 converge at **Exit,** Piazza San Francesco da Paola 39–40 (© **348-7814698**), daily from 10pm to 3am. Live rock or pop is often presented. In summer, tables are placed outside fronting the beautiful square. Bus: 108, 118, 122, or 124.

10 Easy Excursions

Palermo is graced with a number of satellite attractions that can be explored easily as side trips. Monreale, with its cathedral, is such an important sight that it is considered among greater Palermo's major attractions. In summer, there are the beaches of Mondello Lido. For a preview of what to see and do on the periphery of Palermo, refer to chapter 5, "Side Trips from Palermo."

If you don't have time to range far in your explorations, however, you can take an excursion to 600m (2,000-ft.) Monte Pellegrino, towering over the city.

MONTE PELLEGRINO

The parkland and nature preserve of the crown-shaped Monte Pellegrino looms over north Palermo. This green oasis and haven from the heat is where the Palermitani retreat on a summer day. During his visit, Goethe pronounced it "the most beautiful headland on earth." Avoid heading up this promontory on a Sunday, however, when half of the world's cars seem to have the same goal.

The mountain rises sharply on all sides except to the south. The headland here, known for its autumnal gold color, was occupied by the Carthaginian general Hamilcar Barca in the First Punic War and defended between 247 and 244 B.C. before it fell to the Romans.

You can reach the mountain from Piazza Generale Casino in Palermo, close to Fiera del Mediterraneo, the fair and exhibition grounds. From here, take Via Pietro Bonanno, following the signs toward the Santuario di S. Rosalia (see below).

After a 14.5km (9-mile) drive to the north, you will reach the peak of Monte Pellegrino. Along the way to the top, you'll be rewarded with some of Sicily's most **panoramic views** , taking in the old city of Palermo and a sweeping vista of Conca d'Oro, the coastline. The paved road you see today dates from the 1600s, when it was a footpath for people climbing the mountain.

The chief attraction of Monte Pellegrino is **Santuario di Santa Rosalia** (© **091-540326**), a cave where the patron saint of Palermo lived. As you near the top (past endless souvenir shops hawking kitsch), you'll approach a belvedere, dominated by a statue of St. Rosalia. If you stop here, you're treated to a **magnificent view** of the sea.

Santa Rosalia holds a special place in the hearts of the Palermitani, who have affectionately nicknamed her *La Santuzza,* or little saint. You enter the sanctuary through a little chapel constructed over a cave in the hillside, where the bones (read: alleged bones) of Rosalia were found in 1624.

Goethe has already given us his approval, finding the setting "so natural and pleasing one can hardly help expecting to see the saint breathe and move about." Supposedly a niece of William II, St. Rosalia lived and died as a hermit on this mountain, retreating here in 1159.

Inside, a 17th-century statue of the saint, the work of Gregorio Tedeschi, is covered by a gilded silver mantle. Before the statue you'll find a massive pile of euros, a gift to her from the faithful. We suspect that someone else hauls in the loot at night—not the saint herself.

(*Fun Fact* **The Legend of Santa Rosalia**
_____

No one knows for sure who Santa Rosalia was. She's more legend than real woman. She was born in 1130, supposedly to a patrician Norman family said to have been descended from Charlemagne. Never a swinger, she was a very pious young lady. Unable to stand the pressures of hedonistic Palermo and its wicked ways, she fled to a cave in Monte Pellegrino in 1159 and died there in 1166.

When the Black Death swept over Palermo in 1624, the story goes, the figure of Rosalia appeared to a hunter. She directed him to her remains in the cave and ordered him to bring her bones to Palermo. She was then carried in a procession through the streets and properly buried.

After that, the plague disappeared. Ever since, Rosalia—now Santa Rosalia—has been revered as the patron saint of the city.

A festival held in her honor, every year on July 15, is a major social and religious event in Palermo. You can join the faithful on September 4, when the true believers walk barefoot from Palermo to the saint's sanctuary.

As a curiosity, note the thin spikes of flattened "steel cobweb" hanging from the ceiling. This isn't contemporary art; it's done to direct the water seeping from the ceiling into a container. The liquid is supposedly miraculous, and is highly prized by devout followers of the saint.

Admission is free, and the sanctuary (in theory, at least) is open daily from 7:45am to 6pm. Frequent Masses may disrupt your visit.

Note the little pathway leading to the left of the chapel. If you take it, after about 30 minutes you'll be at a cliff-top promontory with a view and a statue of the saint. The pathway to the right of the sanctuary leads to the top of Pellegrino, a leisurely hike of about 40 minutes. Families use the grounds and trails on Pellegrino as a picnic site.

If you're not driving, you can take bus no. 812 from Piazza Sturzo (Politeama) in Palermo (trip time: 30 min.). You can take the bus back or else descend from the mountain along the **Scala Vecchia,** a stepped path that winds down the mountain by the sanctuary going all the way to the Fiera del Mediterraneo fairgrounds.

5

Side Trips from Palermo

In spite of the fact that Palermo holds Sicily's greatest artistic monuments and treasures, it is also a city of noise and pollution. One of the pleasures of a visit to the island's capital is to escape it. A side trip makes a welcome respite.

At your doorstep are any number of treasures, ranging from the golden sands of **Mondello Lido** to **Ustica,** an offshore volcanic island of mysterious origins. The cathedral town of **Monreale** contains an ecclesiastical compound greater than anything in Palermo. But that's not all: You can also wander at leisure through the decaying aristocratic villas of **Bagheria** and later stroll among the ruins of the Greco-Roman town of **Solunto.**

1 Bagheria: Decaying Villas

14km (8½ miles) E of Palermo

In the 18th and 19th centuries, Bagheria became the summer retreat of the noble class, who built magnificent villas here to escape the scorching heat of Palermo. The agriculturally rich setting, on the southern slopes of Mount Catalfano at the eastern extension of the Gulf of Palermo, was home to citrus plantations and vineyards. The novelist Dacia Maraini, in her memoir, *Bagheria,* recalled "the atmosphere of a summer garden enriched by lemon groves and olive trees, poised between the hills, cooled by the salt winds."

As family fortunes disappeared and dynasties faded, however, Bagheria fell into a splendid decay. Many of its villas still exist, but ugly modern buildings and factories have encroached upon this once bucolic locale.

In the latter part of the 20th century, Bagheria earned the dubious distinction of being a center of Mafia activities. You can just imagine the international deals plotted behind the decaying walls of Bagheria's heavily guarded villas.

GETTING THERE

Several trains on the Palermo–Messina line stop at Bagheria, which also lies on the Santa Flavia–Solunto–Porticello line. Buses, operated by AST, also run here from Palermo, leaving from both the Stazione Centrale and Piazza Lolli. By car from Palermo, taking the coastal route (113) via Ficarazzi is easier than going to the trouble of getting on the autostrada (A19).

VILLA VIEWING

Villa Cattolica ✦   Visit this baroque villa for a combination of antique architecture and modern art. It was originally constructed by Giuseppe Bonanni Filangeri, prince of Cattolica, and completed in 1736, during the Ottocento vogue for ostentatious country villas. An art gallery, **Galleria Comunale d'Arte Moderna e Contemporanea,** was established here in 1973. Most of the works in the gallery were donated by Renato Guttuso, a neo-realist painter born in 1912 and the island's best-known modern artist. A staunch anti-Fascist during the Mussolini era, and later anti-Mafia, Guttuso evokes Picasso in some of his

USTICA

Ustica ↖

Ustica

Palermo ↓

AREA OF DETAIL

Palermo Mt. Etna Messina

SICILY

Agrigento Syracuse

--- Ferry Service
↖ Beach
🏛 Ruins

Tyrrhenian Sea

Capo Gallo

Mondello **Mondello Lido**

Punta Ráisi

Terrasini

Golfo di Palermo

Carini

Palermo

Solunto

A29

Montelepre

Sta. Flavia

Monreale

Bagheria

Vilabate

Particino

Altofonte

Misilmeri

A19

0   5 Mi
0   5 Km

Piana

works. Beginning in 1958, the artist fell heavily under the influence of Expressionism, abandoning realism for strong colors and daringly decisive lines. His Jazz Age portraits and still lifes evoke the 1930s, while his works from the 1970s are startlingly sensuous. Note Gattuso's portrait of French Impressionist Paul Cézanne. Gattuso died in 1987, and his sculptor friend Giacomo Manzù designed a surreal "blue capsule" tomb for him. Set among scrubby cacti and citrus trees in the shadow of the villa, the tomb evokes the blue of the Sicilian sky.

After visiting the museum, you can walk through the gardens and see Gattuso's tomb as well as a *Camera dello Scirocco,* an artificial cave built under a seigniorial mansion that provided refuge on days when the scorching winds from Africa swept across the land.

Villa Consolare 9. ☎ **091-943902.** Admission 4.50€ ($5.40) adults, 2.25€ ($2.70) students and children under 18. Tues–Sun 9:30am–7pm.

Villa Palagonia ✿✿

This is one of the most bizarre monuments of baroque decadence in Europe, known around the world as the "Villa of Monsters." When Goethe came this way, he was appalled by its "bad taste and folly." It was designed in 1705 by Tommaso Maria Napoli for Francesco Gravina, prince of Palagonia. But it was hideously decorated by the prince's eccentric grandson, the hunchbacked Ferdinando Gravina Alliata.

Francesco ordered that a series of tufa statues be inserted along the top of the wall in front of the facade. Of the original 200 statues, some 60 remain. Goethe

Hometown Boy Makes Good: *Cinema Paradiso*

The filmmaker Giuseppe Tornatore was born in Bagheria on May 27, 1956. Before making films, he was an award-winning still photographer and later a director of TV documentaries. In 1985, he made his feature movie debut with the film *Il Camorristal (The Professor)*. But it wasn't until 1989 that he received world acclaim for *Cinema Paradiso* (aka *Nuovo Cinema Paradiso*), a nostalgic and unabashedly sentimental tribute to the influence of movies on a young boy's life, shot on location in Tornatore's hometown of Bagheria.

The film won a Grand Jury Prize at the Cannes Film Festival and an Oscar as Best Foreign Film of the Year. In 2002, Tornatore restored 52 minutes to his 1989 film and re-released it, entitled *Cinema Paradiso— The New Version*. Among other changes, the film has an entirely different, mood-altering last act. New ending or old, the director's films are said to "touch the soul of Sicily."

described this parade of hideous figures as "beggars of both sexes, men and women of Spain, Moors, Turks, hunchbacks, deformed persons of every kind, dwarfs, musicians, Pulcinellas." He also commented on the depictions of animals: "deformed monkeys, many dragons and snakes, every kind of paw attached to every kind of body, double heads and exchanged heads."

In addition to his hunched back, Ferdinando was said to have a deformed mind. His wife was known to have had many lovers, and so he ordered artisans to make frightening caricatures of these men to embarrass his wife and her male harem. He also created an eccentric interior, with spikes hidden under inviting velvet seats and sets of lovely Chinese porcelain glued together in a sticky mess. Mirrors were often built into the walls to distort the figures of visitors—thus, the hunchback got his revenge on those who stood tall and straight. A Hall of Mirrors remains, although in disrepair.

Unfortunately, most of the decorations that so infuriated Goethe are gone today, and the entire villa, while richly evoking the glories of its baroque past, is in sad need of a major restoration.

Piazza Garibaldi (at the end of Corso Umberto I). © 091-932088. Admission 4€ ($4.80) adults, 2€ ($2.40) students and children under 18. Apr–Oct daily 9am–1pm and 4–7pm; Nov–Mar daily 9am–1pm and 3:30–5:30pm.

2 Solunto: Evocative Ruins

3km (1¾ miles) NE of Bagheria, 18km (11 miles) E of Palermo

Set high on the slopes of Monte Catalfano, the ruins of the city of Solunto may not be the most impressive in Sicily, but they are evocative, and the panoramic view of the sea and the beautiful setting amid aromatic wildflowers make the trip appealing. At a location 374m (1,227 ft.) above the bay, Solunto was the Carthaginian town of Solus and was actually founded as early as the 8th century B.C. Along with Palermo and Mozia, it was one of three Phoenician colonies in Sicily.

In 397 B.C., Dionysius of Syracuse destroyed the city. The present ruins are from the small city that existed here in the mid–4th century B.C. In time, Solunto

Travel Tip: He who finds the best hotel deal has more to spend on facials involving knobbly vegetables.

Hello, the Roaming Gnome here. I've been nabbed from the garden and taken round the world. The people who took me are so terribly clever. They find the best offerings on Travelocity. For very little cha-ching. And that means I get to be pampered and exfoliated till I'm pink as a bunny's doodah.

travelocity®

1-888-TRAVELOCITY / travelocity.com / America Online Keyword: Travel

Plan your vacation

- flights, hotels, car rentals
- cruises & vacation packages
- destination guides
- fare alerts
- go to yahoo.com, click travel

was captured by the Romans, its dwellers fleeing their homes sometime during the 2nd century A.D.

The conquerors would not leave poor Solunto alone, even when it was nearly empty of life. The Saracens, for reasons known only to them, practically destroyed what remained after the Roman destruction.

GETTING THERE

Bagheria (p. 118) is generally the gateway for visitors continuing on to Solunto. By train, Solunto is one stop beyond Bagheria on the Santa Flavia–Solunto–Porticello line. Once you get off the train, go over the tracks and head toward the sea. In 300m (984 ft.), you'll see a signpost pointing to the ruins. From here, it's another 15- to 20-minute hike to the site.

Motorists generally arrive first in Bagheria. Solunto is signposted from Piazza Garibaldi at the entrance to Villa Palagonia in Bagheria. You can also reach Solunto by taking SS113 east from Palermo toward Porticello.

EXPLORING THE RUINS ℱ

On the way to the **Parco Archeologico di Solunto (Solunto Archaeological Garden),** you'll pass an **Antiquarium** just inside the gate. Everything of any real value was hauled off to Palermo a long time ago, but you might stop in for a look at some artifacts removed during excavations, including bas-reliefs, statuettes, ancient coins, and architectural fragments.

Immediately to the north lie the ruins of the **Terme,** the old thermal baths, with a mosaic floor remaining. Brick supports from below held up the rooms, allowing hot air to circulate.

The Terme fronts Via della Terme. If you head north and then right, you'll be walking along the main street of Solunto, **Via Dell'Agorà** ℱℱ. The first ruin of any interest is the so-called **Gymnasium,** actually a patrician house with a peristyle and atrium more or less intact. Partially restored in 1866, the building has a trio of Doric columns and a partial roof. Directly east of it is an even more impressive patrician house, **Casa di Leda** ℱ, with a wall frescoed with a scene of Leda and her amorous swan. This house was built around a peristyle with an elaborate cistern system for collecting rainwater. In one room you can see the remains of a fresco similar to those discovered in the ruins of Pompeii.

The **Agorà,** the center of public life in old Solunto, lies east of Casa di Leda. Directly north of the square are the ruins of the **Odeon,** a small theater, and to its immediate east the larger ruins of what must have been an impressive theater in Hellenistic times, although not much remains today.

Admission is 3.10€ ($3.70). The park is open Monday through Saturday from 9am to 6pm (closes at 3:30pm in winter), Sunday from 9am to 1pm. Call ℭ **091-904557** for more information.

WHERE TO DINE

Antica Pizzeria Solunto/La Grotta/Abu Simbel SICILIAN/PIZZA   Set on the uppermost promontory of Bagheria, with views over the ruins of Solunto and the nearby hamlet of Porticello, this is the most panoramic restaurant in the district. It has an outdoor terrace and two floors of seating, tended by a jaded staff. Frankly, the food and the service could both be better, but the view and the ambience here go a long way toward the creation of a magical Sicilian evening.

Parco Archeologico di Solunto. ℭ **091-903213.** Reservations not necessary. Pizzas 5€–8€ ($6–$9.60); main courses 6€–14€ ($7.20–$17). AE, DC, MC, V. Fri–Wed 7:30pm–1am; Sun 1–3pm.

3 Monreale: A Magnificent Cathedral ★★★

10km (6 miles) SW of Palermo

This hilltop town has one of the greatest cathedrals in all of Italy and a panoramic view over the bay, Conca d'Oro. In the distance you can see the rise of Palermo.

During Norman rule, the kings chose Monreale as their royal hunting ground. When William II launched the celebrated cathedral and attached a royal residence and a monastery to it, Monreale was put on the maps of the world.

Since that time, pilgrims from virtually everywhere have flocked here to see this wonder. Even if you have to miss all the other sights in the Palermo environs, try to schedule 2 or 3 hours to make the trek to Monreale. It dwarfs other sights in this chapter and is, in fact, one of the major attractions of southern Italy.

GETTING THERE

From Palermo, take bus no. 389, departing from Piazza Indipendenza, which 40 minutes later will drop you off at Monreale's Piazza Vittorio Emanuele. During the day, three buses per hour leave for Monreale, costing 1€ ($1.20) one-way. Motorists can approach Monreale by Corso Calatafimi from Porta Nuova in Palermo.

MONREALE DUOMO ★★★

Arabo-Norman art and architecture reached the pinnacle of its beauty in this cathedral, launched in 1174 by William II. Like the grand Alhambra in Granada, Spain, the Duomo hides behind a relatively drab facade, giving little indication of the riches inside. William issued orders "to spare no expense" as he set about to out-razzle-dazzle the glory of Palermo's Cappella Palatina (p. 86), which was the crowning architectural achievement of his grandfather Roger II. Today, the Monreale Duomo is the last and most stunning of the Norman churches of Sicily and is viewed as one of the architectural wonders of the Middle Ages.

The facade lies between two towers, one of which was never finished. Interlacing Arabic arches crown an 18th-century classical portico. If you stand on the Via dell'Arcivescovado, you can see where the original royal palace was absorbed by the Archbishop's Palace.

Bonanno Pisano, the sculptor and architect who created the Leaning Tower of Pisa, designed the cathedral's splendid **bronze doors** ★★ in 1185. He created 46 bas-reliefs of biblical scenes from both the Old and New Testaments. Beneath a portico from the 1500s, the lateral entrance is also graced with bronze doors, the 1179 work of Barisano da Trani, depicting saints, battles, animals, and scenes from the life of Christ. It is through this door that you enter the Duomo.

Once you step foot inside the golden interior, your eye won't know where to look first. The **mosaics** ★★★ here evoke the Cappella Palatina in Palermo, but on a much grander scale. This splendiferous cycle of 12th- and 13th-century art occupies the aisles, the choir, the transepts, and all of the nave, vividly bringing to life scenes from the Old and New Testaments. Craftsmen from Venice were brought in to create some of these mosaics, which show an amazing attention to detail. ***Christ Pantocrator*** ★ dominates the middle apse with majestic splendor; this is the most imposing of all such figures in any church on the island. Overall, there are more than 2,000 mosaics here—even more than in St. Mark's in Venice. The mosaic cycle is the second largest on earth, topped only by Istanbul's Hagia Sofia.

Impressions

Anyone who comes to Palermo without seeing Monreale arrives on a donkey and leaves as an ass.

—Old Sicilian saying

In the north apse, **Cappella del Crocifisso** is gloriously baroqued to its teeth. The **treasury** shelters various precious objects and reliquaries, along with other ecclesiastical artifacts such as vestments, silverware, and goldsmithery dating back to the Middle Ages or the Renaissance.

The plan to make this a Norman royal pantheon was never carried out, although you can see the porphyry sarcophagus of William I (d. 1166) and William II (d. 1190) before the entryway into the Cappella di San Benedetto, whose decoration dates from the 16th century.

Well worth the steep climb uphill from the cathedral is an ascent to the **terraces**. Once you reach the top, you're rewarded with a sweeping vista over the cloisters with another stunning **view of the apses**. From the more elevated terrace is a **dramatic panorama** to the sea and the bay of Conca d'Oro.

Descending from the terraces, you can visit the **cloisters**, which represent the flowering of Islamic architecture in Sicily. Devout Sicilians often refer to these cloisters as a "preview of Paradise." Pointed arches link 228 twin columns, each with a different design, many decorated with mosaics or reliefs. Each of the splendid **Romanesque capitals** is imaginatively conceived and carved. The artisan who depicted Adam and Eve hiding their genitalia in shame definitely had a sense of humor.

In the southwest corner is a **mini-cloister,** with one of the most delightful fountains in town. A dozen lionlike mouths gush water into the basin below.

Piazza Guglielmo il Buono. ✆ 091-6404413. Free admission to cathedral. Cloisters 4.50€ ($5.40); treasury 2.05€ ($2.45); ascent to terraces 1.55€ ($1.85). May–Sept daily 8am–6pm; Oct–Apr 8am–12:30pm and 3:30–6pm.

WHERE TO STAY

Baglio Conca d'Oro *Finds* This 18th-century paper mill at Borgo Molara was completely restored in 1998 and turned into a retreat of old-fashioned charm with 21st-century comforts. Guest rooms are modernized and come with small bathrooms with shower stalls. Most units open onto panoramas of the beautiful bay of Conca d'Oro, Monreale itself, or the Gulf of Palermo. In the antique red-brick building, the use of dark wood and Oriental rugs adds to the allure. You'll find this a convenient base for exploring both Palermo and Monreale.

Via Aquino 19, Borgo Molare 90126. ✆ 091-6406286. Fax 091-6408742. www.baglioconcadoro.it. 27 units. 136€–162€ ($163–$194) double; 164€–190€ ($197–$228) suite. AE, DC, MC, V. Located 3km (1¾ miles) from Monreale. From Palermo, take Viale Regione Siciliana and follow signs to Sciacca and N624. **Amenities:** Restaurant; bar; 24-hr. room service. *In room:* A/C, TV, minibar, hair dryer, safe.

WHERE TO DINE

Drop in at **Bar Italia,** Piazza Vittorio Emanuele (✆ **091-6402421**), near the Duomo. The plain cookies are wonderfully flavorful; in the morning, order a croissant and a cappuccino, Monreale's best. Open Wednesday through Monday from 5am to 1am.

Peppino SICILIAN For a modest meal, consider this simple trattoria that's positioned within a maze of narrow streets, about 4 blocks uphill (and west) from the cathedral. During clement weather, the preferred seating is on the cobble-covered terrace. Inside, you'll find a pizza oven and a TV that's likely to be blaring the latest football matches. The straightforward cuisine is typical of what you might find in the home of a local family: roulades (thin slices of veal that are stuffed, rolled, and fried), lamb or veal cutlets, and Spaghetti alla Norma (somehow eggplant always tastes better in Sicilian pastas). Your best bet might be the catch of the day, which is usually grilled along with roasted vegetables.

Via B. Civiletti 12. ⓒ 091-6407770. Reservations not necessary. Main courses 7€–8.50€ ($8.40–$10.20). AE, DC, MC, V. Fri–Wed 12:30–2pm and 7:30pm–midnight.

Taverna del Pavone ⭐ SICILIAN/ITALIAN The most highly recommended restaurant in Monreale faces a small cobblestone square, about a block uphill from the cathedral. Inside, you're likely to find a friendly greeting, an artfully rustic environment that's akin to an upscale tavern, and tasty Sicilian food. We delighted in the zucchini flowers braised in a sweet-and-sour sauce; a delightful *pennette* with fava-bean sauce; and the house-made *maccheroni,* which was loaded with country cheese and absolutely delicious. For dessert, the most soothing choice might be *semifreddo*—whipped cream folded into ice cream, given extra flavor with baked almonds.

Vico lo Pensato 18. ⓒ 091-6406209. Reservations recommended. Main courses 8.50€–14€ ($10–$17). AE, DC, MC, V. Tues–Sun 12:30–2:30pm and 7–10:30pm.

4 Mondello: Fun at the Beach

12km (7½ miles) W of Palermo

When the summer sun burns hot, when the old men on the square seek a place in the shade, and when *bambini* tire of their toys, it's beach weather. For Palermo residents, that means Mondello Lido. Before this beachfront town started attracting the wealthy class of Palermo, it was a fishing village, and you can still see rainbow-colored fishing boats bobbing in the harbor. A good sandy beach stretches for about 2km (1¼ miles), filled to capacity on July and August days. *Tip:* Some women traveling alone find Mondello more inviting and less intimidating than Palermo.

GETTING THERE

To reach all of the locations below by bus, take no. 806 to Mondello, leaving from Piazza Sturzo in the center of Palermo, close to Teatro Politeama. By car, take Viale Regina Margherita from the northern end of Parco della Favorita, going through the dreary suburb of Pallavicino beneath the western slope of Monte Pellegrino. On your way back, you can drive from Valdesi, at the southern tip of Mondello, along the Lungomare Cristoforo Colombo toward the heart of Palermo, going via the rock-strewn coastline at the foot of Monte Pellegrino.

HITTING THE BEACH

As a seaside resort in Sicily, Mondello is outclassed only by Taormina. But if you find yourself in Palermo in July or August, **Mondello Lido** ⭐⭐ is the place to be. The wide, sandy beach extends for 2km (1¼ miles) from Monte Pellegrino to Monte Gallo.

Opening onto a half-moon-shaped bay between Monte Pellegrino and Capo Gallo, Mondello is the place for showing off your most daring swimwear and for living the good life, including lots of late-night staggering along with the young Palermitani from bar to bar (largely in the center, around **Piazza Mondello**).

Otherwise, Mondello Lido holds little of historic interest. What remains of the original fishing village lies at the far north of the bay—but it's hardly worth the trek. Between the wars, Mondello was a snobbish retreat for the upper crust, evoking the most fashionable parts of the French Riviera. After World War II, it more democratically became a "beach for everyone."

In the center of the beach, rising from concrete piers above the surface of the water, and connected to the Sicilian "mainland" with a bridge, you can still see the *kursaal,* a whimsical bathhouse (now a restaurant, **Charleston Le Terrazze;** p. 128) designed in the Art Nouveau style and adorned with sea dragons and other mythological creatures.

WHERE TO STAY

Albergo Conchiglia d'Oro *(Value* Situated a 6-minute walk inland from the Lido (beach) in a residential neighborhood loaded with bougainvillea and private homes, this well-maintained hotel has a setting that's calmer and more sedate than those of other hotels close to the oceanfront frenzy. It's sometimes favored by Palermo-based business travelers who appreciate the easy parking after a day in the big sweaty city. Guest rooms are contemporary and somewhat generic-looking, though very comfortable; each has a small bathroom with shower. The hotel's garden—in the midst of which is a swimming pool—is one of the most appealing in Mondello. The beach is private. The in-house restaurant is large, airy, and welcoming, serving a good regional cuisine.

Via Cloe 9, 90151 Mondello, Palermo. ⓒ 091-450032. Fax 091-450359. 50 units. 65€–92€ ($78–$110) double. AE, DC, MC, V. Free parking. **Amenities:** Restaurant; bar; outdoor pool. *In room:* A/C, TV.

Mondello Palace Hotel ☆☆ This is the most prestigious hotel in Mondello, set on its own private beach. It's favored by resort-goers and business travelers who prefer the relative peace of Mondello to the crush of Palermo. Modern and minimalist, it has an appealing kind of simplicity—a hint of the 1950s-derived glamour of *la dolce vita.* Originally built in 1953, it sits on prime real estate that's separated from the sands of the Lido only by a garden, an iron fence, and a busy oceanfront boulevard. The mix of privacy and seclusion on one side of the hedge and the crush of holiday-making flesh on the Lido is very appealing. Guest rooms are conservative, contemporary, and comfortable. Most contain private balconies; the luxurious bathrooms have combination tub-showers.

Viale Principe di Scalea, 90151 Mondello, Palermo. ⓒ 091-450001. Fax 091-450657. www.mondellopalace hotel.it. 93 units. 158€–200€ ($190–$240) double; 110€ ($132) supplement for sitting room. Extra bed 60€ ($72). AE, DC, MC, V. **Amenities:** Restaurant; bar; outdoor pool; watersports; gym; room service; babysitting; laundry service; dry cleaning. *In room:* A/C, TV, minibar, hair dryer.

Splendid Hotel La Torre ☆ *(Value* Tucked away at the distant edge of Mondello's fishing port, this postmodern building rises in stark contrast to the low cement structures that line the harbor. Inside the hotel, you'll find clean lines, oak floors, skylights, sweeping views of the sea, and mobs of European tourists, many of them on group tours. Originally built in 1959 and last renovated in 2002, the hotel has a hip but busy staff and midsize guest rooms filled with comfortable, bland-looking furnishings and combination tub-showers. One highlight is this hotel's location, on a rocky peninsula jutting into the sea at the edge of the harbor. Terraces descend several steps to sweeping views over the water and the sands of the Lido, about a half-mile away. Also on-site are a park, garden, and solarium.

Via Piano Gallo 11, 90151 Mondello, Palermo. ⓒ 091-450222. Fax 091-450033. www.latorre.com. 169 units. 124€–155€ ($149–$186) double; 155€–205€ ($186–$246) triple. AE, DC, MC, V. **Amenities:** Restaurant;

"This Thing We Have": Men of Dishonor

In Sicily, they don't call it the Mafia (from the Arabic mu'afah, or "protection"). They call it Cosa Nostra, literally "our thing," but more accurately "this thing we have." Its origins are debated, but the world's most famed criminal organization seemed to grow out of the convergence of local agricultural overseers working for absentee Bourbon landowners—hired thugs, from the peasant workers' point of view.

Members of the Sicilian Mafia (or "Men of Honor," as they like to be called) traditionally operated as a network of regional bosses who controlled individual towns by setting up puppet regimes of thoroughly corrupt officials. It was a sort of devil's bargain between the regional bosses and the national Christian Democrat Party, which controlled Italy's government from World War II until 1993 and, despite its law-and-order rhetoric, tacitly left Cosa Nostra alone as long as its bosses got out the party vote.

The Cosa Nostra trafficked in illegal goods, of course, but until the 1960s and 1970s its income was derived mainly from funneling state money into its own pockets, low-level protection rackets, and ensuring that public contracts were granted to fellow mafiosi (all reasons that Sicily has experienced grotesque unchecked industrialization and modern growth at the expense of its heritage and the good of its communities). But the younger generation of Mafia underbosses got into the highly lucative heroin and cocaine trades in the 1970s, transforming the Sicilian Mafia into a major player on the international drug-trafficking circuit. This ignited a clandestine Mafia war that, throughout the late 1970s and 1980s, generated lurid headlines of bloody Mafia hits. The new generation was wiping out the old and turning the balance of power in their favor.

This situation gave rise to the first of the Mafia turncoats, disgruntled ex-bosses and rank-and-file stoolies who opened up and told their stories, first to police prefect Generale Alberto Dalla Chiesa (assassinated in 1982) and later to crusading magistrates Giovanni Falcone (murdered in May 1992) and Paolo Borsellino (murdered in July 1992), who staged

piano bar; saltwater outdoor pool; tennis court; 24-hr. room service; babysitting; laundry service; dry cleaning; solarium; rooms for those w/limited mobility. In room: A/C, TV, dataport, minibar.

Villa Esperia ⭐ (Finds)   Set on a busy commercial boulevard in the center of Mondello, this charming hotel occupies a majestic villa built around 1890. Touches of stateliness remain, thanks to high ceilings, a walled-in garden, and a Liberty-era decor that's more or less authentic to the late 19th century. Rooms are small to medium in size, with vague references to the 19th century, tiled bathrooms with showers, and lots of cozy comfort. Those facing the street can be noisy, although air-conditioning and double layers of glass both help. Four of the rooms are in a comfortable annex that was originally conceived as a stable. The pleasant on-site restaurant has a glassed-in terrace.

Viale Margherita di Savoia 53, 90146 Mondello, Palermo. ⓒ 091-6840717. Fax 091-6841508. www.hotelvillaesperia.it. 22 units. 99€–150€ ($119–$180) double. Discounts of about 20% in midwinter. Rates the "maxi-trials" of mafiosi that sent hundreds to jail. It was the magis-trates' 1992 murders, especially, that attracted public attention to the dishonorable methods that defined the new Mafia and, perhaps for the first time, began to stir true shame.

On a broad and culturally important scale, it is these young mafiosi, without a moral center or check on their powers, who have driven many Sicilians to at least secretly break the unwritten code of *omertà*, which translates as "homage" but means "silence," when faced with harboring or even tolerating a man of honor. The Mafia still exists in Palermo, the small towns south of it, and the provincial capitals of Catania, Trapani, and Agrigento. Throughout the rest of Sicily, however, its power has been slipping. The heroin trade is a far cry from construction schemes and protection money, and the Mafia is swiftly outliving its usefulness.

Even in Palermo, the grip of *Cosa Nostra* seems to be loosening. In the closing days of 2000, the city hosted a United Nations conference on combating organized crime. Palermo's mayor, Leoluca Orlando, pro-claimed that his fragile city was "battling a great evil" and paid hom-age at the conference to those who died fighting the Mafia. As local officials have worked to fight the mafiosi's corruption and stifling of Sicilian society, their efforts have been hailed as a Palermo Renaissance.

Today, civic groups and schools conduct programs to help people, especially young Sicilians, loosen the stronghold of the *Cosa Nostra*. We never thought we'd see it in Sicily, but the **Museo Civico di Palazzo Provenzano,** Via Orfanotrofio 7, Central di Cultura Polivalente (© 091-8464907), exhibits photographs documenting Mafia atrocities, right outside Palermo in the sleepy village of Corleone. (Corleone, of course, is a name familiar to all *Godfather* fans: It was depicted as the home of Salvatore Rina, the "boss of all bosses." Rina lived here for nearly a quarter of a century, as Italy's most wanted man.) Admission is free; hours are Tuesday through Sunday from 9am to 1pm and 3:30 to 6:30pm. **GALLO** (© 091-6171141), Via Balsamo 4, Palermo, runs buses to Corleone; a one-way ticket costs 4.20€ ($5.05).

include breakfast. AE, DC, MC, V. **Amenities:** Restaurant; bar; outdoor pool. *In room:* A/C, TV, dataport, hair dryer.

WHERE TO DINE

Bye Bye Blues ★★ *Finds* SICILIAN   Savvy locals all know of this place, an innocuous-looking private house that's set alarmingly close to a busy street in the tranquil neighborhood of Valdesi. The cuisine is among the finest in the greater Palermo area, though it falls just short of the viands concocted at Charleston (see below). The casual, relaxing dining room is run by Antonio, who used to work on American cruise ships, and his wife, Patrizia, who inherited time-tested Sicil-ian recipes from her mother and grandmother. The kitchen shapes raw materi-als from the surrounding countryside into dishes filled with flavor and passion. We were won over by the mussel soup with potatoes and pumpkin flowers; the extraordinary pasta with prawns; and the grilled calamari, a fragrant delight. If the watermelon gelatin tart is too experimental for you, finish with the hot chocolate cake.

Via del Garofalo 23. ⓒ **091-6841415.** Reservations required. Main courses 7€–10€ ($8.40–$12). AE, DC, MC, V. Wed–Mon 8pm–midnight. Closed Nov 1–15.

Charleston Le Terrazze ★★★ SICILIAN/INTERNATIONAL No restaurant in Mondello—or Palermo, for that matter—achieves the culinary perfection of this long-established citadel of fine cuisine. It's housed in the most charming building in town, built in 1913 on concrete pilings above the sea, just offshore from the Lido and connected to the "mainland" by bridge. Conceived as an Art Nouveau fantasy and crowned with artful depictions of sea monsters, it's the setting for this most memorable of Mondello restaurants. If weather permits, sit on the terrace that's open to the stars; otherwise, you'll dine in a high-ceilinged room that evokes the Gilded Age. Meals feature classy fare that artfully combines fish or meat with exceedingly fresh vegetables, excellent wines, and attentive service. The marinated swordfish is done to elegant perfection, the prosciutto with seasonal fruit is hard to resist, and the risotto with shellfish is a savory delight. Dessert might be an almond parfait or crepes suzettes.

Stabilimento Balneare, Viale Regina Elena, Mondello. ⓒ **091-450171.** Reservations required. Main courses 10€–14€ ($12–$17). AE, DC, MC, V. Daily 1–3:30pm and 8:30–11:30pm. Closed Wed Oct–Mar.

5 Ustica: A Volcanic Island

57km (36 miles) NW of Palermo

Rising from the waters of the Tyrrhenian Sea and linked to the capital by hydrofoil and ferry, this holiday resort goes by the touristic name of the "Black Pearl of the Mediterranean." In this case, the name fits, as the volcanic island is composed of dark, petrified, rather foreboding-looking lava. The Romans, in fact, named it *ustum* ("burnt"), because it looked to them like a large black rock.

Both this turtle-shaped island and its main port are called Ustica. A visit here is a trip to unknown, offbeat Sicily. Even many Palermitans, who live a short ferry ride away, have never visited Ustica.

The village of Ustica is set on a tufa ledge between two inlets, lying in the shadow of Capo Falconara, whose summit is crowned with the remains of a fortress erected by the Bourbons.

The history of the island is ancient; it was once inhabited by the Phoenicians. In time they were followed by the Greeks, who named the island Osteodes ("ossuary"), in memory of the skeletons of 6,000 Carthaginians, mutineers who were brought here and abandoned without food or water.

Saracen pirates raided the island over the years, carrying off the prettiest ladies. Attempts to colonize it in the Middle Ages failed because of raids by Barbary pirates. The Bourbons repopulated it in 1762 with people from the Aeolian Islands and Naples. They constructed a trio of towers to defend the island against pirates.

As late as the 1950s, Ustica was a penal colony, a sort of Alcatraz of Sicily. Antonio Gramsci, the theorist of the Italian Communist Party, was once imprisoned here. And, in one of the most secret meetings of World War II, British and Italian officers met here in September 1943 to discuss a switch in sides from Mussolini to the Allies.

Ustica is tiny, only 8.6 sq. km (3.3 sq. miles). The top of a submerged volcano, it is the oldest island in the Sicilian outer archipelago—even older than the

Aeolian islands, one of which is Lipari, which it resembles. Because its jagged coastline is riddled with creeks, bays, and caves, Ustica is best explored by a rented boat (see below) circling the island.

In 1987, Sicily designated part of the island a national marine park, and today its clear waters and beautiful sea, filled with aquatic flora and fauna, attract snorkelers and scuba divers from around the world. Divers are also drawn to its ancient wrecks and the now-submerged city of Osteodes, a mile west of the island, which sank into the sea in unrecorded times.

Ustica has a population of some 1,370 islanders. Visit them in such idyllic months as June or September; a trip here in July or August is so hot, it's like a journey to Hades.

ESSENTIALS

GETTING THERE Hydrofoils and ferries operate daily from Palermo's Stazione Maríttima to Ustica. The ferry is the cheapest and slowest transport, costing 12€ ($14) each way and taking 2½ hours. The hydrofoil, at a cost of 17€ ($20), does it in half the time. For tickets for either transport, go to **Siremar,** at Via Francesco Crispi 118 in Palermo (© **091-336632**), and on Piazza Bartolo in Siremar (© **091-8449002**). Hydrofoil service runs from April to December; ferries run year-round, but not on Sundays in winter.

GETTING AROUND Arrival from Palermo is at Ustica village, the only port and home to 90% of the islanders. The heart of the village is reached by climbing a flight of steps from the harbor. You'll emerge onto the main square of town—actually a trio of interlocking squares that include the piazzas of Bartolo, Umberto I, and Vito Longo. We recommend that you take care of any shopping needs before you leave Palermo; otherwise, you'll have to buy it here, as whatever Ustica has to offer is found in this area.

Once you arrive, you can always do as the locals do and rely on your trusty feet. Otherwise, take one of the orange minibuses that circumnavigate the island, hugging the coastline. These leave from the center of Ustica village daily

(Moments **Exploring a Watery Wonderland**

J. Y. Cousteau claimed that the waters off the coast of Ustica were among the most beautiful he'd ever seen, ideal for both diving and underwater photography—and we agree. The best spot for diving is the **Grotta del Gamberi,** near Punta Gavazzi, at the southern tip of the island beyond Grotta del Tuono. Nearby is the famous **Sub-Aqua Archeological Trail,** lying off the headland, Punta Gavazzi, with its lighthouse. Many anchors and even Roman amphorae can still be seen in these waters.

The best dive spot on the north coast is **Secca di Colombara,** to the west of Grotta dell'Oro. Here you can see a vast array of gorgonians and Ustica's most beautiful sponges. **Scoglio del Medico** 🐟🐟, or "doctor's rock," lies off the west coast of the island directly north of the bay called Baia Sidoti. This outcropping of basalt, riddled with grottoes and gorges, plunges to murky depths in the Atlantic, and offers a panoramic seascape unequalled anywhere else in Sicily.

on the hour. Figure on 2½ hours for the entire bus ride around the island; a ticket between any two points along the route costs 1€ ($1.20).

Summer boat excursions are run by local fishermen who not only know the most scenic beauty spots, but also will allow you time out for swimming during an island trip. **Hotel Ariston,** Via della Vittoria 5 (*②* **091-8449042**), organizes sightseeing boat trips, rents boats to scuba divers, and hires out motorcycles. Its three-seater boats cost 45€ ($54) a day, gasoline not included. A boat trip around the island, which lets you see the caves and stop at secluded spots for swimming, lasts 2½ hours and costs 15€ ($18). If you'd like to tour on your own—expect rough roads—it costs 24€ to 33€ ($29–$40) a day to hire a motorcycle, with gas and two helmets included.

Scuba divers can go to **Ailara Rosalia,** Banchina Barresi (*②* **091-8449605**), which rents boats for 50€ ($60) a day. You should bring your own diving gear, however.

VISITOR INFORMATION The tourist office is closed. However, you can visit the headquarters of **Parco Marino Regionale,** on the main square of town (*②* **091-8449456**). The staff here can provide information about the marine park. Hours are daily from 8am to 8pm.

FAST FACTS For a medical emergency, call **Guardia Medica** (*②* **091-8449248**). Serious cases are immediately transported to Palermo. The police or **Carabinieri** can be reached at *②* **091-8449049.**

ATTRACTIONS NEAR THE PORT

It's fun just to stroll around the village, taking in views of the bay, Baia Santa Maria. The little town is made more festive by a series of murals that decorate the facades of the buildings.

Directly south of the village stands **Torre Santa Maria,** housing the **Museo Archeologico** (no phone). It's open daily from 9am to noon and 5 to 7pm; admission is 3€ ($3.60). Its most fascinating exhibits are fragments and artifacts recovered from the ancient city of Osteodes, now submerged beneath the sea. Many of the artifacts, such as crusty anchors, were recovered from ships wrecked off the coast. You'll see amphorae, Bronze Age objects from the prehistoric village of Faraglioni, and contents of tombs from the Hellenistic and Roman eras.

To the east of the tower are the ruins of a Bronze Age settlement, **Villaggio Preistorico,** at Faraglioni. Excavations began in 1989 on what was a large prehistoric village dating from the 14th century to the 13th century B.C. The foundations of some 300 stone-built houses were discovered, and the defensive walls of the settlement are among the strongest fortifications of any period known in Italy. It is believed that these early settlers came over from the Aeolian Islands. Admission is free; the site is always open.

If you walk north of Ustica village, you'll come to the remains of the **Rocca della Falconiera,** at 157m (515 ft.). Figure on a 20-minute walk. (Along the way you'll see many cisterns, as water remains a precious commodity on Ustica, even though a desalination plant has been installed.) The defensive tower was constructed by the Bourbons to protect the island from raids by pirates. This site was first settled back in the 3rd century B.C. by the Romans. If you look toward the sea you'll see the lighthouse, **Punta dell'Uomo Morto (Dead Man's Point)** on a cliff, where a cave contains vestiges of centuries-old tombs.

From the fort you can take in a view of **Guardia dei Turchi,** at 244m (800 ft.). This is the highest point on the island. That object you see in the distance, evoking a mammoth golf ball, is in fact a meteorological radar system installed by the Italian government.

The **view** 𝄐 from the fortress ruins stretches from the harbor to the core of the island, with the mountains of **Monte Costa del Fallo** and **Monte Guardia dei Turchi** clearly outlined.

EXPLORING THE ISLAND

Since it is the top of an extinct volcano, Ustica doesn't have sandy beaches. But as you traverse the island, you'll find jumping-off points for swimming. The biggest attraction is the grotto-lined coastline, and because distances are short, hiking is a viable option.

Wildflowers cover the island except in late July and August, when the blistering sun burns them away. You'll also see produce grown by the islanders, such as lentils, figs, capers, grapes, prickly pears, wheat, and almonds.

Of all the caves or grottoes on the island, the most celebrated and fascinating is the **Grotta Azzurra** 𝄐𝄐, the first cave south of Ustica village as you head down the coast by boat. It's named for the more fabled cave in Capri, but both grottoes share an incredible iridescent glow from light reflections from the sea.

Almost as stunning is the next sea cave directly to the south, **Grotta Pastizza** 𝄐. This is a stalactite cave behind a great pyramidal rock. Directly down the coast, another grotto, **Grotta della Barche,** is also intriguing. *Barche* means "boat," and Ustica fishermen anchor in this safe haven during storms.

PARCO MARINO REGIONALE 𝄐𝄐

The Marine National Park was created in 1986, the first marine reserve ever established in Italy. Since Ustica lies in the center of an inward current surging through the Straits of Gibraltar directly from the Atlantic Ocean, its waters are always clean and free of pollution.

Underwater photographers flock to the park to film the stunning **aquatic flora and fauna** 𝄐𝄐𝄐. A splendid seaweed, *Poseidonia oceanica,* is called "the lungs of the sea" because it oxygenates the water. You may also see an array of magnificent red gorgonians, stunning black coral, plentiful turtles (now that they are protected), swordfish, lobster, and *cernia* (a kind of sea perch). Some divers claim to have had close encounters with grouper as big as a Fiat 500.

The park comprises three zones. **A area** extends along the western part of the isle from Cala Sidoti to Caletta and as far as 935m (3,067 ft.) offshore. Swimming is allowed here, but no boats and no fishing. **B area** extends from Punta Cavazzi to Punta Omo Morto, taking in the entire southwest to northeast coastline, and extending out into the sea a distance of 3 nautical miles. Swimming is permitted here. Finally, **C area** is a partial reserve made up of the rest of the coast. Swimming is allowed here, as is fishing.

HIKING AROUND USTICA

You can circumnavigate the island in 3 to 4 hours, depending on your pace. The best hike is along the coastal path heading north of town, where you'll see the Municipio, or island headquarters. Head left here, taking the trail along the north coast that leads past an old cemetery. This hike hugs the steep cliffs on the northern side of the island, part of the Marine Reserve, and the views are stunning.

Eventually you'll come to **Punta di Megna,** on the western coast, on the exact opposite side of the island from Ustica village. The offshore rock so appreciated by scuba divers, **Scoglio del Medico,** can be seen from here.

The road continues along the southwestern coast as far as the battered ruins of the old tower, **Punta Spalmatore,** where you can go swimming. (There is no beach here, however.)

Below this point, at **Punta Cavazzi,** along the southern rim of the island, is **Piscina Naturale** ✦, a sheltered seawater pool and the best place on Ustica for swimming. If there are a lot of tourists on the island at the time of your visit, this "hole" is likely to be crowded with bathers in the briefest of swimwear.

At this point the route no longer follows the coast and cuts inland all the way northeast to Ustica village once again.

WHERE TO STAY

Accommodations are scarce and fill up quickly from April to September. Many islanders rent rooms when the hotels are fully booked, but if you count on that, you're taking a chance. It's far preferable to arrive with a reservation. If you don't have one, go to the Piazza Umberto and start asking around for a *camera,* or room. In winter, many places close down.

Hotel Clelia *Value*   This is the most typical of Ustica's little island inns, situated off Piazza Umberto I, the main square of Ustica village. It was the first little boardinghouse on the island to receive visitors, who began arriving in 1950 during the lean postwar years. It is also one of the island's best bargains. For most of its life, it was a *pensione,* or boardinghouse. But after so many improvements, it has been upgraded by the government to three-star status. Nonetheless, its prices have remained reasonable in spite of the installation of soundproof windows and modern furnishings. Guest rooms are small but comfortable, each with a little shower-only bathroom. Hotel extras include a lovely patio with scenic views, a shuttle bus that makes trips around the island, and scooter and boat rentals. This is one of the few places that remains open year-round.

Via Sindaco I, 29, Ustica 90010. ☎ **091-8449039.** Fax 091-8449459. www.hotelclelia.it. 26 units. 56€–140€ ($67–$168) double. Rates include breakfast. AE, DC, MC, V. **Amenities:** Restaurant; bar; babysitting; laundry service; rooms for those w/limited mobility. *In room:* A/C, TV, minibar, hair dryer, safe.

Hotel Diana ✦ *Finds*   Located on the beach at Contrada San Paolo, this is one of the island's oldest hotels, but it's still in good shape following renovations in 2004. Opened in 1973 at the dawn of tourism on the island, the Diana's most attractive feature is its landscaping, which features fruit trees and wild island plants. The hotel's panoramic position allows some good views from the terraces of its guest rooms. Accommodations are a bit bare-bones but comfortable, with good beds, marble floors, and small bathrooms with both tub and shower. The helpful owner/manager can offer advice on setting up island tours.

Contrada San Paolo, 90010 Ustica. ☎/fax **091-8449109.** www.hoteldiana-ustica.com. 30 units. 62€–90€ ($74–$108) double. AE, DC, MC, V. Closed Sept 25–Apr 30. **Amenities:** Restaurant; bar; outdoor pool. *In room:* A/C, TV.

Hotel Grotta Azzurra ✦✦   This is Ustica's best hotel bet, lying a 5-minute walk from the center. This modern and comfortable choice stands on a wide plateau above the ocean, with a steep drop to a spot for swimming. A natural grotto carved out of a cliff face below gives the hotel its name and its most alluring feature. All of the well-appointed guest rooms open onto sea views; each comes with a small but neat private bathroom with shower. Set among lush gardens, this hotel feels like a Mediterranean retreat, with such resort-style amenities as beach towels and umbrellas. Sports-oriented people can rent scooters and boats for island tours, sailing, and windsurfing. The hotel also attracts a lot of divers. Even if you're not a guest, consider a meal at **La Cala dei Fenici,** known on the island for its refined Sicilian cuisine.

Contrada San Ferlicchio, Ustica 90010. ⓒ **091-8449396.** Fax 091-8449396. www.framon-hotels.com. 51 units. 151€–264€ ($181–$317) double. AE, DC, MC, V. Closed Oct–May. **Amenities:** Restaurant; bar; outdoor pool; hydromassage; babysitting. *In room:* A/C, TV, minibar, safe.

Villaggio Lirial Punta Spalmatore ⚝   Sicily's coastal towns are riddled with self-contained tourist villages, and this is the island's best such choice. Set 4km (2½ miles) from Ustica village on the western coast, it's entirely surrounded by native trees and plants. Most visitors spend their days in the terraced pool area with a panoramic view of the ocean; some guests from Palermo never even leave the grounds. The buildings rise only two floors, and accommodations are in bungalows with small but comfortable guest rooms and shower-only bathrooms. The cuisine is typical resort fare, but much use is made of fresh produce when available. Otherwise, foodstuffs have to be shipped over from Palermo. The wide range in rates depends on when you're here—the highest prices are charged in July and August.

Località Punta Spalmatore, Ustica 90010. ⓒ **091-8449388.** Fax 091-8449472. 399€–763€ ($479–$916) double. Rates include full board and sports activities. AE, MC, V. Closed Sept 14–June 13. **Amenities:** Restaurant; bar; outdoor pool; gym; wellness center; Jacuzzi; sauna; massage. *In room:* A/C, fridge.

WHERE TO DINE

There aren't many places to dine in Ustica. Most of the little trattorie are found in the village around the trio of central squares. The hotels also offer restaurants, with roof terraces opening onto views of the water.

Da Mario USTICAN   In the very center of Ustica village on its heartbeat square, this spot offers good regional fare at reasonable prices. You can sit at a table on the square, watching island life parade before you. Mario can be found in the rear, preparing such dishes as homemade pasta with freshly caught swordfish, grilled fish done to perfection, and roasted squid and spaghetti with fresh crabmeat. And, of course, everything tastes better when washed down with the local Albanella wine.

Piazza Umberto I, 21. ⓒ **091-8449905.** Reservations recommended July–Aug. Main courses 8€–10€ ($9.60–$12). AE, MC, V. Daily 12:30–3pm and 8:30–10:30pm. Closed Jan and Mon from Nov–Mar.

Schiticchio SICILIAN/SEAFOOD   This modest establishment, near town hall in the center of Ustica village, offers a rustic decor, a staff that seems to try harder than average to please its patrons, and good homemade food prepared with the freshest ingredients on the island. Ask about the fresh fish of the day, which is often grilled to perfection. The pizza oven turns out succulent pies, and we delighted in a homemade pasta with a tangy pesto sauce.

Via dei Tre Mulini. ⓒ **091-8449662.** Reservations recommended. Main courses 8€–12€ ($9.60–$14). AE, DC, MC, V. Daily 1–3pm and 7:30pm–2am (until midnight in winter).

Messina & the Tyrrhenian Coast

The coastal road (A20) that runs from Messina westward to the capital at Palermo is one of the most frequented routes in Sicily. You can, of course, drive straight through to Palermo and not see a thing, but if you do, you'll miss some of the treasures of Sicily.

The coast is riddled with sandy beaches, small resorts, and villages. If you have time for only one stopover, make it Cefalù, the premier destination along the coast thanks in part to its famous Romanesque cathedral.

For those who want to cut inland to view a national park, we suggest you set aside a day to explore **Parco Naturale Regionale delle Madonie,** one of Sicily's most important nature reserves.

The best beaches lie to the east of Cefalù. They are sandy, clean, and unpolluted, though filled with visitors in July and August.

The coast also contains some of north Sicily's more impressive ruins, including those at **Himera** (near Termini Imerese) and at **Tyndaris,** west of Milazzo.

1 Messina

233km (145 miles) E of Palermo, 683km (410 miles) SE of Rome, 469km (281 miles) S of Naples

Overlooking the Straits of Messina, with the mainland city of Reggio di Calabria across the sea and to the east, Messina lies at the foot of the Peloritani Mountains. Only 5km (3 miles) separate the city of Messina from the Italian mainland. For most passengers arriving from the mainland, the tacky industrial and port city of Messina is their gateway to Sicily—a shame, really. But since you're here, what the hell? You might as well enjoy what Messina has to offer—and it does have some treasures if you're willing to seek them out.

Sicily's third most populous city wasn't always this dismal. Mother Nature did a better job with Messina than mankind did. However, earthquakes and warplanes have done their damage. Because it has had to be rebuilt over and over, Messina is the most modern city on the island.

Messina was founded in the 8th century B.C. by the Siculans, who named it *Zancle* ("sickle") because of its hooked promontory protecting the harbor. The Greeks from Cumae and Chalcis occupied the site in the 5th century. It fell to the dreaded Anaxilas, tyrant of Reggio, who changed the town's name to *Messána* to honor his native Messenia in the Peloponnesus.

By the 3rd century B.C., Messina had come under Roman influence. Messina's fame in the Middle Ages rested on its position as a launching pad for many of the Crusades. It was a flourishing city until the 17th century, when it lost trading privileges as punishment for protesting against the Spanish viceroys.

Messina boasts one of the deepest and safest harbors in the Mediterranean. With a population of some 275,000, Messina also is one of southern Italy's most

Ionian Sea

Scilla
Torre Faro
Sparta
Villa S. Giovanni
Lazzaro
A3
Straits of Messina
Reggio di Calabria
Scaletta Zanclea
Messina
Ali Terme
Roccalumera
Spadafora
A18
Taormina
Barcellona
Castroreale
Giardini-Naxos
Milazzo
Novara
Giare
Capo di Milazzo
Capo Tindari
Tyndaris
Floresta
Mt. Etna
Gioiosa Marea
Randazzo
A20
Patti
Brolo
Naso
Bronte
Capo d'Orlando
S. Agata di Militello
Troina
Marina di Caronia
Mistretta
SICILY
S. Stéphano di Camastra
Nicosia
S. Ambrogio
Castelbuono
Cefalù
Collesano
Gangi
A20
PARCO NATURALE REGIONALE DELLE MADONIE
Polizzi
MADONIE
Himera
Termini Imerese
Cefalà
Cefalù
Montemaggiore
Alia
A19
Tyrrhenian Sea

Salina
Lipari
Vulcano
AEOLIAN ISLANDS
Filicudi
Alicudi

15 Mi
15 Km

AREA OF DETAIL
Messina
Syracuse
Mt. Etna
SICILY
Palermo
Agrigento
80 Mi
80 Km

Ruins

Not-So-Fun Facts: So You Think *You've* Got Bad Luck?

Aside from the fact that Shakespeare set his *Much Ado About Nothing* in Messina, it has rarely been blessed. Get a load of these disasters.

The Black Death, or bubonic plague, swept over Messina in 1743, killing more than 40,000 people. Forty years later, an earthquake leveled the city. Angered by Sicilian demands for independence, the Bourbon ruler Ferdinand II bombarded Messina to a pulp in 1848. Still reeling from the blows, the city was swept by a cholera epidemic in 1854. It staggered back to its feet by 1894, in time for another devastating earthquake. Messina had barely recovered when, on December 28, 1908, tremors shot through the city once again. Before the day was over, some 85,000 residents were dead. The earthquake was so violent that the coast sank 20 inches into the sea.

Under the dictatorship of Mussolini, the city was rebuilt and stood rather proudly once again. But in1943, with Italy at war with Britain and the United States, Allied bombers were determined to knock out Messina and take Sicily as a prelude to the invasion of southern Italy. Bombs rained from the sky like raindrops falling on a roof; Messina was flattened once again.

bustling cities. Rebuilt after devastation by the 1908 earthquake and the 1943 Allied bombings, it is a city of wide boulevards and low buildings. The structures hug the earth to prevent more danger in the event of another earthquake.

The newest development in Messina was announced in 2002: the Straits of Messina bridge project, which will link the city with mainland Italy. Construction is slated to begin in late 2005 and continue until 2011. If everything stays on track, the first full year of bridge operations will be 2012. Check out www.strettodimessina.it for updates, drawings, and even computer simulations of the new bridge.

ESSENTIALS

GETTING THERE   By Boat   Messina is linked to the Italian mainland by both ferries and hydrofoils crossing the Straits of Messina from either Villa San Giovanni or Reggio di Calabria.

Ferries leave from Villa San Giovanni, which is 12km (7½ miles) north of Reggio and closer to Messina. Ferry services are called *traghetti;* **FS** (© **892021** in Villa San Giovanni) is state-run, while **Caronte** (© **090-3718511**) is independent. Offices for both companies can be found at the harbor where the ferries depart. Both ferries charge a fare of 5€ ($6) to Messina.

If you're leaving from Reggio di Calabria, you can take either a ferry (if you have a car) or a faster hydrofoil. Hydrofoils are operated by **FS** (© **892021**), with offices right at the harbor. The trip takes 25 minutes and costs 2.80€ ($3.35). Ferries are operated by **Meridiano** (© **0965-810414**), which charges .55€ to 1.55 € (65¢–$1.85) for the 40-minute crossing to Messina.

By Plane   The nearest airport to Messina is on the Italian mainland at Reggio di Calabria. **Aeroporto dello Stretto** (© **0965-640517**) is 5km (3 miles) south of Reggio. Once you land at the airport, you can take one of the buses operated by **Cavalieri,** Via 1 Settembre 137 (© **090-771938**), to Messina.

By Train   Eight trains arrive daily from Rome, the trip south taking 8 to 9 hours and costing 52€ ($62) one-way. A train link from Naples takes 4½ hours, costing 44€ ($53). There are also frequent rail links to Palermo, with a dozen or more trains going between Messina and the island's capital, taking approximately 3½ hours and costing 12€ ($14) one-way. The major attraction along the Tyrrhenian coast is Cefalù; trains from Messina go there throughout the day in 2½ to 3½ hours, costing 7.90€ ($9.50). There are also hourly trains between Messina and Taormina, Sicily's major resort to the south, taking 1 hour and costing 3€ ($3.60) each way. For rail information, call © **892021.**

By Bus   For long-distance travel to Messina, we recommend the train, although **SAIS,** Piazza della Repubblica (© **090-771914**), does haul in three buses per week from Naples. The trip takes a grueling 22 hours and cost 30€ ($36) one-way. SAIS buses to Catania depart nine times a week, take 1½ hours, and cost 6.35€ ($7.60) one-way; there are also seven buses per day to Palermo, a 3¼-hour trip that costs 13€ ($16). Many visitors use **Interbus** (© **090-661754**), with offices to the left of the Stazione Centrale. It runs a dozen buses per day to Taormina, taking 1½ hours and costing 4€ ($4.80) one-way.

By Car   From the mainland of Italy, follow A3 south to Reggio di Calabria, getting off at Villa San Giovanni and taking a car ferry across the Straits of Messina to Messina itself. Along the northern coast, travel the A20/SS113 east from Palermo and Cefalù. The A18 from Taormina runs north to Messina.

VISITOR INFORMATION   For information and a map, head to the **Azienda Autonoma per L'Incremento Turistico,** Via Calabria 301 (© **090-674271**), near Piazza della Repubblica and Stazione Centrale. It's open Monday through Friday from 9am to 1:30pm and Monday through Thursday from 3 to 5pm.

ORIENTATION   Messina grew around its harbor, which is shaped like a sickle. You'll see this geographic configuration as you sail into the harbor. The tip of the sickle is marked by a towering statue, **Madonna della Lettera,** atop one of the tall towers of **Forte San Salvatore,** built in 1546 by the Spanish viceroys.

Via Garibaldi, running parallel to the sea, is the main street. It goes through **Piazza del Duomo,** the town's major square. South of this square is the second most important square in Messina, **Piazza Carducci,** site of the university, founded in 1548 and reconstructed in 1927.

To the east, the port is protected by the lighthouse known as the **Lanterna di Raineri,** on the peninsula of the same name. **Via 1 Settembre** leads from the

---

Tips **Rolling On, Rolling Off Across the Sea**

Train or bus travel across the Straits of Messina involves large-scale engineering on a most massive scale: Your train or bus will roll from the terra firma of the Italian mainland directly into the hold of a container ship for transport across the water. Passengers are allowed to remain in their seats on the train or bus, or they can stroll around the ship's upper decks for a breath of fresh air and a visit to the snack bar. A few minutes before landing, passengers head back to their seats on the train or bus, just before it rolls from its berth in the ship's hold onto the highway or railway tracks of Sicily.

sea to the heart of town. The transportation hub of Messina is **Piazza della Repubblica,** in front of Stazione Centrale. Most of the major bus lines converge on this square. To reach the heart of Messina from Piazza della Repubblica, head straight across the busy square and walk directly north along Via 1 Settembre to **Piazza del Duomo,** a square crowned by Messina's cathedral.

If you come by hydrofoil or ferry from Reggio di Calabria, you'll arrive 1km (½ mile) north of Stazione Centrale on Via Vittorio Emanuele II. Those taking a ferry from Villa San Giovanni reach land 3km (1¾ miles) farther on or about 500m (1,640 ft.) north of Fiera, the site of Messina's trade fairs.

GETTING AROUND   Most hotels and attractions lie in the center and are best reached on foot. If you need to go farther afield, **ATM** buses depart from the transportation hub, Piazza della Repubblica. Bus tickets can be purchased at *tabacchi* (tobacco shops) or news kiosks throughout the city; they cost .70€ (85¢) for a ticket valid for 1½ hours or 1.90€ ($2.30) for an all-day ticket. The most useful route is no. 79, which stops at the Museo Regionale and the Duomo.

Taxis are found mainly at the Stazione Centrale, at Piazza Cairoli, and along Via Calabria. For a 24-hour radio taxi, call ☎ **090-6505.**

FAST FACTS: Messina

Currency Exchange   The most convenient currency exchange is **Cambio/ Ufficio Informazioni** (☎ **090-675234**), inside the Stazione Centrale. Open daily from 7am to 9pm. There are also ATMs in the station.

Emergencies   Call ☎ **113** for the police, ☎ **118** for first aid.

Hospitals   Try **Ospedale Policlinico Universitario,** Via Valeria (☎ **090-2211**), or **Ospedale Piemonte,** Viale Europa (☎ **090-2221**).

Internet Access   **Internet Caffè,** Via Garibaldi 72 (☎ **090-662758**), is open Monday through Saturday from 9am to 8pm and charges 3€ ($3.60) per hour.

Luggage Storage   A kiosk at the Stazione Centrale will store your bags for 4€ ($4.80) per day; open daily from 6am to 10pm.

Post Office   The main post office is on Corso Cavour 138 (☎ **090-6015752**). Open Monday through Saturday from 8am to 6:30pm.

EXPLORING THE CITY ON FOOT

As you wander around Messina, you'll come to the ruins of the church of **Santa Maria Alemanna,** built in 1220 by the crusading Teutonic Knights. The church—or what's left of it—stands at the corner of Via dei Mille, off Corso Garibaldi, directly north of Via del Vespiro and to the immediate west of Piazza Cavallotti. It's one of the few Gothic churches on the island, as the Gothic style of architecture never swept Sicily the way it did other parts of Europe. The Messinese seemed to dislike the style, and the unfinished church was left abandoned in the 15th century.

Chiesa SS. Annunziata dei Catalani   When the Messinese saw their beloved church on this square after the 1908 earthquake, they called it a miracle. In an amazing feat, the earthquake stripped away much of the latter-day alterations and additions to the church, leaving its original 12th- and 13th-century architectural style intact. But because the quake leveled the earth on which the church sits, the structure seems to be sinking into the street today. Try to view the church from its western facade, where you'll see a trio of 13th-century doors.

The interior, now used as the chapel for the university, is in red, yellow, and white stone with tall Corinthian columns. The most outstanding feature is the **apse** ✿, a stellar example of the Norman composite style. A nave and two aisles run to the apse, resting under a severe, brick-built cupola. This church is a kind of Arabic-Byzantine hodgepodge: Romanesque architecture blended with such Moorish features as geometrical motifs, with suggestions of the Byzantine.

In back of the church is a famous statue of **Don Juan of Austria,** the "natural" son of the Emperor Charles V and a hero in the 1571 Battle of Lepanto. Amusingly, he's depicted with his foot resting proudly on the head of the Ottoman commander, Ali Bassa. The sculptor Andrea Calamech carved this monument in 1572. Incidentally, an even more famous sailor sailed from Messina to take part in that battle: Miguel de Cervantes, author of *Don Quixote.* Wounded, he was brought back to recover in a local hospital.

Piazza dei Catalani, Via Garibaldi. ℂ **090-6684111.** Free admission. Mon–Sat 9:30–11:30am; Sun 9–11:30am.

Duomo ✿

This Romanesque and Norman cathedral has had a rough time of it since Roger II ordered it built in 1160. Henry VI, the Holy Roman Emperor, attended its consecration in 1197. Earth-shaking events like the 1908 quake and a 1943 Allied firebomb didn't help. The cathedral has more or less been reconstructed from scratch, although some original architectural features remain.

Its **central doorway** ✿ was reconstructed using fragments originally from the 15th century. The lower part of the facade is decorated with 15th-century carvings depicting Sicilian agrarian life. The gray and pink interior has a trio of aisles divided by ogival arches and columns, resting under a trussed and painted ceiling. Many of the Duomo's treasures were re-created, using fragments pulled from the ruins after the Allied bombings.

The statue of **John the Baptist** in the south aisle is attributed to Antonello Gagini in 1525. Dominating the main altar is a copy of the Byzantine **Madonna della Lettera,** the original having been destroyed by the 1943 firebombing. A pupil of Michelangelo, Jacopo del Duca, designed the **Cappella del Sacramento** in the north apse. It holds the cathedral's only original mosaic, a 14th-century work that depicts the Virgin seated with saints, queens, and archangels.

The church's treasure trove is found in its **Tesoro,** which contains valuable candlesticks, chalices, and gold reliquaries. Much of the silverwork was created by artisans from Messina in the 17th and 18th centuries. Displayed for the first time in 3 centuries is the **Manta d'Oro,** or golden mantle, a special cover for the Virgin and Bambino on the Duomo's altar.

Piazza del Duomo. ℂ **090-675175.** Free admission. Guided tours in English 5€ ($6) adults, 3.50€ ($4.20) for children under 18 and seniors over 65. Oct 15–Apr 15 Mon–Sat 9am–1pm; Apr 16–Oct 14 Mon–Sat 9am–1pm and 4–6:30pm.

Orologio Astronomico ✿

The Duomo is upstaged by its 60m (197-ft.) campanile, or bell tower, with its astronomical clock standing to the left of the cathedral facade. Created in 1933 in Strasbourg, France, the clock puts on "the show of shows" at noon every day. With Schubert's *Ave Maria* scraping away on a loudspeaker in a note of high camp, the bronze automata goes into action. A lion waves his banner and roars, while a cock flaps its wing and crows. Dina and Clarenza, the heroines of Messina at the time of the Sicilian Vespers, take turns ringing the bell, and Jesus pops out of the tomb for instant resurrection. Be sure to gather in the square to check out this show.

Piazza del Duomo. Tower open to view 24 hr. Free show at noon.

Fontana di Orione ⋆ Standing in the center of the cathedral square, this elegant fountain was the pre-baroque creation of Giovanni Angelo Montorsoli in 1547. It honors Orion, the city's mythical founder, who is seen surmounting a bevy of giants, nymphs, and crocodile-wrestling *putti.* The fountain was built to honor the construction of the city's first aqueduct. The major figures represent the rivers Nile, Ebro, Camaro, and Tiber.

Piazza del Duomo. Open to view 24 hr.

Museo Regionale ⋆⋆ Situated in a former silk mill from 1914, the Museo Regionale, north of the Duomo, is one of Sicily's finest provincial museums and contains the island's greatest collection of art from the 15th to the 17th century. Its main collection consists of works rescued from the 1908 earthquake.

Its most precious relic to the devout is found in the atrium: a dozen **18th-century gilded bronze panels** that relate the tale of the Holy Letter. As legend has it, during a famine the Madonna sent the Messinese a boat filled with food but devoid of crew. The Virgin is also said to have sent along a letter containing a lock of her hair.

The museum displays many medieval and baroque treasures, including a mosaic of the Virgin and Child, known as *La Ciambretta* and dating from the 13th century. A marble low relief of **St. George** is attributed to Domenico Gagini. For us, there is nothing finer than Antonello da Messina's beautiful but damaged **polyptych** ⋆⋆ of the Madonna with St. Gregory, St. Benedict, and the Annunciation, from 1473. Also on exhibit are two large **Caravaggio masterpieces** ⋆⋆, the work of "the divine" artist during his sojourn in Messina from 1608 to 1609. They represent the Raising of Lazarus and the Nativity.

Antonello da Messina: Hometown Artist

Born around 1430 in Messina, Antonello went on to become one of the greatest masters of the Italian Renaissance and southern Italy's leading painter. Although much of his life remains a puzzle to biographers, it is known that he was very much influenced by the Flemish school, especially by the works of Jan van Eyck. Antonello was the first of the great Italian painters to master the art of working in oil. What is also known is that after many travels across Europe, this brilliant artist returned to his home city of Messina in 1476, remaining here until his death in 1478.

Antonello's works are characterized by their sense of light and attention to detail. Many of his portraits show a three-quarter view of the sitter. His paintings show intense psychological depth and are remarkable for their breakthroughs in texture, shadow, and brilliant light.

While in Sicily, you can see masterpieces of Antonello at Messina's Museo Regionale (see above) and Cefalù's Museo Mandralisca (p. 147).

Greek and Roman antiquities are on view in the newly created garden pavilion. Look for the magnificent 1742 **Senator's Coach** $\mathcal{R}$, with its flamboyantly painted panels. The statues of **Neptune, Scylla,** and **Charybdis** removed from the Fontana di Nettuno (see below) are also on display.

Viale della Libertà. $\textcircled{C}$ **090-361292.** Admission 4.50€ ($5.40). June–Sept Tues–Sat 9am–1:30pm and 4–6:30pm, Sun 9am–12:30pm; Oct–May Tues, Wed, and Fri 9am–1:30pm, Tues, Thurs, and Sat 9am–1:30pm and 3–5:30pm, Sun 9am–12:30pm.

Fontana di Nettuno   This landmark fountain stands on the seafront, at the intersection of Via della Libertà and Via Garibaldi. It's a reconstruction of the heavily damaged fountain created by Montorsoli in 1557. The original of the muscular marble god has been in the Museo Regionale ever since the statue was "castrated" by some roaming youths from Palermo. The sculpture of Neptune is depicted pacifying the sea, guarding the Straits of Messina from those wicked terrors, Scylla and Charybdis. Enjoy this fountain during the day, as the port area here isn't safe at night.

WHERE TO STAY

For such a large city, Messina has a dearth of accommodations; its budget options are a disaster. At some, you might check in with luggage, with no guarantee that your suitcase will be there when you return to your claptrap chambers.

We've recommended only safe accommodations below, and though they offer comfort, they cater mainly to commercial travelers whose expense account might be greater than your vacation budget. Chances are you'll be in Messina for only a night and therefore won't feel the pinch too severely.

EXPENSIVE

Grand Hotel Liberty $\mathcal{R}\mathcal{R}\mathcal{R}$ This is the most elegant, appealing hotel in Messina. In fact, it's one of the finest hotels in Sicily. It originated as a battered rooming house, but the Framon chain transformed it from a sow's ear into one of the most beautiful hotels on the island. Throughout, you'll find rich paneling, marble-inlaid floors, ornate plasterwork, and lavish stained-glass windows. Guest rooms are as plush as anything you'll find in Sicily, with marble-trimmed bathrooms with tub and shower, fine hardwoods, high ceilings, and color schemes of champagne and gold. Thanks to this and to the welcome that's extended with genuine concern to single women traveling alone, the hotel enjoys one of the highest occupancy rates in town.

Via I Settembre 15. $\textcircled{C}$ **090-6409436.** Fax 090-6409340. www.framon-hotels.com. 51 units. 198€ ($238) double; 264€ ($317) suite. AE, DC, MC, V. **Amenities:** Restaurant; 2 bars; concierge; room service; babysitting; laundry service; dry cleaning; nonsmoking rooms; rooms for those w/limited mobility. *In room:* A/C, TV, dataport, minibar, hair dryer.

MODERATE

Jolly Hotel Messina   It isn't as architecturally dramatic, plush, or well-located as its rival, Grand Hotel Liberty, but this boxy-looking *moderno* (ca. 1953) member of the nationwide hotel chain draws goodly numbers of loyal travelers, many of them in town on business. It was the first large-scale modern hotel in Messina, and was once the reigning choice in town. All rooms have double windows for insulation from the roar of traffic, and about half open onto views of the harbor. Units are clean, modern, and a bit banal-looking but very comfortable, each with a tiled bathroom with tub and shower. The in-house restaurant is reviewed under "Where to Dine," below.

Via Garibaldi 126, 98100 Messina. © **090-363860**. Fax 090-5902526. www.jollyhotels.it. 96 units. 137€–162€ ($164–$194) double. AE, DC, MC, V. Free parking. **Amenities:** Restaurant; bar; room service; babysitting; laundry service; nonsmoking rooms; 1 room for those w/limited mobility. *In room:* A/C, TV, dataport, minibar.

Royal Palace Hotel   Built in the 1970s and recognized as a reputable hotel for business travelers, this large, boxy-looking staple of Messina's hotel scene lacks the high-blown style and elegance of its sister hotel, the Grand Hotel Liberty, but both are operated by the same chain. It's a suitable choice, thanks in part to its comfortable guest rooms, its allegiance to streamlined styling, and a genuinely charming lobby bar. Each unit comes with a bathroom with tub and shower.

Via T. Cannizzaro 224, 98123 Messina. © **090-6503**. Fax 090-2821075. www.framon-hotels.com. 107 units. 165€ ($198) double; 240€ ($288) suite. Rates include breakfast. AE, DC, MC, V. **Amenities:** Restaurant; bar; babysitting; laundry service; dry cleaning; nonsmoking rooms. *In room:* A/C, TV, minibar.

WHERE TO DINE

Baked with herbs, sautéed with garlic, or even stewed into a *pesce stucco,* swordfish *(pesce spada)* has the people of Messina hooked. The fish is plentiful in the Straits of Messina, and as you walk along the harbor, you can see the tall-masted swordfish boats *(felucche)* patrolling the narrow channel. May and June are the best months for ordering swordfish.

EXPENSIVE

Jolly Restaurant dello Stretto ⊕ ITALIAN/SICILIAN   This contemporary hotel restaurant has the most panoramic view (in this case, of the wharves that service the ships coming in from Reggio Calabria) in town, along with a floor crafted from mollusk-encrusted russet marble and a sense of *la dolce vita* pizazz. To start, select an array of smoked local fish; there's nothing better on the menu. We were delighted in every way with the breast of chicken with a Sicilian citrus sauce. The staff does very well with even a simple dish such as cream of fresh tomato soup with basil.

In the Jolly Hotel Messina, Via Garibaldi 126. © **090-363860**. Reservations recommended Fri–Sat. Main courses 14€–18€ ($17–$22); set-price lunch 25€ ($30). AE, DC, MC, V. Daily 1–2:30pm and 8–10:30pm.

La Loggia ⊕ ITALIAN/INTERNATIONAL   The town's most appealing hotel features a glamorous dining enclave on its uppermost floor. Beneath a vaulted ceiling that's richly adorned with decorative plasterwork, you'll enjoy superb cuisine presented by a well-trained, formally dressed staff. Much of the allure of this place is thanks to the *maitre flambeur,* who, from a trolley wheeled tableside, can whip together succulent versions of pastas, crepes, and flambéed desserts. Other tasty choices include stuffed eggplant; an especially good saffronstuffed risotto with shrimp; and a wide assortment of the day's freshest fish. *Note:* If you don't have a meal here, opt for a drink at the restaurant bar.

In the Grand Hotel Liberty, Via I Settembre 15. © **090-6409340**. Reservations recommended. Main courses 14€–19€ ($17–$23). AE, DC, MC, V. Mon–Sat 8–10:30pm.

MODERATE

Piero *(Value* SICILIAN   This is one of the town's most recommended restaurants, with a history that goes back to 1959 and an attractive interior that's outfitted with exposed paneling, terra-cotta floors, and a sense of bustling good cheer and workaday efficiency. Menu items may remind many Sicilians of their childhoods: spaghetti with mussels and crabmeat (our favorite), pennette with fresh artichokes, scampi prepared any way you ask for it. Don't overlook the luscious temptations of the antipasti table—it's a serve-yourself buffet that shouldn't be missed.

Via Ghibellina 119. ℭ 090-6409354. Reservations recommended Fri–Sat nights. Main courses 7.50€–20€ ($9–$24). Mon–Sat 12:30–3:15pm and 8–11:30pm. Closed Aug.

INEXPENSIVE

Al Padrino MESSINESE/SICILIAN   Part of the charm of this place is its rough-edged, unpretentious nature. Virtually no effort has been spent on the glaringly white decor (which offers nary a hint of mystery or romance), and tables are hot and cramped, yet Al Padrino has flourished for a quarter of a century in a dreary neighborhood of heavy industry. The impossibly small kitchen churns Messinese-style food that includes a creamy homemade *maccheroni;* eggplant *al padrino* (layered with cheese and herbs); roulades of swordfish; and many different preparations of beef. Flavors are robust and hearty, portions large. Get ready for loud voices, an "in your face" welcome, and an insight into working-class Messina at its most vivid.

Via Santa Cecilia 54–56. ℭ 090-2921000. Main courses 8€–12€ ($9.60–$14). AE, MC, V. Mon–Fri noon–3pm and 7–11pm. Closed Aug.

Casa Savoia *(Value* ITALIAN/SICILIAN   This restaurant, established in 1996 on the site of the since-demolished Teatro della Savoia, is the best budget bet in Messina. Old-fashioned, conservative, and deeply entrenched, with a location just 4 blocks from the harbor, it's decorated with Oriental rugs and antiques, its shelves and tables loaded with bottles of wine. The chef specializes in swordfish, including one succulent version in which the catch is stuffed, rolled, and fried in a roulade. Also tempting is a delectable crescent-shaped pasta that comes simply with fried zucchini and garlic browned in olive oil, a most flavorful combination.

Via XXVII Luglio 36–38. ℭ 090-2934865. Main courses 6€–12€ ($7.20–$14); fixed-price menus 12€–16€ ($14–$19). AE, MC, V. Tues–Sat noon–3pm and 7:30–11:30pm; Sun noon–3pm. Closed 2 weeks in July and 1 week in Jan.

Le Due Sorelle *(Value* SICILIAN   Set beside the square that flanks the front entrance to Messina's town hall, this restaurant occupies a long, narrow room that contains fewer than 10 tables, walls covered with wine bottles, and a carved screen that rises high above the terra-cotta floor. At lunchtime, the place is loaded with municipal office workers, one of whom happens to be the town's mayor. The unpretentious fare includes two different versions of couscous; veal with roasted vegetables; a *padellata di pesce* (panful of fish) with vegetables; and a full roster of house-made desserts.

Piazza Municipio 4. ℭ 090-44720. Reservations recommended on Fri–Sat nights. Main courses 9€–15€ ($11–$18). MC, V. Mon–Fri 1–3pm; daily 8pm–midnight. Closed Aug.

Pasticceria Irrera PASTRIES   Set directly beside Messina's largest and most verdant square, this well-known cafe was established in 1910. The marble bar serves coffee and drinks; the *granita* tastes especially wonderful on warm days; and the pastry shop is widely renowned for its almond-based *Fiori di Mandorlo,* its succulent *Torta Letizia* (made with almonds and vanilla), and a chocolate-covered version of almond paste known as *Le Amarilde.*

Piazza Cairoli 12. ℭ 090-673823. Pastries 1.50€–6€ ($1.80–$7.20). AE, DC, MC, V. Tues–Sat 8am–1:30pm; Tues–Sun 4–8pm.

MESSINA AFTER DARK

If you're here in July or August, head for Piazza del Duomo, the central cathedral square where free concerts devoted to rock, jazz, or classical music are presented. Posters advertise cultural events, and the tourist office (see "Visitor Information," on p. 137) will have details.

(*Tips*   Night Wandering: Do So at Your Own Risk

Some young men in Messina earn a living picking the pockets of foreign men and snatching the purses of foreign women. A woman wandering the streets at night does so at her own risk. Although men aren't as likely to get abducted or raped, they may be at risk of being mugged. The area near the Stazione Centrale, the main rail depot, is the most dangerous part of town—that and the harbor.

If your hotel has a bar, that's often your best and safest bet for a drink. The noisiest (and most fun) *birreria* is **Gli Antenati Pub,** Corso Cavour 109 (© **090-672430**), whose major drawback is that it's closed during the scorching months of June through August. Otherwise, it's a reliable place for a cold beer and pizza. **The Duck,** Via Pellegrino 107 (© **090-712772**), is a British-style pub where you'll encounter U.S. sailors stationed with NATO forces around Messina. It's closed on Mondays and from July 15 to September 15. A place that always seems to be open is **Dolce Vita,** Piazza del Duomo (© **090-670001**), the most central watering hole in town. Try for one of the outdoor tables. Tasty snacks are served here, along with a selection of imported beers.

EASY EXCURSIONS TO THE BEACH

If the streets look a little deserted in July or August, that tells you that the Messinese are hanging out at **Mortelle,** the beach resort 12km (7½ miles) north of the city, at the northeastern tip of the island. The beachfront is a narrow strip of pebble-strewn sand known as the **Lido del Tirreno** (© **090-321001**). Thanks to large numbers of parasols and chaise longues, as well as easy access to beachfront restaurants, it's the best-accessorized beach in and around Messina. Entrance costs 2.50€ ($3) per person; parking is free. A day's rental of a *cabine* goes for 6€ to 8€ ($7.20–$9.60), while a chaise longue and parasol costs 3€ ($3.60).

From Messina, Mortelle is an easy ride on bus no. 79 or 81. Even when the sun goes down, Mortelle continues to stay busy until late at night; be careful not to get run down by cycles and scooters. The area is filled with pizzerie and bars, and in July and August, open-air films are screened at Arena Green Sky, opposite Duc Palme pizzeria.

If you find Mortelle too crowded, continue to the west, where you'll find more sandy beaches and little seaside resorts, the best of which is **Acqualadrone.**

WHERE TO STAY

Grand Hotel Lido di Mortelle *(Kids)*   Set at the Messina end of the best beachfront in Mortelle, this government-rated three-star hotel was built in the late 1970s as the best lodging in town. The simple, airy guest rooms attract holidaymakers from the region, including families with young children. Each unit comes with a small tiled bathroom with shower. Nothing is particularly plush, but in this simple and unpretentious beach resort, no one really seems to mind. Access to the nearby beach is free.

S.S. 113, Mortelle, 98164 Messina. © **090-321017.** Fax 090-321666. www.giardinodellepalme.it. 24 units. 60€–94€ ($72–$113) double; 75€–120€ ($90–$144) triple. DC, MC, V. **Amenities:** Restaurant; bar; outdoor pool; babysitting; laundry service; dry cleaning; nonsmoking rooms. *In room:* A/C, TV, minibar.

WHERE TO DINE

Ristorante Sporting Doddis SICILIAN   This is the biggest and most stylish restaurant in Mortelle, a two-story beachfront complex that encourages its guests to stay on or near the premises for an entire day. It was built in 1957 and retains strong whiffs of sybaritic values and *la dolce vita*. The complex is actually two restaurants, both of which are open to sea breezes and views of the Lido. The more formal of the two is upstairs, where chefs prepare the most tempting array of antipasti in town (including a delectable carpaccio of swordfish) and risotto of tantalizing combinations. On street level, directly beside the beach, is a simpler pizzeria.

S.S. 113, Mortelle. (©) 090-321009. Reservations recommended. Main courses in restaurant 9€–13€ ($11–$16). Pizzas 4€–10€ ($4.80–$12). AE, DC, MC, V. Tues–Sat 4pm–midnight; Sun noon–3pm.

2 Cefalù ★★

81km (50 miles) E of Palermo, 38km (24 miles) NE of Termini Imerese, 170km (106 miles) W of Messina

The major destination along the Tyrrhenian coast, the former fishing village of Cefalù has grown into one of northern Sicily's premier stopovers. It hardly rivals Taormina in appeal, but it's trying. The town was captured in the Oscar-winning film *Cinema Paradiso.*

You can tour Cefalù in half a day and spend the rest of your time enjoying its beach. The town is not only in possession of a great sandy beach; it's also blessed with a Romanesque cathedral and a museum that houses Antonello da Messina's masterpiece *Portrait of an Unknown Man.*

Anchored between the sea and a craggy limestone promontory, Cefalù is a town of narrow medieval streets, small squares, and historic sights. Towering 278m (912 ft.) above the town is La Rocca, a massive and much-photographed crag. The Greeks thought it evoked a head, so they named the village *Kephalos,* which in time became Cefalù.

Known to be inhabited since the 9th century B.C., Cefalù was founded by the Sikels. By the 5th century B.C., it had become the fortified western outpost of Imera. The Byzantine era saw Cefalù thriving as the seat of a Greek bishop. But Saracen raids in the 8th century drove its residents away from the sea to seek refuge on top of La Rocca. Cowering in fear, the inhabitants didn't descend again until 1131, when Roger II ordered that the town be reconstructed along with his grand design for a cathedral.

ESSENTIALS

GETTING THERE   By Train   From Palermo, some three dozen trains head east to Cefalù (trip time: 1 hr.). The cost is 4€ ($4.80) one-way. From Messina, about a dozen trains run daily, costing 8€ ($9.60) and taking about 3 hours. Trains pull into the Stazione Termini, Piazza Stazione (© 892021).

By Bus   SAIS, Via Balsamo 20, in Palermo (© 091-6171141), runs buses between Palermo and Cefalù, charging 4.20€ ($5.05) one-way for the 1½-hour trip.

By Car   Follow route 113 east from Palermo to Cefalù; count on at least 1½ hours of driving time (longer if traffic is bad). Once in Cefalù, park along either side of Via Roma for free, or pay .70€ (85¢) per hour for a spot within one of the two lots signposted from the main street; both are within an easy walk of the town's medieval core.

VISITOR INFORMATION   The **Cefalù Tourist Office,** Corso Ruggero 77 (© 0921-421050), is open Monday through Saturday from 8am to 2pm and 3:30 to 7:30pm, Sunday from 9am to 1pm.

GETTING AROUND   Taxis are the easiest way to get about and take advantage of the city's history-rich environs. **Kefautoservizi** (© **0921-422554**) operates the taxis, most of which can be found clustered at Piazza Stazione or Piazza Colombo.

FAST FACTS: Cefalù

Currency Exchange Go to **Banca Credito Siciliano,** at Via Roma and Via Giglio (© **0921-423922**), near the rail depot. Open Monday through Friday from 8:30am to 1:30pm and 2:45 to 3:45pm. The **Banco di Sicilia,** Piazza Garibaldi (© **0921-421103**), has 24-hour ATM access.

Emergencies For the police, call © **0921-420104;** for first aid, © **0921-424544;** and for Guardia Medica, © **0921-423623.** The latter is open daily from 8pm to 8am and located at Via Roma 15.

Hospital The **Cefalù Hospital** is at Contrada Pietrapollastra (© **0921-920111**).

Internet Access The most central option is **Bacco On-Line,** Corso Ruggero 38 (© **0921-421753**), across from the tourist office; it's open daily from 9am to midnight and charges 2.50€ ($3) per half hour. **Kefaonline,** Piazza San Francesco 1 (© **0921-923091**), at Via Mazzini and Via Umberto, is open Monday through Saturday from 9:30am to 1:30pm and 3:30 to 7:30pm and charges 6€ ($7.20) per hour.

Pharmacies The two most central drugstores are **Cirincione,** Corso Ruggero 144 (© **0921-421209**), open Monday through Friday from 9am to 1pm and 4:30 to 8:30pm, Saturday and Sunday from 4:30 to 11pm; and **Dr. Battaglia,** Via Roma 13 (© **0921-421789**), open Monday through Saturday from 9am to 1pm and 4 to 8pm.

Police The municipal police headquarters are along Via Roma (© **0921-420104**).

Post Office The post office is at Via Vazzana 2 (© **0921-421528**). Open Monday through Friday from 8am to 6:30pm, Saturday from 8am to 12:30pm.

SEEING THE SIGHTS

Getting around Cefalù on foot is easy—no cars are allowed in the historic core. The city's main street is **Corso Ruggero** ⟨★⟩, which starts at Piazza Garibaldi, site of one of a quartet of "gateways" to Cefalù. This is a pedestrian street that you can stroll at leisure, checking out the shops and viewing the facades of its palazzi, even though these are hardly comparable to those found in Palermo's medieval core.

The Romans designed a main street to bisect the village on a north-south axis. Basically that same plan is carried out today. The medieval sector is found to the west, where the poor folks once lived. Noblemen and their families and the rich clergy settled in the posher eastern sector.

Across from the tourist office lies **Osteria Magno,** at the corner of Via Amendola and Corso Ruggero. Constructed in the 1300s but massively altered over the years, this was the legendary residence of Roger II. The palace remains closed but serves occasionally as a venue for temporary art exhibitions. For information on what's happening here, call the tourist office at ⓒ **0921-421050.**

Duomo ☆☆ Set along Corso Ruggero, this magnificent Norman cathedral opens onto a wide square that is the center of town. Legend has it that Roger II ordered this mighty church to be constructed after his life was spared following a violent storm off the coast. Construction stretched on until 1240.

Your first impression may be that you've arrived at a fortress rather than a cathedral. Anchored at the foot of towering La Rocca, the twin-towered facade of the Duomo forms a landmark visible for miles around. Splitting the facade is a two-story portico that had to be rebuilt in the 1400s. We enjoy viewing this splendid facade in the late afternoon, when the building appears bathed in golden light.

To the right of the facade on the south side, you'll find an entrance that may disappoint, if you've already been dazzled by the mosaics of Palermo's Cappella Palatina or Monreale's Duomo. But press on to the apse and vault, where you'll find a stunning array of **mosaics** ☆☆☆ in all their shimmering glory. Completed in 1148, they are the oldest Byzantine-Norman mosaics in Sicily and among the world's most brilliant. The tour de force of the cycle is the Byzantine figure of the Pantocrator in the apse. Since this was a Norman church, Christ is depicted as a blond, not a brunette; but his nose and mouth look Greek, his brows and beard black like a Saracen's.

Regrettably, there's little else to see here. The Duomo seems to be in a perpetual state of restoration, hampered by lack of funds.

Piazza del Duomo. ⓒ 0921-922021. Free admission. Summer daily 8am–noon and 3:30–7pm. Off-season 8am–noon and 3:30–5pm.

Museo Mandralisca *Overrated* We come here just to gaze at the wonder of *Ritratto di un Uomo Ignoto (Portrait of an Unknown Man)* ☆☆, the 1465 work of Antonello da Messina. Unfortunately, the painting is badly framed and a velvet rope requires you to keep your distance. Still, this is clearly a masterpiece by the great Renaissance artist from Messina.

After being dazzled by Antonello, you may find the rest of the exhibitions a disappointment. Baron Enrico Piraino di Mandralisca (1809–64) seemed to have randomly purchased anything that caught his fancy, including coins and medals, artifacts unearthed at digs at Lipari, and even such esoteric items as a Chinese puzzle in ivory. After searching for something intriguing, we did come upon a **4th-century-**B.C. **vase** ☆, depicting a fish vendor and a customer in heated argument. After that, you must face a barrage of 20,000 shells.

Via Mandralisca 13. ⓒ 0921-421547. Admission 4.15€ ($5). Daily 9am–7pm.

La Rocca ☆☆ During the dog days of August, it's a long, hot, sweaty climb up to this rocky crag, but once you're here, the view is panoramic, one of the grandest in Sicily. If you're stout-hearted, count on 20 minutes to approach the ruins of the so-called Temple of Diana and another 45 huffing and puffing minutes to scale the pinnacle.

From Piazza Garibaldi, along Corso Ruggero, a sign—ACCESSO ALLA ROCCA—will launch you on your way. In summer, we recommend taking this jaunt either in the early morning or when evening breezes are blowing.

In Cefalù's heyday, this was the site of the acropolis of Cephaloedium, with a temple dedicated to Hercules on the top. Over the centuries, residents from below used this zone as a stone quarry.

You'll come first to the ruins of the **Tempio di Diana,** which popular tradition has attributed as a temple to the goddess Diana. Now consisting of mammoth trapezoidal blocks, the temple was constructed or reconstructed in various stages from the 9th century to the 4th century B.C.

As you continue to the top, you'll see the restored **ancient Arab** and **medieval fortifications.** From here, you can see all the way to the skyline of Palermo in the west or to Capo d'Orlando in the east. The lookout tower here, now in ruins, was called Torre Caldura and guarded an unfriendly coastline. On a clear day you can't see forever, but you will get a stunning view of the Aeolian Islands.

HITTING THE BEACH

Cefalù's crescent-shaped beach is one of the best along the northern coast. Regrettably, it's always packed in summer. In town, we prefer **Lido Poseidon.** At the best bar here, **Poseidon,** Via Lungomare Giuseppe Giardino (© **0921-424646**), you can rent an umbrella or a deck chair for 6€ ($7.20). Open daily from May to September. **Spiaggia Attrezzata,** in town just off the Lungomare, is another good beach, with brilliant white sand and turquoise shallows. You'll also find free showers here. Other recommended beaches are found west of town at **Spiaggia Settefrati** and **Spiaggia Mazzaforno.**

WHERE TO STAY

If you want to spend the night in Cefalù, and you have wheels, you'll find the hotels outside of town more comfortably satisfying.

Astro Hotel   Originally built in 1969 and intelligently renovated several times since, this is the first hotel many visitors see when they approach Cefalù from its western outskirts. Small-scale and unpretentious, with a hardworking and sensitive staff, it offers well-equipped albeit simple rooms, each with terrazzo or tile floors and a shower-only bathroom. (*Note:* Hot water here means tepid.) About a third of the rooms have balconies. Parking is usually difficult in the traffic-clogged neighborhoods adjacent to the city's car-free inner core, but here it's free and readily available within a walled-in lot directly across the street. The hotel lies just uphill from the private beach, about a 12-minute walk from the medieval core.

Via Roma 105, 90015 Cefalù. © **0921-421639.** Fax 0921-423103. www.astrohotel.it. 30 units. 76€–160€ ($91–$192) double. Rates include breakfast. AE, DC, MC, V. Free parking. **Amenities:** Restaurant; bar; babysitting; laundry service. *In room:* A/C, TV.

Hotel Tourist *(Value)*   Despite its lackluster name, this is a desirable hotel dating from 1970 and last renovated in 2003. It enjoys a tranquil position on the beach, about a 10-minute walk from the center, and is situated to offer scenic views of not only the water but also Cefalù itself. Bedrooms are midsize and simply adorned, each equipped with a shower-only bathroom. The most desirable units have balconies with views of the sea. A private beach lies across the highway from the hotel. The staff is one of the most helpful in the area, serving an excellent breakfast to fortify you for the day ahead.

Lungomare Giardina, 90015 Cefalù. © **0921-421750.** Fax 0921-923916. 46 units. 70€–176€ ($84–$211). AE, MC, V. Rates include breakfast. Free parking. **Amenities:** Restaurant; bar; outdoor pool; laundry service. *In room:* A/C, TV, minibar, hair dryer, safe.

Kalura *(Finds) (Kids)*   Set amid palm trees, Kalura has something of a North African feel to it. This snug retreat is 3km (2 miles) east along the coast on a little promontory, a 20-minute walk from the center of Cefalù (follow the street signs from town to reach it). Run by the same family for nearly 3 decades, it's a friendly, inviting oasis. Guest rooms are well furnished; most open onto a sea view. Nothing is too elaborate here, including the simple shower-only bathrooms. A special park is reserved for children, one reason this is a very family-friendly place. The private beach offers good swimming in unpolluted waters. The hotel is also the most sports-conscious in the area, and can arrange excursions to nearby attractions as well.

Via Cavallaro 13, 90015 Contrada Caldura. (℃ **0921-421354.** Fax 0921-423122. www.kalura.it. 73 units. 130€ ($156) double. Rates include breakfast. AE, DC, MC, V. **Amenities:** Restaurant; 2 bars; outdoor pool; tennis; watersports; mountain bikes; children's park; room service; babysitting; laundry service; dry cleaning; canoes; pedal boats; rooms for those w/limited mobility. *In room:* A/C, TV, hair dryer.

WHERE TO DINE

If you're heading out on an excursion, perhaps to Parco delle Madonie (p. 151), you can pick up the makings for a delightful picnic at **Gatta Gaetano Alimentari e Salumeria,** Corso Ruggero 152 (℃ **0921-423156**). This well-stocked deli offers the best of Sicilian cheeses and sausages, along with cured meats, to-die-for olives, and luscious fruits—everything except bread, which you'll find sold in many places all over town.

For the best cakes and cookies, stop by **Pasticceria Serio Pietro,** V. G. Giglio 29 (℃ **0921-422293**), which also sells more than a dozen flavors of the most delicious gelato in town. The drawback here? The staff never went to finishing school.

MODERATE

Al Porticciolo ✿ SICILIAN   At the seafront end of the old town, nearly adjacent to the old port, this restaurant is set within a cavelike stone-sided room that used to be a storage point for fish (long before the days of refrigeration). During the day, dine indoors in air-conditioned comfort to avoid the heat, but at night (when all traffic is stopped along this street), opt for an outdoor table. The traditional pasta with sardines is well prepared here, but we're also fond of the tagliatelle of octopus, the addictive grilled radicchio, and the country-style kettle of mussel soup—just right for a seafaring town. The *cassata alla Siciliana* (layered sponge cake filled with ricotta, chocolate, and candied fruits) here is among the best we've ever tasted.

Via Carlo Ortolani di Bordonaro 66. (℃ **0921-921981.** Main courses 7€–15€ ($8.40–$18); set-price menus 15€–25€ ($18–$30). AE, DC, MC, V. Thurs–Tues noon–3pm and 7pm–midnight. Closed Nov to mid-Dec.

Kentia ✿✿ ITALIAN   This restaurant manages to evoke a bit more glamour, and a lot more style, than some of its nearby competitors. It's a cool hideaway from the oppressive sun, thanks in part to tiled floors, high masonry vaulting, and an understated elegance. A dozen homemade pasta dishes are prepared daily, and you'd have to walk to Messina to find swordfish as good as that grilled here. We generally stick to the *pesce del diorno* (catch of the day), which can be grilled to your specifications. The chefs also prepare a daily vegetarian fixed-price menu as well as one devoted entirely to fish. We've sampled both and recommend them heartily.

Via N. Botta 15. [tel **0921-423801.** Reservations recommended. Main courses 6€–13€ ($7.20–$16); fixed-price vegetarian menu 15€ ($18); fixed-price fish menu 22€ ($26). AE, DC, MC, V. June–Sept daily 7:30–11pm; Oct–May Wed–Mon 7:30–11pm.

La Brace SICILIAN   This has been a landmark restaurant in Cefalù since 1977. It's near the Duomo, on an impossibly narrow cobblestone street about a block downhill from the center of town. The Sicilian cuisine here has a number of imaginative Asian and other international touches—a surprise in this part of the world. We were won over by the tagliatelle with porcini mushrooms and the mouthwatering *spiedini di pesce spada* (marinated swordfish roasted with sweet peppers and served in a lemony mustard sauce). As a bow to Tex-Mex cuisine, chili con carne appears on the menu, but we much prefer the gratin of octopus. The house dessert, justifiably celebrated locally, is a banana doused with orange liqueur, baked, and then topped with whipped cream.

Via XXV Novembre 10 (off Corso Ruggero). ⓒ **0921-423570.** Reservations recommended. Main courses 5.50€–13€ ($6.60–$16); set lunch 17€–30€ ($20–$36); set dinner 27€–30€ ($32–$36). AE, DC, MC, V. Tues–Sun 1–2:30pm and 7–11:30pm. Closed Dec 15–Jan 15.

Osteria del Duomo ★★ SICILIAN/INTERNATIONAL   The hippest, most sophisticated restaurant in Cefalù is right in front of the town's famous cathedral, at the bottom of steps that have been trod upon by Norman knights and *La Dolce Vita* movie stars alike. Many tables sit in the open air on cobblestones, others under the vaulted ceiling of the air-conditioned interior. We think the chefs here top those at La Brace (Michelin's Cefalù favorite): They will enthrall you with their smoked fish, their seafood salads are the town's best (and the ideal food on a hot summer day), and their truly excellent carpaccio of beef will appeal to serious carnivores. Count on freshly made salads and desserts as well.

Via Seminario 3. ⓒ **0921-421838.** Reservations recommended Sat–Sun. Main courses 8€–15€ ($9.60–$18). AE, DC, MC, V. Tues–Sun noon–midnight. Closed mid-Nov to mid-Dec.

INEXPENSIVE

Al Grabbiano SICILIAN/SEAFOOD   Unlike most of the other restaurants in Cefalù, which are tucked into hideaway alleys within the medieval core, this one sits directly across from the town's most popular beach, allowing sun-kissed diners access throughout the day and evening. The atmosphere evokes a woodsy-looking tavern with breezy access to the outdoors and touches of heavy timbers and exposed stone. Fresh fish, a menu constant, tastes best grilled and served with spinach or fava beans. The mainstay of the north coast, swordfish, is served here with a tasty onion sauce. For us, no pasta in town compares to this place's linguine with shrimp, clams, and mussels. And one of our favorite items is zucchini flowers, which the chefs are skilled at deep-frying or grilling.

Via Lungomare Giardina 17. ⓒ **0921-421495.** Reservations not necessary. Main courses 5€–9€ ($6–$11). AE, DC, MC, V. Daily noon–3pm and 7–11pm.

L'Antica Corte SICILIAN   The authentic Sicilian cuisine served here is market-fresh and satisfying, despite the restaurant's slight touristic bent (the waiters, for example, appear with red bandannas and sashes like those worn by the Saracen pirates of yore). In good weather, try to get a table set under grapevines in the old courtyard. Otherwise, you'll find the air-conditioned seats inside a welcome relief from the heat. The pizzas are among the best in town—try the "Drago," with spicy sausage. Tempting pastas include one with hot peppers *(all'arrabbiata)* and another with shrimp, mushrooms, and a dousing of limoncello. The best bet is the catch of the day, which the chefs flavor with herbs and grill to your specifications.

Cortile Pepe 7, off Corso Ruggero. ⓒ **0921-423228.** Reservations recommended. Pizza 3.60€–9€ ($4.30–$11); menu turistica 12€ ($14); main courses 7€–10€ ($8.40–$12). AE, MC, V. Fri–Wed noon–3pm and 7–11:30pm (Sat–Sun only in Feb and Nov).

Lo Scoglio Ubriaco (The Drunken Rock) SICILIAN   This restaurant is set high atop a rocky cliff at the edge of the old town. Walk in boldly and bypass the less desirable tables in the narrow dining room. Near the back, you'll find a staircase that meanders down onto a terrace perched atop jagged rocks, just above sea level and overlooking the fortifications on either side of the old port. If a table is available, this is where you should sit. Menu items are well prepared, albeit relatively predictable in light of the roughly equivalent food served in the town's other restaurants. A tangy mussel soup might tempt you before you proceed to the mixed grill of either fish or meat. The house-style tagliatelle is understandably a local favorite, served with a well-flavored mussel and cream sauce.

Via Carlo Ortolani di Bordonaro 2–4. (℃) 0921-423370. Reservations recommended. Main courses 6€–12€ ($7.20–$14). AE, DC, MC, V. July–Aug daily noon–2:30pm and 7pm–midnight; Sept–June Wed–Mon noon–2:30pm and 7pm–midnight.

CEFALÙ AFTER DARK

Many townspeople like to go home, eat their catch of the day, and retire early after watching some TV. The liveliest spot in Cefalù is **Bip Bop Pub, Bar & Bistro,** Via Nicolà Botta 4 (℃ **0921-923972**). The rock-'n'-roll music and youthful (or at least young-at-heart) crowd in this English-style pub pull you very far away from the medieval setting of old Cefalù. Opt for a cocktail or beer on tap, crepes, sandwiches, salads, or a plate of pasta. Open daily from 11am to 4am; closed Mondays from October to March.

EASY EXCURSIONS

On Cefalù's doorstep lies an array of some of Sicily's greatest attractions, including a national park, **Parco Naturale Regionale delle Madonie;** the ruins of ancient **Tyndaris** (which date from 1500 B.C.); and the ceramic capital of **Santo Stefano di Camastra,** among many other sights.

You can easily schedule 3 nights for a visit to Cefalù, allowing 1 day to explore the town and another 2 days to see the highlights in the surrounding environs.

PARCO NATURALE REGIONALE DELLE MADONIE 🐾🐾

Since 1989, some 39,679 hectares (8,007 acres) of the most beautiful land in Sicily has been set aside as a national park. The park begins just 6km (3¾ miles) south of Cefalù. You can explore it on your own if you have plenty of time, or let **Barranco Tours** (℃ **0921-421525**) do it for you by guided bus on its "Unknown Sicily" tour. The cost is 40€ ($48) for a full-day excursion, which includes a visit to the Romanesque monastery of Gibilmanna, a working Capuchin monastery with 20 monks.

The park has been called a botanic paradise, as it contains more than half of the 2,600 species known in Sicily. Some of the most ancient rocks and mountains on the island are found here, along with some of the most spectacular peaks. Among them, **Pizzo Carbonara,** at 1,979m (6,493 ft.), is the highest mountain in Sicily outside of Mount Etna.

The park is far from a wilderness—it is inhabited and contains any number of charming villages. To reach it from Cefalù, follow the road directions south for 14km (8¾ miles) to the **Santuario di Gibilmanna.** From the belvedere at this town, in front of the little 17th-century church, you can take in a **panoramic view** 🐾🐾 of the Madonie, including the peak of Pizzo Carbonara.

The Santuario di Gibilmanna is a shrine to the Virgin Mary. The Madonna is said to have shown signs of life in the 18th century when she was restoring sight to blind pilgrims and speech to a mute. Since the Vatican confirmed this claim, Gibilmanna has been one of the most important shrines in Sicily, drawing the devout.

After taking in the view, continue southeast, following the signs to **Castelbuono,** an idyllic town that grew around a *castello* constructed in the 1300s. You can stop over to visit its historic core, **Piazza Margherita.** The church here, **Madrice Vecchia,** dates from the 14th century, when it was built on the ruins of a pagan temple.

If you arrive during the lunch hour, your best bet for a bite to eat is **Romittaggio,** Località San Guglielmo Sud (© **0921-671323**), 5km (3 miles) south of Castelbuono. Specializing in simple mountain food, the restaurant is installed in a monastery from the Middle Ages. In summer, you can request a table in the arcades of the cloister. Meals range in price from 25€ to 32€ ($30–$38). The restaurant is closed from June 15 to July 15 and on Wednesdays year-round.

The road continues south to **Petralia Soprana** ✫✫, at 1,147m (3,762 ft.) the loftiest town in Madonie and one of the best-preserved medieval villages of Sicily, with narrow streets and houses of local stone. A grand belvedere is found at Piazza del Popolo, with a **stunning vista** ✫✫ toward Enna in the east.

At the end of Via Loreto, you can visit the church of **Santa Maria di Loreto,** built on the site of a Saracen fortress and framed by a set of campaniles. In back of the church is **Madonie's greatest panorama** ✫✫✫, with glorious views of volcanic Mount Etna.

The next stopover is **Petralia Sottana,** overlooking the River Imera Valley. This little village, perched on a rocky spur 1,000m (3,280 ft.) above sea level, is the headquarters of the national park service, **Ente Parco,** Corso Paolo Alliata 16 (© **0921-680840**). The office is open Monday through Friday from 9:30am to 1:30pm and 3:30 to 6:30pm.

At this point, head west along S120, stopping at **Polizzi Generosa,** another hilltop magnificently situated on a limestone spur. The **view** ✫✫✫ at Piazza XXVII Maggio is one of the most spectacular in Madonie, taking in its loftiest peaks and the scenic valley of the River Himera.

Here you can begin your journey north back to Cefalù, passing through little **Scillato** until you reach **Collesano,** a holiday resort where the aura of the Middle Ages still lingers.

It is deceptively simple in its exterior, but the **Chiesa Madre,** reached by going up a flight of stairs, is filled with art treasures. This church contains masterpieces by the 16th-century painter Gaspare Vazzano, who signed his name "Zoppo di Gangi"; his cycle of **frescoes** ✫ illustrates scenes from the lives of Jesus Christ, St. Paul, and St. Peter. He also painted another magnificent canvas, *Santa Maria degli Angeli* ✫, found in the north aisle.

After viewing Collesano, you can continue north until you reach autostrada A20, which will take you back to Cefalù, your best base for the night.

CASTEL DI TUSA

This pleasant little town on the sea is only of minor interest. It opens onto one of the most beautiful "bayscapes" on the island, but not a lot happens here. Despite a ruined feudal fortress that rises from the highest hill, Castel di Tusa might pass for an uneventful fishing village surrounded by rocky, scrub-covered landscape. What makes it worthwhile is an overnight stay at one of Sicily's most remarkable hotels (see below). You can also use the hotel as a base for exploring Madonie Park (see above).

You'll really need a car for getting around the area. Take autostrada A20 from Cefalù, which becomes the SS113 for its final stretch to Castel di Tusa, a distance 25km (16 miles) east of Palermo.

Atelier Sul Mare ★★★   Sometimes defined as an "arts-oriented ashram," the most unusual hotel in Sicily occupies a boxy, concrete building that was erected in the 1960s as a conventional hotel with access to a nearby beach. Any vestiges of its original decor were ripped out long ago by the iconoclastic owner, Messina-born Antonio Presti. Today, the hotel artfully combines aspects of Bauhaus architecture, pop art, psychedelics, hints of flagrant and very permissive sexuality, and goodly doses of Italian-based socialist politics.

The black-and-white lobby's only adornments are hundreds of photocopies of articles about the place. About 25 of the guest rooms are comfortable, "conventional" units, each with original art and a sense of whimsy. The other 15 rooms were each decorated by an artist who lived on the premises for several months while completing the work. Examples include a sinuously curved all-black room by Chilean artist Raoul Ruiz, with a circular bed and a square-shaped skylight whose blasts of sunlight represent a spiritual liberty from oppressive governments and cultures. A room decorated in honor of filmmaker and gay activist Pasolini was conceived as a mud-built grotto that might remind you of a miniature mosque.

Via Cesare Battisti 4, 98070 Castel di Tusa. (℃ **0921-334295.** Fax 0921-334283. www.ateliersulmare.com. 40 units. Designer-style room 230€ ($276) double; conventional unit 170€ ($204) double. Rates include buffet breakfast. DC, MC, V. Free parking. **Amenities:** Restaurant; bar; occasional classes in pottery and ceramics. *In room:* A/C, no phone.

SANTO STEFANO DI CAMASTRA

Heading east of Cefalù for 33km (20 miles), you'll approach one of the ceramic capitals of Sicily. A visit here can easily be tied in with a stopover at Castel di Tusa (see above). Santo Stefano lies 13km (8 miles) east of Castel di Tusa.

If you're driving, follow A20 east from Cefalù, which becomes the SS113 on its approach to Santo Stefano. The town is also on the main rail link from Palermo/Cefalù, heading east into Messina.

Santo Stefano lies at the western end of the **Parco dei Nebrodi,** one of the natural beauty spots to the east of Parco delle Madonie (p. 151). Following a disastrous landslide in 1682, the town was laid out in a geometric grid said to have been copied from the gardens of Versailles.

On the approach roads in and out of town, you'll see dozens of vendors hawking ceramics and pottery. The industry grew here because the area in the hinterlands is said to have some of the best clay in Sicily. Most of the pottery styles are traditional, but others are glaringly *moderno.* Would you believe a set of tableware devoted to Princess Di? In this vast array of merchandise, not all is of equal quality. Some items are shoddily made and filled with imperfections. Examine each piece before buying, and be prepared to haggle over prices.

If the many choices overwhelm you, head for the shop we've found the most reliable over the years: **Ceramiche Franco,** Via Nazionale 8 (℃ **0921-337222**). Craftsmanship and skill go into the Franco family's ceramics, which are inspired by various artistic movements in Italy, especially the Renaissance and the baroque. Hours are Monday through Saturday from 9am to 7:30pm.

Before actually buying anything, you might want to familiarize yourself with the area's wares by visiting the **Museum della Ceramica** ★, Via Palazzo (℃ **0921-331110**), in the heart of town in the Palazzo Trabia. The restored palace itself is a thing of beauty, especially its **tiled floors** ★, **antique furnishings** (mainly from the 1700s), and beautifully **frescoed ceilings.** You'll learn how varied ceramics can be and the technique and skills that go into making them. It's open from May to September, Tuesday through Sunday from 9am to 1pm and 4 to 8pm; and from October to April, Tuesday through Sunday from 9am to 1pm and 3:30 to 7:30pm. Admission is free.

TYNDARIS 🎔

At Capo Tindari, approximately 85km (52 miles) from Cefalù, stand the ruins of Tyndaris, on a lonely, rocky promontory overlooking Golfo di Patti. It was known to the ancients since it was founded by Dionysius the Elder in 396 B.C. after a victory over the Carthaginians. For a long time it formed a protective union with its ally, Syracuse, until that eastern Sicilian city fell to the Romans in 256 B.C. Tyndaris has had a rough time of it: It was partially destroyed by a landslide in the 1st century A.D., and then suffered an earthquake in A.D. 365. The Arabs in the 10th century were particularly vicious in destroying its buildings.

The **view** 🎔🎔 alone is almost reason enough to go; it stretches from Milazzo in the east to Capo Calavà in the west. On a clear day, there are stunning vistas of the Aeolian Islands, with Vulcano the nearest.

The most serious excavations of the site began after World War II, although digs were launched much less successfully in the 19th century. Most of the ruins you see today date from the days of the Roman empire, including the **basilica,** whose exact function remains unknown. Just beyond the basilica is a **Roman villa,** which is in rather good condition (you can still see the original mosaics on the floor). Cut into a hill at the end of town is a wide **theater,** built by the Greeks in the late 4th century B.C. The **Insula Romana** contains the ruins of baths, patrician villas with fragments of mosaics, and what may have been taverns or drinking halls. Beyond the entrance to the site on the left is a little **Antiquarium,** exhibiting artifacts dug up on the site. You can also see the ruins of defensive walls constructed during the dreadful reign of Dionysius.

The ruins are open daily from 9am until 1 hour before sunset. Admission is 2.10€ ($2.50) for adults, 1.05€ ($1.25) for students and children. For information on the archeological area, call (📞 **0941-369023**).

The site is also a place of pilgrimage for the devout who flock to the **Santuario di Tindari** (📞 **0941-369003**), which contains a Byzantine Black Virgin, or the *Madonna Nera.* Legend has it that this Madonna washed up on the shores of Tyndaris centuries ago. The sanctuary is open Monday through Friday from 6:45am to 12:30pm and 2:30 to 7pm, Saturday and Sunday from 6:45am to 12:30pm and 2:30 to 8pm. Admission is free.

The site is best reached by private car. From Cefalù, motorists continue east approximately 85km (52 miles) along the main coastal route (A20/SS113). A small tourist office (📞 **0941-241136**), at the site at Piazza Marconi, offers limited information.

3 Termini Imerese

40km (25 miles) E of Palermo

Long known for its thermal waters, this town might merit a couple hours of your time. Although it is used mainly as a base for those wishing to take side trips from here, it does offer a few treasures.

Cáccamo, to the south, is one of the island's biggest and most magnificent bastions, and Himera, to the east, is the site of the ruins of a 7th-century-B.C. Greek settlement. For the dedicated sightseer, both Cáccamo and Himera are more rewarding than Termini Imerese itself, whose name comes from the Latin *Thermae Himerenses,* meaning "Hot Springs of Himera." Among those who came for the cure was the Greek poet Pindar. In a rather fanciful endorsement, Diodorus claimed that the springs were created by three nymphs and that Hercules was the first to enjoy the baths.

The town is split into two sectors—**Termini Bassa (Lower Termini)** and **Termini Alta (Upper Termini).** The upper town comprises most of the spa's historic center, whereas the transportation hub for the area is in the lower town. Once enclosed by fortified walls, the city lost most of its charms to the creeping industrialization that followed the end of World War II, including some hideously ugly petrochemical factories.

ESSENTIALS

GETTING THERE   By Train   Trains arrive from Palermo on the main Palermo–Messina line every hour (trip time: 20 min.). A one-way ticket from Palermo costs 2.65€ ($3.20). For rail information, call ✆ **892021.**

By Bus   Buses run by **SAIS,** Via Balsamo 20, Palermo (✆ **091-6171141**), make frequent runs to Termini Imerese throughout the day. A one-way ticket costs 2.75€ ($3.30).

By Car   From Palermo, head east along A19, the Palermo–Messina autostrada. The exit for Termini Imerese is clearly marked.

VISITOR INFORMATION   The **tourist office,** Via del Municipio 1 (✆ **091-8112690**), is open Monday through Friday from 7:30am to 2:45pm.

EXPLORING THE TOWN

Duomo   Largely rebuilt in the 17th century, this cathedral has been much modified over the years. Its facade, which dates mainly from 1912, was designed to fit a quartet of early-16th-century statues (the present ones are copies). Inside are some treasures, most notably 18th-century sculptures including an 1842 marble relief, *Madonna del Ponte* ⊛, found in the fourth chapel on the right. In the Chapel of San Bartolomeo, look for an elaborate **Venetian rococo sedan chair,** and in the chapel dedicated to the Immaculate Conception, seek out the **wooden statue** by Quattrocchi from 1799. The *Crucifix* at the main altar was painted on both sides by Pietro Ruzzolone in 1484.

Piazza del Duomo. No phone. Free admission. Daily 9am–7pm.

Museo Civico ⊛   Founded in 1873 in an abandoned 14th-century palazzo, this is one of the finest regional museums along Sicily's northern coast. A visit here is like taking a class in the art, archaeology, and natural history of the area.

⌒Moments Palms, Pines, Ficus & Roman Remains

In back of the cathedral, Via Belvedere leads up to a panoramic terrace offering one of the **grandest seascapes** ⊛⊛ along the Tyrrhenian coast. The sea is set against the backdrop of Monte Calógero. From here, you'll also have a vista of the lower town and the port. Try not to let the industrialization spoil this otherwise idyllic vision for you. A short walk to your left leads to the "always locked" church dedicated to **Santa Caterina d'Alessandria** in the 14th century. Continue along at this point to the park, **Villa Palmieri,** laid out in 1845. Here you will see the ruins of an ancient Roman curia. Follow Via Anfiteatro from the park to the ruins of a **Roman amphitheater** from the 1st century A.D.

Prehistory is even represented, with displays of artifacts recovered from nearby caves inhabited in Paleolithic and Neolithic times. The most precious relics are those removed from the ruins of Himera, including the **head of a lion** ✱ that came from the Temple of Victory between 480 and 460 B.C. A large stone slab with Arabic inscriptions may have been mounted over the gates of Termini Imerese during the days of its Saracen rule. You can also see mosaics, sarcophagi, and even the lead pipes used by the Romans for their plumbing (the lead eventually poisoned them). Look for a Byzantine triptych and paintings by Mattia Preti, pupil of Caravaggio. A most impressive triptych, *Madonna and Saints* ✱, is by Gaspare da Pesaro from 1453.

Via del Museo Civico. ✆ **091-8128279.** Free admission. Tues–Sat 9am–1pm and 4–6:30pm; Sun 9am–1pm.

WHERE TO STAY

Grand Hotel delle Terme ✱ This 19th-century hotel stands right over the spring whose famous waters won an endorsement from Plutarch. Even today you can enjoy the same curative waters as the Roman soldiers of yore: In the basement is a thermal spa that offers such treatments as mud therapy. The hotel offers modernized rooms with traditional furnishings, mostly in teak. Half of the guest rooms come with bathrooms with tubs, the other half bathrooms with showers; suites have Jacuzzis. The place is located in the commercial center of the lower town near the port.

Piazza delle Terme 2, 90018 Termini Imerese. ✆ **091-8113557.** Fax 091-8113107. 69 units. 63€–75€ ($76–$90) double; suite 38€ ($46) extra. AE, DC, MC, V. **Amenities:** Restaurant; bar; outdoor pool; gym; spa; sauna; salon; room service; massage; laundry service; dry cleaning. *In room:* A/C, TV, minibar, hair dryer.

WHERE TO DINE

Ristorante Pub Santi e Peccatori SICILIAN/SEAFOOD The best restaurant in town serves up tempting dishes for discriminating palates, often visitors from Palermo, who know of this place's charm and attractively priced cuisine. Sicilians claim that the waters of Termini Imerese make the best pasta in Sicily, and they may be right: We still recall a memorable spaghetti marinara with shrimp, mussels, and—as an added surprise—pistachios. For a main course, we recommend the fresh fish of the day grilled with aromatic herbs.

In the Hotel Il Gabbiano, Via Libertà 221. ✆ **091-8113262.** Reservations not needed. Main courses 6€–12€ ($7.20–$14). AE, DC, MC, V. Wed–Mon noon–5pm and 8pm–4am.

EASY EXCURSIONS

You may opt to spend less time in Termini Imerese and more time in its environs, exploring two of the north coast's most impressive attractions: Himera and Cáccamo.

HIMERA This was the site of a 7th-century Greek settlement, 15km (8 miles) east along the coast. It's famous for the remains of the **Tempio della Vittoria (Temple of Victory)** ✱, situated on a coastal plain at the mouth of the Imera River off route SS113. Frankly, these ruins are not as impressive as those of Solunto outside Palermo (p. 120), but they're worth an hour or so of your time.

In 480 B.C., Himera was the site of one of the major battles of Sicily. The Greeks had settled in the east, the Carthaginians in the west. The Greeks from Agrigento and Syracuse defeated a massive army led by Hamilcar, who was killed in battle. The Tempio della Vittoria was constructed to honor this Greek victory; the labor was supplied by the Carthaginians taken prisoner. The triumph was short-lived, however. In 409 B.C., Hamilcar's nephew, Hannibal, attacked Himera in revenge for his uncle's death. He razed the city, killing most of its inhabitants.

Himera's temple contains little more than its foundation, with no standing columns. Yet the setting and the view make it worth a visit, especially if you have the imagination to bring it alive. If your imagination fails you, you can visit a modern antiquarium that shows diagrams of how the temple looked in its heyday. The remains of two other temples are also found in this archaeological park.

To get to the temple site from Termini Imerese, you can take one of four daily buses run by **Nancini** (© **091-8144497**); the round-trip costs 3.50€ ($4.20). Buses depart from the train station at Termini Imerese. The site charges admission of 2€ ($2.40). It's open Monday through Saturday from 9am until 1 hour before sunset, Sunday from 9am to 1pm. For information, call © **091-8140128.**

CÁCCAMO   The Middle Ages live on at **Castello Cáccamo** ✪, a huge 12th-century fortress overlooking the San Leonardo River Valley. This is the greatest fortress in Sicily and one of the most majestic in all of southern Italy. Dominating the tranquil village of Cáccamo, the feudal castle was built by the Normans on the site of an older Saracen fortress. The entrance is from Via Termitana on a rocky spur.

With its massive towers and battlements, the gray stone castle looks like something Disney might have created, but it's the real thing. It has some 130 rooms, its most impressive being **Sala della Congiura.** You can visit the theater hall, the court chapel, the 17th-century residence of various lords, the gatehouse, the knight's house, the keep, and the guard tower as well as the ramp wall. The castle is rather bare-bones inside, but worth seeing is the **panoramic view** ✪ from the tower, **Torre Mastra.**

Castello Cáccamo, on Corso Umberto (© **091-8103248**), is 12km (8 miles) south of Termini Imerese and 52km (32 miles) southeast of Palermo. If you're taking the Palermo–Catania autostrada, the exit for Cáccamo is signposted, 10km (6 miles) to the south. Buses bound for Cáccamo leave throughout the day from Termini Imerese's main train station. The castle is open daily from 9am to 1pm and 3 to 7pm. Admission is 2€ ($2.40) for adults, free for children under 18.

Don't get your hopes up if you're hungry: Restaurants at Cáccamo are very limited. The finest dining choice in town is **A Castellana,** Piazza Caduti 4 (© **091-8148667**), located in the stables of the castle and serving up hearty, affordable Sicilian fare. The pastas are the best, with more than a dozen varieties prepared fresh every day. The chefs also make 55 different pizzas.

After you visit the castle, take an hour to walk around the medieval village. The highlight is the main square, **Piazza Duomo** ✪, built on two different levels. The higher part contains a spectacular complex of structures, including the 17th-century **Palazzo del Monte di Pietà,** flanked on the right by **Chiesa delle Anime Sante del Purgatorio** and on the left by **Oratorio del Santissimo Sacramento.** The whole square looks like a stage set.

On the western side of the square is the town's most interesting church, **Chiesa Madre,** open Monday through Saturday from 8am to 1pm. Dating from 1090, it was largely rebuilt in the 1400s and given a heavily baroque overlay centuries later. The church contains some treasures, including a painting from 1641 by Mattia Stomer, called the *Miracle of Sant'Isidoro Agricola.*

For information, contact the **Ufficio Turismo del Commune di Cáccamo,** Piazza Duomo (© **091-8103248**). It's open in July and August, Monday through Friday from 7:30am to 2pm, Tuesday through Thursday from 3 to 6pm; and from September to June, Tuesday through Friday from 8am to 2pm, Tuesday and Thursday from 3 to 6pm.

7

The Aeolian Islands

The Aeolian Islands *(Isole Eolie o Lipari)* have been inhabited for more than 3,000 years, in spite of volcanic activity that even now causes the earth to issue forth sulfuric belches, streams of molten lava, and hissing clouds of steam. **Lipari** (36 sq. km/14 sq. miles) is the largest and most developed island, **Stromboli** (13 sq. km/5 sq. miles) is the most distant and volcanically active, and **Vulcano** (21 sq. km/8 sq. miles), with its brooding, potentially volatile cone and therapeutic mud baths, is the island closest to the Sicilian "mainland." The remaining islands (**Salina, Filicudi, Alicudi,** and **Panarea**) offer only bare-bones facilities and are visited mainly by day-trippers, if at all.

Despite the potential for volcanic activity, the area attracts visitors (mainly Germans and Italians) thanks to its crystalline waters that offer prime snorkeling, diving, and spearfishing, and its photogenic beaches composed of hot black sand and rocky outcroppings jutting into the Tyrrhenian Sea. The volcanoes themselves offer hikers the thrill of peering into a bubbling crater.

Ancient Greek sailors believed that these seven windswept islands were the home of Aeolus, god of the winds. He supposedly lived in a cave on Vulcano, keeping the winds of the world in a bag to be opened only with great caution. "All the winds of the world" do seem to converge here at times. Until tourists began to arrive, the Aeolian Islands were one tough place to make a living. Many of its inhabitants long ago emigrated to a better life in the United States or Australia; even today, the islands remain sparsely populated.

Because of frequent ferry and hydrofoil service, the Aeolian Islands are easy to reach from the Sicilian mainland. The conquering hordes descend here in summer, with much overcrowding because of limited accommodations (hence, reservations are important). We prefer the less crowded times of late May, early June, and September. We've also made several winter visits, when most tourist businesses are closed and the island is sometimes bathed in brilliant sunshine. At other times the winds blow furiously, and the islands can be lashed by storms, especially between October and March. The sea can be so turbulent that ferry and hydrofoil service to mainland Sicily is suspended, and you may find yourself stranded.

GETTING THERE Ferries and hydrofoils service all of the Aeolian Islands from the port of Milazzo, on the northeastern coast of Sicily 32km (20 miles) west of Messina. Both **Società Siremar,** Via Dei Mille (✆ **090-9283242;** www.siremar.it), and **Ustica Lines,** Via Rizzo (✆ **090-9287821;** www.usticalines.it), operate ferry and hydrofoil routes.

The Milazzo–Vulcano–Lipari–Salina ferry lines leave Milazzo four to six times daily from 7am to 6:30pm. It takes 1½ hours to reach Vulcano; a one-way ticket costs 5.95€ ($7.15). Lipari is 2 hours from Milazzo; a one-way ticket costs 7.50€ ($9). To reach Stromboli, take the Milazzo–Panarea–Stromboli ferry line, departing

The Aeolian Islands

Milazzo at 7am Tuesday through Saturday, and at 2:30pm Monday, Wednesday, Thursday, Saturday, and Sunday. The Stromboli trip takes 5 hours and costs 11€ ($13) one-way.

For a faster option, take the Milazzo–Vulcano–Lipari–Salina hydrofoil line, which reaches Vulcano in 30 minutes; a one-way ticket costs 12€ ($14). It takes 1 hour to reach Lipari and costs 12€ ($14) one-way. Siremar makes the trip 6 to 12 times daily from 6:05am to 7pm, while Ustica Lines makes six runs daily from 7:30am to 7pm. To reach Stromboli, use the Milazzo–Panarea–Stromboli hydrofoil line, which takes 2½ hours and costs 17€ ($20) one-way.

For more information on ferry and hydrofoil connections, call ℂ **081-3172999** or ℂ **199-123199** (within Italy only).

If you're driving from Messina in the east, take S113 west to Palermo until you come to the turnoff for the port at Milazzo.

1 Lipari ✸✸

37km (23 miles) N of Milazzo, 41km (25 miles) W of Messina

Homer called it "a floating island, a wall of bronze and splendid smooth sheer cliffs." The offspring of seven volcanic eruptions, Lipari is the largest of the Aeolians and is also the name of the island's only real town. It's the administrative headquarters of the Aeolians (except autonomous Salina). The town sits on a plateau of red volcanic rock on the southeastern shore, framed by two beaches: **Marina Lunga,** which functions as the harbor, and **Marina Corta.**

Nearly all activity is centered in Lipari town, which contains the largest concentration of tourist facilities in all of the Aeolian Islands, and as such makes the best base for exploring the entire archipelago. There are also four other villages, including **Canneto,** which is only 2km (1¼ miles) north of Lipari town. **Acquacalda** is found on the northern tip of the island. Inland and to its southwest is **Quattropani.** If you're heading southeast from Quattropani back to Lipari town, you'll pass through the small town of **Pianoconte.**

Marina Lunga and Marina Corta lie on either side of the *castello,* or cliff-top citadel, still surrounded by walls built in the 1500s for defensive purposes. Inside these walls are the Duomo, the archaeological museum (the major sight on the island), and two decaying baroque churches.

The major artery of Lipari town, **Corso Vittorio Emanuele,** goes north-south and is the site of most of the businesses catering to visitors, including bars, banks, and trattorie.

ESSENTIALS

GETTING AROUND   Ferries from Milazzo dock at the deep-water port of Marina Lunga, while hydrofoils pull in at Marina Corta. Much of what there is to see, aside from the island's scenic wonders, lies between these two small ports. Lipari is serviced by a limited bus network.

Buses leave from Marina Lunga about every hour (more frequently in summer), taking you across the island. No point on the island is less than a half-hour ride away. A bus schedule is available at **Urso Guglielmo,** Via Cappuccini 9 (© **090-9811262**), above Marina Lunga. Tickets cost 1.55€ ($1.85) and can be purchased onboard from the driver. Urso buses also operate tours of the island from July to September. Three buses at a time leave at 9:30am, 11:30am, and 5pm, costing 3.70€ ($4.45) for the circuit. Along the way you'll pass the highlights of Lipari's scenery. It's also possible to summon one of the independently operated taxis, most of which are found at Marina Corta.

A final transportation option is to rent a bike (10€/$12 daily) or motor scooter (15€/$18 daily, not including fuel). A security deposit is required: either a large sum, a credit card, or a passport. Two rental outlets are **Da Marcello,** Via Sottomonastero, Marina Lunga (© **090-9811234**); and **Da Tullio,** Via Amendola 22, Marina Lunga (© **090-9880540**).

VISITOR INFORMATION   The **tourist office** in Lipari is at Via Vittorio Emanuele 202 (© **090-9880095**). In July and August, it's open daily from 8am to 2pm, plus Monday through Saturday from 4:30 to 10pm. From September to June, hours are Monday through Friday from 8am to 2pm and 4:30 to 7:30pm, Saturday from 8am to 2pm.

FAST FACTS   **Ferry** and **hydrofoil** tickets are available at Siremar offices at Via Mariano Amendola, Marina Lunga (© **090-9811312**), and at the Terminal Aliscafi, Marina Corta (© **090-9812200**). Hours are Monday through Friday from 9am to 1pm and 4:30 to 7:30pm. The two major **pharmacies** are Farmacia Morsillo, Via Marina Garibaldi 72 (© **090-9811428**), and Meccio Giuseppe, Via Roma Alicudi (© **090-9889689**). For a **hospital** emergency, call © **090-983040;** for **first aid,** © **090-9885267.** For the local *Carabinieri* (army police corps), call © **090-9811333.** The **post office** is at Corso Vittorio Emanuele 207 (© **090/9810051**); open Monday through Friday from 8am to 6:30pm and Saturday from 8am to 12:30pm. For Internet access, go to **Net Cafe,**

LIPARI

Acquacalda **6**
Canneto **2**
Cave di Pomice **3**
Lipari **1**
M. Chirica **8**
M. Pilato **9**
Pianoconte **10**
Porticello **4**
Quattropani **7**
Rocche Rossi **5**

VULCANO

Gelso **14**
Gran Cratere **13**
Porto di Levante **12**
Porto di Ponente **11**

Via Garibaldi 61 (℗ **090-9813527**), which charges 3.50€ ($4.20) per half hour. The major bank is **Banca Monte dei Paschi di Siena,** Via Vittorio Emanuele 209 (℗ **090-9880432**), which has an on-site ATM available 24 hours.

EXPLORING THE ISLAND
CITADEL/UPPER TOWN

Most of the man-made sights of Lipari are centered in this citadel area surrounded by the walls of Lipari's castle. The *castello,* or what remains of it, dates from the 16th century, when it was constructed by the Spaniards. The citadel is approached by heading up Via Garibaldi.

You must traverse long steps cut through thick walls to reach the Upper Town. Part of the area here is an archaeological park (see below), where stratified clues about civilizations dating back to 1700 B.C. have been unearthed. From these ruins, archaeologists have learned much about settlements in other Mediterranean cultures.

Take the steps at Via del Concordato to climb to the **Cattedrale di San Bartolomeo,** which replaced an earlier Norman cathedral destroyed by Barbarossa on his killing rampage in 1544. A Benedictine cloister from the 1100s is all that remains from Redbeard's assault on the cathedral. Today, the cathedral lies behind an impressive baroque facade and is dedicated to St. Bartolomew. A silver statue of the saint, dating from 1728, can be found in the northern transept. The church is open daily from 9am to 1pm.

To the south of the Duomo is the **Parco Archeologico,** its stones going as far back as Neolithic times. You can view Greek and Roman burial grounds here, along with a contemporary Greek-style theater where concerts and ancient plays are performed in July and September (see the tourist office for details). Major finds dug up here are displayed in the archaeological museum (see below). Parco Archeologico is open from April to September, Monday through Saturday from 9am to 7pm; off season, daily from 9am to 4pm. Admission is free.

Museo Archeologico Eoliano 🎭🎭 This is one of southern Italy's greatest archaeological museums, housing one of the world's finest Neolithic collections. It's divided into two buildings: One lies just south of the cathedral in the 17th-century **Palazzo Vescovile,** or bishop's palace, and contains Neolithic and Bronze Age exhibits. The other, the **Sezione Classica,** is on the south side of the Duomo and focuses on the classical and Hellenic periods.

The collection is laid out chronologically, beginning with the Neolithic to Bronze Age discoveries unearthed nearby. You'll see lustrous red ceramics, known as the "Diana style," from 3000 to 2500 B.C.; a display of obsidian, the glasslike black volcanic rock that was crafted into blades used throughout the ancient world before it was eventually replaced by metal; and the only Late Bronze Age (8th c. B.C.) necropolis found in Sicily.

Over in the Sezione Classica section is a rich array of classical and Hellenic artifacts, many dug up in the nearby necropolis. Particularly noteworthy are **burial urns** from Milazzo; archaeologists discovered that in the 11th century B.C., Lipari islanders buried bodies in fetal positions in large jars. The upper level holds a stunning collection of **decorated vases** 🎭🎭, many from the ancient Roman site of Paestum, that depict gods and goddesses, satyrs and courtiers, and scenes of daily life in ancient times. The museum also contains the world's greatest collection of **theatrical masks** 🎭🎭🎭, unearthed in tombs from the 4th century to the 3rd century B.C. Those gruesome grins on the masks of Hercules and Hades will haunt your dreams.

The final and least interesting section of the museum is the **Sezione Epigrafica,** in a smaller adjoining building. It displays engraved stones and the remains of several Greek and Roman burial tombs.

Via del Castello. ✆ **090-9880174.** Admission 4.50€ ($5.40) adults, free for children under 18. Daily 9am–1:30pm and 3–7pm.

LOWER TOWN

After visiting the enclosed citadel, you will have seen the best of Lipari town. The only sight of interest in the lower town is the **Parco Archeologico Contrada Diana,** west of Corso Vittorio Emanuele, the main street. Here you can see the remains of Greek walls dating from the 5th and 4th centuries B.C., as well as the ruins of several Roman villas. Ancient tombstones reveal an eerie necropolis from classical days. The burial grounds are visible off Via Marconi. The park is usually locked, so you can only stroll by and look in. Any major finds discovered here are housed in the archaeological museum in the Upper Town.

AROUND THE ISLAND

Twenty-nine kilometers (18 miles) of road circle the island, connecting all of its villages and attractions. Buses run by **Urso Guglielmo,** Via Cappuccini (✆ **090-9811262**), make 10 circuits of the island per day. The trip to the little towns of Quattropani and Acquacalda, on the north coast, costs 1.55€ ($1.85). Closer destinations cost 1.30€ ($1.55). Buses leave Lipari town from Marina Lunga, opposite the service station.

The major destination is the little town of **Canneto,** 2km (1¼ miles) away, where the best beaches are found. Canneto can be reached by bus or a 30-minute walk. It's on the eastern coast of the island, directly to the north of Lipari town. Just north of Canneto is **Spiaggia Bianca,** named for the white sand that was originally found here, although today it's rather grayish. White sand is an oddity here—the rest of the island's beaches are predominantly black volcanic sand. To reach the beach from Canneto, take the waterfront road, climbing the stairs along Via Marina Garibaldi, then veering right down a narrow cobbled path for 297m (974 ft.). Other than its beaches, nothing in Canneto need detain you.

Buses run north of Canneto, passing the **Cave di Pomice** at Campobianco, located between Spiaggia Bianca and Porticello. Other than tourism, pumice is the principal industry of Lipari. Pumice is used for everything from a building material to an ingredient in toothpaste. Some daring visitors slide down a pumice chute directly into the waters along the north coast.

From Cave di Pomice, you can see **Mount Pilato,** at 476m (1,562 ft.). This is the ancient crater of a volcano that last erupted in A.D. 700. Fields around this crater are the source of the pumice. You can walk to the crater, passing through barren fields locals call *Rocce Rosse,* or the "red rocks," because of the hue of the stone. A path leading to the crater from the northern tip of Campobianco stretches for 1.2km (¾ mile).

The bus stops in the village of **Porticello,** which has a beach. We suggest you avoid it, however, as it's rocky and not very special. If you do stop here, the most rewarding feature is the **panoramic view** ★★ of the other Aeolian Islands such as Alicudi, Filicudi, and Salina.

The island's northernmost little town is **Acquacalda,** or "hot water," a settlement known for its obsidian and pumice quarries. But few people go to the black-sand beaches here because they're rocky and there's also no shade. Acquacalda itself is virtually a one-street town with some snack bars and waterfront dives.

The bus moves along the northern tier of Lipari and then heads southwest to the little town of **Quattropani,** which is to the west of Mount Chirica at 602m (1,975 ft.). In the town, you can make a steep climb to **Duomo de Chiesa Baraca,** where the point of interest is most definitely not the "cathedral," but the **panoramic view** ★ from the grounds of the church. The distance between Quattropani and Acquacalda is 5km (3 miles); some hikers prefer to traverse this route on foot, enjoying scenic vistas at every turn.

There is yet another grand view to be enjoyed before leaving Lipari. West of Lipari town, and reached by buses departing from Marina Lunga, is a lookout point at **Quattrocchi** ("four eyes"). It's 4km (2½ miles) from Lipari town. Once at Quattrocchi, you can make the steep climb to **Quattrocchi Belvedere,** which will reward you with one of the most **panoramic vistas** ★★ in the Aeolian Islands.

WHERE TO STAY
EXPENSIVE
Gattopardo Park Hotel ★★   Set in an 18th-century villa and enveloped by white bungalows, this is the island's most architecturally interesting hotel. In comfort, it also ranks among the top choices on the island. Spacious terraces opening onto scenic views are yet another allure. The hotel provides free minibus service to some of the best beaches on the island, although there's also free swimming from the rocks in a bay nearby. For Aeolian style, this place is unbeatable, with beautifully planted grounds, tiled floors, and wood-beamed ceilings. The furnishings are a blend of antique and modern, the rooms come with small

shower-only bathrooms, and the best units are some of the most comfortable in Lipari. The dining and drinking facilities are among the island's best.

Vico Diana, 98055 Lipari. © **090-9811035.** Fax 090-9880207. www.gattopardoparkhotel.it. 78 units. 112€–248€ ($134–$298) double. Rates include half-board. AE, DC, MC, V. Closed Nov–Feb. **Amenities:** Restaurant; bar; outdoor pool; room service; babysitting. *In room:* A/C, TV, hair dryer.

Giardino sul Mare ✿ This first-class option is only minutes from Marina Corta, opening onto the sea. It's a real Mediterranean resort hotel, with covered terraces for dining and a smallish pool surrounded by chaise longues and umbrellas. Guest rooms are well tended and comfortably furnished, with small shower-only bathrooms. Many European guests spend all their vacation time here except for an occasional island trip. The drinking and dining facilities equal those found at Villa Meligunis.

Via Maddalena 65, 98055 Lipari. © **090-9811004.** Fax 090-9880150. www.netnet.it/conti. 46 units. 60€–140€ ($72–$168) double. Rates include breakfast. AE, DC, MC, V. Closed Oct 30–Mar 21. **Amenities:** Restaurant; bar; outdoor pool; 24-hr. room service; babysitting; laundry service; dry cleaning; rooms for those w/limited mobility. *In room:* A/C, TV, dataport, hair dryer, safe.

Hotel Carasco This hotel enjoys the most dramatic location in Lipari, with its own private stretch of rocks opening onto the water and panoramic views from a bougainvillea-draped pool. The Carasco consists of two buildings that sit on a lonely bluff by the sea. The cool interior, with its terra-cotta floors and dark-wood furniture, contrasts with the bright heat of the outdoors. Each comfortable, well-furnished guest room comes with a ceiling fan, rustic artifacts, and a bathroom with shower or tub; ask for a room with a private balcony. Grace notes include an afternoon tea service and piano music in the lounge after dinner. *Note:* Although citing the beauty of the location, some readers have complained about the food and the service.

Porto delle Genti, 98055 Lipari. © **090-9811605.** Fax 090-9811828. www.carasco.it. 89 units. Half board 70€–120€ ($84–$144) per person. Children under 14 stay free in parent's room. AE, DC, MC, V. Closed Oct 13 to Easter. **Amenities:** Restaurant; bar; outdoor pool; 24-hr. room service; babysitting; laundry service; dry cleaning; all nonsmoking rooms. *In room:* A/C, dataport, minibar, hair dryer.

Villa Meligunis ✿✿ This first-class hotel is as good as it gets in the Aeolian Islands. Less than 45m (148 ft.) from the ferry docks, the appealingly contemporary villa rose from a cluster of 17th-century fishermen's cottages at Marina Corta. It oozes stylish charm, from its lovely fountain to its dramatic rooftop terrace to its wrought-iron bedsteads used by fashion photographers as backdrops. Guest rooms are comfortably furnished with summery pieces and well-maintained bathrooms with either tub or shower. The restaurant serves excellent regional specialties.

Via Marte 7, 98055 Lipari. © **090-9812426.** Fax 090-9880149. www.villameligunis.it. 32 units. 120€–290€ ($144–$348) double; 195€–365€ ($234–$438) suite. Rates include breakfast. AE, DC, MC, V. Free parking. **Amenities:** Restaurant; 2 bars; outdoor pool; 24-hr. room service; babysitting; laundry service; dry cleaning; nonsmoking rooms. *In room:* A/C, TV, dataport, minibar, hair dryer, safe.

MODERATE

Hotel Oriente ✿ Located in the historic center of Lipari town, this hotel is only steps from the archaeological park and 300m (984 ft.) from the port. On a hot day, its shady terrace is one of the best places to be on the island. The interior is like a museum—it's stuffed with knickknacks and artifacts made from wrought iron. The rooms are light and airy, with small tiled bathrooms that have hydromassage showers. A generous breakfast is served in the garden amid bougainvillea and citrus blossoms.

Via Marconi 35, 98055 Lipari. ⓒ **090-9811493.** Fax 090-9880198. www.hotelorientelipari.com. 32 units. 60€–130€ ($72–$156) double; 85€–170€ ($102–$204) triple; 110€–210€ ($132–$252) quad. AE, DC, MC, V. Closed Oct 30–Mar 30. **Amenities:** Bar; room service; babysitting; laundry service; dry cleaning. *In room:* A/C, TV, minibar, hair dryer, safe.

Hotel Poseidon   A favorite with scuba divers as well as discerning travelers in general, this well-run hotel lies off the main street, just 100m (328 ft.) from the sea, with guest rooms opening onto an inviting courtyard. Diving instruction can be arranged, as can equipment rentals, cylinder refills, and guided underwater trips. There is a fresh, breezy Mediterranean feel to this place. The guest rooms are well maintained, with wicker decorations and small tiled bathrooms with showers.

Vico Ausonia 7, 98055 Lipari. ⓒ **090-9812876.** Fax 090-9813295. www.hotelposeidonlipari.com. 18 units. 75€–150€ ($90–$180) double; 100€–190€ ($120–$228) triple. Rates include breakfast. AE, DC, MC, V. Closed Nov 15–Feb 28. **Amenities:** Bar; 24-hr. room service; babysitting; laundry service; dry cleaning; nonsmoking rooms. *In room:* A/C, TV, minibar, hair dryer, safe.

Villa Augustus ⭐ *(Finds*   Set in the historic center, close to the port, this hotel is surrounded by luxuriant gardens with a dramatic roof terrace overlooking the sea. It's just 100m (328 ft.) above the main harbor and 2km (1¼ miles) from the whitish beaches north near the pumice quarries. The hotel is reached along a narrow island road and relatively hidden from the street. Rooms are attractively furnished; preferred, of course, are those with a balcony or terrace. Each unit has a small tiled bathroom with either tub or shower. Attractive features include a reading room, a piano bar, and a solarium.

Vico Ausonia 16, 98055 Lipari. ⓒ **090-9811232.** Fax 090-9812233. www.villaaugustus.it. 35 units. 100€–170€ ($120–$204) double. Rates include breakfast. Closed Nov 1–Feb 28. **Amenities:** Restaurant; 2 bars; room service (7am-10pm); babysitting; laundry service; dry cleaning; solarium. *In room:* A/C, TV, hair dryer.

AT CANNETO

Casajanca ⭐ *(Finds*   It looks like a private home, and for good reason: Before it was converted into this little inn, Casajanca was the home of Ruccio Carbone, a native son who was celebrated as "the poet" of the Aeolian Islands. Rooms are little more than basic, motel-like accommodations, with small, shower-only bathrooms, but there is reasonable comfort here. Furnishings mix contemporary pieces with the occasional antique. The little garden is studded with tropical plantings and tables and chairs. The friendly owners provide a grand welcome to what they call "the inn of everlasting love."

Marina Garibaldi 115, Canneto (Lipari). ⓒ **090-9880222.** Fax 090-9813003. www.casajanca.it. 10 units. 102€–180€ ($122–$216) double; 133€–233€ ($160–$280) triple. Rates include breakfast. AE, DC, MC, V. **Amenities:** Bar; 24-hr. room service. *In room:* A/C, TV, minibar, safe.

WHERE TO DINE

E Pulera ⭐⭐ SICILIAN/AEOLIAN   Owned by the same family that runs the Filippino (see below), this restaurant emphasizes its Aeolian origins. Artifacts and maps of the islands fashioned from ceramic tiles are scattered about. Some tables occupy a terrace with a view of a flowering lawn. Specialties include a delightful version of fishermen's soup, swordfish ragout, and risotto with squid in its own ink. We had one of the most delightful pasta dishes we've ever tasted in the Aeolian Islands: fettuccine with yellow pumpkin, shrimp, and wild fennel.

Via Isabella Vainiches. ⓒ **090-9811158.** Reservations recommended. Main courses 10€–13€ ($12–$16). DC, MC, V. Daily 8pm–midnight. Closed Oct–May 15.

Filippino ★★ SICILIAN/AEOLIAN   It's a pleasant surprise to find such a fine restaurant in such a remote location. Filippino has thrived in the heart of town, near the town hall, since 1910. You'll dine in one of two large rooms or on a terrace ringed with flowering shrubs and potted plants. Menu items are based on old-fashioned Sicilian recipes and prepared with flair. The chef's signature pasta dish is "Aeolian orchids," a curly pasta topped with tomatoes, pine nuts, capers, garlic, basil, mint, and pecorino cheese. We especially enjoyed the swordfish with basil and the eggplant caponata.

Piazza Mazzini. ℃ 090-9811002. Reservations required July–Aug. Main courses 6€–10€ ($7.20–$12). AE, DC, MC, V. Daily noon–2:30pm and 7:30–10:30pm. Closed Mon Oct–Mar.

La Nassa ★ (Finds) SICILIAN/AEOLIAN   At this enchanting restaurant, the delectable cuisine of Donna Teresa matches the friendly enthusiasm of her son Bartolo, who has thousands of interesting stories to tell. The food is the most genuine on the island, prepared with respect for both old traditions and modern tastes. After the *sette perle* ("seven pearl") appetizer, a combination of fresh fish, sweet shrimp, and spices, you can try your choice of fish, cooked to your specifications. Local favorites include *sarago, cernia,* and *dentice,* as delicate in texture as their names are untranslatable. For dessert, try cookies with Malvasia wine.

Via G. Franza 41. ℃ 090-9811319. Reservations recommended. Main courses 8€–18€ ($9.60–$22). AE, MC, V. Apr–June Fri–Wed 8:30am–3pm and 6pm–midnight; July–Oct daily 8:30am–3pm and 6pm–midnight. Closed Nov–Easter.

Ristorante Pizzeria Pescecane (Value) SICILIAN/AEOLIAN   The oldest restaurant on the island is a warm, rustic place located right on the main street of town. It offers tables both inside and out on a terrace. The pastas are savory, especially those made with freshly caught seafood. *Lipparata* is the most regional pasta dish, prepared with capers, olives, anchovies, and tomatoes. Pizzas are also good, especially the Desirée, made with mozzarella, fresh tomato, and ham.

Via Vittorio Emanuele 249. ℃ 090-9812706. Reservations recommended. Main courses 5€–10€ ($6–$12); fixed-price menu 15€ ($18). AE, DC, MC, V. Daily 10:30am–3pm and 6pm–midnight. Closed Nov 1–Dec 31.

LIPARI AFTER DARK

On a summer night, most of the scantily clad visitors congregate around one of the bars with outdoor tables at Marina Corta. The early evening begins at the **Net Cafe,** Via Garibaldi 61 (℃ **090-9813527**), where people come not only to surf the Web, but also to enjoy drinks and burgers, the big-screen TV, and a beautiful garden. **Turmalin** (℃ **090-9811588**) is a summer dance club off Piazza Municipio near the castle. May through August, it's open nightly from 11pm to 6am, charging a cover of 15€ ($18).

Otherwise, nightlife consists of bars and more bars. One of the best is **Rusticheria Vecchia Lipari,** Corso Vittorio Emanuele 46 (℃ **090-9812521**), in the center of town. It offers classic snacks such as *arancini,* little balls of fried rice filled with minced meat and tomato sauce. But it's mainly a pub attracting visitors from 18 to 50. From May to August, hours are 9am to 3am (off season until midnight). Both live and recorded music are featured at **Chitarra Bar,** 5 Salita San Giuseppe (℃ **090-9811554**), drawing a young to middle-aged crowd. In summer, it's open daily from 7pm to 4am (until midnight in winter). It shuts down completely in January and February. A hard-drinking place, **Bar Caffè La Vela,** 2 Piazza San Onofrio (℃ **090-9880064**), is open 24 hours a day in summer, daily from 7am to midnight off season.

2 Vulcano (★(★(★

55km (34 miles) NW of Milazzo, 18km (11 miles) NW of Lipari

Vulcano, the ancient Thermessa, figured heavily in the mythologies of the region. The island was thought to be not only the home of Vulcan but also the gateway to Hades; Ulysses even stopped here in Homer's *Odyssey,* further delaying his return home to Ithaca. Thucydides, Siculus, and Aristotle each recorded eruptions. Other dormant volcanoes (including Vulcano Piano and Vulcanello) exist on the island, but a climb to the rim of the active **Gran Cratere (Big Crater),** or Vulcano della Fosse, draws the most attention. It hasn't erupted since 1890, but one look inside the sulfur-belching hole makes you understand how it inspired the hellish legends surrounding it. The 418m (1,372-ft.) peak is an easier climb than the one on Stromboli, taking just about an hour—though it's just as hot, and the same precautions prevail.

For centuries, the island was uninhabited because of fear of the volcano. Today, however, Vulcano is a stamping ground of the party crowd. Rich Italians from the mainland have erected fancy villas here as second homes. Vulcano's thermal baths, known for their curative powers and said to be especially helpful in relieving rheumatic suffering, also draw visitors.

The Romans had a small colony here, but the Bourbon rulers paid more attention to Vulcano. Under their reign, the whole island became a working farm, with labor provided by convicts shipped over from Lipari. A Welshman, James Stevenson, tried to bring agriculture and vineyards to the island in the 19th century, but most of his efforts failed because of a violent volcanic eruption. The last such explosive action occurred in the years 1888 and 1890, after which the volcano fell silent.

Vulcano is the island closest to the Sicilian mainland. Ferries and hydrofoils stop here before going on to the other islands. If the wind is blowing in the right direction, you can smell the island's prevalent sulfurous fumes. Vulcano also has the best beaches in the Aeolians, if you don't find black volcanic sands off-putting.

ESSENTIALS

VISITOR INFORMATION   The **tourist office** is at Via Porto di Levante (② **090-9852028**), and operates only from June to September, when it's open daily from 8am to 2pm, Monday through Saturday from 4:30 to 10pm.

GETTING AROUND   Most people walk, but a private company, **Scaffidi** (② **090-9853017**), runs buses from the port area to Piano, a village in the southwestern interior of the island, and to Gelso, at the southern tip. Seven buses operate Monday through Saturday; two operate on Sunday. If you'd rather rent a bike or scooter, go to **Da Paolo,** Via Porto Levante (② **090-9852112**), open May through November daily from 8am to 8:30pm. Mountain bikes cost from 5€ to 10€ ($6–$12) per day; scooters range from 15€ to 40€ ($18–$48).

FAST FACTS   The **Banco di Sicilia,** Via Marina Garibaldi 152 (② **090-9811140**), has an ATM and keeps regular banking hours Monday through Friday. Money can also be exchanged at the **Thermessa Agency,** Via Porto Levante (② **090-9852230**), open daily from 6:30am to 8:30pm. You can purchase hydrofoil tickets here as well, or try **Siremar,** Via Roma 74 (② **090-986016**), for both hydrofoil and ferry tickets. For **medical services** from June to September, a doctor is on call at ② **090-9852220.** The island **pharmacy,** Bonarrigo, Via Favaloro 1 (② **090-9852244**), is open daily from 9am to 1pm and 7 to

9pm. The *Carabinieri* can be called at © **090-9852110.** The **post office** is on Via Piano, off Porto di Levante (© **090-9853143**).

EXPLORING THE ISLAND

It might be, as the ancients believed, the entrance to hell. Nonetheless, Vulcano is the most visited of the Aeolian Islands, no doubt because of its proximity to the Sicilian mainland. Only the late, great Fellini could have done justice to a film about visitors flocking here to bathe in the mud.

To reach these fabled mud baths, **Laghetti di Fanghi,** go to the docks and enter along Via Provinciale. Walk over to a 56m (183-ft.) high *faraglione,* or "stack": It's one massive pit of thick, sulfurous gunk that is said to greatly relieve certain skin diseases and rheumatic suffering. Be warned that the mud discolors everything from clothing to jewelry, which is one explanation for the prevalent nudity. In summer, expect to encounter muddy pools brimming with naked, package-tour Germans and other Europeans. Since the mud baths are also radioactive, you are warned not to stay in them for more than 10 to 15 minutes. The water from the sea bubbles up like a giant Jacuzzi nearby, and it's here that mud bathers wash off the gunk. Take care that you don't scald yourself while cleaning yourself off. The beach nearby isn't bad, but the aroma from the mud baths may have you holding your nose if you attempt to sunbathe here. The baths are open from Easter to October, daily from 6:30am to 8pm; admission is 1€ ($1.20).

You can, of course, skip this muddy cauldron altogether and head directly to the dramatic **Spiaggia Sabbie Nere (Black Sands Beach)** ☆, the finest in the archipelago. Regrettably, its black sand gets so hot by midday that flip-flops are a virtual necessity if you plan to while away your day here. This beach is on the distant side of the peninsula from Porto di Levante to Porto di Ponente; get here by going along Via Ponente. Porto di Ponente is a 20-minute walk north from the mud baths.

If you tire of the black sands, leave the beach and take the only road north, which leads to **Vulcanello,** at the northern tip. Locals call this a "volcanic pimple." It erupted from the sea in 183 B.C., spiking its way up through the earth to become a permanent fixture on the island's landscape. As late as 1888, this toylike volcano erupted a final time, creating what the islanders call a *Valle dei Mostri* ("valley of monsters") of bizarrely shaped lava fountains.

THE GRAN CRATERE ☆☆☆

To the south of Porto di Levante lies one of the greatest attractions in the Aeolians, the Gran Cratere. From Porto di Levante, follow Via Piano away from the sea for about 182m (597 ft.) until you see the first of the AL CRATERE signs. Once you do, follow the marked trail; allow 3 hours to make it there and back. *Tips:* This walk is unshaded, so go early in the morning or late in the day; load up on sunscreen and water; and wear sturdy hiking shoes.

Tips What's Where?

A knowledge of street names is worthless, really, because there are no street signs here. Not to worry—the locals who gather at the dock are friendly and experienced at giving directions to visitors, especially since all they ever have to point out are the paths to the crater, the mud baths, and the beach. Oh, and then there's the village center, a drab 1970s eyesore filled with souvenir shops and snack bars.

For your trouble in making this steep, hot climb, you'll be rewarded with **dramatic views** ⚑⚑ of some of the other Aeolian Islands. As you near the mouth of the crater, you see rivulets caused by previous eruptions. At the rim, peer down into the mammoth crater itself. Vapor emissions still spew from the crater, whose lips measure 450m (1,476 ft.) in diameter. The steam is tainted with numerous toxins, so you may not want to hang out here for long.

SOUTH TO GELSO

Most of the tourist activity is concentrated in northern Vulcano, but an offbeat excursion can be made by taking a bus that cuts inland to the remote, almost forgotten villages of **Piano** and **Gelso.** For details on the island buses, see "Getting Around," above.

Islanders who live inland are likely to reside in the remote village of Piano, 7km (4¼ miles) from the port. Piano lies between two peaks, **Mount Saraceno,** at 48m (157 ft.), and **La Sommata,** at 387m (1,270 ft.). There's not much here, and many of the homes are abandoned in the off season. If you continue on the bus to the southernmost village of Gelso, you can view the inland scenery of Vulcano along the way. At Gelso, the end of the line, you'll find some summer-only places to eat and good sea bathing. *Gelso* is Italian for "mulberry," one of the crops cultivated here along with capers.

The best beach is immediately east of Gelso. **Spiaggia dell'Asino** is a big cove reached by a steep path from the village of Gelso. Hydrocycles, deck chairs, and umbrellas can be rented from kiosks on the beach in summer.

Another little road goes to **Capo Grillo,** which has some of the best **panoramic views** ⚑⚑ on the island, with a sweeping vista of the Aeolians.

BOAT EXCURSIONS ON VULCANO

You can rent your own boat at **Centro Nautico Baia Levante,** Porto di Levante (✆ **090-9822197**). With a boat, you can visit the hamlet of Gelso and explore the caves and bays that riddle Vulcano's western shores. Rentals range in price from 120€ to 500€ ($144–$600) per day, fuel not included.

EXCURSIONS TO OTHER ISLANDS

If you'd like to use Vulcano as a base to visit other Aeolian Islands, excursions can be arranged through **Centro Nautico Baia Levante,** Porto di Levante (✆ **090-9822197**), open April through October daily from 8:30am to 8pm. Day excursions, which head for the islands of Lipari, Filicudi, Alicudi, and Salina, begin at 10am and last until 6pm. Because many options are available, the cost can range from 15€ to 80€ ($18–$96) per person. Night excursions begin at 6pm and end at midnight, with similar costs.

WHERE TO STAY

Hotel Conti ⚑   This is the second-best hotel on the island, surpassed only by Les Sables Noirs (see below). Just a few minutes' walk from the port where the hydrofoils and ferries pull in, the hotel opens onto the black sands of Ponente Bay. It's quite Aeolian in architecture, with luxuriant vegetation surrounding the main building and bungalows. Inside, you'll find cool tiled floors and dark wood furnishings. Guest rooms are simply though comfortably furnished, each with a private entrance opening onto the gardens and a small tiled bathroom with shower. The terraces, solarium, and restaurant (which serves excellent Aeolian specialties) all boast sea views.

Via Porto Ponente, 98050 Vulcano. ✆ **090-9852012.** Fax 090-9852064. www.netnet.it/conti. 67 units. 50€–90€ ($60–$108) double. Rates include half board. AE, DC, MC, V. Closed Oct 1–Apr 30. **Amenities:** Restaurant; bar; laundry service; dry cleaning. *In room:* TV, dataport, hair dryer, safe.

Hotel Eolian ★ *Value* This hotel opens onto Ponente Bay. In typical Aeolian style, the main building is surrounded by stucco bungalows and set in a lush garden studded with palms. None of the bungalows has a view of the water—that's reserved for the restaurant and bar—but most guests spend their days beside the sea anyway. Guest rooms are midsize and furnished in a minimalist style; each has a tiled bathroom with shower. Walk down from the terrace of the bar to reach the beach, where you can indulge in various watersports or rent a small boat to explore the more remote parts of the coastline. The thermal sulfurous pool is said to aid poor circulation.

Via Porto Levante, 98050 Vulcano. ✆ **090-9852151.** Fax 090-9852153. www.eolianhotel.com. 88 units. 124€–176€ ($149–$211) double. Rates include breakfast. 148€–214€ ($178–$257) per person with half board. AE, DC, MC, V. Closed Oct–Apr. **Amenities:** Restaurant; bar; 2 outdoor pools; tennis court; babysitting; laundry service; dry cleaning; nonsmoking rooms. *In room:* A/C, TV, dataport, minibar, hair dryer.

Les Sables Noirs ★★ Les Sables Noirs is the most elegant place to stay on Vulcano, offering a surprising level of luxury and excellent service in this remote outpost. Its rooms overlook a black-sand beach and front a panoramic sweep of the Bay of Ponente. The stucco and bamboo touches evoke a Caribbean resort. Accommodations are spacious, comfortably furnished, and decorated in typical Mediterranean style; many units open onto a wide balcony. All have tiled bathrooms, about half with showers and the rest with tubs. There's a solarium as well. Another reason to stay here is the restaurant, which serves impressive regional specialties and opens onto a broad terrace in front of the beach.

Via Porto di Ponente, 98050 Vulcano. ✆ **090-9850.** Fax 090-9852454. www.framonhotels.com. 48 units. 186€ ($223) double; 340€ ($408) suite. AE, DC, MC, V. Closed Oct–Mar. **Amenities:** Restaurant; 2 bars; outdoor pool; babysitting; laundry service; dry cleaning; nonsmoking rooms; solarium. *In room:* A/C, TV, dataport, minibar, hair dryer, safe.

WHERE TO DINE

Da Maurizio AEOLIAN/SICILIAN Known for its shady oasis of a garden and its good food, this local dive is decorated in a typical Aeolian style, with white walls, tile floors, and dark wooden tables. Most of the ingredients are shipped over from Sicily, although the fish is caught locally and some of the foodstuffs are grown on the island. Nothing is finer than the macaroni with lobster. Another superb pasta is made with spinach and served with fried zucchini. Seafood kabobs are also featured, made most often with swordfish or shrimp.

Via Porto di Levante. ✆ **090-9852426.** Reservations recommended. Main courses 8€–15€ ($9.60–$18); fixed-price menu 21€ ($25). AE, DC, MC, V. Daily noon–3pm and 7:30–11:30pm. Closed Nov 1 to the week before Easter.

Il Palmento AEOLIAN/SEAFOOD The terrace opening onto the beach is a potent lure, but so is the cuisine. Although the food never rises to the sublime, it's still good, hearty fare. There is an accurate and thorough understanding of flavor here, especially in the house specialty: spaghetti with chunks of lobster in a zesty tomato sauce. The fish soup with homemade croutons was the best we sampled in Vulcano, and that Sicilian classic, pasta with fresh sardines, was prepared admirably here, with tomato sauce, olive oil, pine nuts, and wild fennel.

Via Porto Levante. ✆ **090-9852552.** Reservations not needed. Main courses 6€–15€ ($7.20–$18); fixed-price menu 20€ ($24). MC, V. Daily noon–4pm and 6pm–12:30am. Closed Nov 1–Mar 30.

Ristorante Belvedere AEOLIAN/SICILIAN   We like to come here for the food, of course, but we also enjoy sitting out on the beautiful terrace with a view of some of the other Aeolian Islands. The seafood dishes are typically superb; we favor the catch of the day grilled with fresh herbs and a squeeze of lemon. Grilled Sicilian lamb is another savory treat. Our all-time favorite pasta here is the homemade ravioli stuffed with ricotta and spinach.

Via Reale 42. ℂ **090-9853047.** Reservations recommended. Main courses 5€–10€ ($6–$12). AE, DC, MC, V. Daily noon–2:30pm and 8pm–midnight. Closed Oct 1–Mar 30.

Vincenzino *Value* SICILIAN/AEOLIAN   This is the most appealing of the trattorie lurking near the ferry port. Known for its hefty portions and affordable prices, it serves clients in a rustic setting. You might begin your meal with spaghetti with crayfish, capers, and a tomato sauce. We're fond of the risotto *alla pescatora,* with crayfish, mussels, and other sea creatures. Another good choice is the house-style macaroni with ricotta, eggplant, tomatoes, and herbs. From October to March, the menu is limited to a simple array of platters from the bar.

Via Porto di Levante. ℂ **090-9852016.** Reservations recommended. Main courses 8€–10€ ($9.60–$12); fixed-price menu 15€ ($18). AE, DC, MC, V. Daily noon–3pm and 7–10pm.

VULCANO AFTER DARK

One of your best bets for a drink is **Ritrovo Remigio,** Porto di Levante, open daily from 6am to 2am. It offers terrace seating overlooking the port at Porto di Levante, where the ferries and hydrofoils from the mainland come in. In addition to its soothing cocktails, it serves excellent pastries and gelato.

The best nightlife—in fact, virtually the only nightlife—is found at **Cantine Stevenson** ⋆, Via Porto di Levante (ℂ **090-9853247**), the former wine cellars of James Stevenson, a virtual Renaissance man who did much to change the face of the island. Born in Wales, Stevenson's many interests led him to Vulcano, where he exported sulfur and pumice. In 1870, he purchased most of the island and planted the first vineyards. Here, in his former wine cellars, live music is featured nightly—whether folk, Sicilian, pop, rock, jazz, or blues—and more than 600 types of wine are sold. The old-style cantina, with seats outside in summer, is open April through September, daily from noon to 3am.

3 Stromboli ⋆⋆⋆

This is the most famous island of the Aeolians for the simple fact that its volcano is still active. The volcano, its single cone measuring 926m (3,038 ft.), has caused the island to be evacuated several times, although today Stromboli maintains a small population and attracts summer visitors.

The island has two settlements. **Ginostra,** on the southwestern shore, is little more than a cluster of summer homes with only 15 year-round residents. **Stromboli,** on the northeastern shore, is a conglomeration of the villages of Ficogrande, San Vincenzo, and Piscita, where the only in-town attraction is the black-sand beach. You won't see volcanic eruptions from any of these villages, as they occur on the northwest side of the volcano.

The entire surface of Stromboli is the cone of a sluggish but still-active volcano. Puffs of smoke can be seen during the day. At night along the **Sciara del Fuoco (Slope of Fire),** lava glows red-hot on its way down to meet the sea with a loud hiss. The main attraction is a steep, difficult climb to the lip of the 92m (302-ft.) **Gran Cratere.** The view of bubbling pools of ooze is accompanied by rising clouds of steam and a sulfuric stench.

The most distant island in the archipelago, Stromboli achieved notoriety and became a household word in the United States in 1950 with the release of the Roberto Rossellini *cinema vérité* film *Stromboli,* starring Ingrid Bergman. The American public was far more interested in the love affair between Bergman and Rossellini than in the film. Although tame by today's standards, the affair temporarily ended Bergman's American film career, and she was even denounced on the Senate floor. Movie fans today are more likely to remember Stromboli from the film version of the Jules Verne novel *Journey to the Center of the Earth,* starring James Mason.

ESSENTIALS

GETTING AROUND   Although several agencies at the port hawk deals ranging from cruises to boat trips, **Strombolandia,** Via Marina (© 090-986390), is the most reliable. From Easter to September, it's open daily from 9am to 1pm and 3 to 7pm. Boat rentals for tours around Stromboli begin at 130€ ($156) a day (fuel extra). You can also rent a scooter here for 20€ ($24) a day (fuel extra). The staff can arrange guided boat excursions to Vulcano, which leave at 6am and return at midnight; the cost is 25€ ($30) per person. Guided excursions to Panarea leave Stromboli at 10am and return at 6pm; the cost is 40€ ($48) per person. The excursion to Filicudi and Alicudi begins at 10am and ends at 6pm, costing 80€ ($96) per person. The agency can also book boat trips around Stromboli, calling at Ginostra and Strombolicchio. Trips last 3 hours and cost 15€ ($18) per person. Trips at night to see Sciara del Fuoco last 2 hours, 20 minutes, and costs 20€ ($24). Most of these excursions leave from the beach at Ficogrande.

FAST FACTS   To book hydrofoil or ferry rides, head for the offices of **Siremar** (© 090-986016) or **Ustica Lines** (© 090-986003), both along the harbor road at the port and easy to spot. Boats arrive from Milazzo from April to September only. From July to September, it's possible to book hydrofoil tickets on Ustica Lines from Stromboli direct to Naples for 57€ to 62€ ($68–$74) per person one-way. Siremar offers year-round boat trips from Stromboli to Naples at 37€ to 44€ ($44–$53) per person. The local **pharmacy** is **Farmacia Bonarrigo Pietro,** Via Favaloro 1 (© 090-9852244), open daily from 8:30am to 1pm and 4:30 to 9pm (8am–midnight in Aug). The **post office** is at Via Roma (© 090-986261), open Monday through Friday from 8am to 1:30pm and Saturday from 8am to 12:30pm.

EXPLORING THE ISLAND

By law, the cone of the volcano, **Gran Cratere** ✮✮✮, can be visited only with a guide. **Guide Alpine Autorizzate** (© 090-986211), charges 15€ ($18) per person and lead groups on the 3-hour one-way trip up the mountain, leaving at 5pm and returning at 11pm. (We don't recommend taking the trip during the day—it's far less dramatic then.) The trip down takes only 2 hours, but you're allowed an hour at the rim. About halfway up is a view of the **Sciara del Fuoco** ✮, which is a strikingly fiery red at night.

Climbing the volcano is the big deal here; otherwise, there isn't much to see in town. Film buffs can follow Via Vittorio Emanuele to the **Chiesa di San Vincenzo,** a church so unremarkable it barely merits a visit. However, just two doors down on the right, near the Locanda del Barbablu, is the **little pink house** where Ingrid Bergman and Roberto Rossellini "lived in sin" during the filming of the 1950 flick *Stromboli.* The house can only be viewed from the outside. You may also want to drop by the little **La Lebrería sull'Isola,** Via Vittorio Emanuele III (℃ **090/986-5755**), a charming bookstore in a typical Stromboli house. Here you can purchase a good map or book in English, send email, and catch up on the local gossip.

On the northeast coast is a striking rock, **Strombolicchio,** a steep basalt block measuring 43m (141 ft.). It is reached by climbing steps hewn out of rock. Once at the top, you'll be rewarded with a **panoramic view of the Aeolians** 🌟🌟, and on a clear day you can see as far as Calabria on the Italian mainland.

WHERE TO STAY

La Locanda del Barbablu 🌟 *(Finds)*   This is a quirky choice, a charming little isolated Aeolian inn with only a few rooms, standing against turn-of-the-20th-century breakfronts. Rooms are small but comfortably furnished, often with four-poster beds encrusted with cherubs and mother-of-pearl inlay. A wide terrace opens onto dramatic views of the volcano and the sea. All units have well-maintained bathrooms with shower-tub combinations. The restaurant is worth a visit even if you're not a guest.

Via Vittorio Emanuele 17–19, 98050 Stromboli. ℃ **090-986118**. Fax 090-986323. 6 units. 120€–200€ ($144–$240) double. AE, DC, MC, V. Closed Nov–Feb.

La Sirenetta Park Hotel 🌟🌟   This is the island's finest accommodation, a well-maintained, government-rated four-star hotel. It's the best equipped, with a scenic terrace, a nightclub, and a restaurant serving the best cuisine of any hotel here. It also has an idyllic location on the Ficogrande Beach in front of Strombolicchio, the towering rock that rises out of the waters at San Vincenzo. Guest rooms are attractively furnished, with tiled floors and an airy feel. All come with private bathrooms—half with showers, half with tubs. The hotel is justly proud of having the island's best pool as well, complete with hydromassage. Facilities include a fitness center and a dive center that also offers waterskiing, sailing, and windsurfing.

Via Marina 33, 98050 Ficogrande (Stromboli). ℃ **090-986025**. Fax 090-986124. www.lasirenetta.it. 60 units. 140€–256€ ($168–$307) double in summer. Rates include breakfast. 180€–300€ ($216–$360) double with half board. Off-season discounts. AE, DC, MC, V. Closed Nov 1 to mid-Mar. **Amenities:** Restaurant; 2 bars; saltwater outdoor pool; tennis court; fitness center; watersports; room service; massage; laundry service; dry cleaning; nonsmoking rooms; rooms for those w/limited mobility. *In room:* A/C, TV, dataport, minibar, hair dryer, safe.

WHERE TO DINE

Il Canneto AEOLIAN   This typical island restaurant was constructed in the old style, with white walls and dark tables. Among the local trattorie, it's nothing fancy, but it's one of the more reliable joints in town. The specialty is always fish caught in local waters. A delectable pasta dish is the macaroni with minced swordfish or whitefish cooked in a light tomato sauce with fresh herbs. Swordfish roulades are also prepared with a certain flair here.

Via Roma 64. ℃ **090-986014**. Reservations recommended. Main courses 9€–15€ ($11–$18). AE, MC, V. Daily 7–11pm. Closed Oct–Mar.

La Locanda del Barbablu 🌟 SICILIAN/ITALIAN   This *locanda,* or inn, has enjoyed a certain renown since the early 1900s, when sailors used to stop here for some R&R en route to Naples. Today, the place is rather chic and has a lovely garden. The food is classically Italian, with no experimentation whatsoever. Excellent dishes include *ravioli di melanzane,* fried ravioli stuffed with eggplant and covered with a tomato sauce; *matarocco,* pasta flavored with tomato sauce, garlic, pine nuts, and fresh basil and parsley; and that old Sicilian reliable, pasta with fresh sardines.

Via Vittorio Emanuele 17–19. (C) **090-986118.** Reservations recommended in summer. Main courses 6€–10€ ($7.20–$12). AE, DC, MC, V. Daily 7:30–11:30pm. Closed Nov 1–Feb 1.

Punta Lena ★★ AEOLIAN   The island's best cuisine is served at this old Aeolian house tastefully converted into a 17-seat restaurant, with a terrace opening onto the sea. The restaurant lies on the beach, a 10-minute walk from the center of town. There is a genuine effort here to cook with fresh products whenever possible. Stick to whatever the fishermen have brought in that day. The gnocchi *alla Saracena,* with whitefish, capers, olives, and tomatoes, is also excellent. The restaurant stocks the island's widest selection of wines.

Marina Ficogrande. (C) **090-986204.** Reservations recommended. Main courses 8€–15€ ($9.60–$18). AE, DC, MC, V. Daily noon–2:30pm and 7–11pm. Closed Nov–Mar.

Trattoria Ai Gechi di Mirabito AEOLIAN   Everything in this warm, airy trattoria is homemade—each dish has that *mamma mia* touch. The menu focuses on freshly caught fish. We sampled a homemade pasta with tomato sauce, capers, onions, garlic, parsley, and lemon zest, followed by fish cooked in white wine and flavored with fresh herbs. This is one of the few restaurants on the island that remains open year-round.

Via Salina 12. (C) **090-986213.** Reservations recommended. Main courses 8€–10€ ($9.60–$12). AE, DC, MC, V. Aug daily 7:30pm–2am; Sept–July daily 12:30–2:30pm and 7:30pm–2am.

STROMBOLI AFTER DARK

As the sun sets and the volcano lights up the sky, it seems that everyone heads for **Bar Ingrid,** Piazza San Vincenzo (C) **090-986385**). Naturally, it's named for Ingrid Bergman. Drinks, beer, and sandwiches are the casual offerings, but mainly people come here to see and be seen. It's open 6 days a week from 6pm to 2am. It closes Monday one week, Sunday the next.

Also popular is **Il Malandrino,** Via Marina (C) **090-986376**), where you can hang out, drink, and even order a pizza. It's open 6 days a week from 5:30pm to 3am. It closes Monday one week, Sunday the next, a rotation it jointly maintains with Bar Ingrid.

For live music, head to **La Tartana,** Via Marina 33, Ficogrande (C) **090-986025**), opening onto the beach. It's open June through September, daily from 9pm to 2am. Patrons come here to dance to disco or enjoy live pop. La Tartana is part of La Sirenetta Park Hotel, right near the port.

Taormina & Mount Etna

Sicily's greatest resort, Taormina, and its fiercest attraction, Mount Etna, can be combined in one powerful trip. Such writers as Goethe and D. H. Lawrence, besotted with the glories of Taormina's panoramic views of the bays beyond and Mount Etna looming in the background, spread word of the area's charm.

Taormina was built on a cliff, Monte Tauro, overlooking the sea. To the surprise of many first-time visitors, Taormina has no beach of its own. To reach the sands, you must take a steep cable-car descent down the hill. But the medieval charm of Taormina makes a stay high on the hill well worth your time.

The official high season lasts from April to October. If you're seeking a holiday by the beach and prefer to enjoy Taormina only on day trips, then **Giardini-Naxos** is your best choice. It has more style than many beach resorts in Sicily, which, frankly, tend toward the tacky. Seen from the terraces of Taormina, Giardini-Naxos opens onto a wide, curving bay with a beach that is justifiably one of the most popular on the island.

There are many possible excursions from Taormina, including a visit to the even loftier **Castelmola** and to the **Alcantara Gorges.** But nothing lures visitors quite like **Mount Etna,** the highest volcano in Europe. It's a potential menace, however: The entire coast of eastern Sicily is dominated by this volcanic peak, which continues to blow its top, sending deadly lava flows in all directions. The main crater is still dangerously active. At press time, Etna was at it again, opening up a new crater near Catania and spewing mile-high columns of smoke and ash into the air.

1 Taormina ★★★

53km (33 miles) N of Catania, 53km (33 miles) S of Messina, 250km (155 miles) E of Palermo

Taormina was just too good to remain unspoiled. Dating from the 4th century B.C., it hugs the edge of a cliff overlooking the Ionian Sea. The sea and even the railroad track lie below, connected by bus routes. Looming in the background is Mount Etna, an active volcano. Noted for its mild climate, the most beautiful town in all of Sicily seems to have no other reason to exist than for the thousands upon thousands of visitors who flock here for dining, bar-hopping, shopping, and enjoying the nearby beaches.

International visitors stroll back and forth along the one main street, Corso Umberto I, from April to October. After that, Taormina quiets down considerably. In spite of the hordes that descend in summer, Taormina has remained charming, with much of its medieval character intact. It's filled with intimate piazzas and palazzi dating from the 15th to the 19th century. You can dine in a different restaurant for every day of the week, linger at the many cafes, and browse the countless stores that sell everything from souvenir trinkets to

Taormina

ACCOMMODATIONS ■

Excelsior Palace Hotel **3**
Grande Albergo Capotaormina **43**
Grand Hotel Atlantis Bay **31**
Grand Hotel Mazzarò Sea Palace **33**
Grand Hotel Timeo **19**
Hotel Isabella **20**
Hotel La Campanella **11**
Hotel Lido Méditerranée **32**
Hotel Monte Tauro **16**
Hotel Victoria **22**

Hotel Villa Diodoro **39**
Hotel Villa Sonia **1**
Palazzo San Domenico **10**
Romantik Hotel Villa Ducale **2**
Villa Belvedere **41**
Villa Fabbiano **40**
Villa Fiorita **36**
Villa Paradiso **15**
Villa Sant'Andrea **35**
Villa Schuler **17**

Casa di Riposo Zuccaro

CASTELMOLA

Salita Bronco

Monte Tauro

Via Leonardo Da Vinci

Via Cappuccini

Castello Saraceno

Via L. Pirandel
Palazzo Corvaja
Teatro Comunale
Via Teatro Greco

Via Circonvallazione

NAUMACHIE

Corso Umberto

Via Roma

Piazza S. Antonio

Duomo

Madonna delle Grazie

Parco Duchi di Cesa

Convento di S. Domenico

Monte Crocefisso

Villagonia

Strada Statale No. 114

Autostrada A18

Via D. Primo

Stazione Taormina Giardini F.S.

Golfo di Naxos

GIARDINI-NAXOS

Torrente Sirina

🏖 Beach

0   1/10 Mile
0   100 meters

ATTRACTIONS ●

Chiesa Santa Caterina **24**
Duomo **8**
Museo Archeologico
di Taormina **9**
Museo Siciliano di Arte e
Tradizioni Popolari **25**
Palazzo Corvaja
(Tourist Office) **25**
Roman Odeon **26**
Teatro Greco
(Greek Amphitheater) **37**
Villa Comunale **18**

DINING ◆

Al Duomo **5**
Al Settimo Cielo
del Paradiso **17**
Bella Blu **29**
Casa Grugno **6**
Club Septimo **30**
Da Saro **28**
Granduca **12**
Il Baccanale **23**
Il Ciclope **7**
La Giara **14**
Maffei's **13**
Osteria Nero D'Avola **4**
Ristorante Angelo a
Mare-Il Delfino **34**
Ristorante da Giovanni **44**
Ristorante La Griglia **21**
Ristorante Luraleo **41**
Ristorante Parco Reale **1**
Ristorante U'Bossu **38**
Tirami Su **27**

antiques for well-heeled visitors. Hotels here tend to be pricey, but the good location can be worth it, as everyone gravitates to the top for dining and diversion—and those side roads from the bottom are quite steep to navigate.

You can always escape the throngs during the day by seeking out adventures: perhaps climbing Mount Etna, walking to the Castelmola, or making a day trip to Syracuse (see chapter 10). In summer, you can hang out at the beaches below the town (although Taormina itself isn't right on a beach). At night, enjoy jazz and disco music or just spend time in a local tavern or restaurant.

Lots of people contributed to putting Taormina on the map. First inhabited by a tribe known as the Siculi, it has known many conquerors, such as the Greeks, Carthaginians, Romans, Saracens, French, and Spanish. Its first tourist is said to have been Goethe, who arrived in 1787 and recorded his impressions in his *Journey to Italy.* Other Germans followed, including Wilhelm von Gloeden, who photographed not only the town but also nude boys crowned with laurel wreaths. His pictures sent European high society flocking to Taormina. Von Gloeden's photos, some of which are printed in official tourist literature to this day, form one of the most enduring legends of Taormina. Souvenir shops still sell the pictures, which, considered scandalous in their day, seem tame—even innocent—by today's standards. In von Gloeden's footsteps came a host of celebs hoping to see what all the excitement was about: Truman Capote, Tennessee Williams, Marlene Dietrich, Joan Crawford, Rita Hayworth, and Greta Garbo. In time, another wave of stars arrived, including Elizabeth Taylor and Richard Burton, Cary Grant, and the woman who turned Grant down, Sophia Loren.

ESSENTIALS

GETTING THERE   By Train   You can make rail connections on the Messina line south. It's possible to board a train in Rome for the 8-hour trip to Messina, where you connect on to Taormina. Call © **892021** for schedules. There are 26 trains a day from both Messina and Catania; trips from either town take 1 to 1½ hours and cost 3.05€ ($3.65) one-way. The Sicilian Gothic train station for Taormina/Giardini-Naxos is a mile from the heart of the resort, below the town. Buses run uphill from the station daily from 9am to 9pm, every 15 to 45 minutes (schedules vary throughout the year); a one-way ticket costs 1.50€ ($1.80). You can also take a taxi for 10€ ($12) and up.

By Bus   You can also take the train as far as Messina and then hop a Taormina-bound bus. There are 15 a day, taking 1½ hours and costing 3€ ($3.60) one-way. For details, call **Interbus** (© **0942-625301**).

BY CAR   From Messina, head south on A18. From Catania, continue north on A18. **Lumbi Parking,** Contrada Lumbi, is signposted off the Taormina Nord Autostrada junction; there's another garage at **Mazzarò Parking,** on Via Nazionale in Mazzarò, in the vicinity of the cable-car station off the coastal road. For 24-hour parking, count on paying 12€ to 15€ ($14–$18).

VISITOR INFORMATION   The **tourist office** is in the Palazzo Corvaja, Piazza Santa Caterina (© **0942-23243**); open Monday through Saturday from 8am to 2pm and 4 to 7pm. Here you can get a free map, hotel listings, bus and rail timetables, and a schedule of summer cultural events staged at the Greek amphitheater. Information is also available at a branch office at Via Tysandros 54 (© **0942-51010**), which keeps the same hours.

SPECIAL EVENTS   The Greek Amphitheater (p. 180) offers theatrical performances from July to September. Churches and other venues are the setting for a festival of classical music from May to September. Each July, an international film festival is held in the amphitheater.

GETTING AROUND   Within the heart of Taormina, use your trusty feet to get about. If you're venturing off on day excursions, a network of buses goes to such places as Giardini-Naxos and Mount Etna.

The more distant parts of Taormina are linked by minibus, which leaves from the terminal at Via Luigi Pirandello in town and costs .50€ (60¢) for a one-way ticket. Most visitors use the minibus that goes from the terminal to Madonna della Rocca, since it passes most of the major hotels. Service is daily from 8am to 7:05pm.

Taxi ranks are found at Piazza Vittorio Emanuele and at Piazza San Pancrazio. These are used primarily if you're leaving the heart of Taormina and venturing into its hinterlands. A typical fare—say, from the center of Taormina to Madonna della Rocca—is 10€ ($12).

Many visitors prefer to rent a car in Taormina and explore at their leisure. A good local company is **Sicily By Car** (© **800-334440**); reservations should be made in advance in high season. The Taormina office is at Via Apollo Arcageta 4 (© **0942-21252**). Vehicles rent for 32€ to 134€ ($38–$161) per day with unlimited mileage. Cars can be picked up in one Sicilian location and returned to another if you plan to explore beyond Taormina, perhaps taking a trip south to Syracuse and Agrigento.

Cable cars from Taormina run to the beaches below at Mazzarò, next to the Mazzarò car park. Service is daily from 8am to 1am in summer, until 6pm in winter. A round-trip ticket costs 2.70€ ($3.25).

If you prefer to get around by moped, **Autonolo "City,"** Piazza Sant'Antonio 5 (© **0942-23161**), rents scooters for 26€ ($31) and Vespas for 40€ ($48) per day. From March to October, it's open daily from 8am to noon and 4 to 8pm.

FAST FACTS: Taormina

American Express   The travel agency **La Duca Viaggi**, Via Don Bosco 39 (© **0942-625250**), handles Amex clients Monday through Friday from 9am to 1pm and 4 to 7:30pm. However, the most comprehensive travel agency in Taormina is **Dr. Silvestri Travel Bureau**, Corso Umberto I, 143–145 (© **0942-23052**). Established in 1905, it offers services ranging from car rentals and airline tickets to currency exchange and bus excursions. It's open Friday through Wednesday from 9am to 1pm and 4 to 8pm.

Currency Exchange   There are dozen of possibilities, especially at the banks along Corso Umberto I and Via Pirandello. **Cambio Valute**, Corso Umberto I, 224, near Piazza Sant'Antonio (© **0942-24806**), has ATMs and is the most convenient; open Monday through Saturday from 9am to 1pm and 4 to 8pm.

Emergency   Dial © **113** or 0942-23232.

Hospital   Serving the entire Taormina area is **Ospedale San Vincenzo**, Piazza San Vincenzo (© **0942-628040**). In an emergency, call **Guardia Medica** (© **0942-625419**), open Monday through Friday from 8am to 8pm, Saturday and Sunday 24 hours.

Internet Access   The best place to go is the **Internet Café**, Calle Umberto I, 214 (© **0942-628839**), which charges 2€ ($2.40) per hour.

Left Luggage A kiosk inside the Taormina/Giardini-Naxos train station is open daily from 8am to 9pm; it charges 4€ ($4.80) per piece over a 24-hour period.

Pharmacy The most central drugstore is **Farmacia Ragusa**, Piazza Duomo 9 (© **0942-23231**), open Thursday through Tuesday from 8:30am to 1pm and 5 to 8:30pm. It posts a schedule of other pharmacies open at other times; this list changes weekly on a rotating basis.

Police Dial © **112** for help.

Post Office The post office is at Piazza Sant'Antonio (© **0942-23230**), at the top end of Corso Umberto I in the vicinity of the hospital. Hours are Monday through Saturday from 8am to 6:30pm.

EXPLORING THE AREA

Many visitors to Taormina come for the beach, although the sands aren't exactly at the resort. To reach the best and most popular beach, **Lido Mazzarò** 🎿🎿, you have to go south of town via a cable car (© **0942-23605**) that leaves from Via Pirandello every 15 minutes. A one-way ticket costs 1.60€ ($1.90). This beach is one of the best equipped in Sicily, with bars, restaurants, and hotels. You can rent beach chairs, umbrellas, and watersports equipment at various kiosks from April to October. To the right of Lido Mazzarò, past the Capo Sant'Andrea headland, is the region's prettiest cove, where twin crescents of beach sweep from a sand spit out to the minuscule **Isola Bella** islet. You can walk here from the cable car in a minute, but it's more fun to paddle a boat from Mazzarò around Capo Sant'Andrea, which hides a few grottoes with excellent light effects on the seaward side.

North of Mazzarò are the long, wide beaches of **Spisone** and **Letojanni,** more developed but less crowded than **Giardini,** the large, built-up resort beach south of Isola Bella. A local bus leaves Taormina for Mazzarò, Spisone, and Letojanni, and another heads down the coast to Giardini.

The **Teatro Greco (Greek Amphitheater)** 🎿🎿🎿, Via del Teatro Greco (© **0942-23220**), is Taormina's most visited monument, offering a view of rare beauty of the seacoast and Mount Etna. In the Hellenistic period, the Greeks hewed the theater out of the rocky slope of Mount Tauro; the Romans remodeled and modified it greatly. What remains today dates from the 2nd century A.D. The conquering Arabs, who seemed intent on devastating the town, slashed away at it in the 10th century. That leaves us with a rather sparse and dusty ruin, less evocative than the Greek theater in Catania. On the premises is an antiquarium containing artifacts from the classical and early Christian periods. Today, the Greek Amphitheater is the site of the annual Taormina film festival. It's open from April to September, daily from 9am to 7pm; and from October to March, daily from 9am to 4pm. Admission is 4.50€ ($5.40) for adults, 2€ ($2.40) for those 18 to 25, and free for seniors over 65 and children under 18. The ruins lie on the upper reaches of Taormina, near the Grand Hotel Timeo.

Behind the tourist office, on the other side of Piazza Vittorio Emanuele, is the **Roman Odeon,** a small theater partly covered by the church of Santa Caterina next door. The Romans constructed this theater around A.D. 21. Much smaller than the Greek theater and with similar architecture, it was discovered in 1892 by a blacksmith digging in the area. A peristyle (colonnade) was also discovered here, perhaps all that was left of a Greek temple dedicated to Aphrodite.

Chiesa Santa Caterina, Piazza Santa Caterina, off Corso Umberto I ((C **0942-23123**), was consecrated to St. Catherine of Alexandria (exact consecration date unknown); it may have been built in the mid–17th century. It sits on a piazza that abuts the highest point of the town's main street, Corso Umberto I. Within its severely dignified exterior are baroque detailing and a trussed wood-beamed ceiling. Chiesa Santa Caterina is the temporary replacement for Taormina's cathedral, which will be closed for some time. Open daily 9am to noon and 4 to 7pm.

Farther along the main drag, **Corso Umberto I** ⭐, you'll arrive at Piazza del Duomo and the **Duomo,** or cathedral, of Taormina. Built around 1400 on the ruins of a church from the Middle Ages, this fortress cathedral has a Latin cross plan and a trio of aisles. The nave is held up by half a dozen monolithic columns in pink marble; a fish-scale decoration graces their capitals in honor of the island's maritime tradition. The Duomo is currently closed for renovations and may remain so for some time. For information, call (C **0942-23123.** The cathedral's role has been assumed by Chiesa Santa Caterina (see above).

Museo Archeologico di Taormina, in the Palazzo Badia Vecchia, on Via Circonvallazione ((C **0942-620112**), is set on the site of the ancient Roman baths. It is a repository for the hundreds of archaeological remnants discovered during excavations in and around the city. Expect pottery shards and lingering artifacts of the ancient Roman world. Admission is 2.60€ ($3.10); it's open Tuesday through Sunday from 9am to 1pm and 4 to 8pm.

The Palazzo Corvaja, one of the most famous palaces in Taormina, contains the tourist office as well as the **Museo Siciliano di Arte e Tradizioni Popolari (Museum of Art and Popular Traditions),** Piazza Santa Catarina at Corso Umberto I ((C **0942-23243**). It's filled with 18th-century oil portraits, painted glass and donkey carts, and embroidery. The most charming pieces in the collection are secular portraits of the mid-19th-century Sicilian bourgeoisie. Entrance to the ground floor of the palace (also the town's tourist office) is free. Admission to the museum is 2.60€ ($3.10). It's open Tuesday through Sunday from 9am to 1pm and 4 to 8pm.

Where Garbo's Big Feet Trod the Sands

The district's most appealing beach club, **Beach Club Paradiso,** Via Lungomare, Letojanni ((C **0942-36944**), lies at the easterly end of the beachfront of Letojanni, a hamlet that receives lots of traffic from hotel guests of Taormina above. It was built on the site of a villa (ca. 1920s) that was the lair of Dr. Gayelord Hauser, a dietitian and confidant of a long list of Hollywood stars that included Greta Garbo. Come here for a half or full day, relax beside a freshwater pool, enjoy a meal at the pleasant restaurant, or swim in the sea on a gravel beach under supervision of a registered lifeguard. Platters of well-prepared food in the open-air restaurant cost from 8.50€ to 15€ ($10–$18). At least some of the clients here might be registered guests at Taormina's Villa Paradiso, which maintains shuttle service between Taormina and this club. The club is open from June to October, daily from 9am to 6pm. The entrance fee of 10€ ($12) includes all-day use of a chaise longue and parasol.

The site of the best temporary art exhibitions is the Palazzo di Santo Stefano, which contains the **Fondazione Mazzullo,** Corso Umberto I, 242–246 (✆ **0942-610273**). Entrance is free, but dates and opening times vary (check with the tourist office). Many of the exhibitions focus on the history of Taormina; others are showcases for modern art. Constructed for the dukes of Santo Stefano, the palace dates from the 15th century and is a rather stunning mix of black lava and white Syracuse stone.

A local sightseeing oddity here is **Villa Comunale,** sometimes called **Parco Duca di Cesarò** 🕊🕊, Via Bagnoli Croce, off Corso Umberto I. One of the most beautiful little parks in all of Sicily, the gardens were the creation of Lady Florence Trevelyan in the late 19th century. This Scottish lady was "invited" to leave Britain after a well-publicized romance with the future king, Edward VII, son of Victoria. She built various amusements in the gardens, including a fanciful stone-and-brick pavilion that might have been conceived as a teahouse. The gardens are open daily from 8:30am to 7pm (6pm in winter); admission is free.

Another flower-filled garden in Taormina is the **Giardino Púbblico (Public Garden),** Via Bagnoli Croce. It overlooks the sea, making it a choice spot for views. You can order drinks at a bar in the park. The garden is open from dawn until dusk.

It's worth a trip to the nearby village of **Castelmola** 🕊, 3km (2 miles) northwest of Taormina. This is one of the most beautiful places in eastern Sicily, with a panoramic view of Mount Etna on clear days. You might also visit the ruined *castello* (castle) on the summit of **Mount Tauro** (390m/1,280 ft.), about 3km (2 miles) northwest of Taormina along the Castelmola road. Hikers can follow a footpath here. Ruins of a former acropolis are visible, but most people come simply for the panoramas.

FARTHER AFIELD TO THE ALCANTARA GORGES

To see some beautiful rapids and waterfalls, head outside of town to the **Gole dell'Alcantara** 🕊 (✆ **0942-985010**), a series of gorges. The waters are extremely cold—uncharacteristic for Sicily, but quite refreshing in August. It's usually possible to walk up the river from May to September (when the water level is low), though you must inquire about current conditions before you do so. From the parking lot, take an elevator partway into the scenic abyss and then continue on foot. You're likely to get wet, so bring your bathing suit. If you don't have appropriate shoes, you can rent rubber boots at the entrance. Allow at least an hour for this trip. From October to April, only the entrance is accessible, but the view is always panoramic. It costs 2.50€ ($3) to enter the gorge, which is open daily from 9am to 5pm. By car, head up SS185 some 17km (11 miles) from Taormina. Or take **Interbus** (✆ **0942-625301**) for the 20-minute trip departing from Taormina at 9:30am. There's only one bus back, leaving at 2:30pm. The round-trip fare is 4.50€ ($5.40). You can also go by taxi from Taormina, but you'll have to negotiate the fare with your driver; try calling Franco Nunzio at ✆ **0942-51094.**

SHOPPING

Shopping is easy—just find **Corso Umberto I,** the main street. The trendy shops here sell everything from lacy linens to fashionable clothing to antique furniture. The more adventurous can veer off the Corso and search out little shops on the side streets.

Bar Pasticerria A Chemi ⭐ Everything in this store comes from Sicily. The array of candies is amazing: Expect at least four kinds of *torrone* (nougat); local honey fortified with slices of dried fruit; and every conceivable kind of marzipan. Bottled Sicilian liqueurs are also available, including a worthy collection of Marsalas and an almond-flavored dessert wine. Corso Umberto I, 102. ✆ **0942-24260.**

Carlo Panarello This shop offers a good selection of Sicilian ceramics, plus deluxe umbrellas, tablecloths, and an eclectic mixture of antique furnishings, paintings, and engravings. Corso Umberto I, 122. ✆ **0942-23910.**

Casa d'Arte Forin The Venetian family who runs this store sells antique prints featuring bucolic scenes of the Sicilian countryside and the Ionian Sea. They also have some excellent reproductions of antique jewelry and furnishings, with an emphasis on Sicilian and Venetian pieces. Corso Umberto I, 148. ✆ **0492-23060.**

Gioielleria Giuseppe Stroscio ⭐ This is the best outlet for antique gold jewelry from 1500 to the early 1900s. It also sells a good selection of modern jewelry. We've seen more helpful staff, however. Corso Umberto I, 169. ✆ **0942-24865.**

Giovanni di Blasi ⭐ Ceramics stores are found all over Sicily, but this is one of the best in terms of quality and design. It specializes in the highly valued "white pottery" of Caltagirone. Corso Umberto I, 103. ✆ **0942-24671.**

Il Quadrifoglio Here you'll find a rich collection of amber jewelry from the Dominican Republic and the Baltic, antique jewelry from estate sales throughout Sicily, antique porcelain from Dresden, and papier-mâché masks that might be suitable for Carnevale in Venice. The venue is artsy, antiquey, and charming. Corso Umberto I, 153. ✆ **0942-23545.**

La Torinese Loaded to the rafters with the agrarian bounty of Sicily, this delicatessen was established in 1936 by—you guessed it—a one-time resident of Torino. Pick up cheeses, sliced meats, pâtés, bread, and pastries for a picnic on any of the city's panoramic outcroppings. There's also an impressive collection of wines, liqueurs, and grappas. Corso Umberto I, 59. ✆ **0942-23321.**

WHERE TO STAY

The hotels in Taormina are the best in Sicily—in fact, they're the finest in Italy south of Amalfi. All price ranges are available, from army cots to sumptuous suites.

If you're coming primarily to hit the beach, at least in July and August, you may want to stay at **Mazzarò,** 5km (3 miles) from the center, and trek up the hill for shopping, nightlife, and dining. Mazzarò is the major beach and has some fine hotels (see the Grand Hotel Mazzarò Sea Palace, later in this chapter). Buses connecting Mazzarò and Taormina leave every 30 minutes daily from 8am to 9pm; the fare is 1.50€ ($1.80). Otherwise, we recommend that you stay in Taormina—it has far more charm than anything down by the sea.

In summer, the curse of Taormina hotels is the noise, not only of traffic but also of visitors who turn the town into an all-night party. If you're a light sleeper and you've chosen a hotel along Corso Umberto, ask for a room in the rear—you'll be trading a view for a good night's sleep.

If you're driving to a hotel at the top of Taormina, call ahead to see what arrangements can be made for your car. Ask for exact driving directions as well as instructions on where to park—the narrow, winding, one-way streets can be bewildering once you get here.

VERY EXPENSIVE

Grande Albergo Capotaormina 🌟🌟🌟   This barren cape was transformed in the 1960s with the addition of the most avant-garde architectural statement in or around Taormina—an oasis of comfort and poshness within a spectacularly inhospitable natural setting. Surrounded by the Ionian Sea on three sides, and with a layout that resembles an irregular pentagon, the hotel contains five floors with wide sun terraces. Elevators take you through 46m (150 ft.) of solid rock to the beach and to a large, free-form pool far below the level of the hotel, directly adjacent to the sea. Guest rooms are handsome and well-proportioned, each with a private terrace and a spacious bathroom with tub and shower.

Via Nazionale 105, 98039 Taormina. ✆ **0942-572111.** Fax 0942-625467. www.capotaorminahotel.com. 202 units. 220€–430€ ($264–$516) double; 490€–1,030€ ($588–$1,236) suite. AE, DC, MC, V. **Amenities:** 3 restaurants; 3 bars; outdoor pool; golf; tennis; gym; seawater Jacuzzi; sauna; watersports program (supplemental charge) including deep-sea fishing and scuba; salon; room service; massage; laundry service; dry cleaning; nonsmoking rooms. *In room:* A/C, TV, minibar, hair dryer, safe.

Grand Hotel Atlantis Bay 🌟   This government-rated five-star hotel has its own private beach along the Taormina coast. Associated with the excellent Mazzarò Sea Palace, but with a less experienced management and a less gifted staff, it blends artfully into a landscape of pebbly beachfronts and cliffs. Great care was taken for an ecologically sensitive approach to the natural surroundings. The result is a jagged and earthy-looking combination of rough-hewn stones, terra-cotta tiles, and primal colors that don't stand out when viewed from afar. There's something stylish and postmodern about this youthful, sports-oriented hotel, with its bubbling aquariums and neo-Roman accessories in the lobby. Many guest rooms feature terraces; all have bathrooms with tub and shower.

Via Nazionale 161, 98030 Taormina Mare. ✆ **0942-618011.** Fax 0942-23194. www.atlantisbay.it. 86 units. 280€–400€ ($336–$480) double; from 450€ ($540) suite. AE, DC, MC, V. **Amenities:** 2 restaurants; 2 bars; outdoor pool; fitness center; concierge; nonsmoking rooms. *In room:* A/C, TV, dataport, minibar, hair dryer.

Grand Hotel Mazzarò Sea Palace 🌟🌟🌟   The leading hotel in Mazzarò opens onto the most beautiful bay in Sicily and has its own private beach. Completed in 1962, this government-rated five-star deluxe hotel has been renovated frequently since, most recently in 2004. From the coastal highway, you won't be able to see very much of this spectacular lodging—only a rooftop and masses of bougainvillea. You'll register on the top floor, then ride an elevator down to sea level for access to a stylish, airy set of marble-sheathed public rooms. The hotel is very elegant, genuinely charming, and well staffed. Big windows let in cascades of light and offer views of the coast. Guest rooms are well furnished, filled with wicker and veneer pieces along with original art and wood or tile floors; most have panoramic views. The bathrooms are clad in marble, each with a shower-tub combination.

Via Nazionale 147, 98030 Mazzarò. ✆ **0942-24004.** Fax 0942-626237. www.mazzaroseapalace.it. 88 units. 300€–450€ ($360–$540) double; 680€–1,380€ ($816–$1,656) suite. Rates include breakfast. AE, DC, MC,

---

Moments   When the Monks Come Out at Night

If you stay at San Domenico, take a walk through the ecclesiastical-looking hallways, chapels, and courtyards late at night, when things are eerily empty and quiet, and when torches flicker exotically in the gardens. That's when the resident ghosts are said to make their appearances. It's the most mystical and otherworldly experience available in any hotel in Sicily.

V. Parking 16€ ($19) nearby. **Amenities:** Restaurant; bar; outdoor pool; fitness center; 24-hr. room service; babysitting; laundry service; dry cleaning; nonsmoking rooms; rooms for those w/limited mobility. *In room:* A/C, TV, dataport, minibar, hair dryer, safe.

Grand Hotel Timeo ★★   Hidden in a tranquil private park just below the Greek Amphitheater, the Timeo opened in 1873 and has hosted everyone from King Umberto II to Liz Taylor. It's perched at the eastern edge of Taormina, on a precarious but panoramic terrace that's flooded with light and views upward to the amphitheater and down across town to the sea. A prestigious member of the Framon chain, it evokes a 19th-century neoclassical villa that manages to be lighthearted and baronial at the same time. It lacks the manorial dignity of the Palazzo San Domenico and has none of its ecclesiastical overlays; you get the feeling that the Timeo was built purely for pleasure, and it carries the aura of a sophisticated and very secular private villa. Guests are treated to a winning combination of old-world elegance and contemporary conveniences. All rooms are spacious and well outfitted, with balconies and marble bathrooms equipped with both tub and shower. Room nos. 301 to 316 enjoy the widest views. The hotel has a private beach with lounge chairs and umbrellas; the staff will arrange tee times at nearby golf courses.

Via Teatro Greco 59, 98039 Taormina. ✆ **0942-23801.** Fax 0942-628501. www.framon-hotels.com. 87 units. 290€–490€ ($348–$588) double; 414€–710€ ($497–$852) suite. Rates include breakfast. AE, DC, MC, V. Free parking. **Amenities:** Restaurant; piano bar; outdoor heated pool; fitness center; Turkish bath; concierge; car-rental desk; shuttle service to the beach; room service; massage; babysitting; laundry service; dry cleaning; nonsmoking rooms; rooms for those w/limited mobility. *In room:* A/C, TV, dataport, minibar, hair dryer, safe.

Palazzo San Domenico ★★★   This is one of the greatest hotels of Italy, with a pedigree so impressive that it evokes a national monument. Having housed such illustrious guests as François Mitterand and Winston Churchill, it's the envy of other hoteliers of Taormina. Set in the heart of the resort's oldest neighborhood, it originated in the 14th century as a semi-fortified Dominican monastery. Today, after generations of meticulous upgrades, it's surrounded by walled-in terraced gardens lit at night by flickering torches.

Don't expect the interior to look cutting-edge and glossy, or as if a team of decorators has just finished moving in the furniture: What you'll find are massive and dignified areas (reception rooms, hideaway chapels, paneled salons) outfitted with museum-quality antiques that have been in place for at least 75 years, a genuinely impressive patina, and a physical setting that no one would ever dare modernize. The result is old-fashioned in the most appealing sense of the word.

Guest rooms are located in either the old monastery part of the hotel, where furnishings are severely dignified and very comfortable, or in the somewhat more opulent "newer" wings, those added in 1897, which evoke the Gilded Age and its aesthetics a bit more richly. All units have bathrooms with shower/tub combinations. Views extend out over the bougainvillea, palms, and citrus trees in the garden to the sea.

Piazza San Domenico 5, 98039 Taormina. © 0942-613111. Fax 0942-625506. www.sandomenico.thi.it. 108 units. 300€–450€ ($360–$540) double; from 750€ ($900) suite. Rates include breakfast. AE, DC, MC, V. Free parking outside; 3 spaces inside (summer only) 15€ ($18). **Amenities:** 4 restaurants; piano bar; outdoor heated pool; gym; concierge; beauty center; 24-hr. room service; babysitting; laundry service; dry cleaning; nonsmoking rooms; rooms for those w/limited mobility. *In room:* A/C, TV, dataport, minibar, hair dryer.

EXPENSIVE
Excelsior Palace Hotel ★★ This government-rated four-star hotel in Taormina is used more aggressively by tour groups than virtually any other hotel in town. It's set on a rocky ridge in the lower reaches of Taormina, midway between a busy piazza and an isolated, somewhat dusty garden. Part of the allure of this place derives from its outrageous facade (ca. 1903), which artfully mimics the grand Moorish architecture you might expect in Marrakesh. Most of the rather formal-looking guest rooms were upgraded in 2001 and inspired by late-19th-century models. Older, not-yet-renovated rooms are a bit more bland but equally comfortable. Private bathrooms come with shower or tub.

Via Toselli 8, 98039 Taormina. © 0942-23975. Fax 0942-23978. www.excelsiorpalacetaormina.it. 88 units. 220€ ($264) double. AE, DC, MC, V. **Amenities:** Restaurant; bar; outdoor pool; babysitting; laundry service; dry cleaning; solarium. *In room:* A/C, TV, dataport, minibar, hair dryer.

Hotel Isabella Only one other hotel, the Victoria, enjoys a location directly on the main street of Taormina; the Isabella is the better-rated of the two. Small-scale and chic in a way that only a boutique hotel can be, it welcomes visitors with a lobby that might remind you of a living room with a peaches-and-cream color scheme. Its pleasing decor was inspired by a sun-flooded English country house. Guest rooms are not particularly large, though cozy and plush. Some have views over the all-pedestrian hubbub of the town's main street; all have tiled shower-only bathrooms. On the rooftop is a solarium.

Corso Umberto I, 58, 98039 Taormina. © 0942-23153. Fax 0942-23155. www.gaishotels.com. 32 units. 110€–164€ ($132–$197) double. Rates include breakfast. AE, DC, MC, V. **Amenities:** Restaurant; bar; free access to beach club with watersports, sunning, and swimming; babysitting; nonsmoking rooms; solarium. *In room:* A/C, TV, minibar, hair dryer, safe.

Hotel Monte Tauro This hotel was built into the side of a hill rising high above the sea. Each room has a balcony with a sea view. Rooms are furnished to a high standard, with tiled bathrooms with shower-tub combinations. Junior suites have Jacuzzis. The social center is the outdoor pool, whose cantilevered platform is ringed with dozens of plants.

Via Madonna delle Grazie 3, 98039 Taormina. © 0942-24402. Fax 0942-24403. www.hotelmontetauro.it. 100 units. 277€ ($332) double; 342€ ($410) junior suite. Rates include breakfast. AE, DC, MC, V. Closed Jan 15–Mar. **Amenities:** Restaurant; 2 bars; outdoor pool; room service; babysitting; laundry service; dry cleaning. *In room:* A/C, TV, dataport, minibar, hair dryer, safe.

Hotel Villa Diodoro ★ This is one of Taormina's better hotels, with tasteful design through and through. There are sunny spots where you can swim, sunbathe, and enjoy the view of mountains, trees, and flowers. The vistas of Mount Etna, the Ionian Sea, and the eastern coastline of Sicily are reason enough to stay here. Guest rooms are elegant and comfortable, with wrought-iron headboards, terra-cotta floors, balconies, and compact bathrooms with shower-tub combinations. From June to October, a shuttle bus runs to the beach at nearby Lido Caparena.

Via Bagnoli Croce 75, 98039 Taormina. © **0942-23312**. Fax 0942-23391. www.gaishotels.com. 99 units. 174€–302€ ($209–$362) double. Rates include breakfast. AE, DC, MC, V. Free parking. **Amenities:** Dining room; lounge; outdoor pool; car rental; 24-hr. room service; babysitting; laundry service; dry cleaning; rooms for those w/limited mobility. *In room:* A/C, TV, minibar, hair dryer, safe.

Romantik Hotel Villa Ducale ★★ This restored old villa is a charming and romantic choice. Villa Ducale sits on a hillside, a 10-minute walk up from the center, in the quiet hamlet of Madonna della Rocca (midway between the heart of the resort and high-altitude Castelmola). It boasts magnificent views of the Mediterranean, the town, and Mount Etna. Each guest room has a veranda, terra-cotta floors, wrought-iron beds, and a compact bathroom with shower-tub combination. The service is warm and helpful. Breakfast is usually served on an outdoor terrace with a gorgeous view.

Via Leonardo da Vinci 60, 98039 Taormina. © **0942-28153**. Fax 0942-28710. www.hotelvilladucale.it. 15 units. 190€–245€ ($228–$294) double; 270€–413€ ($324–$496) suite. Rates include buffet breakfast. AE, MC, V. Parking 10€ ($12). **Amenities:** Lounge; shuttle service to the beach; 24-hr. room service; laundry service. *In room:* A/C, TV, minibar, hair dryer, safe.

Villa Sant'Andrea ★ *Finds* Staying here is like going to a house party at a pretty home. The atmosphere draws return visits by artists, painters, and other discerning guests. The Sant'Andrea lies at the base of the mountain, directly on the sea, and opens onto a private beach. Guest rooms are well maintained and comfortable, though size and decor vary. Many have balconies or terraces; the tiled shower-only bathrooms are small but adequate. A cable car, just outside the front gates, runs into the heart of Taormina.

Via Nazionale 137, 98030 Taormina Mare. © **0942-23125**. Fax 0942-24838. www.framon-hotels.com. 80 units. 220€–310€ ($264–$372) double. Rates include breakfast. AE, DC, MC, V. Parking 15€ ($18). **Amenities:** 2 restaurants; 3 bars; boat rental; room service; babysitting; laundry service; dry cleaning; nonsmoking rooms. *In room:* A/C, TV, dataport, minibar, hair dryer, safe.

MODERATE

Hotel Lido Méditerranée ★ *Value* Less stylish and a bit more dowdy than some of the five-star palace hotels that lie within a 3-minute drive along the coast, this solidly reliable four-star choice offers less expensive rates than those around it. Originally built in 1968 next to a gravel beach, and renovated a few times since, it resembles a private bougainvillea-draped villa. Guest rooms are unpretentious, reminiscent of a simple beachfront hotel in the Caribbean.

Via Nazionale, 98030 Taormina Mare (Spisone). © **0942-24422**. Fax 0942-24774. www.taorminahotels. com. 72 units. 120€–340€ ($144–$408) double. AE, DC, MC, V. Closed Nov to Easter. **Amenities:** Restaurant; piano bar; room service; babysitting; laundry service; dry cleaning; nonsmoking rooms. *In room:* A/C, TV, minibar.

Villa Belvedere With a friendly reception, professional maintenance, and old-fashioned style, this hotel near the Public Garden offers the same view enjoyed by guests at more expensive hotels nearby. Head to the cliffside terrace in the rear to enjoy the vista of the Ionian Sea, the cypress-studded hillside, and smoldering Mount Etna. The small to midsize guest rooms feature functional furniture with a touch of class. Most units have slivers of balconies from which to enjoy views over the neighboring Public Garden to the sea; top-floor rooms have small terraces. Most of the bathrooms have shower-tub combinations. The hotel is located near the cable car and the steps down to the beach.

Via Bagnoli Croce 79, 98039 Taormina. © **0942-23791**. Fax 0942-625830. www.villabelvedere.it. 47 units. 120€–198€ ($144–$238) double; 160€–250€ ($192–$300) suite. Rates include breakfast. MC, V. Parking 7€ ($8.40). Closed late Nov to mid-Dec and mid-Jan to mid-Mar. **Amenities:** 2 bars; outdoor pool; 24-hr. room service; laundry service; dry cleaning; nonsmoking rooms. *In room:* A/C, TV, hair dryer.

Villa Fabbiano ★★ *Finds*   Only Villa Ducale and Grand Hotel Timeo enjoy the same tranquillity and romantic position as this house, situated in a mock castle with an alluring roof garden—it's a charmer in every way. The staff, the service, the accommodations, and the price combine to make this a little gem. Furnishings are well chosen for comfort, tradition, and style, and each guest room is beautifully furnished and inviting. The neatly tiled private bathrooms come with tub or shower. The cuisine at the restaurant is first rate.

Via Pirandello 81, 98039 Taormina. (© **0942-626058.** Fax 0954-23732. www.villafabbiano.com. 27 units. 170€–240€ ($204–$288) double; 240€–325€ ($288–$390) suite. Rates include buffet breakfast. MC, V. Closed Nov–Mar. **Amenities:** Restaurant; outdoor pool; room service; babysitting; laundry service; dry cleaning; nonsmoking rooms. *In room:* A/C, TV, dataport, minibar, hair dryer, safe.

Villa Paradiso ★ *Finds*   This charming boutique hotel originated in 1921 when the grandfather of the present owner bought a villa originally built in 1892. Today, it's the impeccably maintained domain of local patriarch Signore Salvatore Martorana. Set within a warren of narrow streets adjacent to the town's most beautiful public gardens, the Paradiso contains tastefully furnished public rooms outfitted with antiques and fine art. Each of the cozy, individually decorated guest rooms has a balcony, conservative furnishings, and a tiled bathroom with (in most cases) a shower-tub combination. Between June and October, the hotel offers free shuttle service and free entrance to the also-recommended **Paradise Beach Club,** about 6 km (4 miles) to the east, in the seaside resort of Letojanni. The hotel's restaurant, Al Settimo Cielo del Paradiso, serves excellent cuisine on the panoramic rooftop (see p. 181 for a review).

Via Roma 2, 98039 Taormina. (© **0942-23921.** Fax 0942-625800. www.hotelvillaparadisotaormina.com. 35 units. 134€–180€ ($161–$216) double; 170€–216€ ($204–$259) junior suite. AE, DC, MC, V. Parking: 12€ ($14). **Amenities:** Restaurant; bar; lounge; 24-hr. room service; 1 room for those w/limited mobility. *In room:* A/C, TV, hair dryer, safe.

INEXPENSIVE

Hotel La Campanella   This hotel is rich in plants, paintings, and hospitality. It sits at the top of a seemingly endless flight of stairs, which begin at a sharp curve of the main road leading into town. You'll climb past terra-cotta pots and the dangling tendrils of a terraced garden, eventually arriving at the house. The owners maintain clean, simple, homey guest rooms.

Via Circonvallazione 3, 98039 Taormina. (© **0942-23381.** Fax 0942-625248. 12 units. 80€ ($96) double. Rates include breakfast. No credit cards. **Amenities:** Lounge. *In room:* Hair dryer.

Hotel Victoria   It's unusual to find a good government-rated two-star hotel in Taormina, and this one is conveniently positioned smack in the middle of the nighttime action, on the town's all-pedestrian main street. It was established in 1885 within a 300-year-old, four-story building that has been frequently upgraded over the years. Rooms are accessible via a flight of stone steps; they're high-ceilinged, well-maintained, and comfortable, with hints of manorial style. All but a few have air-conditioning; eight have minibars; and all have shower-only bathrooms. Rooms overlooking the Corso Umberto I get more light but also more noise.

Corso Umberto I, 81, 98039 Taormina. (© **0942-23372.** Fax 0942-623567. www.albergovictoria.it. 22 units. 93€–103€ ($112–$124) double. Rates include buffet breakfast. AE, MC, V. Closed Jan–Feb. *In room:* TV, hair dryer.

Villa Fiorita ★ *Value*   This small inn stretches toward the Teatro Greco from its position beside the road leading to the top of this cliff-hugging town. Its imaginative decor includes a handful of ceramic stoves, which the owner

---

Moments An Evening Promenade

We like to stroll at twilight along Corso Umberto I until we reach the resort's most charming small square. **Piazza IX Aprile** ★★ overlooks the sea with the grandest panoramas of Mount Etna looming in the background. One side of the square is open; its other three sides are enclosed by the 17th-century church of San Giuseppe, San Agostino (converted into a library), and Torre dell'Orologio, from the late 1600s. Choose any of the bars with outdoor seating and sit back to enjoy the show—Piazza IX Aprile is the favored rendezvous point for the young men of Taormina to meet ladies.

---

delights in collecting. A well-maintained garden lies alongside an ancient but empty Greek tomb whose stone walls have been classified a national treasure. The guest rooms are arranged in a steplike labyrinth of corridors and stairwells, some of which bend to correspond to the rocky slope on which the hotel was built. Each unit contains antique furniture and a shower-only bathroom; most have private terraces.

Via Luigi Pirandello 39, 98039 Taormina. ✆ 0942-24122. Fax 0942-625967. www.villafioritahotel.com. 26 units. 120€ ($144) double; 160€ ($192) suite. Rates include breakfast. AE, MC, V. Parking 12€ ($14). **Amenities:** Lounge; outdoor pool; 24-hr. room service; nonsmoking rooms. *In room:* A/C, TV, hair dryer, safe.

Villa Schuler ★ *(Value)*   Filled with the fragrance of bougainvillea and jasmine, this hotel offers style and comfort at a good price. Family-owned and -run, it sits high above the Ionian Sea, with views of Mount Etna and the Bay of Naxos. It's only a 2-minute stroll from Corso Umberto I and about a 15-minute walk from the cable car to the beach below. Guest rooms are comfortably furnished, with bathrooms with shower-tub combinations; many have a small balcony or terrace. Breakfast can be served in your room or taken on a lovely terrace with a panoramic sea view. Service is impeccable.

The most luxurious way to stay here is to book the garden villa suite with its own private access. It's spacious and beautifully furnished, with two bathrooms (one with a Jacuzzi). The villa comes with a kitchenette, patio, private garden, and veranda, and costs from 220€ ($264) per day for two, including breakfast.

Piazzetta Bastione, Via Roma, 98039 Taormina. ✆ 0942-23481. Fax 0942-23522. www.villaschuler.com. 26 units, most with shower only. 116€–130€ ($139–$156) double; 130€–170€ ($156–$204) junior suite. Rates include breakfast. AE, DC, DISC, MC, V. Parking 13€ ($16) in garage; free outside. Closed Nov 15–Mar 15. **Amenities:** Bar; lounge; 24-hr. room service; laundry service; dry cleaning; library. *In room:* A/C, TV, hair dryer, safe.

IN CASTELMOLA

Hotel Villa Sonia ★ *(Finds)*   Created in 1974 on the site of an old villa, this stylish brick-and-stone retreat is a short walk downhill from Castelmola's town square. The best-rated and most appealing hotel in Castelmola, it was built on a ridge beside the winding road that accesses the village, with spectacular views from both the front and back sides. Guest rooms feature modern lines and manorial Sicilian touches such as wrought-iron headboards. Each unit has a tiled bathroom with tub or shower; about half have terraces. The restaurant, Ristorante Parco Reale, is especially noteworthy (see p. 194 for a review). Shuttle-bus transfers run twice a day from the hotel to central Taormina.

Via Porta Mola 9, 98030 Castelmola. © **0942-28082.** Fax 0942-28083. www.hotelvillasonia.com. 36 units. 180€–200€ ($216–$240) double; 250€ ($300) suite. Rates include breakfast. AE, DC, MC, V. Free parking. **Amenities:** Restaurant; bar; outdoor pool; fitness room with sauna; babysitting; laundry service; dry cleaning. *In room:* A/C, TV, minibar, hair dryer, safe.

WHERE TO DINE
VERY EXPENSIVE
Casa Grugno ★★★ MODERN SICILIAN/INTERNATIONAL   The most exciting restaurant in Taormina is making a bold statement about modern Sicilian cuisine. Austrian-born chef Andreas Zangerl presides over this increasingly famous place, where the snows of the Austrian Tyrol seem to mingle with the torrid Sicilian scrublands. The setting is a stone-sided house that contains a bar, an ocher dining room outfitted like a trompe l'oeil rendition of Carnevale in Venice, and a walled-in terrace ringed with plants. The hip and alert young staff gets excellent supervision from the town's most successful maître d'hotel, Stephano Lo Guidice.

The sublime food here is reinvented Sicilian cuisine at its finest, a haute cuisine that draws from a pan-European sensibility. The set-price menus might include tuna steak with sweet-and-sour onion and mint sauce; pasta *alla Trapanese* (with almonds, tomatoes, and chile peppers); roasted pigeon with lentils from the offshore island of Pantelleria; and an impeccable version of Parmesan eggplant that might be the most deliciously fragrant dish in this part of town.

Via Santa Maria de Greci. © **0942-21208.** Reservations recommended. Main courses 15€–25€ ($18–$30); set-price menus 52€–75€ ($62–$90). AE, DC, MC, V. Thurs–Tues 7pm–midnight. Closed Nov 2–28 and Feb 1–27 (dates may vary).

EXPENSIVE
La Giara ★★ SICILIAN/ITALIAN   Glossy, airy, and reminiscent of Rome during the heyday of Gina Lollobrigida, La Giara evokes a warmed-over *la dolce vita.* The restaurant is almost excessively formal and has remained predictably stable since its founding in 1953. Views sweep from the veranda's outdoor tables over the bay of Taormina. The Art Deco ambience is also inviting, with marble floors and columns shaped from stone quarried in the fields outside Syracuse. The pastas are meals in themselves; we're especially fond of the ricotta-stuffed cannelloni and the ravioli stuffed with pesto-flavored eggplant. The fresh fish of the day is grilled to perfection, and meats are cooked equally well.

Vico la Floresta 1. © **0942-23360.** Reservations required. Main courses 18€–22€ ($22–$26). AE, DC, MC, V. Apr–July and Sept–Oct Tues–Sun 8:15–11pm (Nov–Mar open only Fri–Sat; Aug open daily).

Maffei's ★ *Finds* SICILIAN/SEAFOOD   Maffei's is very small, with only 10 tables, but it serves the best fish in Taormina. Every day the chef selects the freshest fish at the market, and you simply tell him how you'd like it prepared. We often choose the house specialty, swordfish *alla Messinese,* braised with tomato sauce, black olives, and capers. The *fritto misto* (a mixed fry with calamari, shrimp, swordfish, and sea bream) is made superbly light by good-quality olive oil.

Via San Domenico de Guzman 1. © **0942-24055.** Reservations required. Main courses 10€–15€ ($12–$18). AE, DC, MC, V. Daily noon–3pm and 7pm–midnight. Closed early Jan to mid-Feb.

Ristorante Luraleo *Value* SICILIAN/INTERNATIONAL   Luraleo offers excellent value. Diners can sit either on the flowery terrace or in the rustic dining room with tile accents, flowers, candlelight, and a bountiful antipasti table. The grilled fish is a good choice, as are the tender herb-flavored steak, risotto with salmon and pistachio nuts, and homemade macaroni with tomato, egg-plant, and basil.

Via Bagnoli Croce 32. (✆ **0942-24279**. Reservations recommended. Main courses 15€–25€ ($18–$30). DC, MC, V. Daily 10am–3pm and 6pm–midnight. Closed Wed in winter.

MODERATE

Al Duomo ✿ SICILIAN/MESSINESE   Known for its romantic terrace din-ing (with a view of the square and cathedral), this restaurant prepares its dishes using the freshest local produce and regional ingredients. It's an attractive place, with brickwork tiles and inlaid marble tables. Try the stewed lamb with potatoes and red Sicilian wine; fried calamari sautéed in extra-virgin olive oil; or *rissolé* of fresh anchovies.

Via degli Ebrei 11. (✆ **0942-625656**. Reservations required. Main courses 8€–16€ ($9.60–$19). AE, DC, MC, V. Nov–Mar Mon–Sat noon–2:30pm and 7–11pm; Apr–Oct Thurs–Mon noon–2:30pm and 7–11pm.

Club Septimo ✿ INTERNATIONAL/ITALIAN   In addition to its excellent cuisine, this restaurant and club offers a sweeping view of Taormina and the Ion-ian Sea and is framed with reproductions of ancient Roman columns. It lies on the winding road leading downhill from Taormina, between Campo Sportiva (a soccer field) and Parcheggio Lumbi, the public parking lot. The place has a ritzy feel, especially if you dine on the terrace overlooking the sea—one of the most beautiful settings around. Menus present classic and modern cuisine ideas almost in equal measure. Among the more stimulating dishes is swordfish with mussels, sliced potatoes, and an aromatic touch of saffron. The platter of smoked fish comes with a citrus-flavored olive-oil sauce and warm bread.

Via San Pancrazio 50. (✆ **0942-625522**. Reservations required. Main courses 8€–16€ ($9.60–$19). AE, DC, MC, V. June–Sept daily 7:30pm–midnight (or later).

Il Ciclope *Value* SICILIAN/ITALIAN   This is one of the best of Taormina's low-priced trattorie. Set back from the main street, it opens onto the pint-size Piazzetta Salvatore Leone. In summer, try to snag an outside table. The food is fairly simple, but the ingredients are fresh and the dishes well prepared. Try the fish soup, Sicilian squid, or grilled shrimp.

Corso Umberto I, 203. (✆ **0942-23263**. Main courses 5.50€–13€ ($6.60–$16). AE, DC, MC, V. Thurs–Tues noon–3pm and 6:30–10:30pm. Closed Jan 10–Feb 15 and Wed Oct–May.

Osteria Nero D'Avola ✿ *Finds* SICILIAN   For some real down-home Sicil-ian fare, head to this traditional trattoria in the city center, in back of the Duomo. The chef changes the menu daily and prepares dishes to order. The restaurant stocks more than 200 types of Sicilian wines along with 15 different types of island olive oil. If you have an adventurous palate, start off with home-made pasta with sea urchins or pasta with or tuna roe. Specialties include the best shrimp salad in Taormina and a fillet of tuna with caramelized onions.

Vico de Spuches 8. (✆ **0942-628874**. Reservations recommended. Main courses 10€–15€ ($12–$18). AE, DC, MC, V. June–Sept daily 8:30pm–3am; Oct–May daily 6:30pm–midnight.

Ristorante La Griglia ✿ SICILIAN   One of the city's newer restaurants seems much older, thanks to its country-elegant location within the thick stone walls of what was a private palazzo in the 1600s. Our favorite seats are those against the most distant back wall, where windows overlook one of Taormina's oldest streets, a ravinelike alley known as Via Naumachia, whose walled edges were built by the ancient Romans. Start with one of the best selections of antipasti in town or with a classic island pasta dish—we enjoyed one prepared with swordfish and baby eggplant. The chef will be happy to prepare grilled fresh vegetables for vegetarians. The wine list is wonderful.

Corso Umberto I, 54. ℭ **0942-23980.** Reservations recommended for dinner during midsummer. Main courses 9€–15€ ($11–$18). AE, DC, MC, V. Wed–Mon noon–3:30pm and 7–11pm.

INEXPENSIVE

Al Settimo Cielo del Paradiso ℜ *Value* SICILIAN   It's far from being the most popular restaurant in Taormina, but in some ways it's our undisputed budget favorite, thanks to its superb view, sense of chic, and high-altitude view that seems to sweep over half of Sicily. To reach it, take an elevator from the lobby of the also-recommended hotel, and then dine on a rooftop where Orson Welles and John D. Rockefeller IV once ate. Dishes are likely to include well-crafted versions of pennette or risotto with salmon; succulent salads of grilled prawns with a limoncello sauce; and roulades of grilled swordfish layered with vegetables and herbs. *Note:* You must enter the restaurant between 8 and 9pm, as it has the shortest opening times of any place along the coast.

In the Hotel Villa Paradiso, Via Roma 2. ℭ 0942-23922. Reservations recommended. Main courses 8€–15€ ($9.60–$18). AE, DC, MC, V. Daily 1–2pm and 7:30–9pm.

Bella Blu ℜ SICILIAN/INTERNATIONAL   This chic international spot is a restaurant and pizzeria, as well as a piano bar and disco. In addition to offering fine cuisine, Bella Blu is one of the most entertaining places to be in Taormina after dark. Located a 150m (492-ft.) walk from the center, it has a rich, luxurious aura. Its menus and fine food are based on the freshest of local ingredients. The chef specializes in barbecued and grilled meats flavored with fresh herbs, as well as fresh fish. Sicilian favorites include homemade pasta with fresh sardines in a savory tomato sauce with wild fennel and pine nuts.

Via Luigi Pirandello 28. ℭ 0942-24239. Reservations required June–Aug. Main courses 5€–10€ ($6–$12); fixed-price menu 15€ ($18). AE, DC, MC, V. Daily 10am–3pm and 6–11pm.

Da Saro SICILIAN   This popular restaurant is favored by neighborhood locals as well as mainly European visitors. Much of its charm derives from the animated staff. The surrounding neighborhood, near the Grande Arco Porta Messina, isn't particularly fashionable, and commercial traffic roars by outside. But that doesn't detract from the delicious flavors within—for example, try the spaghetti Don Giuliano, concocted with olives, tuna, and tomatoes. Other choices include prosciutto with olives and a memorable *frittura* (mixed grill) of fish and calamari.

Via Costantino Patricio 24. ℭ 0942-23934. Reservations not necessary. Main courses 8€–14€ ($9.60–$17). AE, DC, MC, V. Daily noon–3:30pm and 7–11pm.

Granduca ℜ *Finds* ITALIAN/SICILIAN   This is the most atmospheric choice in town, entered through an antiques store; it also serves an excellent, carefully executed cuisine. In fair weather, request a table in the beautiful gardens. Our favorite pasta here is spaghetti alla Norma (with tomato sauce, eggplant, and ricotta). If you want something truly Sicilian, ask for pasta with sardines. The best meat dish is the grilled roulades. At night, various pizzas are baked to perfection in a wood-fired oven.

Corso Umberto I, 172. ℭ 0942-24983. Reservations recommended. Main courses 8€–15€ ($9.60–$18). AE, DC, MC, V. Daily 12:30–3pm and 7:30pm–midnight.

Il Baccanale SICILIAN   This trattoria/grill serves what islanders called *Cucina Tipica Siciliana*. A slightly better dining venue than its many competitors that flank it on all sides, this eatery lies at the end of a pedestrian-only street. It's the Taormina

Fun Fact   **The Case of the Bouncing Check**

The writer Truman Capote visited Taormina to finish his novel *Answered Prayers*. One drunken night at the San Domenico, he closed a deal to purchase the offshore island Isola Bella. It's actually a gloriously conical peninsula—small, ringed with sand, and absolutely beautiful. The asking price from a local landowner was $10,000. Everyone was happy with this amazing deal until the check was returned from New York, marked "insufficient funds."

equivalent of a French bistro, with checkered tablecloths and a bustling kitchen visible on an upper balcony. The 30 or so tables spill onto the piazza in front.

Piazzetta Filea 1 (Via Di Giovanni). ✆ 0942-625390. Reservations recommended. Main courses 8€–15€ ($9.60–$18). MC, V. Daily noon–3pm and 6–10pm. Closed Thurs Oct–Mar.

Ristorante U'Bossu SICILIAN/MEDITERRANEAN   Vines twine around the facade of this small restaurant in a quiet part of town. Amid fresh flowers, wagon-wheel chandeliers, and burnished wooden panels, you'll enjoy a meal pungent with the aromas of an herb garden. Specialties include pasta with sardines, swordfish roulades, and *maccheroni alla Turiddu* (with tuna, olives, capers, onions, wild herbs, tomatoes, and fennel). For dessert, nothing can top the zabaglione with fresh strawberries.

Via Bagnoli Croce 50. ✆ 0942-23311. Reservations recommended. Main courses 6€–12€ ($7.20–$14); fixed-price menu 13€ ($16). AE, DC, MC, V. Tues–Sun noon–3pm and 6pm–midnight. Closed Nov 10–Mar 1.

Tirami Su ⭐ *Value* SICILIAN   This is one of the most frequently praised inexpensive restaurants in Taormina, drawing appreciative comments from both residents and visitors. It's small and basic-looking, set beside a busy, narrow commercial street. You'll enjoy dishes that may include beef with mushrooms and cream sauce; swordfish roulades; and spaghetti with seafood.

Via Costantino Patricio. ✆ 0942-24803. Reservations recommended. Pizzas 5€–9€ ($6–$11); main courses 7.50€–14€ ($9–$16). AE, DC, MC, V. Wed–Mon 12:30–3pm and 7:30pm–midnight.

IN MAZZARO
Ristorante Angelo a Mare-Il Delfino MEDITERRANEAN/ITALIAN   This late-19th-century building is in Mazzarò, about 5km (3 miles) from Taormina and a 2-minute walk from the cable-car station. From the flower-filled terrace, you can enjoy views over the bay. Both decor and menu items were inspired by the sea. Specialties include mussels *Delfino* (with garlic, parsley, olive oil, and lemons), house-style steak (with fresh tomatoes, onions, garlic, capers, and parsley), and risotto *pescatoro* (fisherman's rice).

Via Nazionale. ✆ 0942-23004. Reservations recommended. Main courses 7€–15€ ($8.40–$18). AE, DC, MC, V. Daily noon–3pm and 6pm–midnight. Closed Nov–Mar.

IN ISOLA BELLA
Ristorante da Giovanni SICILIAN/ITALIAN   Perched precariously between the coastal road and the cliff that drops vertiginously down to the sea, this restaurant enjoys a view that sweeps over the peninsula of Isola Bella. The glassed-in dining room is simple and airy, accented with blue tile floors and very few adornments other than the view. The flavorful menu items include a fish

soup that might win the approval of Neptune, as well as a mixed grill of fish caught that morning by fishermen working the Ionian Sea. For our pasta fix, we gravitate to pennette with succulent crabmeat. Meat aficionados should find the veal scaloppine with white-wine sauce heartwarming.

Isola Bella. ✆ 0942-23531. Reservations recommended. Main courses 8€–17€ ($9.60–$20). AE, DC, MC, V. Tues–Sun 12:15–3pm and 8–11pm.

IN CASTELMOLA

Ristorante Parco Reale ✯ *Finds* SICILIAN/INTERNATIONAL   Artful and romantic, the best restaurant in Castelmola offers lots of international pizazz. Some members of the staff are Australian, with an offbeat sense of humor that might contribute to your understanding of this very Sicilian venue. The airy and rambling dining room is awash with displays of wine and rolling food trolleys. The menu is constantly changing, but the grilled catch of the day is always done to perfection. We've also loved the risotto with fresh mushrooms; the macaroni with garlic, tomatoes, and ham; and the veal escalope cooked in almond wine.

In the Hotel Villa Sonia, Via Porta Mola 9, Castelmola. ✆ 0942-28082. Reservations recommended for dinner in midsummer. Main courses 8€–15€ ($9.60–$18). AE, DC, MC, V. Daily 12:30–2:30pm and 7–10:30pm.

TAORMINA AFTER DARK

Sicilian cities aren't known for their nightlife. The best—and certainly the most sophisticated—after-dark amusements can be found in Taormina. The resort is also the best spot in Sicily for gay and lesbian visitors. (Incidentally, drinks here are more expensive than elsewhere in Sicily.)

Many visitors are content to relax at cafe tables on outdoor terraces. The most popular form of evening entertainment is the *passeggiata,* or promenade, along the Corso Umberto I. Join it—it's fun.

You might also catch a bus to Giardini-Naxos (p. 196) for a waterfront stroll in the evening. Most bars and clubs there stay open until way past midnight, at least in the summer.

For a nightlife adventure, one of the most popular activities in Taormina is to take a CST bus tour, **Etna Tramonto,** for a sunset trip to the slopes of Mount Etna. The cost is 70€ ($84). Buses run from June to October. Departures are daily at 3:45pm (returning at midnight) from June to August; at 3:15pm (returning at 11pm) in September; and at 2:15pm (returning at 10:30pm) in October. Call ✆ 0942-625301 for tickets and information.

Bar at the Palazzo San Domenico ✯   For a (relatively) inexpensive way to see one of Italy's most legendary hotels, drop by here for a drink. Within a sprawling labyrinth of public areas—some of which evoke the Gilded Age, others the inner sanctums of medieval monasteries—you can order drinks and listen to live piano music. Bar service is technically available daily from 4 to 11:30pm, but the place is most romantic after 9pm, when flickering torches illuminate the gardens. Piazza San Domenico 5. ✆ 0942-613111.

Bar San Giorgio   Perched on the main square of Castelmola, adjacent to a rocky drop-off guaranteed to induce vertigo, this might be the only building in the town's historic core that was able to beat the local building codes and alter its otherwise medieval-looking architecture. The result is a boxy, glass-sided upper story that looks like something from the German Bauhaus. Many visitors opt for coffee or gelati in the ground-floor cafe, but if you prefer to contemplate the Sicilian views that sweep over the surrounding hills, simply negotiate the steep steps that cling to the building's exterior to reach the upper story. The place serves only coffee, sandwiches, and drinks. Open year-round, daily from 7:30am to midnight. Via Porta Mola 9, Castelmola. © 0942-28228.

Bella Blu On a crazy summer day, you can bet that the most fun is being generated by the high-energy 20- and 30-somethings who flock to this previously recommended restaurant/pizzeria (see p. 192 for further details). It's one of the most elegant and popular piano bars and dance clubs in town. The disco is open only on Saturday from 11pm to 2:30am; the piano bar is also open only on Saturday, from 9pm to 2am. Via Luigi Pirandello 28. © 0942-24239.

Caffè Wunderbar We always begin our evening here, as Tennessee Williams did on his yearly visits to Taormina. This bar/cafe is on Taormina's main street, opening onto a panoramic view of the bay and Mount Etna beyond. Ice creams and *granite* (crushed-ice drinks) are served at outdoor tables or inside an elegant salon where you might hear the soft notes of a cafe concert. Open daily from 8:30am to 2:30am; closed Tuesdays from November to February. Piazza IX Aprile 7 (Corso Umberto I). © 0942-625302.

Club Septimo ☞ With some of the loveliest terraces in Taormina, this well-attended nightclub plays disco all night long to a mostly European, 20- to 40-something crowd. Fashion shows and other gala evenings are often staged here. The interior contains all the strobe and ultraviolet lights you could want, along with some of Taormina's most daring apparel. The disco is open June through September, daily from midnight to 5am; and off season, on Saturdays only during the same hours. Via San Pancrazio 50. © 0942-625522. Cover 8€–13€ ($9.60–$16).

La Cisterna del Moro The focal point of this restaurant/pub is a stone-sided cistern, built during the Middle Ages by the Arabs, that's set deep within a basement used for wine storage. A staff member will show it to you upon request, but you're more likely to be drinking and eating on the upper floors. Located in a narrow alley a few steps downhill from Corso Umberto, the club is most fun after 8pm. An attached restaurant, set on a terrace draped in bougainvillea, serves 25 kinds of pizza (including a version with grilled radicchio, smoked cheese, and bacon). Beer is the preferred drink. Open Tuesday through Sunday from noon to 3pm and 7pm to midnight. Via Bonifacio 1. © 0942-23001.

Mocambo Bar ☞ Our favorite outdoor bar in Taormina occupies an enviable location on the main square, smack in the center of the evening hubbub. It was established in 1952, during the peak of *la dolce vita,* when Truman Capote and Tennessee Williams held court at sidewalk tables. You can opt for a seat on the piazza throughout the year, weather permitting, but during colder months many visitors migrate inside, where there's a satirical mural showing a busy night at the Mocambo. There's live piano music every evening between 9pm and 12:30am. Open in summer daily from 8pm to at least 2am; in winter, Saturday and Sunday from 9pm to 12:30am. Piazza IX Aprile 8. © 0942-23350.

Morgana Bar This ultra-hip bar is tucked into one of the narrow alleys that run downhill from Corso Umberto I. Centered around a semicircular bar, it spills onto a candlelit terrace with lighting guaranteed to make anyone look fabulous. Don't expect this place to even begin to hop until around midnight. The clientele is international and attractive, and mating games between regulars and incoming holidaymakers sometimes get serious. Open nightly from 9pm to 5am. Scesa Morgana 4. © 0942-620056.

O-Seven Irish Pub One of our favorite bars in Taormina is a woodsy, sudsy, high-ceilinged affair, staffed with attractive Europeans. It welcomes 20- and 30-somethings from around the world, many flirting and philosophizing with one another over foaming mugs of beer. Open from June to September, daily from 4pm to 6am; from October to May, Thursday through Tuesday from 5pm to 2am. Largo La Farina 6 (at Corso Umberto I). ℭ **0942-24980.**

Re di Bastoni   Favored by locals as a convivial and almost claustrophobically crowded hideaway, this bar gets impossibly loud after 10pm with its live or recorded music reverberating off sienna-colored walls, a beamed ceiling, and oversize paintings. Patrons usually come here late at night, sometimes with their pets, and always with their fetishes, to slurp down the house specialty of strawberry caipirinhas. Open Tuesday through Sunday from 11am to 3am. Sandwiches are the only food served. Corso Umberto I 120. ℭ **0942-23037.**

Shatulle   This cozy counterculture bar was established by an Austrian who gave it the German name *Shatulle,* or "jewel box." Set on an intimate piazza just downhill from Corso Umberto I, it's the self-acknowledged gay, or gay-friendly, hangout of Taormina. You'll find a mix of Europeans and nonconformist locals. Most of the youngish guests opt for seats outside. Open year-round, daily from 5pm to 4am. Piazza Paladini 4. ℭ **0942-626175.**

2 Giardini-Naxos

5km (3 miles) S of Taormina, 47km (29 miles) N of Catania, 54km (34 miles) S of Messina

Many first-time visitors to Taormina are disappointed when they find they have to commute from its hotels to the beach. At Giardini-Naxos, however, you can walk from your hotel room to the sands in short order. You can reach this resort by the sea in just 30 minutes by taking the Giardini-Naxos bus from the hilltop of Taormina.

The beach here opens onto the bay, lying between Capo (Cape) Taormina in the northwest and Capo Schisò in the south. Its point formed by an ancient lava flow from Mount Etna, Capo Schisò was the natural landfall for mariners rounding the toe of Italy on their way from eastern Mediterranean ports.

Thucydides tells us that Naxos was founded in 735 B.C. by Chalcidians under the leadership of the Athenian Thucles, who was the first Greek to land on Sicilian soil. From their base at Naxos, the Greeks branched out to take over more parts of Sicily. The colony at Naxos thrived until Dionysius of Syracuse destroyed it in 403 B.C. Even if you're staying in Taormina, you should set aside some time to visit the archaeological garden that remains here (see below).

Over the years, beach development at Giardini-Naxos has been so great that the resort now competes with Taormina for visitors, although it lacks the older resort's medieval charm. Since the 1960s, it's been catering mainly to package-tour operators from the north of Europe. (As a local said, "Taormina has the class, we have the sands.") Indeed, all the trappings of tourism are evident in this once-tranquil fishing village, with its many sports facilities and amusement parks, handicraft shops, antiques stores, hotels, trattorie, and beachside bars.

Much of the resort continues to function even during the short winter, when the winds can blow cold. Europeans from the frigid north will find Giardini-Naxos's weather balmy almost any time of year.

ESSENTIALS

Giardini-Naxos has a long main street, **Lungomare,** that runs parallel to the sea.

Interbus (ℭ **0942-625301**) runs buses from the terminal in Taormina along Via Luigi Pirandello; a one-way ticket costs 1.50€ ($1.80). Service is daily, every half hour from 8am to midnight.

Giardini-Naxos shares the same rail depot as Taormina (see above). If you're driving from Taormina, take the SS114 south. From Messina, follow autostrada A18 south, exiting at the turnoff for Giardini-Naxos.

The **tourist office,** Via Tysandros 54 (© **0942-51010**), is open Monday through Friday from 8:30am to 2pm and 4 to 7pm, Saturday from 8:30am to 2pm.

EXPLORING ANCIENT RUINS

In a setting of citrus trees and prickly pears, on the headland of Capo Schisò, lie the ruins of the **Naxos excavations** ⭐, the site of the first Greek colony in Sicily. This site has been inhabited since 735 B.C., and has gone through the various tribulations of all such colonies, thriving and prospering until conquered and devastated—only to rise again out of the ashes.

If you're driving, head out on Via Naxos, which becomes Via Stracina. The ancient site lies in the dusty, barren scrubland above Giardini-Naxos. The actual excavations are behind a rusted iron fence facing the uphill (landward) side of the main road leading into Giardini-Naxos. Inside, you'll find the repository of artifacts that remained after Dionysius of Syracuse razed the city in 403 B.C.

This is not Pompeii, so don't be disappointed. What the tyrant didn't raze to the ground, centuries of builders carted off for other structures. Little remains today except some structural foundations and the pavement stones of ancient streets.

The best of what was dug up is displayed in the **Archaeological Museum,** on two floors of an old Bourbon-built fort. The most evocative artifact is a statuette of Aphrodite Hippias from the 5th century B.C. As a curiosity, one exhibit displays objects removed from a surgeon's grave, including a strigil, a speculum used to examine injuries, and tiny ointment jars.

The site is open daily from 9am to 4:30pm. Admission is 2€ ($2.40) for adults, free for children 17 and under. For information, call © **0942-51001.**

WHERE TO STAY

Arathena Rocks Hotel ⭐ *Value*   This government-rated three-star hotel contains one of the most appealing collections of decorative objects along the Taormina coastline. This includes bas-reliefs, sculptures, wrought-iron balustrades, gilded baroque door frames, and hand-painted tilework tastefully assembled into a complete whole. The overall effect is that of a whimsical private villa that happens to rent out rooms. Built in the 1970s atop a jagged strip of eroded lava rocks, it has compensated for its lack of sandy beach with a terraced pool and masses of potted flowers. Its rock-studded beach is private. Rooms are cozy and clean; many contain balconies or loggias. Half of the units have air-conditioning. About half of the bathrooms contain showers, while the rest have tubs.

Via Calcide Eubea 55, 98035 Giardini-Naxos. © 0942-51349. Fax 0942-51690. www.hotelarathena.com. 50 units. 110€–120€ ($132–$144) double. Rates include breakfast. AE, DC, MC, V. Free parking. Closed Nov to Easter. **Amenities:** Restaurant; bar; outdoor pool; free shuttle transfers to Taormina. *In room:* TV.

Hellenia Yachting Club ⭐⭐   Set in the heart of Giardini-Naxos, closer to the town's bars than some of its competitors, this is a gracefully modern hotel whose public areas have some of the most lavish marble decoration anywhere, often with classical Greek touches. Built in 1978 and radically upgraded in 2004, it features a sun terrace (with a pleasant but not overly large pool) and black-lava steps that descend to a private gravel beach. The place has the aura of a private club—perhaps one in Greece that welcomes a nautically minded British clientele. Be warned that guest rooms are not as opulent as the lobby would imply.

They have a sparsely furnished, somewhat cold decor, with hints of 18th-century French styling. Each is equipped with a well-maintained bathroom with tub or shower; half have private balconies. Some units have dataports.

Via Jannuzzo 41, 98035 Giardini-Naxos. © **0942-51737.** Fax 0942-54310. www.hotel-hellenia.it. 112 units. 139€–211€ ($167–$253) double. Rates include buffet breakfast. Free parking. AE, DC, MC, V. **Amenities:** Restaurant; 2 bars; outdoor pool; tennis nearby; fitness room; room service; babysitting; nonsmoking rooms; rooms for those w/limited mobility. *In room:* A/C, TV, minibar, hair dryer, safe.

Hotel Sabbie d'Oro   The on-site restaurant (p. 199) is genuinely charming and more alluring than the hotel that administers it. Nonetheless, this simple lodging is acceptable in every way, though hardly grand. Built in 1990, and named after the public beach (Sabbie d'Oro/Golden Sands) that's just across the street, this government-rated three-star hotel is clean, only a bit battered, and completely unpretentious. Each room has a tiled, shower-only bathroom.

Via Schisò 12, 98035 Giardini-Naxos. © **0942-51227.** Fax 0942-56913. www.hotelsabbiedoro.it. 39 units. 140€–156€ ($168–$187) double. Rates include breakfast. AE, DC, MC, V. Parking: 10€ ($12). **Amenities:** Restaurant; bar; concierge; laundry service. *In room:* A/C, TV, minibar, hair dryer, safe.

Sant Alphio Garden Hotel ✦   This is the biggest and most opulent hotel in Giardini-Naxos. Constructed in 1979 at the northern edge of the resort, its rich style evokes the scope and imagination of Las Vegas. Its centerpiece is a free-form outdoor pool with lavish landscaping and a swim-up bar, set directly adjacent to the best-looking cluster of swimming pools along the Taormina coastline. The hotel is outfitted in contemporary tones of navy and white, with touches of chrome and a jazzy combination of Sicilian and European styling. Bedrooms range from midsize to spacious, each with a well-maintained bathroom with shower or tub. Most visitors opt to spend at least a week here, decompressing from overburdened schedules in other parts of (usually northern) Europe. Come here for a retreat, with the understanding that the medieval attractions of Taormina are just an easy taxi ride away. A private beach lies within a 3-minute walk; tennis, horseback riding, and golf are available through outside concessions.

Marina di Recanati, 98030 Giardini-Naxos. © **0942-51383.** Fax 0942-53934. www.santalphiohotel.com. 124 units. 98€–150€ ($118–$180) double. Rates include breakfast. AE, DC, MC, V. Free parking. **Amenities:** 2 restaurants; 2 bars; outdoor pool with sunken bar; spa with indoor pool; fitness center; Jacuzzi; sauna; steam room; 24-hr. room service; massage; babysitting; laundry service; dry cleaning. *In room:* A/C, TV, dataport, minibar, hair dryer, safe.

Villa Mora ✦✦ *Finds*   A friendly, welcoming couple take special care of guests at this hotel across from the beach and waters of the Ionian Sea. Guest rooms are invitingly comfortable; furnishings range from antique writing desks to painted trunks, giving the place a cozy ambience. Most of the units contain private balconies; each has a shower-only bathroom. The staff takes pride in the aromatic Sicilian cuisine served here, mainly fish and vegetables, using locally grown ingredients.

Via Naxos 47, 98030 Giardini-Naxos. ©/fax **0942-51839.** www.hotelvillamora.com. 17 units. 70€–96€ ($84–$115) double. Rates include breakfast. MC, V. Free parking. Closed Jan 10–Mar 1. **Amenities:** Bar; laundry service; dry cleaning. *In room:* A/C, TV.

WHERE TO DINE

La Cambusa ✦✦ SICILIAN/SEAFOOD   This restaurant attracts both gastronomes and romantics, thanks to an indoor/outdoor setting with a view that sweeps over the beach, the coastline, and hundreds of boats bobbing at anchor.

After dark, the allure is enhanced with dozens of flaming torches. The menu presents classic and modern ideas in equal measure; the cuisine doesn't get better than this in Giardini-Naxos. For a zesty pasta, opt for fusilli with tuna and capers. We can never resist the platter of local smoked fish. Linguine with whitefish sounds dull, but isn't. And the *zuppe di pesce* (fish soup) here is spectacular, prepared with olive oil, lemon juice, and fresh oregano.

Via Schisò 3. © 0942-51437. Reservations recommended for dinner in midsummer. Main courses 8.50€–15€ ($10–$18). AE, DC, MC, V. Daily 12:30–3pm and 7:30pm–midnight. Closed Tues mid-Sept to Oct and Apr–May. Closed Nov–Mar.

Ristorante Sabbie d'Oro SICILIAN   Amicable and laid-back, this restaurant sits in a covered open-air pavilion adjacent to both the beach and the hotel that manages it. You'll dine in a setting that evokes a woodsy tavern, with tables loaded with grappa and a ceiling draped with fishnets and nautical bric-a-brac. The cooks, though not world class, are attentive. You'll enjoy such dishes as a curious marriage of beef and clams; pennette with swordfish and almonds; and macaroni with eggplant and fresh tomatoes.

Via Schisò 12. © 0942-52380. Reservations recommended Sat–Sun. Main courses 8€–15€ ($9.60–$18). AE, DC, MC, V. Daily noon–3pm and 7–11pm.

Ristorante Sea Sound ★★ SICILIAN/SEAFOOD   From a position beside a commercial street in the center of town, adjacent to the Hellenic Yacht Club Hotel, you'll walk for at least 4 minutes along a private footpath flanked by flowering vines. Just when you suspect you've made a wrong turn, you'll see a low-rise concrete bungalow adjacent to the sea. Its focal point is the terrace, surrounded by walls adorned with cheerful pottery. Overall, the place is charming, humorous, and very pleasant; it's almost the equal of La Cambusa. The antipasti selection, ranging from smoked tuna to swordfish, is the best in the area. More than a dozen pastas are made daily, including spaghetti *alla bottarga* (with tuna roe) and risotto with fresh seafood. Meat choices are limited, but dishes such as veal scaloppine in Marsala sauce are competently made.

Via Jannuzzo 37A. © 0942-54330. Reservations recommended. Main courses 11€–20€ ($13–$24). AE, DC, MC, V. Daily 12:30–2:30pm and 7–11:30pm. Closed late Oct to late Mar.

3 Mount Etna ★★

23km (15 miles) SW of Taormina; 31km (19 miles) N of Catania; 60km (37 miles) S of Messina

Looming menacingly over the coast of eastern Sicily, Mount Etna is the highest and largest active volcano in Europe—and we do mean active. The peak has changed in size over the years, but is currently in the neighborhood of 3,292m (10,800 ft.). Etna has been active in modern times (in 1928, the little village of Mascali was buried under its lava), and eruptions in 2001 and 2002 rekindled Sicilian fears. In October 2002, the air was thick and dirty over eastern Sicily as Mount Etna once again spewed out columns of ash that blackened skies as far away as Tripoli, on the coast of North Africa. Although lava flowed down both sides of the mountain, at press time no villages were endangered.

Etna has figured in history and in Greek mythology. Empedocles, the 5th-century B.C. Greek philosopher, is said to have jumped into its crater as a sign that he was being delivered directly to Mount Olympus to take his seat among the gods. It was under Etna that Zeus crushed the multi-headed dragon Typhoeus, thereby securing domination over Olympus. Hephaestus, the god of fire and blacksmiths, made his headquarters in Etna, aided by the single-eyed Cyclops.

The Greeks warned that whenever Typhoeus tried to break out of his prison, lava erupted and earthquakes cracked the land. That must mean that the monster nearly escaped on March 11, 1669, the date of one of the most violent eruptions ever recorded—it destroyed Catania.

Visitors will have to decide whether to ascend Mount Etna from the northern or southern approach. We prefer the north-facing side, partly because it's cooler, more beautiful, and much richer in wildflowers that thrive in the volcanic soil. The north side is also more heavily forested. The south side, because of the eruptions during the last decade, is mostly covered with barren-looking lava flows. Its access routes are more crowded, and its views less appealing. Nonetheless, many visitors to Catania come up Etna's south side (for details, see chapter 9).

If you decide to come up the north side, simply take the highway to its end, Piano Provenzana, which stops at a complex of Alpine-inspired chalets selling souvenirs. During the heat of a Sicilian summer, they appear visibly out of place, but in winter, because of the high altitude (2,700m/8,858 ft.), they function as the centerpiece of a small-scale but thriving ski colony. The ski facilities include five downhill ski lifts and a network of cross-country ski trails.

It is from this artificial-looking Alpine hamlet of Piano Provenzana that you buy tickets for bus excursions to the top of Mount Etna. The round-trip lasts 2 hours and cost 37€ ($44) for adults, 26€ ($31) for children under 16. Departures are whenever business merits, but in summer buses usually leave every hour.

The bus tours are loaded with bio-curious, bio-conscious folks from throughout Europe, especially France, who shoot away on their cameras as the specially equipped bus (more like an armored car) winds its way laboriously uphill, through gravel beds and rocky gullies, past barren, lichen-covered gray-green landscapes. Frankly, it's not all that exciting. At the top, the bus parks near a seismic exploration station, which is mostly abandoned, and visitors walk a bit farther to a point near the top, across gravel-covered landscapes of great brutality. There's no fire and brimstone to see—if there is, and if the crater is active, all bus trips are immediately discontinued. Note that visibility is poor on cloudy days; it's also generally clearer in the mornings.

In Taormina, **CST,** Corso Umberto I, 101 (© **0942-23301**), organizes tours to Etna, offered Monday through Friday in summer. The cost is 70€ ($84) per person. The office is open Monday through Saturday from 8:45am to 12:45pm and 4 to 7:30pm; closed on Saturday from October to April.

A road around the foot of the volcano takes you through magnificent country where the rich soil has spawned many plantations and vineyards. Pistachio trees and prickly pears are commonplace. If you're driving around Etna in the morning, you can usually see the volcano, although it is often hidden in mist after lunch.

THE FOOTHILLS OF MOUNT ETNA

The village of Linguaglossa, 18km (11 miles) west of Taormina, is the best base for excursions to Mount Etna. From here, you can access Piano Provenzana at 1,800m (5,906 ft.), the main ski resort on Etna. It's at Piano Provenzana that four-wheel-drive vans are organized for those wanting to go on excursions to Etna's dangerous summit. Many hikers walk from Piano Provenzana to the cone of Etna in about 3 hours, following the track used by the shuttle vans.

M. Nero
2049▲ Peak, with Elevation in Meters

Gole dell' ■
Alcantara

Taormina

Randazzo○

Castelmola○

Mazzarò

Linguaglossa

**Giardini-
Naxos**○

Capo
Taormina

M. Sta. Maria
1632

Calatabiano○

■ **Naxos**

Maletto

M. Nero
2049

Capo
Schisò

M. La Nave
1273

Piedimonte○

Bronte○

M Ruvolo
1410 ▲

▲3323

Giarre○

la Montagnola
▲ *2640*

M. Turchio
1291 ▲

**PARCO
DELL'ETNA**

M. Piniteddu
1398

A18

*Ionian
Sea*

Adrano○

Biancavilla○

Nicolosi○

Acireale

Paterno○

Misterbianco
○

0   80 Mi

0   80 Km

Palermo○

Mt. Etna

Messina○

SICILY

Catania

Agrigento○

Syracuse○

LINGUAGLOSSA

Before climbing the mountain, you may want to linger in the village of Lingua-glossa. Built from black lava, it is traversed by a main street called Via Roma. At the most distant end of this street is the 17th-century church **Chiesa Madre Madonna della Grazie,** capped with an iron cross and opening onto Piazza Matrice.

Via Roma is covered with large and very heavy black-lava cobblestones. It begins at the **Chiesa di San Francesco de Paola,** known for its lavish baroque frescoes and plasterwork. Via Roma continues to the 17th-century Duomo, which is also known as **Chiesa della SS. Annunziata.** The stately-looking, pink-stucco **Town Hall (Il Municipio)** opens on Piazza Municipio, overlooking a Liberty-style monument dedicated to the Italian dead in World War I.

The tourist office, **Associazione Turistica Proloco Linguaglossa,** Piazza Annunziata 7 (© **095-643094**), is open Monday through Saturday from 9am to 1pm and 3 to 7pm, Sunday from 9:30am to noon. Pick up brochures for area attractions and check out the mini-display that showcases the local geology, including insights on the abundant lava flows.

A bus from Giardini-Naxos (p. 196) leaves for Linguaglossa daily at 2:55pm. If you're driving from Taormina to Linguaglossa, take A18 south. After 12km (7½ miles), take the exit marked FIUMEFREDDO. After 815m (2,674 ft.), turn left and follow SS120 into Linguaglossa.

Where to Dine

Chalet della Ginestre SICILIAN   As you navigate your way uphill through the scrubby pine forests and occasional snows of the north slope of Mount Etna, you'll find this isolated, cement-sided chalet a welcome sight. Set 9km (5½ miles) from the uppermost terminus of the highway, it was built in 2000 and offers a cozy, weatherproof venue for a fortifying meal or drink. Menu items include mixed grill of meat; asparagus with risotto, butter, and sage; and roasted veal. The food is satisfying and filling, nothing more.

Strada Mareneve, Km 10.8. © 0347-8180990. Reservations not necessary. Main courses 5€–9€ ($6–$11); set-price menu 20€ ($24). No credit cards. Oct–Feb daily 12:30–4pm; Mar–Sept daily 12:30–4pm and 8–10pm. Closed 2 weeks in Nov.

Ristorante La Betulle ITALIAN   Everything about this place—the indestructible wooden furniture, easy-to-mop tile floors, tavern-style coziness, and big windows overlooking the mountains—might remind you of an Alpine ski resort farther north. The food is satisfying and served in generous portions—the sort of rib-sticking fare you appreciate in cold climates. Look for homemade soups, fresh salads, pastas, grilled meats, and the occasional fresh fish.

Etna Nord (Linguaglossa). © 095-643430. Reservations not required. Main courses 8.50€–12€ ($10–$14). Daily noon–3pm and 7–9pm. Closed Nov.

RANDAZZO

After you explore Linguaglossa and Mount Etna, you may want to continue west to the intriguing "black town" of Randazzo, 20km (13 miles) away on Route 120. Amazingly, this town, built of lava and with a history going back to antiquity, has never been destroyed by the volcano. Most of its destruction came from man, when the Germans made Randazzo their last stand of resistance in August 1943. That dubious honor caused Randazzo to be bombed by the Allies.

Chiesa di Santa Maria ⚘, Piazza della Basilica 5 (© **095-921003**), is a study in contrasts, its building materials of black lava contrasting with its white trim. Its black-and-white tower is a prime example of brilliant Sicilian masonry. The church dates from the 13th century and contains a 15th-century south portal built in the Catalan Gothic style. The interior opens onto impressive black-lava columns. Open daily from 10am to noon and 4 to 6pm.

The other notable church in town, **Chiesa di San Martino,** Corso Umberto I (© **095-921003**), is open daily from 10am to noon and 4 to 6pm. Its impressive **campanile** ⚘, or bell tower, is from the 13th century, although the church was reconstructed in the 17th century. The black-and-white stone tower makes a dramatic contrast to the church, whose facade is adorned with reliefs of martyrs and saints.

The **tourist office** is at Corso Umberto I, 197 (© **095-7991611**). It's open daily from 9am to 1pm and 2 to 8pm.

Where to Stay

L'Antica Vigna ⚘ *Kids*   Take the SS120 out of Randazzo to get to this stunningly situated little hotel, located 4km (2½ miles) southeast of town at the foot of the volcano. This charming accommodation is actually a converted farm surrounded by 3 hectares (32 acres) of olive trees. The farmyard menagerie includes horses along with the inevitable Sicilian goats. The place is ideal for families with children; there's even a small park set aside for them. Guests are housed in small, comfortable villas, furnished with everything from kitchens to fireplaces. Each unit comes with a small bathroom with tub.

Località Monteguardi Est., 95036 Randazzo. ② **095-924003**. Fax 095-923324. 14 units. 48€ ($58) per person (includes half board). No credit cards. **Amenities:** Restaurant; tennis court. *In room:* No phone.

Where to Dine

Trattoria di Veneziano SICILIAN   Randazzo's most elegant restaurant is separated from the town's medieval zone by a deep valley, along the bottom of which runs a busy boulevard. It's set on the ground floor of an airy, modern building decorated in tones of Chinese red. Among the well-prepared menu items are grilled tenderloin steaks, grilled and smoke-cured ham, salted codfish, grilled sausages, and rigatoni or papperdelle with fresh mushrooms.

Via del Romano 8. ② **095-921418**. Reservations not necessary. Main courses 6€–8€ ($7.20–$9.60). AE, DC, MC, V. Tues–Sat noon–3:30pm and 7–11:30pm; Sun noon–3:30pm.

9

Catania

Often neglected by visitors in their race toward Taormina, the baroque art city of Sicily deserves at least a day or two—and hopefully more—of your time. The capital of the eastern part of Sicily and its second-largest city after Palermo, **Catania** ★★ has had a tormented history of conquest and devastation by nature. It's also one of the richest repositories of baroque architecture in Europe, with treasures well worth seeking out.

The city has suffered natural disasters throughout the centuries. Much of the history of Catania is linked to its volcanic neighbor, **Mount Etna.** It has also been a victim of earthquakes. In 1669, the worst eruption in Catania's history occurred when Etna buried much of the city under lava that literally ran through the streets. Catania had hardly recovered when a massive earthquake leveled much of the city in 1693, creating an economic crisis.

But the people of Catania bounced back, creating an even better city and rebuilding in the harmonious baroque style. Many of the buildings were fashioned from the black lava that had rained down upon it. An aura of the 18th century still lingers over much of the heart of Catania as a direct result of the city's rebuilding program.

Even though much of the city today is in decay, its art treasures, church museums, and Roman ruins make it a rewarding stopover—that and the chance to meet, argue with, converse with, and dine with the Catanian people.

Of course, looming in the background is that menace of a volcano, Mount Etna. If you didn't take our suggestion and visit Etna from a base in Taormina (p. 175), you can do so from the southern slopes, with a base in Catania (see below).

This chapter concludes with our surprise destination: a side trip to **Acireale.** As Sicilian cities go, Acireale is a mere infant, having been founded in 1326. Built on streams of lava, the little city stands on cliffs above the sea and is filled with wonders, especially around its monumental inner core.

1 Essentials

52km (32 miles) S of Taormina, 60km (37 miles) N of Syracuse

Standing in the ominous shadow of Mount Etna, Catania is a city of lava. A bustling port opening onto the Ionian Sea, it's known as the "city of black and white." Black lava and white plaster and marble form major parts of its architectural look.

Catania is the second-largest city in Sicily, with a population of 380,000. It's a lively place, and the seat of a bishop and a great university. In deference to its hometown boy, **Vincenzo Bellini** (1801–35), Catania boasts one of Italy's grandest opera houses, where you can hear the operas and the eternal arias of this virtuoso composer.

Its second hometown boy who made good was **Giovanni Verga** (1840–1922), acclaimed as one of Italy's greatest writers. Known for his naturalistic fiction, he wrote such masterpieces as *Vita dei Campi* and *Mastro Don Gesualdo.*

If we can believe the historian Thucydides (he wasn't always right), Catania was founded in 729 B.C. It's had a rough go of it ever since. In 403 B.C., Dionysius of Syracuse sold off its citizens into slavery. Its patron saint, Agatha, in 253 B.C. had her breasts lopped off and has been carrying them around on a platter ever since—at least in artistic depictions of herself. That was the penalty she suffered for turning down the advances of the Roman praetor, Quintianus. Catania grew up on the Laestrygonian Fields known in Book 10 of the *Odyssey* as the home of the cannibalistic Laestrygones.

The Catania you see today, a city of wide boulevards, is a direct result of those disasters. The architect **Battista Vaccarini** (1702–68) was assigned the task of rebuilding. He decided to turn it into "the city of the baroque," since that was the fashionable architectural statement of the time. Many famous artists were commissioned, and fragments of solidified black lava were used extensively. This lava, and the way it was positioned into the masonry, gave added strength to the walls of various buildings. The result was so successful that in the 18th and 19th centuries Catania was a mandatory stopover for those rich dandies making the "Grand Tour" of Europe. Regrettably, the Allied bombing raids of 1943 did much to damage many monuments.

Grime and neglect have also taken their toll. Today Catania is often called the most degraded city of Europe, largely because of the decay of its once-beautiful historic core. Urban flight to the suburbs is common, with residents leaving behind an inferno of garbage, the despair of poverty, and crime. In fact, Catania vies with Palermo for the dubious distinction of crime capital of Sicily. Sicilians living elsewhere on the island generally express disdain for Catania.

Yet, in spite of its crime and poverty, the city's industry and burgeoning economy have earned it the appellation of "the Milano of the South." And the inner city has seen improvements in recent years, including a few brightly restored antique buildings.

Our verdict on Catania? You'll either love it or hate it. We're among its devotees because we don't judge a city by whether it's pretty or not or even by whether it's well kept. We gravitate to places that bustle with life, and Catania is blessed with plenty of that. In what some critics have called a "rotting urban carcass," we have found joy in its people, pleasure in its food, and spiritual fulfillment in its artistic treasures.

There is no greater symbol of Catania, a city wiped off the map at least seven times, than the hideously ugly but endearing puce-colored elephant in front of the Duomo. It's made entirely of lava spewed from Etna. Somehow this tough little elephant is an appropriate mascot for Catania itself: It symbolizes the city's ability to bounce back from one disaster after another, and even to create art from the lava that destroyed it.

Catania is a cauldron in summer, one of the hottest cities in Italy, with temperatures known to shoot up to 104°F (40°C). Winters are mild, but the best time to visit is spring or autumn.

GETTING THERE   By Plane   Flights from across Italy arrive at **Aeroporto Fontanarossa** (✆ **095-340505**), 7km (4 1/2 miles) to the south. Major links are via Palermo, Naples, and Rome.

Major carriers flying into Catania include the market leader, **Alitalia** (✆ **800/223-5730** in the U.S.; ✆ **8488-65641** in Italy for information on domestic links). You can also fly in on **Meridiana** (✆ **06-478041**) from Milan (but not Rome or Naples). **Air Europe** (✆ **800-454000**) offers service from Milan and Venice. A taxi into the city center costs around 16€ ($19). You can also take an Alibus to the Stazione Centrale, or rail depot, in the heart of Catania. Bus departures between the two points are every 20 minutes from 5pm to midnight. A ticket costs the same as a ride on a city bus (see "Getting Around," below).

Many people fly into Catania but choose to skip the city and go on to Taormina. If that suits you, you can catch a bus just outside the airport that will take you into Taormina in about an hour, for 4€ ($4.80) one-way.

By Train   Arrivals are at the **Stazione Centrale,** Piazza Papa Giovanni XXIII (✆ **095-7306255**). Catania is a 10-hour train ride from Rome, with eight trains arriving daily and costing 49€ ($59). Catania also enjoys links with all the major cities of Sicily: Palermo (trip time: 3½ hr.), costing 12€ ($14); Agrigento (trip time: 4 hr.), costing 12€ ($14); Messina (trip time: 2 hr.), costing 5€ ($6); and Taormina (trip time: 1 hr.), costing 3€ ($3.60). For rail information, call ✆ **892021.**

By Bus   There is no central bus company; all operate independently and in total chaos. Companies are found on Via D'Amico across from the Stazione Centrale. The most useful for visitors include **SAIS Trasporti** (✆ **095-536201**), running 8 buses per day to Agrigento (trip time: 3 hr.), costing 11€ ($13) one-way; and **SAIS Autolinee** (✆ **095-536168**), running 24 buses per day to Messina (trip time: 1½ hr.), costing 6.70€ ($8.05), and 17 buses per day to Palermo (trip time: 2¾ hr.), costing 13€ ($15).

By Car   From Messina, which will probably be your gateway into Sicily, take A18 south, passing Taormina and continuing on to Catania.

VISITOR INFORMATION   **Tourist offices** are found at the Stazione Centrale, Piazza Giovanni XXIII (✆ **095-7306255;** www.apt.catania.it), and at Via Cimarosa Domenico 10 (✆ **095-7306211**), both open daily from 8am to 8pm. There is also a branch at the airport (✆ **095-7306266**), open daily from 8am to 8pm.

CITY LAYOUT

Catania was rebuilt using anti-seismic measures. Its major boulevards were made straight and wide, virtually eliminating anything that had existed from medieval Catania. Broad piazzas punctuate many streets. The aim was to make streets wide enough to allow Catanians to escape in case lava flows through the streets again.

In recent years, unchecked growth has sent Catania crawling up the southern slopes of the ferocious Etna and sprawling across the fertile lands of the Simeto River.

The old center of the city is the **Piazza Duomo,** with the aforementioned fountain of the ancient elephant. Splitting Catania in two parts is its main street, **Via Vittorio Emanuele II,** which begins east at **Piazza del Martini** running west past Piazza Duomo.

Running on a north-south axis, **Via Etnea** ✿ is the grand boulevard of Catania that runs north from Piazza Duomo for 3km (1¾ miles). Along this avenue are the best restaurants and boutiques. Eventually Via Etnea reaches **Villa Bellini,** the beautiful public gardens.

In western Catania, **Via Crociferi** ✿ is the city's gracious street of the baroque, flanked by churches and palazzi.

GETTING AROUND   Traffic is not quite as horrendous as in Palermo, but it's still the second worst in Sicily. Don't even attempt to use a car. Go by bus or taxi. Most of the historic treasures in Catania can be covered on foot.

By Bus   AMT **(Azienda Municipale Trasporti),** Via Plebiscito 747 (✆ 095-7360247), operates a good network of buses, branching out across the city. Tickets cost .80€ (95¢) and are valid for 90 minutes. A ticket valid for a day goes for 2€ ($2.40). You can purchase tickets at *tabacchi* (tobacco stands) and news kiosks. *Tip:* If you take circular bus no. 410, you'll be treated to a round-trip of all the major sightseeing attractions for the cost of a one-way fare. The service is run only by appointment; call ✆ **095-7360247.**

By Metro   The very limited subway system has trains running every 15 to 30 minutes daily from 7am to 8:45pm, costing .80€ (95¢) for a ticket valid for 90 minutes. Metro tickets, like bus tickets, are available from news kiosks and tobacco shops. Service runs from Stazione Centrale at Platform 11 south to Catania Porto and north and northwest all the way to Catania Borgo, the terminus for the Stazione Circumetnea via Caronda 490.

By Taxi   CST (✆ **095-330966**) operates 24-hour taxi service. Taxi ranks are found at the Stazione Centrale and Piazza Duomo.

FAST FACTS: Catania

American Express Amex is represented by **La Duca Viaggi,** Piazza Europa 1 (✆ **095-7222295**). Open Monday through Friday from 9am to 1pm and 4 to 7:30pm, Saturday from 9am to noon.

Currency Exchange Most banks lie in the center along Corso Sicilia; these include **Deutsche Bank,** Corso Sicilia 51 (✆ **095-325831**), and **Banca Banco di Sicilia,** Corso Sicilia 8 (✆ **095-368111**), both open Monday through Friday from 8:30am to 1:30pm and 2:30 to 4pm. You can also exchange currency at the train station and at the Amex office (see above).

Emergencies Call ✆ **113**. For **first aid,** dial ✆ **118**. **Guardia Medica** is at Corso Italia 234 (✆ **095-377122**).

Hospital The major hospital is **Garibaldi,** Piazza Santa Maria del Gesù (✆ **095-7591111**).

Internet Access Your best bet is **Atlantinet,** Via Gradisca 21 (✆ **095-370874**), open Wednesday from 5 to 9:30pm, Thursday through Saturday and Monday through Tuesday from 10am to 1:30pm and 5 to 9:30pm. It charges 2.60€ ($3.10) per hour.

Pharmacies Ask at your hotel for the one nearest you. One night pharmacy is **Croceverde,** Via Gabriele D'Annunzio 43 (✆ **095-441662**), open daily from 4pm to 1am.

Police Dial ✆ **112** or 095-7306711.

Post Office The main post office is at Via Etnea 215 (✆ **095-7155071**), next to the Villa Bellini Gardens. It is open Monday through Saturday from 8am to 6:30pm.

2 Where to Stay

EXPENSIVE

Excelsior Grand Hotel ✦✦✦ No other hotel in Sicily so gracefully manifests the flowing sense of *la dolce vita* modernism as Catania's leading establishment. It brought postwar tourism to Catania with a stately and monumental facade, built in 1954, that's almost a mirror image of the Palazzo di Giustiza (Municipal Courthouse), which lies immediately across Piazza Verga, the most impressive square in Catania. A radical renovation in 2001 retained the best aspects of this hotel's retro, age-of-Sputnik design, and added zillions of new grace notes.

Expect a *moderno*-style lobby in perfect taste, with a resident pianist, deep and comfortable settees, and the kind of bar you'd expect in a posh hotel on Rome's Via Veneto. Half of the bedrooms overlook Piazza Verga and faraway Mount Etna. These standard double rooms are called deluxe rooms, and each comes with a loggia-style balcony. The remainder ("superior rooms") are just as large, plush, and comfortable, but they face the back of the hotel and in most cases lack balconies. Bathrooms are sheathed in marble; those in the deluxe rooms contain showers, while those in the superior units and suites come with tubs as well. The in-house restaurant, **Le Zagare,** is reviewed on p. 213.

Piazza Verga, 95129 Catania. ✆ **095-7476111.** Fax 095-537015. www.thi.it. 176 units. 204€–265€ ($245–$318) double; 349€–568€ ($419–$682) suite. Free parking. Rates include breakfast. AE, DC, MC, V. Bus: 443, 457, 721, or 722. **Amenities:** Restaurant; piano bar; fitness center; steam room; room service; babysitting; laundry service; dry cleaning; nonsmoking rooms; e-mail facilities in the lobby; room for those w/limited mobility. *In room:* A/C, TV, dataport, minibar, hair dryer, safe.

Sheraton Catania ✦ This seaside resort lies in Cannizzaro, 5.6km (3½ miles) north of Catania's center. Set across the highway from the sea, and originally built in 1983, it offers a *moderno* lobby accented with fountains set into artificial grottos, Lucite-trimmed balustrades, and a low-rise atrium that fills the interior with sunlight. This is not a "showcase" Sheraton (it's a member of the Sheraton franchise, but owned by a local investor), and its links to the international chain are relatively loose. It looks a bit dated when compared to more recently renovated places such as the Excelsior. But it's appealing and comfortable, graced with a surprising number of modern paintings. Guest rooms, accessible via a labyrinthine set of low-ceilinged hallways, have big windows, a sense of 1980s design, and generous space. Each has a well-polished tiled bathroom with a tub-and-shower combination.

Via Antonello da Messina 45, 95020 Cannizzaro-Catania. ✆ **095-271557.** Fax 095-271380. www.sheraton catania.com. 170 units. 232€ ($278) double; 538€ ($646) suite. DC, MC, V. Free shuttle bus to town center. **Amenities:** Restaurant; 2 bars; outdoor pool; tennis court; fitness center; health club; Jacuzzi; sauna; 24-hr. concierge; business center; salon; room service; massage; nonsmoking rooms; solarium; rooms for those w/limited mobility. *In room:* A/C, TV, dataport, minibar.

Villa del Bosco ✦✦✦ Guests at Villa del Bosco will enjoy a true taste of the aristocratic life of a landowning Sicilian family during the early 19th century. The stately-looking Bosco is set behind a high wall that separates it from a suburban neighborhood, 5km (3 miles) south of Catania's historic core. It was originally built in 1826 as a private home and converted into a dignified boutique hotel, rich with antiques and a sense of another time. The hotel's social center is an elaborately detailed salon with a bar at one end. Guest rooms are elegant, with four-poster beds, tiled or stone-sheathed bathrooms with tub and shower, and the sense of fragility you might expect in a private home. Its artfully frescoed breakfast room is the most beautiful in Catania. The in-house restaurant, **Il Canile,** is reviewed on p. 214.

Via del Bosco 62, 95125 Catania. © **095-7335100.** Fax 095-7335103. www.hotelvilladelbosco.it. 33 units. 160€–200€ ($192–$240) double; 228€–268€ ($274– $322) suite. AE, DC, MC, V. Bus: 129, 314, or 421. **Amenities:** Restaurant; bar; outdoor pool; laundry service; dry cleaning; nonsmoking rooms; rooms for those w/limited mobility. *In room:* A/C, TV, dataport, minibar.

Villa Paradiso dell'Etna ★★ *Finds* If you need to stay near the Fontanarossa airport, you might want to spend the night here, 11km (7 miles) from Catania. This elegant hotel lies on the slopes of Mount Etna, between the towns of San Giovanni La Punta and Viagrande. Surrounded by gardens, the hotel was opened in 1927 and has been restored to its former glory. Its original furnishings are still here, and the atmosphere of the past lives on splendidly. Guest rooms are beautifully and comfortably furnished with antiques and old prints; all have views of Etna. Most bathrooms have tubs, the rest have showers, and the suites have hydromassage baths. The villa also has a wine cellar, a panoramic roof garden, and a disco on summer Sundays.

Via per Viagrande 37, 95030 San Giovanni La Punta. © **095-7512409.** Fax 095-7413861. www.paradiso etna.it. 34 units. 228€ ($274) double; 353€ ($424) suite. Rates include buffet breakfast. AE, DC, MC, V. From Catania, follow the Catania–Messina motorway in the direction of Etna and San Gregorio. The hotel is signposted at the yellow signs leading to Le Zagare shopping center. **Amenities:** Restaurant; piano bar; lounge; outdoor pool; tennis court; fitness center; sauna; room service; massage; laundry service; dry cleaning; nonsmoking rooms; rooms for those w/limited mobility. *In room:* A/C, TV, minibar, hair dryer, safe.

MODERATE

Albergo Savona A definite cut above the Hotel Centrale Europa, which sits across the street, this solid, well-located hotel lies a 2-minute walk from the Duomo. Converted into a hotel about a century ago, it has three floors of quiet, soundproofed bedrooms with high ceilings, severely dignified yet comfortable furniture, and shower-only bathrooms. Guest rooms are accessed via a grandiose flight of marble-capped stairs flanked with elaborate wrought-iron railings. All units were renovated in 2001. Although some have views of the cathedral, room nos. 102 and 104 are among the most interesting, with views over a medieval-looking courtyard. One of the best aspects of this place is the plush paneled bar, complete with soaring ceiling vaults, deep armchairs, and plenty of dignified style. It doubles as a breakfast room.

Via Vittorio Emanuele 210, 95124 Catania. ©/fax **095-326982.** www.hotelsavona.it. 30 units. 140€ ($168) double; 170€ ($204) triple. AE, DC, MC, V. Bus: 1-4, 2-5, 3-6, or 457. **Amenities:** Bar; nonsmoking rooms; rooms for those w/limited mobility. *In room:* A/C, TV, dataport, minibar, safe.

Hotel Mediterraneo ★ Well designed and unpretentious, with three stars from the local tourist authorities, this is one of Catania's most modern hotels. In 2002, after a well-planned reconfiguration by celebrity architect Romeo Francesco, the place was reincarnated as a member of the Best Western hotel chain. The blue-floored lobby's best features include a tactful, hard-working staff and dramatic murals inspired by the great masterpieces of the Italian Renaissance. Guest rooms are predictably angular, simple, and uncomplicated, with big windows and bathrooms with tub-and-shower combinations.

Via Dottor Consoli 27, 95124 Catania. © **800-5281234** in the U.S., or 095-325330. Fax 095-7151818. www. hotelmediterraneo.it. 64 units. 150€–180€ ($180–$216) double. Rates include breakfast. Parking 10€–18€ ($12–$22) per day, depending on vehicle size. Bus: 431. **Amenities:** Lobby cafe and bar; laundry service; dry cleaning; nonsmoking rooms; rooms for those w/limited mobility. *In room:* A/C, TV, dataport, minibar, hair dryer, safe.

Catania Accommodations & Dining

ACCOMMODATIONS ■
Albergo Savona **5**
Excelsior Grand Hotel **2**
Hotel Centrale Europa **10**
Hotel Collegiata **3**
Hotel Gresi **8**
Hotel Mediterraneo **1**
Jolly Hotel Bellini **2**
Jolly Hotel Catania Ognina **14**
San Demetrio Hotel **9**
Sheraton Catania **2**
Villa del Bosco **11**
Villa Paradiso dell'Etna **11**

DINING ◆
Il Canile **11**
La Marchesana **12**
La Siciliana **14**
Le Zagare **2**
Osteria Antica Marina **6**
Osteria I Tre Bicchieri **4**
Ristorante Piccolo Teatro **13**
Trattoria La Paglia **7**

Piazza S. Domenico

Piazza della Borsa

Anfiteatro Romana

Via Santa Maddalena

V. Crociferi

Via S. Elena

Piazza A. Riccò

Piazza Miracoli

Piazza Vaccarini

Via G. Clementi

Piazza Matteotti

S. Nicolò

Piazza Dante

Via Gesuiti

Via C. Ardizzone

Ex Convento Benedettino

Via Teatro Greco

V. Crociferi

Via Teatro Greco

Piazza S. Francesco d'Assisi

Odeon

Teatro Romano

Museo Belliniano

Via Vittorio Emanuele II

V. S. Anna

Piazza Mazzini

Piazza Machiavelli

Via Recupero

Via Pozzo Mulino

Piazza S. Pantaleone

Via Gisina

Via Garibaldi

Via Castello Ursino

Via del Transito

Via Velis

Via Quartiere Militare

Via Abate Ferrara

Via Naumachia

Via S. Maria dell'aiuto

Piazza Federico Di Svevia

Piazza S. Cristoforo

Via Di Giacomo

Via Gentile

Via Reitano

Castello Ursino

Via del Plebiscito

Via delle Calcare

Via Juvarra

V. Testulla

Via Belfiore

Via P. Platania

Via de Lorenzo

Via Cordai

Via A. Custode

V. Gramignani

Jolly Hotel Bellini   This is the older (ca. 1959), more central of Catania's two Jolly Hotels, sporting only three government stars, a low ranking for a chain more noted for its four- and five-star properties. Detractors find it a wee bit dated; we find it comfortable, well maintained, and, despite a few remaining touches of retro-dowdiness, an acceptable choice. Each room comes with a box-like bathroom with shower stall.

Piazza Trento 13, 95129 Catania. ℂ **095-316933.** Fax 095-316832. www.jollyhotels.it. 159 units. 129€–155€ ($155–$186) double. Rates include buffet breakfast. Bus: 443, 721, or 722. **Amenities:** Restaurant; bar; room service; laundry service; dry cleaning; nonsmoking rooms. *In room:* A/C, TV, minibar.

Jolly Hotel Catania Ognina ⚐   Set at the point in Catania where the city devolves into the seaside strip of beach resorts that eventually lead to such towns as Acireale, this boxy-looking, government-rated three-star hotel is favored by business travelers. A somewhat blasé staff will check you into a contemporary-looking guest room, outfitted with bland but comfortable furniture. About half of the units have harbor views. Each comes with a well-maintained bathroom with shower. There's no on-site restaurant, but a respectable choice of dining options lie within a few minutes' drive or walk.

Via Messina 626–628, 95126 Località Ognina Catania. ℂ **095-7528111.** Fax 095-7121856. www.jollyhotels. it. 56 units. 162€ ($194) double. Rate includes breakfast. Free parking. AE, DC, MC, V. Bus: 334 or 448. **Amenities:** Bar. *In room:* A/C, TV, minibar.

INEXPENSIVE

Hotel Centrale Europa   This age-old government-rated two-star hotel occu-pies a site that's closer to the cathedral than any other lodging in town. It's been here since 1900, still evoking a battered but genteel pensione whose staff has seen thousands of art lovers and business travelers come and go. The small lobby is filled with sepia-toned photos of old Catania. Rooms are very simple and bland-looking, with few frills but acceptably comfortable furniture. More than half overlook the Duomo and the historic buildings around it. Each room is equipped with a bathroom—half with shower, the other half with tub. No meals of any kind, not even breakfast, are served, but the Caffè del Duomo (featured on p. 225 as part of our walking tour of Catania) lies a few steps away.

Via Vittorio Emanuele 167 (Piazza Duomo), 95124 Catania. ℂ **095-311309.** Fax 095-317531. www.hotel centraleuropa.it. 17 units. 80€ ($96) double; 95€ ($114) triple. AE, MC, V. Bus: 1-4, 2-5, 3-6, or 457. *In room:* A/C, TV.

Hotel Collegiata ⚐ *Finds*   All of the floors in this 17th-century building are devoted to private apartments except for two, which contain a series of high-ceilinged guest rooms that, however spartan-looking, are airy, comfortable, and bigger than you'd expect. Each unit comes with a small bathroom with shower. The setting is close to one of Catania's most beautiful churches, La Collegiata, a short walk from the Duomo. The staff is hip and friendly.

Via Vasta 10 (at Via Etnea), 95100 Catania. ℂ **095-315256.** Fax 095-322848. www.lacollegiata.com. 14 units. 80€ ($96) double. Rates include breakfast. AE, DC, MC, V. Bus: 448, 449, or 457. *In room:* A/C, TV, hair dryer.

Hotel Gresi   Small-scale and lacking any bona-fide amenities, this would be nothing more than a tucked-away set of rooms fashioned from a once-private apartment except for the fact that the painted ceilings are as lavishly frescoed as those in any hotel in town. To reach the place, you'll pass through a stately-look-ing courtyard, take a small elevator to the third floor, and register in a high-ceilinged anteroom whose painted ceiling is just one of many more to come. Most of the frescoes date from around 1850 in a style so lovely as to place them

Finds **A Farmhouse Retreat in the Shadow of Etna**

With Mount Etna rising ominously in the foreground, **Azienda Trinità**, 34 Via Trinità, 95030 Mascalucia (ⓒ/fax **095-7272156**; www.azienda trinita.it), is a rural farm dating back to 1609. It lies near the little Etnean town of Mascalucia, renowned for its 16th-century churches. The setting is a botanical park where Etna's lava breeds a collection of indigenous and exotic plants. Visitors can stay on the farm or in one of the newly built apartments. Guest rooms are midsize and cozy, with wooden ceilings with traditional furniture. Each has air-conditioning, TV, and small, shower-only bathroom. Meals are prepared with old Sicilian recipes using as much locally grown produce as possible, including the farm's own citrus fruit, olive oil, artichokes, zagara honey, mandarin liqueur, and baked olives. Half board costs 50€ to 57€ ($60–$68) per person. From the center of Catania, follow the signs to Tangenziale Ovest. Go along this road until you see the exit to Gravina. From here, follow the street signs to Mascalucia Etna.

in almost surreal contrast with the hotel's simple furniture. Each unit is equipped with a small bathroom with shower or tub.

Via Pacini 28, 95124 Catania. ⓒ **095-322709.** Fax 095-7153045. www.gresihotel.com. 23 units. 70€ ($84) double; 90€ ($108) triple. AE, DC, MC, V. Bus: 1-4. **Amenities:** Breakfast lounge. *In room:* A/C, TV.

San Demetrio Hotel ★ *Finds*   Small-scale, personal, and deeply idiosyncratic, this hotel occupies one of the upper floors of a grandiose building near the cathedral; it shares the floor with the branch of the local bureaucracy that fines motorists for parking and traffic violations. (To reach the entrance to the hotel, you pass somewhat scary-looking government offices, traverse a courtyard, and take a claustrophobic elevator to an upper floor.) The hotel was converted from a private apartment in 2000, and it still evokes a private home. It is graced with some of the most beautiful ceiling frescoes of any hotel in Catania. The appealing paintings on the walls are done in a "post-Renaissance kind of modernism." Room no. 22 is particularly charming, but the others compete worthily with early-19th-century grace notes. In contrast, room furnishings are spartan. Each unit has a private bathroom with shower.

Via Etnea 55, 95124 Catania. ⓒ/fax **095-2500237.** www.hotelsandemetrio.com. 7 units. 82€ ($98) double; 110€ ($132) triple; 135€ ($162) quad. Rates include breakfast. MC, V. Free parking. Bus: 448, 449, 457, 722, or 733. **Amenities:** Babysitting; laundry service; dry cleaning. *In room:* A/C, TV, hair dryer.

3 Where to Dine

EXPENSIVE

Le Zagare ★★ CONTINENTAL/SICILIAN   When an army of designers renovated the dining room of the Excelsior Grand Hotel in 2001, they took pains to retain the original lines of its *dolce vita* decor (ca. 1954). The result is a genuinely elegant dining experience complemented by superb food and access to an outdoor terrace lined with flickering candles and flowering shrubbery. Menu items are a cut above the standard fare served in other hotel dining rooms. The best examples include braised scorpionfish in a green-olive sauce; superb sautéed medallions of lobster with fried endive; and scalloped lamb in an aromatic breaded crust with leek slices in a curry sauce. Follow your meal with an after-dinner drink at the piano bar.

In the Excelsior Grand Hotel, Piazza Verga. ℂ **095-7476111.** Reservations recommended. Main courses 18€–25€ ($22–$30). AE, DC, MC, V. Daily 1–3pm and 8–11pm. Bus: 443, 457, 721, or 722.

Osteria I Tre Bicchieri ✿✿✿ CONTINENTAL   This is the finest and most appealing restaurant in Catania. Established in 2000 in partnership with one of the best-respected wine merchants (Benanti, Inc.) in Sicily, it welcomes visitors to a location on a narrow, quiet street 2 blocks northwest of the cathedral.

Note that this building contains two dining venues, the other a well-conceived wine tavern, called **Cantina,** in a woodsy-looking room near the front entrance. Food here includes the likes of fondue, steak tartare, carpaccio, pasta, and crepes, costing from 6€ to 15€ ($7.20–$18).

But the real culinary vision of the place is found in the three high-ceilinged, vaulted rooms outfitted in a graceful 18th-century style, reached by walking through the Cantina and the kind of sliding, high-security door you might expect to see in a bank vault.

Part of the success of this place derives from the culinary vision of Naples-born chef Laquinangelo Carmine, whose creativity is fast becoming legend among local gastronomes. The best pasta we tasted in Catania was his tagliatelle with ragout of sucking pig. He does wonders with fish, especially *triglia,* a local saltwater fish served with onion-stuffed artichokes and a sauce of smoked foie gras. His signature gnocchi comes with a cheese from Ragusa. The wine list includes at least 1,000 Italian vintages, many from Sicily.

Note to wine experts: Make it a point to drop into the wine boutique, which sells both popular and very rare vintages. Best of all, it maintains a resident expert wine steward who really knows what he's talking about.

Via San Giuseppe al Duomo 31. ℂ **095-7153540.** www.osteriaitrebicchieri.it. Reservations required. Main courses 10€–15€ ($12–$18). AE, DC, MC, V. Mon–Sat 8–11:30pm. Bus: 443, 457, 721, or 722.

MODERATE

Il Canile SICILIAN/CONTINENTAL   Elegant and traditional, this restaurant in the Villa del Bosco hotel (p. 208) is very appealing. You can dine in a richly frescoed interior room or take a seat on an outdoor terrace without a hint of Sicilian traffic. Menu items include a *risottini* of porcini mushrooms from the slopes of Mount Etna. We sampled our finest seafood pasta in Catania here and went on to devour a succulent sea bream under an oven-crisp potato crust. The restaurant's name, which translates as "The Kennel," is taken from the pair of 18th-century stone dogs that stand near its entrance.

In the Villa del Bosco, Via del Bosco 62. ℂ **095-7335100.** Reservations recommended. Main courses 13€–15€ ($16–$18). Daily 1–2:30pm and 8–11pm. Bus: 129, 314, or 421.

La Siciliana SICILIAN   Decorated in a classic and rustic style, this restaurant was established in 1968 and is today managed by two sons of the original owner. Located in north Catania, it's set in a 19th-century villa that's furnished in provincial island style. In winter, diners sit in one of four cozy rooms; in summer, tables overflow onto a garden terrace. The cuisine is both innovative and respectful of tradition. We've enjoyed carpaccio of fresh swordfish, grilled stuffed calamari, and risotto with squid ink and fresh ricotta. For dessert, typical local favorites are always on the menu.

Viale Marco Polo 52A. ℂ **095-376400.** Reservations required. Main courses 5€–15€ ($6–$18). AE, DC, MC, V. Tues–Sun 12:30–3pm; Tues–Sat 8–11pm.

INEXPENSIVE

La Marchesana SICILIAN/SEAFOOD ⭐ *Value*   The charm of this place lies in its well-managed simplicity, the genuinely friendly welcome from the staff at the bar near the entrance, and the flavorful cuisine. Outdoor tables fill part of the quiet street during nice weather; otherwise, you can dine in a high-ceilinged, vaulted dining room that manages to stay cool even on hot days. The Didio family, well versed in welcoming diners from the English-speaking world, prepare dishes that include delectable risotto, salads, and a succulent spaghetti with squid, cuttlefish, shrimp, and tomatoes.

Via Mazza 4–8 (at the Piazza San Placido). ✆ 095-315171. Reservations recommended on weekends. Main courses 5€–8€ ($6–$9.60). AE, DC, MC, V. Daily 11am–4pm and 7pm–1am. Bus: 1-4.

Osteria Antica Marina SICILIAN   Only a handful of other restaurants convey as effectively the earthy, grimy, teeming maze of humanity that hauls food in and out of central Catania. Established just after World War II and sheathed with wooden panels, this osteria is set amid the densest concentration of open-air food stalls in town, two labyrinthine blocks south of the cathedral, on a piazza that by day teems with food merchants, but by night is calmer and quieter. You'll be separated from most of the hysteria outside by plate-glass windows and air-conditioning, but at the same time you'll get a sense of the freshness and variety of raw material just a few steps away. Menu items include ultra-fresh homemade pasta, garnished (you guessed it) with seafood and shellfish; every imaginable kind of grilled gilled creature in the Mediterranean; and very fresh cuts of beef, pork, veal, and lamb.

Alla Pescheria di Catania, Via Pardo 29. ✆ 095-348197. Reservations recommended. Main courses 12€–15€ ($14–$18). AE, DC, MC, V. Thurs–Tues 1–3pm and 8pm–12:30am. Bus: 1-4, 2-5, or 3-6.

Ristorante Piccolo Teatro INTERNATIONAL   Set a few steps from the Teatro Massimo is this cozy pub whose battered wood panels and prominent bar might remind you of an Italian beer hall. It attracts after-work business and a pre-theater crowd of young hipsters and hipster wannabes. Expect dishes that include fresh fish (especially swordfish), risotto, and hot-weather favorites such as octopus salad and sorbets. "A dish for the gods," as one habitué described it, is spaghetti with sea urchins, eggs, and extra-virgin olive oil given additional flavor by fresh parsley, garlic, and hot peppers. Pennette with swordfish is made enticing by the addition of eggplant, fresh mint, pine nuts, and hot peppers.

Via Michele Rapisardi 6–8. ✆ 095-315369. Reservations not needed. Main courses 8€–16€ ($9.60–$19). AE, DC, MC, V. Wed–Mon 8pm–12:30am. Bus: 14.

Trattoria La Paglia ⭐ *Finds* SICILIAN   If you like your food ethnic and your atmosphere hale and hearty, you can enjoy the most authentic Catanian dining experience at the site of the lively fish market. If you don't like the day's offerings, one of the staff might step out to the market and buy a fish you like, cooking it to your specifications. Start with *la triaca pasta,* an excellent pasta in fresh bean sauce, or *sarda al beccafico* (sardines fried in bread crumbs with pecorino cheese). We're also fond of the spaghetti whipped with sea urchins in an extra-virgin olive oil with fresh garlic. One local dish that's highly favored is *tonno con cipollata* (broiled tuna with onions and a dash of vinegar). Most of the dishes are based on the sea, and the atmosphere is very rustic.

Via Pardo 23. ✆ 095-346838. Reservations required Fri–Sat. Main courses 4€–7€ ($4.80–$8.40). MC, V. Mon–Sat 12:30–2:30pm and 8–11pm. Bus: 457.

4 Seeing the Sights

Duomo ⊛   The cathedral of Catania, located in the center of the city, is dedicated to the memory of the martyred St. Agatha. The Duomo was originally ordered built by Roger I, the Norman king, but it was destroyed in the earthquake of 1693 and had to be reconstructed. Its **facade** ⊛ is its most enduring architectural legacy, the work of Battista Vaccarini (1702–68), who redesigned the city after the earthquake. For the granite columns of the facade, the architect "removed" them from the city's Roman amphitheater. Only the lovingly crafted medieval apses, made from lava, survived the devastation of that earthquake.

Many opera fans come here to pay their respects at **Bellini's tomb,** guarded by a life-size angel in marble. It's to the right as you enter the Duomo through its right door. The words above the tomb are from *Sonnambula* and in translation read, "Ah, I didn't think I'd see you wilt so soon, flower."

In the **Norman Cappella della Madonna,** also on the right, precious metals envelop a magnificent Roman sarcophagus and a statue of the Virgin Mary carved in the 1400s. To the right of the choir is the **Cappella di Sant'Agata,** to whom the cathedral is dedicated. In the sacristy is a fresco, said to have been created in 1774, that depicts the horrendous eruption of Mount Etna in 1669.

Piazza Duomo, Via Vittorio Emanuele II 163. ⓒ 095-320044. Free admission. Daily 7am–noon and 4:30–7pm. Bus: 448, 449, 457, 722, or 733.

Piazza Duomo   The Duomo is not the only attraction on this landmark square. Lying in the very heart of Catania, the Piazza Duomo was also created by the city's planner, Vaccarini. The baroque elegance of Catania's heyday lingers on here.

The symbol of the city, the **Fontana dell'Elefante** ⊛⊛, was created in 1735. It was obviously inspired by Bellini's monument in Rome's Piazza Minerva. The elephant was hewn from black lava spewed forth by Mount Etna and stands on a Byzantine platform. The elephant is a beast of burden here, carrying on its back an Egyptian obelisk lettered with hieroglyphics celebrating the cult of Isis.

The less-imposing **Fontana dell'Amenano** lies on the south side of the piazza. Water cascades down from its top basin, evoking a sheer veil that caused the Catanians to dub it *acqua a lenzuolo.* On the north side of the square are the facades of **Palazzo degli Elefanti** (today the city hall) and **Palazzo Senatorio.** Unless security forbids it, Palazzo degli Elefanti is usually open Monday through Friday from 8am to 7pm.

Moments The Green Lung of Catania

Escape from the city heat and congestion to **Villa Bellini** ⊛, the "Central Park" of Catania, reached by heading north along Via Etnea. Planted with such exotics as Brazilian araucarias, the park sprawls over several hills. This is one of the most attractive public parks in Sicily, and for some reason maintenance is higher here than it is in most of Catania's public monuments or gardens. The Catanians claim that the fig tree planted here is the world's largest. Unique in Italy is the floral clock and calendar on the hillside. Stand on a hill here and be rewarded with a panoramic view of Mount Etna.

Standing beside the Duomo is the **Badia di Sant'Agata,** again dedicated to the patron saint of Catania. This is another stellar example of Vaccarini's mastery of baroque elegance. This church is one of seven in Catania dedicated to its patroness.

Lying east of Piazza Duomo is **Teatro Massimo** (or Bellini), one of the grandest and richest in Europe (p. 229).

Directly uphill from Piazza Duomo lies the entrance to the **Greco-Roman Theater,** Via Vittorio Emanuele II 266, dating from 415 B.C. The Roman theater, where gladiators battled wild beasts shipped from nearby Africa, was constructed on the site of an even earlier Teatro Greco. At its apex, 7,000 spectators could view the grisly entertainment here. The marble was coated by Mount Etna's eruption in 1669. In back of the theater is a similar but smaller **Odeon,** dating from the 2nd and 3rd centuries A.D. Concerts are sometimes staged here. The site is open daily from 9am to 1:30pm and 3 to 7pm; admission is 2€ ($2.40).

Museo Diocesano   This is dedicated to the cult of St. Agatha, patron saint of Catania. Agatha is also the patroness of all wet nurses, bell-founders, and jewelers. She suffered martyrdom by having her breasts lopped off. The museum is joined architecturally to the Duomo, its windows opening onto Piazza Duomo. Most of the artworks consist of vestments, altar furnishings, and relics from the bishops' palace. This minor museum need occupy no more than an hour of your time. The best of the treasure trove is found in Hall II: Look for a relic arm of St. George as well as St. Cataldo's relic bust attributable to Paolo Guarna, one of the most famous goldsmiths of Catania in the 16th century.

Via Etnea 8. ✆ 095-281635. Admission 4.20€ ($5.05) adults, 2.50€ ($3) children under 18. Tues–Sun 9am–2:30pm and 4–7:30pm. Bus: 448, 449, 457, 722, or 733.

Museo Civico Belliniano ✮✮   One of the trio of nearly adjacent museums honoring local sons (Verga, Emilio Greco, and Bellini museums), this is the most compelling, and the one that most easily evokes an emotional reaction from Catanians, many of whom view it as a national shrine. To reach it, you enter a quiet courtyard off the Piazza San Francesco, then climb to the drab, second-floor apartment where composer Vincenzo Bellini was born in 1801. Bellini is known for such titanic works as *La Straniera, Sonnambula, Norma, I Puritani,* and *I Cavalieri.*

Here you'll see original folios of his operas, his death mask, harpsichords and spinet pianos he rehearsed on as a child, and the coffin in which his body was transferred in 1876 back to Catania from its original burial place in Puteaux, near Paris. Signatures in the guest book read like a who's who of international musicians, ranging from Carlo Muti to Pavarotti. Many of the mementos of his life were donated by Rossini, a devoted latter-day fan of Bellini's brilliant *bel cantos.* If you're an opera fan, you will likely find this museum thrilling.

Note: At press time, this museum was temporarily closed for renovations. Before you visit, call ahead to check on its current status.

Piazza San Francesco 3. ✆ 095-7150535. Free admission. Daily 9am–1pm; Tues–Thurs 3–6pm. Bus: 1-4, 2-5, or 3-6.

Museo Emilio Greco ✮   Larger, plusher, and more obviously well-financed than either the Bellini or the Verga museums, this second-story museum showcases the oil paintings and engravings of Sicilian artist Emilio Greco (1913–95). Many locals are not that familiar with Greco and his abstract nude forms. His fame is mostly derived from accolades he received in New York and Tokyo, not

Catania Attractions

Monumento a
V. Bellini

Piazza
Tesicoro

Corso Sicilia

Piazza
della
Reppublica

Piazza
Spirito
Santo

Via Montesano

Via Puccini

V. Rizzo

Via Don L. Sturzo

Via Giovanni Di Prima

Via Monsignor Ventimiglia

Piazza
Falcone

To Train →
Station ⓘ

Via Fischetti

Via Pistone

Via De Marco

Via Finanze

Piazza
Majorana

Piazza
Manganelli

Via Etnea

Via A. di Sangiuliano

Via S. Orsola

Piazza
V. Bellini

Via Teatro Massimo

Piazza
P. Lupo

Università

Palazzo
S. Giuliano

Teatro
Bellini

Piazza
Università

Via Vittorio Emanuele II

Piazza
Cutelli

Via Serravalle

Fontana
d. Elefante

6

Piazza
Duomo

Duomo

Piazza
S. Placido

Via Museo Biscari

Piazza
Cutelli

Via Porta di Ferro

Via Calì

Piazza
S. Francesco
da Paola

a Garibaldi

Porta
Uzeda

8

9

Palazzo
Biscari

Piazza Duca
di Genova

Piazza
XVII Agosto

Piazza
Benedetto

7

Via Cardinale Dusmet

Piazza
ndirizzo

VILLA
PACINI

Via Cardinale Dusmet

Piazza
Currò

Via Alcalà

Via Cristoforo Colombo

Via del Plebiscito

Via Zurria

Piazza
Alcalà

Via Mullino S. Lucia

Via Fornacial

Porto
Vecchio

Via Grimaldi

Via Cristoforo Colombo

Via Ortolani

Via Parisi

0   80 Mi
0   80 Km

Palermo

Messina

Mt. Etna

SICILY

Catania

Agrigento

0   1/10 Mile

0   100 Meters

Where Gladiators Battled Lions

Lovers of antiquity should head to the Piazza Stesicoro, Via Vittorio Emanuele 260 (② **095-7150508**), for a very evocative site, the ruins of a **Roman amphitheater** dating from the 2nd century A.D. Due to shifting land, the ruins lie below street level, although the gladiator tunnels are still visible. This is one of the largest of all Roman amphitheaters; it is believed that some 17,000 spectators were once entertained here by blood games. Only a tiny part of the theater survives, so you'll have to use your imagination to conjure up the ancient gore. The reason? The Ostrogoths, not devotees of Roman glory, used the amphitheater as a quarry. In fact, the Goths found the Roman gladiator contests too vicious and completely outlawed them. They converted the stones into churches and public monuments. The site is open daily from 9am to 1:30pm and 3 to 7pm. Admission is 2€ ($2.40) for adults, 1€ ($1.20) for students and children 17 and under.

from adulation heaped upon him by other Sicilians. Sure, we admire Emilio Greco, but we couldn't help but wonder why works by other Sicilian artists weren't also on display in this magnificent space.

Note: At press time, this museum was undergoing renovations, with plans to reopen by spring 2005.

Piazza San Francesco 3. ② **095-325706**. Free admission. Mon, Wed, and Fri–Sun 9am–1pm; Tues and Thurs 3–6pm. Bus: 31.

Casa di Verga   This is a memorial to Sicily's national poet, Giovanni Verga (1840–1922), who lived and wrote here for many years. Verga was a firebrand who wrote with poignancy about the plight of underpaid workers during the Industrial Revolution. Climb a flight of worn stairs for access to the battered, dusty, and not-particularly-well-stocked museum that occupies the rooms where he completed some of his works. Despite the artist's powerful literature, you might leave with a sense of sadness that the local municipality has neglected this museum as obviously as it has. We recommend this place only for avid enthusiasts—the Bellini Museum, a few blocks away, is far more interesting.

Via Sant'Anna 8. ② **095-7150598**. Admission 2€ ($2.40) adults, 1€ ($1.20) for ages 18–25, free for children 17 and under. Tues and Thurs–Sat 8:30am–1:30pm; Wed 3–5:30pm. Apr–June Sun 9am–1pm. Bus: 1-4, 2-5, or 3-6.

Museo del Giocattolo (Museum of Childhood) *Kids*   Relatively unpublicized and almost chaotically disorganized, this museum offers exhibits designed to both entertain and shape the creativity of children. The place is so confusing, the staff so unhelpful and inarticulate (even in Italian), that you may feel like Alice in Wonderland. Exhibits include dolls, electric train sets, and whimsical sculptures, many displayed beneath lavish frescoed ceilings from the late 18th or early 19th century.

In the Palazzo Bruca, Via Vittorio Emanuele 201. ② **095-320111**. Admission 3.50€ ($4.20) adults, 2€ ($2.40) for children 3–12. Tues–Sun 9:30am–12:30pm. Bus: 448, 449, 457, 722, or 733.

Palazzo Biscari *★*   Today a private home, this is the most impressive palazzo in the city. To visit, you must call first and make an appointment. Constructed after the 1693 earthquake, the palace flowered in the mid–18th century as the home of Ignazio Paternò Castello, prince of Biscari, who held a passionate interest in art, archaeology, painting, music, and literature. When Goethe and others doing the Grand Tour of Europe passed through Catania, they pronounced Palazzo Biscari the city's grandest attraction.

Partially constructed on the city's old fortress wall, the palace dances with a wealth of *putti* and caryatids. Balconies are the stunning work of Francesco Battaglia and his son, Antonino. In the courtyard is a grand stairwell, and on the second floor are the major reception rooms. The room at the far end has frescoes by Sebastiano Lo Monaco.

Prince Biscari installed an archaeological museum in his palace, but the collection has been moved to Castello Ursino (see below). Classical concerts are sometimes staged in the palace (check with the tourist office).

Via Museo Biscari 10–16. © 095-321818. Free admission (donation appreciated). Call to arrange a visit. Bus: 1-4, 457, or 733.

Castello Ursino & Museo Civico ⟨⟩   This castle, west of Piazza Duomo, was once the proud fortress of Frederick II in the 13th century. When it was originally built, the grim-looking fortress, surrounded by a moat, stood on a cliff overlooking the Ionian Sea. But Mount Etna's lava has shifted the land over the centuries. Now landlocked, Castello Ursino is reached by going through a rough neighborhood where caution is advised.

The castle was built on a square plan with a keep 30m (99 ft.) high on each corner and semicircular towers in the middle on each side. If you walk along the perimeter, you can still see the old moats and even some Renaissance windows imbedded in the south side.

The castle's *pinacoteca* **(library)** has an interesting (though hardly spectacular) series of paintings that date back to the 1400s. Most of the work is from Sicily or southern Italy, including Antonello de Saliba's polyptych of the **_Madonna Enthroned with Saints Francis and Anthony_** ⟨⟩; De Saliba was a pupil of the legendary Antonello da Messina. One of the best-known Catanian artists was Michele Rapisardi, who is represented by two lovely studies: the **_Head of the Crazed Ophelia_** and a **depiction of the Sicilian Vespers.** Surely the saddest **_Grieving Widow_** in all of Catania was that depicted by another home-grown artist, Giuseppe Sciuti. The art of Lorenzo Loiacono is also worth noting for his vivid, even theatrical efforts.

Moments **Something Fishy This Way Comes**

One of the largest, most bustling, and certainly most colorful fish markets *(pescheria)* in the Mediterranean is held Monday through Saturday mornings in a narrow warren of streets behind the Duomo. We doubt if even the late Cousteau could identify some of these creatures from the murky depths. "If it swims, we Catanians eat it," a local fishmonger told us.

Octopus, squid, eels, shellfish, and other writhing, twitching creatures are sold here. You can buy fresh mussels and sea urchins to eat on the spot. Vegetable and fruit stalls also spill into the offshoot lanes. The bloody butchers' tables surely inspired the paintings of Francis Bacon.

Housed inside are Prince Biscari's **archaeological collection** (see above), along with objects from San Nicolò Monastery, and some of the best Sicilian painted carts on the island.

Piazza Federico di Svevia. © **095-345830**. Free admission. Tues–Sat 9am–1pm and 3–7pm; Sun 9am–1pm. Bus: 429.

Chiesa di San Nicolò All'Arena   This is the largest and spookiest church in Sicily, stretching for 105m (345 ft.) with transepts measuring 42m (138 ft.). The cupola is 62m (204 ft.) high. Begun in 1687 by Giovanni Battista Contini, it was reconstructed in 1735 by Francesco Battaglia. Stefano Ittar designed the dome; the facade, with its mammoth columns, was left unfinished in 1796 but remains impressive. Catanians call it "mastodonic" because the pillars stick up like tusks. The interior is rather bare-bones. A beautiful 18th-century organ with 2,916 pipes is found behind the main altar. A meridian line was laid in the transept floor in 1841 to catch the sunlight precisely at noon. But because of the shifting volcanic land, today it catches the sun at 12:13pm. Sadly, the church will never be completed. Sporadic renovations try to keep it propped up, but the efforts seem doomed to failure.

The adjoining **Monastereo di San Nicolò All'Arena** is the second-largest monastery in Europe, rivaled only by Mafra, outside of Lisbon. This old Benedictine complex, dating from 1703, is part of Catania University, but frankly, it's in really bad shape. Depending on conditions at the time of your visit, you may or may not be able to enter.

Piazza Cavour. © **095-438077**. Free admission. Thurs 5–7:30pm; Sun 11am–1pm. Bus: 429 or 432.

WALKING TOUR   HISTORIC CATANIA

Start	Castello Ursino.
Finish	Piazza Università.
Time	4½ hours, including brief visits inside churches and monuments.
Best Times	Mornings before noon, when the food market is at its busiest.
Worst Times	After dark, when the alleyways of the old town are unsafe.

Begin your tour amid the palms and palmettos of the piazza in front of the massive and forbidding-looking:

❶ Castello Ursino

Built on ancient Greek foundations, its soaring, severe-looking interior has some of the most impressive stone vaulting in Catania. The inside is devoted to a municipal museum that contains everything from archaeological remnants to 19th-century landscapes and portraits. When the *castello* (castle) was built in 1239, it directly fronted the sea, although since then, lava flows from Etna raised the ground level to the point where it now lies some distance inland. Look for patterns of both menorahs and crosses set into the medieval masonry, a hallmark left by the masons.

After your visit, with your back to the *castello,* walk diagonally to the right, across Piazza Federico de Svevia, heading to a point immediately to the left of the iron fence that fronts the railway tracks. Pass through an alley that funnels into an unnamed triangular piazza, and from there continue onto Via Auteri. At Via Auteri 26, note the 18th-century facade of the privately owned **Palazzo Auteri.** Said to be haunted, and long ago divided into private apartments (none of which can be visited), it's just one

Walking Tour: Historic Catania

1 Castello Ursino
2 Outdoor Fish, Meat & Produce Market
3 Chiesa Santa Maria dell'Indirizzo
4 Terme dell'Indirizzo
5 Porta Carlo V
6 Fontana dei 10 Canales (Fountain of the 10 Rivers)
7 Piazza Duomo
8 Via Garibaldi
9 Caffè del Duomo
10 Palazzo degli Elefanti
11 Fontana dell'Elefante
11 Duomo
12 Museo Diocesano (Catania Diocese Museum)
13 Porta Uzeda
14 Palazzo Bruca
15 Museo Emilio Greco
16 Museo Civico Belliniano
17 Chiesa San Francesco Immacolata
18 Casa di Verga
19 Roman amphitheater
20 Via Crociferi
21 Chiesa di San Nicolò All'Arena
22 Collegiata (Santa Maria della Consolazione)
23 Piazza Università

example of the many grand buildings dotting this historic neighborhood.

From Via Auteri, turn right onto Via Zappala Gemelli, site of the beginning of Catania's:

❷ Outdoor Fish, Meat & Produce Market

We can't even begin to describe the cornucopia of sights, sounds, and smells that rise from this warren of narrow streets. Pay attention to your footing: Don't slip on the slime from fish guts or rotting vegetables.

Continue downhill, through the souks, to the bulk that rises on the right-hand side of Via Zappala Gemelli, the:

❸ Chiesa Santa Maria dell'Indirizzo

Its elegant baroque facade—punctuated with a garish-looking neon sign declaring VIVA MARIA—stands above a square (Piazza dell'Indirizzo) that rises above that part of the food market specifically dedicated to meats. This is not a showcase church destined for the art books or tourist trade. It's the parish church of the meat- and fish-market district, with an evocatively battered interior, crumbling stucco, and scads of dusty baroque/rococo ornamentation. Opening hours are erratic, but are usually daily from 8am to noon and 3 to 6pm.

After your visit, walk to the church's southern side (the one on the left as you face it from the teeming meat market outside). Here, separated from the square by an iron fence, lies the ancient Roman ruins of the:

❹ Terme dell'Indirizzo

Constructed by the ancient Romans of black volcanic rock and terra-cotta brick, with only a few of its original vaults and arches still intact, these baths are best admired from the outside of the fence. Look also for a tiny domed Greek-cross building, constructed of black lava. It's virtually never open except for qualified archaeologists. It's the ugliest monument on this tour—and the rocks have been cited as unsafe for climbing.

After your visit to the ruined baths, descend along basalt cobblestones in front of the Church of Santa Maria dell'Indirizzo. They lead downhill into the bowels of the rest of the food market. The largest open space in the market—a mass of parasols, blood, humanity, and grime—is the **Piazza Pardo** (also known as the Via Pardo), at the edge of which is the hard-to-see facade of a highly recommended restaurant, **Osteria Antica Marina** (reviewed on p. 215).

With your back to the restaurant, turn left, noting the massive soaring archway, built of dark lava rock, on either side of which the food market teems wildly. It's the:

❺ Porta Carlo V

Punctuating the entranceway to the indoor section of the city's food markets, this is one of the rare structures of Catania that survived the earthquake of 1693. Pass beneath it and then turn left. After a few steps, you'll emerge into the open air again, into a neoclassical, traffic-free square filled with more food vendors selling, in this case, fish. Your map might identify it as the Piazza A. di Benedetto, but there is no sign. Most of the buildings date from the early 1600s. At the distant edge of this piazza, at the top of a short flight of stone steps, is a small stone obelisk marked **Fontana dell'Amenano.** Built in 1867, it marks the location of a powerful underground river.

Visible at the bottom of a steep masonry-sided chasm from the obelisk's rear side is the:

❻ Fontana dei 10 Canales (Fountain of the 10 Rivers)

For years, this was the only water source in this neighborhood, and many local residents remember when a flood of water from this underground canal was diverted, thanks to conduits and channels, to an aboveground curtain of water used liberally by everyone in the food market. Today, because of urban renovations and difficulties with the plumbing, the waters remain mostly underground.

From here, walk to the top of the previously mentioned stone steps for a view over the:

❼ Piazza Duomo

At the edges of this piazza sit several of the monuments visited as part of this walking tour.

But before your visits, look left (westward) along the wide, upward-sloping vista of the:

❽ Via Garibaldi

At the most distant point on the street's faraway horizon, beyond the masses of people and cars, note the decorative triumphal arch that was built to celebrate the marriage, in 1768, of the Spanish king Ferdinand de Bourbon and Princess Carolina of Austria. About a century later, in 1862, it marked the processional route of Garibaldi for his triumphant entrance into Catania during the agonizing process of unifying Italy into a coherent political whole. The event marked Garibaldi's utterance, for the first time, of what eventually became a unifying political slogan, *"O Roma, o morte"* ("Give me Rome or give me death").

TAKE A BREAK

Caffè del Duomo, Piazza Duomo 12 (✆ 095-7150556), is the most charming of the cafes flanking the square. Built in the late 1800s, it has a marble counter, hints of the Belle Epoque, and a lavish *tavola calda* (hot table) adjacent to the bar. You can choose from at least 15 different snack items, most priced between 1€ and 2.50€ ($1.20–$3). The cafe also sells some of the most artful almond candies in Catania, shaped like berries, pears, and apples. For a quick pick-me-up at the bar, do as the locals do and ask for seltzer water doctored with a tantalizingly scoop of fruit-flavored *granita.* Open daily from 5:30am to midnight.

After your refueling stop, walk across Piazza Duomo to the:

❾ Palazzo degli Elefanti

This palace is now the Municipio, or town hall, of Catania. From its central balcony, Mussolini once gave one of his rabble-rousing speeches. If it's open, walk into the building's central courtyard, where you'll see lava-rock foundations; bas-relief wall friezes dedicated to Catania's patron saint (St. Agatha); and a pair of 18th-century ceremonial coaches that are used every February to carry Catania's ecclesiastical and secular dignitaries (including the mayor) down the city thoroughfares for the Festival of St. Agatha. If the security guard allows it, proceed into the second courtyard. Here, note the wall-mounted 19th-century copy of an ancient Greek sundial. Proud Sicilians claim that the ancient Romans learned the art and science of sundials from the Greek colonists of Sicily. Regrettably, unless you're on official civic business, the rest of city hall is usually closed to casual visitors.

After your visit, cross the Piazza Duomo and take time to admire:

❿ Fontana dell'Elefante

This fountain was created from black lava and is Catania's most famous monument. It stands on a Byzantine platform and carries on its back an ancient Egyptian obelisk covered with hieroglyphics. On top of that is an iron ornament that includes, among other symbols, a cross devoted to the patron saint, Agatha.

Piazza Duomo is dominated, naturally, by the:

⓫ Duomo

Begun by King Roger in 1902 and rebuilt by Caccarini after the earthquake, this cathedral used many ancient monuments of Catania in its construction, including stones from Roman theaters. Pause to admire its lugubrious baroque facade with granite columns. Norman apses can be viewed from Via Vittorio Emanuele. The church was built over the ruins of a vaulted Roman bath, and inside, a Romanesque basilica lies under the Duomo's nave. The cathedral is a pantheon of some Aragonese royalty.

After you exit from the cathedral, turn immediately left (with your back to the Duomo's entrance) and walk a few steps to a building that functioned for many generations as a seminary for theologians and is now the:

⓬ Museo Diocesano (Catania Diocese Museum)

Located at Via Etnea 8, this museum gives insight into the lavish traditions associated with one of Sicily's most powerful undercurrents of religious ecstasy, the Cult of St. Agatha. Inside, you'll see photos of modern-day religious processions as well as the massive silver sledge that holds the iconic effigy of St. Agatha, which is hauled through the streets every February as part of the mystical rites associated with this powerful cult.

After your visit, with your back to the entrance of the Diocese Museum, turn left and walk a few paces to the south, passing beneath the massive ceremonial stone portal known as:

⓭ Porta Uzeda

Originally built by Sicily's Spanish overlords during the early 18th century, this archway contains some interesting shops selling folkloric pottery. On its opposite side is a pleasant and verdant park, **Villa Pacini,** where you rest for a few moments.

Now retrace your steps back into Piazza Duomo, walking diagonally across it toward Via Vittorio Emanuele, which flanks its northern edge. Continue westward. A point of minor interest en route is at Via Vittorio Emanuele 175, immediately adjacent to the Hotel de l'Europe. Here, note the **hidden doorway,** crafted from wood, whose panels were painstakingly designed to look like a continuation of the stone mullions of the building that contains it.

Continue west along the Via Vittorio Emanuele to one of Catania's quirkiest museums. Concealed behind a massive wall and an imposing doorway is the:

⓮ Palazzo Bruca

The palace, at Via Vittorio Emanuele 201, contains the **Museo del Giocattolo (Museum of Childhood),** reviewed on p. 220. This once private and still elegant palace is prefaced with an enormous, walled-in courtyard surrounding a heroic fountain of Hercules. If you're in the mood for another refueling stop, stop at the museum's cafe (hours are erratic) for pastries and cold drinks, which can be consumed in the panoramic rooftop or in the street-level entrance area.

After your visit, exit back onto Via Vittorio Emanuele and continue walking westward past some lesser churches and lots of baroque facades. Stop at the point where the street opens onto Piazza San Francesco, site of three important attractions, each noted below. You'll recognize the square thanks to the contemporary-looking statue devoted to Cardinal Dusmet, a 19th-century benefactor of Catania's poor. The inscription on its base translates as "Because we have bread, we give it to the poor."

The three attractions flanking the square include:

⓯ Museo Emilio Greco

Located at Piazza San Francesco 3, this archive-cum-museum displays the major artistic contributions of Catania citizen **Emilio Greco** (1913–95). He is most famous for his grand sculpture. For more information, see p. 217.

Accessible via the same entranceway on the western edge of the square is the more interesting:

⓰ Museo Civico Belliniano

The great **Vincenzo Bellini** (1801–35) was born in this house, which displays memorabilia and portraits. For details, see the review on p. 217.

Facing both of these museums at the eastern edge of Piazza San Francesco is:

⑰ Chiesa San Francesco Immacolata

The most interesting objects inside this church are the six massive, richly gilded candelabra—most at least 3.3m (11 ft.) high and incredibly heavy—that are proudly displayed in the nave. Carved at the beginning of the 20th century, they're carried on the shoulders of the faithful during the Feast Day of St. Agatha. The largest and heaviest of them was carved in 1913, gilded in 1935, and donated to the church and to St. Agatha by the city's bakers' guild.

After your visit, continue westward along Via Vittorio Emanuele, turning left in 2 short blocks onto Via Santa Anna. On that street, you'll find the small-scale baroque facade of the tiny Chiesa Santa Anna (it's almost always closed to casual visitors) and, a few buildings later, on the left, the former home of one of Sicily's most famous writers:

⑱ Casa di Verga

Known for his naturalistic fiction, **Giovanni Verga** (1840–1922) became one of Sicily's greatest writers. He was celebrated in his day, making friends with such greats as Emile Zola. Much of Catania turned out for his 80th birthday, where Luigi Pirandello appeared as orator. For details of the building at Via Sant'Anna 8, see the review on p. 220.

Retrace your steps to Via Vittorio Emanuele and turn right, back toward the Piazza San Francesco. En route, along that street's northern edge, see the deceptively modern-looking stone entrance to one of Catania's most cherished archaeological treasures, the:

⑲ Roman amphitheater

Draped with ivy, and overlooked by a ring of 17th-century buildings and apartments, this charming theater at Via Vittorio Emanuele 260 is an ancient oasis concealed in the midst of an urban neighborhood. During classical times, it held as many as 17,000 spectators for plays and—to a lesser extent—water games, when boats would float on waters funneled in from then-nearby streams and aqueducts. It was also a site for gladiator contests. Ironically, part of the theater's graceful crescent-shaped seating structure is blocked by a black-lava bridge added during the early 17th century as the base for the since-demolished Via Grotte, once a densely populated street within this residential neighborhood.

Via Grotte, most of its bridgelike foundations, and all of its buildings were demolished in the 1950s by Catania's historic buildings committee as a means of returning the ancient theater to some semblance of its original purity. Vestiges of the street remain within the circumference of the Roman theater, however, cutting surreally across one edge of the theater's sweeping crescent-shaped bleachers.

Since Via Grotte was demolished, some former residents of the neighborhood have returned from prolonged sojourns in North America, Australia, or Argentina, and have been shocked to find their childhood playgrounds (the Via Grotte and its offshoots) no longer in place.

Come with stamina, a good sense of balance, and sturdy walking shoes. Sandals are not recommended because of the steep, uneven steps, which lead visitors through ghostly tunnels that wind their way through and beneath the bleacher stands.

A smaller theater, the **Odeon,** is accessible near the back side of the Roman theater. To reach it, follow signs from the theater and walk uphill through some tunnels and steep vaulted stairs.

After your visit, return to Piazza San Francesco, stand in front of its mammoth church, and turn uphill to face the lowest end of one of the most richly embellished baroque streets in Catania:

⑳ Via Crociferi

Above its downhill entrance is a soaring stone bridge, **L'Arco San Benedetto,** which allowed nuns, many of whom were in seclusion, to access the buildings on either side of this street during the convent's heyday in the 17th to 19th centuries. Via Crociferi is so authentically baroque that it was filmed by Franco Zeffirelli for *Storie di une Copinere* his cinematic tale of love gone awry during the baroque age.

In order of their appearance on this fabled but relatively short street, you'll see the following churches, convents, or monasteries: (1) **San Benedetto,** (2) **San Francesco Borgia,** (3) **San Giuliano,** and others whose facades aren't marked with name or number.

Three blocks from where you first entered Via Crociferi, turn left onto Via Gesuiti. Walk 4 blocks to reach Piazza Dante and the mammoth, never-completed:

㉑ Chiesa di San Nicolò All'Arena

The biggest church in Sicily was never completed and is almost ringed in scaffolding to keep it from falling down. Immediately adjacent is an abandoned monastery once intended as a library. Surrealistically large, this complex is Catania's symbol of the folly of large-scale projects gone awry. For more information, see p. 222.

Retrace your steps to Via Crucifero, turn left for about a block, then turn right (downhill) onto Via San Giuliano. You'll be walking down the steep slope of a dormant volcanic crater that's associated with the geology of nearby Mount Etna. After 2 blocks, turn right onto Via Etnea and walk 2 blocks. On the right is a church with a baroque concave facade:

㉒ Collegiata (Santa Maria della Consolazione)

This royal chapel from 1768 is one of the masterpieces of the Catanese late baroque style, based on plans by Angelo Italia. The facade was completed by Stefano Ittar, and the vaults inside were frescoed by Giuseppe Sciti. It's dearly beloved to many Catanians who attended religious celebrations here during their childhoods.

After your visit, continue another block south along Via Etnea to the:

㉓ Piazza Università

This elegant urban piazza is often the site of political demonstrations. One side is devoted to the back of the previously visited Municipio (town hall), the other side to the symbolic headquarters of the University of Catania. The university was founded in 1434, but the bulk of it lies in a modern educational complex 3km (2 miles) to the east, in the suburbs. The square was constructed at the request of the duke of Camastra. It's dominated by the **Palazzo Sangiuliano,** built in 1745, and by the main university building, **Palazzo dell'Università,** which was finished at the end of the 1700s. One of the richest libraries in Sicily is housed in the **Università degli Studi di Catania,** founded by Alphonese of Aragon in 1434.

5 Shopping

Dolci di Nonna Vincenza   Come here for marzipan and almond-based candies, made from recipes developed generations ago. You'll pay about 7€ ($8.40) per pound. The shop is on a quiet piazza, across from the main facade of the San Placido church. Piazza San Placido 7. ✆ 095-7151844. Bus: 3-6, 259, or 334.

L'Artigianato Siciliano   Chances are you'll eventually wander beneath the Porta Uzeda during your stay in Catania, either on our walking tour or as part of your logical exploration of the Piazza Duomo, which it fronts. Beneath it are vaulted spaces loaded with the fancifully hand-painted pottery skillfully made in Caltanizzetta, a city in central Sicily that has churned out tons of the stuff during the past centuries. Look for gaily decorated serving dishes, candelabra painted like members of the 19th-century bourgeoisie, and all manner of art objects. Via Etnea 2 (beneath Porta Uzeda). ✆ 095-345360. Bus: 448, 449, 457, 722, or 733.

Marella Ferrera ⭐⭐ Catania-born Marella Ferrera is the most successful women's clothing designer to emerge from Sicily. She's known for fashions that makes women look like goddesses or lionesses, sometimes with outrageous flounces or appropriately inappropriate slits in indiscreet places. Prices begin at about 800€ ($960) for ready-to-wear, and from 3,100€ ($3,720) for couture. The shop evokes a cross between an Italian garden and a boudoir, with bolts of lace bursting from antique chests and paintings that evoke dream sequences in a style that could have been inspired by Dalí. Viale XX Settembre 25-27. ℂ 095-446751. Bus: 443, 721, or 722.

6 Catania After Dark

Lapis and *Ciao Catania* are monthly bulletins issued by the tourist office, and available at hotels and bars throughout Catania. They document any special concerts or festivals, movies, or nightclubs (such as they are).

Music lovers should head for the **Teatro Massimo** ⭐, sometimes called Teatro Bellini in honor of the hometown composer. It's at Piazza Teatro Massimo, Via Perotta Giuseppe 12 (ℂ **095-7306111**). Some of Italy's best operas and concerts are presented here, with tickets costing from 11€ to 70€ ($13–$84). Nothing is grander than hearing Bellini's *Norma* or *La Sonnambula* on its home turf. The opera and ballet seasons extend from mid-January to right before Christmas, whereas the concert season runs from mid-October to late May. The box office is open Monday through Saturday from 9:30am to 12:30pm and 5 to 7pm. Bus: 429.

Pubs and dance clubs rule the night. One such option is **Royal Pub Ceres,** Via San Giuseppe al Duomo 17–21 (ℂ **095-7152294**), on a block northwest of the Duomo. This woodsy-looking English pub comes complete with a carved Victorian-style bar and a crowd of good-looking people under 35. Its reputation for beers on tap is unequalled in Catania. The venue sometimes spills onto the narrow street outside. The place rocks daily from 7am (for that early libation) to 2am. Bus: 448, 449, 457, 722, or 733.

In the same vicinity, another popular after-dark rendezvous occurs at **Mr. Bahia Pub,** Via Alessi 16 (ℂ **095-2500083**), a 5-minute walk northwest of the Duomo. This is a wide-open, airy club whose architects inserted stainless-steel bar-tops and catwalks into an older, stately building. The result is a bustling room suitable for cocktails, snacks, and meeting the scads of 20- and 30-somethings who flood here late at night. Part of the venue moves onto the quiet piazza outside. Open Friday through Wednesday from 5:30pm to 3am; closed for 2 weeks in August. Bus: 448, 449, 457, 722, or 733.

Bar Nievsky, Scalinetta d'Alessi 13 (ℂ **095-313792**), is the most visible of Catania's limited number of counterculture bars, where—if labels like this were still fashionable today—Marxists, Communists, anarchists, and leftists of any ilk feel genuinely welcome. It's also the self-acknowledged haven for bikers, radical feminists, gay liberationists, and avant-garde painters. It sprawls across a multi-level labyrinth of early-20th-century rooms. Entrance is via a flight of steps from the Chiesa San Placido, a 5-minute walk northwest of the Duomo. Most people come here to drink, but the bar also serves macrobiotic salads and sandwiches. Bus: 448, 449, 457, 722, or 733.

7 Side Trips from Catania

The looming menace of **Mount Etna** attracts those who did not explore the volcano from its northern tier (p. 199). In addition to Etna, the town of **Acireale,** like Catania, is adorned with baroque treasures—but here you can enjoy the sights without the traffic and the people.

MOUNT ETNA ☆☆☆

Few who visit Catania can resist the temptation to explore Europe's most active volcano, Mount Etna, northwest of the city. At 3,292m (10,800 ft.), it is the highest volcano in Europe and one of the largest in the world. Taormina (see chapter 8) is the base for exploring it from the north. From the south, Catania is ideal for flirting with this still-active volcano.

For a good view of this ferocious mountain, take one of the **trains** that circumnavigate the base of the volcano. Trains are boarded at Via Caronda 352/A (℗ **095-541250**), in Catania off Viale Leonardo da Vinci. A tour from Catania, lasting 3 hours, 20 minutes, costs 6€ ($7.20).

A **bus** leaves from the Stazione Centrale in Catania at 8:15am daily, bound for Rifugio Sapienza (see below). The bus returns to Catania in theory at 4pm—but always check schedules locally, as they vary. The round-trip costs 6.10€ ($7.30).

You can also **drive** one of the many southern approaches to Etna from Catania. The quickest and most convenient route is to head northwest of Catania by following the road signs to Tangenziale Ovest. Drive along this road until you see the exit to Gravina. At Gravina, continue northwest along the road directing you to Mascalucia. Once there, you will see signs pointing to Nicolosi. At Nicolosi, follow a small road to the north for the final lap to Rifugio Sapienza.

In either Rifugio Sapienza, a little village on the southern slope of Mount Etna, or the little town of Nicolosi, you can book guided Jeep tours of Mount Etna for a cost of 38€ ($46). The trip lasts 2 to 3 hours and takes you as close as you can get to the top without walking. In Nicolosi, tickets can be purchased at **Funivia dell'Etna** (℗ **095-911158**), Monday through Friday from 9am to 1pm and 5:30 to 8pm, Saturday from 9am to 1pm. Nicolosi is connected with Rifugio Sapienza by frequent shuttle-bus service. You can also purchase tickets in Rifugio Sapienza at **Contrada Cantoniera** (℗ **095-915321**), open daily from 9am to 4pm.

More private tours can also be organized at Rifugio Sapienza. For information on these, call the **tourist office** in Nicolosi at Via Garibaldi 63 (℗ **095-911505**).

From Rifugio Sapienza, it's possible to hike up to the **Torre del Filosofo (Philosopher's Tower),** at 2,920m (9,580 ft.). The trip there and back takes about 5 hours. At the tower, you'll have a panoramic sweep of Etna, its peaks and craters hissing with steam. This is a difficult hike and not for the faint of heart. The climb is along ashy, pebbly terrain, and once you reach the tower, you have another risky 2-hour hike to the craters. The craters can erupt unexpectedly (as they did in the early 1990s, killing 11).

Tours should only be taken with a guide who knows current conditions. If Etna shows signs of erupting or even "belching," guided tours are suspended. On the return from Torre del Filosofo to Rifugio Sapienza, you'll pass Valle de Bove, the original crater of Etna.

ACIREALE

Located 16km (10 miles) north of Catania, this makes for one of the most satisfying day trips along the eastern coast of Sicily. Many people find Acireale more interesting than those rather dull lava fields of Mount Etna.

Overlooking the Ionian Sea, Acireale lies in a fertile valley of Mount Etna surrounded by citrus groves. The town stands on seven streams of lava and has long been known for its hot springs and spa facilities. Like Catania, it is a city of the baroque, with many of its greatest treasures from the 17th century. The same 1693 earthquake that destroyed Catania also did major damage in Acireale.

The "Aci" in the town's name comes from the mythical river said to have been created in the wake of the death of Acis, the handsome youth in love with the graceful Nereid Galatea. Acis was, according to the story, slain by the jealous Polyphemus, the savage of Cyclops.

To reach the town, most visitors arrive by car. Drive north of Catania until you see the cutoff to the right leading to the sea and Acireale. Buses also run throughout the day from Catania.

Before walking about the town, stop at the **tourist office,** Via Scionti 15 (© **095-891999**), for a town map. Hours are Monday through Friday from 8am to 2pm, Tuesday and Thursday from 4 to 7pm.

SEEING THE SIGHTS

Piazza del Duomo ⚜ is the monumental baroque heart of Acireale, containing its most impressive attractions. Filled with gelato parlors and cafes, the square is dominated by its cathedral, the **Duomo** ⚜. Originally built in the late 16th century, the church has suffered abuse from Etna, and the present building has been vastly altered and reconstructed. Note the lavish tiled and cusped bell towers and the fine baroque portal, which leads into an interior with frescoed vaults. At the east end are beautiful frescoes by **Pietro Paolo Vasta** (1697–1760), a home-grown artist. In the right transept is the Cappella di Santa Venera, dedicated to the patron saint of Acireale. Hours are daily from 8am to noon and 4 to 7pm; call © **095-601797** for more information.

Another important church on the square is **Basilica dei Santi Pietro e Paolo,** identified by its landmark bell tower. Although it was constructed in the 17th century, its facade is from the 18th century. The church's greatest artworks are by Pietro Paolo Vasta. Open daily from 8am to noon and 4 to 7pm. For more information, call © **095-601834.**

The 17th-century **Palazzo Comunale** is a rather bizarre example of the Spanish/Sicilian baroque style. Its wrought-iron balconies are held up by monsters and gargoyles. The entrance to the palace is on Via Lancasteri, right off Piazza del Duomo. Admission is free; hours are Monday through Friday from 8am to noon.

A final church worth visiting is **Basilica di San Sebastiano** ⚜, Piazza Vigo (© **095-601313**), one of the loveliest of all the baroque churches on the island. We prefer it to the treasures of the Duomo. It boasts a magnificent **balustrade facade** ⚜, adorned with statues representing scenes from the Old Testament. In the transept and chancel are frescoes by Pietro Paolo Vasta (there's that name again) that depict episodes from the sad life of St. Sebastian, the saint to whom this church is dedicated. Get to the church by way of Corso Vittorio Emanuele, just beyond Piazza del Duomo. Open daily from 8am to noon and 4 to 8pm.

After Piazza del Duomo, the next most impressive baroque square of Acireale is **Piazza San Domenico,** at the end of Via Cavour. Dominating this small square is the splendid baroque facade of the **Church of San Domenico.** The most beautiful building here is the 17th-century **Palazzo Musmeci,** celebrated locally for its graceful balconies and rococo windows.

Since the days of the Greeks and most definitely the Romans, the sulphur-rich Etna "volcanic waters" have lured visitors to Acireale. The tradition continues at **Terme di Acireale,** Via della Terme 47 (© **095-7686111**). Every illustrious person passing through Sicily in the 18th and 19th centuries seems to have taken the waters here, which are said to have miraculous powers to treat rheumatism, gynecological disease, skin diseases, and periodontal diseases. You can also come for massages and mud treatments, each costing 24€ ($29). There is talk—so far, just that—of modernization. Open daily from 7am to 12:30pm.

SHOPPING

Most islanders who visit Acireale go home with marzipan, as the town is famous for this confection. The best are sold at **El Dorado,** Corso Umberto 5 (© 095-601464), open Monday through Friday from 6am to midnight. It also makes the town's best chocolate cakes. A good competitor is **El Castorina,** Piazza del Duomo (© 095-601546); try *cassata Siciliana,* the island's most celebrated cake, and some divine almond granita. Open Monday through Saturday from 7am to 1am.

WHERE TO STAY

Aloha D'Oro ☆   This hotel was constructed in 1968 using materials and techniques evocative of the old farmhouses surrounding Mount Etna. Architectural grace notes include wooden windows, arches, handmade tiles, and wrought-iron adornments. This offbeat and very comfortable choice is one of the better stopovers between Taormina and Catania. The complex includes a main building, called the *castello,* and another 33 accommodations in outlying units. Opt for a room with a view, which in this case means in the rear, looking out onto the Ionian Sea and a government-protected nature reserve. Half of the neatly tiled bathrooms have tubs, while the rest have showers. The hotel is within walking distance of a good sandy beach and the thermal baths.

Via dei Gasperi 10, 95024 Acireale. © 095-7687001. Fax 095-606984. www.hotel-aloha.com. 113 units. 80€–140€ ($96–$168) double. Rates include breakfast. AE, DC, MC, V. Free parking. **Amenities:** 3 restaurants; bar; 2 outdoor pools (1 heated, with Jacuzzi); sauna; wellness center; room service; babysitting; laundry service; dry cleaning; all nonsmoking rooms. *In room:* A/C, TV, dataport, minibar, hair dryer.

Grande Albergo Maugeri ☆ *Value*   Located close to the Duomo, this is your best bet for an overnight stopover in the heart of town. Many guests here use Acireale instead of Catania or Taormina as a base for exploring Mount Etna. Rated four stars by the government, the hotel opened in 2001 across from Villa Garibaldi Park. The traditionally furnished bedrooms come with modern bathrooms, half with showers and the rest with tubs. The restaurant serves the best hotel cuisine in Acireale. The **Maugeri "Well-Being" Center** offers spa treatments ranging from massages to pedicures.

Piazza Garibaldi, 95024 Acireale. ©/fax 095-608666. www.sicilytourist.com/hotelmaugeri. 45 units. 165€ ($198)double. 100€ ($120) per person half board. AE, DC, MC, V. Free parking. **Amenities:** 2 restaurants; bar; limited room service; laundry service; dry cleaning. *In room:* A/C, TV, minibar, hair dryer.

WHERE TO DINE

All'Antica Osteria *Value* SICILIAN/PIZZA   This rustic restaurant-cum-pizzeria prepares an array of local delicacies and specializes in grills, especially grilled seafood from the Ionian Sea. The chefs turn out such dishes as *maccheroni All'Antica Osteria* (homemade pasta flavored with a creamy pesto, Parmesan cheese, and fresh tomatoes). *Stocco* is a white fish cooked *alla Messinese*—with carrots, potatoes, raisins, celery, and pine nuts. The small, well-priced wine list offers some local gems.

Via Carpinati 34. © 095-7634135. Reservations recommended. Main courses 7€–9€ ($8.40–$11); fixed-price menu 13€–20€ ($16–$24). AE, DC, MC, V. Daily noon–4pm and 7pm–2am.

Kids   The Images of Lost Dreams

Although the art of Sicilian puppetry is rarely seen today, Acireale still carries on this ancient tradition, and the town is known for its puppet shows and theater. Sicilian families journey here to give their kids a treat (most adults enjoy the shows, too). Shows are staged at **Teatro dell'Opera dei Pupi,** Via Galatea 89 (© **095-606272**), from July to September on Thursdays and Sundays at 9 and 10:30pm. Tickets, which cost 10€ ($12), must be purchased just before the show, as there is no box office open during the day.

Al Molino SEAFOOD/SICILIAN   This local favorite is adjacent to an antique water mill on the Lungomare, the boardwalk along the sea, a short walk from the center of Acireale. Outside is a small garden with a wooden grape arbor. Inside, the decorations are appropriately nautical. Since the menu is based on fresh fish, it can vary from night to night. You might begin with Acireale's best bowl of fish soup or a homemade pasta made with fish. Raw marinated shellfish is another specialty. Using old-fashioned recipes, the restaurant is better than ever.

Via Molino 106. © **095-7648116**. Reservations recommended. Main courses 8€–10€ ($9.60–$12). AE, DC, MC, V. Thurs–Tues 1–3pm and 8pm–midnight. Closed 2 weeks in Nov or Dec.

La Grotta di Carmelo ⟲⟲ SEAFOOD/SICILIAN   Here's a chance to dine in a cave with a rock-face wall—hence the name of the joint. Much of the structure was built from black-lava rock from Mount Etna. But this is no touristy gimmick. Its tables are in demand more than any other in town, in large part thanks to its excellent seafood, much of it plucked fresh from the Ionian Sea. Start with a savory bowl of fish soup; it doesn't get much better than this. Our pasta favorite is homemade and served with squid ink along with tomatoes, garlic, olive oil, and hot peppers. The cooks are experts at grilling fish to your specifications; locals tend to prefer it a bit rarer than the average American. The delicately steamed fish with lemon and olive oil is memorable. Desserts, wine, and service are all first-rate.

Via Scala Grande 36. © **095-7648153**. Reservations required. Main courses 8€–15€ ($9.60–$18). AE, MC, V. Wed–Mon 1–3pm and 7–11pm. Closed Oct 15–Nov 1.

Syracuse & the Southeast

One of the centers of ancient Western civilization, southeastern Sicily is a sightseeing mecca filled with glorious, evocative ruins. The area's chief town is **Syracuse,** one of the most important cities of the ancient world of Magna Graecia (Greater Greece).

We'll even go out on a limb and suggest that if you're forced to choose between Agrigento (see chapter 12) and Syracuse, opt for the latter, whose wealth and size were once unmatched by any other city in Europe.

Those with extra leisure time should also explore the baroque city of **Noto** and its surrounding sites, populated by Bronze Age people between 2,000 and 1,500 B.C.

Today, many of the sights of this sunbaked land are decaying. Noto, especially, is in peril. Earthquakes have caused massive damage to monumental, centuries-old buildings. But a trip through towns that knew great glory centuries ago is one of the most rewarding jaunts to take in Sicily, not to mention all of Italy.

1 Syracuse ✶✶✶ & Ortygia Island ✶✶✶

182km (110 miles) S of Messina, 87km (52 miles) S of Catania, 330km (198 miles) SE of Palermo, 256km (154 miles) E of Agrigento

Of all the Greek cities of antiquity that flourished on the coast of Sicily, Syracuse (Siracusa) was the most important, a formidable competitor of Athens. In its heyday, it dared take on Carthage and even Rome.

Colonists from Corinth founded Syracuse on the Ionian Sea in about 735 B.C. Much of its history was linked to despots, beginning in 485 B.C. with Gelon, the tyrant of Gela, who subdued the Carthaginians at Himera. Syracuse came under attack from Athens in 415 B.C., but the main Athenian fleet was destroyed and the soldiers on the mainland were captured. They were herded into the **Latomia di Cappuccini** at Piazza Cappuccini, a stone quarry. The "jail," from which there was no escape, was particularly horrid—the defeated soldiers weren't given food and, packed together like cattle, were allowed to die slowly.

Dionysius I was one of the greatest despots, reigning over the city during its greatest glory in the 4th century B.C., when it extended its influence as a sea power. But in A.D. 212, the city fell to the Romans under Marcellus, who sacked its riches. In that attack, Syracuse lost its most famous son, the Greek physicist/mathematician Archimedes, slain in his study by a Roman soldier.

Although the ruins of Syracuse will be one of the highlights of your trip to Sicily, the city itself has been in a millennia-long decline. Today, it's a blend of often unattractive modern development (with supermarkets and high-rises sprouting along speedways) and the ruins of its former glory.

A lot of what you'll want to see is on the island of **Ortygia,** which is filled with not only ancient ruins but also crafts shops and boutiques. From the mainland, Corso Umberto goes to the Ponte Nuova, which leads to the island. Parking is a

Syracuse & the Southeast

Brucoli

80 Mi
80 Km

Palermo
Messina
Mt. Etna
SICILY
AREA OF
DETAIL
Agrigento
Syracuse

Villasmundo

Augusta

Pedagaggi

Melilli

*Golfo
di Augusta*

**Megara
Hyblaea**

Sortino

Peninsola magnisi

Ferla

Marina di Melilli

Sta. Panagia

Cassaro

124

Solarino

Belvedere

**Castello
Eurialo**

**Syracuse
(Siracusa)**

Floridia

Palazzo
Alacreide

Canicattini
Bagni

A18

*Peninsola
della Maddalena*

Lido Arenella

**Cava Grande
Del Cassible**

Villa Vela

Ognina

Testa
dell'Acqua

Cassibile

287

Fontane Bianche

Castelluccio

S. Corrado
di Fuori

115

Monte Renna

Avola

Noto

**Villa Del
Tellaro**

Calabernardo

E45

S. Paolo

Lido di Noto

Eloro

*Golfo
di Noto*

Rosolini

**Riserva Naturale
di Vendicari**

Ispica

*Ionian
Sea*

S. Lorenzo
Vecchio

Marzamemi

Pozzallo

Pachino

Capo Passero

Beach

Portopalo
di Capo Passero

Capo delle Forniche

5 Mi
5 Km

235

serious problem on Ortygia, so if you drive, leave your car in one of the garages near the bridge and then walk over and explore the island on foot. Allow yourself at least 2 hours to explore, plus another hour to shop along the narrow streets. You'll also want to sit on **Piazza del Duomo,** off Via Cavour—one of the most elegant squares in Sicily.

The ancient sites are a good half hour's walk back inland from Ortygia, past a fairly forgettable shopping strip, so you might want to take a cab (they're easily found at all the sites). You'll find buses on Ortygia at Piazza Pancali/Largo XXV Luglio. The harbor is lined with 18th- and 19th-century town houses.

Syracuse is a cauldron in summer. Do as the locals do and head for the sea. The finest **beach** is about 19km (12 miles) away at **Fontane Bianche;** bus nos. 21 and 22 leave from the Syracuse post office, Piazza delle Poste 15. If you're driving, Fontane Bianche lies to the south of the city (it's signposted); take SS115 to reach it. The same buses will take you to **Lido Arenella,** only 8km (5 miles) away but not as good a beach.

ESSENTIALS

GETTING THERE   From other major cities in Sicily, Syracuse is best reached by **train.** It's 1½ hours from Catania, 2 hours from Taormina, and 5 hours from Palermo. Usually you must transfer in Catania. For information, call ℂ **892021.** Trains arrive in Syracuse at the station on Via Francesco Crispi, centrally located between the Archaeological Park and Ortygia.

From Catania, 23 Interbus **buses** per day make the 1¼-hour trip to Syracuse. The one-way fare is 4.50€ ($5.40). Call ℂ **0931-66710** in Syracuse, or 095-7461333 in Catania, for schedules.

By **car** from Taormina, continue south along A18 and then on E45, past Catania. Allow at least 1½ hours.

VISITOR INFORMATION   The **tourist office** is at Via San Sebastiano 43 (ℂ **0931-67710**), open Monday through Friday from 8:30am to 1:30pm and 3 to 6pm, Saturday from 8:30am to 1:30pm. There's another office in the historic center at Via della Maestranza 33 (ℂ **0931-65201**), open Monday through Friday from 8:15am to 2pm and 2:30 to 5:30pm, Saturday from 8:15am to 2pm.

SPECIAL EVENTS   Some of the most memorable cultural events in Sicily are staged in May and June of even-numbered years, when actors from the Instituto Nazionale del Dramma Antico present **classical plays** by Aeschylus, Euripides, and their contemporaries. The setting is the ancient Teatro Greco (Greek Theater) in the Archaeological Park. Tickets cost about 25€ ($30). For information, contact **INDA,** Corso G. Matteotti 29, 96100 Siracusa (ℂ **0931-67415**).

CITY LAYOUT   The chief attraction, **Isola di Ortygia,** is linked to mainland Syracuse by a bridge, **Ponte Umbertino.** The city's main street, **Corso Umberto,** runs from this bridge directly to the train station and crosses **Piazza Marconi,** a square from which most of the buses depart. Another main street is **Via Montedoro,** which runs parallel to and to the immediate north of Corso Umberto.

Other than Ortygia, Syracuse's grand attraction is the **Parco Archeologico della Neapolis.** To get to this garden of ruins from the heart of Syracuse, head north along **Corso Gelone.**

If you'd like to drive along the boulevard fronting the Ionian Sea, head up the **Dionisio Grande** for panoramic scenery. This route will also take you to the **Latomia dei Cappuccini,** one of the most ancient of the limestone quarries that

---

Moments **Syracuse from the Sea**

We like to see this ancient city the way the Greeks first came upon it—from the sea. Motor launches operated by **Selene** (© **0931-790132**) take you on a **panoramic trip** 🌟🌟 around Porto Grande and Ortygia. It lasts an hour, and the scenes of the ancient ruins are evocative and inspiring. The most memorable boat trips occur around twilight, when the monuments are floodlit.

---

supplied blocks of limestone for the construction of the major buildings and monuments of Syracuse.

Off Via Cavour is **Piazza del Duomo,** one of the city's most elegant squares. A 5th-century temple that the Greeks dedicated to Athena became in time a Christian cathedral, or duomo.

From Piazza del Duomo, **Via Picherali** heads southwest to the sea and the **Fountain of Arethusa,** a freshwater spring beloved by the ancient Greeks, who claimed that this was where the nymph Arethusa was turned into a fountain.

The oldest street in town, **Via della Maestranza,** is a sightseeing attraction in its own right. It passes the island's most aristocratic residences, mostly baroque in style. The two most interesting palaces, which can be admired from the outside, are **Palazzo Interlandi Pizzuti,** at no. 10, and **Palazzo Impellizzeri,** at no 17.

On the southernmost tip of Ortygia rises **Castello Maniace,** named in honor of George Maniakes, the Byzantine who with aid from Norman soldiers captured the city from the Muslims. Rebuilt by Frederick II in 1239, this castle is now a military barracks and is off-limits to the public. You can sail by the castle, however, if you take a boat tour (see "Syracuse from the Sea," below).

GETTING AROUND

Syracuse is served by a network of **buses** following circular routes, which means that many places will be quite a ways from a bus stop. Buses leave from the center of Syracuse for Piazza della Posta, which lies across the bridge on Ortygia Island. The best place to catch a bus in Syracuse proper is Piazza Marconi (also called Foro Siracusano). The most frequented routes are nos. 21 to 23, which also stop at the rail depot.

Sometimes it's better to call a **taxi** (© **0931-69722**). The fare from the train station to Ortygia is about 10€ ($12).

FAST FACTS: **Syracuse**

Emergency Dial © **113.**

Internet Your best bet is **La Bottega di Jenny,** Via Trieste 24 (© **0931-480193**), close to the post office. It charges 5.20€ ($6.25) per hour. Open Sunday through Friday from 8am to 8:30pm, Saturday from 8am to 12:30pm.

Luggage Storage A kiosk in the train station along Via Francesco Crispi is open from 7am to 10pm, charging 4€ ($4.80) per piece.

Medical In case of medical emergency, **Guardia Medica,** Contrada La Piz-zuta 20 ((C) **0931-484629**), is open Monday through Friday from 8pm to 8am, Saturday and Sunday from 2pm to 8am. The regular hospital is the **Ospedale Generale Provinciale,** Via Testaferrata ((C) **0931-724111**), near the end of Corso Gelone.

Pharmacy The **Farmacia Zecchino,** Viale Zecchino 199 ((C) **0931-783384**), is open Monday through Saturday from 8:30am to 1pm and 4:30 to 8pm. A list of pharmacies open at night is posted in the window.

Police Call (C) **0931-481511.**

Post Office The post Office is at Riva Posta 15 ((C) **0931-796011**), open Monday through Friday from 8am to 7pm, Saturday from 8am to 12:30pm. There is also a currency exchange here.

SEEING THE ANCIENT SITES

Take bus no. 1 to reach these sites.

Parco Archeologico della Neapolis 🐱🐱🐱   Syracuse's Archaeological Park contains the town's most important attractions, all on the mainland at the west-ern edge of town, to the immediate north of Stazione Centrale. The entrance to the park is down Via Augusto.

On the Temenite Hill, the **Teatro Greco (Greek Theater)** 🐱🐱🐱, Viale Teocrito, was one of the great theaters of the classical period. Hewn from rock during the reign of Hieron I in the 5th century B.C., the ancient seats have been largely eaten away by time, but you can still stand on the remnants of the stone stage where plays by Euripedes were mounted. Today, the Italian Institute of Ancient Drama presents classical plays by Euripedes, Aeschylus, and Sophocles. In other words, the show hasn't changed much in 2,000 years.

Outside the entrance to the Greek Theater is the most famous of the ancient quarries, **Latomia del Paradiso (Paradise Quarry)** 🐱🐱, one of four or five from which stones were hauled to erect the great monuments of Syracuse in its glory days. Upon seeing the cave in the wall, Caravaggio is reputed to have dubbed it the "Ear of Dionysius" because of its unusual shape. But what an ear—it's nearly 60m (200 ft.) long. You can enter the inner chamber of the grotto, where the tearing of paper sounds like a gunshot. Although it's dismissed by some scholars as fanciful, the story goes that the despot Dionysius used to force prisoners into the "ear" at night, where he was able to hear every word they said. Nearby is the **Grotta dei Cordari,** where rope-makers plied their craft.

A rather evocative but gruesome site lies on the path down into the Roman amphitheater. The **Ara di Lerone,** or Altar of Heron, was once used by the Greeks for sacrifices involving hundreds of animals at once. A few pillars still stand, along with the mammoth stone base of this 3rd-century-B.C. monument. The longest altar ever built, it measured 196m by 23m (653 ft. by 75 ft.).

The **Anfiteatro Romano (Roman Amphitheater)** 🐱 was created at the time of Augustus. It ranks among the top five amphitheaters left by the Romans in Italy. Like the Greek Theater, part of it was carved from rock. Unlike the Greek Theater with its classical plays, the Roman Amphitheater tended toward gutsier fare. Gladiators faced each other with tridents and daggers, and slaves were whipped into the center of a battle to the death between wild beasts. Either way, the victim lost: If his opponent, man or beast, didn't do him in, the crowd would

Via A. Von Platen

Via le Teocrito

Viale Luigi Cadorna

Piazza della Vittoria

Museo Archeologico Regionale Paolo Orsi (Paolo Orsi Regional Archeological Museum)

Catacombe di San Giovanni & Chiesa di San Giovanni

Museo del Papiro

Santuario della Madonna delle Lacrime

Via del Santauro

Via S. Sebastiano

Via S. Simeone

Via C. Bruno

Via le Teocrito

Via Demostene

Via Testaferrata

Via Terracati

Corso Gelone

Via Augusto

Via Romagnoli

PARCO ARCHEOLOGICO DELLA NEAPOLIS

Latomia del Paridiso (Paradise Quarry)

Longo Anfiteatro

Via Cavallari

Anfiteatro Romano (Roman Amphitheater)

Viale Paolo Orsi

Via Zappala

Grotta dei Cordari

Biglietteria (Ticket Office)

Via Paradiso

Ara di Lerone (Altar of Heron)

Via G. E. Rizzo

Teatro Greco (Greek Theater)

often scream for the ringmaster to slit his throat. The amphitheater is near the entrance to the park, but you can also view it in its entirety from a belvedere on the road.

Via Del Teatro (off the intersection of Corso Gelone and Viale Teocrito). (C) **0931-66206**. Admission 4.50€ ($5.40). Apr–Oct daily 9am–6pm; Nov–Mar daily 9am–3pm.

Museo Archeologico Regionale Paolo Orsi (Paolo Orsi Regional Archaeological Museum) ⭐⭐⭐ One of the most important archaeological museums in southern Italy surveys the Greek, Roman, and early Christian epochs. Crafted from glass, steel, and Plexiglas, and designed as an ultramodern showcase for the objects unearthed from digs throughout Sicily, this is the kind of museum that reinvigorates an appreciation for archaeology. Its stunning modernity is in direct contrast to the sometimes startling portrait busts and vases unearthed from around the island. Laid out like a hexagon, the museum is set in a garden dotted with ancient sarcophagi.

Section A takes us back before the dawn of recorded history. We're always fascinated by the skeletons of prehistoric animals found here, including dwarf elephants. Many artifacts illustrate life in Paleolithic and Neolithic times. Look for the stunning red-burnished **Vase of Pantalica** ⭐.

Section B is devoted to Greek colonization. The celebrated **Landolina Venus** ⭐⭐ is here, without a head but alluring nonetheless. After all these centuries, the anatomy of this timeless Venus is still in perfect shape. A Roman copy of an original by Praxiteles, the statue was found in Syracuse in 1804. When he visited the town in 1885, Guy de Maupassant fell in love with this Venus and left a vivid description of her. Although it's not the equal of the Landolina Venus, the singular limestone block of a **Mother-Goddess** ⭐ suckling twins dates from the 6th century B.C. and was recovered from a necropolis.

Section C brings the sub-colonies and Hellenistic centers of eastern Sicily alive once more. It's a hodgepodge of artifacts and fragments, including votive terra-cottas, sarcophagi, and vases from Gela. Interspersed among some rather dull artifacts are stunning creations such as an enthroned male figure from the 6th century B.C., a horse and rider from the same era, a terra-cotta goddess from the late 6th century B.C., and a miniature 6th-century-B.C. altar with a relief depicting a lion attacking a bull. You can also seek out three rare wooden statues from the 7th century B.C. (found near Agrigento).

In the gardens of the Villa Landolina in Akradina, Viale Teocrito 66. (C) **0931-464022**. Admission 4.50€ ($5.40). Mon–Sat 9am–6pm; Sun 9am-1pm.

Museo del Papiro Located near the Paolo Orsi museum (see above), these galleries devoted to papyrus are unique in Italy. That's because Syracuse has the only climate outside the Nile Valley in which the papyrus plant can flourish. The word "paper," of course, comes from papyrus. But the plant has far more uses than making paper. Papyrus was used in the construction of lightweight boats, ropes, baskets, wigs, and fabric (papyrus sandals were all the rage in ancient Egypt). The most delicate part of the stalk might once have served as food. The most intriguing exhibit is of documents dating from the era of the pharaohs, featuring fragments from the Egyptian Book of the Dead.

Viale Teocrito 66. (C) **0931-61616**. Free admission. Tues–Sun 9am-1pm.

Catacombe di San Giovanni (Catacombs of St. John) ⭐⭐ Evoking the more famous Christian burial grounds along Rome's Appian Way, the Catacombs of St. John contain some 20,000 ancient tombs, honeycombed tunnels of empty coffins that were long looted of their "burial riches" by plundering grave robbers.

In Roman times, Christians were not allowed to bury their dead within the city limits, so they went outside the boundaries of Syracuse to create burial chambers in what had been used by the Greeks as underground aqueducts. The early Christians recycled these into chapels. Some faded frescoes and symbols etched into stone slabs can still be seen. Syracuse has other subterranean burial grounds, but the Catacombs of St. John are the only ones open to the public.

You enter the "world of the dead" from the **Chiesa di San Giovanni,** now a ruin. St. Paul is said to have preached on this spot, so the early Christians venerated it as holy ground. Now overgrown, the interior of the church was abandoned in the 17th century. In its heyday, it was the cathedral of Syracuse.

The church's roots go back to the 6th century, when a basilica stood here, but it was eventually destroyed by the Saracens. The Normans reconstructed it in the 12th century, but in 1693 an earthquake destroyed it. A baroque church was then built, but was left in ruins by the earthquake of 1908. All that remain are roofless Norman walls and about half of the former apse. A beautiful rose window is still visible on the facade of the Norman church.

Underneath the church is the **Cripta di San Marciano (Crypt of St. Marcian),** constructed on the spot where the martyr is alleged to have been beaten to death. His Greek-cross chamber is found 5m (16 ft.) below the ground.

Warning: Make sure that you exit well before closing. Two readers who entered the catacombs after 5pm were accidentally locked in.

Piazza San Giovanni, at end of Viale San Giovanni. No phone. Admission 3.50€ ($4.20) adults, free for children 15 and under. Tues–Sun 9am–12:30pm and 2:30–4:30pm. Closed Feb.

Santuario della Madonna delle Lacrime
The "Our Lady of Tears" sanctuary is one of the most bizarre monuments or churches in all of Sicily. Designed to evoke a gigantic teardrop, the structure was created by two Frenchmen, Michel Arnault and Pierre Parat, in 1994. It houses a statue of the Madonna that supposedly wept for 5 days in 1953. Alleged chemical tests showed that the liquid was similar to that of human tears. Pilgrims still flock here.

Although criticized by architectural purists, the contemporary conical structure dominates the skyline, rising 74m (243 ft.) with a diameter of 80m (262 ft.). The **interior** is rather amazing. You might get dizzy looking up at the vertical windows stretching skyward to the apex of the roof.

Lacrime is new, but just to the south of the sanctuary, on Piazza della Vittoria, you can stand and see the fenced-off excavations of an array of ancient Greek and Roman houses and streets.

Via Santuario 33. © 0931-21446. Admission 1.55€ ($1.85). Daily 7:30am–8pm.

Santa Lucia al Sepolcro
The original church here was constructed on the site where in A.D. 304 St. Lucy (Santa Lucia) was said to have been martyred. Dating from the Byzantine period, the church was vastly altered in the 12th century and completely reconstructed in the 17th century. Beneath this sanctuary is a vast labyrinth of dank catacombs dating from the 3rd century, most of which, even today, have not been explored and are closed to the public. You can, however, visit the sanctuary. The famous Caravaggio painting depicting the burial of Santa Lucia once hung here, but is now in the Palazzo Bellomo museum.

Indeed, there isn't much left to see of this church since all its former treasures have been hauled off. The doorway and apses are from Norman days, and a

Syracuse Attractions

SICILY

80 Mi
80 Km

Messina
Mt. Etna
Syracuse
Palermo
Agrigento

Riviera Dionisio Il Grande

Porto Piccolo

Via Torino

Via Bignami

Piazza
Santa
Lucia

Via Gorizia

Via Agrigento

Via Montalcone

Via Sant'Agneses

Via dell'Arsenale

Via Agacoce

Via Von Platen

Viale Luigi Cadorna

Viale Teocrito

Museo
Archeologico
Regionale

Santuario
della Madonna

Piazza
della
Vittoria

Via Dante

Viale Montedoro

Via Sebastiano

Via Eumelo

Via Bruno

Vi di Naale

Corso Gelone

Viale Teracati

Corso Gelone

Piazza
della
Repubblica

Via Romagnoli

PARCO ARCHEOLOGICO
DELLA NEAPOLIS

Viale Augusto

Piazza
Aldo Moro

Via Brenta

Train
Station

Viale Paolo Orsi

Via Elorina

Ionian Sea

ORTYGIA ISLAND

Via Meastranza

Via Roma

Via Minerva

■ Duomo

Piazza del Duomo

Corso Matteotti

Via Caovur

V. Picherali

V. Capodieci

Castello Maniace

■ Maniace

Corso Umberto I

Via Bengasi

Molo St. Antonio

Porto Grande

Castello Maniace **19**
Catacombe di San Giovanni **3**
Fonte Arethusa **18**
Latomia di Cappuccini **6**
Museo Archeologico Regionale
  Paolo Orsi **5**
Mueso del Papiro **5**
Palazzo Bellomo **17**
Palazzo Beneventano del Bosco **10**
Palazzo del Senato **13**
Palazzo Impellizzeri **15**
Palazzo Interlandi Pizzuti **16**
Parco Archeologico della Neopolis **2**
Piazza Archimede **14**
Piazza del Duomo **12**
Piazza Pancali **8**
Santa Lucia **11**
Santa Lucia al Sepolcro **7**
Santuario della Madonna delle Lacrime **4**
Teatro Greco **1**
Tempio di Apollo **9**

0   0.25 Km
0   1/4 Mi

lovely rose window is from the 14th century. A granite column to the right of the presbytery marks the spot where Syracusans believe Santa Lucia suffered decapitation. Under the reign of Frederick III in the 16th century, the present ceiling was constructed with painted beams, reproducing a thick constellation of "stars" alternating with rose petals and small crosses.

Adjacent to the basilica and linked to it by a spooky 12th-century catacomb is a little baroque chapel containing the tomb of the martyred saint. She is long gone, however. In 1039, the Byzantine general Giorgio Maniace ordered that her corpse be sent to Constantinople. During the Crusades, the Venetians claimed the remains and shipped them back to Venice, where they remain today.

A marble statue placed under the sepulcher's altar is of particular, though morbid, fascination. From May 6 to 8, 1735, eyewitnesses reported that this statue miraculously "sweated" profusely.

The sanctuary lies at the northern end of one of the loveliest squares in Syracuse, Piazza Santa Lucia, lined on three sides by rows of trees.

Via Gignami 1. ✆ 0931-67946. Free admission. Daily 9am–noon and 4–7pm.

ORTYGIA ISLAND ✮✮✮

Ortygia, inhabited for many thousands of years, is also called the *Città Vecchia* (Old City). It contains the town's Duomo, many rows of houses spanning 500 years of building styles, most of the city's medieval and baroque monuments, and some of the most charming vistas in Sicily. In Greek mythology, it's said to have been ruled by Calypso, daughter of Atlas, the sea nymph who detained Ulysses (Odysseus) for 7 years. The island, reached by crossing the Ponte Nuova, is about a mile long and half again as wide. Take bus no. 21 or 23 to get here.

Heading out the Foro Italico, you'll come to the **Fonte Arethusa** ✮, also famous in mythology. The river god Alpheius, son of Oceanus, is said to have fallen in love with the sea nymph Arethusa. The nymph turned into this spring or fountain, but Alpheius became a river and "mingled" with his love. According to legend, the spring ran red when bulls were sacrificed at Olympus.

At Piazza del Duomo, the **Duomo** ✮ of Syracuse, reached by heading down Via Minerva from Piazza Archimede, illustrates more than any other structure in town the changing colonizations and architectural styles that have dominated the city over the centuries. The present cathedral incorporates architectural fragments from a 5th-century-B.C. temple honoring Athena. In its heyday, this Greek temple was spoken of in revered tones by the people of the Mediterranean. From miles away, sailors could see the golden statue of Athena shining like a beacon. Twenty-six of the temple's **Doric columns** ✮ are still in place. In 1693, an earthquake caused the cathedral's facade to collapse, and in the 18th century structure was rebuilt in the baroque style.

Once inside, look in the first bay on the right for a beautiful **font** ✮ fashioned from a Greek marble krater. It is held up by seven stunning 13th-century wrought-iron lions. The Duomo is also rich in statues adorning its chapels, including one honoring patron saint Lucia. Entry to the Duomo is free; it's open daily from 8am to noon and 4 to 7pm.

The irregular **Piazza del Duomo** ✮ is especially majestic when the facade of the cathedral is dramatically caught by the setting sun or when floodlit at night. Acclaimed as one of the most beautiful squares in Italy, it's filled with fine baroque buildings. They include the striking **Palazzo Beneventano del Bosco,** with its lovely courtyard, and the **Palazzo del Senato,** with an inner courtyard displaying a senator's carriage from the 1700s. At the far end of the square stands another church, **Santa Lucia.**

The other important landmark square is **Piazza Archimede,** with its baroque fountain festooned with dancing jets and sea nymphs. This square is directly northeast of Piazza del Duomo, forming the monumental heart of Ortygia. It, not the cathedral square, is the main piazza of the old city. Original Gothic windows grace the 15th-century **Palazzo Lanza** here. As you move about Ortygia, you'll find that Piazza Archimede is a fine place from which to orient yourself. Wander the narrow streets wherever your feet will take you, and when you get lost, ask for directions back to Piazza Archimede.

Palazzo Bellomo ⭐⭐ This elegant 13th-century palace is today the home of the **Museo Regionale di Arte Medievale e Moderna,** which contains one of the great art collections of Sicily, dating from the high Middle Ages through the 20th century. It's located next to St. Benedict's Church close to Fonte Aretusa.

The palazzo is from the Swabian era and was enlarged in the 15th century by the powerful Bellomo family. The art is arranged chronologically on two floors. Much of it was rescued from deconsecrated monasteries and churches.

We like to gaze upon two exquisite masterpieces: *The Burial of St. Lucia* (1608) ⭐, by the "divine" Caravaggio, and Antonello da Messina's exquisite *Annunciation* (1474) ⭐. Caravaggio, the master of light, created a stunning canvas of grieving figures, graced with the serene expression of the martyr and the raw nudity of the gravediggers. The saint's death sleep was meant to signify her glorious rebirth in heaven. Though damaged, the *Annunciation* remains powerful in its imagery and majesty.

On the ground floor of the palazzo is an array of sculpture from the Middle Ages and the Renaissance, the most outstanding of which are from the Gagini school, including the tomb of Giovanni Cardinas, by Antonello Gagini, and a masterful *Madonna of the Bullfinch,* by Domenico Gagini. Look for the 17th- and 18th-century Sicilian carriages in the loggia.

The collection of Sicilian **decorative arts** ⭐ is full of charm and whimsy. It includes marble intarsia panels, ecclesiastical objects, 18th-century statuettes, church vestments, terra-cotta figurines, ceramics, and silver- and goldsmithery.

Via Capodieci 16. ✆ **0931-69511.** Admission 2.50€ ($3). Mon–Sat 9am–6:30pm; Sun 9am–1:30pm.

The Tears of an Abandoned Mistress

One of the most evocative boat rides in and around Syracuse is along the **River Cyane,** 5km (3 miles) west of the city along Via Elorina. From May to September, a 2-hour boat trip can take you to the source of this river. Here you will see a pool that, according to legend, was formed by the tears shed by Cyane, a nymph attending her mistress, Persephone, who was abducted by Hades (Pluto in Roman mythology), leaving Cyane alone.

Along the way you'll see clusters of papyrus plants. The original plants were a gift from Ptolemy to Hieron II. The boat also goes by the meager ruins of **Olympeion,** a temple erected at the end of the 6th century.

Boat rentals cost between 8€ to 15€ ($9.60–$18) per person, depending on the number of passengers. For tickets and information on departure times, call ✆ **0931-69076.** To reach the departure site, take bus no. 21, 22, or 23 from Piazza della Posta and get off at Ponte delle Fiane.

Tempio di Apollo   At the Piazza Pancali on the island of Ortygia, this Greek temple dating from the 6th century B.C is the oldest peripteral (having a row of columns on each side) Doric temple in the world. The inscription says that the temple honors Apollo. However, after Cicero came to Syracuse, he wrote that the temple was dedicated to Artemis. Regardless, the temple faced a rocky future—it was first turned into a Byzantine church before the Saracens took over and converted it into a mosque. Later, under Norman rule, it was turned back into a church. On a square across the bridge to Ortygia, the fenced-off ruins can be viewed at any time.

SHOPPING

Enoteca Capriccio   This well-recommended shop inventories the town's largest collection of Sicilian wines, with a good selection from the Piedmont and Tuscany as well. Bottles are priced from 4€ to 100€ ($4.80–$120). The most sought-after wines include a 1988 "Regaleali" cabernet sauvignon, priced here at around 100€ ($120) per bottle. Via Dell'Amalfitania 11. ℂ 0931-464918. Bus: 21 or 22.

Galleria Bellomo ⭐   Located across the narrow medieval street from the Museo Bellomo, this is an art gallery with a twist: It sells colorful still lifes and landscapes painted on papyrus that's manufactured on the premises. Part of the charm of this place involves a free demonstration of how this water-logged reed is soaked, pressed, and layered between linen sheets to painstakingly produce the substance upon which the day-to-day business of ancient Egypt was conducted. Prices range from 5€ ($6) for a simple postcard to 800€ ($960) for an original work of art suitable for framing. Via Capodieci 15. ℂ 0931-61340. Bus: 21 or 22.

Old Times/Davies of London Antiquario   This shop's entrance is set on the innermost rim of an antique courtyard, immediately adjacent to the Ortygia Island branch of Syracuse's tourist office. Inside is a wide array of mostly English art objects and porcelain, hauled down to Syracuse from estate sales in Britain by an expatriate who fell in love with southern Sicily many years ago. Via Cavour 18/20. ℂ 0931-60977. Bus: 21 or 22.

WHERE TO STAY

The best place to stay here is on Ortygia, at either the Grand Hotel or the Albergo Domus Mariae (see below). The island has far more character and charm than "mainland" Syracuse. On the downside, both of these hotels might be booked to capacity, especially in summer. In that case, we've included some backup choices.

EXPENSIVE

Grand Hotel ⭐⭐⭐   Originally built in 1905, this is the best hotel in Syracuse, with a very appealing mix of modernity and old-world charm. It's set directly on the waterfront, near Ortygia's main access bridge to the Italian "mainland," in a stately four-story building containing lots of inlaid marble and polished Belle Epoque hardwoods. The vaulted cellar has a bar with comfortable sofas and a collection of remnants—some museum-quality—unearthed from this site during long-ago excavations. Guest rooms are contemporary and comfortable, with color schemes of beige and champagne. In some of the suites, duplex setups include interior staircases of polished steel. All units boast state-of-the-art bathrooms with shower-tub combinations. The in-house restaurant, **La Terrazza,** is reviewed on p. 252. The bus station is only 100m (328 ft.) away.

Viale Mazzini 12, 96100 Siracusa. ⓒ **0931-464600**. Fax 0931-464611. www.grandhotelsr.it. 58 units. 225€ ($270) double; from 280€ ($336) suite. Rates include breakfast. AE, DC, MC, V. Free parking. **Amenities:** Restaurant; 2 bars; babysitting; laundry service; dry cleaning; 1 room for those w/limited mobility. *In room:* A/C, TV, dataport, minibar, hair dryer, safe, radio.

Grand Hotel Villa Politi   For decades after its inauguration in 1862, the Grand Hotel Villa Politi (not to be confused with Syracuse's Grand Hotel, described above) was one of the three most elegant and sought-after hotels in Sicily, rivaled only by Palermo's Villa Igiea and Taormina's Palazzo San Domenico. Today, it's a lot less prestigious, evoking, at least from the outside, either a hospital or a battered public school. But if you know what you're getting beforehand, *and* if you understand some of its history, you'll probably be content to stay on its unusual premises. The hotel is awkwardly located in a residential neighborhood that's connected by roaring boulevards, after a 10-minute drive, to the Archaeological Park. It's situated above what was used thousands of years ago as a rock quarry, the historic Latomie dei Cappuccini. The result is bizarre, even surreal, incorporating a dry, dusty garden with a deep chasm almost at the hotel's foundation, all of it surrounded by the urban encroachments of the 21st century. Most of the rooms reflect the somewhat dowdy tastes of someone's well-heeled but not widely traveled Sicilian aunt: lace curtains, high ceilings, comfy beds, and a definite sense of the south Italian bourgeoisie. Some rooms have Jacuzzis; some have dataports. Overall, the hotel lacks the excitement and good location of other choices like the Grand Hotel on Ortygia Island.

Via MP Laudien 2, 9610-0 Siracusa. ⓒ **0931-412121**. Fax 0931-36061. www.villapoliti.com. 192€–245€ ($230–$294) double; 366€ ($439) suite. Rates include breakfast. AE, DC, MC, V. Free parking. Bus: 1 or 4. **Amenities:** 2 restaurants; bar; 24-hr. room service; outdoor pool; laundry service; nonsmoking rooms; solarium. *In room:* A/C, TV, minibar, hair dryer, safe.

Holiday Inn Originally built in 1965 as an AGIP hotel, this box-shaped structure is set between a gas station and the eastern edge of the Parco Archeologico. Everything about it was designed for quick and uncomplicated access for business travelers; as such, it offers reasonably good value without a shred of historic association or antique charm. Guest rooms are chain-motel efficient, each with a writing desk, a shower-only bathroom, and bland but efficient international styling.

Viale Teracati 30, 96100 Siracusa. ⓒ **0931-440440**. Fax 0931-67115. www.holiday-inn.com/siracusaitaly. 83 units. 190€ ($228) double. AE, DC, MC, V. Free parking. Bus: 8. **Amenities:** Restaurant; bar; concierge; laundry service; dry cleaning; nonsmoking rooms. *In room:* A/C, TV, dataport, minibar, hair dryer.

Hotel Roma   A block from the city's magnificent cathedral, this government-rated four-star hotel opened in the much-renovated shell of a hotel that was originally built in the 1880s. The lobby's vaulted ceiling is crafted from chiseled stone blocks and ringed with Belle Epoque columns. Most of the well-appointed, very comfortable guest rooms have elaborate marquetry floors, original lithographs, and comfortable furniture vaguely inspired by Art Deco. Only a few of the bathrooms contain tubs; most offer a modern shower instead. About four of the rooms have computers. Overall, this is a fine hotel choice, with a location in the heart of monument-laden Ortygia Island.

Via Minerva 10, 96100 Siracusa. ⓒ **0931-465626**. Fax 0931-465535. www.hotelroma.sr.it. 45 units. 190€ ($228) double; 243€ ($292) junior suite. AE, DC, MC, V. Parking 6€ ($7.20) per day. **Amenities:** Restaurant; bar; laundry service; dry cleaning; rooms for those w/limited mobility. *In room:* A/C, TV, dataport, minibar, safe.

MODERATE

Albergo Domus Mariae *Finds* This small-scale hotel originated in 1995 when a Catholic elementary school was transformed into a decent, well-managed

Syracuse Accommodations & Dining

ACCOMMODATIONS ■

Albergo Domus Mariae **17**

B&B Airone **18**

Grand Hotel **11**

Grand Hotel Villa Politi **5**

Holiday Inn **3**

Hotel Bellavista **4**

Hotel Como **8**

Hotel Gutkowski **16**

Hotel Panorama **2**

Hotel Relax **1**

Hotel Roma **21**

Il Limoneto **1**

Jolly Hotel **7**

Park Helios Hotel **2**

DINING ◆

Antico Caffè Minerva **20**

Da Mariano **23**

Darsena da Ianuzzo **10**

Don Camillo **19**

Gambero Rosso **9**

Il Mandarino **13**

La Siciliana **12**

La Terrazza **11**

Le Baronie **15**

Minosse di Visetti **14**

Ristorante Jonico-a
  Rutta e Ciauli **6**

lodging. It's owned by an order of Ursuline nuns, and although the desk staff and porters are likely to be laypersons, its manager is a hardworking, habit-clothed member of the order. This is the only hotel in Syracuse with its own chapel and a genuinely contemplative reading room. There's also a rooftop terrace for sunbathing. Rooms are fairly priced, with modern furniture and a no-nonsense approach to decor. Each has a tiled bathroom with shower. There are no attempts to foist religious education on guests—for most purposes, this is a conventional hotel, without any evangelistic mission. *Note:* The signs for this place are so small as to be almost invisible, especially if you're driving along the waterfront promenade that flanks it. Here's a tip: It's set directly across a tiny waterfront piazza from the baroque facade of San Filippo Neri Church.

Via Vittorio Veneto 76, 96100 Siracusa. ℂ/fax 0931-24854. www.sistemia.it/domusmariae. 17 units. 120€–130€ ($144–$156) double. Rates include breakfast. AE, DC, MC, V. Free parking. **Amenities:** Restaurant; 24-hr. room service; laundry service; dry cleaning. *In room:* A/C, TV, dataport, minibar, hair dryer.

Jolly Hotel   A major stop for tour groups, the six-story Jolly is part of the chain that's Italy's answer to Holiday Inn. You get no surprises, just your basic motel room (albeit slightly worn), with good beds and small tiled bathrooms. At least the view of the sea is panoramic. The location is on a dull but busy shopping street, about a 20-minute walk from Ortygia.

Corso Gelone 45, 96100 Siracusa. ℂ 800/221-2626 in the U.S., 800/237-0319 in Canada, or 0931-4611111. Fax 0931-461126. www.jollyhotels.it. 100 units. 99€–184€ ($119–$221) double. Rates include breakfast. AE, DC, MC, V. Free parking. **Amenities:** Restaurant; lounge; room service; laundry service; dry cleaning; nonsmoking rooms. *In room:* A/C, TV, dataport, minibar, hair dryer, safe.

Park Helios Hotel   The biggest hotel in Syracuse is architecturally uninspiring in its *moderno* statement, except for the private balconies, but it's still a solid, reliable choice. It offers airy, comfortably furnished guest rooms with tiled floors and mostly shower-only bathrooms. The service is good, though we found the restaurant rather mediocre. For the money, though, the place isn't a bad option.

Via Filisto 80, 96100 Siracusa. ℂ 0931-412233. Fax 0931-38096. www.parkhotel-helios.it. 182 units. 98€ ($118) double. AE, DC, MC, V. Free parking. **Amenities:** Restaurant; bar; outdoor pool; room service; babysitting; laundry service; dry cleaning; nonsmoking rooms; solarium. *In room:* A/C, TV, minibar, hair dryer.

INEXPENSIVE

B&B Airone   This converted old palazzo lies right in the historic center of Ortygia. It's the best bed-and-breakfast in the area, drawing young people, often backpackers, from all over the world. Furnishings are bare-bones yet comfortable, and the price is right. Only three of its units have private bathrooms, the others sharing a well-scrubbed hallway bathroom that's generally adequate for the purpose.

Via Maestranza 111, 96100 Siracusa. ℂ 0931-69005. www.bedandbreakfastsicily.com. 6 units. 50€ ($60) double without bathroom; 100€ ($120) double with bathroom. Rates include breakfast. No credit cards. **Amenities:** Lounge. *In room:* No phone.

Hotel Bellavista   This family-run hotel lies in the commercial center, close to the archaeological zone. It was built in 1956 and last renovated in 2001. The spacious lounge has leather chairs and semitropical plants. Guest rooms are informal and comfortable; most are furnished with traditional pieces and have sea-view balconies and tidy shower-only bathrooms. There's an annex in the garden for overflow.

Via Diodoro Siculo 4, 96100 Siracusa. ℂ 0931-411355. Fax 0931-37927. www.hotel-bellavista.com. 47 units. 97€ ($116) double; 126€ ($151) triple. Rates include breakfast. AE, DC, MC, V. Free parking. **Amenities:** Restaurant; bar; lounge; gym; sauna; 24-hr. room service. *In room:* A/C, TV, dataport.

Hotel Como *(Value)* *(Kids)* This small hotel, not far from the historic core, is one of the city's best bargains. It's located in the square at the train station and is convenient for those arriving on trains from Catania. It's little more than a utilitarian lodging, but many of the rooms are quite spacious and comfortably furnished. Each comes with a small, shower-only bathroom. Since some of the units are triples, this is a favorite with families, often from other parts of Sicily. Plus, its low-slung design and sense of style set the place apart from a typically tacky train-station hotel.

Piazza Stazione 13, 96100 Siracusa. ℂ **0931-464055.** Fax 0931-464056. www.hotelcomo.it. 20 units. 94€ ($113) double; 116€ ($139) triple; 148€ ($178) suite. Rates include breakfast. AE, DC, MC, V. **Amenities:** Bar; laundry service; dry cleaning; 1 room for those w/limited mobility. *In room:* A/C, TV, minibar.

Hotel Gutkowski Modern, unpretentious, and with a distinct sense of being alive to the creative arts scene of Syracuse, this small hotel opened in 1999 in a waterfront town house on Ortygia. Don't expect any particular luxury, as everything here is utilitarian and a bit less comfortable than rooms at the nearby Domus Mariae. It nonetheless has a welcoming atmosphere. The only meal offered is breakfast, which is served in a spartan-looking room next to the reception desk.

Lungomare Vittorini 26, 96100 Siracusa. ℂ **0931-465861.** Fax 0931-480505. www.guthotel.it. 15 units. 90€ ($108) double. Discounts of 10% available Oct–Mar. Rates include breakfast. AE, DC, MC, V. Free parking. **Amenities:** Laundry service; dry cleaning. *In room:* A/C, TV, minibar.

Hotel Panorama Near the entrance to the city, on a rise of Temenite Hill, this bandbox-modern hotel sits on a busy street about 5 minutes from the Archaeological Park. Rated four stars by the government, it is close to where Greek plays are presented every summer. It's not a motel, but it does provide free parking. The small guest rooms are pleasant and up-to-date following a 2004 renovation, with comfortable but utilitarian furniture and small, shower-only bathrooms.

Via Necropoli Grotticelle 33, 96100 Siracusa. ℂ **0931-412188.** Fax 0931-412527. www.hotelpanoramasr.it. 51 units. 90€–150€ ($108–$180) double. Rates include continental breakfast. AE, MC, V. Free parking. Bus: 13. **Amenities:** Restaurant; bar; 24-hr. room service; laundry service; dry cleaning; 1 room for those w/limited mobility. *In room:* A/C, TV, dataport, minibar, hair dryer, safe.

Hotel Relax This Mediterranean-style hotel lies 2km (1¼ miles) from the center in a rather tranquil residential area. On the grounds are a garden, pool, and solarium, making it a good choice for those who don't want to stay in the center of hot, dusty Syracuse. Guest rooms are light and airy, furnished in a minimalist yet comfortable fashion. About half of the bathrooms are equipped with showers; the rest have tubs. Suites are a good buy, but there are only two and they must be reserved in advance. The restaurant serves typical but quite good Sicilian and international cuisine.

Viale Epipoli 159, 96100 Siracusa. ℂ **0931-740122.** Fax 0931-740933. www.hotelrelax.it. 59 units. 105€ ($126) double; 135€ ($162) suite. Rates include breakfast. AE, DC, MC, V. Free parking. Take any bus marked BELVEDERE. **Amenities:** Restaurant; bar; outdoor pool; room service; laundry service; dry cleaning; solarium; rooms for those w/limited mobility. *In room:* A/C, TV, dataport, hair dryer.

Il Limoneto *(Value)* *(Kids)* What a discovery! This place brings you close to the heart of Sicily. The tranquil retreat of orange groves and orchards lies 9km (5 miles) from the center of Syracuse along SP14 Mare-Monti. You can stay at this estate and visit not only Syracuse but also Noto (p. 256) and Ragusa (p. 263). Much of the food served here is grown on the grounds, and guests are invited to pick their own fruit. We enjoyed the hotel's house-party atmosphere, with guests gathering in the evening for wine and conversation. If you like the outdoors, this is the best choice in the area—you can take an aerobics class, or even archery instruction. Guest rooms are comfortably furnished in a farmhouse-rustic style. Families can opt for a room with a mezzanine, stashing the kids upstairs. Each bathroom comes with a tiled shower. Two units have air-conditioning.

Via del Platano 3, 96100 Siracusa (Contrada Magrentino). ℭ 0931-717352. Fax 0931-717728. limoneto@ tin.it. 8 units. 40€ ($48) double. Rates include breakfast. Dinner 18€ ($22) per person extra. DC, MC, V. Free parking. Closed Nov. Take the Palazzolo bus from Syracuse's central station. **Amenities:** Restaurant. *In room:* No phone.

WHERE TO DINE

For just a drink, snack, or coffee, head for the elegant **Antico Caffè Minerva,** Via Minerva 15 (ℭ **0931-22606**), in the vicinity of the Duomo. Open Thursday through Tuesday from 7am to 1am.

Note: Only a few of the restaurants below lie on a bus line.

EXPENSIVE

La Terrazza ⊛ ITALIAN/SICILIAN   Set on the top floor of Ortygia's highest-rated hotel, this restaurant features a *dolce vita* ambience, formal service, and big-windowed views that sweep from the outdoor terrace way, way across Syracuse's bay. There's something festive about this place, and the fine food includes starters like smoked salmon with mint sauce; jumbo shrimp with citrus sauce; and an antipasti platter containing smoked turkey. Equally alluring are the main courses, such as risotto with monkfish and saffron. The cuisine is admirably authentic and satisfying, prepared with the freshest of ingredients.

On the top floor of the Grand Hotel, Viale Mazzini 12. ℭ 0931-464600. Reservations recommended. Main courses 10€–16€ ($12–$19). AE, DC, MC, V. Daily 12:30–2:30pm and 7:30–10:30pm.

Ristorante Jonico-a Rutta e Ciauli ⊛ SICILIAN   This is one of the best restaurants in the area for typical Sicilian cuisine and wines. It's right on the sea, not far from Piazzale dei Cappuccini. The decor is pure Liberty (Art Nouveau) style. The antipasti array is dazzling, and the homemade pastas are superb—try pasta *rusticana,* with eggplant, cheese, ham, and herbs. Swordfish appears here in roulades with raisins, pine nuts, and bread crumbs. The dessert specialty is *cassatine Siciliane* (mocha-chocolate ice cream capped with sprinkles of coffee-flavored chocolate, all floating in a lake of English custard). A roof garden has a pizzeria serving typical Sicilian pizza.

Riviera Dionisio il Grande 194. ℭ 0931-65540. Reservations recommended. Main courses 6€–10€ ($7.20–$12); pizzas 4€–7.50€ ($4.80–$9). AE, MC, V. Wed–Mon noon–3pm and 8–10:30pm.

MODERATE

Don Camillo ⊛ SEAFOOD/SICILIAN   This is one of the city's finest dining rooms, built near the historic center on the foundation of a 15th-century monastery that collapsed during an earthquake in 1693. The rather classy joint is full of atmosphere, with vaulted ceilings and potted plants. The cuisine is among the most creative in town, featuring lighter versions of time-tested Sicilian recipes. If you're a devotee of sea urchins (and not everyone is), the delectable morsels are particularly fresh-tasting here. All kinds of fish are served, and the catch of the day can be prepared almost any way you like it. More than 450 different wines are on offer.

Via Maestranza 96. ℭ 0931-67133. Reservations recommended. Main courses 9€–11€ ($11–$13). AE, DC, MC, V. Mon–Sat 12:30–2:30pm and 7:30–10:30pm. Closed Nov.

Gambero Rosso SICILIAN/MEDITERRANEAN/SEAFOOD This large restaurant is housed in an old tavern near the bridge to the Città Vecchia. The dining room extends onto a terrace facing the port. Two reliable choices are *zuppa di pesce* (fish soup) and *zuppa di cozze* (fresh mussels in a tasty marinade). The meat dishes feature a number of choices from the kitchens of Lazio, Tuscany, and Emilia-Romagna.

Via Eritrea 2. ✆ **0931-68546.** Reservations recommended. Main courses 5€–12€ ($6–$14). AE, MC, V. Fri–Wed 11am–3pm and 7:30pm–midnight.

La Siciliana ✦ *Value* SICILIAN Recommended by many local newspapers, and popular for its good food and reasonable prices, this restaurant originated in the 1920s as a simple *tavola calda* (hot-table snack bar). Today, it occupies a site along a dignified residential street near the northern tip of Ortygia Island. The pizzas from the wood-burning oven are superb—so much so that many locals call ahead for takeout. More elaborate meals might include well-prepared versions of *cavatelli a modo nostro* (pasta with ham, cream, peas, and olives); grilled cutlets; and grilled swordfish with herbs and capers.

Via Savoia 17. ✆ **0931-68944.** Reservations recommended Fri–Sat night. Main courses 6€–12€ ($7.20–$14); pizzas 3.50€–7€ ($4.20–$8.40). DC, MC, V. Tues–Sun noon–4pm and 6pm–midnight. Bus: 20.

Minosse di Visetti ✦ *Finds* ITALIAN This well-run restaurant is more formal and a lot more sedate than many of its quasi-hysterical competitors on Ortygia Island. It's set on an obscure alley in the heart of town, occupying a trio of paneled dining rooms. The restaurant entered the annals of local history in 1993, when it was selected as the dinner venue for the Pope on the occasion of his inauguration of the Our Lady of Tears sanctuary (p. 241). The chef wins praise for his fresh mussels with cherry tomatoes. The spaghetti with seafood is marked by intense, refined flavors. And the fish soup is one of the best in town.

Via Mirabella 6. ✆ **0931-66366.** Main courses 9€–17€ ($11–$20). MC, V. Tues–Sun noon–3pm and 7–11pm. Closed 2 weeks in July. Take any minibus leaving Piazza delle Poste and get off at Via Mirabella.

INEXPENSIVE

Da Mariano SICILIAN Set on a cobble-covered alley, much too narrow for a car, a short block downhill from the Museo Bellomo, this hideaway has simple plastic tables and chairs, red-checkered tablecloths, and a good reputation. It offers only 70 seats in a cavelike warren of vaulted rooms that you'll find either charmingly intimate or impossibly claustrophobic. The chef's use of fresh ingredients is a compelling reason to dine here. We sampled a delightful homemade cavatelli with wild boar sauce. Many dishes, such as baked rabbit, Sicilian tripe, and perfectly sautéed calves' liver, are full of good old country flavor. The grilled swordfish was immensely tasty, as was a farfalle pasta with braised radicchio.

Vicolo Zuccolà 9. ✆ **0931-67444.** Reservations recommended. Main courses 6€–8€ ($7.20–$9.60). MC, V. Wed–Mon 1–3pm and 8–11:30pm. Closed 3 weeks in July.

Darsena da Ianuzzo ITALIAN/SICILIAN Well located, almost immediately adjacent to the older of the two bridges leading from the Sicilian "mainland" to Ortygia Island, this stylish enclave overlooks the artfully ratty harborfront life that gives Ortygia such color. A veranda overlooks the Ionian Sea. We've enjoyed some good meals here, but be warned: This is not the friendliest oasis in town. Only time-tested local recipes are served: One specialty is a savory fish soup; another is spaghetti in a mass of little sea urchins. Another excellent dish is *conchigliette al ragù di pesce,* or minced fish in a rich tomato sauce.

Riva Garibaldi 8. ℂ **0931-66104**. Reservations recommended. Main courses 6€–8€ ($7.20–$9.60). AE, DC, MC, V. Thurs–Tues noon–3pm and 7:15–11pm.

Il Mandarino CHINESE   After too much Sicilian food, you might take a cue from the many locals who pack into this elegant Chinese restaurant. Its exterior is gaily and charmingly decorated with twinkling lights. Inside, you'll find red and gold lanterns and big tables that seem to correspond exactly to the size of large Sicilian families. Among the best menu items are squid and prawns on a hot iron platter; pork in hot chili sauce; and myriad preparations of duck, pork, chicken, and beef.

Via Savoia 12. ℂ **0931-22898**. Reservations not necessary. Main courses 4.50€–7€ ($5.40–$8.40). AE, MC, V. Daily noon–3pm and 7:30pm–midnight.

Le Baronie 🏵 *Finds* SICILIAN   Expatriate Americans and longtime friends of ours living in Syracuse turned us on to this delightful trattoria in an old Sicilian villa. Laid out like a hexagon, it's set in a garden dotted with ancient sarcophagi and offers both patio and interior dining. The restaurant serves traditional island cuisine, but adds many creative touches. The result is highly personal, inventive food. Try tucking into gnocchi *alla tancredi* (with radicchio, Parmesan, cream, butter, and olive oil). Our favorite pasta—and it's a delight—is linguine *del vicere* (with those trusty urchins again, plus olive oil, garlic, and Parmesan). The chefs take justifiable pride in their *pesce spada d'Almeria* (swordfish steaks served in a sauce made of green pepper, butter, and brandy).

Via Gargallo 24. ℂ **0931-68884**. Reservations recommended. Main courses 7€–10€ ($8.40–$12). DC, MC, V. Tues–Sun noon–3pm and 7:30pm–midnight.

SYRACUSE AFTER DARK

Much of the nightlife in summer takes place in satellite villages, particularly along the coast. Unless specifically stated, hours can be irregular; check before heading to one of the hot spots, especially those out of town.

In Syracuse itself, you can visit **La Nottola,** Via Gargallo 61 (ℂ **0931-60009**), on a small street near Via Maestanza. This stylish jazz club/piano bar/disco attracts a well-dressed younger crowd.

Peter Pan Caffè Letterario 🏵, Via Castello Maniace 46–48 (ℂ **0931-468937**), is a cocktail bar and wine tavern that even has books, giving it some claim to fame as a "literary cafe." Many patrons are students from the local university who lounge on comfy sofas. It occasionally features live music such as jazz or pop. Open June through September, daily from 7pm to 3am; and October through May, daily from 4:30pm to 3am.

Doctor Sam, Piazza San Rocco 4 (ℂ **0931-483598**), is the premier counter-culture bar of Syracuse, with a hip, youthful, and high-energy clientele that tends to be interested in tattoos, motorcycles, piercings, Rastafarian music, rock 'n' roll, and—under the right circumstances—romance. Open April through September, nightly from 7pm to 4am. Closed Wednesdays from October to March.

Syracuse has a number of other worthy bars and cafes, including **Bar Bonomo,** Corso Gelone 48 (ℂ **0931-67845**), which is more of a bar/bakery. Its gelato is some of the best in town. The spacious **Bar del Ponte,** Piazza Pancali (ℂ **0931-64312**), is near Syracuse's most famous fountain and serves all kinds of drinks, snacks, and excellent gelato. Tables overflow onto the square in fair weather. Also in the vicinity of the fountain is the fashionable bar **Lungo la Notte,** Lungomare Alfeo 22 (ℂ **0931-64200**), open only at night. The panoramic setting overlooking the harbor attracts a young clientele.

ON THE OUTSKIRTS

The region's best disco is **La Piscina,** Viale Scala Greca (© **0931-753633**). It contains a walled garden, a pool that at night seems mostly ornamental, and a crowd that's older than you'll find at the student hangouts closer to the town center. Take bus no. 5, 6, 8, 25, or 26. Another option is the **Discotecca Malibu,** Via Elorina 172 (© **0931-721888**), about 6km (3½ miles) southwest of town on SS115, where a younger crowd dances all night at a seaside pavilion that evokes its California namesake. In midsummer, head for the **Sporting Club Terrauzza,** Via del Galeone (© **0931-714647**), centerpiece of the village of Terrauzza. Located about 10km (6 miles) southwest of Syracuse, it's where vacationers at the local beaches show up to mingle with local 20-somethings.

SIDE TRIPS FROM SYRACUSE

For specific locations, refer to the "Syracuse & the Southeast" map, on p. 235.

CASTELLO EURIALO *⊛*   This boat-shaped structure is one of the most formidable Greek fortresses to have survived from ancient times, set 9km (5½ miles) northwest of Syracuse along Via Epipoli, in the Belvedere district. The castle was adapted and fortified by Archimedes, the famous mathematician who was born in Syracuse in 287 B.C.

The castle was believed impregnable, but such was not the case. The Romans conquered it without a struggle. The approach road crosses the **Wall of Dionysius,** which once stretched for 27km (17 miles) across the Epipolae high plateau, enclosing the northern tier of Syracuse. Two parallel walls were built of limestone blocks, the center filled with rubble. The walls, launched by Dionysius the Elder in 401 B.C. after the Athenian siege, were finished in 385 B.C.

As you survey the ruins, know that they are the most complete of any Greek military work extant. Three ditches precede the west front of the fortress. The main castle consisted of a keep, barracks, and cisterns. A warren of underground passages was cut through the fortress. From the castle precincts, you can enjoy a **panoramic view** *⊛* back to Syracuse.

Take bus no. 11, 25, or 26 from the Archaeological Park to reach the site, which is open daily from 9am to sunset. Admission is free. For information, call © **0931-711773.**

MEGARA HYBLAEA   If you don't suffocate passing through the industrial horror, *Zona industriale,* with its polluting oil refineries, you'll reach ancient Megara Hyblaea, near the major port of Prilo along the coast of southeastern Sicily. The Greeks built the city to open onto the Gulf of Augusta, whose shoreline now contains the largest concentration of chemical plants in Europe. Pollution has killed nearly all marine life in the bay, and the air in this area is contaminated.

Should you be a serious-enough archaeologist, and if you have persisted this far, you'll come upon the ruin of what was Megara Hyblaea, 16km (10 miles) to the north of Syracuse and reached along SS114. Yellow signposts direct you to the excavations, which are open Monday through Saturday from 9am to 2pm and Sunday from 9am to 1pm. Admission is free.

The Megarians arriving in ships from Greece founded Megara Hyblaea in the 8th century B.C., making it one of the oldest of all Greek settlements in Sicily. It was leveled by the tyrant Gelon in 483 B.C. By 340 B.C., Timoleon had founded a second city, but it, too, fell to conquerors, this time the Romans in 214 B.C. Serious excavations of the site began in 1949 and continue to this day.

Outside the old town walls are the remains of a necropolis. After a look, you can walk into the heart of the ruins, exploring foundations of buildings from both the Archaic period (indicated by red iron posts) and the Hellenistic era (green posts). Of particular interest is a Hellenistic house from the 4th century B.C. (the entry is marked by iron steps). Nearly two dozen chambers were arranged around two patios.

To the left of the old *agora,* or marketplace, are the ruins of Hellenistic baths, with a boiler still discernible in the rubble. Nearby is a small Doric temple in bad shape, which dates from the 4th century B.C. You can also view the Hellenistic west gate with its two square towers.

Although Megara Hyblaea is the finest and most complete model of an Archaic city still extant, all the valuable artifacts dug up here have been transferred to the museums of Syracuse.

2 Noto ★★

31km (19 miles) SW of Syracuse, 55km (34 miles) E of Ragusa

Justifiably the most popular day trip from Syracuse is to the little town of Noto, which is set amid olive groves and almond trees on a plateau overlooking the Asinaro Valley. Noto dates from the 9th century and knew Greek, Roman, Byzantine, Arab, Norman, Aragonese, and even Spanish culture before 1692, when an earthquake destroyed it. The town was constructed somewhat like a stage set, with curvilinear accents and wrought-iron balconies. Many Sicilian artists and artisans have worked hard to rebuild Noto into a baroque gem, with uniform buildings of soft limestone. It's even more magical at night, with all the buildings lit up—you may want to stay for dinner and then stroll around, or even stay overnight.

Mercifully, traffic has been diverted away from the main street, **Corso Vittorio Emanuele,** to protect its fragile buildings, on which restoration began in 1987—and not a moment too soon. Your best approach is through the monumental **Porta Reale (Royal Gate),** crowned by three symbols—a dog, a swan, and a tower, representing the town's former allegiance to the Bourbon monarchy. From here, take **Corso Vittorio Emanuele,** going through the old patricians' quarter. The rich-looking, honey-colored buildings along this street are some of the most captivating on the island. This street takes you to the three most important piazzas (see below).

ESSENTIALS

GETTING THERE   By Train   Noto is reached by trains (usually nine per day) heading southwest from Syracuse, which has good rail connections with the rest of Italy. The ride takes 30 minutes and costs 2.65€ ($3.20) one-way. The train station is on Via Principe di Piemonte, a 20-minute walk west of the historic core. For schedules, call ℃ **892021.**

By Bus   Interbus (℃ **0931-66710**) offers 13 buses per day from Syracuse; the trip takes 50 minutes and costs 3€ ($3.60) one-way. The bus station is on Piazzale Marconi, near Giardini Pubblici just east of the center, a 5-minute walk to Porta Reale and the main street, Corso Vittorio Emanuele.

By Car   Head southwest along Route 115.

VISITOR INFORMATION   To get your bearings, stop first at the **tourist office,** at Piazza XVI Maggio, Villetta Ercole, in front of San Domenico Church (℃ **0931-573779**), to pick up a map. Open from May to September, daily from

9am to 1pm and 3:30 to 6:30pm; from October to March, Monday through Friday from 8am to 2pm and 3:30 to 6:30pm.

STROLLING THROUGH A BAROQUE CITY

The main thoroughfare, **Corso Vittorio Emanuele,** cuts through a trio of squares, each with its own church. The main axis begins at **Porta Reale,** a giant gateway to Noto patterned on a Roman-style triumphal arch, except this one dates from the 19th century rather than ancient times. The three squares are Piazza Immacolata, Piazza Municipio, and Piazza XVI Maggio.

If it's a hot day, you can rest in the **Giardini Pubblici,** immediately to the right of Porta Reale opening onto Viale Marconi. These public gardens are filled with palm trees and flowering bougainvillea. Don't bother trying to figure out all those local figures honored by marble busts. Even most of the people of Noto today have forgotten those guys of dubious achievement.

Heading west on Corso Vittorio Emanuele, you'll first approach **Piazza Immacolata.** The square is dominated by the handsome facade of **Chiesa di San Francesco all'Immacolata** (📞 0931-573192), which contains notable artworks rescued from a Franciscan church in the old town. The major work of art here is a painted wooden *Madonna and Child* from 1564, believed to be the work of Antonio Monachello. The most impressive aspect of this church is its grandiose flight of steps. Open daily from 8:30am to noon and 4 to 7:30pm.

Immediately to the right of the church as you face it is the **Monastereo del Santissimo Salvatore,** which can be admired from the outside. The building, today a seminary, is characterized by windows adorned with "potbellied" wrought-iron balconies. The elegant tower is the hallmark of the fine 18th-century facade.

The next square is **Piazza Municipio** 🐾, the most majestic of the trio. It's dominated by the **Palazzo Ducezio,** a graceful town hall with curvilinear elements enclosed by a classical portico. The upper section of this palace was added as late as the 1950s. Its most beautiful room is the Louis XI–style **Hall of Representation** *(Salone di Rappresentanza),* decorated with gold and stucco. On the vault is a Mazza fresco representing the mythological figure of Ducezio founding Neas (the ancient name of Noto). The custodian will usually allow you a look around on the ground level during regular business hours; admission is free.

On one side of the square, a broad flight of steps leads to the **Duomo,** flanked by two lovely horseshoe-shaped hedges. The cathedral was inspired by models of Borromini's churches in Rome and was completed in 1776. In 1996, the dome collapsed, destroying a large section of the nave, and it's still under repair.

On the far side of the cathedral is the **Palazzo Villadorata,** graced with a classic facade. Its six extravagant **balconies** 🐾🐾 are supported by sculpted buttresses of galloping horses, griffins, and grotesque bald and bearded figures with chubby-cheeked cherubs at their bellies. The palazzo is divided into 90 rooms, the most beautiful being the **Yellow Hall** *(Salone Giallo),* the **Green Hall** *(Salone Verde),* and the **Red Hall** *(Salone Rosso),* with their precious frescoed domes from the 18th century. The charming **Feasts Hall** *(Salone delle Feste)* is dominated by a fresco representing mythological scenes. In one of its aisles, the palazzo contains a *pinacoteca* (picture gallery) with antique manuscripts, rare books, and portraits of noble families. The building is under renovation and its status can change suddenly; check with the visitor center before heading here or call 📞 0931-835005 for up-to-date information. Currently, the building is open Monday through Saturday from 9am to 1:30pm and 3:30 to

Like Venice, a City in Peril

The collapse of the dome of the Duomo in 1996 sent a dangerous signal racing through this little baroque city. After literally centuries of decay and neglect, the monuments of Noto are in grave danger. Complicating matters, much of the regional material—white tufa stone—is soft and not meant to last through the ages like marble; unless it is constantly maintained, it can rapidly deteriorate. The only reason many of the buildings of Noto are still standing is because of wooden supports, and for some buildings it looks as if scaffolding is here to stay. Noto is hampered by lack of money, even though restoration is proceeding—but at a snail's pace, in some critics' view. What's the hope? That Noto will be approved as an addition to UNESCO's World Heritage Site list. This would mean funds for ongoing restoration. Until enough money is found, Noto continues to decline, with many of its most precious monuments in peril.

6:30pm; admission is 2€ ($2.40). Guided tours in English are available for 3.10€ ($3.70).

The final main square is **Piazza XVI Maggio,** dominated by the convex facade of **Chiesa di San Domenico** ⊛, with two tiers of columns separated by a high cornice. The interior is filled with polychrome marble altars, but the church appears to have been shut indefinitely as it's in really bad shape. At least you can admire its facade. Directly in front of the church is a public garden, the **Villetta d'Ercole,** named for its 18th-century fountain honoring Hercules.

Right off Corso Vittorio Emanuele is one of Noto's most fascinating streets, **Via Nicolaci** ⊛, lined with magnificent baroque buildings.

In summer, Noto is also known for some fine **beaches** nearby; the best are 6km (3½ miles) away at **Noto Marina.** You can catch a bus at the Giardini Pubblici in Noto; the one-way fare is 2€ ($2.40). Call ✆ **0931-836123** for schedules.

WHERE TO STAY

Camere Belvedere   Set at the highest elevation of the historic district, this elegant stone structure opens onto the "balcony of the city," a short walk from the crumbling Duomo. From its terrace, you're treated to a panoramic view of the baroque city, and on a clear day, you can see all the way to the seashore at Noto Marina and up to Portopalo, the extreme southeastern tip of the island. Constructed of ancient stones from other buildings, the belvedere is traditional all the way. Its guest rooms are sparsely furnished yet comfortable, resting for the most part under wood-beamed ceilings. Each unit comes with a small, shower-only bathroom. Even though it's in the middle of a town, there is a rustic aura to this place.

Piazza Perelli Cippo 1, 96017 Noto. ✆/fax **0931-573820.** www.camerebelvedere.com. 4 units. 50€–60€ ($60–$72) double. No credit cards. Free street parking. **Amenities:** Bar; breakfast room; solarium. *In room:* A/C, minibar.

La Sumalia Residence   This ancient mansion, a real discovery, lies in the hills less than 1km (½ mile) from the center of Noto. From its panoramic perch, a view of the Gulf of Noto and the town unfolds. The property, which dominates a valley planted with almond and olive trees, has been restored and renovated with a number of its original architectural features intact. The small guest rooms have wood-beamed ceilings; rustic, comfortable furnishings; and small, shower-only bathrooms. Guests can take breakfast on the terrace and use the communal kitchen.

Contrada San Giovanni, 96017 Noto. ©/fax 0931-894292. www.lasumasumalia.com. 5 units. 50€–60€ ($60–$72) double. Rates include breakfast. AE, DC, MC, V. Bus departs from Piazza Marconi in Noto for Contrada San Giovanni. **Amenities:** Bar. *In room:* A/C, TV, no phone.

Villa Canisello 🌟 *(Finds* Surrounded by lush vegetation, this offbeat discovery offers the chance to stay in a restored 19th-century farmhouse just a 10-minute walk from the historic core of Noto. You'll enter a world of peace and tranquillity here. The property has been restored with sensitivity, with tasteful decor throughout. The lounge in the garden is used as a reading room as well, and the public rooms display local crafts. Guest rooms are small but beautifully kept, each with a private entrance and a small, shower-only bathroom. Some have air-conditioning; the rest have ceiling fans.

Via Pavese 1, 96017 Noto. © 0931-835793. Fax 0931-837700. www.villacanisello.it. 6 units. 65€–80€ ($78–$96) double. No credit cards. Free parking. **Amenities:** Bar; breakfast room. *In room:* TV, fridge, no phone.

Villa Favorita/Villa Giulia 🌟 *(Finds* These two 18th-century residences have been beautifully restored and filled with modern comforts. Located between Noto and Noto Marina (the beach area), they provide the best-equipped lodgings in the area. Under the same management, and very similar in style, they actually lie 10km (6¼ miles) apart, but on the same road. Palm trees grace the grounds, and the look is one of elegance and serenity. Guest rooms are comfortably though somewhat austerely furnished. Each unit comes with a small bathroom with either tub or shower. The dining rooms are handsomely appointed, and the cuisine of regional and international dishes is some of the best in the area.

Contrada Falconara, 96017 Noto. © 0931-812912. Fax 0931-812812. www.hotelvillafavorita.it. 73 units. 92€ ($110) double. AE, DC, MC, V. Free parking. From May–Sept, a bus leaves Piazza Marconi in Noto and heads for Marina di Noto, stopping at both hotels. **Amenities:** Restaurant; bar; outdoor pool; 24-hr. room service; rooms for those w/limited mobility. *In room:* A/C, TV, dataport.

Villa Mediterranea 🌟 This is your best bet if you'd prefer to visit historic Noto on a day trip but stay on the best beach while in the area. This cozy hotel is set right along the seafront, in its own gardens with a pool. The beach is accessible through a private gate. The public lounges are stylishly furnished. Guest rooms contain comfortable beds, tiled floors, and tidy shower-only bathrooms. In the tradition of beach hotels, there is no attempt to overdecorate here.

Viale Lido, 96017 Noto Marina. ©/fax 0931-812330. www.villamediterranea.it. 15 units. 70€–130€ ($84–$156) double. Rates include breakfast. AE, DC, MC, V. Free parking. Closed Nov 1–Dec 19 and Jan 8 to mid-Mar. **Amenities:** Bar; outdoor pool; laundry service; dry cleaning. *In room:* A/C, TV.

WHERE TO DINE

Al Buco 🌟 *(Finds* SICILIAN Of the restaurants we recommend in Noto, this is one of the easiest to reach, positioned only a few steps downhill from the town's main thoroughfare, Corso Vittorio Emanuele. Descend a flight of modern marble steps into a simply furnished interior that's kept cool by thick masonry walls and a location that's partially below the street's grade. The deep-fried zucchini blossoms here are the best we've ever had in Sicily. Fresh grilled tuna is a delight in its simplicity. Japan meets Sicily in the raw swordfish marinated in citrus sauce. Meat eaters don't get the same loving care fish devotees do, although our steak was perfectly cooked and served in a pepper cream sauce.

Via Giuseppe Zanardelli 17. ✆ 0931-838142. Reservations recommended. Main courses 7€–12€ ($8.40–$14). MC, V. Sun–Fri noon–3:30pm and 7pm–midnight.

Il Barocco SICILIAN   The most whimsical, charming, and lighthearted of Noto's restaurants occupies what was built in the 1700s as the stable block for a historic palace nearby. Tables sit beneath vaulted ceilings, beside walls that patrons have "autographed" in heavy markers with often personalized messages for the extroverted owner, Graziella. Seafood is well handled, especially a delightful plate of calamari and a *fritto misto* (mixed fry) of shrimp and fish.

Via Cavour 8 (at Ronco Sgadari). ✆ 0931-835999. Reservations recommended. Main courses 7€–10€ ($8.40–$12); set-price menu 10€ ($12). MC, V. Daily noon–3:30pm and 5–11:30pm.

Neas *Value* SICILIAN   Reach this family-run restaurant by walking through a medieval-looking courtyard, then pass into vaulted rooms whose stonework was set in place during the 1730s. There's outdoor seating if you want it, but during the heat of a Sicilian day, most diners opt for the restaurant's cool inner recesses. The most typical of Sicilian dishes in Noto are served here, but just because they're typical doesn't mean they aren't good—quite the contrary. We launched our meal with a plate of roasted sardines, and took delight in pennette pasta garnished with swordfish and clams.

Via Rocco Pirri 30. ✆ 0931-573538. Reservations not necessary. Main courses 8€–12€ ($9.60–$14). AE, MC, V. Tues–Sun 10am–3pm and 7pm–midnight.

NOTO AFTER DARK

Café Sicilia   Small-scale, cozy, and prefaced with outdoor chairs and tables, this is Noto's most enduring cafe/bar. Part of its allure comes from architectural adornments in place since 1892. Its clientele seems reluctant to take coffee or drinks anywhere else. The absolutely luscious pastries include a bomb-shaped *savarin al Marsala.* Jars of Sicilian honey and liqueurs are available for sale. Corso Vittorio Emanuele 125. ✆ 0931-835013.

La Fontana Vecchia   Set at the monumental end of Noto's main walkway, this popular and well-positioned bar has a huge terrace and a reputation for being mobbed most evenings after sunset. Established in 1996, but with a turn-of-the-20th-century design that might make you think it's much older, it has a helpful and good-looking staff, a wide selection of cocktails, and *granite* that taste fantastic when a scoop is dissolved in soda water. Open April through September, daily from 7am to midnight, and October through March, daily from 7am to 10pm. 150 Corso Vittorio Emanuele. ✆ 0931-839412.

SIDE TRIPS FROM NOTO

CAVA GRANDE DEL CASSIBILE 🌟🌟   The "Grand Canyon of Sicily" is a bit of a misnomer, but this remote section of the Iblei mountain range attracts hikers and nature buffs alike. To reach the site, drive north of Noto for 19km (12 miles) on Route 287 in the direction of the town of Palazzolo Acreide. When you reach the village of Villa Vela, with its Art Nouveau villas, you will be near the gorge's site. A little secondary road is signposted to Cava Grande. Go to the end of the road, where there is a car park with a stunning **panoramic vista** 🎯 over the Cava Grande gorge: a canyon 250m (820 ft.) deep and some 10km (6¼ miles) long between towering limestone cliffs.

The ancients used the gorge as a burial ground, and thousands of tombs have been discovered here, dating from the 11th to the 9th century B.C. The most important artifacts were removed and taken to Syracuse museums.

If you descend into the gorge, allow at least 45 careful minutes. Figure on doubling your time for the climb back. The most stunning aspect of Cava Grande is a series of **natural rock pools** 🎯 that were created by the Cassibilie River. You can swim, if you like. On a hot day, it's almost the most refreshing place to be in inland Sicily. The site is always open.

ELORO   The countryside surrounding this ancient city is lonely and lovely today, but it was one of the first cities founded by Syracuse back in the 7th century B.C. The location, overlooking the sea, is even more idyllic because it's set on a hill near the mouth of the Tellaro River.

What remains today only vaguely suggests what the little city must have looked like in its heyday. The ruins are in the early stages of excavation. So far, a bit of the ancient city walls have been unearthed. You can also see the ruins of a temple dedicated to Demeter (Ceres in Roman mythology). In the direction of the river lie the ruins of a theater which have also been dug out. The foundation of a temple believed to have been dedicated to Asclepius can also be viewed.

The admission-free site is open Monday through Saturday from 8am to 1 hour before sunset. To reach it by car, drive 11km (7 miles) southeast of Noto. Follow the signposts to the beach town of Noto Marina. Eloro lies immediately to the south.

VILLA DEL TELLARO   In 1972, a Roman villa dating from the 4th century A.D. was discovered with some of its magnificent polychrome mosaics still intact. Its location is 7km (4 miles) west of the principal Noto/Pachino highway beside the Tellaro River. It is believed that this villa was once as richly adorned as the celebrated Villa Romana del Casale in the vicinity of Piazza Armerina (p. 269).

Constructed around a square peristyle, the building was obviously occupied by someone who had a lot of money and a taste for the exotic. The mosaics depict everything from erotica to the slaying of animals during a hunt.

Only the most serious archaeologists may want to seek out this place, which is located near the village of Caddeddi, signposted 1km (½ mile) off the main road. The ruins of the villa lie beneath a farmhouse. The on-site farmer will show you through; a tip is expected. If you drop in, arrive at a reasonable hour (9am–4pm).

RISERVA NATURALE DI VENDICARI 🎯🎯   Created as a government-protected nature reserve in 1984, this stretch of coast south of the Tellaro River is one of the beauty spots of southeastern Sicily. Open daily from 9am to dusk, with free entry, it covers 574 hectares (1,418 acres) of lovely marshland that is an oasis for migratory birds and serious birders. Guides are available at the **office** (© **0931-462452**) at the park entrance.

What you see depends on the season. In winter, all sorts of ducks can be spotted, ranging from the mallard to the red-crested pochard. In fall, you'll see the white egret, black stork, and even European flamingo. Most birds only check in and then fly away to other climes, with the exception of the black-winged stilt, the Kentish plover, and the reed warbler, which all breed here.

The reserve is always open, but it's best to go in the early morning or closer to twilight; don't forget binoculars. To get here from Noto, drive southeast to the coast. Then take the road south—signposted PACHINO—until you come to the marked entrance to the reserve.

If you first visited Eloro (see above), continue driving south for 5km (3¾ miles), where you'll see the **Torre Vendicari,** an abandoned Norman tower. This artifact from Sicily's conquerors of yesterday overlooks a beautiful crescent of golden sand near old salt pans. It's a great place to log some time on the beach.

Motorists with the time can continue all the way to the extreme southeastern tip of Sicily, at **Capo Passero.** You'll pass first through the pleasant town of Pachino before reaching the cape, which lies 7km (4⅓ miles) south of Pachino. An important tuna fishing grounds, the cape rewards you with a **panoramic view** out to sea.

Ragusa & Piazza Armerina

Few foreign visitors cut into the inland trails of central Sicily to discover the treasures they hold. Sicily's coastline, with its Greek ruins, ancient cities, and fabulous beaches, is just too alluring, especially on a hot summer day. But even a short visit will give you a taste of the mountainous interior of this fascinating island, a land that is more representative of traditional Sicily than its port towns and villages.

In this short jaunt, we penetrate the wilds of central Sicily to discover one of the grandest Roman villas ever unearthed. Celebrated for its stunning mosaics, **Villa Romana del Casale,** outside the town of **Piazza Armerina,** is definitely worth the trek inland. It's one of the highlights of antiquity and may be Sicily's greatest single man-made attraction.

For another look at inland Sicily, visit the two cities of **Ragusa Superiore** and **Ragusa Ibla.** After Noto, Ragusa Ibla is one of the most stellar examples of the Sicilian baroque.

1 Ragusa ⊛

267km (166 miles) SE of Palermo, 138km (86 miles) E of Agrigento, 104km (65 miles) SW of Catania, 79 km (49 miles) SW of Syracuse

Ragusa is really two towns in one: an upper town, **Ragusa Superiore,** mapped out after a devastating earthquake in 1693, and **Ragusa Ibla,** constructed on an isolated spur. Ibla, in glaring contrast to the modern city, is one of the best-preserved old towns in Sicily, and well worth a day of your valuable time. The two parts of town are linked by a steep winding road or else by steps. Even if Ragusa Ibla weren't fascinating, the site would make an interesting trip because of the craggy valley that separates the two towns. It is a vista of winding pathways and plant-filled cliffs.

From the twin towns, panoramas of the countryside unfold. The landscapes around Ragusa are among the most memorable (and eerie) in Sicily. Many are crisscrossed with low-lying stone walls, pieced laboriously together without mortar, and lying in impoverished solitude beneath the punishing sun. These are the landscapes most often evoked in Sicilian literature and cinema, an oft-filmed terrain that has positioned Ragusa and its outlying districts in the forefront of Italian filmmaking.

If all this weren't enough, you can take a 30-minute, 7.5km (4½-mile) drive to **Marina di Ragusa,** a thriving beach resort. Many visitors prefer to anchor here, visiting Ragusa Ibla for the day. Unlike the historic core of Ragusa Ibla, Marina di Ragusa is relatively modern, with its long, narrow, and unusually sandy beach strip. A boardwalk is lined with shops, bars, and restaurants. A party atmosphere prevails here in summer, when, by 10pm, the action is just getting started.

ESSENTIALS

GETTING THERE   From the east, Syracuse is often the rail gateway into Ragusa, with three trains per day making the 2-hour journey for a cost of 5.85€ ($7) one-way. It's also possible to take one of three trains per day from Palermo; the 5-hour trip costs 14€ ($16) one-way. There are no direct trains from Palermo—it is necessary to change trains in Caltanissetta, Catania, or Gela.

Ragusa also has a bus link with Syracuse. AST (*©* **0932-681818**) runs seven buses per day on the 2-hour run; the fare is 5.80€ ($6.95) one-way.

The train and bus stations in Ragusa are at Piazza del Popolo and the adjoining Piazza Gramsci.

Motorists touring southeastern Sicily who visited our last stopover in Noto (p. 256) can continue southwest along Route 115 to the town of Ispica, at which point the highway swings northwest toward Ragusa.

VISITOR INFORMATION   The **tourist office,** Via Capitano Bocchieri 33 (*©* **0932-221511**), is open Monday through Friday from 9am to 1:30pm and Tuesday and Thursday from 4 to 6pm.

FAST FACTS   In case of **emergency,** dial *©* **113.** For a **medical emergency,** dial *©* **118.** The local hospital is **Ospedale Civile,** Via da Vinci (*©* **0932-600111**). Call the **police** at *©* **112.** The **post office,** at Piazza Matteotti (*©* **0932-232287**), is open Monday through Saturday from 8am to 6:30pm.

GETTING AROUND   If you don't want to make the steep climb linking Ibla with Superiore, you can take city bus no. 3 departing from in front of the cathedral or from Piazza del Popolo; the fare is .60€ (70¢) one-way. It's a hair-raising ride. The bus will let you off in Ibla at Piazza Pola or Giardini Iblei, most central for exploring the medieval and baroque town.

EXPLORING THE TWO TOWNS

If your time is limited, you can skip the upper town (Ragusa Superiore) and spend all your hours in Ragusa Ibla, as the older town holds far more intrigue. Those with more time can hike through the upper town, looking for the attractions that follow.

RAGUSA SUPERIORE

The long main street, **Corso Italia,** cuts through the upper town and makes for Ragusa's best promenade. The main attraction here is **Cattedrale di San Giovanni,** Via Roma 134 (*©* **0932-621658**), dating from the 18th century and dedicated to St. John the Baptist. Pause on the elegant square in front of the cathedral and look uphill to admire its decorative facade, which is made asymmetrical by a campanile on its western side. Its front elevation contains a wide terrace. The inside is ornate, especially the stucco decorations in the cupola. The Latin cross interior is notable for its two orders of pillars, each made of locally quarried asphaltite. Open daily from 7am to noon and 4 to 7pm.

Museo Archeologico Regionale Ibleo, Palazzo Mediterraneo, Via Natalelli (*©* **0932-622963**), lies off Via Roma, within an easy walk of the Duomo, near the Ponte Nuovo bridge. The museum is rich in artifacts unearthed from ancient colonies in the province. The collection is at its best in remnants of the civilization that flourished in Greek days at Rovine di Camarina, 16km (10 miles) northwest of Marina di Ragusa. Assaulted by the Carthaginians, the colony was finally leveled by the Romans as early as 598 B.C. Some of the artifacts at the museum in Ragusa are from a temple here once dedicated to Athena. Various necropolis reconstructions hold great interest. Hours are daily from 9am to 1:30pm and 4 to 7:30pm; admission is 2.10€ ($2.50).

RAGUSA IBLA 🐦🐦

We prefer to reach the old town by taking a long stairway, **Santa Maria delle Scale** 🐦, heading down from Ragusa Superiore to the historic core of Ibla. Take this walk for the **panoramic vistas** 🐦🐦 alone, some of the finest in southeastern Sicily.

All right, so the town is in deep decay, but it's a nostalgic remnant of yesterday. Wander its narrow streets, checking out its crumbling baroque palaces.

Head east until you come to the **Duomo di San Giorgio** 🐦, Piazza del Duomo (✆ **0932-220085**), which is open daily from 9am to noon and 4 to 7pm. Characterized by an impressive neoclassical dome, this is one of the best examples of Sicilian baroque in the south of Sicily, dating from the 18th century. The facade is a trio of tiers and looks like nothing so much as a glamorous wedding cake. In contrast, the interior may come as a disappointment, as it's quite plain.

Continuing east from the Duomo, you'll come to the **Chiesa di San Giuseppe** ⟨★⟩, Via Torre Nuova 19 (② **0932-621779**), open daily from 9am to noon and 4 to 7pm. It dates from 1590, and its oval-domed interior contains beautiful galleries and striking pavement crafted of black asphalt interspersed with majolica tiles. Among the notable artworks is the painting *Glory of St. Benedict,* by Sebastiano Lo Monaco (1793). At press time, the church was closed for renovations; call ahead to see if it has reopened.

If you continue walking all the way east through Ragusa Ibla, you'll reach beautiful public gardens, **Giardino Obleo** ⟨★⟩, which are studded with religious buildings, notably **Chiesa di San Giacomo,** dating from the 14th century. It was struck by a 1693 earthquake, and much of the damage was never repaired. If it's open, you'll get to see a beautiful **triptych** ⟨★⟩ by Pietro Novelli, depicting the Madonna flanked by St. Agatha and St. Lucy.

At the edge of the gardens, enjoy the **panoramic view** ⟨★⟩ sweeping across the Valley of Irminio. The gardens are the perfect place for a picnic and can be visited daily from 8am to 8pm; there's no entry fee.

WHERE TO STAY
RAGUSA SUPERIORE

Mediterraneo Palace ⟨★⟩   A healthy hike from the center of medieval Ragusa, this government-rated four-star hotel is a boxy concrete structure, but it's the finest lodging for miles around. It offers a high level of comfort, with attractively and comfortably furnished guest rooms (each with bathroom with tub and shower). The decor is so modernized and minimalist that you could be anywhere from Nigeria to Alaska. Those who like to eat in will find good on-site dining and drinking facilities.

Via Roma 189, 97100 Ragusa. ② **0932-621944**. Fax 0932-623799. www.mediterraneopalace.it. 92 units. 120€ ($144) double; 240€ ($288) suite. AE, DC, MC, V. Parking 11€ ($13). **Amenities:** Restaurant; bar; limited room service; laundry service; dry cleaning; rooms for those w/limited mobility. *In room:* A/C, TV, minibar, hair dryer.

Montreal   Set in the modern part of Ragusa, a hellish climb from the medieval quarter, this completely renovated hotel is short on style but big on creature comforts. The location is 10 minutes by car from the baroque-style Ragusa Ibla, the historic center. Guest rooms are without frills but contain sturdy furniture and small tiled bathrooms (most with shower only). The Montreal is a favorite with businesspeople visiting Ragusa to hawk their wares.

Via San Giuseppe 8 (at Corso Italia), 97100 Ragusa. ②/fax **0932-621133**. www.chshotels.com/ragusa.htm. 50 units. 90€ ($108) double; 110€ ($132) triple. AE, DC, MC, V. Parking 6€ ($7.20). **Amenities:** Restaurant; bar; room service; laundry service; dry cleaning; nonsmoking rooms; rooms for those w/limited mobility. *In room:* A/C, TV, dataport, minibar.

MARINA DI RAGUSA

Eremo della Giubiliana ⟨★★⟩ ⟨Finds⟩   About a quarter mile inland from the barren highway, midway between Ragusa (7km/4½ miles to the north) and Marina di Ragusa, this stone estate is set in sun-blasted solitude against a landscape crisscrossed with low limestone walls. Maintained by local tenant farmers for at least a thousand years, the walls enclose grazing lands for cows and sheep. No other hotel we've seen in Sicily is as deceptive in the way it contrasts a baronial, severely dignified exterior with a walled-in compound of verdant greenery and lighthearted posh. Inside the compound, expect water fountains, lemon and almond trees, a kitchen garden burgeoning with life, and a truly unusual restaurant (reviewed on p. 269).

To enter the compound, which functioned as a fortified monastery during the 1400s, you must navigate some signposted country roads that meander between the aforementioned stone walls, across a parched landscape that hasn't changed much in 300 years. After shouting your name into a microphone, you and your car will be "buzzed" in through massive iron gates that swing open, soundlessly, to reveal a walled-in world that might have been the home of a forbidding Sicilian *don* during the 19th century. Today, it's a warm, historically poignant hotel of discreet luxury and meticulous architectural detail. Guest rooms are cozy and as artfully authentic as rooms in a private home. Each unit comes with a private bathroom with shower.

This is the only hotel in Sicily that maintains a private airstrip. One-day airborne excursions to offshore islands such as Lampedusa and Pantelleria cost 430€ ($516) for up to three passengers, with a chauffeured private car and lunch on the islands included.

Contrada Giubiliana, 97100 Ragusa. ℂ **0932-669119.** Fax 0932-633891. 11 units and 5 self-contained cottages. 240€ ($288) double; 450€ ($540) suite; 204€ ($245) cottage. Rates include breakfast. Half board 250€ ($300) for 2 persons in double or triple, 250€ ($300) in cottage. AE, DC, MC, V. From Ragusa, take SP25 southwest toward Marina di Ragusa. Eremo is signposted at Km 7. **Amenities:** Restaurant; bar; outdoor pool; laundry service; dry cleaning. *In room:* A/C, TV.

Hotel Terraqua ⭐ This is the most appealing hotel in the seaside resort of Marina di Ragusa. Configured as a cement-and-glass cube dotted with balconies, it was built in the 1980s, and identifies itself mainly as a beachfront hotel with clean rooms and frequent breezes. It usually shows its guests a good, albeit somewhat anonymous, time. Don't expect any personalized service from the staff—they're familiar with hordes of holiday-makers coming and going. But as a base for exploration of the neighborhood, including Ragusa Ibla, the hotel is a worthwhile choice. Guest rooms have tile floors, shower-only bathrooms, and a beach-going simplicity. The hotel is not directly on the sands of the beach—it's inside its own walled garden, a 5-minute walk from the water. It also has the best and biggest pool in town.

Via delle Sirene 35, 97010 Marina di Ragusa. ℂ **0932-615600.** Fax 0932-615580.www.shr.it. 77 units. 135€ ($162) double; 175€ ($210) junior suite. Rates include buffet breakfast. AE, DC, MC, V. Free parking. **Amenities:** Restaurant; bar; outdoor pool; tennis court; outdoor Jacuzzi; babysitting; laundry service; dry cleaning; solarium. *In room:* A/C, TV, dataport, minibar, hair dryer.

WHERE TO DINE
RAGUSA SUPERIORE

La Pergola ⭐ SICILIAN This elegant restaurant offers the finest dining in the modern town of Ragusa. It's decorated in a style evocative of the late 19th century, with a Belle Epoque aura, marble floors, and comfortable chairs. Dishes are full of flavor and prepared with a certain flair, as exemplified by the swordfish in lemon sauce with capers and toasted pine nuts. Succulent ravioli is filled with porcini mushrooms, chestnuts, ricotta cheese, and a whiff of marjoram. The best tortellini in town is served here, with fresh shrimp and a saffron sauce.

Contrada Selvaggio. ℂ **0932-686430.** Reservations recommended. Main courses 6.80€–12€ ($8.15–$14); fixed-price menus 25€–30€ ($30–$36). AE, MC, V. Wed–Mon noon–2:30pm and 8–11:30pm.

RAGUSA IBLA

Il Barocco SICILIAN The name comes from the elaborate baroque-style doorway, crafted in the 1600s, that dominates the restaurant's small, high-ceilinged dining room. (In fact, you might get the feel that the restaurant is rather uncomfortably crammed into the anteroom of a very grand palazzo or church.) Tiles and wrought iron decorate the interior, and plastic tables and chairs spill onto the pavement in front. (Don't confuse this restaurant with the gelateria, under the same name and management, about a block downhill.) Menu items are not as creative as what you'll find at either of Ragusa's more prestigious eateries (Il Duomo and Locanda Don Serafino), and the staff can be blasé, but food items are flavorful and filling. The best examples include lamb cutlets, crepes with ricotta and spinach, and a dessert specialty of orange mousse.

Via Orfanotrofio 29. © 0932-652397. Reservations recommended. Main courses 7€–13€ ($8.40–$16). AE, DC, MC, V. Thurs–Tues 12:30–2:30pm and 7:30pm–midnight.

Il Duomo ★★ SICILIAN   Set on an impossibly narrow street, uphill and about a block behind the cathedral, this is generally considered the finest restaurant in Ibla. Inside, the small rooms are outfitted like private parlors in a 19th-century country-Victorian style, some with views that sweep over the dry hillsides of southern Sicily. Come here for the intensely patriotic cuisine of Ciccio Sultano, a native *Ragusano* who commits himself passionately to the perpetuation of old-time traditions. Several varieties of bread are baked each day, using old-fashioned, increasingly hard-to-find strains of wheat. At least 20 types of olive oil are on display, and if you ask for help, a staff member will advise you on which variety is best with which particular bread or platter. Menus are based on the changing seasons, and many dishes make ample use of such local products as cherry tomatoes, pistachios, bitter almonds, wild fennel, and mint. We were dazzled by gnocchi with a Ragusan cheese, zucchini, cream, and fresh mussels.

Via Bocchieri 31. © 0932-651265. Reservations recommended. Main courses 9€–17€ ($11–$20); fixed-price menus 40€–45€ ($48–$54). AE, DC, MC, V. Tues–Sat noon–2:30pm and 7–11pm (also open Sun in Aug). Closed Feb.

La Bettola SICILIAN   Located a short walk through narrow winding streets from the town's cathedral, this restaurant shows few hints of any changes that might have been made since the days of Mussolini. That, coupled with the 1940s-era decor, provides much of its charm. Tables and chairs are arranged on a large piazza in front, amid potted flowers and ample doses of old-fashioned Italy. On one visit, the chef told us to leave matters in his hands, which turned out to be capable indeed. We were treated to homemade penne with fresh ricotta, followed by a tender, herb-infused chicken breast and delectable roulades stuffed with ham and onions.

Largo Camerina 7. © 0932-653377. Reservations recommended. Main courses 6.20€–7€ ($7.45–$8.40). MC, V. Mon–Sat 12:30–2:30pm and 7:30–11:30pm.

Locanda Don Serafino ★★★ SICILIAN   This is one of the finest restaurants in southern Sicily. It's set in a 17th-century palace in a labyrinth of intricately vaulted cellars, where the temperature remains cool in summer and comfortable even on the coldest days of winter. Any of the lavishly decorated tables presents a charming venue for lunch or dinner, but the most awe-inspiring are found in the deepest part of the labyrinth, a monastic-looking stone-sided room lined with wines selected personally by the owner. You'll enjoy dishes that may include *zuppe di pesce Don Serafino,* ravioli with a porcini mushroom sauce, fresh fish cooked to perfection, and herb-and-garlic-infused lamb cutlets.

Via Orfanotrofio 39. © 0932-248778. Reservations recommended. Main courses 13€–18€ ($16–$22); fixed-price menu 40€–48€ ($48–$58). AE, DC, MC, V. Wed–Mon 12:30–2:30pm and 5:30–11:30pm.

MARINA DI RAGUSA

Eremo della Giubiliana SICILIAN   Even if an overnight stay at this hotel isn't practical, we heartily recommend it for its fine cuisine and its eerily antique location. The setting is inside a walled compound that originated in the 1400s as a fortified monastery and later evolved into a manorial home for some very tenacious landowners. Meticulously restored to its full limestone glory, and permeated with a discreet poshness, it serves well-prepared meals in a high-ceilinged room whose massive timbers are supported by soaring masonry arches. Lunches are relatively simple, consisting of a medley of omelets, salads, and *focaccia* (sandwiches stuffed with smoked fish, prosciutto, or local cheeses). Dinners are more elaborate, featuring orecchiatta with walnut sauce; roasted quail with spices; couscous; tuna carpaccio; and very fresh salads usually culled from the hotel's walled-in garden. Come here as much for the sightseeing as for the food, and make an effort to see the surrounding landscape in the glare of daylight.

Contrada Giubiliana. ⓒ **0932-669119.** Reservations recommended. Lunch platters 5€–9€ ($6–$11); main courses 8€–15€ ($9.60–$18); fixed-price Sun lunch 35€ ($42). AE, DC, MC, V. Daily 1–3pm and 7:30–10pm.

Ristorante/Pizzeria La Falena *Value* SICILIAN   Short on style but good in the kitchen, this rustic trattoria is known for its fresh fish, tasty pizzas, and welcoming reception. It attracts a beach-loving crowd for home-style dining, indoors or out. Our table was impressed by the pasta with shrimp and arugula, the tortellini with ham and cream, and especially the savory rice dish with fresh shrimp, mussels, virgin olive oil, and garlic.

Via Porto Venere. ⓒ **0932-239321.** Reservations required Sat–Sun. Main courses 7€–12€ ($8.40–$14). AE, DC, MC, V. Wed–Mon 12:30–2:30pm and 7:30pm–12:30am. Closed Jan.

RAGUSA AFTER DARK
RAGUSA IBLA

Belle Epoque   Set in a tucked-away corner of the square directly in front of the cathedral, this place will welcome you for either daytime gelato or nighttime beer and cocktails. The homemade ice creams are likely to include *nocciola* (hazelnut), *pesca* (peach), and *arancia* (orange). From July to September, it's open daily from 7am to 11pm or later. The rest of the year, it's closed on Monday. Via Convento, near Piazza Duomo. ⓒ **0339-7528402.**

MARINA DI RAGUSA

Victoria Pub   Set directly across the street from the beach, this is the largest pub in Marina di Ragusa and one of the most whimsically decorated. The pseudo-Victorian decor includes pithy quotes from Shakespeare, expired New Jersey license plates, and banners advertising everything from Jack Daniels to Newcastle Ale. The crowd tends to be young, on the make, and into rock 'n' roll. Open April through October, nightly from 10pm to 4am; November through March, Saturday and Sunday from 8pm to 4am. Lungomare Andrea Doria 20. ⓒ **0339-2409247.**

2 Piazza Armerina

84km (52 miles) SW of Catania, 181km (113 miles) SW of Messina, 164km (102 miles) SE of Palermo, 103km (64 miles) NW of Ragusa, 134km (84 miles) NW of Syracuse

Art lovers journey from all over Europe and America to see the ruins of an extraordinary Roman villa at Casale, basing themselves in the little town of Piazza Armerina. Once known only as "Piazza," the town gets its name from Colle Armerino, one of a trio of hills on which it was constructed. The town is actually two-in-one: the original "Piazza," a village that dates from the heyday of the Saracens in the 10th century; and a 15th-century "overflow" town that extended to the southeast as early as the 15th century.

Graced with impressive but decaying palazzi, the town itself is worth a visit for at least an hour or two, although most tour buses rush through here delivering their passengers directly to Villa Romana del Casale.

ESSENTIALS

GETTING THERE   One bus a day from Syracuse makes the 3-hour trip for 8€ ($9.60) one-way. Seven buses per day leave from Ragusa, making the 3-hour journey at a cost of 6€ ($7.20) one-way.

If you're driving from Ragusa, where we launched our inland tour of Sicily, continue north along Route 194, following the signs to the town of Caltagirone. At the town of Vizzini, continue northwest along Route 124 to Caltagirone. From here, the road will be signposted northwest all the way to Piazza Armerina.

VISITOR INFORMATION   The **tourist office,** Via Cavour (© **0935-680201;** www.aziendaautonomapiazza.com), is open Monday through Friday from 8am to 2pm, plus Wednesday from 3 to 6:30pm.

GETTING AROUND   If you've arrived in Piazza Armerina by bus, you can take yet another bus (no. B) to reach the Roman villa at Casale. From April to September, **Piccola Società Cooperative** (© **0935-85605**) runs buses to the site daily from 9 to 11am and 4 to 6pm (trip time: 15 min.). A one-way ticket costs 1.50€ ($1.80).

SEEING THE SIGHTS

Piazza Armerina is set on a plateau some 700m (2,297 ft.) above sea level. The city was founded during the Norman era, and today is filled with mansions showing both baroque and Renaissance architectural influences. Its historic **medieval quarter** ⊀ is graced with many beautiful churches, the most impressive of which is the Duomo, crowning the highest point in town at 720m (2,364 ft.).

The **Duomo,** Via Cavour (© **0935-680214**), is open daily from 8:30am to noon and 3:30 to 7pm. The old town's maze of narrow streets sprouted around this cathedral. The bell tower is from 1490, a surviving architectural feature of an even earlier church. The present building was inaugurated in 1627, the facade dating from 1719 and the dome from 1768. The facade is adorned with pilasters and columns, and the grand central door is surmounted by a large, square window topped by an eagle. The interior is spacious and filled with light. Among the best-known works of art here is the ***Virgin delle Vittorie*** ⊀, above the main altar at the far end of the nave in a 17th-century tabernacle. It is believed to have been given by Pope Nicholas II to Count Roger, ruler of Sicily. An impressive **wooden cross** ⊀ dating from 1455 is on view in the small chapel to the left of the chancel. Its back depicts a scene of the Resurrection which has been much reproduced in art books on Sicily.

Villa Romana del Casale ⊀⊀⊀   Located 6km (3½ miles) from Piazza Armerina, this magnificent villa is one of the largest dwellings of its kind to have survived from the days of the Romans. Its 40 rooms are "carpeted" with 11,340 sq. m (122,063 sq. ft.) of some of the greatest, most magnificent mosaics in western Europe.

It is obvious that a wealthy patrician built this mansion, and some scholars have even suggested that it was the hunting lodge of Maximanus, the "co-emperor" of Diocletian. The exact date of the villa's construction is hard to ascertain,

Caltagirone: A Ceramics Side Trip

A lovely drive 30km (18 miles) southeast of Piazza Amerina takes you to **Caltagirone,** an enchanting little town that earthenware potteries built. Glazed pottery is offered at shops throughout the town, whose most celebrated attraction is **Scala di Santa Maria del Monte** 🌟🌟, a stunning set of ceramic steps leading from old town to new town. There are 142 lava stair treads graced with majolica tiles—no two alike—that evoke everything from Moorish designs to baroque patterns.

As you go along, you'll encounter **Branciforti** 🌟, Scala di Santa Maria del Monte 3 (✆ **0933/24427**), which sells stunning ceramics in deep shades of blue with swirling arabesques. To learn more about ceramics, head for the little **Museo della Ceramica,** on Via Roma (✆ **0933-21680**), open daily from 9am to 6:30pm and charging an admission of 2.80€ ($3.35). Later you can relax in the shade of the **Giardino Pubblico,** a public garden nearby.

The **tourist office** is in Palazzo Libertini, Piazza Umberto (✆ **0933-53809**). Parking is available in a public lot near Chiesa San Francesco di Paola, approached before you reach Piazza Umberto. You can purchase parking tickets at various bars and tobacco shops throughout town.

If you'd like to spend the night, the **Grand Hotel Villa San Mauro,** Via Portosalvo 10 (✆ **0933-26500**), has 91 first-class rooms for 190€ ($228) per night. The best place to eat is **La Scala,** Scala di Santa Maria Monte 8 (✆ **0933-57781**), where meals cost around 35€ ($42). It's near the base of the famous stairs, and may be unique for the mountain stream running through it.

---

however—perhaps the end of the 3rd century A.D. or the beginning of the 4th century. The complex was destroyed by fire in the 12th century and over the years was buried in mudslides. Parts of the villa were unearthed in 1881.

Many of the mansion's walls are still standing, but most visitors come to take in the mosaics on the floors and the surviving wall paintings. Many of the mosaic scenes are mythological. Since this was a hunting lodge, most of the tableaux involve the pursuit of wild animals.

Rooms branch out from a central courtyard, or peristyle. Among the discernible rooms still left are the **Terme,** or steam baths, which supplied water and also heated the villa with steam circulating through cavities in the floors and walls. In the **Sala delle Unizioni,** slaves are depicted massaging the bodies of their masters.

The Peristylium, directly east of the peristyle, contains the splendid **Peristylium mosaic** 🌟🌟, which can be viewed on all sides of the portico. It's a romp of birds, plants, wild animals, and more domesticated creatures such as horses. Adjoining it is the **Salone del Circo** 🌟🌟, the narthex (portico) of the Terme. Its name comes from the scenes of the Roman circus depicted in its mosaics. The chariot race at Rome's Circus Maximus can clearly be seen.

Directly south of the peristyle is the **Sala della Piccola Caccia** 🌟🌟🌟, "The Room of the Small Hunt," with mosaics depicting everything from a sacrifice to the goddess of the hunt, Diana, to the netting of a wild boar.

To the immediate west of the peristyle is the **Ambulacro della Grande Caccia** 𝒜𝒜𝒜, "The Corridor of the Great Hunt," measuring 60m (197 ft.). The mosaics discovered here are among the most splendid from the ancient world. One of the most dramatic scenes depicts wild animals, ranging from the rhino to the elephant, being loaded onto a ship.

In a salon at the northwest corner of the peristyle is the most amusing room of all: **Sala delle Dieci Ragazze**, "The Room of the 10 Girls." Wearing strapless two-piece bikinis, the young women are dressed for gymnastic exercises. Their outfits would be appropriate for a beach in the 21st century.

Directly north of the peristyle is the **Triclinium** 𝒜𝒜𝒜, a large central space that spills into a trio of wide apses. This was probably the dining area, and it's known for its magnificent rendition of the Labors of Hercules. In the central apse, the mosaics depict "The Battle of the Giants," five mammoth creatures in their death throes after being attacked by the poisoned arrows of Hercules.

Among the final salons is the **Vestibolo del Piccolo Circo** 𝒜𝒜, or "Vestibule of the Small Circus," depicting circus scenes such as chariot racing; and the **Atrio degli Amorini Pescatori** 𝒜𝒜, with mosaics illustrating fishing scenes.

Cubicolo della Scene Erotica 𝒜 features a polygonal medallion depicting a panting young man locked in a tight embrace with a scantily clad seductress. Yes, there is a gratuitous bottom shot.

The site is open daily from 8am to 30 minutes before sunset. Admission is 4.50€ ($5.40).

WHERE TO STAY

Mosaici da Battiato (see "Where to Dine," below), also rents rooms.

Hotel Ostello del Borgo   This small hotel in the historic center occupies a wing of the ancient monastery of San Giovanni, once filled with Benedictine nuns and dating from the 14th century. It is the most atmospheric place to stay in the area. The small to midsize guest rooms are well maintained and equipped with small shower-only bathrooms. All the sights, including several restaurants, lie within easy reach of the front door.

Largo San Giovanni 6, 94015 Piazza Armerina. ℭ **0935-687019.** Fax 0935-686943. 20 units. 57€ ($68) double. Rates include breakfast. MC, V. **Amenities:** Breakfast room. *In room:* TV, no phone.

Park Hotel Paradiso   This modern hostelry has the best location for those who want to be near the main attraction in the area, Villa Romana del Casale. Located right outside of town and surrounded by a forest, this is a well-kept building with comfortably furnished guest rooms. Each bathroom has either a shower or a hydromassage tub. The hotel has good on-site dining and drinking facilities, so you don't have to wander around Piazza Armerina at night.

Contrada da Ramaldo, 94015 Piazza Armerina. ℭ **0935-680841.** Fax 0935-683391. www.parkhotel paradiso.it. 95 units. 95€–110€ ($114–$132) double; 150€–180€ ($180–$216) suite. Rates include breakfast. AE, DC, MC, V. Free parking. Located 1km (½ mile) beyond Chiesa di Sant'Andrea. **Amenities:** Restaurant; 2 bars; outdoor pool; gym; fitness center; sauna; laundry service; dry cleaning; nonsmoking rooms; solarium; rooms for those w/limited mobility. *In room:* A/C, TV, dataport, minibar, hair dryer, safe.

WHERE TO DINE

Al Fogher 𝒜 *Finds* SICILIAN   This rustic restaurant, 3km (1¾ miles) north of Piazza Armerina, serves dishes based on local recipes. If you like to eat well but shun flashiness, you will instinctively warm to the cuisine here. The carpaccio of swordfish or tuna will get you started off beautifully. The chef's creativity is further expressed in such dishes as risotto with pumpkin, ricotta and goose liver seasoned with fresh rosemary, and pork in a pepper sauce under a pistachio crust. The wine cellar is one of the best in the area, with 400 different local and international choices.

Contrada Bellia, Strada Statale 117. © **0935-684123**. Reservations recommended. Main courses 10€–35€ ($12–$42). AE, DC, MC, V. Tues–Sun 12:30–2:30pm; Tues–Sat 8–11pm.

Mosaici da Battiato SICILIAN   This classic countryside restaurant lies 3km (1¾ miles) west of Piazza Armerina, en route to the famous mosaics. Unless a tour group has stopped off here (a frequent occurrence), this is a good place to order some of the best homemade Sicilian dishes in the area. We began with a delectable pennette with rich cream, fresh tomatoes, and mushrooms. The rigatoni alla Norma is another succulent choice, made with recently harvested eggplant along with vine-ripened tomatoes. Most plates are reasonably priced, except the copious meat platter of grilled specialties—for trenchermen only.

The restaurant also rents 24 well-maintained, simply furnished guest rooms, each with a shower-only bathroom. A double costs 50€ ($60); a triple room goes for 65€ ($78).

Contrada Casale Ovest. © **0935-685453**. Reservations recommended. Main courses 5€–10€ ($6–$12); fixed-price menu 15€ ($18). MC, V. Open 24 hrs. Closed Nov 26–Dec 26.

Trattoria La Ruota SICILIAN   Opt for a table on the open-air terrace of this atmospheric restaurant, which was created from a defunct water mill. You'll be served a typical Sicilian lunch (the only meal offered) evocative of the plains of central Sicily. The good, homemade country cooking may include tagliatelle *alla Boscaiola* (with minced beef in a zesty tomato sauce laced with cream, fresh peas, and mushrooms); stewed rabbit with olives, capers, and tomatoes; and homemade grilled pork sausages.

Contrada Casale Ovest. © **0935-680542**. Reservations recommended. Main courses 6€–8€ ($7.20–$9.60); fixed-price menus 11€–16€ ($13–$19). AE, MC, V. Daily noon–3pm.

Agrigento & Selinunte

Two of the great cities of Magna Graecia—or what's left of them—can be explored along Sicily's southern coast. Both Agrigento and Selinunte knew greater glory than they experience today, but the remains of what they used to be are still relatively rich in spite of the looters and conquerors who have passed through. Of the two, Agrigento is the far greater attraction.

Once known as the Greek city of Akragas, **Agrigento** has seen many conquerors in its day, from the Romans to Byzantines and Arabs. The year 1087 saw the arrival of the Normans.

Agrigento's remarkable series of Doric temples from the 5th century B.C. are unrivaled except in Greece itself. All of the modern encroachments, especially the hastily built and often illegal new buildings, have seriously dimmed the glory of Agrigento, but much is left to fill us with wonder.

Selinunte, in contrast, was never built over as Agrigento was, and holds extensive remains of the acropolis, though none quite equal the charm of Agrigento's Valley of the Temples.

As you stand in the midst of a carpet of mandrake, acanthus, capers, and celery growing wild at Selinunte, you'll have to work hard to imagine what the city must have looked like at the apex of its power.

1 Agrigento ✶✶✶ & the Valley of the Temples ✶✶✶

129km (80 miles) S of Palermo, 175km (109 miles) SE of Trapani, 217km (135 miles) W of Syracuse

Agrigento's amazing **Valley of the Temples (Valle dei Templi)** is one of the most memorable sights of the ancient world. Greek colonists from Gela (Caltanissetta) called this area Akragas when they established a beachhead in the 6th century B.C. In time, the settlement grew to become one of the most prosperous cities in Magna Graecia. A great deal of that growth is attributed to the despot Phalaris, who ruled from 571 to 555 B.C. and is said to have roasted his victims inside a brass bull. He eventually met the same fate.

Empedocles (ca. 490–430 B.C.), the Greek philosopher and politician (also considered by some the founder of medicine in Italy), was the most famous son of Akragas. He formulated the theory that matter consists of four elements (earth, fire, water, and air), modified by the agents of love and strife. In modern times, the town produced playwright Luigi Pirandello (1867–1936), who won the Nobel Prize for Literature in 1934.

Like nearby Selinunte, the city was attacked by war-waging Carthaginians, beginning in 406 B.C. In the 3rd century B.C., the city changed hands between the Carthaginians and the Romans until it finally succumbed to Roman domination by 210 B.C. It was then known as Agrigentium.

The modern part of Agrigento occupies a hill; the narrow casbah-like streets show the influence of the conquering Saracens. Heavy Allied bombing during World War II necessitated much rebuilding. The result is, for the most part,

Agrigento

Stairs

1/4 Mi
0.25 Km

Via Imera

Via Gioeni

V. Degli Angeli

Via delle Mura

Via Girolamo

Via Plebis Rea

Via Gioeni

Via Giardinello

Via Aprile

Via Fodera

Via Atenea

V. Matteotti

Chiesa del Purgatorio

Piazza Ravanusella

Via Duomo

Duomo

V. Barone

Piazza Pirandello

Piazza Sinatra

Museo Civico

Museo Diocesano

Iargo S. Giacomo

Oblati

Seminario Vescovile

Via Recinto

Via Garibaldi

Viale Pietro Nenni

Via Dante

V. Cicerone

Piazza Vittorio Emanuele

Piazzale A. Moro

Piazza Marconi

S. Caolgero

Viale de Vittoria

Via Crispi

Statioze Centrale F.S.

V. Pirandello

Via Callicratide

Via Manzoni

Via Dante

SICILY

Palermo
Messina
Mt. Etna
Syracuse
Agrigento

80 Mi
80 Km

ACCOMMODATIONS ■
Colleverde Park Hotel **8**
Costazzura **1**
Foresteria Baglio della Luna **4**
Grand Hotel dei Templi **8**
Grand Hotel Mosé **8**
Hotel Kaos **1**
Hotel Tre Torri **8**
Hotel Villa Athena **8**
Hotel Villa Eos **1**

DINING ◆
Ambasciata di Sicilia **6**
La Forchetta **2**
Restaurant at the Hotel
Villa Athena **8**
Ruga Reali **5**
Trattoria dei Templi **8**

ATTRACTIONS ●
Abbazia di Santo Spirito **7**
Duomo **3**

275

uninspired and not helped by all the cement factories in the area. But below the town stretch the long reaches of the Valley of the Temples, where you'll see some of the greatest Greek ruins in the world.

Visit Agrigento for its past, not for its modern incarnation. However, once you've been awed by the ruined temples, you can explore the *centro storico*, with its tourist boutiques hawking postcards and T-shirts, and enjoy people-watching at a cafe along Via Atenea. When it gets too hot (as it so often does), flee to a beach at nearby **San Leone.**

ESSENTIALS

GETTING THERE   The main rail station, **Stazione Centrale,** Piazza Marconi (© 892021), is downhill from Piazzale Aldo Moro and Piazza Vittorio Emanuele. The train trip from Palermo takes 1½ hours and costs 7€ ($8.40) one-way; there are 14 trains daily. From Syracuse, you must first take one of four daily trains to Catania; the 6-hour trip costs 16€ ($19) one-way. Three trains a day make the trip from Ragusa to Agrigento, at a cost of 9.20€ ($11) one-way. This is an extremely awkward connection, as you have to change trains at Gela and then at Canicattì. Depending on the train, the trip can last from 5 to 9 hours.

Cuffaro (© 0922-403150) runs four buses per day from Palermo; the trip takes 2 hours and costs 7.20€ ($8.65) one-way. The company also has service from Syracuse, which takes 5 hours and costs 16€ ($19) one-way. By car from Syracuse, take SS115 through Gela. From Palermo, cut southeast along S121, which becomes S188 and S189 before it finally reaches Agrigento. Allow about 2½ hours.

VISITOR INFORMATION   The **tourist office,** Piazzale Aldo Moro 7 (© 0922-20454), is open Sunday through Friday from 8am to 1pm and 3 to 8pm, Saturday from 8am to 1pm. Another tourist office is at Via Empedocle 73 (© 0922-20391), open Monday through Friday from 8am to 2:30pm and Wednesday from 3:30 to 7pm.

SPECIAL EVENTS   The **Settimana Pirandelliana** is a festival of plays, operas, and ballets staged in Piazza Kaos during 1 week in July or August. The tourist office can supply details; tickets cost 7.50€ to 15€ ($9–$18).

GETTING AROUND   Agrigento is served by a network of orange **TUA buses** (© 0922-412024). A ticket selling for 1€ ($1.20) is valid for 1½ hours. Bus no. 2 or 2/ runs to the beach at San Leone. Bus nos. 1, 2, and 2/ make frequent runs to the Valley of the Temples, and bus no. 11 goes to Casa di Pirandello. For **taxi** service in Agrigento, call © 0922-21899 or 0922-26670.

FAST FACTS   In an **emergency,** call © **113,** or the *Carabinieri* at © 0922-596322. The hospital for the greater area is **Ospedale Civile,** Via Rupe Atenea 1 (© 0922-492111). The most central drugstore is **Farmacia Averna Antonio,** Via Atenea 325 (© 0922-26093), open daily from 9am to 1:30pm and 5 to 8:30pm. For Internet access, go to **Michele Lorgio Fotografo,** Via Cesare Battista 11 (© 0922-29660), open Monday through Saturday from 9am to 1pm and 5 to 8pm. It charges 5€ ($6) per hour. The **post office,** Piazza Vittorio Emanuele (© 0922-551111), is open Monday through Friday from 8:10am to 6:30pm and Saturday from 8:10am to 1:20pm. Currency can be exchanged here.

WANDERING AMONG THE RUINS

Many writers are fond of suggesting that the Greek ruins in the **Valley of the Temples (Valle dei Templi)** be viewed at dawn or sunset, when their mysterious aura is indeed heightened. Regrettably, you can't get very close at those times. Instead, search them out under the cobalt-blue Sicilian sky. The backdrop is idyllic, especially in spring, when the striking almond trees blossom.

Ticket booths are found at the west and east entrances (© **0922-497341**); they're 4.50€ ($5.40) for adults and free for those under 18. Hours are daily from 8:30am to 7pm. Board a bus or climb into your car to investigate. Riding out the Strada Panoramica, you'll first approach (on your left) the **Temple of Juno (Tempio di Giunone)** 🐾🐾, erected sometime in the mid–5th century B.C. Many of its Doric columns have been restored. As you climb the blocks, note the remains of a cistern as well as a sacrificial altar in front. The temple affords good views of the entire valley.

The **Temple of Concord (Tempio della Concordia)** 🐾🐾🐾, which you'll come to next, ranks with the Temple of Hephaestos in Athens as the best-preserved Greek temple in the world. With 13 columns on its side, six in front, and six in back, the temple was built in the peripheral hexastyle. You'll see the clearest example in Sicily of an inner temple. In the late 6th century A.D., the pagan structure was transformed into a Christian church, which might have saved it for posterity, although today it's been stripped down to its classical purity.

The **Temple of Hercules (Tempio di Ercole)** 🐾🐾 is the oldest, dating from the 6th century B.C. Badly ruined (only eight pillars are standing), it once ranked in size with the Temple of Zeus. At one time the temple sheltered a celebrated statue of Hercules. The infamous Gaius Verres, the Roman magistrate who became an especially bad governor of Sicily, attempted to steal the image as part of his temple-looting tear across the island. Astonishingly, you can still see black sears from fires set by long-ago Carthaginian invaders.

The **Temple of Jove/Zeus (Tempio di Giove)** ⭐ was the largest in the valley, similar in some respects to the Temple of Apollo at Selinunte, until it was ruined by an earthquake. It even impressed Goethe. In front of the structure was a large altar. The giant on the ground was one of several telamones (male caryatids) used to support the largest Greek temple in the world.

The so-called **Temple of Castor and Pollux (Tempio di Dioscuri),** with four Doric columns intact, is composed of fragments from different buildings. At various times it has been designated as a temple honoring Castor and Pollux, the twin sons of Leda and deities of seafarers; Demeter (Ceres), the goddess of marriage and of the fertile earth; or Persephone, the daughter of Zeus and the symbol of spring. *Note:* On some maps, this is called Tempio di Castore e Polluce. The temples can usually be visited daily from 8:30am until 1 hour before sunset. City bus nos. 1, 2, and 3 run to the valley from the train station in Agrigento.

MORE ATTRACTIONS

The **Museo Regionale Archeologico (Regional Archaeological Museum)** ⭐, near San Nicola, on Contrada San Nicola at the outskirts of town on the way to the Valle dei Templi (📞 **0922-401565**), is open Tuesday through Saturday from 9am to 7:30pm, Sunday and Monday from 9am to 1:30pm. Admission is 4.50€ ($5.40), free for children under 18. Its most important exhibit is a head of one of the telamones (male caryatids) from the Tempio di Giove. The collection of Greek vases is also impressive. Many of the artifacts on display were dug up when Agrigento was excavated. Take bus no. 1, 2, or 3.

Casa di Pirandello (Pirandello's House), Contrada Caos, Frazione Caos (📞 **0922-511826**), is the former home of the 1934 Nobel Prize winner, known for his plays *Six Characters in Search of an Author* and *Enrico IV.* Although Agrigentans back then might not have liked his portrayal of Italy, all is forgiven now, and Pirandello is the local boy who made good. In fact, the Teatro Luigi Pirandello at Piazza Municipio bears his name. His *casa natale* is now a museum devoted to memorabilia pertaining to the playwright's life. His tomb lies under his favorite pine tree, a few hundred yards from the house and grounds, which are open Monday through Saturday from 9am to 1pm and 2 to 7pm. Admission is 2€ ($2.40). The birthplace lies outside of town in the village of Caos (catch bus no. 1 from Piazza Marconi), just west of the temple zone.

THE CHURCHES OF AGRIGENTO

Abbazia di Santo Spirito ⭐ There is one good reason to venture into the tacky modern city itself. Although this 13th-century church is rotting away, it is still a worthy goal, as you'll realize when you stand at its impressive Gothic entrance surmounted by a rose window. The single nave is adorned with a baroque interior of fantastic stucco work with **four high reliefs** ⭐ believed to have been created by Giacomo Serpotta. The scenes depict *The Adoration of the Magi, The Nativity, The Presentation of Christ at the Temple,* and *The Flight into Egypt.* Take the exit to the right of the facade to look at the cloisters. Here you'll note a **lovely entrance** ⭐ into the chapter house, lined with Gothic arcades. A handsome doorway leads through a pointed arch. On each side are elaborate windows in the Arabo-Norman style. The nuns in the adjoining convent still sell a sweet confection called *kus-kus,* composed of chocolate and pistachio nuts.

Via Porcello at Via Santa Spirito. ✆ **0922-20664.** Free admission. Tues–Sat 9am–1pm and 4–7pm; Sun 9am–1pm. No bus.

Duomo ✪ Founded in the 12th century, the cathedral of Agrigento has faced rough times. There are still remnants from the early Norman days, particularly the windows, but most of the church was reconstructed in the 13th and 14th centuries. It was vastly restored in the 17th century, and later rejuvenated from the effects of a landslide in 1966. The bell tower, or campanile, is graced with a series of Catalan Gothic single lancet windows. The tower is from 1470 but was never completed, which gives the cathedral a strange, disturbing look, as if it were the victim of a windstorm. The **beautiful interior** ✪ rests under an **impressive wooden ceiling** ✪, the tie beams adorned with scenes from the lives of various saints. This work was carried out in the 16th century. The Duomo itself is dedicated to a Norman, San Gerlando, the town's first archbishop. His tomb is set in the right wing of the transept. Guides are fond of positioning you under the apse, where you can clearly hear even the whispers of people at the other end of the nave 80m (262 ft.) away. Standing in odd contrast to the rather somber chapels is the choir, a baroque romp of angelic angels and golden garlands.

Piazza Don Minzoni, off Via del Duomo. ✆ **0922-490011.** Free admission. Tues–Sun 10am–1pm and 4–6pm. No bus.

WHERE TO STAY
VERY EXPENSIVE

Foresteria Baglio della Luna ✪✪ *Finds* In 1995, one of the most historic medieval sites in Agrigento was meticulously restored by a local antiques dealer. The resulting country inn has housed glamorous types who appreciate its stylish ways and its isolation from the crowds. The first impression you'll get is of a squarish medieval tower, ringed by a protective wall, in a well-landscaped compound that rises above a dusty, sun-blasted setting west of Agrigento. Originating in the 1200s as a watchtower, then rebuilt in the 1500s by Emperor Charles V, it eventually evolved into an aristocratic manor house that controlled hundreds of acres of the surrounding fields and orchards. You'll enter an immaculately maintained cobble-covered courtyard, off of which lie the stylishly decorated guest rooms. Each evokes a romantic lodging in an upscale home, and many have antique headboards, flowered upholsteries, and marble-clad bathrooms with showers and tubs. Some have faraway views of Agrigento's Greek temples. Hotel Villa Athena (see below) may have a closer view of the temples, but this place far surpasses it in charm and hospitality. To miss the experience of dining in the hotel's restaurant, **Ristorante Il Dehor**—the very best in this part of Sicily—would be unfortunate.

Note: This place can be hard to spot from the SS640. Look for the squarish medieval tower on the northern edge of the SS640, about 4.8km (3 miles) west of Agrigento, and turn at the exit marked SPIAGGIA DI MADDALUSA.

Contrada Maddalusa (S.S. 640), Valle dei Templi, 92100 Agrigento. ✆ **0922-511061.** Fax 0922-598802. www.bagliodellaluna.com. 24 units. 245€–270€ ($294–$324) double; 350€–501€ ($420–$601) suite. Half board 45€ ($54) extra per person. AE, DC, MC, V. Bus: 1 or 3. **Amenities:** 2 restaurants; room service; babysitting; laundry service; dry cleaning; nonsmoking rooms. *In room:* A/C, TV, dataport, minibar, hair dryer.

EXPENSIVE

Hotel Villa Athena ★ *Overrated*   This 18th-century villa rises from the landscape in the Valley of the Temples, less than 3km (1¾ miles) from town. It's worn and overpriced, but its location at the archaeological site is so dramatic that we like to stay here anyway, if only to see the ruins lit up at night from our room. Guest rooms are clean, with little style, and the tiled bathrooms have shower-tub combinations and aging though still functioning plumbing. Ask for a room with a view of the temple, preferably one with a balcony. The perfect choice would be no. 205, which frames a panorama of the Temple of Concord. During the day, guests sit in the paved courtyard, enjoying drinks and fresh breezes. Even if you're not staying here, try to walk through the garden at night for an amazing view of the lit temple. You can also park here during the day and take a 10-minute walk along a trail to the temples.

Frankly, this could be a great hotel with a major overhaul. The staff is known for being the unfriendliest in Agrigento, yet the setting is so compelling that there are those of us who can overlook the drawbacks. At any rate, it remains the most popular and most famous hotel in Agrigento—be sure to reserve at least a month in advance—although celebrities now check in elsewhere. Because of its incomparable location and because of its drawbacks, this is the only hotel in this guide that rates both a star and an overrated icon.

Via Passeggiata Archeologica 33, 92100 Agrigento. ℂ **0922-596288.** Fax 0922-402180. www.hotelvilla athena.com. 40 units. 210€–260€ ($252–$312) double. Rates include breakfast. AE, DC, MC, V. Free parking. Bus: 2 or 2/. **Amenities:** Dining room; 2 bars; outdoor pool; room service; laundry service; dry cleaning. *In room:* A/C, TV, minibar.

MODERATE

Colleverde Park Hotel ★★   Sheathed in a layer of ocher-colored stucco, this is one of our favorite hotels in Agrigento, partly for its verdant garden, partly for its helpful staff, and partly for its location convenient to both the ancient and the medieval monuments of Agrigento. Renovated in 2003, it has the finest hotel garden in town, a labyrinth of vine-covered arbors, terra-cotta terraces, and enormous sheets of white canvas stretched overhead as protection from the glaring sun. The hotel's eminently tasteful glass-sided restaurant is the site of many local wedding receptions. The decor throughout is discreetly elegant, providing refuge from the hysteria that sometimes permeates Agrigento, particularly its roaring traffic. Guest rooms have tiled bathrooms (all with shower-tub combinations), lots of exposed wood, charming artwork, and big windows that in some cases reveal views of the temples of Concordia and Juno.

Via Panoramica dei Templi, 92100 Agrigento. ℂ **0922-29555.** Fax 0922-29012. www.colleverdehotel.it. 48 units. 120€–170€ ($144–$204) double. Rates include breakfast. AE, DC, MC, V. Free parking. Bus: 1, 2, or 3. **Amenities:** Restaurant; bar; laundry service; dry cleaning; nonsmoking rooms; rooms for those w/limited mobility. *In room:* A/C, TV, minibar, hair dryer, safe.

Grand Hotel dei Templi ★   Don't confuse this relatively conservative government-rated four-star hotel, which was originally built as a member of the upscale Jolly Hotel chain, with the more radical-looking three-star Grand Hotel Mosé next door. Originally built in an airy, high-ceilinged style in the mid-1970s, it's dignified and a lot more restrained, with less of a "let's party with *or* without the kids" motif, than what you'll find next door. It offers a pool surrounded by a wall, a tactful and reserved staff, and guest rooms that are contemporary looking and comfortable—simple to the point of being a touch banal. Each unit comes with a small private bathroom with shower and tub. The high-ceilinged, extremely tasteful public areas reflect the best design standards of *la dolce vita* years.

Via Leonardo Sciascia, Villaggio Mosé, 92100 Agrigento. ☎ **0922-610175.** Fax 0922-606685. www.grand hoteldeitempli.com. 146 units. 155€ ($186) double; 186€ ($223) triple. Rates include breakfast. AE, DC, MC, V. Free parking. Bus: 3/. **Amenities:** 2 restaurants; bar; outdoor pool; room service; babysitting; nonsmoking rooms; rooms for those w/limited mobility. *In room:* A/C, TV, dataport, minibar.

Hotel Kaos *(Kids)*   Set 2km (1¼ miles) southwest of the Valley of the Temples is this midsize hotel, which boasts a flowery garden, private beach, children's playground, and rooms opening onto the Mediterranean. The complex was formed by converting the residence of a former nobleman and two outbuildings once used to house servants. Many of the comfortable, well-furnished bedrooms have terraces; some units open onto the garden. Accommodations are well maintained and suitable for families, with tiled bathrooms containing both tub and shower. Unusual for a hotel of this size, Kaos contains three restaurants, each serving regional cuisine that features fresh produce.

Contrada Cumbo, Villaggio Pirandello, 92100 Agrigento. ☎ **0922-598622.** Fax 0922-598770. 105 units. 130€–155€ ($156–$186) double; 156€–186€ ($187–$223) triple. AE, DC, MC, V. Free parking. **Amenities:** 3 restaurants; bar; outdoor pool; 2 tennis courts; babysitting; laundry service; dry cleaning. *In room:* A/C, TV, minibar.

Hotel Tre Torri   Though it's near an unattractive commercial district 7km (4½ miles) south of Agrigento, this is among the area's busiest hotels. Behind a mock-medieval facade of white stucco, chiseled stone blocks, false crenellations, and crisscrossed iron balconies, Tre Torri is a favorite with Italian business travelers. Renovated in 2004, the small guest rooms are comfortable, with modern furnishings and compact tiled bathrooms with shower units.

Strada Statale 115, Viale Canatello, Villaggio Mosè, 92100 Agrigento. ☎ **0922-606733.** Fax 0922-607839. www.htretorri.com. 118 units. 150€ ($180) double. Rates include breakfast. AE, DC, MC, V. Free parking. Bus: 3. **Amenities:** 4 restaurants; 3 bars; 2 pools (1 indoor); fitness center; sauna; limited room service; laundry service; dry cleaning; nonsmoking rooms; nightclub; solarium; rooms for those w/limited mobility. *In room:* A/C, TV, dataport, hair dryer.

INEXPENSIVE

Costazzura   A government-rated three-star hotel, this is a sleek modern choice, with enough comfort but little charm. It's located in San Leone, the seaside resort of Agrigento, 3km (1¾ miles) from the Valley of the Temples. Guests here can combine the beach with a tour of ancient monuments on the side. Bedrooms are comfortably furnished though a bit stark; each has a private balcony and a tiled bathroom with tub-and-shower combination. On-site is a good family-run restaurant specializing in Mediterranean dishes.

Via delle Viole 2, San Leone, 92100 Agrigento. ☎ **0922-411222.** Fax 0922-414040. 32 units. 85€–118€ ($102–$142) double; 120€–150€ ($144–$180) triple. AE, DC, MC, V. Free parking. **Amenities:** Restaurant; bar; room service; laundry service; dry cleaning; nonsmoking rooms. *In room:* A/C, TV, dataport, safe.

Grand Hotel Mosé *(★★)*   This government-rated three-star hotel (not to be confused with the more formal four-star Grand Hotel immediately next door) is a well-designed architectural oddity that evokes a touch of Las Vegas. It sits beside the main traffic artery of Mosé Villaggio, a modern suburb stretching to the north of medieval Agrigento. Sheathed in stucco with the same honey tones as the sandstone used to build the Valley of the Temples, it's theme-ish and imaginative, with a responsive staff and a bubbly kind of zest that can be a lot of fun. Guest rooms are simple, colorful, and slightly spartan-looking, like something you might expect in a Club Med. Most of the units have tiled floors, shower-only bathrooms, wrought-iron headboards, and touches of manorial Sicilian flair. The most dramatic are the units on the hotel's rooftop, which are designed on the outside like mud-walled huts in a North African casbah, and which inside evoke a simple officer's barracks on the edge of the Sahara. The free-form pool is one of the most appealing in Agrigento.

Viale Leonardo Sciascia, Villaggio Mosé, 92100 Agrigento. © **0922-608388**. Fax 0922-608377. www.ias hotels.com. 102 rooms. 100€–140€ ($120–$168) double. Rates include breakfast. AE, DC, MC, V. Free parking. Bus: 3/. **Amenities:** Restaurant; bar; outdoor pool; boutiques; babysitting; laundry service; dry cleaning, solarium; nonsmoking rooms. *In room:* A/C, TV, minibar, hair dryer.

Hotel Villa Eos ☆ *Value* Small and personalized, but isolated in a barren stretch of land between the SS640 and the sea about 4.8km (3 miles) southwest of Agrigento, this ramshackle hotel evokes a rambling, contemporary-looking private home, thanks in part to its well-meaning staff and small scale. It sits in an oasis of greenery with views over the sea. Guests here generally opt to swim in the hotel pool rather than head for the beaches, which require a taxi or bus ride. Rooms are simple, modest, and comfortably furnished. Some, but not all, have minibars. One unit contains a tub; the rest have showers. Frankly, the hotel is best for those with cars—you may be guaranteed peace and quiet here, but the location is something of an inconvenience if you want to avail yourself of the area's many nearby attractions and dining options.

Contrada Cumbo, Villaggio Pirandello, 92100 Agrigento. © **0922-597170**. Fax 0922-597188. 10 units. 100€–150€ ($120–$180) double. Rates include breakfast. AE, DC, MC, V. Free parking. Bus: 1. **Amenities:** Restaurant; bar; outdoor pool; tennis court; babysitting; laundry service; dry cleaning. *In room:* A/C, TV.

AT THE BEACH RESORT OF SAN LEONE

Dioscuri Bay Palace ☆☆ The setting is more lavish than those of many nearby competitors, and this is a good choice if you want to be housed in comparative luxury close to Agrigento's beachfront. A member of Sicily's well-recommended Framon chain, this modern hotel rises three floors above a small bay at the northwestern tip of the boardwalks of Agrigento's waterfront resort of San Leone. Rooms are contemporary and comfortable, with tiled bathrooms and shower-tub combinations.

Lungomare Falcone e Borsellino 1, 92100 San Leone (Agrigento). © **0922-406111**. Fax 0922-411297. www.framon-hotels.com. 102 units. 226€ ($271) double; 328€ ($394) suite. Rates include breakfast. AE, DC, MC, V. Bus: 2 or 2/. **Amenities:** 2 restaurants; 2 bars; outdoor pool; Jacuzzi; car-rental desk; room service; babysitting; laundry service; dry cleaning; nonsmoking rooms; rooms for those w/limited mobility. *In room:* A/C, TV, dataport, hair dryer, safe.

Hotel Akragas This is one of the most appealing budget-priced hotels of San Leone, located on the busy main road leading from Agrigento. It isn't particularly near the water, and other than its restaurant, it has very few amenities—but in light of its reasonable prices, no one seems to care. The boxy-looking 1950s structure is a pleasant place that's completely unpretentious, family-friendly, and conducive to low-key holidays near the beach. Rooms are spartan, clean, and comfortable, with small shower-only bathrooms. The restaurant here is substantial; set-price menus cost 30€ ($36).

Viale Emporium 16–18, 92100 San Leone (Agrigento). © **0922-414082**. Fax 0922-414262. hotelakragas @libero.it. 12 units. Sept–July 75€ ($90) double. Rates include breakfast. In Aug, half board required at 110€ ($132) double, with breakfast and either lunch or dinner. AE, DC, MC, V. Free parking. Bus: 2 or 2/. **Amenities:** Restaurant. *In room:* A/C, TV.

WHERE TO DINE

Ambasciata di Sicilia *&* SICILIAN   This restaurant has been a city staple since the end of World War I, when a local family decided to celebrate the cuisine of their native Sicily in the form of this intensely vernacular trattoria. The cramped setting is accented with panels from antique donkey carts, frescoed ceiling beams, and marionettes salvaged from some long-ago street performance. In nice weather, the preferred seats are outside on four platforms built on the steeply sloping alley. (Some guests have commented that the flocks of birds that fly over the city rooftops far below are among the most soothing and mystical sights in Agrigento.) Menu items are based on 19th-century recipes. Stellar examples include beef roulades; an excellent sampling of antipasti *(antipasti rustico);* and linguine *al'Ambasciata* (prepared with meat sauce, bacon, calamari, and zucchini).

Via Gianbertoni 2, off Via Atenea. ℭ **0922-20526.** Reservations not required. Main courses 5.50€–10€ ($6.60–$12). AE, MC, V. Sept–July Tues–Sun 12:30–3:30pm and 7–11:30pm. Daily in Aug (same hours). Closed 2 weeks in Nov.

La Forchetta SICILIAN/AGRIGENTESE   This pleasant and unpretentious restaurant sits directly on the piazza in front of the golden sandstone facade of the Chiesa San Francesco (ca. 1788), 1 block down a steep flight of stairs from the town's main pedestrian thoroughfare, Via Atenea. In fine weather, tables are strewn across the square in front; otherwise, dining is limited to only 10 tables that completely fill a modest, pine-sheathed room decorated with grainy-looking photographs of Agrigento around 1911. Prices are low, portions are generous, and the cuisine focuses on the kind of two-fisted agrarian specialties that have fed many generations of workers. Hearty examples include six kinds of fresh fish, pasta with swordfish and herbs, pan-fried pork cutlets, and herb-flavored roasted lamb chops. All buses coming into town stop nearby, as La Forchetta is in front of the bus depot.

Piazza San Francesco 11. ℭ **0922-596266.** Reservations recommended Fri–Sat nights. Main courses 6€–8€ ($7.20–$9.60). AE, MC, V. Mon–Sat 1–3:30pm and 7pm–midnight.

Restaurant at the Hotel Villa Athena *&* CONTINENTAL   The formally dressed staff here tends to be brusque, despite a long tradition of welcoming visitors from far away. But the site can be so magical, at least for first-timers to Agrigento, that a midsummer dinner on the outdoor terrace can be a memorable experience unaffected by food, staff, weather, or circumstances. If you opt for lunch here, it will be served in a crescent-shaped stone-and-stucco building whose curtains are usually closed against the noon glare. But it's at dinner that the true magic emerges: Views sweep from the torch-lit terrace to the nearby Temple of Concordia (which literally looms before you) in ways unmatched by any other establishment in Agrigento. In fact, whenever the city wants to impress representatives from Parliament or the world of Italian fashion, the dinner that's held to celebrate their arrival is invariably conducted at this restaurant. Begin, perhaps, with a duet of smoked salmon and swordfish or else a fresh shellfish salad. We're fond of the sea bass flavored with saffron. The special risotto is made with pumpkin flowers, lobster, zucchini, and vodka. A "fantasy" of ice creams and sherbets is served to end the repast.

Via Passeggiata Archeologica 33. ℭ **0922-596288.** Reservations required. Main courses 10€–20€ ($12–$24). AE, DC, MC, V. Daily 12:30–2:30pm and 7:30–9:30pm (until 10pm June–Sept). Bus: 2 or 2/.

Ruga Reali SICILIAN   Tables here spill onto one of Agrigento's most beautiful squares, high in the medieval center's upper zones. It's a short walk downhill from the cathedral, where there aren't a lot of other restaurants. We usually prefer the outdoor terrace, but if it's cold, rainy, or unbearably hot, descend into one of the nearby cellars, built in the 1400s as a stable, where other tables await. The appetizing, well-prepared dishes include pasta with squid ink and shrimp; veal piccata with Marsala; and steamed calamari with peas.

Piazza Pirandello (Piazza Municipio), Cortile Scribani 8. ℂ **0922-20370.** Reservations not necessary. Main courses 7€–15€ ($8.40–$18). Set-price menu 16€ ($19). AE, DC, MC, V. Thurs–Fri and Sun–Tues noon–3pm; Thurs–Tues 8pm–1am. Also open daily for lunch and dinner mid-July to Aug. Closed mid-Oct to mid-Nov.

Trattoria dei Templi ⭐ SICILIAN   This charming, discreet, and extremely well-managed restaurant sits at the bottom of the hill between medieval Agrigento and the Valley of the Temples. Inside, you'll find brick-trimmed ceiling vaults, a polite crowd of diners from virtually everywhere in Europe, and excellent food that's served on hand-painted china. Menu items, served with efficiency by a staff of young, well-trained waiters, include *cavatelli valle dei Templi tipa Norma* (pasta with eggplant and cheese); *panzerotti della casa* (big ravioli stuffed with whitefish and served with a seafood sauce); and local fish with herbs, white wine, lemon juice, capers, olives, and orange zest.

Via Panoramica dei Templi 15. ℂ **0922-403110.** Reservations recommended. Main courses 15€–20€ ($18–$24). AE, DC, MC, V. Daily 12:30–3pm and 7:30–11pm. Closed Sun July–Aug and Fri Sept–June. Bus: 1, 2, or 3.

AT THE BEACH RESORT OF SAN LEONE

Il Pescatore ⭐ SICILIAN/SEAFOOD   Set right on the waterfront of Agrigento's beach resort of San Leone, this is the most famous of the 10 or so restaurants that flank it on either side. It's noted for its skillful preparations of fish, and also for a rough-and-tumble staff whose brusqueness is legendary—but which, almost perversely, has added to the restaurant's fame. The interior is more beautiful than you might expect, thanks to the four dining rooms' beamed ceilings and Romanesque-style columns and capitals salvaged from older buildings. Spaghetti with baby clams is always a smooth lead-in to a meal here, as is the *zuppa di cozze* (kettle of fresh mussels). Homemade bucatini comes with fresh sardines whipped into the pasta, and sole meunière is featured regularly.

Lungomare Falcone e Borsellino, San Leone. ℂ **0922-414342.** Reservations recommended. Main courses 10€–15€ ($12–$18). AE, DC, MC, V. Tues–Sun 12:30–3:30pm and 7:30–11:30pm. Bus: 2 or 2/.

Leon d'Oro SICILIAN/SEAFOOD   Set in an undistinguished, cement-sided modern building that originated as a garage and car-repair shop, this restaurant is uncomfortably close to the busy boulevard that funnels most of the traffic from Agrigento into San Leone. Its festive-looking interior, however, reveals one of the most respected restaurants in town. Expect savory dishes based on time-tested recipes. Our favorite is *rotolini Emporium* (pasta with shrimp, tomatoes, fresh vegetables, and a pecorino cheese sauce).

Via Emporium 102, San Leone. ℂ **0922-414400.** Reservations recommended. Main courses 8€–15€ ($9.60–$18). AE, DC, MC, V. Tues–Sun 12:30–3:30pm and 7:45–11:30pm. Closed 2 weeks in Nov. Bus: 2 or 2/.

Ristorante Il Dehor ⭐⭐⭐ SICILIAN/INTERNATIONAL   Set within the thick medieval walls of the Foresteria Baglio della Luna hotel (p. 279), 5km (3 miles) west of Agrigento, this is the finest restaurant in Agrigento, and one of the best in all of Sicily. Its excellence is the work of chef Damiano Ferraro, an Agrigento-born, London-educated culinary genius who has reinvented aspects of traditional Sicilian cuisine in ways that elicit rave reviews from discerning diners from throughout Europe. Guests dine on an outdoor terrace or in one of two rooms that are ringed with important 19th-century paintings and tapestries.

The 40€ ($48) set menu is traditional Sicilian and a bit cliché-ridden, but the 45€ ($54) tasting menu truly shows off the genius of this most talented chef. The appetizers are the best along the southern coast of Sicily—just wait until you sample the octopus and shrimp with new potatoes in a bisque flavored with escargot butter, or the sea scallops with king prawns on cannellini beans with candied lemon in a sea urchin sauce. We could return here every night for the pastas, like tortellini of spiny lobster in a *jus* of summer truffles. Wild salmon is served in a consommé of cherry tomatoes with little ravioli of melted fennel and chopped garlic. Desserts don't get much better than the chocolate fondant with a pistachio parfait and two sauces.

In the Foresteria Baglio della Luna hotel, Contrada Maddalusa (S.S. 640), Valle dei Templi 92100. ℂ 0922-511061. Reservations required. Main courses 10€–16€ ($12–$19); set-price menus 40€–45€ ($48–$54). AE, DC, MC, V. Mon 7:30-9:30pm; Tues–Sun 12:30–2pm and 7:30–9:30pm. Bus: 1 or 3.

2 Selinunte

122km (76 miles) SW of Palermo, 113km (70 miles) W of Agrigento, 89km (55 miles) SE of Trapani

Guy de Maupassant called the splendid jumble of ruins at Selinunte "an immense heap of fallen columns, now aligned and placed side by side on the ground like dead soldiers, now having fallen in a chaotic manner." Regardless of what shape they're in, the only reason to visit Selinunte is for its ruins, not for the unappealing modern towns (Mazara del Vallo and Castelvetrano) that have grown around it.

One of the superb colonies of ancient Greece, Selinunte traces its history to the 7th century B.C., when immigrants from Megara Hyblaea (Syracuse) set out to build a new colony. They succeeded, erecting a city of power and prestige adorned with temples. But that was calling attention to a good thing. Much of Selinunte's history involves seemingly endless conflicts with the Elymi people of Segesta (p. 288). Siding with Selinunte's rival, Hannibal virtually leveled the city in 409 B.C. The city never recovered its former glory and ultimately fell into decay.

ESSENTIALS

GETTING THERE   Selinunte is on the southern coast of Sicily and is best explored by **car,** as public transportation can be awkward. From Agrigento, take Route 115 northwest into Castelvetrano; then follow the signposted secondary road marked SELINUNTE, which leads south to the sea. Allow at least 2 hours from either Palermo or Agrigento.

If you prefer to take the **train** from Palermo, Trapani, or Marsala, you can make rail connections to Castelvetrano on the southern coast of Sicily, 23km (14 miles) from the ruins. Once at Castelvetrano, board a bus for the final lap of the journey to Selinunte. Rail fares are reasonable; the one-way trip from Palermo to Castelvetrano, for example, costs 6€ ($7.20) and takes 2 hours.

Lumia buses (ℂ 0922-20414) run to Castelvetrano from the cities of Agrigento, Marsala, and Trapani; call for schedule information. Buses arrive in Castelvetrano in front of the rail depot. From here, you must go the rest of the way by a bus operated by **Autoservizi Salemi** (ℂ 0923-981120); the one-way fare for the 20-minute trip is 1€ ($1.20).

VISITOR INFORMATION The **tourist office,** Via Caboto Giovanni (© **0924-46251**), near the archaeological garden, is open Monday through Saturday from 8am to 2pm and 3 to 8pm, Sunday from 9am to noon and 3 to 6pm.

EXPLORING THE ARCHAEOLOGICAL GARDEN ☆☆

Selinunte's temples lie in scattered ruins, the honey-colored stone littering the ground as if an earthquake had struck (as one did in ancient times). Some sections and fragments of temples still stand, with great columns pointing to the sky. From 9am to 1 hour before sunset daily, you can walk through the monument zone. Some of it has been partially excavated and reconstructed. Admission is 4.50€ ($5.40) for adults, free for children under 18.

The temples, in varying states of preservation, are designated by letters. They're dedicated to such mythological figures as Apollo and Hera (Juno); most date from the 6th and 5th centuries B.C. Near the entrance, the Doric **Temple E** contains fragments of an inner temple. Standing on its ruins before the sun goes down, you can look across the water that washes up on the shores of Africa, from which the Carthaginian fleet emerged to destroy the city. **Temple G,** in scattered ruins north of Temple E, was one of the largest erected in Sicily and was also built in the Doric style. The ruins of the less impressive **Temple F** lie between Temples E and G. Not much remains of Temple F, and little is known about it.

After viewing Temples E, F, and G, all near the parking lot at the entrance, you can get in your car and drive along the Strada dei Templi west to the Acropoli (or walk there in about 20 minutes). The site of the western temples was the **Acropoli,** which was enclosed within defensive walls and built from the 6th century to the 5th century B.C.

The most impressive site here is **Temple C.** In 1925, 14 of the 17 columns of Temple C were re-erected. This is the earliest surviving temple of ancient Selinus, built in the 6th century B.C. and probably dedicated to Hercules or Apollo. The pediment, ornamented with a clay Gorgon's head, lies broken on the ground. Temple C towers over the other ruins and gives you a better impression of what all the temples might have looked like at one time.

Also here is **Temple A,** which, like the others, remains in scattered ruins. The streets of the Acropoli were laid out along classical lines, with a trio of principal arteries bisected at right angles by a grid of less important streets. The Acropoli was the site of the most important public and religious buildings, and it was also the residence of the town's aristocrats. If you look down below, you can see the site of the town's harbor, now overgrown. After all this earthquake damage, you can only imagine the full glory of this place in its golden era.

WHERE TO STAY NEARBY

The site of the ruins contains no hotels, restaurants, or watering holes of note. Most visitors come here on a day trip while based elsewhere. But there is a handful of accommodations in the seafront village of Marinella, less than 2km (1¼ miles) east of Selinunte. To reach Marinella, you'll travel along a narrow country road.

Hotel Alceste This concrete structure is about a 15-minute walk from the ruins. Guest rooms have small tiled bathrooms with shower-and-tub combos. Most visitors, however, stop only for a visit to the plant-filled courtyard, where in summer there's musical entertainment, dancing, cabaret, and theater. In July and August, the hotel hosts what may be the highest percentage of academics of any accommodations in Sicily; they come from universities throughout the world. The somewhat shy and very kind owner, Orazio Torrente, is charming, as is his family. The airy, bustling restaurant is open daily for lunch and dinner, and is sometimes filled with busloads of visitors from as far away as Milan. Main courses cost from 7€ to 10€ ($8.40–$12).

Via Alceste 21, 91022 Marinella di Selinunte. ℂ 0924-46184. Fax 0924-46143. www.hotelalceste.it. 30 units. 87€ ($104) double; 115€ ($138) triple. Rates include breakfast. AE, DC, MC, V. **Amenities:** Restaurant; lounge; 24-hr. room service; laundry service; dry cleaning; all nonsmoking rooms. *In room:* A/C, TV, dataport, hair dryer, safe.

WHERE TO DINE NEARBY

Hotel Alceste, recommended above, is also a good choice for dining.

Ristorante Bruno (Ristorante Africa) SICILIAN   Set across the street from the Hotel Alceste, in a very clean, cement-sided building completely open to the air and light of the quiet surrounding neighborhood, this restaurant serves excellent food and the best antipasti in town. The result of a holiday romance oh-so-many years ago, it's managed by Swiss-born and multilingual Ester Weidmann and her Selinunte-born companion, Bruno Veneziano, who jointly prepare excellent fish and an antipasti buffet with the kinds of salads, fish, and vegetables that tempt many diners to make it a meal unto itself. Pizzas are also appealing, with choices such as "pizza Africa," laden with mozzarella, tuna, onions, and pepperoni.

Via Alceste 24, Marinella. ℂ 0924-46456. Reservations not necessary. Pizzas 4€–10€ ($4.80–$12); main courses 6€–10€ ($7.20–$12). AE, DC, MC, V. Fri–Wed noon–2:30pm and 7:30–11:30pm. Open daily July–Aug. Closed Nov–Feb.

13

Western Sicily

In the early days of 20th-century tourism to Sicily, the western part of the island was easily dismissed. On our first visit a long time ago, we were even discouraged from going there by a tourist official in Palermo. "What is there? A few Greek ruins and maybe some Mafia boys running about? Stay in Palermo, where we will wine and dine you."

Even today, most foreign visitors land in the east. But we have come to regard the western coast as one of our favorite areas for discovery. Much of Sicilian history was shaped along these shores, and much is left that is ancient, including the magnificent ruins at **Segesta,** whose temple has remained virtually intact for 2,500 years.

No hilltop medieval town, not even Taormina, equals **Erice.** And in spite of unfortunate modern building on its periphery, **Trapani** still has a historic core with a jumbled maze of narrow streets. Finally, **Marsala,** to the south, is known as the center for the making of world-famous dessert wines.

1 Segesta ★★★

30km (19 miles) E of Trapani, 75km (47 miles) SW of Palermo

There's only one reason to come to Segesta: to see a single amazing temple in a lonely field. For some visitors, that's reason enough because it's one of the best-preserved ancient temples in all of Italy. The trip here takes about an hour from Palermo, and makes a good brief stop en route to Trapani (covered on p. 295).

Segesta was the ancient city of the Elymi, a people of mysterious origin who are linked by some to the Trojans. As the major city in western Sicily, it faced conflicts with the rival power nearby, Selinus (Selinunte). From the 6th to 5th century B.C., there were near-constant hostilities. The Athenians came from the east to aid the Segestans in 415 B.C., but the expedition ended in disaster, eventually forcing the city to turn for help to Hannibal of Carthage.

Twice in the 4th century B.C., Segesta was besieged and conquered, once by Dionysius and again by Agathocles. Segesta, in time, turned on its old but dubious ally, Carthage. Like all Greek cities of Sicily, it ultimately fell to the Romans.

ESSENTIALS

GETTING THERE Nearly a dozen **trains** per day make the run from Trapani (p. 295) to the depot at Segesta, Segesta Tempio. A one-way ticket costs 2.65€ ($3.20). The station is only a 1km (½-mile) walk from the Doric temple. Segesta is also reached by **AST bus** (✆ 0923-31020), leaving from Piazza Montalto in Trapani; the 25-minute ride costs 3€ ($3.60).

By **car,** take the autostrada (A29) running between Palermo and Trapani. The exit at Segesta is clearly marked.

A JOURNEY INTO ANTIQUITY

The **Tempio (Temple) of Segesta** ⭐⭐⭐ is one of the world's most perfectly preserved survivors from the days of antiquity. Unlike the sprinkling of columns in most Sicilian archaeological gardens, this is a full temple of scope and dimension, with its columns relatively intact. It stands on a 304m (997-ft.) hill, on the edge of a deep ravine carved by the Pispisa River.

The site is made all the more majestic by the deep valley that envelops it. In the fading gold and pink sunlight of a Sicilian afternoon, you can stand here and absorb the full view, the setting framed by the distant peaks of Monte Barbaro and Monte Bernardo. It is perhaps the most **magnificent view** ⭐⭐⭐ in all Sicily.

Constructed in the 5th century B.C., the well-preserved temple is supported by 36 Doric columns that in turn support its entablatures and pediments. Because the interior architectural elements are lacking, professors of antiquity believe that the temple was never finished due to a war with Segesta's archenemy, Selinunte.

The site is open daily from 9am to 7pm; admission is 4.15€ ($5) for adults and 2.10€ ($2.50) for children under 18. The ticket office closes an hour before the temple park closes.

After visiting the temple, you can take a bus to the large **Teatro** ✸, or theater, at the top of Mount Barbaro at 431m (1,414 ft.). The one-way fare costs 1.05€ ($1.25), and buses depart at the rate of two per hour during the day.

Dating from the 3rd century B.C., the theater was constructed during the Hellenistic period. A semicircle with a diameter of 63m (207 ft.), it was hewn right out of the side of the mountain. In ancient days, the theater could hold as many as 4,000 spectators, and the site is still used for the staging of both modern and classical plays presented from mid-July to August every other year.

2 Erice ✸✸✸

96km (60 miles) SW of Palermo, 14km (8½ miles) NE of Trapani, 45km (28 miles) NW of Marsala, 330km (205 miles) W of Messina

Originally established some 3,000 years ago, Erice is an enchanting medieval city. From its thrilling mountaintop setting, two sheer cliffs drop 743m (2,478 ft.) to vistas across the plains of Trapani and down the west coast of Sicily. On a clear day, you can even see Cape Bon in Tunisia, but the Sicilian aerie of Erice is often shrouded in mist that only adds to its mystique (or misery, especially in winter, when temperatures can plummet below Sicilian norms and snow is not uncommon).

Erice is a lovely place to spend an afternoon wandering the medieval streets, with their baroque balconies and flowering vines, and drinking in the vistas. The southwest corner of town contains the **Villa Balio** gardens, originally laid out in the 19th century. Beyond the gardens, a path winds along the cliff's edge up to Erice's highest point, the **Castello di Venere,** today little more than crumbling Norman walls surrounding the sacred site where a temple to Venus once stood.

ESSENTIALS

GETTING THERE If taking the **train** from Palermo, you'll pull into the station at Trapani (p. 295). **AST buses** (🕿 **0923-21021**) to Erice depart from Trapani's Piazza Montalto, at the rate of 11 per day. Service is year-round, daily from 6:40am to 7:30pm. The trip lasts 50 minutes and costs 2.50€ ($3) one-way.

By **car** from Trapani, head out on the Via Fardella to the end of the street. At some point near the end of the wide boulevard, you'll see signs pointing the way to Erice. Follow A29 all the way to Erice.

DISCOVERING A MEDIEVAL TOWN

Erice's chief attraction is the **medieval town** ✸✸✸, although there are some individual points of interest worth seeking out as you make your way along its cobblestone streets. The historic core of Erice forms a triangle, with the southeastern corner framed by the **Castello di Venere** (see below). In the southwestern corner is the **Chiesa Matrice,** near Porta di Trapani, the best place to park your car before you walk into the medieval center. The access road to Erice affords **panoramic vistas** ✸✸ of Trapani plains and the sea.

After leaving Porta di Trapani, your first discovery will be immediately to the northeast. **Chiesa Matrice di Erice,** Via Vito Carvini (🕿 **0923-869123**), is the main church of Erice. Not quite a cathedral, it was constructed in 1314 using stones from the ancient Temple of Venus that once stood here. Its merlon-topped walls speak of the church's former role as a fortress and a place of worship. The rose window on the church facade is a thing of beauty, as is its Gothic porch.

If you climb the church's campanile, or bell tower, you'll be rewarded with a stunning view across the Gulf of Trapani to the Egadi Islands. Ordered built by

Frederick of Aragon, the former watchtower has impressive Gothic mullioned windows. The church is open Monday through Friday from 9:30am to 12:30pm and 3:30 to 5:30pm, Saturday and Sunday from 9:30am to 1pm and 3:30 to 6pm.

If you walk north from the church, you can follow **Mura Elimo Puniche** 🐸, the Elimo Punic walls constructed by the Elimini (8th–6th c. B.C.) around the northeastern flank of Erice. Any attack on the town had to come from this direction, which was exposed. The best-preserved part of the walls lies along Via dell'Addolorata, stretching from Porta Carmine to Porta Spada, which is at the far northern end of the massive fortifications.

At Porta Spada, the end of your "wall walk," you'll find yourself at **Chiesa di Santa Orsola,** a 1413 church with its original Gothic rib-vaulting still on view in the nave. Directly to the east of this church is the **Quartiere Spagnola.** Launched in the 17th century but never finished, this "Spanish Quarter" building is no grand sight, but a **panoramic vista** 🐸 unfolds from here over the Bay of Cofano.

In the historic core of Erice stands the **Museo Civico Antonio Cordici,** Piazza Umberto I, at Corso Vittorio Emanuele (ⓒ **0923-869172**), open Monday through Friday from 9am to 1:30pm, Monday and Thursday from 2:30 to 5:30pm, and Sunday from 9am to 2pm; admission is free. Named for a local historian, the building was originally a library dating from 1867. In its entrance hall is a magnificent 1525 relief of the *Annunciation* 🐸 by Antonello Gagini, one of his most impressive pieces of art. Upstairs are displays of the more intriguing artifacts from archaeological digs in the area, including a small Attic head of Venus dating from the 5th century B.C.

Heading east, you'll come first to **Giardino del Balio** 🐸, initially constructed by the Normans as a forward defense for their castle (see below). The gardens take their name from a former Norman governor and were mapped out in 1870 by Count Agostino Pepoli. Situated on the summit of a hill, the gardens open onto one of the most **spectacular views** 🐸🐸 in western Sicily, embracing the peaks of Monte Cofano with distant views of the Egadi Islands. On a clear day you can see all the way to Cap Bon in Tunisia, a distance of 170km (106 miles). The gardens are always open; entrance is free.

Saving the best for last, you'll come to **Castello di Venere,** or Castle of Venus, built atop Mount San Giuliano on the same spot where in ancient times a temple to the goddess stood. Dating from the 12th century, the present *castello* was constructed as a defensive fortification by the Normans. Massive and majestic, it became the seat of Norman authority in the west. It's still encircled by mammoth medieval towers. Above the entrance to the castle, note the coat of arms of Charles V and an original Gothic window. The castle provides an even more **memorable view** 🐸🐸🐸 than does the adjoining Giardino del Balio; you can see the plains of Trapani and the Egadi Islands to the southwest. In fair weather, you can even spot the offshore island of Ustica (p. 128).

After all the looting, burning, and destruction this castle has witnessed over the centuries, little is left of the ruins. But that view still makes it worthwhile. The castle is open daily from 9am to 8pm year-round, with no admission fee.

SHOPPING

Altieri 1882   This small, charming shop lies a few steps uphill from the heart of Erice, Piazza Umberto I. It sells coral jewelry, silver frames, and Sicilian pottery, some of it produced locally. Via Cordici 14. ⓒ **0923-869431.**

Bazar del Miele ⊛   This is one of the most impressive food shops in Sicily, with some items that are esoteric even by local standards. You'll see 15 different honeys; several preparations of anchovies; Marsala wines, arranged by vineyard, year, and degree of sweetness; and liqueurs, including a pale-green one made from fermented pistachios. The array of cheeses and almond-based candies is the most comprehensive in town. Via Cordici 16. (C) **0923-869181.**

Ceramica Ericina ⊛   Erice craftspeople are as famous for their rugs as they are for their ceramics. This is basically a ceramics store, but we also found the best selection of Erice carpets here. These highly valued rugs are rigorously hand-woven, the most traditional colors being red, yellow, and blue. Sometimes the colors are broken up by even brighter hues, with both floral and geometric designs in zigzags and diamonds. There is also a good selection of Sicilian lace here. Via Vittorio Emanuele 7. (C) **0923-869140.**

Nino Marchese   The pottery and stoneware sold here is of a more monumental stature, with more historical antecedents, than what's available in competing shops nearby. Most items are faithful copies of religious and "portrait" porcelain from 18th-century Sicily. Look for wall-mounted containers for holy water, votive candles, and vases and pitchers molded and painted to resemble Moors, Sicilian noblemen, poets, and troubadours. Corso Vittorio Emanuele 39. (C) **0923-869660.**

WHERE TO STAY
EXPENSIVE

Hotel Elimo ⊛   Set in the lower reaches of Erice's historic core, a few steps from the Hotel Moderno (see below), this arts-conscious hotel was built 400 years ago as a private palazzo and transformed into accommodations in 1986. Its public areas feature an appealing combination of old frescoed ceiling beams, antique masonry, Oriental rugs, and contemporary-looking leather sofas, all nestled around a library-style TV den that adds considerable coziness to the space. The best views, seen through the enormous windows of the restaurant, sweep over the golden plains of western Sicily. We prefer this hotel's conventional guest rooms, which tend to be large and have well-styled modern furniture. Avoid the duplex suites, which some visitors find uncomfortably claustrophobic. In the main building, the bathrooms have both tubs and showers; in the annex, the bathrooms have showers only.

Via Vittorio Emanuele 75, 91016 Erice. (C) **0923-869377.** Fax 0923-869252. 22 units. 170€ ($204) double; 220€ ($264) suite. AE, DC, MC, V. **Amenities:** Restaurant; bar; laundry service; dry cleaning. *In room:* A/C, TV, minibar.

MODERATE

Hotel Baglio Santa Croce ⊛ *(Finds*   This is a most delightful discovery and, for many, the most idyllic way to enjoy the pleasures of historic Erice without staying in the crowded center. Not far from town, this converted farmhouse dates back to 1637 and lies on the slope of Mount Erice, opening onto the Gulf of Cornino. The original architectural materials, including wooden beams, have been retained. The delightful terraced gardens have panoramic vistas, and the atmosphere is one of charm and grace. Guest rooms are simply but comfortably furnished with tiled floors and wooden beams, along with olive-wood pieces and wrought-iron beds. Each unit comes with a small bathroom with shower. The on-site restaurant serves good country cooking.

SS187, Km 300 (Contrada Ragosia), 91019 Erice. (C) **0923-891111.** Fax 0923-891192. www.bagliosanta croce.it. 24 units. 96€–112€ ($115–$134) double. Rates include breakfast. AE, DC, MC. Free parking. Located 2km (1¼ miles) east of Valderice on N187. **Amenities:** Restaurant; bar; outdoor pool; laundry service; dry cleaning. *In room:* TV.

Hotel Moderno ⚜ It's cozy, it's warm, and it has a lot of charm, but don't let this hotel's name fool you: The kind of modernism it was named for dates from just after World War II, when a 19th-century stone house and, later, the 14-room annex across the street were converted into one of central Erice's most appealing hotels. Rooms in the annex are bigger than those in the hotel's main core. Regardless of their location, all units have hints of 19th-century styling, the occasional antique, and bentwood, brass, and wicker furniture. About a dozen of the rooms open onto private balconies or terraces. All come with immaculate tiled bathrooms with tub-shower combos. If you arrive on a cold day, you're likely to be welcomed by a blazing fire. The on-site restaurant is highly regarded.

Via Vittorio Emanuele 67, 91016 Erice. ℂ 0923-869300. Fax 0923-869139. www.hotelmodernoerice.it. 41 units. 95€–115€ ($114–$138) double. Rates include breakfast. AE, DC, MC, V. Free parking. **Amenities:** Restaurant; bar; lounge; babysitting; laundry service; dry cleaning. *In room:* A/C, TV, minibar.

INEXPENSIVE

Hotel Belvedere San Nicola ⚜ *Kids* Positioned about 731m (2,398 ft.) downhill from the fortifications that surround medieval Erice, this inn stands in an isolated location that slopes down to views over the shoreline of Trapani. It markets itself as a family-friendly country inn that's less expensive than hotels in Erice's historic core. Built in 2000 adjacent to a community of Mediterranean-style town houses (mostly second homes and timeshares for holiday-making Europeans), it resembles a postmodern version of a thick-walled, big-windowed farmhouse. None of the compact, tile-floored guest rooms has air-conditioning, but thanks to Erice's high altitude and constant breezes, you won't need it. Some rooms have high, sloping ceilings, and all have an efficient, no-frills styling. The social center is the large outdoor pool.

Contrada San Nicola, 91016 Erice. ℂ 0923-860124. Fax 0923-869139. www.pippocatalano.it. 10 units. 80€ ($96) double. Rates include breakfast. AE, DC, MC, V. **Amenities:** Restaurant; bar; outdoor pool; horseback riding grounds; *bocce* court; children's playground. *In room:* TV, hair dryer.

Hotel Ermione ⚜ *Kids* Opening onto panoramic views of the Egadi Islands, this dramatically perched hotel lies only 700m (2,296 ft.) from the heart of Erice. Builders in the 1960s chose this breezy location to erect a hotel overlooking the Tyrrhenian Sea, and today most of the midsize guest rooms open onto these vistas. Units have tiled bathrooms (most with showers, a few with tubs). Because many of the accommodations are triples or quads, this is an ideal family choice. Old-style Sicilian furniture—not necessarily antiques—grace the public areas. You can park your car in the free lot, then take a complimentary hotel van into the center of Erice. With its beautiful views of the sea, the hotel's restaurant is a worthy choice even if you're not staying here.

Via Piuneta Comunale 43, 91016 Erice. ℂ 0923-869138. Fax 0923-869587. www.ermionehotel.com. 47 units. 80€–100€ ($96–$120) double; 90€–110€ ($108–$132) triple; 130€–160€ ($156–$192) quad. Children under 12 stay free in parent's room. Rates include breakfast. AE, DC, MC, V. Free parking. **Amenities:** Restaurant; bar; room service; laundry service; dry cleaning. *In room:* TV.

WHERE TO DINE

Monte San Giuliano ⚜ *Finds* SEAFOOD/TRAPANESE To reach this garden hideaway, negotiate your way through a labyrinth of narrow stone alleys that begin a few steps downhill from Erice's Piazza Umberto I, then pass through an iron gate and wander beyond stone walls and shrubbery to the restaurant's terraces and dining rooms. The setting is very rustic, typical of Erice. The freshest and finest seafood is served here. That the Arabs once ruled the land is evidenced in the seafood couscous. Our favorite pasta is something to savor: *busiate* (a homemade pasta) made with *pesto alla Trapanese*, which in this case means garlic, basil, fresh tomatoes, and—surprise—almonds.

Vicolo San Rocco 7. 🕐 **0923-869595.** Reservations recommended. Main courses 7.50€–13€ ($9–$16). AE, DC, MC, V. Tues–Sun 12:15–2:45pm and 7:30–10pm. Closed Jan 7–21.

Osteria di Venere TRAPANESE/SICILIAN   This local dive has a staff not trained in the social graces, but it serves excellent regional cooking nonetheless. A mix of visitors and locals feasts nightly off the fat of the land. Start, perhaps, with the homemade pasta of the day. It's often made with a spicy sauce of garlic, tomatoes, fresh basil, and toasted almonds in the Trapanese style. The chef's namesake pasta, *alla Venere,* is made with tomatoes, eggplant, swordfish, and a surprising touch of mint. The menu is based mainly on meat in winter, with fish predominating in summer.

Via Roma 6 at Piazza San Giuliano. 🕐 **0923-869362.** Reservations required. Main courses 5€–15€ ($6–$18). DC, MC, V. Thurs–Tues 12:30–2:30pm and 8–10:30pm.

Ulisse SICILIAN   Enter this airy indoor/outdoor dining room by walking up a series of ramps and stairs that seem to go on forever, past hidden pockets of greenery loaded with hibiscus and palmettos. At the top of your climb is a family-managed restaurant lined with paintings by local artists. Pizzas are available here, but only at dinnertime, and they're less popular than the well-prepared fresh fish, meat, and pasta platters for which the place is best known. We had the best spaghetti with lobster we've enjoyed in western Sicily. A pasta favorite with locals is pappardelle (wide noodles) with fresh mushrooms.

Via Chiaramonte 45. 🕐 **0923-869333.** Reservations not required. Main courses 7€–15€ ($8.40–$18). AE, DC, MC, V. Sept–May Fri–Wed noon–3pm and 8pm–midnight; June–Aug daily noon–3pm and 8pm–midnight.

PASTRIES

Erice is renowned throughout Sicily for its pastries. These delectable goodies were carefully refined over the years by nuns based in Erice convents from the 14th to the 18th century. Even if you're dining in one of the restaurants in the central core, skip dessert and head to one of the best pastry shops in town.

Pasticceria Grammatico   Maria Grammatico is a former nun who became famous in Italy when she wrote *Bitter Almonds,* the story of her life. Co-authored with Mary Taylor Simeti, the book told of her recollections and recipes from a Sicilian girlhood spent in a convent. Her almond creations have made her celebrated in these parts, especially her crunchy almond cookies, rum-filled marzipan balls, and confections fashioned from chocolate-covered almond paste. The almond-paste creations are works of art, shaped into a variety of forms such as whimsical animals. The pastry shop also sells liqueurs such as a green, minty Marsala.

Via Vittorio Emanuele 14. 🕐 **0923-869390.** Pastries from 1€ ($1.20). No credit cards. Daily 7am–10pm.

Impressions

In Italy, the pleasure of eating is central to the pleasure of living. When you sit down to dinner with Italians, when you share their food, you are sharing their lives.

—Fred Plotkin, *Italy for the Gourmet Traveler* (1996)

Pasticceria Michele Il Tulipano ⟨☕⟩ This is the most spectacular bakery in Erice, with a stand-up coffee and drinks bar where you can eat the goods on-site. Established on the town's main street in the early 1980s, it devotes itself to the intricately decorated pastries, many flavored with almonds or chocolate, that have made southern Italy famous. The most spectacular pastry we had in all of Sicily was a *casatella,* a deep-fried fritter stuffed with sweetened ricotta, that's typical of the Trapani region. It tastes best with espresso and perhaps a glass of almond-flavored water.

Via Vittorio Emanuele 10–12. ⓒ **0923-869672.** Pastries from 1€ ($1.20). No credit cards. Daily 7:30am–9pm (until 2am July–Aug).

3 Trapani

100km (64 miles) SW of Palermo, 14km (8½ miles) SW of Erice, 150km (94 miles) NW of Agrigento

The major city along the western coast of Sicily, Trapani may be your gateway to the west thanks to its superior transportation links to the rest of Sicily and its easy road links with Palermo.

Trapani lies below the headland of Mount Erice, with the Egadi Islands visible most days off its shore. Trapani is also the capital of its own province, which embraces the medieval hill town of Erice (see above). This most westerly of Sicilian provinces covers a land of great natural beauty, including a coastline that has many long beaches of white sand such as the one at San Vito lo Capo.

The city stands on a sickle-shaped promontory stretching into the sea. Its economy is based largely on fishing and winemaking along with salt mining, with tourism growing annually. A maze of narrow streets makes up its historic core, but it has none of the charm of Erice. If you have only a day for the west, your time is better spent in Erice to the north. But if you have an extra day, consider devoting it to historic Trapani, once a Phoenician outpost. Trapani's most dubious reputation is as a major Sicilian center of the Mafia.

Drepanon, as it was once called, was the key port in the Carthaginian defense of the island at the time of the Punic Wars. The Romans, led by Catulus, captured the city in 241 B.C., marking its decline. It regained some of its lost prestige during the 9th century when the Saracens landed to conquer it. Three centuries later they were followed by the Normans.

It was here in 1272 that Edward I of England pulled into port fresh from the Crusades to learn that he'd inherited the throne. More conquerors were to come, including Peter of Aragon, who landed here in 1282.

Architecturally, the worst blows to Trapani were the Allied bombardments in 1940 and 1943. The entire historic district of San Pietro was razed. Regrettably, the new Trapani bounced back with the building of several ugly modern blocks—think Soviet Union in the heyday of the Cold War. As a result of all this destruction, Trapani has fewer historic sites to visit than most Sicilian cities of its size—but there are some nuggets.

GETTING THERE By Plane The not very busy **Florio Airport** (ⓒ **0923-842502**) is served by daily flights from Rome and the offshore island of Pantelleria. It's located in Birgi on the road to Marsala, 15km (9 miles) from the center of Trapani. Buses, which leave from Piazza Malta, are timed for the arrivals and departures of the planes.

By Train Most trains, at the rate of 10 per day, make the 2-hour run from Palermo; a one-way ticket costs 6.80€ ($8.15). There are also 15 trains per day from Marsala, taking 30 minutes and costing 2.65€ ($3.20) one-way. Trains pull in at the **Piazza Stazione** (© 0923-28071), where luggage storage is available. For general rail information in Italy, call © **892021.**

By Bus   AST (© 0923-21021) runs 11 buses per day to Erice, departing from Piazza Montalto in Trapani. The one-way ride takes 50 minutes and costs 2.50€ ($3).

By Ferry   Trapani is a major embarkation point for ferries and hydrofoils *(aliscafi).* Most departures are for the offshore Egadi Islands of Marrettimo, Levanzo, and Favignana. Service is also available to Ustica, Pantelleria, and even Tunisia in North Africa. Ferries depart from the docks near Piazza Garibaldi. Tickets are available from **Siremar** (© 0923-545455) and **Ustica** (© 0923-22220).

By Car   From Palermo, follow A29 all the way southwest into Trapani. From Marsala, head north along Route 115 to Trapani.

VISITOR INFORMATION   The not very helpful **tourist office,** Piazza Saturno (© 0923-29000), is open Monday through Saturday from 8am to 8pm, Sunday from 9am to noon.

FAST FACTS   Your hotel will point you to the nearest **pharmacy.** Pharmacies operate on a rotational system for night hours, with at least one open every night of the week. More serious medical needs are attended to at **Ospedale Sant'Antonio Abate,** Via Cosenza, in the northeast of the city (© 0923-809111). For Internet access, head to **Phone Center GGE,** Stazione Marittima (© 0923-549840), where the rate is 5€ ($6) per hour. The **post office,** Piazza Vittorio Veneto (© 0923-28914), is open Monday through Saturday from 8am to 6:30pm. The biggest and best travel agency is **Francesca Badalucco,** 91 Via Ammiraglio Staiti (© 0923-542470), across the street from Trapani's harbor. The agency knows all the boat schedules and can sell tickets from Trapani to any of Sicily's offshore islands. It also sells boat tickets from, say, Palermo to Genoa, or from Palermo or Trapani to Corsica.

EXPLORING TRAPANI

Most visitors head first for the *centro storico* ⍟, the medieval core lying on the headland jutting into the sea. The most ancient part of this "casbah" was constructed in a typical North African style around a tightly knit maze of narrow streets. Originally these streets lay behind protective walls that guarded against sudden invasions from the sea.

The most intriguing street is **Via Garibaldi** (also known as Rua Nova, or "New Road"), which is flanked with churches and palaces. The Aragonese laid out this street in the 18th century. The best shops in the old town line **Via Torrearsa,** which leads down to a bustling **fish market** *(pescheria)* where tuna—caught in waters offshore—is king. The spacious central square, **Piazza Vittorio Emanuele,** laid out in 1869 and planted with palm trees, is a relaxing oasis.

The pedestrianized main street of Trapani is **Corso Vittorio Emanuele,** sometimes called Rua Grande by the Trapanese. Many elegant baroque buildings are found along this street, which makes for a grand promenade. At the eastern end of the street rises the **Palazzo Senatorio,** the 17th-century town hall, done up in pinkish marble.

Along the way, you can visit the **Cattedrale** (© 0923-432111), open daily from 8am to 4pm. Built on the site of an earlier structure from the 14th century, the cathedral is dedicated to San Lorenzo (St. Lawrence) and has a 1743 facade. Artworks inside include a *Crucifixion* by Giacomo Lo Verde, a local artist, on the building's south side, fourth altar.

Another important church is **Chiesa Santa Maria del Gesù,** on Via San Pietro, with a facade that incorporates both Gothic and Renaissance features, dating from the first half of the 16th century. Its major work of art is a beautiful *Madonna degli Angeli* (Madonna with Angels), a glazed terra-cotta statue by Andrea della Robbia. Regrettably, the church is often closed.

Also worthy but perpetually closed is **Chiesa di Sant'Agostino,** Piazzetta Saturno, adjacent to the tourist office. This church is known for its lovely rose window from the 14th century, and even more so for occasional concerts staged here. Ask at the tourist office for details.

Another church in the heart of old town, **Chiesa del Purgatorio,** is in the 17th-century baroque style. In theory, it's open daily from 8:30am to 12:30pm and 4 to 8pm. It's across from Stazione Marettima, 1 block up from Piazza Garibaldi. The entire atmosphere of this church remains medieval, with suffocating incense and otherworldly music. It houses the single greatest treasure in Trapani, however: the *Misteri* ✿, 20 life-size wooden figures from the 18th century depicting Christ's Passion. Every bloody detail, including the Crucifixion, is shown.

A once major attraction, **Torre di Lingny,** built in 1671 as a defensive bastion on the tip of Trapani's "sickle," has closed its doors "for a very, very long time"—so we were told.

Villa Margherita lies between old and new Trapani. These public gardens offer a welcome respite from a day of tramping the cobblestone streets. Fountains, banyan trees, and palms rustling in the wind make for an inviting oasis. **Luglio Muscale Trapanese,** a festival of opera, ballet, and cabaret, is staged here in July, with nightly shows at 9pm. A kiosk inside the park gates sells tickets for 5€ ($6). For information, call ✆ **0923-21454.**

Modern Trapani has two sights worth a visit; otherwise, you can skip it without cultural deprivation. **Santuario dell'Annunziata** ✿ is a 14th-century convent whose cloisters enclose the major museum of Trapani (see below). The 14th-century church was forever altered in the 18th century by new decorators, although its Gothic portal remains, surmounted by a lovely rose window. The **chapels** ✿✿ are a treasure and include two dedicated to the fishermen of Trapani who risk their lives daily to harvest the sea. The major chapel to seek out is the **Cappella della Madonna,** with its sacred Virgin and Bambino, attributed to Nino Pisano in the 14th century. The bronze gates to the chapel are from 1591. On its left flank is **Cappella dei Marinai,** a tufa structure crowned by a dome and built in the Renaissance style.

Adjacent to the church is Trapani's major museum: **Museo Regionale Pepoli** ✿, Via Conte Agostino Pepoli 200 (✆ **0923-553269**), open Monday through Saturday from 9am to 1:30pm and Sunday from 9am to 12:30pm. Admission is 2.50€ ($3). The former Carmelite convent has been converted into a showcase of regional art that emphasizes archaeological artifacts but also has a worthy collection of statues and coral carvings. The artistic Gagini family is better represented here than any other artist. Especially striking is *St. James the Greater,* by Antonello Gagini. The folk-art figurines are noteworthy, including a brutal depiction of the biblical legend of Herod's search for the Christ Child. Other works of art include a moving 14th-century *Pietà* ✿ by Roberto di Oderisio and some impressive triptychs by anonymous artists.

SHOPPING

Cinzia Gucciardo   This is one of the few stores in Trapani that specializes in jewelry crafted from coral gathered in nearby waters. Inventories include necklaces, bracelets, and coral-crafted votive portraits of saints that are larger and more elaborate than anything else in Trapani. There's also a collection of 19th-century engravings and art objects, most of them focusing on 18th-century selections, usually in music rooms or salons. Corso Vittorio Emanuele 23-25. ℭ 0923-25542.

Gioielleria Enzo Catania   This might be the most elegant shop in town, the kind of place where a security system "buzzes" you inside after you're checked out by the staff through a plate-glass window. Inside, you'll find clocks, silver picture frames and chalices, religious icons, and impressive gold, silver, and platinum jewelry. Corso Vittorio Emanuele 39-41. ℭ 0923-21148.

Libreria del Corso   One of the town's best bookstores sells Italian-language (and to a lesser degree, English-language) books, many of them about Sicily and its art treasures. Corso Vittorio Emanuele 61. ℭ 0923-26260.

WHERE TO STAY

Crystal Hotel ℛ   A member of the respected Framon chain, this is the most architecturally dramatic and urban-style hotel in Trapani. Constructed in the early 1990s, it's the most distinctive ultramodern building in town, characterized by an all-glass facade that curves above a piazza directly in front of the town's rail station. (Few trains come into Trapani every day, so the neighborhood is very quiet.) Guest rooms are comfortable and efficiently organized. Each unit comes with an immaculate bathroom with shower. Overall, this is a worthy choice and a modern refuge in the midst of an otherwise antique city.

Piazza Umberto I, 91100 Trapani. ℭ 0923-20000. Fax 0923-25555. www.framon-hotels.com. 70 units. 150€–200€ ($180–$240) double; 250€ ($300) suite. Rates include breakfast. AE, DC, MC, V. Free parking. **Amenities:** Restaurant; bar; babysitting; laundry service; dry cleaning; nonsmoking rooms. *In room:* A/C, TV, dataport, minibar, safe.

Hotel Russo   Newer buildings have since taken over this hotel's role as the town's preeminent lodging, and by many standards the design (ca. 1950) and five-story ocher-fronted facade looks slightly outmoded. But a quick view of its art-filled lobby, and a quick understanding of its solid sense of respectability, will make you feel that you're about to stay at one of the most deeply entrenched hotels in western Sicily. There are marble and tile floors throughout, an amusing set of frescoes in the breakfast room, and a sense of old-fashioned Trapani everywhere. Rooms are clean, comfortable, and without any particular sense of drama or theatricality. Each unit comes with a small tiled bathroom with shower.

Via Tintori 4, 91100 Trapani. ℭ 0923-22163. Fax 0923-26623. 35 units. 76€–85€ ($91–$102) double. AE, DC, MC, V. **Amenities:** Babysitting; laundry service; dry cleaning. *In room:* A/C, TV.

Hotel Vittoria   Set on the waterfront road, a short distance from the center of town, this hotel is less preferable to the Crystal but still acceptable in every way. The second-best hotel in town is a well-built, solid structure lacking any particular architectural charm or style. Nevertheless, it is exceedingly comfortable, and the staff is helpful. Guest rooms are furnished in a minimalist way, though the beds are inviting, and each unit comes with a small bathroom. Only three bathrooms contain tubs; the rest have showers.

Via Francesco Crispi 4, 91100 Trapani. ℭ 0923-873044. Fax 0923-29870. www.hotelvittoriatrapani.it. 65 units. 89€ ($107) double. AE, DC, MC, V. Free parking. **Amenities:** Breakfast lounge; bar; room service. *In room:* A/C, TV, dataport, minibar, hair dryer.

WHERE TO DINE

Ai Lumi Tavernetta 𝔊 SICILIAN   Many locals cite this artfully rustic tavern, established in 1993 on the ground floor of what used to be an important family-owned palazzo, as one of Trapani's best restaurants. It's located 2 blocks from the cathedral and features a long, narrow dining room capped with a series of medieval-looking brick arches. During the 17th century, it functioned as a stable, but today the venue is filled with wines from virtually everywhere, dark furniture, and a clientele that includes actors, politicians, and journalists. And, thanks to thick masonry walls and air-conditioning, it's a cool retreat from the blazing heat outside. The cuisine grows more proficient each time we visit. Flavorful dishes include roast lamb in a citrus sauce, local rabbit that's larded and then roasted, and seafood pasta with shrimp and calamari that tasted so fresh, they could have just leapt from the boat.

Corso Vittorio Emanuele 75. 𝒞 **0923-872418.** Reservations recommended Fri–Sat nights. Main courses 6.50€–15€ ($7.80–$18). AE, DC, MC, V. Sept–June Mon–Sat 1–3:30pm and 8–11pm; daily in Aug (same hours). Closed July.

P & G 𝘝𝘢𝘭𝘶𝘦 SICILIAN/SEAFOOD   This restaurant, one of the best in town, is located near the train station across from the public gardens of Villa Margherita. It's also near the historic center, Via Fardella, and the shopping district. The decor is simple but classic, and service is among the finest in town. A highly recommended house specialty is *busiate,* the homemade pasta of the region, served with tomatoes, lots of garlic, anchovies, and almonds. Since North Africa is just across the sea, expect a wickedly delicious couscous prepared with fresh fish. Desserts are luscious, so save room.

Via Spalti 1. 𝒞 **0923-547701.** Reservations recommended. Main courses 5€–15€ ($6–$18). AE, DC, MC, V. Mon–Sat 10am–3:30pm and 7pm–midnight.

Ristorante da Peppe SICILIAN   Often convivial meals are served in this one-room restaurant, where large murals and a blue-green color scheme brighten up the varnished wood and white plaster. Menu items feature a well-rehearsed, oft-repeated medley of mostly Sicilian dishes, such as spaghetti with squid and squid ink; three kinds of couscous; risotto paella (a Sicilian adaptation of the famous dish of Valencia); and a time-honored favorite, *spaghetti rustica,* with swordfish, tuna, salmon, dried tomatoes, Abruzzi herbs, and bread crumbs.

Via Spalti 50. 𝒞 **0923-28246.** Reservations recommended Fri–Sat nights. Main courses 6€–13€ ($7.20–$16); fixed-price menus 12€–20€ ($14–$24). AE, DC, MC, V. Daily 1–11pm.

Taverna Paradiso 𝔊 SICILIAN   This tavern, established in 1996 in an old warehouse on the seafront, is the town's most prestigious restaurant. The warren of medieval-looking stone rooms are stylishly decorated with rustic artifacts that show off the antique masonry to its best advantage. The food is excellent, and prices not nearly as high as you might expect from a place of this quality. Care and precision go into every dish, especially the house specialties: a maritime version of the North African couscous; spaghetti with tangy sea urchins; and a marvelous pasta dish with lobster, shrimp, and fresh artichokes. In winter, well-flavored meat and poultry dishes are likely to be featured when fish catches are slim due to rough waters.

Lungomare Dante Alighieri 22. 𝒞 **0923-22303.** Reservations recommended. Main courses 9€–15€ ($11–$18). AE, DC, MC, V. Mon–Sat 1–3:30pm and 8–11:30pm.

4 Marsala

134km (83 miles) NW of Agrigento, 301km (187 miles) W of Catania, 124km (77 miles) SW of Palermo, 31km (19 miles) S of Trapani

Evoking a North African town with its tangle of narrow streets and alleys, Marsala is the home of the world-famous Marsala wine, a rival of port and Madeira. The wine was first popularized in 1770 when an Englishman, John Woodhouse, came ashore from a British ship that had been forced to anchor here during a violent storm. Woodhouse headed for a local tavern, and the rest is history.

The name Marsala dates from the port's occupation by the Saracens, who called it *Marsa el Allah,* or "Port of God." But it was the Carthaginians who founded the town on Cape Lilibeo (also called Cape Boeo) in 396 B.C. after fleeing nearby Mothia, which had been destroyed by armies from Syracuse. Marsala then fell to the Romans after a siege that lasted a decade (250–241 B.C.). The year 47 B.C. saw the arrival of Julius Caesar, who pitched camp here en route to North Africa.

One of the most famous events in Italian history occurred here on May 11, 1860, when Garibaldi and his brigade of 1,000 red-shirted men arrived to liberate Sicily from the Bourbons.

In 1943, Marsala sustained heavy damage from Allied bombers before their land invasion of Sicily.

Today, Marsala is a thriving little town on Cape Boeo, the westernmost tip of Sicily. Many of its hotels and restaurants are filled with businesspeople trading in Marsala wine. Although Erice (p. 290) is a more popular attraction, Marsala merits a day if you can spare it.

GETTING THERE　Multiple **trains** per day run south from Trapani (14 per day Monday through Friday, 10 on Saturday, and 11 on Sunday). The one-way trip costs 2.65€ ($3.20) and takes 30 minutes. For schedules, call ℂ **892021.**

Buses for Marsala leave from Piazza Montalto in Trapani at the rate of three per day. The one-way trip costs 3€ ($3.60) and lasts 35 minutes. For schedules, call ℂ **0923-21021.**

By **car,** head south from Trapani along Route 115.

VISITOR INFORMATION　The **tourist office,** Via 11 Maggio 100 (ℂ **0923-714097**), is open Monday through Saturday from 8am to 1:45pm and 2:10 to 8:10pm, Sunday from 9am to noon.

GETTING AROUND　For a **taxi,** call ℂ **339-5497849.**

FAST FACTS　In an **emergency,** call the *Carabinieri* at ℂ **112.** The most convenient drugstore is the **Marsala Pharmacy,** Corso 11 Maggio 126 (ℂ **0923-953254**). When it's closed, a notice is posted listing what other pharmacies are open. For medical care, the **Guardia Medica** (ℂ **0923-782343**) is at the Hospital San Biagio, Via Colocasio 10 (ℂ **0923-782343**).

EXPLORING THE TOWN

The heart of this wine-producing town is the **Piazza della Repubblica,** site of the Chiesa Madre (see below) and the Palazzo Senatorio, dating from the 18th century and nicknamed "Loggia."

Branching off from this square is the main street, **Via 11 Maggio,** flanked by the town's most splendid palazzi. In the heyday of the Roman empire, this street was called *Decumanus Maximus.* From Piazza della Repubblica, **Via Garibaldi** heads south to **Porta Garibaldi,** a magnificent gateway crowned by an eagle. Garibaldi is honored because it was at Marsala that he and 1,000 volunteers, dressed in red shirts, landed from Genoa. Their aim was to overthrow the Bourbon rulers, thus liberating the "Kingdom of the Two Sicilies."

The largest church in Marsala is **Chiesa Madre,** Piazza della Repubblica (© **0923-716295**), open daily from 7:30am to 9pm. Originally constructed during the Norman occupation, it was massively rebuilt in the 1700s. The original church here was dedicated to St. Thomas à Becket. The dome collapsed in 1893 and was partially reconstructed in the 20th century. The facade is decorated with statues and flanked by two small campaniles (bell towers), completed as late as 1956. The three-nave interior is graced with slender pillars and contains many art treasures, including 15th- and 16th-century sculptures by the Gagini brothers. Seek out, in particular, the lovely *Madonna del Popolo* in the right transept, a 1490 creation of Domenico Gagini.

In back of the Chiesa Madre is the entrance to **Museo degli Arazzi,** Via Garraffa 57(© **0923-712903**), open Monday through Saturday from 9am to 1pm and 4 to 6pm, Sunday from 9am to 1pm; admission is 1.50€ ($1.80). Its main attraction is a collection of eight **Flemish tapestries** ✿, made in Brussels between 1530 and 1550. The skillfully created tapestries depict such scenes as the capture of Jerusalem and the war fought by Titus against the Jews in A.D. 66 to 67.

Marsala's other major museum, **Museo Archeologico di Baglio Anselmi,** at Lungomare Boéo (© **0923-952535**), is open daily from 9am to 1:30pm, plus Wednesday and Friday through Sunday from 4 to 7pm. Admission is 2.10€ ($2.50). The museum is installed in a former warehouse for bottles of Marsala. Its chief attraction is the remains of a well-preserved **Punic ship** ✿ discovered in 1971 off Isola Longa, north of Marsala. It measures 35m (115 ft.) long and was artfully reconstructed in 1980. The ship may have been originally constructed for the Battle of the Egadi Islands in 241 B.C.; it's amazing to think that a vessel dating back to the First Punic War is still around in any form. Once manned by 68 oarsmen, this is the only known such war vessel ever uncovered.

Open for a look 24 hours a day is the **Insula di Capo Boeo,** at the end of Viale Vittorio Emanuele. Here are the ruins of a trio of Roman *insulae* (apartment complexes), including that of a spacious villa dating from the 3rd century B.C. Around the *impluvium* (basin built into the floor) you can see a quartet of mosaics depicting "The Battle of the Wild Beasts." Also here are the ruins of *terme* (baths) and salons containing mosaics. The head of Medusa is clearly visible.

Don't Even Mention Port in This Town

If you'd like to watch Marsala grapes crushed and turned into the town's "sweet nectar," Marsala wine, head for the **Cantine Florio,** Lungomare Via Florio (© **0923-781111**), which offers free guided tours of the winery. The 30-minute tours are offered Monday and Thursday at 11am and 3:30pm, Friday at 11am.

Devotees of Marsala also flock to **Cantina Sperimentale Istituto Regionale della Vite e del Vino,** Via Trapani 218 (© **0923-737511**), open daily from 7:30am to 2pm and Tuesday and Wednesday from 3 to 7pm. You are allowed to sample a number of experimental wines here.

SHOPPING

Oviesse　Set within about a block from the town's showcase church (Chiesa Madre), this is the department store that every local resident knows. Its enormous inventories include housewares, clothing, camping gear, and gift items. It's the kind of mass-market department store where you can acquire whatever objects you might have lost or forgotten on your way to Marsala, usually at prices a lot less expensive than in smaller but more stylish boutiques. Via Sebastiano Cammereri Scurti. © **0923-951767.**

WHERE TO STAY

Delfino Beach Hotel　Although not fully complete, this is the closest thing to a large-scale resort in Marsala. Set 5km (3 miles) south of town, behind a neobaroque facade across a busy highway from the beach, it was designed as a compound of cement-sided buildings within a walled garden, centered on a splashy-looking core that evokes a highly theatrical stage setting. Regrettably, part of the original dream here went sour, and there's a sense of incompleteness about the place thanks to the scaffolding, piles of sand, cement mixers, and occasional clouds of dust.

　　Plans originally called for the construction of 100 rooms and enough amenities to afford the hotel a government-rated four-star status, but in its present state, tourist authorities have given it only three stars. The existing accommodations include 16 apartments located near the main building. The hotel restaurant (p. 303)—which is better maintained and more pulled together than the hotel itself—and its beachfront lie a dusty 10-minute walk across the busy highway from the hotel's core. Frankly, despite the Vegas-inspired pool and nearby access to the beach, we prefer the Hotel President (see below), closer to the center of town.

Lungomare Mediterraneo 672, 91025 Marsala. © **0923-751076.** Fax 0923-751647. www. delfinobeach.com. 50 units. 83€–115€ ($100–$138) double. Rates include breakfast. AE, DC, MC, V. **Amenities:** Restaurant; bar; outdoor pool; laundry service. *In room:* A/C, TV, dataport, minibar, hair dryer.

Hotel Acos　This boxy-looking, government-rated three-star hotel was originally built in 1959 as a member of the now-defunct AGIP chain. It's set in back of a gas station on one of the town's busiest boulevards, on the south side of Marsala's commercial core. Favored by business travelers, it has a serviceable but not at all stylish lobby with a cramped coffee bar in one corner, and an unpretentious restaurant (**San Carlo**) immediately adjacent. The small to midsize guest rooms were renovated in 2000 and feature efficient contemporary furniture and tiled bathrooms, mostly with shower-tub combinations.

Via Mazara 14, 91025 Marsala. © **0923-999015.** Fax 0923-999132. www.acoshotel.com. 41 units. 75€ ($90) double; 105€ ($126) suite. Rates include breakfast. AE, DC, MC, V. **Amenities:** Restaurant; bar; laundry service. *In room:* A/C, TV, minibar.

Hotel President ♠　Modern and pleasingly designed, this is Marsala's best and most prestigious hotel, with a whiff of jazzy insouciance that might have been inspired by Las Vegas. You may be surprised to learn that this favorite stopover of business travelers is rated only three stars by the local tourist authorities, since it looks very much like it deserves four. The entrance is prefaced with a row of palms; inside, a sheathing of travertine marble adds a touch of sober dignity. Guest rooms are located in two five-story towers, connected at the bases by a granite-floored lobby strewn with leather sofas and chairs. Guest rooms are comfortable, sunny, and relatively large, each with a bathroom that—with three separate kinds of marble sheathing and shower-tub combinations—looks like a testimonial to the stonemason's art.

Via Nino Bixio 1, 91025 Marsala. ℂ 0923-99333. Fax 0923-999115. 128 units. 126€ ($151) double and suites. AE, DC, MC, V. **Amenities:** Restaurant; 2 bars; outdoor pool; health club; room service. *In room:* A/C, TV, minibar.

WHERE TO DINE

Ristorante Delfino *✿* SEAFOOD/SICILIAN   This restaurant lies adjacent to the beachfront and across the highway from the hotel that bears the same name. It was established in the 1960s and has done rip-roaring business ever since. The setting is a very large, always bustling series of terrazzo-floored, slightly battered dining rooms, with a row of large windows and a terrace overlooking the sea. A huge array of antipasti, plus a steamy hardworking kitchen that's open to view, greet visitors as they enter. The fish soup is the best in town, but the homemade *bucatini* pasta in a tuna and mint sauce may be your starter of choice. Several kinds of carpaccio, often flavored with balsamic vinegar, are presented nightly. The chef is justifiably proudest of his wide variety of fresh fish, much of which is exhibited in a display case near the entrance.

Delfino Beach Hotel, Lungomare Mediterraneo 672, 91025 Marsala. ℂ 0923-998188. Reservations not necessary. Main courses 8€–16€ ($9.60–$19); pizzas 4€–7€ ($4.80–$8.40); set menu 15€ ($18). AE, MC, V. Daily 8:30am–11pm. Closed Tues Oct–Mar.

Tenuta Volpara *✿* *Finds* SICILIAN   Follow a labyrinth of winding country roads, then pass between a stately pair of masonry columns, to reach Marsala's quintessential country inn—a jumble of light, noise, and energy in an otherwise isolated rural setting, 5.6km (3½ miles) south of the city center. Vast and echoing, with one of the largest dining rooms in western Sicily, it was rebuilt in 1993 on the site of a ruined tavern that had been here for centuries. Many of your fellow diners might be here as part of a wedding reception or baptism, which adds to this place's sense of fun. Beneath soaring stone arches, you'll dine on such items as steak braised in a Barolo wine sauce, homemade sausages roasted with an herb-flavored liqueur, fettuccine with fresh mushrooms, and the dessert specialty, *zabina,* a pastry laced with ricotta cheese.

Situated in an annex somewhat removed from the bustle of the restaurant are 18 motel-style guest rooms, each with a shower-only bathroom, air-conditioning, minibar, TV, and phone. With breakfast included, a double costs 65€ ($78).

Contrada Volpara. ℂ 0923-984588. Fax 0923-984667. Reservations recommended Fri–Sat nights. Main courses 5€–10€ ($6–$12); set-price menu 20€ ($24). AE, DC, MC, V. Daily 1:30–3pm and 8:30pm–midnight. Closed Mon Oct–Mar.

Trattoria Garibaldi *Value* SICILIAN/SEAFOOD   Located in the historic center near the cathedral, this unpretentious restaurant has been feeding locals well since 1963. Patrons come here, some once or twice weekly, to enjoy the dishes, which despite their low prices are made with fresh, quality ingredients. The chef is justly proud of his array of antipasti, including succulent mussels and sea urchins, the latter dish an acquired taste for many. We especially like his *bisiate* (a local homemade pasta) served with fresh fish. He also does a couscous with fish, inspired by Morocco across the sea. The signature dessert is *Cappidruzzi,* fried ravioli filled with ricotta. There's also an impressive list of Sicilian wines, all at affordable prices.

Piazza dell'Addolorata 35. ℂ **0923-953006.** Reservations recommended. Main courses 5€–11€ ($6–$13). MC, V. Mon–Fri noon–3pm and 7:30–10pm; Sat 7:30–10pm; Sun noon–3pm.

IN THE ENVIRONS

Trattoria delle Cozze Basirico *★ Finds* SEAFOOD   Set on the southern outskirts of the town of Mazara del Vallo, about 5km (3 miles) from the center, this restaurant might remind you of an oversize railway car that just happens to serve vast amounts of seafood to hundreds of diners every night throughout the summer. Don't expect grandeur; this is a gutsy, two-fisted place whose walls are open to the sea breezes. The overworked staff is coyly clad in exaggerated sailor costumes. There are no printed menus here: A fast-talking waiter will tell you that the only options are selections from the buffet-style antipasti table, several different preparations of mussels, and steamed octopus in either lemon or tomato sauce. Drinks of choice include wine or beer, a suitable accompaniment for the restaurant's widely acknowledged specialty, mussels.

Litoranca Bocca-Torretta. ℂ **0923-942323.** Reservations not accepted. Main courses 7€–20€ ($8.40–$24). AE, DC, MC, V. May–Sept daily 8pm–midnight. Closed Oct–Apr. Mazara del Vallo is reached by heading southeast of Marsala along Route 115 for 22km (13½ miles).

MARSALA AFTER DARK

Many locals, especially young people, drop in at **E & N Café,** Via XI Maggio 130 (ℂ **0923-951969**), if for no other reason than to enjoy the most delectable cannoli in town. Located on the most important commercial street of the historic center, the cafe is a bit small, but inviting. It's known for its *tavola calda* (panini, fresh rolls, and the like), as well as for its delicious ice creams. Note the showcase of marzipan fruit, which the friendly staff will convert into a "marzipan smoothie" for you. Four tables are placed outside, where you can sit and watch Marsala parade in front of you. In fair weather, the cafe is open daily from 7:30am to 2am, which is considered very, very late for sleepy Marsala. In winter, hours are Thursday through Tuesday from 7:30am to 11pm.

Appendix A:
Sicily in Depth

Sicily is a land unto itself, proudly different from the rest of Italy in its customs and traditions. On the map, in fact, the toe of the Italian boot appears poised to kick Sicily away from the mainland, as if it didn't belong to the rest of the country. The largest of the Mediterranean islands, it's separated from Italy by the 4km (2½-mile) Straits of Messina, a dangerously unstable earthquake zone, making the eventual construction of a bridge doubtful.

Although the island's economy is moving closer to those of Europe and the rest of Italy, its culture is still very much its own. Its vague Arab flavor reminds us that Sicily broke away from the mainland of Africa, *not* Italy, millions of years ago. Its Greek heritage lives on as well. Although there are far too many cars in Palermo, and parts of the island are heavily polluted by industrialization, Sicily is still a place where life is slower, tradition is respected, and the myths and legends of the past aren't yet forgotten.

Sicily has been inhabited since the Ice Age, and its history is full of natural and political disasters. It has been conquered and occupied over and over: by the Greeks in the 6th to 5th centuries B.C., then the Romans, the Vandals, the Arabs (who created a splendid civilization), the Normans, the Swabians, the fanatically religious House of Aragón, and the Bourbons. When Garibaldi landed at Marsala in 1860, he brought an illusion of freedom, soon dissipated by the patronage system of the Mafia. Besides the invaders, the centuries have brought a series of plagues, volcanic eruptions, earthquakes, and economic hardships to threaten the interwoven culture of Sicily.

The land has a deep archaeological heritage and is full of sensual sights and experiences: verdant vineyards and fragrant citrus groves, horses with plumes and bells pulling gaily painted carts, masses of blooming almond and cherry trees in February, Greek temples, ancient theaters, complex city architecture, and aromatic Marsala wine. In summer, the *sirocco* (hot wind) whirling out of the Libyan deserts dries the fertile fields, crisping the harvest into a sun-blasted palette of browns. Beaches are plentiful around the island, but most are rocky, crowded, or dirty. The best are at Mondello, outside Palermo, and around Taormina in the east.

1 The Natural Environment

Of all the islands of the Mediterranean, Sicily is the largest, spread across 40,965km (25,398 miles), and lying halfway between Gibraltar and the Suez Canal. It is surrounded by several archipelagos, the most important of which are the Aeolian Islands (see chapter 7), with such touristed spots as Stromboli, Lipari, and Vulcano. Other island groups include Egadi, Pantelleria, and Pelagie, the latter centered at Lampedusa.

Bounded by the Tyrrhenian Sea to its north, the Sicilian Sea to its southwest, and the Ionian Sea on its eastern coast, Sicily is separated from southern Italy by the Straits of Messina. Though it's the country's largest region, Sicily is only the fourth highest in population.

Impressions

To have seen Italy without having seen Sicily is not to have seen Italy at all, for Sicily is the clue to everything.

—Johann Wolfgang von Goethe

Sicily enjoys a Mediterranean climate—it's the first part of Italy to heat up in the spring and the last to grow chilly in winter. It also suffers the longest, hottest summers, with July a scorcher.

An island of rivers, Sicily is also volcanic, the most threatening menace being Mount Etna, on the eastern coast. Some of the islands in the various archipelagos also have volcanoes, notably Stromboli, but most are long dormant.

The island is split by four mountain groups. First and foremost are the so-called "Sicilian Alps," the Apennines, actually a continuation of the same mountain range that begins in Calabria on the mainland. These mountains stretch along the north coast, beginning at the Straits of Messina and going west to the Torto River. The Apennines are divided into a trio of ranges, including Peloritani, Nebrodi, and Madonie. Of the three, we recommend at least an exploration of Madonie, the most fascinating for touring.

Another mountain range is found in western Sicily to the west of the Platani and Torto rivers. The third member of the trio lies at the core of Sicily, looking out to the coast of North Africa 140km (87 miles) away, scene of so many embarkations of island conquerors. The southern and western half of Sicily, in terms of topography, is more similar to the Atlas Mountains of North Africa than the Sicilian mainland.

The ancient Greeks, among the first major settlers, called Sicily *Trinacria,* or triangle, because of its triangular shape. The island coastline covers much ground, a distance of 1,000km (621 miles). The smoothest and most uninterrupted flank stretches from the Straits of Messina to the Gulf of Palermo, overlooking the city of Palermo, Sicily's capital. The southern coast begins in the southeast at Capo Passero on the Golfo di Noto and heads west along the Golfo di Gela, coming to an end at Capo Lilibeo south of Marsala of winemaking fame.

The eastern coast, opening onto Mare Ionio, or the Ionian Sea, begins at Capo Passero and heads north to Messina, bypassing the cities of Catania and Syracuse. Gólfo di Catania is the most important body of water in the east, providing the island's largest plain with a seafront.

As the coastline nears Messina, it becomes a series of towering cliffs broken up by a network of craggy inlets. For the visitor, the most stunning sea- and landscapes are found around the resort of Taormina and the small city of Acireale, north of Catania.

FLORA & FAUNA   The deforestation of the island has been a disaster since as far back as Roman times. Once rich in forests that provided it with abundant water, Sicily had vast tracts of woodland razed over the years to turn the island into the grain belt of the Roman Empire. This massive deforestation has left Sicily with a more foreboding climate—hot and dry.

The ancient Greek settlers brought with them the cultivation of the grape and the olive tree. The Arab conquerors brought date palms from Africa and encouraged the cultivation of citrus groves.

Typical Mediterranean flora, including the strawberry tree and myrtle, is found all over the island. Broom bushes set the countryside alive in spring, with miles of sunflower-yellow coloring. The spiny shrub, the so-called "bastard olive," grows wild almost everywhere.

Island fauna have been horrendously affected by the gradual deforestation of Sicily. Other than sheep grazing in country fields, it is rare to see much wildlife as you travel the country roads of Sicily. Along the coast, of course, there is still plenty of birdlife, notably cormorants and seagulls. The viper is the only poisonous snake on the island, frightening tourists as it suns itself at various archaeological sites in summer.

The western coast dwellers of Sicily, who for centuries have depended on the mammoth schools of tuna for their livelihoods, are now facing diminishing returns. Huge Japanese trawlers in international waters are capturing more and more of these fish for shipment to the markets of Tokyo.

2 History 101: Past & Present

EARLY COLONIZERS

Of the Mediterranean, Plato wrote that conquerors flocked to its coastline like "frogs gathering at a pond"—an apt comparison for Sicily itself. Much of the history of this largest of Mediterranean islands is unknown. Perhaps many tales from the *Odyssey* were set in what is now Sicily, adding to its allure as a land of myth and legend.

For 6,000 years, conquerors from both Europe and Africa have tried to turn Sicily into a colony. Sicilians are so used to foreign occupation that the most nationalistic of islanders even today believe they are living under "occupation" by mainland Italy and under the control of Rome.

Archaeology provides much of the evidence of early colonization. Of course, indigenous people already existed on Sicily when the Greeks arrived. The Siculi people, for whom Sicily was named, came from the Calabria peninsula on the mainland, settling in the eastern and southern central parts of the island. Tribes of Sicani from Iberia occupied the western frontiers, and the people of Elimi, claiming descent from the Trojans, inhabited the medieval hilltop town of Erice, on the west coast.

Dateline

- **734 B.C.** Corinthians found Syracuse.
- **480 B.C.** Syracusans overrun the Carthaginian beachhead at the Battle of Himera.
- **415 B.C.** Athens sails a Great Armada against Syracuse but is defeated.
- **409 B.C.** Carthage attacks and destroys Selinunte and Himera.
- **211 B.C.** Syracuse is sacked as Romans declare victory.
- **535** Belisarius annexes Sicily to the Eastern Roman Empire.
- **827** Saracens' invasion of Sicily launched.
- **1032** Roger seizes Palermo, launching the Norman dynasty.
- **1190–97** Henry, a Hohenstaufen, rules Sicily after defeating the Normans.
- **1231** Frederick II issues the anti-feudal Constitution of Melfi.
- **1282** A rebellion—the so-called Sicilian Vespers—breaks out in Palermo, spreading across the island.
- **1302** Peace treaty between the Angevins and the Aragonese gives Sicily to the Spaniards.
- **1513** Spanish Inquisition introduced.
- **1693** Earthquake destroys much of eastern Sicily, including Catania.
- **1713** Treaty of Utrecht assigns Sicily to House of Savoy.

continues

Arriving from Carthage, the Phoenicians—the last of the pre-Hellenistic invaders—settled into Solunto near present-day Palermo. The ruins of their settlement can be explored today (p. 120). The Phoenicians also founded Palermo, the capital of Sicily, calling it *Panormus.* The Chalcidians landed in the east to establish what is modern-day Messina, and the Megarians founded the colony of Megara Hyblaea, the ruins of which can be explored north of Syracuse, once you pass through an industrial blight.

In time these tribes came in for Hellenization. Naxos, near today's Taormina, was launched around 735 B.C. by mariners, a group of Chalcidians from Greece. You can explore these ruins today (p. 197). Around the same time (734 B.C.), the Corinthians laid the first stones on the island of Ortygia, calling their city *Syracoussai,* which in time became today's Syracuse.

North of Syracuse, Megara Hyblaea (p. 255) was founded in 728 B.C., followed in 628 B.C. by the founding of Selinunte (p. 285), still among the great archaeological ruins of Sicily. The last of the great Greek cities, Agrigento, was founded in 581 B.C., its Valley of the Temples today remaining one of the great attractions of southern Italy (p. 274).

- **1734** Spanish reclaim Sicily under Bourbon king, Charles I.
- **1812** A liberal constitution spells the doom of the feudal system.
- **1816** Ferdinand abrogates the constitution, creates Kingdom of the Two Sicilies.
- **1860** Garibaldi's forces chase out the Bourbons, as Sicilians vote for unification.
- **1908** Earthquake in Messina takes 80,000 lives.
- **1943** Allied armies under Patton and Montgomery capture Sicily from the Nazis.
- **1946** Sicily granted limited independence.
- **1951** A massive immigration from the island begins, eventually totaling one million Sicilians.
- **1980s–1990s** In spite of a campaign against it by the government, the Mafia maintains a strong influence on the island.
- **2002** Mount Etna announces itself once again, belching smoke and fire and threatening tourist facilities near Catania.
- **2004** Sicilian Mafia rebuilds, but faces competition from Calabria.

The growing power of Carthage in North Africa brought fear to Sicily. By the 7th century B.C., Carthage had allied itself with the Phoenicians against the Greek settlers. The colonies of Magna Graecia, or Greater Greece, thrived on trade. As the Greek colonies grew more powerful in Sicily, they fought each other out of greed and jealousy—all of which laid the groundwork for the "rule of the tyrants."

THE RULE OF THE TYRANTS

In ancient times, the word "tyrant" described men who grabbed power instead of inheriting it, as in a royal lineage. Tyrants ruled over the Greek city-states of Sicily. The year 480 B.C. proved pivotal in the island's history. That was when the Carthaginians mounted a massive attack on the western possessions of Greece, including Sicily. Hamilcar, the African commander, sailed into Sicily's northern coast with an army of 300,000 mercenaries carried in 3,000 transport ships. The Carthaginian general besieged Himera outside Termini Imerese, and the tyrant of the area, Thereon, appealed to Syracuse for help. Syracuse sent 55,000 men marching across the heart of Sicily. Hamilcar asked for help from Selinunte on the south coast.

The Carthaginians fell for a variation of the old Trojan horse trick, mistaking the Syracuse forces for reinforcements from Selinunte. When their ranks opened, some 150,000 soldiers were slain and their ships torched. As a result, the winner of that battle, Gelon, the tyrant of Syracuse, became a towering figure in the Greek world. Seven decades would pass before Carthage would return to pillage Sicily.

The defeat of the Carthaginians led to a golden age for Sicily, as such classical figures as Archimedes, Theocritus, and Empedocles became household names. Plato and Aeschylus dropped in from Greece. The largest of the Greek temples were constructed in Agrigento, the biggest amphitheater in Syracuse. The period of growth and expansion was set back only by infighting among the city-states.

Syracuse was clearly the dominant power in Sicily, so much so that it dared challenge the supremacy of Athens itself. In response, in 415 B.C. Athens sent the largest armada ever assembled to subdue Syracuse. The Great Expedition from the east met with failure, and 7,000 soldiers from Athens were taken prisoner. The great city of Syracuse reached the apex of its power.

THE REVENGE OF CARTHAGE

The grandson of the defeated Hamilcar, the great Hannibal, arrived on the southern coast of Sicily with his mercenaries in 409 B.C., seeking revenge over his ancestor's defeat at Himera on the northern coast. He destroyed what had been a great city, Selinunte, its modern-day ruins a testament to his victory. Selinunte faded into history forever.

Hannibal then headed north to seek his revenge against Himera, where his grandfather had been defeated. He won a great victory and tortured and murdered all the male survivors of Himera.

Hannibal came back in full force once again, and in 406 B.C destroyed Agrigento (then called *Akragas*). At the time, Akragas was surpassed only by Syracuse in power and influence. During the siege a plague swept through his camp, and Hannibal succumbed to it. His successor, Himilkon, took over for the Carthaginians, offering his son, Moloch, as a sacrifice to the gods to show he meant business. After 8 months of siege, Akragas fell to the Carthaginians.

Blaming the generals in Syracuse for the defeat of Akragas, the demagogue Dionysius seized power in 405 B.C. and became one of the most famous of all the tyrants. The Carthaginians moved on Syracuse, but the plague swept over their forces and the remaining army returned to Africa.

THE ROMANS IN SICILY

The Greek hold over Sicily was coming to an end. With Carthage subdued, a new menace rose to threaten imperial Sicily: Rome. Sicily was largely spared during the First Punic War (264–241 B.C.), but the people of Syracuse sided with Carthage during the Second Punic War, in 213 B.C. For this, the newly emerged powers of Rome did not forgive Sicily, and in 211 B.C. the Romans conquered the island. In its defeat, Sicily became a "sub-colony," and the formerly proud inhabitants of the island became slaves or servants, living in poverty. Slave revolts broke out periodically but were brutally suppressed by the Romans, who used the island as a breadbasket after felling its trees.

In the 3rd century A.D., when Sicilians were finally granted citizenship in the Roman Empire, it was a little late. The barbarians from the north were on the march.

BARBARIANS, BYZANTINES & THE SARACENS

As the Roman Empire collapsed to the invading Visigoths in A.D. 410, Sicily came under increasing attack from the Vandals, who launched warships from the coastline of Tunisia. The barbarian invasion of the island was short-lived, but for a while Sicily was temporarily reunited with Italy under the Ostrogoth Theodoric.

In A.D. 535, the Byzantine general Belisarius occupied Sicily. Amazingly, for a brief time in A.D. 663 Syracuse became the center of the eastern Byzantine empire.

The Arabs, Berbers, and Spanish Muslims—known collectively as the Saracens—had become increasingly attracted to the prize of Sicily. By 700, the island of Pantelleria had fallen to them. By 827, a full-fledged Arab invasion of Sicily was successfully mounted. Their landing was at Mazara del Vallo, in the south. Four years later, Palermo fell to the Saracens, and by A.D. 965, the invading African forces had moved east to the Straits of Messina.

The Arabs made Palermo the capital of their new Sicilian empire, decorating it with gardens, mosques (some 300 in all), palaces, and domes. Unlike the Roman occupation, Sicily actually prospered under the Arab rulers, who made substantial breakthroughs in agriculture, introducing citrus trees, date palms, cotton, and other crops. Even religious tolerance was practiced, and many Christians abandoned their faith to Muslim beliefs.

But the Saracen rule, like so many others, would be short-lived. Because of internal Arab bickering, the Byzantine general George Maniakes decided that Sicily once again was ripe to be plucked. Although his forces never got much beyond Syracuse, a new menace loomed: The Normans were about to move in on Sicily, an island they regarded as a glittering prize.

THE MEN OF THE NORTH

If a visitor should wonder why there are so many blondes in Sicily today, it's because of the Norman conquest of the island. In 1061, an Arab emir in Messina called on Roger Hauteville for help in putting down a rebellion among fellow Saracens. Big mistake. The Normans came, they saw, and they conquered, although it took them another 3 decades to subdue the entire island.

Amazingly, the Normans sometimes enlisted the aid of the resident Arabs to fight other Arabs. At one of the series of bloody battles, the Normans ended up firmly entrenched in Palermo, making it their capital in 1072.

Although the Normans were to stay less than a century, ruling with a series of five kings, they left an architectural legacy that remains a distinctive feature on the Sicilian landscape, especially in Palermo. Sometimes they took over an already existing Arab mosque and turned it into an "Arabo-Norman" style of church. By 1200, the Arabic language was fading, giving way to French and Italian.

Count Roger or Roger I (1031–1101) launched the Norman-Sicilian dynasty. He was followed by Roger II (1105–54), one of the great kings of Europe in the Middle Ages, who brought together some of the most creative forces in the Mediterranean and who was also a big patron of the arts. In addition, he extended his Sicilian kingdom to embrace parts of North Africa, southern Italy, and Malta. Weaker kings, such as William the Bad (1154–66), followed.

THE REIGN OF THE HOHENSTAUFENS

When the Norman king, William II (1166–89)—called William the Good—died in 1189 at the age of 36, the throne went to Tancred, his illegitimate son. The ascension to the throne was challenged by King Henry VI, a German Hohenstaufen, or Swabian. Tancred hung on until his death in 1194, surviving a sacking of Messina in 1190 by Richard the Lion-Hearted on his way to join the Third Crusade.

William III succeeded Tancred, but the Hohenstaufen fleet docked at Messina, and the short-term king was imprisoned and would eventually die in a castle. Henry (later to become the Holy Roman Emperor Henry VI) was declared king of Sicily in 1190.

Henry was to die of dysentery in 1197, the throne passing to Frederick I of Sicily, his son, who was only 3 years old. His mother, Constance, ruled for him. When he grew up, he proved to be a strong king, especially against such island rebels as the Arabs. As a promoter of science, medicine, and law, he was called *Stupor Mundi,* or "Wonder of the World." Under Frederick, Palermo became the most important city in Europe, a cultural center with no equal in the Western world. In 1231, he issued the anti-feudal Constitution of Melfi, stripping the barons of much of their power. At his death in 1250, Sicily entered a period of decline.

A French pope eventually awarded the title of King of Sicily to Charles of Anjou, the brother of Louis IX, the French king. Under Charles, in 1266 Angevin forces fought and beat the armies of the Hohenstaufen rulers. Once in power, Charles of Anjou launched a punishing attack against those islanders who had supported the Hohenstaufens.

THE WAR OF THE VESPERS

The abject poverty and the stern rule of the Angevins sparked an uprising, known as the Sicilian Vespers, which began on Easter Sunday 1282. What sparked the uprising is not known for certain. One story has it that a gang of French troops raped a teenage girl; another that a French soldier insulted a local woman in Palermo.

At any rate, the tolling of a church bell for evening services, or Vespers, at the Chiesa di Santo Spirito set off a riot. Every French soldier in sight was slaughtered, the rebellion fanning out to eventually cover the island. Any Frenchman unable to pronounce the word *cicero* correctly was massacred.

There were many patriots, to be sure, but the general rioting and slaughter was also a time for many islanders to settle old scores with their enemies. A group of noblemen called upon Peter of Aragon for help. He landed in Tripani 5 months after that initial violent outbreak on Easter Sunday. In only a few days, he was proclaimed king.

The actual War of the Vespers was fought between the armies of Aragon and the forces of Angevin, who used Naples as their base. It was to last for 21 years. Slowly but effectively, Spain tightened its noose around Sicily. The rope would not be untied for 5 centuries.

RULE BY THE SPANIARDS

In 1302, the Peace of Caltabelotta concluded the war between the Vatican-leaning Angevins and the imperial Aragonese. Sicily was divided into two kingdoms, the Angevins retaining the territories in mainland Italy (such as Naples), but with Sicily itself going to the Spaniards. The Aragonese kings, based in Palermo, would rule the island directly until 1458.

Isolated in the Mediterranean, Sicily virtually "sat out" the great artistic and cultural movements sweeping mainland Europe in the 14th and 15th centuries. The Renaissance of Italy had virtually no impact in forgotten Sicily. Only one great artist arose from this depression: Antonello da Messina (1430–79), who had been inspired by Flemish art during his travels to the north.

If anything, feudal bonds were tightened as Sicily drifted back into the Middle Ages. The Spanish Inquisition, introduced to Sicily in 1513, virtually silenced any inquiring minds.

THE 17TH & 18TH CENTURIES

As Spain drifted into its own long decline in the 17th and 18th centuries, so did its colony of Sicily, ruled by indifferent viceroys. Political corruption was rampant throughout the land.

In the hinterlands of Sicily, brigand bands, protesting against vast estates and their cruel owners, rose up to strike back. Calling themselves the *Mafia,* these outlaws butchered livestock, burned crops, and slaughtered local bailiffs to protest the outmoded feudal system.

As if the feudal system and its inherent evils weren't enough, in the 17th century Sicily was plagued by natural disasters. Mount Etna erupted in 1669, causing massive damage to the east coast and destroying Catania. The eruption was followed in 1693 by earthquakes along the same coastline, which killed about 5% of Sicily's population. Sicily was also struck by outbreaks of the plague.

Politically, the island became a pawn among the powers of Europe. After the death of Charles II of Spain in 1700, that country was plunged into the Wars of the Spanish Succession. In 1713, Sicily passed into the hands of the House of Savoy, according to the terms of the Treaty of Utrecht. In 1720, it was traded to the Austrians for Sardinia.

The Spanish came back in full force in 1734, reclaiming Sicily and placing it under the Bourbon king Charles I (1734–59). Charles I was to visit Sicily only once. In time he gave up the kingdom to assume the title of King Charles III of Spain. He was followed by Ferdinand IV, who held power as Ferdinand IV of Naples in 1806. The island's so-called noblemen, living parasitically off the people of Sicily, tightened their feudal grips on the island, as new ideas unleashed by the French Revolution brought in winds of change.

THE COMING OF NAPOLEON

The little colonel, Napoleon, never actually invaded Sicily, although his rearranging of the maps of Europe had an impact on the island. When Napoleon conquered Naples in 1799, Ferdinand IV was forced out when the crown went to Napoleon's brother, Joseph. Ferdinand fled to Sicily, where he was protected by British troops. Under pressure from the island commander of British forces, Lord William Bentinck, Ferdinand was compelled in 1812 to draw up a constitution for Sicily similar to that which governed Britain.

This document spelled the death of the feudal life, as a two-chamber Sicilian Parliament was formed in Palermo. The court established in Palermo was to be free of the one presiding in Naples.

Once Napoleon was defeated in 1815, Ferdinand went back to Naples and abrogated the constitution. The British departed, and Ferdinand assumed control again, declaring himself Ferdinand I, King of the Two Sicilies (that is, Naples and Sicily) in 1816. He repealed all reforms.

In protest, Sicily rebelled, but the rebellion was put down with the aid of mercenaries from Austria. Ferdinand died in 1825, and conditions only worsened under Ferdinand II (1830–59), who was named *Re Bomba* after his 5-day bombardment of Messina to quell insurrections there and in Palermo in 1848. In spite of the failures of the rebellions, the spirit of revolution remained. By 1860, the name Garibaldi was being whispered across the island.

REVOLT & THE ARRIVAL OF GARIBALDI

On April 4, 1860, an island-wide revolt against the Bourbon regime broke out. Seizing upon the news, the revolutionary leader Giuseppe Garibaldi decided the time to strike was at hand. Along with his famous *mille,* 1,000 red-shirted soldiers, he arrived at Marsala on the west coast of Sicily on May 11, 1860. He set about to conquer the island, aided by the peasants who joined his army.

A Bourbon army of 15,000 soldiers was defeated at Calatafimi on May 15, and within 2 weeks the capital at Palermo had fallen. By the time Garibaldi declared victory at the port of Milazzo on July 20, the Bourbons were in serious retreat. For the first time since 1282, Sicily was no longer under the yoke of the Bourbon regime.

On October 21 of that same year, an island-wide referendum was conducted. The results were staggering. Some 99% of the voters had opted to follow Garibaldi's plan and unify with mainland Italy. Many poor Sicilians not allowed to vote were cynical of the results, viewing the Piedmontese House of Savoy as the new "occupier" of the island.

FASCISM & WARS

Under the House of Savoy, Sicily indeed found itself in the same poor position it had endured over the centuries under many conquerors. The so-called aristocracy remained firmly in charge of the economy, and the peasants got nothing, not even the right to vote. In 1866, Turin crushed a rebellion in Palermo, just as previous rulers had done.

The *Mafiosi,* which later became the dreaded Mafia of the 20th century, acted as regent for the bailiffs, or landowners, extracting exorbitant rents from the peasant farmers. In desperation, some 500,000 Sicilians felt compelled to leave the island to settle in Australia, North America, and South America. Many of these people came from Messina, which was devastated in the earthquake of 1908, with some 80,000 lives lost.

The 20th century brought more grim realities, with the Italian conquest of Libya in 1912, followed by World War I, which devastated the economy of Sicily and took the lives of many of its young men.

The aftermath of World War I, which Italy lost to the Allied victors, was followed in 1922 by the emergence of Benito Mussolini, who had gained power in Rome. The island of Sicily was anything but his bastion of power, so the Italian dictator decided to crack down on Sicily's *Mafiosi,* a move that simply drove the criminals underground.

Mussolini sent his agent Cesare Mori to restore law and order to Sicily. To do so, Mori won the support of the landed gentry. To reward these large estate holders for their help, he reversed all agrarian reforms of the past decades. Amazingly, by the 1920s Sicily found itself plunged back into a feudal system.

By the 1930s, Mussolini took a page from the ancient Roman conquerors' playbook and came to regard Sicily as a breadbasket to feed his armies in his quest for empire. Wheat production on the island increased, but at great expense to the land, which suffered from erosion and soil depletion.

Suddenly, Sicily found itself caught up in a new war, World War II. Softening it for an invasion with aerial bombardments, the Allies attacked most of Sicily's major cities. Catania, Messina, and Palermo were heavily bombed.

In July 1943, General Patton and the American Seventh Army landed at Gela on the southern coast, as Montgomery's British forces put ashore at a point to the east. The Sicilians offered little resistance, but the Nazis fought back with venom, hoping to delay the Allied advance until they could move their men and equipment across the Straits of Messina into Calabria.

Palermo fell to the Allied advance, followed by Messina. On September 3, as the Germans escaped to southern Italy, Sicilian authorities signed an armistice, becoming the first region of Italy to fall to the Allies, long before the invasion of

Normandy in 1944. Amazingly, the Allies were greatly helped by the Mafiosi, who were eager to rid Sicily of the Fascists who had tried to wipe them out.

49TH STATE FOR THE U.S.?

With the devastation of World War II behind it, Sicilians reviewed their modern link with the Italian mainland, with thousands deciding the union had been a disaster. A Separatist movement gained hold, demanding complete independence for the island.

Sicilian Communists called for massive land redistribution. In an unlikely marriage, the landed gentry allied itself with the Mafia to keep a lid on "dangerous left-wing uprisings" throughout the land.

In 1946, bowing to pressure, the government in Rome agreed to give Sicily limited independence. Regional autonomy called for Sicily to have its own assembly and president. The role would be similar to what Scotland enjoys with England.

Many of the Separatists were even lobbying to be linked to the United States, becoming the 49th state. But with the coming of the elections of 1951, the Separatists faded into history.

For most of the latter part of the 20th century, Sicily was dominated by the Christian Democrats. This is the party more or less of the Catholic church, with center-of-right leanings—a very conservative bunch. In an unspoken, almost hidden alliance, the Christian Democrats worked with the Mafia, as *clientilismo*—political patronage—became the rule of the land. Many a developmental fund ended up in the pocket of a Mafia don.

Even in the late 20th century and early 21st century, the Mafia has remained a strong influence on the island, in spite of a campaign against it by the governments presiding in the 1980s and 1990s. In 2004, the annual report to the Interior Ministry to the Parliament in Rome claimed that the Mafia in Sicily was experiencing "a moment of renewal to overcome a structural crisis following the arrest of many top-ranking elements." The report also concluded that the so-called *Cosa Nostra* was trying to "regain credibility and competitiveness." The Ministry report ominously concluded that the Cosa Nostra was pressing ahead with its traditional activities, such as gaining control of public-works contracts and practicing widespread extortion of Sicilian businesses for "protection" money.

Still, the more famous Cosa Nostra is facing competition from a rival syndicate: the 'ndrangheta of Calabria, that section of the mainland forming the "toe" of the Italian peninsula. Moving in on traditional Cosa Nostra territory, the 'ndrangheta has increased its hold on cocaine trafficking and has strong ties with Colombian drug cartels.

One novel approach to dealing with the Cosa Nostra is taking place in the town of Corleone, which gave its name to Marlon Brando's jowly don. Corleone has been confiscating the property of some of the more notorious Mafiosi and making this blood-soaked land bloom. Agronomists are planting melons, lentils, wheat, grapes, and chickpeas on estates once owned by the Mafia. And how is the mob striking back at this agricultural bounty? Retaliation has been relatively minor at this point; at one time, mob members let loose a herd of hungry sheep to devour wheat fields.

Looking forward, while it is estimated that some one million people left Sicily over a 20-year period beginning in 1951, today North Africans in hopes of a better life arrive by the boatload on such southern-tier islands as Lampedusa and Pantelleria.

3 Art & Architecture 101

For decades, scholars have claimed that if you want to uncover the history of Western civilization, you need look no further than the island of Sicily. The original melting pot is a showcase of art and architecture of the Mediterranean, as each conqueror brought a different style and artistic statement to the island over 10,000 years of history. From the earliest graffiti found in caves to the glorious Doric temples at Agrigento to the pinnacle of Sicilian baroque in Catania, each wave of civilization has left its mark. Sometimes the styles of two different occupiers have been uniquely blended—witness the marriage of Arabic and Norman art and architecture into an "Arabo-Norman" style.

The bad news is that much of Sicily's artistic legacy has been damaged by volcanic explosions, earthquakes, and a range of man-made forces, from Hannibal's invading troops from North Africa to the Allied bombardments of 1943, which routed the Nazi occupiers. Much that remains is threatened by decay.

The Mafia hasn't helped either. The looting of the island's treasures for sale abroad to wealthy, anonymous buyers has taken a vast toll on Sicily's artistic heritage.

PREHISTORIC ART

Artists have been at work in Sicily since prehistoric times, as rock paintings and graffiti discovered at Palermo and Messina reveal. Even in the Neolithic period, the first indigenous cultures, such as those who settled Lipari, were turning out artful **ceramics** and **terra cotta,** many of which remain to this day (see the Museo Archeologico Eoliano in Lipari, p. 162).

The most remarkable **cave paintings** were those found at Grotta del Genovese on Levanzo, one of the Egadi Islands off the western coast of Sicily. Discovered by accident in 1949, Paleolithic wall paintings and Neolithic drawings are anywhere from 6,000 to 10,000 years old. Most of the drawings are of wild animals, such as deer and horses. Even the mighty tuna traditionally found in these waters show up here.

THE LEGACY OF THE GREEKS

From the 8th century on, the Greeks settled Sicily in waves, leaving great contributions to architecture before they were replaced by other conquerors. Much of their heritage was destroyed by pillagers, but much still remains to delight us. The Greeks left a legacy of some of the best-preserved **temples** in the Western world, especially those at Agrigento in the Valley of the Temples, those in the ruined city of Selinunte, those in the archaeological gardens at Syracuse, and (best of all) the magnificent and still-standing Temple at Segesta. The temples constructed in Sicily were more innovative than even those of classical Greece.

The archaeological museums of Sicily are filled with artifacts from the Greek occupation: painted **ceramics** and **amphorae, sculptures** and **metopes,** and **bronzes** and **carved ornaments** for temple buildings.

The apogee, however, of Greek architectural contribution to Sicily is the **Doric temple,** which stood on a three-stepped base, its inner chamber housing a statue of the god to whom the temple was dedicated.

THE COMING OF THE ROMANS

Unlike the Greeks, the Romans did not leave a great artistic legacy in Sicily, except for the **Roman villa (Villa Romana)** at Casale, outside the town of Piazza Armerina (p. 270). The vast polychrome floor mosaics at this 40-room villa from the 3rd century A.D. are worth the trek across Sicily. Other traces of

Roman architecture can be found in the amphitheaters of Taormina and Syracuse, as well as in Syracuse's Christian catacombs.

ARTISTIC FLOWERING UNDER THE NORMANS

Subsequent conquerors such as the Byzantines and the Arabs made little artistic impact on Sicily until invited back by later conquerors, the Normans. The Byzantines transformed Greek temples into Christian basilicas, while the Arabs built palaces, private residences, and religious buildings with such Asian characteristics as domes piercing the roofs. The Arab-Norman artistic expression—called the Arab or "Arabo-Norman" style—represented a flowering of art and architecture.

From the 11th century on, the Normans began to transform Sicily, and much of their achievement remains today. This trio of different cultures—Norman, Arabic, and Byzantine—created what came to be called the "Sicilian Romanesque" style.

The Normans erected **cathedrals,** or **duomos.** Their achievements—the cathedrals at Monreale and Cefalù and the Palazzo dei Normanini in Palermo—remain among the greatest sightseeing attractions on the island today.

Roger II (1131–54) launched the first major Sicilian cathedral at Cefalù, using a Latin cross plan with a chevron pattern. Pointed arches and angled columns particular to Sicily, as opposed to mainland cathedrals, still characterize this landmark church. The mosaic decorations in its interior alone would make this one of Sicily's greatest churches.

The mosaics in the cathedral at Monreale are even more stunning and beautiful. It was at Monreale that Sicily reached the apex of its contribution to medieval art in Europe. The Monreale duomo also contains the most examples of Norman sculpture on the island, more than 200 slender columns with twin capitals. Each of these capitals is graced with a singular composition.

Palermo also has a splendid cathedral and important **churches** of the period, such as Martorana and San Giovanni degli Ermeti, along with the Arab-influenced **palaces** of La Cuba and La Zisa.

But the Normans lavished the most attention on the seat of their power, the mammoth Palazzo dei Normanni in Palermo. This sumptuous palace became the seat of the Hauteville dynasty. Using a palace originally constructed by the Arabs in the 9th century, the Normans greatly extended it between 1132 and 1140. The crowning architectural glory of this palace is the **Cappella Palatina (Palatine Chapel),** with its Arab-inspired cupola and a stunning modern honeycomb ceiling based on Arab designs.

With the passing of the Normans and the arrival of the Hohenstaufen rulers in the 13th century, the great flowering of Sicilian art slowly died. The Hohenstaufens were more interested in fortifications and castles than in art. The Dark Ages of Sicilian art had descended on the island and would last for 4 centuries.

SICILY SLEEPS THROUGH THE RENAISSANCE

At the height of the Renaissance, Sicily remained under Spanish occupation. That may explain why Sicily virtually slept through the Renaissance, which began in Florence and swept across the rest of Italy. Although no great architectural heritage remains in Sicily from this era, painting and sculpture dominated the artistic firmament, revealing mainly Spanish but also Flemish influences.

Sicily's greatest artist, **Antonello da Messina** (1430–79), emerged during this period, initially inspired by the Flemish school and later showing the influence of his encounters with Piero della Francesca and Giovanni Bellini in Venice. One painting more than any other exemplifies his work: *Portrait of an Unknown Man,* in the Cefalù Museo Mandralisca. His other notable works, the greatest of Renaissance art in Sicily, are the *Polyptych of St. Gregory,* in the Museo Regionale in Messina, and the *Annunciation,* in the Palazzo Bellomo in Syracuse.

The **Gagini family** of sculptors and architects moved down from Lake Lugano and had an enormous impact on Sicily. The founding father of the Gagini school was Domenico Gagini (1420–92), who often worked in conjunction with his son, Antonello, born in Palermo in 1478. Their sculpture still adorns many of the churches of Palermo, and a Gagini school flourished in Sicily until the mid-1600s.

THE EXPLOSION OF THE BAROQUE

The baroque style swept Sicily, awakening the island from a long slumber since the Normans departed centuries earlier. That observer of all things Italian, Luigi Barzini, saw the baroque as a metaphor for "a frenzied search for consolation and revenge against crude and overbearing foreign devils."

The baroque came into vogue as a result of a devastating earthquake in 1693 in eastern Sicily that leveled such cities as Catania. The style of their reconstruction was baroque, whose founding father in Sicily was **Rosario Gagliardi** (1700–70). He designed the magnificent **Cattedrale San Giorgio** at Ragusa Ibla. Islanders combined the Spanish-inspired version of the baroque with Sicilian decorative and structural elements to create their own unique style.

The baroque city that emerged after the earthquake in Catania was created in part by **Giovanni Battista Vaccarini** (1702–69), who devoted 3 decades of his life to pulling a new Catania out of the ashes.

Noto, in southeastern Sicily, is another city that was rebuilt in the baroque style after the earthquake. The unity of the baroque style here remains unequaled anywhere else on the island.

In the west in Palermo, the baroque style came under the influence of Spanish dons who preferred *Spagnolismo,* or a love of ostentation. The **Quattro Canti** crossroads of the city remains today as the most lavish example of the dons' taste for overly adorned squares and streets. Private palaces, or palazzi, were also richly adorned, with sculptures ranging from angels to nymphs to gargoyles.

The master of the Palermitan oratories, **Giacomo Serpotta,** born in Palermo in 1656, specialized in adorning church oratories with molded plasterwork in ornamental frames. You can see one of his masterpieces today, Palermo's **Oratory of the Rosary,** in the church of Santa Zita—about which the author Paul Duncan once claimed: "You can almost hear the chortling, farting, and giggling of the *putti*."

CONTEMPORARY ART

Now that the 20th century has ended, it can safely be said that few books will be written on modern art and artists in Sicily. The one exception is **Renato Guttuso** (1911–87). Painting in a style often called visceral, Guttuso became renowned around the world for his nudes, landscapes, and still lifes. Visitors to Palermo today need only drive just outside the city to the **Galleria Comunale d'Arte Moderna e Contemporanea,** at the town of Bagheira (p. 118), to see the best examples of Guttuso's work as well as his on-site tomb.

4 La Cucina Siciliana

Good food is one of the main reasons to go to Sicily, especially now that the so-called "Mediterranean diet"—a cuisine comprised of fresh vegetables, fruit, fish, and olive oil—is being touted as healthy fare. But few heart-healthy diets are as enchanting as Sicilian fare, whether served up in modest trattorie or star kitchens.

A MELTING-POT CUISINE

Island fare is a blend of the cuisines of Sicily's many conquerors and cultures. The lush citrus groves around Catania were originally planted by the Arabs. Even those magnificently intricate pastries and rich desserts are a direct result of the Arab invasions, which brought a taste of North Africa to the shores of Catania.

In time, subsequent invaders, including Norman rulers and Spanish viceroys, left their own legacy of "aristocratic food," often as part of huge banquets prepared by enormous staffs and presented by a legion of servants. These extravagant excesses were in direct contrast to the diet of the fishermen, the land-tillers, and other working people who set a simple table based mainly on fish and the bountiful harvest of vegetables from the Sicilian countryside.

THE TYPICAL SICILIAN DIET

Sicily is blessed with some of the finest raw culinary materials in Italy. Using this incredible array of fresh ingredients from the sea and field, the chefs of Sicily fashion a delectable display of enticing platters, many of them better and more original than those found anywhere on the mainland of Italy.

STARTERS   Sicilian antipasti make a fine meal by themselves. Our favorite opening to a meal is the island specialty *caponata,* eggplant and caper salad. It's made with eggplants, sweet bell peppers, cauliflower, fresh tomatoes, olives, fat capers, onions, and celery in a sweet-and-sour sauce of vinegar and sugar.

Another savory starter is *arancini di riso,* little rice balls stuffed with peas, cheese, and meat, then coated with bread crumbs and deep-fried. These rice balls are strangely addictive, as is *bottarga,* the dried and salted roe of gray mullet or tuna, which is pressed into loaves, cut into paper-thin slices, and dressed with lemon-laced virgin olive oil.

We could begin any meal in Sicily with an *insalata di mare,* a deluxe seafood salad of boiled squid, tasty bits of octopus, fat shrimp, and chopped fresh vegetables with a dressing of olive oil flavored with lemon juice or vinegar.

PASTA ALLA SICILIANA   For your *primi,* or first course, especially if you've skipped the antipasti, you'll be treated to delicious pasta and rice dishes or even couscous, the latter deriving from Sicily's centuries-old links with North Africa. Most pasta dishes are adorned with fresh fish or vegetables, such as *spaghetti alla Norma,* pasta with eggplant. Fishermen in particular love the classic *pasta con le sarde,* a simple but savory pasta with fresh sardines, served in a tomato sauce and wild fennel and given added zest with raisins, pine nuts, and capers. For us, there is nothing finer than *spaghetti alle vongole veraci.* This pasta is served with fresh clams steamed in wine with garlic, fresh parsley, and olive oil. Notice that instead of the relatively mild Parmesan, many islanders sprinkle *caciocavallo,* a particularly strong cheese, on their pasta dishes.

VEGETABLES & FRUITS   Luscious local vegetables, used liberally in pastas and main courses, include vine-ripened tomatoes, spring-green zucchini, yellow onions, tangy capers, fat garlic cloves, many varieties of olives, multicolored peppers, and broccoli—each among the most flavorful in Italy.

On a visit to a citrus grove on the slopes of Mount Etna north of Catania, we were treated to some of the sweetest-tasting and most vividly colored blood-red oranges known to humankind (and we've lived in both Florida and California).

BOUNTY OF THE SEA   Naturally, fresh fish and crustaceans—including sea urchins, mussels, cockles, and whitebait—are the dominant feature at most tables. The traditional *musseddu,* salted and fried tuna, is used to flavor many salads. The most popular fish dishes are tuna from the west and swordfish from the Straits of Messina. For most gastronomes, fish is best served *alla griglia* (simply grilled) or else *arrosto* (roasted). After a sea harvest, you'll find what might be the world's best *zuppa di cozze* **(mussel soup)** resting in a bowl in front of you. Or try *cozze alla marinara,* fresh mussels steamed in wine with garlic and parsley. *Involtini di pesce spada,* grilled roulades of swordfish, are covered with bread crumbs and sautéed in olive oil. Sicilians are also fond of anchovies, using them in such dishes as *sfincione,* thick island pizza topped with anchovies, onions, and tomatoes. Many Sicilians don't consider *sfincione* pizza—it's sold in focaccerias, in bakeries, or perhaps from street vendors, but never in a pizzeria.

MEATS   Traditionally, Sicilian cuisine is based largely on vegetables and the catch of the day harvested from coastal waters. But you can also fill your plate with marvelous meat specialties, including our favorite, a simple but tasty concoction called *costoletta alla Siciliana* **(thinly sliced veal with Parmesan and chopped garlic),** which is dipped in bread crumbs and sautéed. One of the better-known meat dishes is *falsomagro,* meaning "false lean." This rich, bountiful dish, a family favorite, is composed of a large slab of beef wrapped around Sicilian sausages, perhaps prosciutto, raisins, pine nuts, grated cheese, and even a boiled egg or two. The treat is tied with a string and stewed in a savory tomato sauce.

One Sicilian dish now served around the world is *pollo alla Marsala* **(chicken in Marsala wine).** A variation on this famous dish is veal Marsala, which originated among western Sicily's English families living here in the 19th century. Appearing on almost every menu is some form of *involtini,* a roulade made from grilled or roasted chicken or sliced beef, stuffed with a vegetable or meat filling. Sometimes a leafy vegetable such as radicchio is added to the filling.

SWEET STUFF   One of the most succulent of the byproducts derived from the sweet blood-red oranges (and from Sicily's tangerines, lemons, and figs as well) is *frutta candita,* a sugared and preserved confection that explodes with flavor in your mouth and that is well worth the effort of taking home with you. Equally tempting are the fabulously lifelike replicas of pears, grapes, or apples concocted from almond paste and sugar. The colors used in their fabrication and the realism with which they're crafted make them appear as if they had just been picked. In some cases, for added realism, the artisans add hints of a tiny bruise or blemish in each of the confections, partly for charm, partly for whimsy, and partly, we think, to show off their skills. Many of these techniques were originally developed by monks or nuns in monasteries or convents during the 17th and 18th centuries.

Sicilians are also known for their *gelato,* often produced in exotic flavors. (Have you ever had a velvety, creamy mulberry?) In summertime, you can order right from a street vendor a *granita di anguri,* a delectable, slushy watermelon ice. Sicily makes some of the best granita in the world, using purées of fresh fruit pulp—and not just watermelon, but *limone* (lemon), *fragola* (strawberry), and *pesca* (peach), among other flavors. Of course, they also do splendid chocolate, coffee, and vanilla versions.

Islanders point with justifiable pride to their desserts, one of the high points of dining in Sicily. Nothing is grander than a *cassata alla Siciliana,* Catania's most famous cake. It's a layered sponge cake sweetened with Marsala or orange liqueur and filled with ricotta cheese, chunks of chocolate, and candied island fruits. A different cake, *cassata al galleto,* is made with a vanilla-flavored frozen custard and, perhaps, candied fruits, chocolate bits, hazelnuts, or pistachios.

Finally, never leave Sicily without sampling one of its classic *cannoli,* a crunchy tube of pastry filled with ricotta and studded with candied fruits, bits of chocolate, and the inevitable pistachios.

THE WINES OF SICILY

Sicily is celebrated for its wines. The most famous wine, **Marsala,** comes from the west coast from the city of the same name. Marsala is a fortified wine whose alcoholic content is about 20%; it's Sicily's version of port or sherry. A typical Marsala is amber yellow in color with wonderful depths of orange. With its special bouquet, it has a pleasing fragrance, both velvety and fruity, coming in both brut and sweet versions.

Moscata wines usually carry the designations *della Zucco, di Noto,* or *di Pantelleria* (an offshore western island). Moscata is made from the Muscat grape, which is sometimes fortified with Zibibbo or Corinto. Most often it is a golden or light amber dessert wine. It can also be sparkling—then it's called *spumante.*

Malvasia wine is associated with the volcanic island of Lipari. It is golden yellow, turning to amber, with a delightful aroma, both generous and strong. **Novello** is the island's nouveau wine, sold just months after the grapes are harvested and pressed. This is a red wine, both robust and fruity. **Faro,** which means "lighthouse," is a wine produced around Messina. It is a vivid ruby red, with a nutty flavor and fine bouquet; it's a good wine for roasts.

Appendix B:
Glossary of Italian
Terms & Phrases

1 Basic Vocabulary

English	Italian	Pronunciation
Thank you	**Grazie**	*graht*-tzee-yey
You're welcome	**Prego**	*prey*-go
Please	**Per favore**	*pehr* fah-*vohr*-eh
Yes	**Si**	see
No	**No**	noh
Good morning or Good day	**Buongiorno**	bwohn-*djor*-noh
Good evening	**Buona sera**	*bwohn*-ah *say*-rah
Good night	**Buona notte**	*bwohn*-ah *noht*-tay
How are you?	**Come sta?**	*koh*-may *stah*
Very well	**Molto bene**	*mohl*-toh *behn*-ney
Goodbye	**Arrivederci**	ahr-ree-vah-*dehr*-chee
Excuse me (to get attention)	**Scusi**	*skoo*-zee
Excuse me (to get past someone)	**Permesso**	pehr-*mehs*-soh
Where is . . . ?	**Dovè . . . ?**	doh-*vey*
the station	**la stazione**	lah stat-tzee-*oh*-neh
a hotel	**un albergo**	oon ahl-*behr*-goh
a restaurant	**un ristorante**	oon reest-ohr-*ahnt*-eh
the bathroom	**il bagno**	eel *bahn*-nyoh
To the right	**A destra**	ah *dehy*-stra
To the left	**A sinistra**	ah see-*nees*-tra
Straight ahead	**Avanti (*or* sempre diritto)**	ahv-*vahn*-tee (*sehm*-pray dee-*reet*-toh)
How much is it?	**Quanto costa?**	*kwan*-toh *coh*-sta
The check, please	**Il conto, per favore**	eel kon-toh *pehr* fah-*vohr*-eh
What time is it?	**Che ore sono?**	kay *or*-ay *soh*-noh
When?	**Quando?**	*kwan*-doh
Yesterday	**Ieri**	ee-*yehr*-ree
Today	**Oggi**	*oh*-jee
Tomorrow	**Domani**	doh-*mah*-nee
Breakfast	**Prima colazione**	*pree*-mah coh-laht-tzee-*ohn*-ay
Lunch	**Pranzo**	*prahn*-zoh
Dinner	**Cena**	*chay*-nah
Monday	**Lunedì**	loo-nay-*dee*
Tuesday	**Martedì**	mart-ay-*dee*
Wednesday	**Mercoledì**	mehr-cohl-ay-*dee*

English	Italian	Pronunciation
Thursday	**Giovedì**	joh-vay-*dee*
Friday	**Venerdì**	ven-nehr-*dee*
Saturday	**Sabato**	*sah*-bah-toh
Sunday	**Domenica**	doh-*mehn*-nee-kah

2 Numbers

1	**uno** (*oo*-noh)		30	**trenta** (*trayn*-tah)
2	**due** (*doo*-ay)		40	**quaranta** (kwah-*rahn*-tah)
3	**tre** (tray)		50	**cinquanta** (cheen-*kwan*-tah)
4	**quattro** (*kwah*-troh)		60	**sessanta** (sehs-*sahn*-tah)
5	**cinque** (*cheen*-kway)		70	**settanta** (seht-*tahn*-tah)
6	**sei** (say)		80	**ottanta** (oht-*tahn*-tah)
7	**sette** (*set*-tay)		90	**novanta** (noh-*vahnt*-tah)
8	**otto** (*oh*-toh)		100	**cento** (*chen*-toh)
9	**nove** (*noh*-vay)		1,000	**mille** (*mee*-lay)
10	**dieci** (dee-*ay*-chee)		5,000	**cinque milla** (*cheen*-kway *mee*-lah)
11	**undici** (*oon*-dee-chee)		10,000	**dieci milla** (dee-ay-chee mee-lah)
20	**venti** (*vehn*-tee)			
21	**ventuno** (vehn-*toon*-oh)			
22	**venti due** (*vehn*-tee *doo*-ay)			

3 Architectural Terms

Ambone   A pulpit, either serpentine or simple in form, erected in an Italian church.

Apse   The half-rounded extension behind the main altar of a church; Christian tradition dictates that it be placed at the eastern end of an Italian church, the side closest to Jerusalem.

Atrium   A courtyard, open to the sky, in an ancient Roman house; the term also applies to the courtyard nearest the entrance of an early Christian church.

Baldacchino (also ciborium)   A columned stone canopy, usually placed above the altar of a church; spelled in English *baldachin* or *baldaquin*.

Baptistery   A separate building or a separate area in a church where the rite of baptism is held.

Basilica   Any rectangular public building, usually divided into three aisles by rows of columns. In ancient Rome, this architectural form was frequently used for places of public assembly and law courts; later, Roman Christians adapted the form for many of their early churches.

Campanile   A bell tower, often detached, of a church.

Capital   The top of a column, often carved and usually categorized into one of three orders: Doric, Ionic, or Corinthian.

Cavea   The curved row of seats in a classical theater; the most prevalent shape was that of a semicircle.

Chancel   Section of a church containing the altar.

Cornice   The decorative flange defining the uppermost part of a classical or neoclassical facade.

Cortile   Courtyard or cloisters ringed with a gallery of arches or lintels set atop columns.

Crypt   A church's main burial place, usually below the choir.

Cupola   A dome.

Duomo   Cathedral.

Grotesques   Carved and painted faces, deliberately ugly, used by everyone from the Etruscans to the architects of the Renaissance; they're especially amusing when set into fountains.

Hypogeum   Subterranean burial chambers, usually of pre-Christian origins.

Loggia   Roofed balcony or gallery.

Narthex   The anteroom, or enclosed porch, of a Christian church.

Nave   The largest and longest section of a church, usually devoted to sheltering or seating worshipers and often divided by aisles.

Palazzo   A palace or other important building.

Piano Nobile   The main floor of a palazzo (sometimes the 2nd floor).

Pieve   A parish church.

Portico   A porch, usually crafted from wood or stone.

Pulvin   A four-sided stone that serves as a substitute for the capital of a column, often decoratively carved, sometimes into biblical scenes.

Putti   Plaster cherubs whose chubby forms often decorate the interiors of baroque chapels and churches.

Stucco   Colored plaster composed of sand, powdered marble, water, and lime, either molded into statuary or applied in a thin concretelike layer to the exterior of a building.

Telamone   Structural column carved into a standing male form; female versions are called *caryatids.*

Thermae   Roman baths.

Transenna   Stone (usually marble) screen separating the altar area from the rest of an early Christian church.

Tympanum   The half-rounded space above the portal of a church, whose semicircular space usually showcases a sculpture.

4 Menu Glossary

Abbacchio   Roast haunch or shoulder of lamb baked and served in a casserole and sometimes flavored with anchovies.

Agnolotti   A crescent-shaped pasta shell stuffed with a mix of chopped meat, spices, vegetables, and cheese; when prepared in rectangular versions, the same combination of ingredients is identified as ravioli.

Amaretti   Crunchy, sweet almond-flavored macaroons.

Anguilla alla veneziana   Eel cooked in a sauce made from tuna and lemon.

Antipasti   Succulent tidbits served at the beginning of a meal (before the pasta), whose ingredients might include slices of cured meats, seafood (especially shellfish), and cooked and seasoned vegetables.

Aragosta   Lobster.

Arancini di riso   Rice balls stuffed with peas, cheese, and meat, then coated with bread crumbs and deep-fried.

Arrosto   Roasted meat.

Baccalà   Dried and salted codfish.

Bagna cauda   Hot and well-seasoned sauce, heavily flavored with anchovies, designed for dipping raw vegetables; literally translated as "hot bath."

Bocconcini   Veal layered with ham and cheese, then fried.

Bollito misto   Assorted boiled meats served on a single platter.

Bottarga   Dried and salted roe of gray mullet or tuna, which is pressed into loaves, cut into paper-thin slices, and dressed with lemon-laced virgin olive oil.

Braciola   Pork chop.

Bresaola   Air-dried spiced beef.

Bruschetta   Toasted bread, heavily slathered with olive oil and garlic and often topped with tomatoes.

Bucatini   Coarsely textured hollow spaghetti.

Cacciucco ali livornese   Seafood stew.

Caciocavallo   A semi-hard cow's-milk cheese with a particularly strong flavor, often used by Sicilians on pasta dishes instead of parmigiano.

Calzone   Pizza dough rolled with the chef's choice of sausage, tomatoes, cheese, and so on and then baked into a kind of savory turnover.

Cannelloni   Tubular dough stuffed with meat, cheese, or vegetables and then baked in a creamy white sauce.

Cannoli   Crunchy tubular pastry filled with ricotta and studded with candied fruits, bits of chocolate, and pistachios.

Caponata   Antipasti made with eggplants, capers, bell peppers, cauliflower, tomatoes, olives, onions, and celery in a sweet-and-sour sauce of vinegar and sugar.

Cappelletti   Small ravioli ("little hats") stuffed with meat or cheese.

Carciofi   Artichokes.

Carpaccio   Thin slices of raw cured beef, sometimes in a piquant sauce.

Cassatta al galleto   Cake made with vanilla-flavored frozen custard and, perhaps, candied fruits, bits of chocolate, hazelnuts, or pistachios.

Cassatta alla siciliana   A richly caloric dessert that combines layers of sponge cake, ricotta cheese sweetened with Marsala or orange liqueur, and candied fruit, bound together with chocolate butter-cream icing.

Costoletta alla siciliana   Thinly sliced veal cutlet dredged in bread crumbs, fried, and flavored with Parmesan and chopped garlic.

Cozze   Mussels.

Fagioli   White beans.

Falsomagro   Large slab of beef wrapped around Sicilian sausages, perhaps prosciutto, raisins, pine nuts, grated cheese, and even a boiled egg or two; then tied with string and stewed in a savory tomato sauce.

Fave   Fava beans.

Foccacia   Ideally, concocted from potato-based dough left to rise slowly for several hours and then garnished with tomato sauce, garlic, basil, salt, and pepper and drizzled with olive oil.

Fontina   Rich cow's-milk cheese.

Frittata   Italian omelet.

Fritto misto   A deep-fried medley of whatever small fish, shellfish, and squid are available in the marketplace that day.

Frutta candita   Sugared and preserved confection derived from fruits such as blood-red oranges, tangerines, lemons, and figs.

Fusilli   Spiral-shaped pasta.

Gelato (produzione propria)   Ice cream (homemade).

Gnocchi   Dumplings usually made from potatoes *(gnocchi alla patate)* or from semolina *(gnocchi alla romana)*, often stuffed with combinations of cheese, spinach, vegetables, or whatever combinations strike the chef's fancy.

Gorgonzola   One of the most famous blue-veined cheeses of Europe—strong, creamy, and aromatic.

Granità   Flavored ice, usually with lemon or coffee.

Insalata di frutti di mare   Seafood salad (usually including shrimp and squid) garnished with pickles, lemon, olives, and spices.

Involtini   Thinly sliced beef, veal, or pork, rolled, stuffed, and fried.

Involtini di pesce spada   Grilled roulades of swordfish, covered with bread crumbs and sautéed in olive oil.

Minestrone   A rich and savory vegetable soup usually sprinkled with grated parmigiano and studded with noodles.

Mortadella   Mild pork sausage, fashioned into large cylinders and served sliced; the original lunch-meat bologna (because its most famous center of production is Bologna).

Mozzarella   A nonfermented cheese, made from the fresh milk of a buffalo (or, if unavailable, from a cow), boiled, and then kneaded into a rounded ball, served fresh.

Mozzarella con pomodori (also caprese)   Fresh tomatoes with fresh mozzarella, basil, pepper, and olive oil.

Musseddu   Traditional Sicilian salted and fried tuna, used to flavor many salads.

Osso buco   Beef or veal knuckle slowly braised until the cartilage is tender and then served with a highly flavored sauce.

Pancetta   Herb-flavored pork belly, rolled into a cylinder and sliced—the Italian bacon.

Panettone   Sweet yellow-colored bread baked in the form of a brioche.

Panna   Heavy cream.

Pansotti   Pasta stuffed with greens, herbs, and cheeses, usually served with a walnut sauce.

Pappardelle alle lepre   Pasta with rabbit sauce.

Parmigiano   Parmesan, a hard and salty yellow cheese usually grated over pastas and soups but also eaten alone; also known as *granna*. The best is *Parmigiano-Reggiano*.

Peperoni   Green, yellow, or red sweet peppers (not to be confused with pepperoni).

Pesto   A flavorful green sauce made from basil leaves, cheese, garlic, marjoram, and (if available) pine nuts.

Piccata al Marsala   Thin escalope of veal braised in a pungent sauce flavored with Marsala wine.

Piselli al prosciutto   Peas with strips of ham.

Pizza   Specific varieties include *capricciosa* (its ingredients can vary widely, depending on the chef's culinary vision and the ingredients at hand), *margherita* (with tomato sauce, cheese, fresh basil, and memories of the first queen of Italy, Marguerite di Savoia, in whose honor it was first made by a Neapolitan chef), *napoletana* (with ham, capers, tomatoes, oregano, cheese, and the distinctive taste of anchovies), *quattro stagione* (translated as "four seasons" because of the array of fresh vegetables in it; it also contains ham and bacon), and *siciliana* (with black olives, capers, and cheese).

Pizzaiola   A process in which something (usually a beefsteak) is covered in a tomato-and-oregano sauce.

Polenta   Thick porridge or mush made from cornmeal flour.

Polenta de uccelli   Assorted small birds roasted on a spit and served with polenta.

Polenta e coniglio   Rabbit stew served with polenta.

Polla alla cacciatore   Chicken with tomatoes and mushrooms cooked in wine.

Pollo alla Marsala   Chicken cooked in Marsala wine.

Pollo all diavola   Highly spiced grilled chicken.

Ragù   Meat sauce.

Ricotta   A soft bland cheese made from cow's or sheep's milk.

Risotto   Italian rice.

Salsa verde   "Green sauce," made from capers, anchovies, lemon juice and/or vinegar, and parsley.

Saltimbocca   Veal scallop layered with prosciutto and sage; its name literally translates as "jump in your mouth," a reference to its tart and savory flavor.

Salvia   Sage.

Scaloppina alla Valdostana   Escalope of veal stuffed with cheese and ham.

Scaloppine   Thin slices of veal coated in flour and sautéed in butter.

Semifreddo   A frozen dessert; usually ice cream with sponge cake.

Seppia   Cuttlefish (a kind of squid); its black ink is used for flavoring in certain sauces for pasta and also in risotto dishes.

Sfincione   Sicilian pizza-like treat, topped with anchovies, onions, and tomatoes; sold in focaccerias and bakeries (but never in a pizzeria).

Sogliola   Sole.

Spaghetti   A long, round, thin pasta, variously served: *alla bolognese* (with ground meat, mushrooms, peppers, and so on), *alla carbonara* (with bacon, black pepper, and eggs), *alla Norma* (with eggplant), *al pomodoro* (with tomato sauce), *al sugo/ragù* (with meat sauce), and *alle vongole* (with clam sauce).

Spiedini   Pieces of meat grilled on a skewer over an open flame.

Strangolaprete   Small twisted nuggets of pasta, usually served with sauce; the name is literally translated as "priest-choker."

Stufato   Beef braised in white wine with vegetables.

Tagliatelle   Flat egg noodles.

Tonno   Tuna.

Tortelli   Pasta dumplings stuffed with ricotta and greens.

Tortellini   Rings of dough stuffed with minced and seasoned meat, and served either in soups or as a full-fledged pasta covered with sauce.

Trenette   Thin noodles served with pesto sauce and potatoes.

Vermicelli   Very thin spaghetti.

Vitello tonnato   Cold sliced veal covered with tuna-fish sauce.

Zabaglione/zabaione   Egg yolks whipped into the consistency of a custard, flavored with Marsala, and served warm as a dessert.

Zuccotto   A liqueur-soaked sponge cake, molded into a dome and layered with chocolate, nuts, and whipped cream.

Zuppa di cozze   Mussel soup.

Zuppa inglese   Sponge cake soaked in custard.

Index

See also Accommodations and Restaurant indexes, below.

ACCOMMODATIONS

RESTAURANTS

A Guide for Every Type of Traveler

FROMMER'S® COMPLETE GUIDES

For independent leisure or business travelers who value complete coverage, candid advice, and lots of choices in all price ranges.

These are the most complete, up-to-date guides you can buy. Count on Frommer's for exact prices, savvy trip planning, sightseeing advice, dozens of detailed maps, and candid reviews of hotels and restaurants in every price range. All Complete Guides offer special icons to point you to great finds, excellent values, and more. Every hotel, restaurant, and attraction is rated from zero to three stars to help you make the best choices.

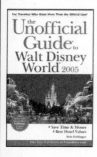

UNOFFICIAL GUIDES

For honeymooners, families, business travelers, and anyone else who values no-nonsense, *Consumer Reports*–style advice.

Unofficial Guides are ideal for those who want to know the pros and cons of the places they are visiting and make informed decisions. The guides rank and rate every hotel, restaurant, and attraction, with evaluations based on reader surveys and critiques compiled by a team of unbiased inspectors.

FROMMER'S® IRREVERENT GUIDES

For experienced, sophisticated travelers looking for a fresh, candid perspective on a destination.

This unique series is perfect for anyone who wants a cutting-edge perspective on the hottest destinations. Covering all major cities around the globe, these guides are unabashedly honest and downright hilarious. Decked out with a retro-savvy feel, each book features new photos, maps, and neighborhood references.

FROMMER'S® WITH KIDS GUIDES

For families traveling with children ages 2 to 14.

Here are the ultimate guides for a successful family vacation. Written by parents, they're packed with information on museums, outdoor activities, attractions, great drives and strolls, incredible parks, the liveliest places to stay and eat, and more.

Visit Frommers.com

WILEY
Now you know.

FROMMER'S® COMPLETE TRAVEL GUIDES

Alaska
Alaska Cruises & Ports of Call
American Southwest
Amsterdam
Argentina & Chile
Arizona
Atlanta
Australia
Austria
Bahamas
Barcelona, Madrid & Seville
Beijing
Belgium, Holland & Luxembourg
Bermuda
Boston
Brazil
British Columbia & the Canadian Rockies
Brussels & Bruges
Budapest & the Best of Hungary
Calgary
California
Canada
Cancún, Cozumel & the Yucatán
Cape Cod, Nantucket & Martha's Vineyard
Caribbean
Caribbean Ports of Call
Carolinas & Georgia
Chicago
China
Colorado
Costa Rica
Cruises & Ports of Call
Cuba
Denmark
Denver, Boulder & Colorado Springs
England
Europe
Europe by Rail
European Cruises & Ports of Call

Florence, Tuscany & Umbria
Florida
France
Germany
Great Britain
Greece
Greek Islands
Halifax
Hawaii
Hong Kong
Honolulu, Waikiki & Oahu
India
Ireland
Italy
Jamaica
Japan
Kauai
Las Vegas
London
Los Angeles
Maryland & Delaware
Maui
Mexico
Montana & Wyoming
Montréal & Québec City
Munich & the Bavarian Alps
Nashville & Memphis
New England
Newfoundland & Labrador
New Mexico
New Orleans
New York City
New York State
New Zealand
Northern Italy
Norway
Nova Scotia, New Brunswick & Prince Edward Island
Oregon
Ottawa
Paris
Peru

Philadelphia & the Amish Country
Portugal
Prague & the Best of the Czech Republic
Provence & the Riviera
Puerto Rico
Rome
San Antonio & Austin
San Diego
San Francisco
Santa Fe, Taos & Albuquerque
Scandinavia
Scotland
Seattle
Shanghai
Sicily
Singapore & Malaysia
South Africa
South America
South Florida
South Pacific
Southeast Asia
Spain
Sweden
Switzerland
Texas
Thailand
Tokyo
Toronto
Turkey
USA
Utah
Vancouver & Victoria
Vermont, New Hampshire & Maine
Vienna & the Danube Valley
Virgin Islands
Virginia
Walt Disney World® & Orlando
Washington, D.C.
Washington State

FROMMER'S® DOLLAR-A-DAY GUIDES

Australia from $50 a Day
California from $70 a Day
England from $75 a Day
Europe from $85 a Day
Florida from $70 a Day
Hawaii from $80 a Day

Ireland from $80 a Day
Italy from $70 a Day
London from $90 a Day
New York City from $90 a Day
Paris from $90 a Day
San Francisco from $70 a Day

Washington, D.C. from $80 a Day
Portable London from $90 a Day
Portable New York City from $90 a Day
Portable Paris from $90 a Day

FROMMER'S® PORTABLE GUIDES

Acapulco, Ixtapa & Zihuatanejo
Amsterdam
Aruba
Australia's Great Barrier Reef
Bahamas
Berlin
Big Island of Hawaii
Boston
California Wine Country
Cancún
Cayman Islands
Charleston
Chicago
Disneyland®
Dominican Republic
Dublin

Florence
Frankfurt
Hong Kong
Las Vegas
Las Vegas for Non-Gamblers
London
Los Angeles
Los Cabos & Baja
Maine Coast
Maui
Miami
Nantucket & Martha's Vineyard
New Orleans
New York City
Paris

Phoenix & Scottsdale
Portland
Puerto Rico
Puerto Vallarta, Manzanillo & Guadalajara
Rio de Janeiro
San Diego
San Francisco
Savannah
Vancouver
Vancouver Island
Venice
Virgin Islands
Washington, D.C.
Whistler

FROMMER'S® NATIONAL PARK GUIDES

Algonquin Provincial Park
Banff & Jasper
Family Vacations in the National
 Parks

Grand Canyon
National Parks of the American
 West
Rocky Mountain

Yellowstone & Grand Teton
Yosemite & Sequoia/Kings
 Canyon
Zion & Bryce Canyon

FROMMER'S® MEMORABLE WALKS

Chicago
London

New York
Paris

San Francisco

FROMMER'S® WITH KIDS GUIDES

Chicago
Las Vegas
New York City

Ottawa
San Francisco
Toronto

Vancouver
Walt Disney World® & Orlando
Washington, D.C.

SUZY GERSHMAN'S BORN TO SHOP GUIDES

Born to Shop: France
Born to Shop: Hong Kong,
 Shanghai & Beijing

Born to Shop: Italy
Born to Shop: London

Born to Shop: New York
Born to Shop: Paris

FROMMER'S® IRREVERENT GUIDES

Amsterdam
Boston
Chicago
Las Vegas
London

Los Angeles
Manhattan
New Orleans
Paris
Rome

San Francisco
Seattle & Portland
Vancouver
Walt Disney World®
Washington, D.C.

FROMMER'S® BEST-LOVED DRIVING TOURS

Austria
Britain
California
France

Germany
Ireland
Italy
New England

Northern Italy
Scotland
Spain
Tuscany & Umbria

THE UNOFFICIAL GUIDES®

Beyond Disney
California with Kids
Central Italy
Chicago
Cruises
Disneyland®
England
Florida
Florida with Kids
Inside Disney

Hawaii
Las Vegas
London
Maui
Mexico's Best Beach Resorts
Mini Las Vegas
Mini Mickey
New Orleans
New York City
Paris

San Francisco
Skiing & Snowboarding in the
 West
South Florida including Miami &
 the Keys
Walt Disney World®
Walt Disney World® for
 Grown-ups
Walt Disney World® with Kids
Washington, D.C.

SPECIAL-INTEREST TITLES

Athens Past & Present
Cities Ranked & Rated
Frommer's Best Day Trips from London
Frommer's Best RV & Tent Campgrounds
 in the U.S.A.
Frommer's Caribbean Hideaways
Frommer's China: The 50 Most Memorable Trips
Frommer's Exploring America by RV
Frommer's Gay & Lesbian Europe
Frommer's NYC Free & Dirt Cheap

Frommer's Road Atlas Europe
Frommer's Road Atlas France
Frommer's Road Atlas Ireland
Frommer's Wonderful Weekends from
 New York City
The New York Times' Guide to Unforgettable
 Weekends
Retirement Places Rated
Rome Past & Present

Travel Tip: He who finds the best hotel deal has more to spend on facials involving knobbly vegetables.

Hello, the Roaming Gnome here. I've been nabbed from the garden and taken round the world. The people who took me are so terribly clever. They find the best offerings on Travelocity. For very little cha-ching. And that means I get to be pampered and exfoliated till I'm pink as a bunny's doodah.

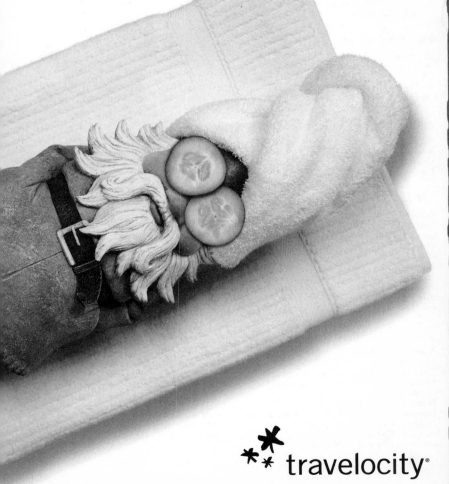

travelocity®

1-888-TRAVELOCITY / travelocity.com / America Online Keyword: Travel

Travel Tip: Make sure there's customer service for any change of plans — involving friendly natives, for example.

One can plan and plan, but if you don't book with the right people you can't seize le moment and canoodle with the poodle named Pansy. I, for one, am all for fraternizing with the locals. Better yet, if I need to extend my stay and my gnome nappers are willing, it can all be arranged through the 800 number at, oh look, how convenient, the lovely company coat of arms.

travelocity®